The Social Circulation
of the Past

The Social Circulation of the Past

English Historical Culture
1500–1730

DANIEL WOOLF

OXFORD

UNIVERSITY PRESS

*This book has been printed digitally and produced in a standard specification
in order to ensure its continuing availability*

OXFORD
UNIVERSITY PRESS

Great Clarendon Street, Oxford OX2 6DP

Oxford University Press is a department of the University of Oxford.
It furthers the University's objective of excellence in research, scholarship,
and education by publishing worldwide in

Oxford New York

Auckland Cape Town Dar es Salaam Hong Kong Karachi
Kuala Lumpur Madrid Melbourne Mexico City Nairobi
New Delhi Shanghai Taipei Toronto
With offices in
Argentina Austria Brazil Chile Czech Republic France Greece
Guatemala Hungary Italy Japan South Korea Poland Portugal
Singapore Switzerland Thailand Turkey Ukraine Vietnam

Oxford is a registered trade mark of Oxford University Press
in the UK and in certain other countries

Published in the United States
by Oxford University Press Inc., New York

ISBN 0-19-925778-7

For

PAUL CHRISTIANSON

Preface

EARLY MODERN SCHOLARS were inclined to find datable origins for every-thing, and were often uncomfortable with the notion that some things simply could not be so dated. Looking back over the genesis of this book it is still pos-sible, even after nearly twenty years, to identify, if not a precise point of origin, then at least some key moments in its development. The first of these was the evening late in 1983 when I attended Keith Thomas's now famous Creighton Lecture on 'The Perception of the Past in Early Modern England', a brief but incisive study that, in its printed form, has never strayed far from my desk. Following close upon my having completed a D.Phil. dissertation on early Stuart historians, the contents of this lecture persuaded me (somewhat brashly given who was giving the lecture) that there might be more to the topic than this. Was it the case, I began to ask, that the likes of Camden and Selden whom I had been studying for several years might not represent the sum and total measure of historical culture in early modern England? The second moment occurred some months later when I began noticing for the first time a surprising number of references to what we now call oral tradition in the works of Tudor and Jacobean antiquaries now prin-cipally celebrated for their contributions to the advance of historical scholarship based on rigorous documentation of sources. A third occurred in the Essex Record Office nearly a decade later still, on reading through the extensive correspondence of William Holman, a minor early eighteenth-century antiquary of Halstead, complete with its references to antiquities furnished by common folk, and to details of family genealogy furnished by local (and especially female) writers that I had not been expecting to see. There were many other such moments of discovery along what has been a long and winding road. The book as planned up to the mid 1990s would have been much longer than it already is, since it also once included an extensive discussion of the reading and circulation of history books. It took a further, rather difficult moment to realize that the two projects, though clearly related, were really separate studies, and my work on the latter subject has in fact preceded the present volume into print by some time as *Reading History in Early Modern England*. Even now, at the end of the process, I am acutely conscious that there are topics relevant here that space and time have not allowed me to treat at all, and others that might have merited more extensive consideration than I have been able to give them.

I am grateful to the editors or publishers of a number of journals or presses for permitting me to reprint, albeit often in much revised form, materials that first appeared in the following essays:

'In Praise of Older Things: Notions of Age and Antiquity in Early Modern England', in *Historians and Ideologues: Essays in Honor of Donald Kelley*, ed. J. H. M.
Salmon and Anthony Grafton (Rochester: University of Rochester Press, 2001),
123–52.

'A Feminine Past? Gender, Genre, and Historical Knowledge in England,
1500–1800', *American Historical Review*, 102/3 (June 1997), 645–79.

'Little Crosby and the Horizons of Early Modern Historical Culture', in Donald
R. Kelley and David Harris Sacks (eds.), *The Historical Imagination in Early Modern
Britain* (Cambridge: Cambridge University Press, 1997), 93–132.

'The Dawn of the Artifact: The Antiquarian Impulse in England, 1500–1730', *Studies
in Medievalism*, 4 (1992), 5–35.

'Of Danes and Giants: Popular Beliefs about the Past in Early Modern England',
Dalhousie Review, 71 (Summer 1991), 166–209.

'Memory and Historical Culture in Early Modern England', *Journal of the
Canadian Historical Association*, NS 2 (1991), 283–308.

'The "Common Voice": History, Folklore, and Oral Tradition in Early Modern
England', *Past and Present*, 120 (Aug. 1988), 26–52.

Some portion of this book is devoted to the topic of memory, and especially to
memories (real or derived from literary culture) of the Middle Ages. Regrettably
my own now middle-aged memory does not adequately recall every person who
has assisted me in some way towards the completion of this project over the years,
including various persons who kindly provided references, and whose contributions are acknowledged in the notes as they occur. In Britain, Sir Keith Thomas's
interest in the project has already been mentioned, and I am grateful for his encouragement at various stages; John Morrill has been similarly supportive and
encouraging. Adam Fox kindly allowed me to read his own doctoral thesis before
it appeared in print, and proved a wonderful collaborator on a volume that has
appeared shortly before this one. In the United States, Fritz Levy offered useful
and often critical comment on some of the earlier work represented here, and
his *Tudor Historical Thought* is another title (too long out of print) I keep close
at hand. Several fellow Canadian historians of Britain have rendered advice,
including Ian Dyck, Ian Gentles, and especially Robert Tittler. The Tittler Tudor
sofa has provided refuge for scholars in Montreal for many years. But for Bob's
stringent advice in the late 1980s that I explore local record office material (only
a selection of which I have been able to use here) the book would have been finished
long ago, and been much shorter; it is for him to judge whether it is better. A
debt to another fellow Canadian (like me, by naturalization) and former teacher
is reserved for the dedication, publication of this volume coinciding happily with
the occasion of his retirement. Several early modern Europeanists have also
stimulated me at various points, in particular Don Kelley, Zachary Schiffman
(in whose Chicago home I enjoyed several vigorous arguments about historical

consciousness and, more importantly, also discovered that I liked jazz), John Salmon, and Fernando Cervantes. I have derived some valuable perspective on my own subject (as well as considerable pleasure) through periodic exchanges over the past decade with several students of modern European historiography (Chris Lorenz and Georg Iggers most especially) and through the laborious but thoroughly instructive process of editing a multi-authored reference work on historical writing around the globe. Jane Arscott also provided early encouragement and support for the project. I must also add a bittersweet acknowledgement: Gerald Aylmer maintained his interest in my work long after any official duties to a former D.Phil. student abated. He died very suddenly in 2000, with much left to offer both scholarship and humanity, and is sorely missed by his many students and friends. I like to think he would have approved of the final product but I can imagine arguing with him over sherry on one or two points.

Members of several seminars have offered critiques of earlier versions of various chapters. Among these I must mention Peter Lake's seminar at Princeton University (1996) and Mark Kishlansky's at Harvard (1993). I must also acknowledge the departmental seminars at my two former institutions Dalhousie University (where, it is frightening to recall, a summary of the book in different form was the subject of my assistant professor 'job talk' in 1987 and where a great deal of the book was written and researched) and McMaster University, as well as my current home, the Department of History and Classics of the University of Alberta, where, as a visitor, I gave talks on the topic in 1989 and 2000. Among my former colleagues I thank Cynthia Neville and Jack Crowley at Dalhousie, both of whom stayed in touch on the project after I left their company, and Sara Mendelson, Graham Roebuck, Jim Alsop, and Virginia Aksan at McMaster for their general interest in the research of a colleague among them rather intermittently during an all-too-brief posting in Hamilton. I enjoyed, and I hope profited from, sparring with John Pocock and Joe Levine at the Woodrow Wilson Centre conference, a decade ago, where I first publicly evinced my reservations about a history of historical scholarship in the early modern period that concentrated only on the scholars and on the achievements now regarded as having led to modern historical methods. I have had the great fortune to have several perceptive and helpful graduate students over the years, Greg Bak, Ruth McClelland-Nugent, Kathryn Brammall, Aki Beam, and Krista Kesselring. I am indebted, too, to two anonymous reviewers, whose thoughtful and helpful comments have, I hope, produced a better book. Ruth Parr has been an enormously supportive commissioning editor, and I thank her and her many colleagues at Oxford University Press for seeing the book through the editorial and publication stages.

A great deal of the research here occurred in places normally out of the way of intellectual historians and especially historiographers: I have to thank the Social Sciences and Humanities Research Council of Canada for two successive grants between 1990 and 1996 in support of my frequent trips to Britain. The School of Historical Studies of the Institute for Advanced Study in Princeton awarded me a year's membership in 1996–7, and much of the writing and rewriting of an early draft of the work was completed, among other tasks, during that period. I am also very grateful to the many librarians and archivists who assisted me in my research while using their facilities and who have patiently answered queries from me before and since.

I am also indebted for permission to cite privately owned papers on deposit in record offices, in particular to Mr B. Whitlock Blundell for family materials in the Lancashire Record Office and to the Society of Antiquaries of Newcastle-upon-Tyne for documents in the ZAN series at the Northumberland Record Office. The Society of Antiquaries of London and its librarian Mr B. Nurse afforded me generous access to its rich holdings.

My three children, Sarah, Sam, and David, and my parents Margaret and Cyril continue to take an interest in these somewhat arcane pursuits. I should also like to acknowledge the invaluable example and encouragement Stuart Woolf has provided to a younger family member over many years, including giving me my very first history book nearly forty years ago.

Contents

Part IV. The Past Remembered

A Note on Conventions

CONTRACTIONS FROM MANUSCRIPT sources have occasionally been modernized for clarity; in other respects spelling is retained as in the original. Dates are Old Style, but the year is calculated from 1 January. On occasion, where clarity requires it, dates are written 1687/8. Place of publication of all works is London except where otherwise indicated.

List of Figures

The illustrations listed above are reproduced by kind permission of the following:

4.1. The Abbot Hall Art Gallery, Kendal, Cumbria

4.2, 4.3, 4.4, 4.5, 6.1, 9.1, 9.2, 9.3, and 9.5. The Mills Memorial Library, McMaster University, Hamilton, Ontario

5.1, 6.2, 6.3, 7.1, and 7.2. The Killam Memorial Library, Dalhousie University, Halifax, Nova Scotia

5.2. Hampshire Record Office

7.3. The British Library

7.4. Canon Roger Daley

9.4. The Guildhall Library, Corporation of London

Abbreviations

BL	British Library
Bodl.	Bodleian Library, Oxford
Blundell, *Cavalier's Notebook*	William Blundell (1620–98), *Crosby Records. A cavalier's note book; being notes, anecdotes, & observations of William Blundell of Crosby, Lancashire, esquire, captain of dragoons . . . in the royalist army of 1642*, ed. T. Ellison Gibson. (London, 1880)
CKS	Centre for Kentish Studies, Maidstone
Coll. Arms	College of Arms, London
Crosby Records	*Crosby Records: A Chapter of Lancashire Recusancy. Containing a relation of troubles and persecutions sustained by William Blundell, of Crosby Hall, Lancashire, esq. (1560–1638)*, ed. T. E. Gibson (Manchester: Chetham Society, 1887)
CSPD	*Calendar of State Papers Domestic*
CUL	Cambridge University Library
DNB	*Dictionary of National Biography*
Dugdale, *Life, Diary and Correspondence*	*The Life, Diary and Correspondence of Sir William Dugdale, Knight, Sometime Garter Principal King of Arms*, ed. W. Hamper (London, 1827)
EETS	Early English Text Society
ES	extra series
Evelyn, *Diary*	*The Diary of John Evelyn*, ed. E. S. de Beer, 6 vols. (Oxford, 1955)
HRC	Harry Ransom Humanities Research Center, University of Texas, Austin
Hearne, *Remarks and Collections*	*Remarks and Collections of Thomas Hearne*, ed. C. E. Doble, D. W. Rannie, and H. E. Salter, 11 vols., Oxford Historical Society (Oxford, 1885–1921)
Hist. MSS Comm.	Great Britain, Historical Manuscripts Commission
Leland's Itinerary	*The Itinerary of John Leland in or about the Years 1535–1543*, ed. Lucy Toulmin Smith (London, 1907–10; repr. 5 vols., Carbondale, Ill., 1964)

Nichols, *Literary Illustrations*	John Nichols, *Illustrations of the Literary History of the Eighteenth Century*, 8 vols. (1817–58)
n.s.	new-style date
NS	new series
OS	original series
Pepys, *Diary*	*The Diary of Samuel Pepys*, ed. R. Latham and W. Matthews, 11 vols. (London and Berkeley, Calif., 1970–83)
Pevsner, *BE*	N. Pevsner, *The Buildings of England* (Harmondsworth, 1951 *et seq.*)
PRO	Public Record Office, London
PS	Parker Society
Rec. Soc.	Record Society
REED	*Records of Early English Drama*
RO	Record Office
SAL	Society of Antiquaries, London
STC	A. Pollard and G. Redgrave, *A Short-Title Catalogue of Books Printed in England, Scotland, & Ireland and of English Books Printed Abroad, 1475–1640*, 2nd edn., ed. W. A. Jackson, F. S. Ferguson, and Katharine F. Pantzer, 3 vols. (1976–91)
TRHS	*Transactions of the Royal Historical Society*
VCH	*Victoria History of the Counties of England*
Wanley, *Diary*	*The Diary of Humfrey Wanley, 1715–1726*, ed. C. E. Wright and Ruth C. Wright, 2 vols. (1966)
Wanley, *Letters*	*Letters of Humfrey Wanley: Palaeographer, Anglo-Saxonist, Librarian, 1672–1726: with an appendix of documents*, ed. P. L. Heyworth (Oxford, 1989)
Wood, *Life and Times*	*The Life and Times of Anthony Wood, Antiquary, of Oxford, 1632–1695, described by himself*, ed. A. Clark, 5 vols., Oxford Historical Society, vols. xix, xx, xxvi, xxx, xl (Oxford, 1891–1900)
Wing	Donald Wing, *A Short-Title Catalogue of Books Printed in England, Scotland, Ireland, Wales, and British America, and of English Books Printed in Other Countries, 1641–1700*, rev. edn., 3 vols. (New York, 1972–88)

Introduction

EARLY MODERNISTS, ESPECIALLY those interested in the evolution of the discipline of history, have long taken a special pride in their chosen period. During this age the foundations of modern scholarly and critical techniques are thought to have been laid, and a recognizable sense of distance from the ancient past is held to have been achieved. Renaissance historical thinkers have enjoyed a particularly privileged position, whether engaging in epistolary conversation with dead ancients in the manner of Petrarch; adapting the historical style of Livy to tell the story of Florence as did Leonardo Bruni; scouring the ruins of late medieval Italy for its architecture and archaeology as did Flavio Biondo; or ransacking the past for political examples as did Niccolò Machiavelli. The 'Renaissance sense of the past',[1] often devoted to branches of knowledge such as ancient chronology that now seem arcane, is in many ways as alien to us as the 'medieval' sense that preceded it. In other ways, however, it appears strikingly familiar. Many of the problems faced by philologers from Lorenzo Valla and Angelo Poliziano or Politian in the fifteenth century through Joseph Scaliger and Isaac Casaubon in the late sixteenth, to Richard Bentley at the end of the seventeenth, still concern us methodologically. Many of the issues of both literary style and scholarly research confronted by narrative historians from Bruni to Edward Gibbon anticipate, in broad terms, matters still debated in historical journals. Because of this family resemblance, we have more often than not been tempted to make early modern historians, philological scholars, and antiquaries our direct ancestors, applauding their anticipations of modern concerns and explaining away the features of their works that seem dated or even retrograde.[2]

---

[1] The phrase is used most famously in Peter Burke's short study, *The Renaissance Sense of the Past* (1969), but has been widely adopted elsewhere.

[2] This is manifestly *not* the view of medievalists, for whom the chronicle is the definitive historical form of their period, but who have, till recently, also searched within it for signs of a 'critical spirit', 'rigorous method', 'recourse to documents', 'scepticism to report and myth', and so on. For examples of this approach see B. Smalley, *Historians in the Middle Ages* (1974); V. H. Galbraith, *Kings and Chroniclers: Essays in English Medieval History* (1982); and M. McKisack (a medievalist writing about sixteenth-century antiquarianism rather than the medieval chronicle), *Medieval History in the Tudor Age* (Oxford, 1971). A general survey of early English historical literature may be found in A. Gransden, *Historical Writing in England*, 2 vols. (Ithaca, NY, 1974–82). For a more holistic and less progressivist approach, see the perceptive essay by R. W. Southern, 'Aspects of the European Tradition of Historical Writing: The Sense of the Past', *TRHS*, 5th ser., 23 (1973), 243–63. For two largely persuasive attempts to situate the chronicle within its contemporary literary and cultural contexts as much as within methodological history, see N. F. Partner, *Serious Entertainments: the Writing of History in Twelfth-Century England* (Chicago, 1977); G. M. Spiegel, *Romancing the Past: The Rise of Vernacular Prose Historiography in Thirteenth-Century France* (Berkeley and Los Angeles, 1992). Finally, the most thorough treatment of the chronicler and his environment, still regrettably untranslated, is Bernard Guenée's book, *Histoire et culture historique dans l'Occident médiéval* (Paris, 1980).

Yet even if we acknowledge our debt to the scholars and historians of earlier centuries, we are not a good deal closer to comprehending how they themselves conceived of their role, nor are we very near to an understanding of why their accomplishments were deemed significant by their own or subsequent generations. If *Britannia*, William Camden's pioneering exploration of his country's ancient and medieval remains, had not immediately resonated with an affluent gentry readership, would it have found its way into several further editions by the time of his death and become the vade mecum of seventeenth-century antiquarian interests? On a different front, would the painstaking reconstruction of ancient chronology by Joseph Scaliger (and by his English critic Thomas Lydiat and his Anglo-Irish imitator James Ussher) have had much significance if it did not speak to a tremendous contemporary concern with such matters as the precise age of the world and the dates of the major ancient empires—a subject that preoccupied some of the most learned Europeans from the Reformation to the lifetime of Sir Isaac Newton?[3] Should anyone really have wondered whether or not Sir John Hayward's life of King Henry IV contained veiled references to Queen Elizabeth and the earl of Essex? What, aside from the genius of Shakespeare and Marlowe, accounts for the enormous if relatively brief popularity of the history plays? Why should villagers and townsmen have been ready to recount to travellers from John Leland to Celia Fiennes the numerous and often conflicting stories they had inherited regarding the origins of local landmarks and the practice of immemorial customs—and why were the travellers themselves interested? In fact, a great many people of varying degrees and disparate backgrounds cared very much about various aspects of their individual and collective pasts, though not necessarily the same aspects, nor all for the same reasons. Why this should be so has not yet been adequately explained nor, I would argue, fully contextualized.

Not surprisingly, we are much better acquainted with the upper echelons than with those below. There can be little doubt that the sixteenth and seventeenth centuries witnessed an enormous efflorescence in historical interest among European social elites. In England, one has but to compare history's relatively marginal connection to the university and scholastic curriculum in 1500 with the status it enjoyed by 1730. By that time Oxford had been filling its Camden professorship for just over a century, and both universities had recently established Regius professorships in modern history to cover times beginning in late antiquity.[4] By nearly any standard of measurement, the advancement of history from a minor genre represented either in inaccessible manuscript chronicles or the relatively small number of rediscovered ancient historians is truly impressive.

---

[3] A. Grafton, 'Joseph Scaliger and Historical Chronology: The Rise and Fall of a Discipline', *History and Theory*, 14 (1975), 156–85; id., *Joseph Scaliger: A Study in the History of Classical Scholarship*, 2 vols. (Oxford, 1983–93), esp. vol. ii; F. E. Manuel, *Isaac Newton, Historian* (Cambridge, Mass., 1963).

[4] M. Feingold, 'The Humanities', in N. Tyacke (ed.), *The History of the University of Oxford* iv: *Seventeenth-Century Oxford* (Oxford, 1997), 327–57, on history-teaching at Oxford; K. Sharpe, 'The Foundation of the Chairs of History at Oxford and Cambridge: An Episode in Jacobean Politics', *History of Universities*, 2 (1982), 127–52.

This rise in history's stock within the cultural marketplace has itself been linked to a number of factors such as increased literacy and the advent of the printing press, but the nature of this relationship is itself far from clear. For example, while the press has often been heralded as an engine of cultural change,[5] most recent histories of the book, of print culture, and of reading have strangely remained at a distance from the history of history. There is a reason for this. Students of the history of history are willing to credit print with making the wares of historians more available to readers, but this is a somewhat grudging concession. At bottom, most historiographers are more interested in the techniques, methods, ideologies, and intellectual influences that underlie the creation of a particular historical text than they are in its subsequent reproduction and dissemination. Print plays an important but subordinate role to the Renaissance's all-purpose reagent, humanism, and to its major achievement, the rediscovery of antiquity. The philological foundations of later German *Quellenkritik* are thought to have been laid by the likes of Valla and Politian, just before the advent of movable type. Since the Renaissance awareness of anachronism commenced even earlier, with Petrarch, Bruni, and Bembo (and, in the visual arts, with their contemporaries among painters and sculptors), print could not have 'caused' the new sense of the past. The printing press assisted in the spread of historical works; it enabled the standardization of corrected ancient texts; and it promoted education, especially in the classical historians. But it was not, on this view, essential in and of itself to the creation of historical knowledge, to the advancement of the methodological practices by which such knowledge was obtained, or to the refinement of evidentiary principles whereby the value of such knowledge was evaluated.[6]

HUMANISM AND HISTORY REVISITED

(In contrast to the influence of the press, a more strictly intellectual influence, conveniently summarized under the rather open-ended term 'humanism') has for a very long time borne most of the weight of explanation for the emergence of early modern historical writing from its medieval past. In particular humanism is associated closely with the attainment of a sense of distance from antiquity analogous to the development of perspective in painting, and with a related capacity to grasp the nature of long-vanished things through the graphic signatures they

---

[5] Most notably in the flurry of publications on books and publishing that have appeared since Elizabeth L. Eisenstein's mammoth study *The Printing Press as an Agent of Change*, 2 vols. (Cambridge, 1979), and in the cultural historiography of Henri-Jean Martin, Robert Darnton, Natalie Zemon Davis, Roger Chartier, and others, a bibliography sufficiently well known not to need detailed citation here.

[6] The impact of print on historical reading and writing is the subject of my recent book, *Reading History in Early Modern England* (Cambridge, 2000). Though it concentrates principally on a later period, there is useful information on historical publication in R. Sweet, *The Writing of Urban Histories in Eighteenth-Century England* (Oxford, 1997).

(left in the form of language, properly categorized and its major texts purged of error through rigorous philological spadework) The fit between humanist scholarship and education, on the one hand, and changes in historical outlook, on the other, is difficult to resist. Since the humanists were concerned with restoring the purity of ancient texts, their methods seem highly 'historical'. Since they also admired and emulated ancient rhetoric, their literary output marks a sharp departure from the structure and style of medieval chronicles.[7] And since they were focused squarely on the reconstruction and imitation of the past, an interest in the genre of history, and in theories of historical change,[8] was perhaps inevitable.

It is not an overstatement to say that these connections have shaped and coloured virtually every account of early modern historiography written in the past hundred years. When Eduard Fueter wrote his then definitive survey of the history of European historiography in the early 1900s, he spent a great deal of space on the early modern era, and considered humanism as the leading factor in dragging history up the next notch on the evolutionary ladder. His account has been more or less repeated (with obvious changes in emphasis owed to national allegiance or personal knowledge), by J. T. Shotwell, J. W. Thompson, and H. E. Barnes, an American triumvirate who all wrote surveys of the history of history in the first half of the century. It still figures prominently in the most recent survey by Ernst Breisach, though that work correctly pays much more attention to social and political context.[9] Most powerfully, the many essays and lectures of Arnaldo Momigliano, one of the twentieth century's outstanding classicists and a historiographer of great influence, have made the debts of early modern historiography to its classical antecedents into an almost unassailable orthodoxy.[10]

[7] W. J. Brandt, *The Shape of Medieval History: Studies in Modes of Perception* (New Haven, Conn., 1966) remains a stimulating evaluation of the structure of medieval chronicles and the mentalities underlying them.
[8] D. R. Kelley, 'The Theory of History', in C. B. Schmitt and Q. Skinner (eds.), *The Cambridge History of Renaissance Philosophy* (Cambridge, 1988), 746–61.
[9] E. Fueter, *Geschichte der neuren Historiographie* (1st pub. 1911), 2nd edn. (Munich and Berlin, 1936), 1–333; J. T. Shotwell, *An Introduction to the History of History* (New York, 1922); J. W. Thompson, *A History of Historical Writing*, 2 vols. (New York, 1942); H. E. Barnes, *A History of Historical Writing*, 2nd edn. (1st pub. 1937; New York, 1963); E. Breisach, *Historiography: Ancient, Medieval, and Modern*, 2nd edn. (Chicago, 1994). In his anthology *Versions of History from Antiquity to the Enlightenment* (New Haven, Conn., 1991), Donald R. Kelley devotes over 200 pages, nearly half the volume, to selections originating in the period from the end of the Middle Ages to the early Enlightenment.
[10] A. Momigliano, *Studies in Historiography* (New York, 1966); id., *Essays in Ancient and Modern Historiography* (Middletown, Conn., 1977); id., *The Classical Foundations of Modern Historiography* (Berkeley and Los Angeles, 1990); but cf. the recent critique by M. S. Phillips, 'Reconsiderations on History and Antiquarianism: Arnaldo Momigliano and the Historiography of Eighteenth-Century Britain', *Journal of the History of Ideas*, 58 (1996), 297–316. The importance of the classical heritage continues to be stressed by Momigliano's leading former student Anthony Grafton, but with several critical differences: the focus of Grafton's many books, for instance *Commerce with the Classics: Ancient Books and Renaissance Readers* (Ann Arbor, 1997) is on the adaptation and re-adaptation of classical philology and rhetoric (including historical scholarship) than on its straightforward 'heritage'. Grafton also correctly stresses the political, religious, and social pressures that made scholars into hardened polemicists, rather than disinterested intellectuals serving only the advancement of learning: cf. his *The Footnote: A Curious History* (Cambridge, Mass., 1997).

   As the font of historical philology and neoclassical rhetoric, humanism is even more clearly stressed in North American-authored studies of early modern history-writing, explicitly in those concerned with Italy (Felix Gilbert, Mark Phillips, Donald Willcox, Nancy Struever, Eric Cochrane, and others),[11] Germany (Gerald Strauss),[12] and in most of those that deal with France (Donald R. Kelley, George Huppert, Julian Franklin, and Zachary S. Schiffman).[13] Like Polydore Vergil and the migrant scholars of the early sixteenth century, the idea of humanism as both necessary and sufficient condition for the emergence of modern historical consciousness has successfully crossed the Channel and entered into accounts of English historiography. In different ways, the earlier accounts of Renaissance English historical thought during the period by F. Smith Fussner, F. J. Levy, Arthur B. Ferguson, and (more recently) Graham Parry and myself tell very similar tales.[14] In this account humanism provided the necessary potion for restoring medieval annalistic dross into neoclassical-hence-modern historical gold, even if it was gold that still needed a century or two of scholarly refinement.[15]

   The two most prolific modern scholars of early modern English historiography, J. G. A. Pocock and Joseph M. Levine, have in different ways discussed the development, in the wake of Continental humanism, of principles for comparing not only texts, but entire ages. For Pocock, the measure of English historiography's achievement is that, in the face of an anachronistic and ahistorical common-law view of the past, a select number of legal scholars were able both to pose and find a solution to a key problem in modern medieval scholarship,

[11] F. Gilbert, *Machiavelli and Guicciardini: Politics and History in Sixteenth-Century Florence* (Princeton, 1965); M. S. Phillips, *Francesco Guicciardini: The Historian's Craft* (Toronto, 1977); D. J. Wilcox, *The Development of Florentine Humanist Historiography in the Fifteenth Century* (Cambridge, Mass., 1969); E. Cochrane, *Historians and Historiography in the Italian Renaissance* (Chicago, 1981); N. S. Struever, *The Language of History in the Renaissance* (Princeton, 1970). Other endeavours in the same enterprise include M. P. Gilmore, *Humanists and Jurists: Six Studies in the Renaissance* (Cambridge, Mass., 1963) and D. Hay, *Annalists and Historians* (London and New York, 1977).

[12] G. Strauss, *Historian in an Age of Crisis: The Life and Work of Johannes Aventinus, 1477–1534* (Cambridge, Mass., 1963). Consider the title of a much earlier work, P. Joachimsen, *Geschichtsauffassung und Geschichtsschreibung in Deutschland unter dem Einfluss des Humanismus* (Leipzig, 1910; repr. Aalen, 1968).

[13] D. R. Kelley, *Foundations of Modern Historical Scholarship: Language, Law and History in the French Renaissance* (New York, 1970); G. Huppert, *The Idea of Perfect History: Historical Eruditon and Historical Philosophy in Renaissance France* (Chicago and Urbana, 1970); J. H. Franklin, *Jean Bodin and the Sixteenth-Century Revolution in the Methodology of Law and History* (New York, 1963); Z. S. Schiffman, *On the Threshold of Modernity: Relativism in the French Renaissance* (Baltimore, 1991).

[14] F. S. Fussner, *The Historical Revolution: English Historical Writing and Thought, 1580–1640* (1962); F. J. Levy, *Tudor Historical Thought* (San Marino, 1967); A. B. Ferguson, *Clio Unbound: Perception of the Social and Cultural Past in Renaissance England* (Durham, NC, 1979); id., *Utter Antiquity* (Durham, NC, 1993); G. Parry, *The Trophies of Time: English Antiquarians of the Seventeenth Century* (Oxford, 1995); D. R. Woolf, *The Idea of History in Early Stuart England: Erudition, Ideology, and the 'Light of Truth' from the Accession of James I to the Civil War* (Toronto, 1990).

[15] The tendency to judge past historiography by modern standards is not unique to early modernists. As Stephen Bann has forcefully remarked, the thrust of much historiographical writing in the last century is towards distinguishing good from bad past historical practice, 'as if Dr Jekyll had written his autobiography and carefully set a distance between his own eminent career and the disreputable doings of a certain Mr Hyde'. Stephen Bann, preface to M. Myrone and L. Peltz (eds.), *Producing the Past: Aspects of Antiquarian Culture and Practice 1700–1850* (Aldershot, 1999), p. xviii.

the meaning of feudalism and the implications of that system for seventeenth-century law and politics.[16] Levine even more explicitly makes humanism the central feature connecting the age of Valla with that of Gibbon, in a collection of essays significantly entitled *Humanism and History*. The classical tradition and the perfection of methods for its study and literary presentation provide the backdrop to his subsequent reconstruction, from textual and epistolary evidence, of the most celebrated intellectual dispute of England's Augustan age, the Battle of the Books. The essential problem, as Levine sees it, is explaining, 'how and why English historiography found its modern method'.[17]

This 'how and why' is certainly a problem worth solving. Nor is there anything wrong with proceeding in like manner, if the methodological and discursive practices of scholars and historians, then and now, are seen as lying at the heart of history's 'rise' in the past five centuries. The explanations for the changes in the nature and functions of historical writing in the early modern era that Pocock, Levine, and others have collectively provided are, in the main, persuasive in so far as the future *discipline* of history is concerned. It seems beyond dispute that early modern scholars, historians, philologers, and antiquaries were indeed inspired by their exposure to ancient works and by the learning inherent in a humanist *paedeia* to make more careful assessments of texts and documents, and, as a by-product of this close study, to acquire an enhanced sensitivity to social change. We now have a workable, thorough and generally satisfying set of books and articles answering pretty clearly the question how history as a literary form and a methodological practice evolved between the end of the Middle Ages and the mid-eighteenth century.[18]

The difficulty is that these sorts of questions are not the only ones that can or should be asked in connection with English historical thought during the early modern period. What we now need to know is what turned the English, who were not, by contemporary Continental standards, remarkably interested in their national history in 1500, and only marginally more so, Shakespeare notwithstanding, three generations later, into a people thoroughly absorbed in history at the start of the Hanoverian era (so absorbed by it, in fact, that history presented through much of the eighteenth century the only serious contender with the novel for dominance of civilized reading and conversation). For this we need to look a bit nearer the ground for explanations, using a more open-ended definition of the

---

[16] J. G. A. Pocock, *The Ancient Constitution and the Feudal Law: A Study of English Historical Thought in the Seventeenth Century—a Reissue with a Retrospect* (1st pub. 1957; Cambridge, 1987); Pocock's most recent discussion of English historiography is his major ongoing study of Gibbon's *Decline and Fall of the Roman Empire: Barbarism and Religion*, 2 vols. published to date (Cambridge, 1999).

[17] J. M. Levine, *Humanism and History* (Ithaca, NY, 1987), quotation at p. 9; id., *The Battle of the Books: Literature and History in Augustan England* (Ithaca, NY, 1991); id., *The Autonomy of History, Truth and Method from Erasmus to Gibbon* (Chicago, 1999); id., *Between the Ancients and the Moderns: Baroque Culture in Restoration England* (New Haven and London, 1999).

[18] L. Braudy, *Narrative Form in History and Fiction: Hume, Fielding and Gibbon* (Princeton, 1970); P. Hicks, *Neoclassical History and English Culture from Clarendon to Hume* (New York, 1996); K. O'Brien, *Narratives of Enlightenment: Cosmopolitan History from Voltaire to Gibbon* (Cambridge, 1997); M. S. Phillips, *Society and Sentiment: Genres of Historical Writing in Britain, 1740–1820* (Princeton, 2000).

past than that embraced by 'history' in its narrower definition as those aspects of the past that someone deliberately chooses to select, organize, and represent in a coherent literary form.

The various polemical ends to which the past was put offer part of the solution, but while there will be occasion to refer to such uses in the present book, I have avoided making this a major theme. To do so would have added considerably to an already lengthy study, and would plough over, probably unsatisfactorily, material that others have cultivated well. Pocock, for example, has elucidated the ideological significance of key historical events such as the Norman Conquest and the calling of the first parliaments in seventeenth-century debates over matters constitutional.[19] Kevin Sharpe has demonstrated compellingly the uses to which the past was put in matters of policy through a detailed study of the antiquary Sir Robert Cotton.[20] Arthur B. Ferguson, though veering on occasion into rather anachronistic conclusions, makes controversy the organizing principle of his monograph, *Clio Unbound*, clearly demonstrating that historical thought could reach new levels of clarity in the appeal to the past to make an argument.[21] Certainly polemical purposes underlay such endeavours as the rifling through 'divers and sundry chronicles' in Henry VIII's reign for evidence to support the break with Rome. Later in the sixteenth century, the same impulses drove the antiquarian endeavours of Archbishop Matthew Parker and his associates. In the early seventeenth century, a rather consensual narrative historiography was shaken in 1618 by John Selden's *History of Tithes*, a book that linked antiquarian erudition, historical narrative, and rhetorical argument for the first time in England and, as at least some of Selden's critics realized, threatened to make history a matter of 'interpretation'. The ideological fissures became canyons in the 1640s, and thereafter historical narrative and, to a less explicit degree, antiquarian scholarship, were driven in large measure by partisan concerns. Older worries about truth and reliability in the face of open ideological and methodological disagreement now returned with a vengeance.[22] The Restoration continued this tendency. Recent books by Justin Champion and Adrian Johns have demonstrated just how fundamental historical argument remained, whether its practitioners were defending the Anglican Church from enemies to the right and left, or cleverly reconstructing the history of the printing trades for a very specific purpose, to undermine the

[19] Pocock, *Ancient Constitution*; cf. P. G. Burgess, *Absolute Monarchy and the Stuart Constitution* (New Haven, 1996); id., *The Politics of the Ancient Constitution: An Introduction to English Political Thought, 1603–1642* (Basingstoke, 1992); C. Kidd, *British Identities before Nationalism: Ethnicity and Nationhood in the Atlantic World, 1600–1800* (Cambridge and New York, 1999); M. S. Zook, *Radical Whigs and Conspiratorial Politics in Late Stuart England* (University Park, Pa., 1999); J. R. Greenberg, *The Radical Face of the Ancient Constitution: St. Edward's 'Laws' in Early Modern Political Thought* (Cambridge, 2001).

[20] K. Sharpe, *Sir Robert Cotton 1586–1631: History and Politics in Early Modern England* (Oxford, 1979). Cf. Paul Christianson's study of another major antiquary in *Discourse on History, Law and Governance in the Public Career of John Selden, 1610–1635* (Toronto, 1996).

[21] Ferguson, *Clio Unbound*, pt. 2.

[22] Woolf, *Idea of History in Early Stuart England*, chs. 7 and 8, *passim*.

well-established monopoly of the Stationers' Company.[23] Paradoxically, a consequence of frequent disagreement as to the meaning, significance, value, or even factual details of certain key events in English history assisted in establishing these as mental landmarks in national consciousness. The Norman Conquest, Magna Carta, the Reformation, the Armada, and, later, the civil wars and Glorious Revolution, became common currency for dispute, collectively defining a shared agenda for historical debate that endured for much of the next three centuries.

Studies such as Ferguson's strongly suggest that to get at the heart of English historical consciousness we must move beyond study of the great historians and antiquaries of the period, however erudite and influential they appear to have been. Yet even if we simply move down the intellectual ladder to lesser-known writers, and provide studies of *their* texts, we will not be moving very far ahead; we would simply be asking the same set of questions again, substituting one slightly larger set of individuals for another. In this book, I wish to propose a different approach that does not undervalue conceptual, literary, and methodological innovations, but that looks beyond authors and their texts to the ambient cultural noise from which such innovations emerged.[24]

HISTORICAL CULTURE

The familiar terms 'historical writing', 'historiography', and even 'historical thought', all three of which will be used in different contexts in the present study,

---

[23] J. A. I. Champion, *The Pillars of Priestcraft Shaken: The Church of England and its Enemies, 1660–1730* (Cambridge, 1992); Adrian Johns, *The Nature of the Book: Print and Knowledge in the Making* (Chicago, 1998), ch. 5.

[24] This is not the first attempt to excavate the social foundations that give rise to historiography. A comparative perspective—not employed in the present study—has also been proposed at various times. J. G. A. Pocock, 'The Origins of Study of the Past: A Comparative Approach', *Comparative Studies in Society and History*, 4 (1961–2), 209–46, points to the benefits to be drawn by studying not only *what* the historians of a particular era said about their past but also the social, religious, and political grounds that encouraged or permitted them to say it. A more recent effort in the same direction is Donald Brown's *Hierarchy, History, and Human Nature* (Tucson, Ariz., 1988). This is an ambitious and suggestive work, by a social anthropologist, that melds Pocock's approach with experiences gleaned from anthropological fieldwork. Brown's book is impressive in its usage of Indian, south-east Asian, and oriental sources to obtain a broader picture of the relations between society and history, thereby meeting some of Pocock's desiderata. But it is fatally flawed by its author's subscription to an extreme and Eurocentric positivism. This is clearest in Brown's thesis that there are epistemologically more 'sound' (Brown's term, *passim*) historiographies in some (open-caste or class) societies and 'unsound' in others (closed-caste and rigidly hierarchical) societies, as opposed simply to different ways of perceiving and representing the past. The goal seems to be simply to explain, yet again, how the West got it right. Similar problems weaken J. H. Plumb's otherwise stimulating *The Death of the Past* (1969); see p. 14, wherein Chinese historians are praised but their tradition seen as of less value than Western 'critical historiography', a view belied by the work of many Sinologists, notably Benjamin Elman in *From Philosophy to Philology: Intellectual and Social Aspects of Change in Late Imperial China* (Cambridge, Mass. and London, 1984). Most recently, the postcolonial writer Ashis Nandy has turned this equation on its head, suggesting that historical consciousness is in essence little more than a modern Western imperialistic construct, which has imposed its violent and nationalist understanding of the past on the non-historical third world: A. Nandy, 'History's Forgotten Doubles', *History and Theory*, theme issue, 34 (1995), 44–66.

are terminologically inadequate to the task at hand. All denote phenomenal expressions or superstructures of a cultural tendency in England towards greater awareness of the past, and they are not the only such expressions. One can measure a people's interest in its past, at any time period, not only through their formal historiography, but also through other genres entirely, and through manuscript references to the past tucked away in diaries, genealogies, and letters. One can measure it not only through the content of history books written but also through the number of books published and the number of persons reading those books. One can measure it, as has been done with notable success for modern Britain,[25] through an interest in such matters as heritage, or the urge towards traditional values now being contested in British schools and driven largely by the residual legacy of Thatcherism. This has been done with even greater thoroughness by French scholars investigating their own country's reconstruction of its past and the institutional shaping of collective memory.[26]

As an umbrella term to capture what is being described in the present book, I have chosen the phrase 'historical culture'.[27] This is nothing more than a convenient shorthand for the perceptual and cognitive web of relations between past, present, and future. A historical culture gives rise to, nurtures, and is itself ultimately influenced by the formal historical writing of an era, but it also manifests itself in other ways, including many that look decidedly suspicious from the point of view of other periods. Thus the willingness of Tudor antiquaries to give credence as a 'source' to oral tradition, the subject of Chapter 10 below, or the desire of certain worthies to trace their family ancestry back to the remotest antiquity (Chapter 4), now appear odd from the point of view of our own historical culture, especially when judged according to the academic protocols by which the boundaries and practices of that culture are now more stringently policed. In short, any civilization has a historical culture (or possibly multiple cultures) specific to its time and circumstances, even those not especially interested in 'history' as such, as pre-Islamic India is often supposed to have been.[28]

A historical culture consists of habits of thought, languages, and media of communication, and patterns of social convention that embrace elite and popular, narrative and non-narrative modes of discourse. It is expressed both in texts and in commonplace forms of behaviour—for instance, the resolution of conflicts

[25] P. Wright, *On Living in an Old Country: The National Past in Contemporary Britain* (1985); R. Samuel, *Theatres of Memory* (London and New York, 1994); D. Lowenthal, *The Past is a Foreign Country* (Cambridge, 1985); id. and M. Binney (eds.), *Our Past Before Us: Why Do We Save It?* (1981).
[26] P. Nora (ed.), *Les Lieux de mémoire*, 3 vols. (Paris, 1984), of which a partial English translation is *Realms of Memory: Rethinking the French Past*, ed. L. D. Kritzman and trans. A. Goldhammer (New York, 1996); J. Revel and L. Hunt (eds.), *Histories: French Constructions of the Past*, trans. A. Goldhammer *et al.* (New York, 1995). For an English-speaking scholar's perspective on some of this, see R. Gildea, *The Past in French History* (New Haven, Conn., 1994).
[27] For a fuller definition see D. R. Woolf, 'A High Road to the Archives? Rewriting the History of Early Modern English Historical Culture', *Storia della storiografia*, 32 (1997), 33–59. My usage is closer to that of Bernard Guenée's work, cited above, than it is to the semiological analysis of Sande Cohen in *Historical Culture: On the Recoding of an Academic Discipline* (Berkeley, 1986).
[28] Nandy, 'History's Forgotten Doubles', 58–60.

through reference to a widely accepted historical standard such as 'antiquity'. The defining characteristics of a historical culture are subject to material, social, and circumstantial forces that, as much as the traditionally studied intellectual influences, condition the way in which the mind thinks, reads, writes, and speaks of the past. Above all, the notions of the past developed within any historical culture are not simply abstract ideas, recorded for the benefit of subsequent generations (and early third-millennium cultural historians). Rather, they are part of the mental and verbal specie of the society that uses them, passing among contemporaries through speech, writing, and other means of communication. This motion or process of exchange of elements of a historical culture may be called for convenience its 'social circulation'. If this book is concerned at one level with defining early modern historical culture rather than treating historical writing *per se*, so it is preoccupied at another with tracing the social circulation of that culture *within* early modern England and the channels through which this occurred, rather than with the linear transmission of select proto-modern ideas about and practices of historiography from that day to ours.

To assert that a country such as England had, at a particular juncture, a discernible historical culture within which various aspects of the past were identified and circulated by contemporaries is not, however, to paint a static picture. This should be expected given the length of the period under study, nearly a quarter-millennium from the Renaissance to the dawn of the Enlightenment. There are, as suggested above, extraordinary changes in some key aspects of discourse about the past between the beginning of the sixteenth century and the early eighteenth century. One of these, the changing perception of time, has been well studied in recent years but should here be noted briefly. By any standard, a major characteristic of modernity is its enforcement, through the state, of a uniform measurement of time. Since the sixteenth century, this has been gradually brought into effect through a centralized and national calendar of the sort David Cressy, Ronald Hutton, and Robert Poole have studied,[29] and by the growing influence of artificial means of keeping daily time. The eventual result, already emerging in the seventeenth century, was a single social time that overlapped with and gave shape to the sense of subjective personal time. The calendar, disseminated through print in the form of almanacs, also worked toward the homogenization of time, a process that Poole has recently chronicled from the Elizabethan age to the late eighteenth century. Lord Chesterfield's 1752 statute brought England's year into line with the Gregorian calendar and imposed 1 January as the legal new year's day (it had already been a day for giving new year's gifts), wiping out eleven days as it did so.[30] Well before this, however, English letter-writers and

---

[29] D. Cressy, *Bonfires and Bells: National Memory and the Protestant Calendar in Elizabethan and Stuart England* (1989); R. Hutton, *The Rise and Fall of Merry England: the Ritual Year, 1400–1700* (Oxford and New York, 1994); R. Poole, *Time's Alteration: Calendar Reform in Early Modern England* (1998). I am indebted to Robert Poole for allowing me to read much of his book prior to publication.

[30] Poole, *Time's Alteration*, 128 ff.

diarists were already surrendering to European convention, giving their dates in both styles, and in both years. 'In all dates, between the first of January and the 24th of March inclusive,' the Huguenot Francis Misson observed, 'they mark the double year in this manner, 169⁶₅.'[31]

Changes in the perception and measurement of time are manifested in a variety of commonplace features of early modern civilization, for instance in an increased interest in punctuality, and a greater emphasis on the commercial value of time. The equation of time and money has been seen by Jacques Le Goff and E. P. Thompson, among others, as critical to the development of commercial culture and subsequently of industrial capitalism.[32] A more acute awareness of temporality can also be found in the greater care taken to preserve the memory and record of the exact times and days of events such as crimes, births, funerals, marriages, and even more banal occurrences (the brawls or accidents that appear in court depositions). This was again something already enjoined by medieval law as a necessity for valid indictments, but it increased dramatically in the early modern era through urbanization and the growth of central and local bureaucracy. The seventeenth century's domestication of clocks and watches impressed on the family and the individual the same obsession with the hours that had previously had meaning only in corporate and public institutions.[33] Meanwhile, the keeping of parish registers, begun in 1538, provided an officially sanctioned, if often sporadically kept, record of the local population, sometimes turning into an informal chronicle of events.[34]

Other notable changes within the period have received less attention. Among those dealt with in the present book, perhaps the most remarkable is the progressive subordination of oral and mnemonic modes of commemorating and transmitting information to scribal/mechanical ones. The means of preserving the past are now fundamentally graphic, and have been since 1600, but it was not always so. It would perhaps be more accurate to say that writing achieved during the early modern era that authenticity as a medium for the past which it now enjoys, whereby document is privileged over tradition, text over memory, record over oral anecdote, and written bond over verbal agreement.[35] Oral modes of commemoration and transmission have never disappeared, and interest in them has recently experienced resurgence as academic historiography applies itself to

---

[31] François or Francis Misson, *M. Misson's Memoirs and Observations in his Travels over England*, trans. J. Ozell (London, 1719), 366.

[32] J. Le Goff, *Time, Work and Culture in the Middle Ages*, trans. Arthur Goldhammer (Chicago and London, 1980), 29–52; E. P. Thompson, 'Time, Work-Discipline, and Industrial Capitalism', *Past and Present*, 38 (1967), 56–97 (repr. in his *Customs in Common: Studies in Traditional Popular Culture* (New York, 1993), 352–403). The entire topic is reviewed, and the Le Goff thesis qualified somewhat, in G. Dohrn-van Rossum, *History of the Hour: Clocks and Modern Temporal Orders*, trans. T. Dunlap (Chicago and London, 1996).

[33] D. S. Landes, *Revolution in Time: Clocks and the Making of the Modern World* (Cambridge, Mass., 1983); C. M. Cipolla, *Clocks and Culture, 1300–1700* (repr. New York, 1977).

[34] Woolf, *Reading History in Early Modern England*, 74–5.

[35] On this last point especially I am indebted to Tim Stretton for furnishing me with a copy of his essay in progress, 'Words and Bonds and the Clash Between Law and Equity, 1580–1620'.

non-literate societies, but the beginnings of a long period of eclipse can be found in the seventeenth century.[36]

A similarly neglected topic is the progressive saturation of public and private discourses, oral and written, by historical references. Modes of speech, behaviour, and performance have explicit, often casual reference to historical episodes and persons. This was true in a more limited sense during the Middle Ages and the Renaissance (then with the exemplary function noted above, and predominantly on biblical or classical subjects). But it becomes much more frequent, and wider-ranging during and after the seventeenth century. Historical references and allusions creep into early modern discourse in ways that range far beyond formal history-writing. They can be found in both elite and popular story-telling, in jokes, in sermons, and in political debates. At the same time certain historical rituals (coronations, mayoral installations, public anniversary celebrations, and so on) are made more consciously allusive to and repetitive of the past, as they seek to emulate 'olden times' or to comply with 'time-hallowed tradition'. The physical remnants of the past, no longer simply the casual 'survivals' that blend in smoothly with the present and help to validate (often erroneously) the longevity of its institutions, begin to become exotic, foreign curiosities and even, where aesthetic principles permit, *objets d'art*. Instead of being put to utilitarian purposes, produced in evidence to resolve legal disputes, or made to serve some contemporary function, they are now to be collected and cherished in private cabinets, conserved and displayed to the respectable public through museums. The changes in attitude that occur, often in a single generation, can be quite subtle. The second earl of Peterborough, for instance, was said always to wear a dagger of Henry VIII on his person, emphasizing a personal connection to the past. His son-in-law, Sir John Germain, had no such wish to adorn himself with this weapon, whose pastness now rendered it 'other'. Instead, Germain displayed it in his cabinet of marvels, as he might a Roman coin or rare jewel: possessable, but out of fashion as an ornament, and thus more remote from his daily life.[37] It is matters such as these that will concern us in ensuing chapters.

The argument of this book can be summarized thus: that there was indeed a distinctive 'historical culture' during the early modern period; that it was not static but changing; and that both the culture itself and the changes thereto were sustained or effected by a process of social circulation, both horizontally among persons of roughly similar social and economic status, and vertically between persons of very different status. Connected with this more general argument are the following corollary propositions:

1. That during the early modern era, from roughly 1500 to the early decades of the eighteenth century, the English developed a more or less coherent—which

---

[36] A. Fox, *Oral and Literate Culture in England 1500–1700* (Oxford, 2000) is the fullest study of this subject.

[37] According to the account of Mary, Countess Cowper, who was shown Peterborough's collections by Germain in 1716: *Diary of Mary Countess Cowper*, ed. S. Cowper (London, 1864), 71–2.

does not mean 'uncontested'—historical sense of a *national* past.[38] This includes not merely the particular history of England itself and its relations with its British and Continental neighbours/enemies, but also the place of England, and eventually Britain,[39] within a world history that includes the classical and pre-classical eras.

2. That this national past was commemorated in, collected from, and rearticulated in various forms (narrative history, antiquarianism, chorography, philology on the 'factual' side; historical drama and verse on the 'fictional side') through a variety of media, written, oral, and printed.

3. That the media for commemorating the past were hierarchically arranged by the end of the seventeenth century, such that oral tradition and popular memory lost the status of authority that they had as sources of *history*, even while retaining them for local matters of custom—though here, too, in increasing conflict with the statute-making powers of the centralized state.

4. That these developments in turn owe less to narrowly conceived intellectual innovations such as the rediscovery of the ancients, or to the brilliant insights and heroic labours of individual historical authors than they do to social factors such as England's transition into a more clearly stratified society with an educated elite and a marginalized 'vulgar' culture, and to a broader shift in mentality such as the sense of change stimulated by observable alterations to the social and physical environment. These cultural changes did not occur instantaneously, nor even all at the same rate. On occasion the mid-seventeenth century appears to offer a convenient dividing-line between two rather different sets of assumptions and perceptions, but this is at best an arbitrary line admitting of exceptions on both sides.

In pursuing these lines of enquiry, I have striven not so much to tell a story about historiography, leading somewhere, as to paint the cultural landscape against which historiography developed; that landscape was itself unstable and looked much different in 1700 than it had a century or so earlier. To put it another way, I am not much concerned herein with the question of 'how historiography found its modern method', nor with discussing, except as it relates to the book's

---

[38] Bernard S. Cohn offers a brief definition as to what might characterize a 'modern' society, in terms of its shared attitudes to the past. 'I would speculate that a society is modern when it does have a past, when this past is shared by the vast majority of society, and when it can be used on a national basis to determine and validate behaviour.' B. S. Cohn, 'The Pasts of an Indian Village', in D. O. Hughes and T. R. Trautmann (eds.), *Time: Histories and Ethnologies* (Ann Arbor, 1995), 21–30, at p. 29. On the opposite of this 'sharing', namely the jockeying for control of a finite past by segments of a society, see A. Appadurai, 'The Past as a Scarce Resource', *Man*, NS 16 (1981), 201–19.

[39] L. Colley, *Britons: Forging the Nation, 1707–1837* (New Haven, 1992), is an important work dealing with the forging of a British, as opposed to English or Scottish, identity in the eighteenth century, and pointing to the construction of a historical past shared among English, Scots, and Welsh. However, much of this integration was preceded in the late sixteenth and seventeenth centuries by the development of a distinctively 'English' historical past. But cf. the treatment of ethnic identities in Kidd, *British Identities before Nationalism, passim*.

central themes, the essence of that method. Rather, I wish to explore a number of contexts within which the social circulation of the past occurred (many of which might appear to have precious little to do with historical writing *per se*) and how, within and through those circulatory occasions, a distinctive historical culture emerged by 1730 that was qualitatively different from the one that existed two centuries previously.

To carry out this design involves expanding the scope of the enquiry to include materials beyond formal historical writing; exploiting both published and unpublished sources containing references to the past in general and to history in particular; focusing on the overall development of English culture, rather than merely on the origins of a modern academic discipline; and looking at the problem over a more extended period than the few decades or so typically embraced in such works. In this account, many familiar names such John Leland, William Camden, Humfrey Wanley, or William Stukeley, among the antiquaries, will appear frequently, along with other, less familiar figures. The latter include Abraham de la Pryme, author of an informative diary of parish life at the end of the seventeenth century; William Holman, an inquisitive nonconformist minister who left a remarkable archive, now in the Essex Record Office; and several generations of the Blundells, a recusant family of Little Crosby, Lancashire, each of whom had particular historical interests arising from their home manor and a strong sense of religious persecution. Balancing more traditional sources to be found in printed texts or in major manuscript repositories such as the British and Bodleian libraries, family and other local archives have proved especially useful, providing a means of escape from a London- or university-centred perspective.

Although the various chapters all relate to the problematic outlined here, it has proved useful to group them into four major sections. Part I examines the general habits of mind that promoted a sense of the past, and more particularly some of the contexts within which this sense evolved. The particular aspects of that sense which have been selected for study here, and which are not the only possible aspects that could be so studied, include the various environmental and material reminders of temporal change and mutability, and changing attitudes to *deliberate* human change under such names as 'innovation' and 'improvement'. In Part II, this contextual discussion is spun in a different direction, towards consideration of a single major social issue, family ancestry and its proper valuation. This involved virtually every family above the level of yeoman (and some below) in direct confrontation with its past. English views of ancestry, together with the institutional framework for the validation of claims to hereditary honour and social status, mutated quite significantly in the long period under discussion. An unintended by-product of this change, rather than a deliberate consequence, was the development by the end of the seventeenth century of genealogy as a recognizable ancillary to history.

In Part III the growth of the antiquarian movement is examined. This is not, once again, by way of celebrating its methodological achievements in philology, palaeography, and numismatics, important as those were, but rather to explore the ways in which historical knowledge and historical objects alike circulated through society, fuelling historical consciousness rather in the same way that the movement of money and goods fuels an economy. Here, less attention is paid to the individual contributions of the major antiquaries of the period than to asking how and why they were able to conduct their research and communicate it. We must also ask how the collection and display of the 'trophies' of time figured in the refashioning of civilized society, a society that turned the past into a field for recreation and a source of visible and tangible aesthetic pleasure. The recovery of coins, urns, and ancient statuary owed a good deal to the literally ground-breaking work of ploughboys and day-labourers, something that is generally overlooked, and the final chapter in this part illustrates a particular variety of social circulation, namely the participation by both literate and non-literate in an 'archaeological economy'. At the same time these chapters note the advent of a visual dimension in the perception and representation of the past. This in turn encouraged a crucial shift in antiquarian practice, away from the interpretation of the physical world exclusively through the lens of philology, towards a much greater reliance on direct observation of objects and their comparison and categorization, without reference to classical categories and textual authorities.[40]

From the tangible and visible we move in Part IV to the spoken and remembered. These chapters pick up on the subject of elite/popular intercourse in a related context: the recollection and circulation of popular beliefs and perceptions. Keith Thomas drew the outlines of this in a suggestive lecture in 1983.[41] The present treatment builds on Thomas's work to deal with the place of memory in commemorating such perceptions; with local beliefs about particular places or persons; and, finally, with the striking change in attitude towards such beliefs among early modern antiquaries, the contemporary equivalents of our anthropologists. In reprinting here, in much-revised versions, three essays first published between 1988 and 1993, I argue that a distinctively English, national historical culture, the culture of what 'every schoolboy knows' was created at a cost. By 1700, the world of scholarship had marginalized both intellectually and socially the sort of 'local knowledge' which those sixteenth-century elite visitors had previously found useful and informative. Their successors, from about the mid-seventeenth century, found such information largely repugnant, vulgar, and superstitious, and they gave scant credence to its oral provenance. This change in judgement and taste has at least as much to do with the changing nature of relations between elite and popular culture as it does with the influence of a humanist classical education. Such an education was shared by John Leland, an early sixteenth-century antiquary who used oral information freely, and Thomas Hearne, his

---

[40] Among the many treatments of late seventeenth-century antiquarian activities, see especially M. Hunter, *John Aubrey and the Realm of Learning* (1975). This is especially good in addressing the multifaceted interests of late Stuart scholarship.

[41] K. Thomas, *The Perception of the Past in Early Modern England* (Creighton Lecture, 1983).

eighteenth-century editor, who disparaged both oral sources and the errors that they perpetuated. The conventions of historical scholarship and writing had undoubtedly changed a good deal in the two centuries that separate Leland from Hearne. But the changes in the social, political, and cultural worlds that those two scholars inhabited were incomparably more profound.

Part I

THE PAST AND THE PRESENT

CHAPTER ONE

Consciousness of Change

The times, the times are chang'd.

(John Fletcher, *The tragoedy of Rollo, duke of Normandy* (Oxford, 1640),
I. i, p. 3)

ANXIETY ABOUT THE accelerating pace of change has been a defining mark
of modern culture for over a century. Long before the post-atomic doomsday
scenarios of the 1950s and 1960s, and the current frenetic developments in information technology, Henry Adams, attempting to measure the 'velocity' of history according to the laws of thermodynamics, expressed the view that the world
would 'break its neck' from over-acceleration by 1950. As a modern historian commented a few years before the computer revolution of the 1980s, 'nothing defines
our age more than the furious and relentless increase in the rate of change'.[1] This
chapter will deal with the experience of change between the sixteenth and early
eighteenth centuries, when the pace was far slower than in Henry Adams's time,
but also more noticeable than it had been in the past.

A sense of change, regardless of whether it is understood to be a positive or a
negative, has always been taken as a precondition of the ability to think historically. Without change, write Diane O. Hughes and Thomas R. Trautmann, 'there
is no temporal reality; and it is no accident that the most drastic recognitions
of change—the fall of Rome, the French Revolution—seem to evoke the most
powerful historical narratives'; it is change, together with chronological sequence
and a sense of coherence, that marks most modern historical writing as an
attempt to reduce the confusion of discrete events into narrative, a point also made
by Hayden White.[2] R. W. Southern has made similar observations in a slightly
different vein, commenting on the connection between flourishing historical studies and a perception of chaos and disruption in the present that threatens to alien-
ate the individual from his own time. 'So far as there is a central tradition in our
historical writing, it arises from this recurrent need to understand and stabilize
the present by reviving the experience of the past', Southern suggests, pointing

[1] A. M. Schlesinger Jr., 'The Modern Consciousness and the Winged Chariot', in B. S. Gorman
and A. E. Wessman (eds.), *The Personal Experience of Time* (New York, 1977), 267–88, at pp. 268–9,
whence comes also the quotation from Henry Adams.
[2] D. O. Hughes and T. R. Trautmann (eds.), *Time: Histories and Ethnologies* (Ann Arbor, 1995),
Introduction, p. 5; H. White, 'The Value of Narrativity in the Representation of Reality', in his *The
Content of the Form* (Baltimore, 1987).

out that the years after the Norman Conquest mark one such period of reaction to change, and the six decades between 1560 and 1620 another.[3]

Michel de Certeau has asserted that 'Modern Western history essentially begins with differentiation between the *present* and the *past* . . . historiography separates its present time from a past.'[4] It has been orthodoxy for rather longer that Europe first acquired a more profound sense of distance from the past and an awareness of change during the Renaissance.[5] In the literary world, humanists had much to do with this, beginning as early as Petrarch, and there is a happy coincidence, noted by the great art historian Erwin Panofsky, between the achievement of a sense of historical anachronism and the beginnings of visual realism in the arts, especially in narrative history painting. In Panofsky's famous phrase, the Renaissance first achieved the reintegration of classical form with classical content, taking ancient material already known to the Middle Ages but now representing it in a manner that more closely reflected the original reality. Greeks and Romans now became ancient statesmen, soldiers, and philosophers, more or less appropriately garbed, rather than medieval knights, just as humanist historians adopted classical models to write their accounts of civic history, and philologers strove to restore Latin to a Ciceronian purity. The correspondence between past entity and modern image was never mechanical nor narrowly literal. The theory of narrative painting from Alberti in the fifteenth century to Richardson and Reynolds in the eighteenth century permitted creative manipulation and imaginative juxtaposition of characters, stretching literal historical truth in the interests of aesthetic principles.[6] A parallel debate in poetics raised the issue of just *how* literal-minded dramatists, poets, and even historians themselves had to remain—how far rhetoric could be allowed artfully to twist the facts to a higher didactic or poetic end. Yet there can be no doubt that humanism achieved much in both the visual and literary worlds by way of promoting both a general awareness of change, a more highly developed sense of period, and an understanding of a past reality that required both scholarly knowledge and imaginative apprehension in order to be re-created meaningfully in the present.

The problem with this explanation is that it generally peers no further than the doctrines of humanism and the insights of a brilliant few, without questioning why this understanding of historical period and temporal difference came about. It is tough to imagine the Renaissance without Petrarch, Bruni, and Valla, each of whom contributed in different ways to humanist historical thought. But their great insights into the changes wrought by a millennium of medieval life and thought were not, it must surely be agreed, the product of divine revelation or sheer genius alone. It has long been recognized, for instance, that Bruni's own classicization

---

[3] R. W. Southern, 'Aspects of the European Tradition of Historical Writing: 4. The Sense of the Past', *TRHS*, 5th ser., 23 (1973), 243–63. My only disagreement with Southern's perceptive article is that it does not take into account the more radical change in historical writing and thought wrought by the civil war, nor the deeper, and socially more widely spread, perceptions of cultural change in realms beyond the political.

[4] M. de Certeau, *The Writing of History*, trans. T. Conley (New York, 1988), 2–3.

[5] The classic brief account of this is P. Burke, *The Renaissance Sense of the Past* (1969).

[6] D. Irwin, *Neoclassicism* (1997), 132, on neoclassical efforts at historical accuracy.

of political discourse, and in turn the full-scale humanist history of Florence that marked the high point of his later career, were inspired by a profound sense of political instability induced by his city's near conquest at the hands of the Visconti between 1397 and 1402. Similar concerns would animate the thoughts about past and present, history and political action, of Machiavelli and Guicciardini amid a similar series of crises a century later.[7]

All of these authors wrote political historiography of the classical humanist variety, so it is not surprising that when we look for external influences we turn first to their political careers and contexts, and to the political concepts and vocabulary—the linguistic context advocated by Professors Pocock and Skinner. But not all thought about the past was either cast in classical categories or necessarily concerned with politics. It is making humanism do double duty to assign it, in addition, responsibility for the general sense of change that had emerged across Europe by the mid-seventeenth century. It is possible, without taking anything away from the *intellectual* achievements of Italian, French, German, and English humanists in the literary, religious, and political spheres, to argue for a more general sense of change that developed at the same time as humanism, but sprang from quite other sources. This chapter will deal with the general reorientation of English thought in the sixteenth and seventeenth centuries towards the acceptance and even promotion of useful change, as a response to the inescapable fact of actual, observable change in the material and cultural environment. In the next chapter, the tensions between oldness and novelty will be explored more directly, together with the ambivalent attitude of commentators to the religious, moral, and cultural implications of change.

CHANGE AND THE MATERIAL ENVIRONMENT

Throughout the pre-industrial age, technological developments were slowly but subtly altering the domestic and external environments. Alterations to the landscape, or to the economic base of an area, inevitably excited comment; fen drainage, new mining techniques, and the development of some medium-scale industries could alter a local community's relationship with its natural environment. The court of sewers at Boston decided in 1554 that a drain called the Old Syke, issuing from Holland fen, was not sufficiently wide or deep, and locals were commanded to undertake appropriate repairs. In such circumstances, the change could be viewed simply, in the phrasing of a Henrician statute, as providing 'reformacion and amendement' to restore an object to its original, pristine form and remove ruin and decay; it was not necessary to conceive of change as creating something new.[8]

---

[7] H. Baron, *The Crisis of the Early Italian Renaissance*, rev. edn. (Princeton, NJ, 1966).

[8] *Records of the Commissioners of Sewers in the Parts of Holland, 1547–1603*, ed. A. M. Kirkus, Lincolnshire Rec. Soc., 54 (1959), 12, 27; *Statutes of the Realm*, III. 368–72, 23 Hen. VIII, cap. 5. This is rather the same distinction that permits property-owners in some countries today to deduct from income the cost of doing extensive renovations, such as the repair of an old porch, whereas its complete replacement by a new one would have to be accounted as a taxable capital gain.

In other cases, however, tradition won out over technology. When a Devonshire landowner constructed a gravel weir in order to improve his irrigation, the parish of Fennyton complained that this diversion of the river from 'his right and aunciente course' was causing the decay of bridges, and they secured an order from the judges of assize for the raising of banks to return the river to its former course.[9] Abraham de la Pryme, whose Flemish grandfather had lost a small fortune on the draining of the Great Level Fen sixty years earlier, was raised to believe that such technological tampering was against nature. The flood of the fen in 1697 reinforced his belief 'that one time it will come to its ancient state again, which will be the ruin of all those that have land therein'.[10] Changes in the natural environment, or in the techniques of its control, were observable to a far wider spectrum of the population, though most of our evidence derives from the comments of the literate. Michael Drayton lamented the deforestation of England in the preceding two centuries, while technical developments such as fen drainage or the damming of rivers were perceived as interfering with the ancient course of nature, as well as interfering with the traditional relationship of local people to the landscape.[11]

We are apt to divide early modern statements about the position of the present with respect to the past into those asserting the inevitability of decline and those advocating the possibility of improvement. This is rather an artificial and simplistic division, since even the most vociferous exponents of either view felt a strong ambivalence. Not all writers agreed that *all* things were either better or worse than in former times. Few commentators could be cheerier than Robert Reyce when it came to enumerating the contemporary virtues of his native Suffolk. Reyce saw the world as 'nothing butt a shop of all change', and repeated the topos that these were 'unfaithfull times' and took it as given that 'in the latter times . . . the earth through extreme age is become less fruitfull then in former times'. Yet human ingenuity had developed to counteract nature, and new techniques of tillage and fertilization had, he believed, made his an age 'wherein all things are so improved'. Though some things, such as his shire's reputation for dairying, had decayed, it was only natural that 'things should [not] be so currant as they were wont to bee in times past'.[12]

It was possible to distinguish between technical progress and moral decline, and to imagine both occurring simultaneously. The Devon antiquary Thomas Westcote thought that human nature had grown considerably worse in the century before he wrote: charity, piety, and 'thoughtful deeds' had declined; along with many others, he blamed this on the pillaging of the monasteries. On the other hand, when he observed his native county he was filled, like Robert Reyce

---

[9] *Western Circuit Assize Orders*, ed. J. S. Cockburn, Camden Soc., 4th ser., 17 (1976), 5–6.

[10] *The Diary of Abraham de la Pryme, the Yorkshire Antiquary*, ed. C. Jackson, Surtees Soc., 54 (1870), 168.

[11] Michael Drayton, *Poly-Olbion*, ii. 145–8, in *Works of Michael Drayton*, ed. J. W. Hebel, 2nd edn., 5 vols. (Oxford, 1961), iv. 33.

[12] Robert Reyce, *Suffolk in the XVIIth Century*, ed. F. Hervey (1902), 40 f., 45, 52, 58.

a few years earlier, with respect for the environmental improvements that had been made in the preceding century or so: 'Viewing the now present state, comparing it with those former ages we have spoken of, you cannot but marvel, admire, yea! wonder at the strange metamorphosis for the better.' Where ravenous beasts once had preyed, there were now houses, churches, and entire towns; valleys of thistles had been transformed into fields full of sheep and cattle. George Owen made similar comments about his native Wales; he believed that the century of the Tudors had wrought such marvellous changes 'that if our ffathers weare nowe lyvinge they wowld thinke it som straunge countrey inhabited wth a forran nation, so altered is the cuntrey and cuntreymen . . . from evill to good, and from good to better'.[13]

Environmental change might only be slowly noticed in the countryside. In London and the other towns which expanded between 1500 and 1700, it was more commonplace, and more speedily noted. The economic and agrarian changes of the sixteenth century ensured that there were social winners and losers among families and communities. While some towns, such as Bristol and Norwich, prospered, others, such as Coventry and Hull, decayed from their former status as prosperous communities, and many smaller villages disappeared altogether. Inevitably, observers tended to magnify the depths to which things had sunk over the previous century or so. The villagers of Dunwich in Suffolk had it by 'common fame and report' in the early seventeenth century that 'before the towne came to decay, there belonged thereunto, two and fifty religious houses, as parish churches', as well as priories, hospitals, chapels, and windmills.[14] The Somerset antiquary Thomas Gerard was particularly struck by the decay of Ilchester from a bustling medieval commercial centre of ten parishes into a small village without a franchise. Imagining 'the former glory of this place, and seeing it now' put him in mind of his contemporary John Weever's comment concerning decayed Verulam, 'Here's a Citty in a grave.'[15] The parishioners of Stock in Essex, which had long lost its status as a major pottery-producing community, continued to refer to their loamy soil as 'brick-and-pot earth' in the reign of George I.[16]

Old buildings were now used for purposes that maligned the memories of their founders. John Stow, on seeing a stone and timber house in the London parish of Allhallows, which then belonged to Sir Edward Coke, was saddened by its recent

[13] Thomas Westcote, A view of Devonshire (written c.1630; 1st edn., Exeter, 1845), 37; George Owen, 'Dialogue of the government of Wales', in The Description of Penbrokeshire, ed. H. Owen, Cymmrodorion Rec. Soc., 4 vols. (1892–1936), iii. 56; M. Aston, 'English Ruins and English History: The Dissolution and the Sense of the Past', Journal of the Warburg and Courtauld Institutes, 36 (1973), 232–55.

[14] John Weever, Ancient funerall monuments within the united monarchie of Great Britaine, Ireland, and the islands adjacent (1631), 718.

[15] Thomas Gerard, The particular description of the county of Somerset, ed. E. H. Bates, Somerset Rec. Soc., 15 (1900), 205–6; Leland remarked on the decay of this town a century earlier: Leland's Itinerary, i. 156.

[16] Essex RO D/Y/1/1/87 (Holman papers), unfoliated (Thomas Cox to Rev. William Holman, 14 Dec. 1716).

decline into a place for 'poulterers, for stabling of horses and stowage of poul-
try', and its renting out to 'strangers, and other mean people'. The same sense
of decayed grandeur would drive Edward Gibbon, surveying ruined Roman tem-
ples two centuries later, to write the *Decline and Fall of the Roman Empire*.[17] The
ruins of a Devon castle both exhilarated and depressed Tristram Risdon, reminding him of his own mortality:

> If castles made of lime and stone decay,
> What surety is in bodies made of clay?[18]

While the social and economic developments of the sixteenth and seventeenth
centuries unfolded, the buildings in which people lived changed with them;
rising food prices gave producers, even below the level of the gentry, surplus funds
to invest in their own domestic comfort. Among the most obvious mutations
were the materials used for building themselves, though these continued to vary
by region.[19] W. G. Hoskins's 'great rebuilding' of rural England in the period
1560–1640 was answered in the Restoration and Hanoverian periods by a similar
makeover in towns as the ornate carving of the Renaissance was renounced for
the simplicity of columns and classical ornamentation. Tile and slate supplanted
pebble and turf or thatch for roofs. Dr Borsay has shown that at least twenty-
four provincial towns built new halls or mayor's residences between 1655 and 1730,
but the trend towards establishing civic identity through the construction of central halls had already been well established under the Tudors and early Stuarts.[20]
Much of this rebuilding was by accretion, helped along by the occasional urban
cataclysm. Few changes in urban prospect were quite as radical or dramatic as
those occasioned by the Great Fire in 1666, when most of old inner London was
razed, its medieval and Tudor parish churches to be replaced by Wren's classicism. Other towns, however, experienced serious blazes that permitted thorough
rebuilding and changes in street planning: Warwick's destructive fire in 1694
destroyed much of its vernacular architecture, but a classically designed modern
provincial city soon arose from medieval and Tudor ashes.[21]

---

[17] John Stow, *The Survey of London*, ed. H. B. Wheatley (1912; repr. 1980), 147; cf. his similar comments on the decay of the church of St Michael the Archangel in Cornhill since the seizure of its
lands by the Edwardian regime, ibid. 175–6. For an earlier example of Gibbon's more famous sentiments, see Henry Savage's comment about Quakers using the kitchen of the ruined Glastonbury Abbey
as a meeting house, Bristol RO MS 36074 (88), p. 147.

[18] Tristram Risdon, *The chorographical description or survey of the county of Devon* (1811), 196.

[19] Pevsner, *BE: Shropshire* (1958), 27–9; M. Airs, *The Making of the English Country House
1500–1640* (1975), 111. As Airs observes, the first edition of Harrison's *Description of England* (1577)
notes a lack of wood only in the fenlands; by the second edition a decade later, that scarcity, attributed to new building, was extended to 'northerne parts'.

[20] F. Heal, *Hospitality in Early Modern England* (Oxford, 1990), 164; P. Borsay, *The English Urban
Renaissance: Culture and Society in the Provincial Town 1660–1770* (Oxford, 1989), 54–5, 325–8; R. Tittler,
Architecture and Power (Oxford, 1991), *passim*.

[21] Bodl. MS Tanner 142 ('Churches & parishes in London consumed by the late dreadfull fire' (n.d.)),
fos. 18[r], 25[r]. The church of St Dionys Backchurch parish, for instance, was completely rebuilt, and
paid for, by the beginning of 1679—a relatively short period if one remembers that most medieval

These alterations to the look, size, and orientation of urban buildings between the mid-sixteenth and mid-eighteenth centuries both encouraged and signified a heightening of historical awareness. They also promoted the gradual development of a sense of 'period', though we should exercise some caution in reading contemporary accounts of environmental, as much as moral, change, since these were often affected as much by attitudes and circumstances as by 'objective' observation. John Stow (1525–1605) lived through an extraordinary half-century of reconstruction in which many of the buildings of his childhood were either destroyed or refashioned to suit changing tastes. His understanding of the layers of architecture that enveloped his world, rather than a university humanism to which he lacked access, gave Stow both his tremendous sense of the past and his enthusiasm for the Middle Ages. He had an ability, unequalled among his contemporaries, of comparing the past and present as they appeared to him in the streets and stone walls of his beloved London, in order to make 'the alteration . . . easily appear'.[22] His nostalgic recollection of the past—rather selective, as both Ian Archer and Patrick Collinson have noted—was as much a function of his advanced age (he was in his seventies when he penned the *Survey of London*) as of the religious conservatism of which he has sometimes been charged. As Collinson notes, 'Old men hate change.'[23]

Stow's comments summarized, with a sentimental spin, several decades of urban change. But even in the briefer compass of a few years, it was possible to note smaller-scale differences in housing, other buildings and structures, and the layout of the city. Comparable observations could be made in provincial towns and parishes. Richard Carew, who had a less pessimistic outlook on the present, nevertheless noted alterations in the style of Cornish housing at the close of the sixteenth century. He also commented on the gradual encroachment of the sea on the Cornish coast at Land's End; Tudor fishermen had 'drawn up peeces of doores and windowes' in their nets, remnants of a time when the shore extended further out. Within parishes, old people could remember changes from the days of their youth, and even older changes knowledge of which passed down by tradition.[24]

churches were built over many more years. Cf. T. F. Reddaway, *The Rebuilding of London after the Great Fire* (1940); J. E. N. Hearsey, *London and the Great Fire* (1965); Borsay, *English Urban Renaissance*, pp. vii, 45–6. For examples of fires, principally during the civil wars, and the destruction they caused, see S. Porter, *Destruction in the English Civil Wars* (1994), 13–14, 17, 71, 88–9.

[22] Stow, *Survey of London*, 74; C. Platt, *The Great Rebuildings of Tudor and Stuart England: Revolutions in Architectural Taste* (London and Bristol, P., 1994); W. G. Hoskins, 'The Rebuilding of Rural England, 1570–1640', *Past and Present*, 4 (1953), 44–59; J. E. Crowley, *The Invention of Comfort: Sensibilities and Design in Early Modern Britain and Early America* (Baltimore, 2000), 58–62; R. Tittler, *The Reformation and the Towns in England* (Oxford, 1998), 254–69; id., *Architecture and Power: The Town Hall and the English Urban Community, 1500–1640* (Oxford, 1991); B. L. Beer, *Tudor England Observed: The World of John Stow* (Phoenix Mill and Stroud, England, 1998), 127–46.

[23] I. Archer, 'The Nostalgia of John Stow', in D. L. Smith, R. Strier, and D. Bevington (eds.), *The Theatrical City: Culture, Theatre and Politics in London, 1576–1649* (Cambridge, 1995), 17–34; P. Collinson, 'John Stow and Nostalgic Antiquarianism', in J. F. Merritt (ed.), *Imagining Early Modern London: Perceptions and Portrayals of the City from Stow to Strype, 1598–1720* (Cambridge, 2001), 27–51.

[24] Richard Carew, *The survey of Cornwall* (1602), fo. 3. For tradition and the oral circulation of historical knowledge, see below, Ch. 10.

A tradition in the parish of Myddle in 1700 had it that 'there was noe peiws in churches before the reformation', but the local antiquary, Richard Gough, who had consulted 'certaine antient cases in law-books', knew this to be an error.[25] In the same year, Abraham de la Pryme generalized from the example of his own parish of Hatfield Chase, Yorkshire, magnifying the prosperity of the poorer sort:

The town itself, tho' it be but little yet tis very handsom & neat, the manner of the buildings that it formerly had were all of wood, clay and plaster, but now that way of building is quite left of, for every one now from the richest to the poorest will not build unless with bricks: so that now from about 80 years ago, (at which time bricks were first seen, used & made in this parish) they have been wholy used & now there scarce is one house in the town that dos not if not wholy yet for the most part consist of that lasting & genteel sort of building.[26]

John Aubrey—who also observed a decline of foxes and martins since his grandfather's day—waxed nostalgic about the social uses of pre-Reformation architecture. As highly sensitive to changes in the environment as he was to changes in popular culture, he noted, with some exaggeration, the increase in glass windows since his childhood, so that 'Now, the poorest people that are upon almes, have it.'[27]

The rebuilding trend accelerated in the seventeenth and eighteenth centuries through the advent of Palladian, baroque, and finally Gothic styles, which were overlapping rather than successive.[28] The flights of taste from Gothic to neoclassicism and back again from the early seventeenth to early nineteenth centuries reflect more than simply changing preferences for the shape of the material environment; they are indicative of tides in attitudes towards antiquity and the Middle Ages.[29] The decision taken in 1624 to build the library of St John's College, Cambridge with Gothic rather than Jacobean windows, was a deliberate

---

[25] Richard Gough, *The History of Myddle*, ed. D. Hey (1980), 77.

[26] BL MS Lans. 897 (Abraham de la Pryme, 'History and Antiquities of Hatfield Chase, Yorkshire', c.1700), fo. 40^r.

[27] John Aubrey, *Wiltshire. The Topographical Collections of John Aubrey, FSA*, ed. J. E. Jackson (Devizes, 1862), 5, 8. Aubrey may have been the first Englishman actually to write a treatise on changes in medieval architecture complete with pictures, in the fourth section of his unpublished *Monumenta Britannica*: H. M. Colvin, 'Aubrey's *Chronologia Architectonica*', in J. Summerson (ed.), *Concerning Architecture* (1968), 1–12.

[28] E. Mercer, 'The Houses of the Gentry', *Past and Present*, 5 (1954), 11–32, argues that the first wave of Palladianism under Inigo Jones's influence remained a court phenomenon, rejected by the country and by London urban builders who preferred traditional and imitation Gothic. This is persuasively revised, however, by Giles Worsley, who stresses Jones's wider and earlier influence: *Classical Architecture in Britain: The Heroic Age* (New Haven and London, 1995), 4, 14.

[29] J. Isaacs, 'The Gothick Taste', *Journal of the Royal Institute of British Architects*, 59/9 (July 1952), 336–40; Worsley, *Classical Architecture in Britain*, 178–9, and id., 'The Origins of the Gothic Revival: A Reappraisal', *TRHS*, 6th ser., 3 (1993), 105–50; P. Thompson, 'The Survival and Revival of Gothic Architecture', *Apollo*, 76 (May 1962), 283–7; M. Girouard, 'Elizabethan Architecture and the Gothic Tradition', *Architectural History*, 6 (1963), 23–38. For the development of the word 'Gothic' as a style, see A. E. Longueil, 'The Word "Gothic" in Eighteenth Century Criticism', *Modern Language Notes*, 38 (1923), 453–60 and, with special reference to architecture, E. S. de Beer, 'Gothic: Origin and Diffusion of the Term; the Idea of Style in Architecture', *Journal of the Warburg and Courtauld Institutes*, 11 (1948), 149–62. For later Gothicism amid an era of industrial progress, see C. Dellheim, *The Face of the Past: The Preservation of the Medieval Inheritance in Victorian England* (Cambridge, 1982).

one, ascribed by Giles Worsley to the strength of antiquarian learning at the universities and to a clerical distaste for radical change. Like the determination of Christopher Wren, fifty years later, to put a Gothic tower on a Tudor gatehouse at Christ Church, this was the self-conscious act of men who 'like the best the old fashion of church windows, holding it most meet for such a building'. This is a very early example of a carefully conceived attempt to imitate a past clearly perceived as remote and dead. Worsley has shown that there were many others, though they must still be distinguished from many instances of unconscious Gothic 'survivals', late hangovers from the Middle Ages.[30]

Being surrounded by old objects by no means necessitated an appreciation of their aesthetic and historical qualities. Often quite the opposite was true. Buildings and other structures were routinely demolished and cannibalized in order to provide the materials for replacements, often with a lack of sensitivity to their past that appalled a tiny minority but which otherwise encountered little interference in those pre-Heritage Trust days. The worst enemy of the ancient Roman roads, remarked both William Camden and Sir Thomas Browne, was not time but 'the countrie people digging gravell out of them'.[31] Medieval structures fared no better. John Percival noted of Colchester Castle in 1701 that 'the proprietors are every day pulling it down to sell the materials, the bricks again for building, and the Flints for paving their Streets or mending their highways'. The ruins of Glastonbury Abbey were still providing scavengers with building material a century after the monastic dissolution. An old tower at Lowicke, standing on property disputed by Sir Thomas Haggerston and Sir John Swinburne, was pulled down in 1700 by labourers in Haggerston's employ so that the stones could be used 'to build a barne for some of his tenants'.[32]

Although antiquaries would decry the deliberate vandalism of funeral monuments and works of art, the remnants of the past were in less danger from either concerted iconoclasm or popular ignorance than from the determination of estate owners to keep their properties in good repair while reusing resources such as stone and brick, as John Neale did when he paid a labourer £3. 1s. 4d. for 'taking down an old brick wall' in his garden and laying the foundation of a new one. The minute book of repairs to the church of St Dunstan in the West, London, in the early 1660s, records stones being salvaged from the foundation, sorted from rubbish, and reused.[33] In 1743 the Society of Antiquaries would log, as the sole

---

[30] B. Sprague Allen, *Tides in English Taste (1619–1800): A Background for the Study of Literature*, 2nd edn., 2 vols. (New York, 1958), i. 47–54, ii. 43–86; N. Pevsner, *The Englishness of English Art* (1956), 56–7; Girouard, 'Elizabethan Architecture', 36; Worsley, *Classical Architecture in Britain*, 175–95, and id., 'Origins of the Gothic Revival', for the argument that Gothic revivalism (as opposed to unconscious survival) can be found as early as the 1550s.

[31] *Letters of Sir Thomas Browne*, in *Works of Sir Thomas Browne*, ed. G. L. Keynes, 2nd edn., 4 vols. (Chicago, 1964), iv. 314 (Browne to Dugdale, 11 Dec. 1658, citing Camden).

[32] *The English Travels of Sir John Percival and William Byrd II*, 47; Northumberland RO, ZSW/510/1 (John Gardner to Sir John Swinburne, 3 June 1700).

[33] Bodl. MS Top. Essex f. 1, fo. 39ᵛ (Neale of Alborough Hatch, Essex), 26 Sept. 1683; CUL MS Add. 4144 (minute book of St Dunstan in the West, 1659–63), fo. 10ʳ, 5 July 1661.

entry on its rather short list of the 'preservers of antiquities', brave Betty Bruce, who had implored her father to spare a Roman circular building on his land near Falkirk, known locally as 'Arthur's O'on' or oven, which he had determined to dismantle for material to build a park wall. Although Betty would be married in the building a few days afterwards, her father eventually had his way and 'pulld it down in earnest, to mend a mill-dam', to the outrage of the antiquarian community.[34] Antiquarian scruples were not always so deeply felt when it came to putting the remnants of the past back into daily use. The habitual smoker John Batteley, archdeacon of Canterbury from 1687 to 1708, and a great lover of Roman objects, was not above keeping his tobacco in a Roman urn. His more learned junior, William Wotton, saw no difficulty in ingratiating himself with the archdeacon by sending him an even bigger urn, dug up at Sandy in Bedfordshire, 'which will hold three or four pounds of tobacco'.[35]

Religious buildings had a special aura that did not apply to secular objects and structures. The same horror at the misuse of sacred property that informs Henry Spelman's gruesome *History and Fate of Sacrilege* emerges from the diary of William Blundell the younger, one-time royalist officer and fervent Catholic. Blundell recounts a cautionary tale he himself had heard from a clergyman. The story itself concerns a cross at Tewkesbury, pulled down by a puritan minister 'long before the general ruin of crosses through England'. A puritan townsman of low status having made use of the stones from the cross for erecting a wall around his well, and even devoting some 'wherein had been pictures of Our Lady and St. John' to the manufacture of troughs, was justly rewarded by his wife and children being struck blind, and himself soon after drowning in his own well.[36] Objections such as this were no more successful at restraining the reuse of ecclesiastical fabric than they were at restoring ecclesiastical revenues. The maintenance of church fabric was a constant problem as those older buildings not destroyed outright by fire or civil war depredations simply decayed. The great concern of the Caroline regime for physical improvements to the conditions of churches in the 1630s has recently been demonstrated,[37] and the problem of what accountants now call accumulated deferred maintenance continued to worsen during the second half of the seventeenth century and afterwards. The chapel of St Mary in Kingston upon Thames, where a number of Anglo-Saxon kings were buried, collapsed into rubble in 1730 when one of its arches gave way, the victim of grave-digging inside the church.

[34] SAL Antiquaries MS 268, fo. 76ᵛ; J. Nichols, *Bibliotheca Topographica Britannica* (1780–90), vol. iii, pp. 385–6; I. G. Brown, ' "Gothicism, Ignorance, and a Bad Taste": The Destruction of Arthur's O'on', *Antiquity*, 48 (1974), 283–7. William Stukeley's account of this monument would inspire the Scottish antiquary Alexander Gordon (who, moving to London in 1736, succeeded Stukeley as secretary to the Society of Antiquaries) to publish his *Itinerarium Septentrionale,* a lavishly illustrated collection of Roman and Danish antiquities in Scotland and the north of England.
[35] Nichols, *Literary Illustrations,* iv. 99 (Wotton to Batteley, 9 July 1704).
[36] Blundell, *Cavalier's Notebook,* p. 103. (This William Blundell, known as 'the Cavalier', should not be confused with his same-named grandfather William Blundell the elder; both are mentioned frequently in the present book.) The *locus classicus* of such cautionary tales involving former ecclesiastical property is Henry Spelman, *The History and Fate of Sacrilege* (1698 but written in the 1630s); cf. A. Walsham, *Providence in Early Modern England* (Oxford, 1999), 109.
[37] K. Sharpe, *The Personal Rule of Charles I* (New Haven and London, 1993), 308–28.

The similar fate of Greenwich church, the roof of which fell in 1710 after grave-digging undermined a pillar, led the antiquary Samuel Gale to call for an end to burials beneath church floors.[38]

The fate of the remains of old buildings raised the connected issue of what we would now call 'recycling', the deliberate adaptation of older materials into new structures. This was a commonplace and accepted practice where construction was concerned, and rights to salvage were treated like any other property right, actionable at law. A Star Chamber case during the reign of Henry VIII documents the illegal pulling down of church bells and a porch and the sale of its windows, the defendants having allegedly 'pulled downe & converted the same to there owne uses'.[39] The use of some stone from the precincts of Bristol Cathedral for the building of 'certen superfluous and ruinouse walles of stone' was the subject of a case in the Court of Requests from 1559 to 1563.[40] The destruction of church buildings for the use of their materials was a long-standing source of concern to ecclesiastical authorities, and after the Restoration those who wished to demolish decayed chapels and other structures were required to petition for a faculty to do so. In 1709 the incumbent of the parish of Little Wratting, Suffolk, Thomas Rant, allied himself with his patron, Sir Edward Turnor or Turnour, a Middle Temple lawyer who wanted to pull down his decayed family chapel in the church rather than undertake expensive repairs ordered by the bishop of Norwich, Charles Trimnell. In exchange for assisting Turnour with the preparation of the petition for such a faculty, Rant sought the use of the chapel's materials for rebuilding the church's chancel.[41]

The dissolution of the monasteries had provided an impetus to materials recycling, since at one blow not only was an enormous amount of property transferred from clerical to gentry hands, but the abandonment and destruction of numerous smaller and many larger abbeys left large quantities of building material available for reuse, either in foundations or for more refined purposes.[42] Stone from Reading Abbey and two non-monastic buildings was used in construction at Windsor in the 1550s; the windows from Rewley Abbey church near Oxford wound up in Hampton Court, as did much of the brickwork, transported down the Thames to become a bowling alley.[43] Some specific governmental thrift

---

[38] Nichols, *Literary Illustrations*, iv. 500 and n. (Samuel Gale to unknown correspondent, n.d. (after 1730)).

[39] PRO STAC 2/34/66 (Edward Duke v. Richard Savile and Thomas Watson). Only a reply to the answer by Savile survives, the original bill and answer now being lost; the relevant index erroneously records Savile as 'Richard Smith'.

[40] PRO REQ 2/271/25 (Sharington v. John Cottrell, prebendary of Bristol).

[41] *The History of the King's Works*, iii: *1485–1660*, ed. H. M. Colvin 2 pts. (1975–82), pt. 1, 293; C. E. Welch, 'The Turnour Chapel at Little Wratting', *Proceedings of the Suffolk Institute of Archaeology*, 27 (1958), 37–40.

[42] D. M. Woodward, ' "Swords into Ploughshares": Recycling in Pre-Industrial England', *Economic History Review*, 2nd ser., 38 (1985), 175–91. Glass was among the most reused of materials, because of its expense.

[43] Colvin, *History of the King's Works*, iii, pt. 1, 319, 68, 71, 73, 94, 132, 137, 236, 290, 295, 352, 375, 468, 475, 528, 536, 575–6; pt. 2, 21. Henry VIII also took over some eleven religious houses across the country either as they were, or with slight changes, as royal houses: ibid, pt. 2, 3.

measures mandated the reuse of old materials in major projects. A Tudor statute dealing with Royal works at Calais had included a clause prohibiting the long-standing practice of carpenters claiming the salvageable old timber from demolished buildings. The 1609 Orders issued for officers of the works required that on the demolition or collapse of any of the king's buildings, all materials be stored for reuse as far as possible. The reused materials were to be valued and entered in the accounts in order to estimate future building costs more accurately; those materials not reused by the Crown were to be sold and account made of the profits.[44]

It is easy to lose sight of this point amid the growing enthusiasm of Renaissance and seventeenth-century antiquaries for the recovery and preservation of ancient buildings. A clear tension existed between a growing reverence for decaying edifices and the need to keep them functional in a contemporary society for which they had not been designed or, alternatively, the need to put their pieces to good use. Ultimately, in any conflict between physical exigency and an attachment to the past, the former was likely to win. A correspondent warned the bishop of Exeter in 1623 that a project to put a gate through the town wall to the bishop's house might be dangerous since the walls were 'old, thin, high, ill-builded, no ways flanked but by some old decayed towers'. The narrow, winding, streets of old London, John Graunt pointed out in 1672, were 'unfit for the present frequencie of coaches'.[45] Throughout the Tudor era various statutes and proclamations enforced the rebuilding or demolition of crumbling structures which posed a public nuisance. One of the early acts of Mary Tudor's first parliament ordered the rebuilding of the decaying St Eden's church in York, defaced under Edward VI, which now posed 'a greate decaye to sundrye stretes of the said citie'.[46] The quarter sessions and borough court records of the sixteenth to eighteenth centuries are full of examples of persons presented and fined for allowing structures under their charge, roads, bridges, weirs and churches, to fall into ruin.[47] The decay and destruction of buildings of great age was the darker side of rebuilding, and another daily reminder of the changing environment. As we will see further on, it would also have a profound influence on antiquarian sensibilities during the seventeenth century since it raised quite separate questions of taste and aesthetic judgement.

FASHION AND CONSUMPTION

An important factor behind the enhanced sense of change was provided by fluctuations and new developments in domestic consumption. Food and clothing,

[44] Colvin, *History of the King's Works*, pt. 1, 112, 164; *Statutes of the Realm*, iii. 646. Old bricks were used for refurbishment at Windsor Castle in the 1630s: M. W. Thompson, *The Decline of the Castle* (Cambridge, 1987), 158.

[45] Hist. MSS Comm. *The Manuscripts of the Earl Cowper, K.G., preserved at Melbourne Hall, Derbyshire*, 3 vols. (1888–9), i. 136; John Graunt, *Natural and political observations . . . made upon a bill of mortality* (1672), ed. W. F. Willcox (Baltimore, 1939), 4.

[46] 1 Maria st. 2, c. xv, *Statutes of the Realm*, iv. 216–17.

[47] For instance the several farmers and a widow presented at Michaelmas Sessions at Chelmsford, 1654, for having allowed the Shelley Common Bridge to fall into a 'great decay': Essex RO Q/SR 362/37.

because of their obvious relevance to everyone, serve as particularly useful indicators of the growing sense that society and culture were in a state of flux. It is true that there was no such thing as 'fashion' in the modern sense of a constantly changing and commercially manipulated clothing industry, and recent work has shown that changes in clothing and other consumables did not occur as frequently as some contemporaries claimed. Contemporary comments on the subject ought also not to be taken at face value, for instance Gervase Markham's Jacobean denunciation of 'new and fantastic fashions' for women, or the Dutch traveller Emmanuel van Meteren's claim that the English, being 'very inconsistent and desirous of novelties', changed their fashions every year.[48] Joseph Addison remarked that 'There is not so variable a thing in nature as a lady's head-dress. Within my own memory I have known it rise and fall above thirty degrees.'[49] These are literary exaggerations. But even if one applies appropriate caution, there is no doubt that recurrent alterations in dress were an observable phenomenon well before Addison's day, by which time England was also evolving decisively into a 'consumer society'.[50]

Fashion, Fernand Braudel once wrote, is 'a search for a new language to discredit the old, a way in which each generation can repudiate its immediate predecessor and distinguish itself from it'. In the seventeenth and eighteenth centuries, change in fashion certainly accelerated, at the very time when it was expected to symbolize stability and social order. Braudel has suggested that the use of 'traditional' costumes for public rituals creates a conscious link with the past in the face of radical changes to more day-to-day dress; the ceremonial clothing of the English monarchy, for instance, has remained virtually unchanged since the fifteenth century.[51] As Thomas Middleton had his dramatic narrator point out in one play, no fashion was ever entirely new, only different from what immediately preceded it:

> Fashions, that are now call'd new,
> Have been worn by more than you;
> Elder times have used the same,
> Though these new ones get the name.[52]

In the sixteenth and seventeenth centuries, fashion enjoyed a cycle quite independent of changes in other material possessions. Henry Peacham the younger

---

[48] Gervase Markham, *The English Housewife*, ed. M. Best (Kingston and Montreal, 1986), 8.

[49] *The Spectator*, 98 (22 June 1711), ed. D. F. Bond, 5 vols. (Oxford, 1965), i. 413. The country, he went on to claim a few weeks later, was often out of fashion, lagging behind the court and the city (*Spectator*, 119 (17 July 1711)), ed. Bond, i. 487.

[50] N. McKendrick, J. Brewer, and J. H. Plumb, *The Birth of a Consumer Society* (Bloomington, Ind., 1982), esp. pp. 34–99 (on fashion) and pp. 265–85 (on leisure); cf. J. Thirsk, 'The Fantastical Folly of Fashion: The English Stocking Knitting Industry, 1500–1700', in *The Rural Economy of England: Collected Essays* (1984), 235–57; W. Hooper, 'Tudor Sumptuary Laws', *English Historical Review*, 30 (1915), 433–49.

[51] F. Braudel, *Capitalism and Material Life, 1400–1800*, trans. M. Kochan (New York, 1973), 236.

[52] Middleton, *The Mayor of Queenborough*, in *Works of Thomas Middleton*, ii. 6, discussed in M. Heinemann, *Puritanism and Theatre: Thomas Middleton and Opposition Drama under the Early Stuarts* (Cambridge, 1980).

thought clothes had become extremely decorous since Henry VIII's time. The many unsuccessful attempts by Elizabethan and Stuart governments to regulate dress and diet through sumptuary laws and proclamations suggest, at first sight, that he was correct, and had he lived only two decades longer he would have seen even more profound changes as the tide of French fashions swept over Restoration England. But the same complaints, and similar laws, had been made in the early sixteenth century after comparable experiences with ostentatious foreign garments late in the fifteenth century. Peacham was not wrong, but his perspective was limited to the memory of his own and the previous generation, and he saw alteration in dress as a fever of innovation that had struck in recent times, rather than as a series of historical changes dating back centuries.[53]

Commentators frequently decried fashion, as they did innovation of any kind. One Jacobean ballad blamed the decline of 'Happy England' when 'Pitty was porter at every mans gate' on conspicuous consumption of luxury clothing:

> For gorgious array,
> Now beareth such sway
> That by her continuance,
> All things decay.

Another tells the sad tale of a young gallant who squanders his inheritance on 'a merry progresse to London to see fashions'. It was recognized that this was primarily a sin of those who could afford it, the gentry and nobility. But what affected the elite had consequences further down the social ladder: the same balladeer was distressed by the increased use of coaches in recent times, because they put servants out of work.[54] Thomas Fuller considered the gentry 'more floating after fine fashions' than their social inferiors in the yeomanry, whom he regarded as more traditional and austere in dress, and hence 'the surest landmark whence foreigners may take aim of the ancient English customs'. Lawyers, members of an otherwise conservative profession, were peculiarly disposed to adopting new styles of dress, according to the Elizabethan law student John Manningham, who recorded that 'in tymes past the counsellours wore gownes faced with satten, and some with yellowe cotten, and the benchers with jennet furre; nowe they are come

---

[53] 'An acte for the Reformacion of Excesse in Apparaile' (1 & 2 Phil. and Mary, c. 2), *Statutes of the Realm*, iv. 239; Henry Peacham, *The truth of our times* (1638), 65–70; J. Youings, *Sixteenth-Century England* (1984), 110–11; N. B. Harte, 'State Control of Dress and Social Change in Pre-Industrial England', in D. C. Coleman and A. H. John (eds.), *Trade, Government and Economy in Pre-industrial England* (1976), 132–65; D. Yarwood, *English Costume from the Second Century B.C. to 1952* (1952), 100–72; G. Clinch, *English Costume from Prehistoric Times to the End of the Eighteenth Century*, 2nd edn. (Wakefield, England, and Totowa, NJ, 1975), 53–114; C. W. and P. Cunnington, *Handbook of English Costume in the Seventeenth Century* (1955), *passim*; E. Ewing, *Everyday Dress 1650–1900* (1984), 7–36. A useful essay on many of these matters is Sara Warneke, 'A Taste for New fangleness: The Destructive Potential for Novelty in Early Modern England', *Sixteenth Century Journal*, 26 (1995), 881–96.

[54] Anon., *Pitties lamentation for the cruelty of this age* (1616), in *The Pepys Ballads*, ed. H. E. Rollins, 8 vols. (Cambridge, Mass., 1929), i, no. 17, stanzas 1, 7, 8; *A Merry Progresse to London to see Fashions*, facs. repr. in *Catalogue of the Pepys Library at Magdalene College, Cambridge: The Pepys Ballads*, ed. W. G. Day (Cambridge, 1987), facs. vol. i, pp. 198–9.

to that pride and fa[n]tastincknes that every one must have a velvet face'.[55] Richard Verstegan took the imitation of French, Italian, and Spanish fashions in the early seventeenth century as an indication that 'this age of ours [is] more given to change, than any other former tyme whatsoever'. Samuel Purchas thought that any traveller who had been away from England for the past three decades would think he had arrived back in the wrong country, so much had fashions changed. James Whitelocke commented in the early 1600s that the picture of his father Richard (taken in 1563 when Richard was 30 years old) showed him in a Spanish cape, ruff, a cap, and doublet, all in heavy black cloth, of which his son thought 'This apparell now wolde be thoughte overgrave in an elder by ten yeares.'[56] Nicholas Barbon thought that changes in clothing were so rapid that man dressed 'as if he lived in a perpetual spring; he never sees the autumn of his clothes'; yet he approved of this and even argued that the promotion of new fashions would be an economic boon, since it would help provide a livelihood for cloth workers, who were suffering from the competition of foreign artisans and, increasingly, machines.[57]

THE AGRARIAN ENVIRONMENT

Food was another aspect of the material environment that provoked thought about change. 'In the beginning of the world', said Hugh Latimer, 'mankind ate nothing but herbs, and roots, and sallads, and such gear as they could get.' He dated the consumption of fish and flesh to the Deluge.[58] More obvious than such supposed ancient additions to the human diet were those alterations notable within far shorter periods of a few centuries, or even a few decades. New consumables such as tobacco, and more widely available drink, spurred one satirist into the remark that,

> This age of men to that excesse is growne
> That was I think in Sodome never knowne.

Cambridge University authorities, sharing James I's dislike of tobacco, passed a decree against drinking alcohol and smoking in 1606, which claimed that the abuse of these substances, 'not heard of in former better times' had grown out of control.[59] William Harrison believed that melons, cucumbers, radishes, and other root plants had been 'plentiful in this land, in the time of the first Edward', and had declined in the fourteenth and fifteenth centuries, but were reviving in his own

---

[55] Thomas Fuller, *The holy state* (1642), 106; *The Diary of John Manningham of the Middle Temple, 1602–1603*, ed. R. P. Sorlien (Hanover, NH, 1976), 81.

[56] Richard Verstegan (alias Rowlands), *A restitution of decayed intelligence* (London and Antwerp, 1605), 197 f.; Samuel Purchas, *Purchas his pilgrim. Microcosmus or the historie of man* (1619), 261; *Liber Famelicus of Sir James Whitelocke, a Judge of the Court of King's Bench, in the Reigns of James I and Charles I*, ed. J. Bruce, Camden Soc., os 70 (1858), 5.

[57] Nicholas Barbon, *A Discourse of Trade*, ed. J. H. Hollander (Baltimore, 1903), 33.

[58] Hugh Latimer, *The sixth sermon, preached on the first Sunday in Advent, 1552, in Works of Hugh Latimer*, ed. George Elwes Corrie, 2 vols., PS 27–8 (Cambridge, 1844–5), ii. 14.

[59] R.C., *The times whistle*, ed. J. M. Cowper, EETS, os 48 (1871), 55; *REED: Cambridge*, ed. A. H. Nelson, 2 vols., (Toronto, 1989), i. 409.

day; another popular tradition held that there had been little fruit in the country before the reign of Henry VIII. The increase in foreign exploration and travel led to the transplanting of a number of new plants and vegetables in the course of the sixteenth century. As early as 1548, the herbalist William Turner included in his *The names of herbes* a list of 'Names of newe founde Herbes, whereof is no mention in any olde auncient wryter'.[60]

The seventeenth century witnessed the introduction and diffusion of a variety of new crops, including tobacco (home-grown, amid considerable controversy, as well as colonially imported), liquorice, and dyeing plants such as madder and woad.[61] The consumption changes observed by Harrison in the 1570s were even clearer a hundred years or so later, when fruit and vegetables were a part of the regular diet of the moderately affluent, who were also now eating considerably less red meat. In one of his many satirical jabs at Augustan nostalgia, Addison purported to demonstrate a decline since the Middle Ages, accentuated after 1560, from a hearty diet of beef in favour of 'under-age' animals such as lamb and veal. 'The tables of the ancient gentry of this nation were covered thrice a day with hot roast beef', Addison suggested. The 'unparalleled victories' against the French under Queen Anne were won not on the playing fields of Eton, as Wellington would much later proclaim, but on the tables of the common people who, Addison wrote, 'do still keep up the tast of their Ancestors'.[62]

Other agricultural changes were also observable. The Quaker grocer William Stout noticed in the late seventeenth century a variety of alterations since his youth, for instance in the system of market transportation in the north-west, away from coastal ships and in favour of wagons.[63] Experiments such as floating water-meadows were attempted to increase agricultural yields, and some older forms of improvement made a comeback. The use of chalk or 'marl' as a fertilizer since Roman times had, thought Gervase Markham, fallen out of fashion at the end of the Wars of the Roses. But it underwent a revival in the late sixteenth and seventeenth centuries.[64] In the later seventeenth century, John Aubrey considered the agrarian changes of Wiltshire over recent decades, observing that before the civil war wheat had been grown rarely, locals eating mainly barley bread. 'Since the aforesaid time, they have changed that course of husbandry . . . and now they spend twenty bushels of wheat to one of barley.' He also observed that wheeled ploughs had come in 'about 1630', while wagons had not been used commonly

---

[60] William Harrison, *The Description of England*, ed. G. Edelen (Ithaca, NY, 1968), 203, 265; N.F., *The fruiterer's secrets* (1604), cited in M. Campbell, *The English Yeoman* (repr., 1983), 181; William Turner, *The names of herbes* (1548), ed. J. Britten, English Dialect Soc., 34 (1881; repr. 1965), 82 ff.

[61] J. Thirsk, 'Seventeenth-Century Agriculture and Social Change', in *The Rural Economy of England*, 183–216, at p. 195; id., 'New Crops and their Diffusion: Tobacco-Growing in Seventeenth-Century England', ibid. 259–85; A. Grafton, *New Worlds, Ancient Texts: The Power of Tradition and the Shock of Discovery* (Cambridge, Mass. 1992), 167–76, for contemporary reactions to tobacco.

[62] Addison in *The Tatler*, 148 (21 Mar. 1709/10), ed. D. F. Bond, 3 vols. (Oxford, 1987), ii. 335–6.

[63] *The Autobiography of William Stout of Lancaster 1665–1752*, ed. J. D. Marshall (Manchester and New York, 1967), 95.

[64] Gervase Markham, *The inrichment of the weald of Kent* (1625), 4; W. Johnson, *Folk-Memory, or the Continuity of British Archaeology* (Oxford, 1908), 213–17.

in the southern parts of the shire before about 1655. 'Before that they altogether did use carts which are now grown quite out of fashion.'[65] With all this came a literature of agrarian improvement: one has but to compare Tudor manuals such as Tusser's or Fitzherbert's, which are essentially formularies of existing agrarian practice, with the genre of works that began to appear in the mid-seventeenth century to notice a distinct difference in orientation. Works such as Walter Blith's popular *The English Improver or a New Survey of Husbandry* (1649) and its revised third edition, *The English Improver Improved* (1652) were followed by Robert Sharrock's *An Improvement to the Art of Gardening* (1694), and the potato pioneer John Houghton's *A Proposal for the Improvement of Husbandry* (1691).

The climate had been cooling at the start of the 'Little Ice Age', and comments about the weather also indicate a sense of biological change, though such alterations were more often attributed to the will of providence than to spontaneous natural forces. Tristram Risdon, for instance, ascribed the migration of herring from Norwegian waters to the coast of Devon to divine benevolence rather than to climatological change. Godfrey Goodman, less optimistic, was convinced that the cooling was part of a steady decline since antiquity, and that fruits no longer ripened as well as they once did, while seasons were more extreme and 'in these times, our dayes are increased a full houre in length, before the nativitie'. Food itself, he thought, had steadily become more 'delicate' to fit the weaker stomachs of modern men: 'We must have warme and delicious brothes to comfort our decayed nature.' Even George Hakewill, who did not believe that these changes signified a permanent condition of decay, noted the frequency of the complaint that summers had become colder and damper in recent decades.[66] The climate began to warm again near the end of the seventeenth century (by which time techniques had developed for observing and recording weather patterns), and this too demanded comment. One member of the Royal Society observed an 'extraordinary alteration' in temperature in America and Ireland. Within the past fifteen years, he noted, ''twas not unusual to have frost and deep snows of a fortnight and three weeks continuance'; in the past two or three years, however, 'we have had scarce any frost or snow at all'.[67]

LANGUAGE

A further reminder of social change could be found in words themselves, and in the manner of their speaking, as distinct from the things they signified. As

[65] John Aubrey, 'Natural History of Wiltshire' (MS, written 1684–5), cited in *Seventeenth-Century Economic Documents*, ed. J. Thirsk and J. P. Cooper (Oxford, 1972), 177–9.

[66] Risdon, *The chorographical description . . . of Devon*, 351; Godfrey Goodman, *The fall of man* (1616), 351–3, 357, 381; George Hakewill, *An apologie of the power and providence of God in the government of the world* (Oxford, 1627), 112.

[67] Anon., 'Remarks concerning the gradual alteration of the temperature of the air', in Royal Society, *The Philosophical Transactions and Collections, to the End of the Year 1700*, ed. J. Lowthorp, 3rd edn., 3 vols. (1722), ii. 42.

several generations of experts on humanism and Renaissance art have recognized, few things caused a greater sense of distance from the past than the realization that language was not immutable.[68] Latin, which the humanists had so effectively restored to Ciceronian purity as to kill it as a living tongue, had by 1700 begun its long period of decline as a standard international language of elite communication outside the relatively narrow channels of the European philosophical, philological, and scientific communities. Antiquaries from the late sixteenth century on made the evolution of English a high priority in their studies, and by the late seventeenth century it was realized that linguistic change could take place over the shorter span of decades. Swift pilloried such recent developments as the use of abbreviations in polite conversation and writing, and the coinage of new words like 'mob' and 'banter'; he declined to insert current oaths in his satire on conversation because they were 'children of fashion . . . in some sense, almost annuals' and likely to change with the seasons. Elsewhere he warned that the failure of his own age to solidify Renaissance improvements of the native language would make it impossible for future historians to say much about the early eighteenth century beyond a mere chronicle of events.[69] Spelling, which was largely unfixed in the early sixteenth century, gradually approached a degree of standardization, especially in print, during the century and a half separating Shakespeare from Samuel Johnson. When Sir John Percival and William Byrd visited Dr Thomas Gale in 1701, the latter showed them some English and French letters from Henry VIII to Anne Boleyn, which Percival thought 'very dull & ill spelt even for the time they were wrote in'.[70]

Changes in speech were even more obvious, and the standardization of modern spoken English in the later seventeenth century made it tempting to relegate rusticisms and traces of ancient tongues to the realm of the provincial and rude.[71] Aubrey observed that 'There were (no doubt) severall dialects in Britaine as we see there are now [in] England: they did not speake alike all over this great Isle; just as the South, or North-Welchmen doe now.' A thousand years, he thought, could make a 'great alteration in pronunciation which will much disguise words, as we well know how names of men and places are so by the vulgar'.[72] When the

---

[68] D. R. Kelley, *Foundations of Modern Historical Scholarship: Language, Law and History in the French Renaissance* (New York, 1970); A. Grafton, *Forgers and Critics: Creativity and Duplicity in Western Scholarship* (Princeton, 1990). The best study of this in the context of English historical thought is A. B. Ferguson, *Clio Unbound: Perception of the Social and Cultural Past in Renaissance England* (Durham, NC, 1979), 312–45.

[69] Jonathan Swift, *Swift's Polite Conversation*, ed. E. Partridge (New York and Oxford, 1963), 11, 27, 30–1; id., *A Proposal for Correcting, Improving and Ascertaining the English Tongue* (1712), in *The Prose Works of Jonathan Swift*, ed. H. Davis, 16 vols. (Oxford, 1957–74), iv. 18.

[70] *The English Travels of Sir John Percival and William Byrd II: The Percival Diary of 1701*, ed. M. R. Wenger (Columbia, Mo., 1989), 114; BL MS Lans. 937, fo. 39ᵛ (Kennett collections), 1 May 1684.

[71] A. Fox, *Oral and Literate Culture in England, 1500–1700* (Oxford, 2000), 51–111; A. Bryson, *From Courtesy to Civility: Changing Codes of Conduct in Early Modern England* (Oxford, 1998), 151–92; C. Davies, *English Pronunciation from the Fifteenth to the Eighteenth Century* (1934); E. J. Dobson, *English Pronunciation, 1500–1700*, 2 vols. (Oxford, 1957); id., 'Early Modern Standard English', *Transactions of the Philological Society* (1955), 25–54.

[72] Bodl. MS Aubrey 5 ('An Interpretation of Villare Anglicanum'), fo. 17ʳ; M. Hunter, *John Aubrey and the Realm of Learning* (1975), 170.

duchess of Cornwall visited Land's End at the end of the seventeenth century, she was attended by Cornishmen speaking that region's language, including an ancient hermit. 'Smiling at his rustick simplicity', she asked him for 'some memorable instance of his language' which he proceeded to demonstrate 'like an ancient bard'.[73] Sir Peter Leycester, placing his own study of Cheshire dialect within the context of European works by Giovanni Botero and others, thought that

The English continued their native language, notwithstandinge the greate and longe commixture with the Normans: but much altered since Chaucer's tyme under Kinge Richard the Second: especially since Henry the eighths tyme downward, it is soe intermingled with Latine and ffrench wordes, besides some old wordes retayned from the Normans, anciently, that it is now become a new language, and much of the ancient English tongue quite lost and perished amonge us.[74]

Swift made much the same point about the incursions of French upon English under Edward the Confessor, William I, and especially Henry II, in his *A Proposal for Correcting, Improving and Ascertaining the English Tongue*, though he thought many words had been deported back to Paris since the time of Spenser and Shakespeare. On the opposite side of the political spectrum, however, Addison suggested that this process was now being continued as the modern French wars brought in more new words. 'The present war has so adulterated our tonge with strange words, that it would be impossible for one of our great-grandfathers to know what his posterity have been doing, were he to read their exploits in a modern news paper.'[75]

POPULATION AND ECONOMY

The population of some towns, especially London (by Continental standards England's only real city through most of the sixteenth century but the largest in Europe by 1700), had increased dramatically over time. Although observant contemporaries might notice such growth even within the period of their own lives, the greatest changes had happened over the longer span of several centuries. 'The most undeniable proof of the increase of mankind in England', thought Nicholas Barbon, was Domesday Book, which suggested that the country's population had doubled since the late eleventh century.[76] Such increases were most noticeable in large communities, especially London. Gregory King, the pioneering political arithmetician who worked out figures for London's growth over a sixteen-century period, concluded that the city had grown from 4,000 or 5,000 at the time of Julius Caesar's invasion to 530,000 in his own time. From this rate of growth

---

[73] Bodl. MS Carte 269 (Edward Lhwyd's account of 'The duchess of Cornwall's progresse to see ye Land's end'), fo. 40ᵛ.
[74] Cheshire RO, DDX 180 (Sir Peter Leycester, 'A Short View of Greate Brettaine and Ierland from the Beginninge', 1670), fos. 21ʳ, 48 ff.
[75] *The Prose Works of Jonathan Swift*, ed. Davis, iv. 7, 87–95; *The Spectator*, 165 (8 Sept. 1711), ed. Bond, ii. 149.
[76] Barbon, *Discourse of Trade*, ed. Hollander, 25.

he was able to project forward to 1900, at which time he estimated the population would pass the 2 million mark.[77] One of King's readers, the prominent northerner Sir John Lowther, noted prophetically that the total population of the world might double again over the next fourteen centuries, causing overcrowding and violence. Lowther attempted to calculate the number of persons to die since the Creation, and made the by now obvious connection between rising population and steady inflation. 'I conclude that as people double faster now than they did in former ages, soe the rents of lands must alsoe rise proportionably and the number of yeares purchase alsoe.'[78]

Population increase occasioned other social changes that registered with contemporaries—overcrowding, increased migration from the countryside, and recurrent outbreaks of plague to name but a few. Perhaps no type of change, however, affected more people (and was more conducive to speculative attempts at measurement) than alterations in the economy. In our own time, we are used to monthly and weekly reports on our own national economy, tracing subtle rises and falls in trade, production, consumption and, above all, cost. Price changes invite comment because, unlike other economic indices, they tend to exhibit a general, linear pattern of upward movement, and also because they affect the ordinary individual's perception of his or her own recent past. Few persons now living in an industrialized Western country cannot have had the experience of recalling days, a decade or so earlier, when a given item cost less, whether it be a mundane item of daily life such as postage stamps or milk, or more exotic commodities such as fur coats and sports cars. Inflation thus plays an important role in shaping the ways in which individuals periodize their own lives. The ubiquitous, steady rise in prices that sixteenth-century England encountered had a comparable effect on contemporaries, and it further stimulated general awareness of mutability.

Except for a few brief periods (that of the mid-Tudor currency debasement among them) the pace of economic change was far less rapid in early modern England than it is now, and was consequently harder rather than easier for contemporaries to explain. Inflation was clearly observable from the 1540s on, though it took some time for the realization to sink in that a steady rise in prices was not simply the consequence of short-term 'dearth' or of the commercial machinations of evil men, and longer still for social commentators to recognize that this rather unwelcome economic visitor had come to stay. The mid-Tudor *Discourse of the common weal*, now generally attributed to Sir Thomas Smith, suggests that as early as the 1550s, men were aware of the problem of rising prices.

---

[77] *Two Tracts by Gregory King*, ed. G. E. Bennett (Baltimore, 1936), 26. John Graunt made similar observations: *Natural and Political Observations made upon the Bills of Mortality* (1662), ed. W. F. Willcox (Baltimore, 1939), 64–5, 76, commenting also on the decay and disappearance of 'old wooden dark houses' which were being replaced by new ones built in imitation of Continental architecture. For the activities of the political arithmeticians, see I. Hacking, *The Emergence of Probability* (Cambridge, 1975), 99–110.

[78] Cumbria RO, Carlisle, D/Lons/W.1/31 (Lowther papers), memorandum book, p. 60.

Sporadic fluctuations in the price of staple commodities, and even of luxury goods, were nothing new; after the sharp depression caused by the Black Death and its enormous reduction in the population, prices had slowly crept back up to something approximating their pre-plague levels. But a general rise in the prices of most commodities that was both very sharp and then sustained over a long period had not been experienced in England in recent memory, and it naturally excited comment. Most early remarks on the problem lack the conceptual framework of the *Discourse*: the tendency was, at least initially, to blame price rises on dearth occasioned by malevolent individuals engaged in sinister practices such as coin-clipping, or the 'forestalling and regrating' of goods. Still wedded to the notion that all commodities had a 'just price', mid-sixteenth-century commentators were unconditioned to inflation as an ordinary condition of social existence. For our purposes, the adequacy of contemporary explanations of the problem in economic terms is of less consequence than the growing frequency of comments about price rises, which were increasingly attended by a sense of historical change.

At the start of the price rise in the 1540s, after Henry VIII had debased the coinage for a second time in his reign, contemporaries had no reason to expect that this presaged an endless upward trend. The London chronicler Charles Wriothesley noted in September 1546 that some foods had actually dropped in price during the preceding months; wheat was then selling at the rate of 10s. a quarter, and malt at 5s., 'which was before the peace at high prices, by reason the harvest was faire, and also there is a great plentie thereof in Englande'.[79] Wriothesley was not mistaken: prices could still rise and fall from season to season or year to year, and from place to place, according to factors such as politics and the harvest. The prospect of rising prices as the long-term rule rather than the exception had not yet dawned upon him, or most others, in contrast to the economic speculation that would be commonplace by the end of the seventeenth century. A few years later, in 1550, the reformer and social critic Robert Crowley noted the changing price of coal, convinced that it should and would eventually be restored to its 'just price':

> A lode that of late yeres for a royall was solde,
> Wyll coste nowe xvi.s of sylver or golde.
> God graunt these men grace theyr pollyng to refrayne,
> Or els bryng them backe to theyr olde state agayne.[80]

But by the mid-1550s and early 1560s, after several efforts at restoring the coinage to its pre-1540 degree of fineness, prices stayed high, and even continued to rise, though at a less marked rate. It was only then, when a generation had grown up within an inflationary economy, that it finally struck some observers that the old

---

[79] Charles Wriothesley, *A chronicle of England during the reigns of the Tudors, from A.D. 1485 to 1559*, ed. W. D. Hamilton, 2 vols., Camden Soc., NS 11, 20 (1875–7), i. 175.
[80] *A Discourse of the Commonweal of this realm of England* (1581), ed. M. Dewar (Charlottesville, Va., 1969), 18–21, 39–41; 'Of the Colier of Croydon', *Epigrams* (1550), in *Select Works of Robert Crowley*, ed. J. M. Cowper, EETS ES XV (1872), 20.

days were gone: as an early economic tract, the *Discourse of the common weal* is interesting not simply because it notes the general rise in prices and offers several explanations for them, but because its author recognized that the refinement of the coinage was not returning prices to their old level.

Most Tudor commentators lacked the perceptiveness and the knowledge of the *Discourse*'s author. By the early seventeenth century, inflation had already established itself as an accepted, if resented, fact of life. Ordinary commodities such as fuel and food continued to rise in real terms until the middle of the seventeenth century. Once this had become a general pattern, it could then arouse comment not just as a relatively recent development but as a historical phenomenon, buttressing arguments for the decline of the world from the good old days. Godfrey Goodman pointed to the decay of the coinage and the attendant price rise—neither of which was in fact as severe in his time as fifty years earlier—as evidence of man's worsening condition, while an early Stuart balladeer recalled for his readers the days when

> A bushell of wheat for sixe pence was sold,
> An oxe for a marke fat from the stall:
> A score of fat lambes for an angell was told.[81]

This trend continued through the seventeenth century. In 1689 William Stout, who saw the worst inflation of his own day as a relatively recent consequence of warfare with France, found that prunes, which had previously 'sould three pounds for fowrepence' could not now be had for less than 40s. a hundredweight 'which now turned to the butcher's profit'. Resin, previously 10s. a hundredweight, advanced to 6d. or 8d. a pound, until a replacement source was found in New England.[82]

The occasional temporary collapse of prices in certain commodities such as wool or cloth which occurred at times of depression, such as the 1620s and early 1680s, also stimulated comment on change, perhaps because this type of deflation was now so exceptional. Wool prices began to come down about 1600, after a hundred years of steady increases, and did not recover through most of the next century.[83] Aubrey, blaming the fall in the value of wool on the decay of trade with the Turks in the 1680s, noted that his own sheep farm was 'worse by £60 per annum than it was before the Civil Wars'.[84] Complaints about the scarcity of money—the opposite situation from that experienced during the days of Tudor debasement —became commonplace during the economic crisis of the Restoration, though one leading commentator on the issue, Sir Josiah Child, dismissed them as

---

[81] Goodman, *The fall of man*, 373–7; Anon., *Pitties lamentation for the cruelty of this age* (1616), *The Pepys Ballads*, ed. Rollins, i, no. 17, stanza 12.

[82] *Autobiography of William Stout*, 94–5.

[83] Thirsk, 'Agriculture and Social Change', 184; A. H. John, 'The Course of Agricultural Change, 1660–1760', in L. S. Pressnell (ed.), *Studies in the Industrial Revolution, Presented to T. S. Ashton* (1960), 125–56.

[84] John Aubrey, *Natural History of Wiltshire*, quoted in Thirsk and Cooper (eds.), *Seventeenth-Century Economic Documents*, 179.

unwarranted over-reaction, 'it being natural for men to complain of the present, and commend the times past; so said they of old, "The former days were better than these" '. He recalled complaints of inflation in his youth, observing how it was 'the very same persons that now complain of this, and commend that time'.[85] Such cool arguments would not have persuaded John Evelyn, who commented in 1694 that several executed coin-clippers had together brought prices 'to such a strange exorbitance ... beyond that any age can shew example'.[86]

Thomas Sprat, future bishop of Rochester and historian of the Royal Society, was an unabashed optimist on the subject of economic change, seeing the inflation of his own time as a sign of prosperity and population, and a mark of the hundredfold increase in trade since the Saxon and Danish invasions.[87] His poorer brethren among England's parochial clergy can hardly be blamed for not echoing his enthusiasm. Particularly hard hit by inflation in the century or so after the Reformation, and having lost much of that economic control over their own affairs which they had enjoyed in the pre-Reformation era, they were frequent harpers on the price rise. 'Wee cannot live now as our predecessors did an hundred yeeres ago', complained one early Stuart preacher. Another, Foulke Robartes, thought that a shilling's-worth of corn could have sufficed a family for a week a century or so earlier, but not in his day, when 'prices have beene raysed as often againe as Jacobs wages have been changed, ten and ten times'. Richard Eburne urged the restoration of tithe payment in kind because, by his calculation, prices had increased twelvefold relative to the tithe's monetary value.[88]

By the mid-seventeenth century at the latest, the sustained price rise of the past century had entered popular lore. A rhyme current among the poorer sort at Chippenham, Wiltshire, in the 1660s recalled that

> When Chipnam stood
> In Pewnsham's wood
> Before it was destroyed,
> A cowe might have gonne for a groate a yeare,
> But now it is denoyed.

[85] Josiah Child, *A new discourse of trade* (1693), p. xxxviii.

[86] Evelyn, *Diary*, v. 186; for another comment on coinage debasement and its effects during the 1690s, see *Autobiography of William Stout*, 113–17. A sharp decrease in the price of gold led Gilbert Burnet, observing a treasure trove of gold medals in the collection of the elector of Mainz, to wonder why its owner, some five centuries earlier, would 'bury all this under ground, especially in an age in which so much gold was ten times the value of what [it] is at present': *Dr Burnet's Travels* (Amsterdam, 1687), book III, p. 32.

[87] T. Sprat, *The History of the Royal Society*, ed. J. I. Cope and H. W. Jones (St Louis, Mo., 1958), 400.

[88] Thomas Myriell, *The Christian's comfort* (1623), 53; Foulke Robartes, *The revenue of the gospel is tithes* (Cambridge, 1613), 84; Richard Eburne, *The royal law* (1616), 57; C. Hill, *Economic Problems of the Church, from Archbishop Whitgift to the Long Parliament* (Oxford, 1956); F. Heal, *Of Prelates and Princes: A Study of the Economic and Social Position of the Tudor Episcopates* (Cambridge and New York, 1980); C. Cross, 'The Incomes of Provincial Urban Clergy, 1520–1645', in R. O'Day and F. Heal (eds.), *Princes and Paupers in the English Church 1500–1800* (Leicester, 1981), 65–89. Under-endowed livings were a particular cause of grief in the inflationary context: M. L. Zell, 'Economic Problems of the Parochial Clergy in the Sixteenth Century', in O'Day and Heal (eds.), 20–43, at p. 32.

Aubrey, who recorded this rhyme, encountered at least one elderly man who recalled 'when he was a boy about 60 yeares since, the goeing of a cowe in the Pewsham Forest for 4 d a yeare, and pigges cost nothing the goeing: the order was how many they could winter might summer'.[89]

Contemporary perceptions along these lines were not always accurate. Bernard de Mandeville thought that 'There is no Intrinsick Worth in Money but what is alterable with the Times.' In this he represented the mature mercantilist understanding of the fluidity of specie that had become well established by the early eighteenth century. He was much less successful in measuring actual inflation, observing that the day-labourer of his own time now scorned to do for 16*d*. what 'Thirty Years ago his Grandfather did chearfully for half the money'.[90] Others such as Gregory King and Josiah Child, however, were more attentive to detail. Child thought that the memories of England's aged would provide a valuable measure of economic change over the previous half-century, wishing in particular to demonstrate that a general increase in the money supply, though it had driven prices upwards, had also brought about a higher standard of living:

And if this be doubted, let us ask the aged, whether five hundred pounds portion with a daughter sixty years ago, were not esteemed a larger portion than two thousand pounds now: And whether gentlewomen in those days would not esteem themselves well cloathed in a serge gown, which a chamber maid now will be ashamed to be seen in . . .

An ancient embroiderer informed Child, no doubt with some exaggeration, that he had made hundreds of doublets for knights and gentlemen who sixty years earlier would have been unable to afford them; money had become much more readily available, so much so that 'We with ease can pay a greater tax in one year, than our fore-fathers could in twenty.'[91]

Child's comments on the prices of luxuries, and his general belief that 'we have now much more money in England than we had twenty years past' provide an important reminder that whatever sensitivity to change economic fluctuations caused still tended to be mainly of a long-term nature. Although people would notice such things as a local jump in bread prices readily enough, on the whole it was difficult to detect steady change except over a period of years or even decades. The political arithmeticians of late Stuart England, like their Tudor humanist predecessors, lacked the statistical means to measure economic change over shorter intervals. Thus Child rested his case for the increase in money on long-term past trends, believing that the further back he looked the greater the support for his position—though in the end he restricted his enquiry to the previous twenty years, 'which is within most mens memories'.[92] The perception of any kind of historical change inevitably depends upon the speed of communications and the ability to

---

[89] John Aubrey, *Wiltshire. The Topographical Collections of John Aubrey, FRS*, ed. J. E. Jackson (Devizes, 1862), 67.

[90] Bernard de Mandeville, *The Fable of the Bees*, ed. F. B. Kaye, 2 vols. (Oxford, 1924; Liberty Classics facs. repr., Indianapolis, 1988), i. 301.

[91] Child, *A New discourse of trade*, 10.   [92] Ibid. pp. xxxv f.

gather information. Sir Julius Caesar was able to note in 1616, after the debacle of Alderman Cockayne's project, that there were 'twice as many people needing work as 14 years since'.[93] We would now be able to say, with the greater confidence deriving from a faith in serial statistics, that 'unemployment rose last month'. Yet only the speed at which such changes are detected and quantified has changed; the sensitivity to economic change itself we have inherited from the early modern era.

This chapter has suggested that economic, social, and environmental alterations over the short and medium term were sufficiently commonplace, and occurred with such increasing frequency, that it was very difficult to escape an awareness of mutability in general and of the difference between present and past. The capacity to articulate that difference, and the process whereby change can occur either sharply or 'by little and little' has sometimes been seen as a necessary, if not a sufficient, condition of 'modern' historical consciousness.[94] Alterations wrought by nature, by time, or by broad social forces such as commerce clearly constituted a significant stimulus to discussion of change. So, too, did more obviously human alterations, such as religious reformation, or changes in manners. Not surprisingly, considerations of such matters often invoked moral judgement as to their value or harmfulness. The language used to defend or attack such changes oscillated between two qualitative poles—'old' and 'new'—that, respectively, bore a positive or negative relation to the past. Discussions of matters of social importance, framed in this manner, regularly invoked words like 'antiquity' and 'innovation', value-laden terms that require more detailed exploration in the next chapter.

[93] Thirsk and Cooper (eds.), *Seventeenth-Century Economic Documents*, 198.
[94] For the most compelling statement of this in the English context, see Ferguson, *Clio Unbound*.

CHAPTER TWO

Old and New

THE EARLY MODERN era is noteworthy for its great reverence for things that were very old, whether books, institutions, traditions, or even personal belongings.[1] This respect for the objects (and, generally, the people) of the past manifested itself in a variety of ways. One of these was the growth of antiquarianism, which will concern us in ensuing chapters. But antiquarianism differs from the respect for antiquity from which it emerged in one critical respect: it extracted pieces of the past into modern scholarly works or display settings, for study or decoration rather than daily use; it exoticized an oldness previously deemed normal, even banal. Moreover, antiquarianism must be understood within a much larger mental context as a single aspect of a wider set of assumptions held in one form or another by most men and women from the fifteenth to the early eighteenth centuries. The most fundamental of these were: that old was better than new; that the older something was the better; and that the authority or legitimacy of a belief, practice, or institution, or even of an individual, was a function of its longevity and antiquity. Yet even these principles admitted of nuances, contradictions, and contested definitions, depending upon the context—and attitudes to innovation and novelty were not unaffected by two centuries of profound material, intellectual, and social change.

IN PRAISE OF OLDER THINGS

It was proverbial wisdom that the old, and especially the continuous or traditional old, was simply better, its survival into the present investing it with authority, as a number of late Renaissance writers pronounced in an enormous variety of contexts. Archbishop Tobie Matthew declared that new friends were not as valuable as old ones, a point repeated by John Selden.[2] The best wine, said Robert Burton, who was repeating a commonplace, comes out of old vessels, and even old grain, aged for twenty weeks or so, was better for making bread and

---

[1] K. Thomas, 'Age and Authority in Early Modern England', *Proceedings of the British Academy*, 62 (1976), 1–46; D. Herlihy, 'Vieillir à Florence au Quattrocento', *Annales ESC*, 24 (1969), 1338–52; trans. as 'Growing Old in the Quattrocento', in P. Stearns (ed.), *Old Age in Preindustrial Society* (New York, 1982), 104–18. Sections of this chapter have been previously published in my essay, 'In Praise of Older Things: Notions of Age and Antiquity in Early Modern England', in A. Grafton and J. H. M. Salmon (eds.), *Historians and Ideologues: Essays in Honour of Donald R. Kelley* (Rochester, NY, 2001), 123–53.

[2] *The Correspondence of Dr Matthew Hutton, Archbishop of York*, ed. J. Raine, Surtees Soc., 17 (1843), 95; *Table-talk: being the discourses of John Selden, Esq.*, ed. R. Milward, 2nd edn. (1698), 63.

beer than newly harvested corn, according to a belief repeated by Thomas Tusser. Part of the great medical efficacy of the waters of Bath, thought one medical writer, derived from their great antiquity.[3] Richard Hooker attempted to explain reverence for the old in religious terms, as an approximation of the divine: the more ancient something was, the closer it approached the 'infinit continuance of God'.[4] To Francis Junius, paraphrasing Quintilian, respect for the old was simply a function of a human instinct for imitation in all spheres of learning: the painter and the husbandman alike naturally follow the examples set by their predecessors, while creating innovative works that add originality and individuality to such imitation.[5] George Hakewill thought antiquity likely to best modernity in any argument because of a natural predisposition towards the former. 'Such is the advantage which antiquity hath against the present times, that if wee meete with any thing which excells, wee thincke it must bee ancient, or if with any thing that is ancient, it cannot but excell: nay therefore we think it excells because wee thinke it ancient though it be not so.'[6] 'Antiquity', wrote one seventeenth-century reader in his commonplace book, is to be 'reverenced and idolized'. But the same reader also recognized the perils inherent in idolatry, that 'dangerous wickedness may be done upon pretext of antiquity'.[7]

As the ambivalence of this last comment suggests, to take at face value this apparent tendency to value the old, in whatever setting, over the new is to reify an ideal that often broke down in practice. It has already been seen that old buildings and monuments could be torn down unceremoniously for either economic or religious reasons. The reality of life in early modern England is that everywhere such ingrown assumptions as the intrinsic value of oldness were being assailed increasingly by a social, cultural, and technological environment in which new things and new events were increasingly evident to the senses, rupturing the experience of time, widening the fissure of past and present, and rendering visible what had once been a seamless connection between the current and the traditional.

THE MEANING OF ANTIQUITY

The appeal to the past saturates early modern discourse, public and private. It was sufficient, through much of the period, to argue on behalf of something by pointing out its antiquity. Yet the words 'antiquity' and 'ancient', which occur

[3] Robert Burton, *The Anatomy of Melancholy*, ed. F. Dell and P. Jordan-Smith (New York, 1927), 497; Thomas Tusser, *Five Hundred Points of Good Husbandry*, ed. G. Grigson (Oxford, 1984), 46; John Jones, *The Bathes of Bathes Ayde* (1572), fos. 2–6; cf. the same author's *The Benefit of the Auncient Bathes of Buckstones* (1572), where he advances similar arguments on behalf of the Buckstone baths near Manchester.

[4] Richard Hooker, *Of the Laws of Ecclesiastical Polity*, V, 69.1, in *The Folger Library Edition of the Works of Richard Hooker*, ed. W. Speed Hill, 7 vols. in 8 pts. (Cambridge, Mass., 1977–98), ii. 359–60.

[5] Francis Junius, *The painting of the ancients* (1638), 8; Quintilian, *Institutio Oratoria*, X, ii, 1–12, ed. and trans. H. E. Butler, 4 vols. (London and New York, 1922), iv. 75–81.

[6] George Hakewill, *An Apologie of the Power and Providence of God in the Government of the World* (1627), 24.

[7] BL MS Sloane 517 (anon. commonplace book), fo. 100ʳ.

much more frequently in early modern speech than in modern, could have a variety of meanings, depending on the contexts in which they were used. For a start, the word 'ancient' was used much more loosely than it is today. To be 'ancient' did not, in fact, require that something or someone be very old at all: antiquity as a *quality* (as opposed to 'Antiquity' as a particular historical period) was relative rather than absolute. In Coventry, by the middle of the sixteenth century, the former officers of a craft were commonly known as 'the most auncient persones', having survived twenty years of membership in that craft. The Elizabethan popular writer Thomas Deloney describes the widow, who was not old, of Jack of Newberry's master as 'a very comely ancient woman'.[8] A century later, Locke made 'oldness' a function of relative age and expected longevity:

Thus having setled in our thoughts the idea of the ordinary duration of a man to be seventy years, when we say a man is young, we mean, that his age is yet but a small part of that which usually men attain to. And when we denominate him old, we mean, that his duration is run out almost to the end of that which men do not usually exceed.[9]

'Old' was often no more than a tag used to distinguish one object, person, or place from another: negotiations between two Suffolk families of the mid-sixteenth century describe the piece of land at issue as 'the olde shepes bridge', a referent clearly understood by both parties. A barren parcel of waste known simply as 'the olde' was the issue of a Worcester tithe dispute in 1561, and one of Yarmouth's 'havens' or harbours, constructed in the reign of Edward VI, was known as the 'Old Haven' by 1619, when it had been replaced by an Elizabethan harbour.[10] 'Old' might also be used in the sense of 'sitting' or 'incumbent': thus in 1644 William Dowsing the iconoclast distinguished between 'new' and 'old' churchwardens, in noting local resistance to his visitation at Ufford in Suffolk.[11]

The brief expanse of time required to cloak something in the garb of antiquity was partly a function of the relatively low level of literacy in early modern

---

[8] C. Phythian-Adams, 'Ceremony and the Citizen: The Communal Year at Coventry 1450–1550', in P. Clark and P. Slack (eds.), *Crisis and Order in English Towns* (1972), 57–85, at p. 59; Thomas Deloney, *The pleasant history of John Winchcomb [or] Jack of Newbery*, 11th edn. (1630), sig. A3ᵛ. The town meetings of Braintree and Finchingfield regularly denominate certain citizens by the tag 'old', in many cases presumably to distinguish them from like-named kin and descendants: F. G. Emmison, *Early Essex Town Meetings: Braintree, 1619–1636; Finchingfield 1626–1634* (London and Chichester, 1970), 34, 112, 118, 123, 129. For use of the term 'old' to describe simply one servant as to be distinguished from a maid, presumably young, see the will of the London tailor William Mason (6 Oct. 1540), who left a feather bed, some sheets, and a pillow to 'Margarite, my olde woman': *London Consistory Court Wills 1492–1547*, ed. Ida Darlington, London Rec. Soc. Publications, 3 (1967), 74.

[9] John Locke, *An Essay Concerning Human Understanding*, ed. P. H. Nidditch (Oxford, 1975), ii. xxvi, 327.

[10] Acquittance between Lord Keeper Nicholas Bacon and John and Edmund Barnyard, 16 Oct. 1570, in *The Papers of Nathaniel Bacon of Stiffkey*, i: *1556–1577*, ed. A. H. Smith *et al.*, Norfolk Rec. Soc., 46 (1978–9), 17; Henry Manship, *The History of Great Yarmouth*, ed. C. J. Palmer (1854), 84; R. H. Helmholz, *Roman Canon Law in Reformation England* (Cambridge, 1990), 98. Locals at Great Sampford, Essex, commonly referred to it as 'Old Sandford' in the seventeenth century to distinguish it from nearby Little Sampford: see the recognizances for midsummer general sessions at Chelmsford, 1654, Essex RO Q/SR 361/84.

[11] *The Journal of William Dowsing of Stratford, Parliamentary Visitor*, ed. C. H. Evelyn White (Ipswich, 1885), 29.

England. As literacy increased, and with it the dominance of a learned sense of remote, chronological time, as opposed to dateless immemorial past, so 'antiquity' in common parlance gradually acquired its modern meaning as something genuinely centuries old. Throughout the later Middle Ages, and well into the early modern era, something ancient was legally regarded as only a few decades old, and perhaps less. The medieval civilian Azo and a number of canonists had regarded 'age-old' custom as that of forty years' duration. As Michael Clanchy points out, this was not so much a consequence of the relative brevity of life as of the 'shortness of memory unaided by writing and under constant social pressure'.[12] Evidence from modern non-literate societies bears this out: among the Nuer, for instance, Evans-Pritchard found that the furthest extent of historical time was fifty years.[13] Even in the more literate society of early modern England, where print was rapidly multiplying the available documents of the past, something could be ancient simply if it had endured forty or fifty years, and often less. This notion of antiquity marked the efforts of Charles I to restore the court to its 'ancient splendour'. After an era of frequent disorder and laxity under King James, his successor was advised to 'resume the ancient forms' of ceremony and formality, many of which dated back only to the reign of Elizabeth.[14]

Within the local environment of town, manor, or village, the word 'ancient' could simply refer to a customary practice of dateless origin. Disputes in court records over 'ancient' property lines, paths, and waterways have provided fodder for social and legal historians for decades, and only a few examples need be adduced here. Several men were presented at Wiltshire quarter sessions in April, 1612, for having 'turned the water out of his auncyent course' in the parish of Rowde by damming it, thereby creating an inconvenience to travellers. Another Wiltshire case, from 1646, involved a struggle between a widow and her neighbour, who had diverted an 'antient watercourse' from its normal path to his own house, through her own property, and had beaten the widow's daughter when she tried to 'keep the water in its auncient course'. Those who appealed to antiquity in this sense did not normally ponder the origins of a practice or custom: it mattered

---

[12] M. T. Clanchy, 'Remembering the Past and the Good Old Law', *History*, 55 (1970), 172; but compare the position of P. J. Geary, who has demonstrated the degree to which archives not only stored writings but eliminated much material in the process of selection and pruning: *Phantoms of Remembrance: Memory and Oblivion at the End of the First Millennium* (Princeton, 1994), ch. 3 (pp. 81–114).

[13] E. E. Evans-Pritchard, *The Nuer* (Oxford, 1940), 105.

[14] Hist. MSS Comm., *The Manuscripts of the Earl Cowper, K.G., Preserved at Melbourne Hall, Derbyshire*, 3 vols. (1888–9), i. 382. Many court offices were reviewed and obliged to demonstrate their antiquity: the marshals and sewers of the hall, for instance, protected their position by having the lord chamberlain issue them a certificate declaring them to have endured 'with little alteration' since the time of Henry I: ibid. i. 198. Where there was no or ambiguous documentation, antiquity could easily be contested: at some date before 1621, the Crown tried to stop the meeting of the Court of Roundhedge, the court for Enfield Chase, Middlesex, on the grounds that it was 'a newe devysed court'; but 'by reporte of anncient men present when the said court should have bin holden, yt had bin a court for the said chace tyme out of mynd' Hist. MSS Comm. *Calendar of the Manuscripts of the Most Hon. the Marquis of Salisbury, K.G., &c. &c. &c., Preserved at Hatfield House, Hertfordshire*, 24 vols. (1883–1976), xxii. 139 (n.d.).

less *how* old something was, than that it *was* old.[15] Because of this, the notion of something enduring 'time out of mind' had by the end of the Middle Ages assumed great weight in judicial decisions, and was frequently appealed to by those forced to have recourse to the law. In 1617, to give just one example, a group of husbandmen who regularly brought coal every Saturday for sale at Leicester market complained to city aldermen that they had been expelled from Leicester Forest by the inhabitants of nearby Branston, though they had gathered coal there on Friday nights 'tyme out of mynde'.[16]

Since the whole notion of 'antiquity' was thus relative rather than absolute, virtually anything could be said to be 'ancient' after only a few years (or even if it were simply a replica of something ancient: the townsmen of Tudor Faversham referred oxymoronically to the making of a 'new ancient staffe' when they needed to replace their old ceremonial staff).[17] Sir Thomas Egerton believed that, although Queen Elizabeth had filled the office of chamberlain in the Exchequer of Chester with noblemen in recent years, it had 'in ancient time' (that is, in the previous reigns) been occupied by men of lower origins.[18] 'Ancient' or 'old' were often no more than coded signifiers for value and legitimacy, like 'noble' or 'true'; they could be used with reference to very recent times or to very old times, often by the same writer. Thus Richard Bancroft, attacking the Presbyterians in the 1590s, refers at one point to the ancient Fathers of the Church and at another to an 'auncient councell' of the Church which was held seven years earlier, in 1586, and he compares a recent statement of Thomas Cartwright to one of 'his antient stile' in order to show his opponent contradicting himself. His contemporary, William Harrison, uses the phrase 'in old time' frequently in his *Description of England*, at different places referring to the Romano-British period, the Anglo-Saxon era, a more recent period 'within three or hundred year past', or even the youth of the old men living in his parish.[19] Following correction of a subsidence

[15] *Records of the County of Wiltshire*, ed. B. H. Cunnington, Wiltshire Rec. Soc. (1932), 35, 157–8. Similar language is used in estate dealings to describe the legal status of land according to 'ancient' tenure, that is to say, long-standing and outside the memory of man: 'The land is auncyent copyhold and well approved by your evydence': his surveyor William Hornby to Nathaniel Bacon of Stiffkey, 18 Dec. 1583, *The Papers of Nathaniel Bacon of Stiffkey*, ed. Smith, ii. 268. In contrast, legislation had to be more concerned about defining specific chronological boundaries to which measures applied. The major point at stake during second reading of a bill on pulling down weirs in order to safeguard salmon fry was how far back to apply it, that is, whether weirs set up in the last century or only in the past sixty years should be brought down. *Proceedings in Parliament 1614 (House of Commons)*, ed. M. Jansson, *Memoirs of the American Philosophical Society*, 172 (Philadelphia, 1988), 309 (21 May 1614).

[16] *Records of the Borough of Leicester*, ed. H. Stocks (Cambridge, 1922), 168. In at least one case, involving a question of disputed marriage, the antiquity of a church window was presented to a jury at assizes and accepted: William Burton, *The Description of Leicestershire* (1622), 'To the reader'.

[17] Centre for Kentish Studies, Maidstone Borough Archives, MS FA FAc/9 Bundle 2. I owe this reference to the kindness of Robert Tittler, to whom I am also grateful for sharing in advance of publication a relevant chapter in his book *The Reformation and the Towns in England: Politics and Political Culture, c.1540–1640* (Oxford, 1998).

[18] W. J. Jones, 'The Exchequer of Chester in the Last Years of Elizabeth I', in A. J. Slavin (ed.), *Tudor Men and Institutions* (Baton Rouge, 1972), 123–70, at p. 133.

[19] Richard Bancroft, *A Survey of the Pretended Holy Discipline* (1593), 207, 448; William Harrison, *The Description of England*, ed. G. Edelen (Ithaca, NY, 1968), 61, 125, 197, 200, 215, 438.

problem in 1537, the privy chamber at Greenwich Palace was fitted with a new ceiling which included new battens 'after the anttycke facion'. In this instance, 'anttycke' did not denote, as it would later, the deliberately and consciously old-fashioned or 'historical', but precisely the opposite, traditional and normal.[20]

There were, of course, important contexts within which not just oldness but degree of oldness mattered urgently, even desperately. Some of these now appear to us as naive, simple-minded, even childish, rather like the 'my father is stronger than yours' boast of a 10-year-old boy. The ongoing squabble between Oxford and Cambridge over which university was older, a recondite controversy which began in the early sixteenth century and was still argued in the early eighteenth,[21] provides a well-known example. It is difficult to explain if one does not under-stand just how great a value was placed by contemporaries on oldness. Yet such quarrels should be regarded as neither vacuous nor scholastic since the issues were often concrete: in a dispute over customs jurisdiction between Bristol and Gloucester in 1582, Bristol asserted precedence because it claimed to have been founded by Brennus or Brennius in 3574 BC, while Gloucester, so Bristol claimed, was a mere stripling founded by Claudius Caesar in AD 45.[22] Although much higher stakes depended on it, the defence of Protestants against the Catholic assertion that their Church was a sixteenth-century innovation ('Where was your Church before Luther?') involved essentially the same strategy, comparing the post-patristic origins of much Catholic belief and practice unfavourably with their own, which originated with Christ or even at the beginning of time.[23]

More than most arenas of argument, religion demanded that proponents set their rhetorical battalions on the high ground of antiquity. Apologists for the Elizabethan Church were nevertheless placed in a difficult position simply by having to deny the validity of many Catholic innovations while asserting against puritan critics that some legitimate beliefs and practices had originated at times later than the founding of the Church. 'The faith, zeale and godlines of former times is worthylie had in honour', conceded Richard Hooker, without also con-ceding that 'nothing may bee which was not then; or that nothing which then was may lawfully since have ceased'.[24] The belief that the best law was that which

[20] *The History of the King's Works*, iii: *1485–1660*, ed. H. M. Colvin, 2 pts. (1975–82), pt. 2, 104, 132, 148. On the other hand, it could also be used to describe architectural or decorative innovation, for instance the Italianate-style borders on the numerous parts of Hampton Court that were built in the 1530s.

[21] Thomas Hearne and William Wotton discussed the issue in 1705: Hearne, *Remarks and Collections*, i. 47.

[22] PRO, SP 46/17, fo. 83[r]. I owe this reference to Robert Tittler.

[23] See *The Diary of John Manningham of the Middle Temple, 1602–1603*, ed. R. P. Sorlien (Hanover, NH, 1976), 156, 188, for such an argument. Antiquity did not, however, always invest legitimacy. The parish of Pitney brought a case against Sir John Strangways at Wells quarter sessions in 1646 for the levying of certain local rates on his property; this had already been determined by an order of 1640, but in this case the 'antiquity of the said order' proved a liability; the order was so 'old' that the court had to 'revive and confirm it' for it to be enforced. *Quarter Sessions Records for the County of Somerset*, iii: *Commonwealth, 1646–60*, ed. E. H. Bates Harbin, Somerset Rec. Soc., 28 (1912), 24.

[24] Hooker, *Laws*, IV, 2.3 (*Works*, i. 278); A. B. Ferguson, *Clio Unbound: Perception of the Social and Cultural Past in Renaissance England* (Durham, NC, 1979), 171–224, for a discussion of the position of Church apologists and their greater awareness of historical change.

had, for all practical purposes, always existed, paralleled the argument that Christianity itself was timeless and had existed since the creation of the world, though there had been no Christians; it was therefore sufficient argument against Catholicism, in the view of puritans such as William Loe, to show that, unlike true Christianity, popery 'was not so from the beginning'.[25] Donald Lupton singled out St Ignatius of Antioch for special reverence because he was so ancient that, like the Apostles, he had seen Jesus in person.[26]

Argument from antiquity was a central feature of many of the ecclesiastical and political debates of the early modern era, and it was used to great effect in local causes. The projected reformation of the canon law in 1552 dealt specifically with 'proof from antiquity' and provided guidelines to judges as to what sorts of authority, written and oral, should be given weight. 'In proving boundaries and ancient matters, rumors, and witnesses concerning what was said and heard, ancient books guarded and found without any suspicion can lead [the judge] to a limited belief, so that he may rightly pass sentence in favor of the man who thus proved his case, unless stronger proofs of the other party require otherwise.'[27] The origins of antiquarian research owed much to the routine labours of lawyers and judges, required to work through mounds of evidences and evaluate their age and authority in adjudicating on disputes over boundaries, property, and tithes. One example is provided by Sir Roger Manwood, chief baron of the Exchequer and a warden of the stone bridge at Rochester, who drew up 'A true discourse of the auncient woodden and present stone bridge at Rochester'. This was intended to clarify how the bridge came to be built (as a replacement for an earlier wooden one) and at whose expense, and how repairs had generally been carried out. Manwood wrote his discourse in response to a special session of the Privy Council held in February 1575, at which the government had required all records on the bridge to be produced for Manwood and an appointed committee.[28]

RESISTANCE TO THE NEW

For all the manifest interest in the 'new' that is evident in the seventeenth century, it remains an axiom in early modern intellectual history that innovation and novelty were words that invariably met with mistrust. Certainly they are among those terms whose connotations have radically changed since the seventeenth

[25] John Woolton, the Elizabethan bishop of Exeter, makes such an argument for the radical antiquity of Christianity in his *The Christian Manual* (1576), repr. PS 52 (Cambridge, 1851), 15; William Loe, *The Mystery of Mankinde* (1619), 12.

[26] Donald Lupton, *The Glory of their Times* (1640), 15.

[27] Text of 'Concerning Trials', cap. 26: 'The Proof from Antiquity', in *The Reformation of the Ecclesiastical Laws of England, 1552*, ed. J. C. Spalding, Sixteenth Century Essays and Studies, 19 (Kirksville, Mo., 1992), 197.

[28] SAL MS 159 (collections of John Thorpe for Rochester), fos. 1–37ᵛ. This is an early eighteenth-century copy of an original Latin treatise by Manwood dated 1586; it includes evidence from the Tower records and the *Rotuli parlamentorum*.

century. Although novelty retains something of its original association with
frivolity (as in the sense of 'novelty' stores), innovation now has a generally positive valence, like 'progress', of which it is commonly seen as an engine. In contrast, comments in the sixteenth and seventeenth centuries about the evils of
innovation are so frequent that few instances need be adduced here. The author
of a popular Elizabethan madrigal was merely echoing a commonplace when he
decried change as the consequence of human wickedness and of a natural crav-
ing for innovation:

> The love of change hath changed the world throughout;
> And what is counted good but that is strange?
> New things wax old, old new, all turns about,
> And all things change except the love of change.[29]

Half a century later, the royalist gentleman Roger Whitley, generalizing amid
trying times, would note in his commonplace book the political truism that 'all
innovacion and change in government is very bad & dangerous'.[30]

It is not the case that early modern thought accepted no change as good; rather,
it recognized the fact of change and distinguished between that which was good
and that which was bad. Deliberate but moderate change might be acceptable under
certain circumstances, particularly if it restored a desirable prior situation—the
English Reformation was built on this idea. Richard Hooker thought that things
which had decayed could be altered, but expressed a dislike of new things on the
principle that they were unproven: 'there are fewe thinges knowne to be good,
till such time as they grow to be ancient'.[31] On the whole, however, that narrower,
non-restorative type of change known as innovation, now a virtue, was then a
vice, a deliberate and often gratuitous violation of tradition and order. In John
Donne's polemic *Ignatius his Conclave*, Ignatius Loyola, the founder of the
Society of Jesus, debates with Machiavelli, Columbus, and Copernicus as to who
among them is the most troublesome innovator, and the devil gathers around
him the souls of 'all which had invented any new thing, even in the smallest
matters'.[32] Contemporaries acknowledged that the psychological instinct in
favour of novelty was in some ways more forceful, given human weakness, than
the learned fear of it. 'Men's nature is still desirous of news, variety, delights',
observed Robert Burton, 'and our wandering affections are so irregular in this
kind, that they must change, though it be to the worst.' Though the world itself
was in her dotage, argued the preacher George Benson, she was 'ever in childbed,
in travell every month of newe fashions, of newe sinnes, of new vanities: of all
new things, save only of the new man'. Robert Shelford speculated that even if a
perfect liturgy were established by common consent, 'it would not long be liked,

[29] Richard Carlton, *Madrigals for five voyces* (1601), repr. in E. H. Fellowes, *English Madrigal Verse 1588–1632*, 2nd edn. (Oxford, 1967), p. 77, no. 1.
[30] Bodl. MS Eng. hist. e. 312, p. 47, and MS Eng. hist. e. 310, p. 77, *sub* 'Innovation'.
[31] Hooker, *Laws*, IV, 14.5 (*Works*, i. 340); V, 39.3 (ii. 159); V, 7.3 (ii. 37).
[32] John Donne, *Ignatius his Conclave* (1610), 18, 92–3.

except it might roll as mens wits roll; that is, as continually to alter, as the winde bloweth and the weather changeth'.[33]

One can find criticisms of innovation in almost every sphere of debate or controversy throughout the sixteenth and seventeenth centuries, from the great to the relatively trivial. Among the fears articulated by John Stubbs in opposing Queen Elizabeth's prospective match with the duke of Alençon in 1579 was that a Valois consort would bring in French surveyors and the end of old English measurements. Courtyards would be 'measured by the foot; our houses by the stories, windows, and chimneys, and accordingly new rents raised upon them'.[34] The economist Edward Misselden, attacking the proto-mercantilist views of Gerard Malynes, defended the traditional monopoly structure of the English cloth trade against 'the danger and inconvenience of innovations' which would damage the economy far more than the depression the country was suffering.[35] Local governments jealously guarded their traditional practices, protected by custom and charter, against dangerous innovation, though sometimes these came into conflict. In a dispute at Chester in the early seventeenth century over the proper number of aldermen and common councillors to be chosen, the city was faced with an apparent contradiction between long-standing practice and a recently granted charter. After much debate they elected to follow the 'ancient custom' and yield no room for 'innovation'.[36] Even in everyday life, innovation could be frowned upon as an infringement on personal status and privilege. When Sir Thomas Bodley's first librarian, Thomas James, proposed a change in the methods for cataloguing books, his employer sharply reminded him of their agreement that 'no innovation might be made without my privitie'.[37]

Like its obverse, the defence from antiquity, the argument against innovation was a motivating force in politics and religion from the Reformation to the end of the seventeenth century. To suggest that something was an improvement was, generally speaking, insufficient; it had to be shown as a manifest return to a socially sanctioned past whose authenticity was not in doubt. Catholic polemicists throughout the sixteenth century regarded Protestant reformers as innovators, devoted to what one called the 'abolishing of the auncient doctrine of Christ' in favour of 'apish noveltie'.[38] The reformers returned fire by arguing that their own religion dated back much further and therefore represented true, ancient tradition. In 1537, at the height of the Henrician Reformation, Archbishop Cranmer reproved a Kentish JP, who was enforcing popish practices such as saint-worship

[33] Burton, *Anatomy of Melancholy*, 294; George Benson, *A sermon preached at Paules Crosse the seaventh of May MDCIX* (1609), 41; Robert Shelford, *Five pious and learned discourses* (Cambridge, 1635), 41.

[34] John Stubbs, *The discovery of a gaping gulf* (1579), ed. L. Berry (1968), 90.

[35] Edward Misselden, *The circle of commerce* (1623), 63.

[36] *Calendar of Chester City Council Minutes, 1603–1642*, ed. Margaret J. Groombridge, Lancashire and Cheshire Rec. Soc., 106 (1956), p. 25 (23 Sept., 1606).

[37] *Letters of Sir Thomas Bodley to Thomas James: First Keeper of the Bodleian Library*, ed. G. W. Wheeler (Oxford, 1926), 117.

[38] Thomas Harding, *A Confutation of a booke intituled An apologie of the church of England* (Antwerp, 1565), fos. 257, 323[v].

and relics and obstructing obedience to the Bishops' Book, for confusing the new and old:

> truly you and your servants be so blinded, that you call old that is new, and new that is old . . . But in very deed the people be restored by this book to their old good usages, although they be not restored to their late abused usages; for the old usage was in the primitive church, and nigh thereunto when the church was most purest, nothing less so to phantasy of ceremonies, pilgrimage, purgatory, saints, images, works, and such like, as hath these three or four hundred years been corruptly taught.[39]

Heinrich Bullinger's treatise *Antiquissima Fides et vera religio*, which argues that Protestantism was 'no new-fangled faith', was translated by Miles Coverdale as *The olde fayth* and went through several editions. The first Edwardian prayer book tried to strike a balance between the repudiation of old customs and the inclination of hardliners such as Bishop Hooper to 'be so new fangle that they would innovate all thing'.[40]

The fear of innovation was thus a visceral response that even some contemporaries realized could be carried to extremes; like most such reactions, it could be controlled and even overcome. Ambrose Fisher, defending the liturgy of the Established Church, criticized puritans for the repudiation of all innovations simply because they were perceived as popish. 'Will you reject printing and gunnes, because they were found out by papists?' he asked. Innovation was permissible in things indifferent to salvation, such as the use of music and the cross in services, though he admitted that such changes, 'without important necessitie', could be harmful to church and state.[41] By the later seventeenth century, the knee-jerk defence of oldness for its own sake and repudiation of novelty were becoming less easy to sustain. Samuel Butler satirized both in *Hudibras*, where a lady refuses to free the imprisoned knight because she has no warrant for it in 'authentical romance':

> And I'de be loath to have you break
> An ancient custom for a freak,
> Or innovation introduce
> In place of things of antique use.[42]

Thomas Pope Blount, politician and essayist, would make a defence of novelty central to his argument against superstitious reverence of antiquity, and in favour of a notion of artistic and technological progress. 'It is not therefore an offence, to introduce new things, unless that which is introduced prove

---

[39] Cranmer would adopt the same line a few years later with Queen Mary, pointing out the paradox whereby 'that which they call the old is the new, and that which they call the new is indeed the old': *Miscellaneous Writings and Letters of Thomas Cranmer*, vol. ii of *Works of Thomas Cranmer*, ed. J. E. Cox, 2 vols., PS 15–16 (Cambridge, 1844–6), ii. 351, 355, 450.

[40] Miles Coverdale, *The olde fayth* (1541), in *Writings and Translations of Myles Coverdale*, PS 13 (Cambridge, 1844), 6; another edition of Bullinger's work appeared in 1624 under the title *Look from Adam, and behold the Protestants' faith and religion*, in *The two liturgies . . . of King Edward VI*, PS 29 (Cambridge, 1844), 155–7.

[41] Ambrose Fisher, *A defence of the liturgie of the church of England* (1630), 144, 149.

[42] Samuel Butler, *Hudibras*, pt. 2, canto I, lines 789–92, ed. J. Wilders (Oxford, 1967), 123.

pernicious in it self', he wrote. 'If novelty should always be rejected, neither would arts have arrived to that perfection, wherein now we enjoy them, nor could we ever hope for any future Reformation.'[43] The great inventions of the age, the compass, printing press, and gunpowder, lent support to those who wished to argue that things had changed for the better, though not all men were convinced, in the case of powder and print, that these were good things. Against an older view, put most articulately in Polydore Vergil's enormously popular *De Rerum Inventoribus*, a book which found ancient inventors for virtually everything, there was developing a much more historical sense of culture and technology as cumulative and progressive. This view did not ignore the past as 'obsolete' but venerated it precisely because it threw the accomplishments of recent times into perspective. William Lisle borrowed from Vasari's famous teleology of modern art to make a point about the historical study of language. 'Cimabue and Giotto came far short of Dominico, and he of Michael Angelo, miracle of both those arts' of painting and sculpture, he wrote, 'yet all had their due and respective praise, because perfection starts not up suddenly with invention, but growes by certaine degrees.'[44] The older and inferior should be studied to cast light on the perfection of its descendants, Lisle suggested, thereby providing a justification for his treatise on old English, from which the language of his own day had developed.

There was a conflict in late medieval and Renaissance mentalities between a desire, on the one hand, to soften the shock of the new by categorizing it instead as old, revived, or rediscovered and more radical tendencies that, on the other hand, actually admitted the possibility of new things. This tension grew more pronounced as the seventeenth century wore on and the speed of technological improvement made it increasingly difficult to assert that the ancients had known everything worth knowing. It can be seen in the thought of Francis Bacon, which totters uneasily between two very different notions of 'modernity', one which repudiates the recent past in favour of the more distant past, of which it is a restoration and continuation, and another, more radical conviction that his own time represented an improvement on, and break with, even the accomplishments of the ancients.[45] It can be seen again, later in the seventeenth century, in the physician John Radcliffe's remark to his old friend Obadiah Walker, wherein authority is assigned to its appropriate sphere and not permitted to contradict common sense. 'Fathers, and councils, and antique authorities, may have their influence in proper places,' Radcliffe told Walker, 'but should any of them all, though covered with dust 1,400 years ago, tell me that the bottle I am now drinking with some of your acquaintance is a wheelbarrow, and the glass in my hand a salamander, I should ask leave to dissent from them.'[46]

---

[43] Thomas Pope Blount, *Essays on Several Subjects* (1691), ch. 4, pp. 80–1.
[44] William Lisle, *Divers ancient monuments in the Saxon tongue* (1638), sig. e4–f.
[45] Charles Whitney, *Francis Bacon and Modernity* (New Haven, Conn., 1986), 1–19 and *passim*.
[46] *Memoirs and Correspondence of Francis Atterbury, D.D., Bishop of Rochester*, ed. F. Williams, 2 vols. (1869), i. 29 (Radcliffe to Walker, 25 May 1688).

Less illustrious writers than Bacon or Radcliffe also testify to this ambivalence. Gabriel Plattes believed that 'invention' should not be 'lightly regarded', citing the ox-drawn plough as an instance of technological and economic progress. But he also defined invention in the conventional way as the *re*discovery of ancient arts, 'hidden since the worlds beginning' and now graciously restored to man by providence.[47] The author of a treatise on fen drainage argued in favour of this 'improvement' by appealing to history for earlier instances; such innovations had helped the common weal in the past, and the 'consent of so many ages, wise and politike princes and assemblies of parliament' dictated that such projects be continued. An Elizabethan treatise on gardening asserted that that art had only recently reached perfection, yet its author still felt obliged both to praise and to refer to older, classical practices. Whatever the aesthetic attractions or historical interest which classical or Renaissance gardens may now hold for us as models of landscape, we would now regard the horticultural techniques used in their creation as obsolete, at least in a practical sense. Seventeenth-century people could not so easily jettison the skills and methods of antiquity.[48]

THE IDEA OF HISTORICAL DECLINE

Closely related to the belief that novelties and innovations violated the traditional order of things was the idea that the world and everything in it was in an advanced state of decay, of which a principal sign was a steady decline in morals and manners. Almost every Western society has tended to romanticize or glorify the past, recent or remote: our own is no exception, as the political discourse of North American and British neo-conservatism over the past two decades demonstrates. But in a culture so firmly focused on the past and tradition rather than on potential progress into a future, the sense of decay could assume much more importance.

Since the Augustan debates of ancients and moderns (with which the present chapter will conclude), Western culture has operated under a set of practical rules and moral measures deduced from an assumption of general secular progress and a capacity for moral improvement. Political philosophers of the eighteenth century, building on the civic humanist tradition of the Renaissance, made manners, comportment, and even 'politeness' critical elements in their analysis of the social world.[49] Even in the religious sphere this can be seen in the philanthropic and educative societies such as the SPCK that flourished in the eighteenth century. At a more popular level it occurs in the greater popular appeal of Methodism, with its ethos of self-help, over the predestinarianism of the sixteenth and

[47] Gabriel Plattes, *A discovery of infinite treasure, hidden since the worlds beginning* (1639), sig. C3ᵛ.
[48] H.C., *A discourse concerning the drayning of fennes* (1629), sig. A2; Thomas Hill, *The arte of gardening* (1563; repr. 1608), 5, 17.
[49] A. Bryson, *From Courtesy to Civility: Changing Codes of Conduct in Early Modern England* (Oxford, 1998), 42–74.

seventeenth centuries. Progress, in eighteenth-century terms, could be either slow, organic, and incremental, as in the thought of a Burke, or sharp and radical, as for a Paine or Wollstonecraft. But the overall assumption of progress, the belief in a forward-moving social arrow leading from barbarism to civility, is a feature of Augustan and Georgian thought that was very largely foreign to the sixteenth and early seventeenth centuries.[50] Though there were indeed suggestions, even then, of progress in various spheres such as the arts and sciences, these have to be measured against a general assumption that the natural condition of beings in time was one of decline.

The idea that the natural world was itself in a continual state of decay had been inherited from antiquity by the early Christians, and had been given its classic formulation by authors such as St Cyprian and Lactantius. It had been a more or less constant theme in medieval historical writing, and many Renaissance thinkers had taken it up. Its literary expressions are legion, and have been amply discussed elsewhere.[51] They go hand in hand with a culture that appears in many ways to have been obsessed with death, the inescapable decay and ultimate annihilation of the body.[52]

A prominent part of the long-standing theme of historical decline, challenged only sporadically in the Middle Ages by such visionaries as Joachim of Fiore, was the idea that mankind had *literally* declined in physical stature, longevity, and prowess. This was natural enough to a culture that took the ages of Methuselah and the other patriarchs literally, and accepted the gigantic stature of other biblical and some classical figures.[53] John Donne, whose melancholic comments on his own times in *The first anniversarie* are sufficiently well known not to require repetition, thought that 'the patriarchs in the Old Testament had their summer day, long lives; we are in the winter, short lived'. Henry Peacham concurred, though he did not have to look back as far as the patriarchs for evidence of the superiority of past times: 'the age of man very much declineth', he wrote, and men 'are not halfe so strong & vigorous as they were in the memory of our

[50] D. Spadafora, *The Idea of Progress in Eighteenth-Century Britain* (New Haven and London, 1990), is the best analysis of progress in the eighteenth century, with appropriate attention to its seventeenth-century roots. Among older accounts of the idea, the following remain most useful: W. W. Wagar, 'Modern Views of the Origins of the Idea of Progress', *Journal of the History of Ideas*, 28 (1967), 55–70; J. Delvaille, *Essai sur l'histoire de l'idée de progrès jusqu'à la fin du XVIIIe siècle* (Paris, 1910); J. B. Bury, *The Idea of Progress: An Inquiry into its Origin and Growth* (1920).

[51] G. L. Davies, *The Earth in Decay: A History of British Geomorphology 1578–1878* (New York, 1969), 27–94; S. Toulmin and J. Goodfield, *The Discovery of Time* (New York, 1965).

[52] J. Huizinga, *The Waning of the Middle Ages* (1924; repr. Harmondsworth, 1976), 124–35; A. Esler, *The Aspiring Mind of the Elizabethan Younger Generation* (Durham, NC, 1966), 47–50; for the *artes moriendi*, see R. Chartier, *The Cultural Uses of Print in Early Modern France*, trans. L. G. Cochrane (Princeton, 1987), 32–70; C. Gittings, *Death, Burial and the Individual in Early Modern England* (1984), 22, 34–5; R. Houlbrooke, *Death, Religion, and the Family in England, 1480–1750* (Oxford, 1998). The paraphernalia of death are the subject of N. Llewellyn, *The Art of Death: Visual Culture in the English Death Ritual, c.1500–c.1800* (1991).

[53] For example, William Harrison, 'The Description of Britaine', in R. Holinshed, *The First and Second Volumes of Chronicles* (1587), 12–13, in which the fact of diminishing stature is mentioned, though Harrison asserts that 'hugeness of bodie is not to be accompted of as part of our felicitie'.

fathers'.[54] Several decades later Ralph Palmer was convinced that the shrinkage in stature was continuing, and was directly attributable to human moral failure. Reading *Gulliver's Travels* appears to have given him a horrifying vision of mankind's eventual destiny. 'The luxurys and debaucherys of every age is driving us on towards pygmeism, and if we stop not short, but proceed as fast as we have done, I know not but that (if the world shall last long enough), we or our posterity may become actual Lyllyputians.'[55]

The new natural philosophy of the Restoration, for all its Baconian admiration of experiment and observation over inherited assumption, was obliged for over a century to fit its findings into this paradigm, with varying success. The decay of natural bodies was not in itself a problem, nor was it irreconcilable with the new experimental science of the seventeenth century. The plenitude and wonder of nature and its mutability and impermanence were perfectly compatible. It was possible, for instance, to admit the existence of individual 'monsters or individuals of extraordinary growth' throughout history while denying 'that there ever was a time when men were generally larger than at present'.[56] John Evelyn, member of the Royal Society, and a fervent attender of sermons in later life, heard one preacher present the view, first advanced by the Caroline writer George Hakewill, 'that we ought to rely on the providence of God, discovering the wonderfullnesse of it from the Creation, & Government of the World'. Barely two weeks later, however, he paid rapt attention to a sermon on 'this declining age of the world'.[57]

One can trace the origins of the eighteenth-century idea of progress in the discussions of decay and mutability a century earlier, but the relationship is more complex than a straightforward intellectual pedigree would suggest. George Hakewill's *Apologie of the Power and Providence of God* asserted that things in nature and civilization neither improved nor declined but stayed much the same as they had always been. In contrast to his contemporary, Francis Bacon's, more radical vision of overall improvement in the arts and learning, Hakewill did not, as is sometimes erroneously asserted, believe in progress, either moral or technological, but rather in a pattern of 'vicissitude'—drawn from the sixteenth-century Frenchman, Le Roy—whereby a number of 'progresses', or gradual improvements over time in the past, were offset by periodic decays. While man might, he conceded, have declined in longevity, he had improved in many other ways. Hakewill even questioned the reliability of certain classical formulations of the idea of decay: St Cyprian, he reminded readers, had lived in the late third

---

[54] Francis Shakelton, *A blazyng starre or burnyng beacon, seene the 10 of October laste* (1580), sig. A5ʳ, is among the earliest English statements of the belief that physical prowess, longevity, and stature had declined; *The Sermons of John Donne*, ed. G. R. Potter and E. M. Simpson, 10 vols. (Berkeley and Los Angeles, 1953–8), vol. ii. no. 9, p. 199; Henry Peacham, *The truth of our times* (1638), 189 ff.

[55] SAL MS 20 (Ralph Palmer, 'Gigantologia' (c.1730)), fo. 18ʳ.

[56] Edward Lhwyd, paraphrasing Robert Plot, in R. T. Gunther, *Early Science in Oxford*, xiv: *Life and Letters of Edward Lhwyd* (Oxford, 1945), 200–1.

[57] Evelyn, *Diary*, iv. 156–7.

century during an age of particularly severe persecution, and might have had an entirely different outlook had he survived into the era of Constantine.[58]

Hakewill, who cites Jean Bodin frequently, followed the French philosopher in dismissing the Hesiodic notion of the gold, silver, brass, and iron ages, ascribing the theory of decay to 'the morosity and crooked disposition of old men, always complaining of the hardnesse of the present times, together with an excessive admiration of antiquitie, which is in a manner naturall and inbred in us'.[59] The association of excessive nostalgia with old age would be mimicked by eighteenth-century defenders of progress such as the physician Peter Shaw, and Restoration and Augustan thinkers picked up on the suggestion that the idea of decline was a natural but mistaken belief, increasingly easy to contradict by example.[60] John Lee alias Warner, archdeacon of Rochester, drew up sermon notes designed to show that 'every succeeding age attests to the wickedness of the former'.[61] Samuel Dale, an Augustan antiquary with a profound admiration for the achievements of the Romans and no soft spot for the nobility of the ancient Britons, who had been 'involved in the darkest errour and wholy ignorant of the true God', saw their liberation from Druidic tyranny as part of a longer evolution of the native British towards civilization and religion.[62]

THE DECAY OF COMMONWEALTHS

Since polities were the creations of declining and flawed humanity, it was equally commonplace to believe that they would, in time, decay. One had only to look to history for evidence of this, and political writers from Machiavelli to James Harrington to Charles Davenant believed that the pattern of decay was so reliable that the study of past examples could be used to predict the causes of decline in the future, and perhaps arrest them. Davenant, one of the founders of political arithmetic, believed that no empire had ever decayed, 'but the seeds of its destruction may have been observed long before in the course of its history'. Decays in a country's wealth and prosperity could similarly be 'foreseen early by such as bend their study to matters of this nature, for where the causes are apparent, we may judge easily of the effects'.[63] The negative face of this lay in the acknowledgement that all political bodies must inevitably decline. 'Where is now the innumerable company & puyssaunce of Xerxes and Caesar, where are the great

[58] Hakewill, *Apologie*, 50 f., 271.
[59] Elnathan Parr, 'Short and godly admonitions concerning time', *Abba father*, p. 26, in his *Workes*, 3rd edn. (1632); Jean Bodin, *Method for the Easy Comprehension of History*, trans. B. Reynolds (New York, 1945), 302; Hakewill, *Apologie*, 22.
[60] Spadafora, *Idea of Progress in Eighteenth-Century Britain*, 38.
[61] Bodl. MS Eng. th. e. 176 (sermon notes of John Warner the older and younger), fo. 6ᵛ.
[62] Bodl. MS top. gen. c. 66 (Samuel Gale, 'Of ye Religion of ye Ancient Britons', *c*.1710), fos. 123–130ᵛ.
[63] *Two Manuscripts by Charles Davenant*, ed. A. P. Usher (Baltimore, 1942), 93–4.

victoryes of Alexander and Pompey, where is now the rychesse of Cresus & Crassus?' asked John Fisher in 1509.[64] 'The naturall body hath his infancy, his youthfulnes, his confirmed, declyning, and decrepit age', wrote Edward Forset, the Jacobean political writer; 'so hath each Commonwealth, his beginning, his enlarging, his puissance, his drowping, his decay and downfall.'[65]

Beliefs about the instability and decay of bodies politic endured through the period, but they were most apparent in periods of extreme crisis and stress, such as the mid-sixteenth century, the end of Elizabeth's reign, and especially the 1640s and 1650s, when the collapse of censorship allowed the idea to be put to radical, as opposed to merely critical, uses. The Levellers and Diggers framed their democratic and socialist platforms as a return to an earlier age of simplicity and equality; they wanted a revolution, but the very word 'revolution' then implied a return to an earlier state of affairs. For Richard Overton and William Walwyn, this involved a recovery of Anglo-Saxon freedom, an escape from the 'Norman yoke', as they termed the legal system enforced on England since the Conquest. John Lilburne refused to acknowledge the authority of the judges at his treason trial in 1649, whom he claimed were 'no more but Norman intruders', and argued for the resumption of the judges' powers by the jurymen whom, he believed, had exercised them in freer times.[66] Gerrard Winstanley viewed the victory of the parliamentary army simply as the restoration of ancient social justice: 'When the Norman power had conquered our forefathers, he took the free use of our English ground from them, and made them his servants.'[67] As the seventeenth century wore on, however, an increasing number of individuals ceased to trouble to perform the mental gymnastics necessary for the framing of the outrageously new as the acceptably old. John Warren, an Essex minister, made no such apology for the abolition of monarchy in 1649:

Did you never see an old house translated into a new form before? Has Rome sometime the lady of the world bin changed in point of government so oft, and is it such an horrid thing that England changes once in five or six hundred yeeres? is any civill government

[64] John Fisher, *Treatyse concernynge . . . the seven penytencyall psalmes* (1509), in *English Works of John Fisher*, pt. 1, ed. J. E. B. Mayor, EETS es 27 (1876), 145–6; Fisher returned to this theme in his sermon at the funeral of Henry VII, ibid. 270.

[65] Edward Forset, *A comparative discourse of the bodies naturall and politique* (1606), 41.

[66] Richard Overton and William Walwyn, *A Remonstrance of Many Thousand Citizens . . . to their House of Commons* (1646), repr. in *Leveller Manifestoes of the Puritan Revolution*, ed. D. M. Wolfe (New York, 1944), 123–30; C. Hill, 'The Norman Yoke', in his *Puritanism and Revolution* (1958), 50–122; S. Kliger, *The Goths in England: A Study in Seventeenth and Eighteenth Century Thought* (Cambridge, Mass., 1952), 112–209, 253–87, now largely superseded by R. J. Smith, *The Gothic Bequest: Medieval Institutions in British Thought, 1688–1863* (Cambridge, 1987); T. A. Green, *Verdict According to Conscience: Perspectives on the English Criminal Trial Jury, 1200–1800* (Chicago, 1985), 173.

[67] On the other hand, Winstanley had no great fear of innovation: he called unashamedly for the removal of '*old* oppressing laws and customs'. These were not merely Norman laws, for Winstanley pushed the historical origins of property back far beyond the Conquest to the Fall. Winstanley, *The law of freedom in a platform, or true magistracie restored*, in *Works of Gerrard Winstanley*, ed. G. H. Sabine (New York, 1965), 501, 506, 559, 573, 587 (my italics); *The New Law of Righteousnes* (1649), ibid. 159; *The True Levellers Standard*, ibid. 252.

eternall? . . . If God will turne all things upside downe, who are we that should stand against him?[68]

On the whole, the language of political dissent as much as that of political conservatism continued to look to the past for its arguments. Whether 1066 had been a conquest or not, and whether England as a result was an absolute monarchy, was as much a question in 1679 and 1689 as it had been in the 1620s—perhaps more so, since few men of the Restoration, whatever their dissatisfaction with the later Stuarts, wished to repeat the unsettling experiments of the 1650s. In the famous 'Brady controversy' near the end of the century both the royalist historian Robert Brady and his Whig opponents turned alike to the past for the answers to pressing political questions. Where they differed was on what exactly the past had to say. For Brady, it provided unanswerable proof that the English constitution, and parliament with it, derived from the will of the Norman conqueror and his heirs. His Whig arch-rival and critic William Petyt believed just as sincerely that William I had confirmed and abided by the laws of Edward the Confessor, thereby maintaining and subordinating the monarchy to a legal system which dated back time out of mind.[69] More radical republicans such as Henry Neville and Algernon Sidney alternately lauded republican Rome as the age of liberty and virtue, or yearned for the hardy freedom of the German woods described in Tacitus's *Germania*. They blamed the disappearance of England's 'gothic' liberty on the growth of luxury and, following the teachings of Machiavelli and Justus Lipsius, the decline of the armed citizen.[70]

MANNERS AND MORALS

Another manifestation of the idea of decay applied less to the natural world of mutable bodies (human or otherwise) than to the social world of behaviour. The belief that manners and morals had changed for the worse, and were continuing to decline, amounted to a cliché throughout the sixteenth and seventeenth centuries. Like most commonplaces it was repeated frequently and generally with so little thought that we should guard against taking every utterance of it as evidence of either a melancholic zeitgeist or a passive submission to fatalism. Mary, Lady

---

[68] John Warren, *The potent potter* (19 Apr. 1649), in *The English Revolution: Fast Sermons to Parliament*, ed. R. Jeffs (1970), XXXII, 299–300.

[69] J. G. A. Pocock, *The Ancient Constitution and the Feudal Law: A Study of English Historical Thought in the Seventeenth Century. A Reissue with a Retrospect* (Cambridge, 1987), 182–228. Cf. J. Greenberg, *The Radical Face of the Ancient Constitution: St. Edward's 'Laws' in Early Modern Political Thought* (Cambridge, 2001), which appeared after the present work had been completed.

[70] C. Robbins, introduction to *Two English Republican Tracts* (Cambridge, 1969), 54–6; J. G. A. Pocock, *The Machiavellian Moment: Florentine Political Thought and the Atlantic Republican Tradition* (Princeton, 1975), 388, 393, 416, 441, 493–4; for Lipsius see G. Oestreich, *Neostoicism and the Early Modern State* (Cambridge, 1982), pt. 1; A. A. N. McCrea, *Constant Minds: Political Virtue and the Lipsian Paradigm in England, 1584–1650* (Toronto, 1997). For Sidney, see Jonathan Scott, *Algernon Sidney and the Restoration Crisis, 1677–1683* (Cambridge, 1991).

Chudleigh traced the steady decline of kindness, justice, and integrity from earliest times in 'the first Histories' down to her own day, concluding that 'there's
hardly anything left that looks like the Work of God', but in the same breath she
grudgingly conceded that her own age 'encreases in Politeness, in Fineneses of
Learning', and devoted a lengthy set of essays to the improvement of morals, which
she cannot have deemed an unachievable goal.[71]

One's opinion of contemporary manners naturally depended on one's own point
of view, which in turn was often dictated by social status: it was the elites of
seventeenth-century England who tried to reform the morals of their subordinates, not the other way around. 'It is nowe a common speach', observed one
Elizabethan, 'that the world is bad.' The assertion as bald fact of the judgement
that the present times were inherently, inescapably corrupt and sinful was frequently heard from the lips of those devoted to the improvement of mankind as
an injunction to try harder, or at least to be more contrite. The cleric and moral-
ist Robert Shelford subtitled his early work on the education of youth 'A treatise
very necessarie for all parents in this corrupt and declining age of the world'. The
puritan lawyer Edward Hake spoke from the same position, comparing the
morals of contemporary women with those of antiquity, to the discredit of those
'in this our extreme, and to [sic] impious time', while the preacher Samuel
Hieron attacked 'the beguiling enticements of this excessive age'.[72]

Cicero's anti-Catilinian ejaculation O tempora! O mores! was a much-quoted
line, and it reminds us that complaints against contemporary manners do not
originate in the Reformation; they are part of almost any culture with a sense of
its own past, historical, legendary, or mythical. In England a strong tradition of
decrying the morality of the day runs from Gildas in the sixth century, through
Chaucer and Piers Plowman in the fourteenth, to Reformation moralists such as
Robert Crowley (the first publisher of Langland's poem) in the mid-sixteenth.[73]
Nevertheless, the Reformation seems to have more fervently reinforced this
notion if only because Protestants knew that they had less excuse for impiety and
sin than their superstitious ancestors. The claim was often made by Elizabethan
and early Stuart writers and preachers that the Reformation, whatever its necessity, had led to a decline in charity and hospitality because of its assertion of the
inefficacy of good works towards salvation, and because it had occasioned the
ruin of the monastic houses. This is a charge that modern scholarship on both
subjects has largely dispelled, but we are interested here in contemporary

[71] Mary, Lady Chudleigh, 'Of Calumny', in Essays of Several Subjects in Prose and Verse (1710), in
The Poems and Prose of Mary, Lady Chudleigh, ed. M. L. Ezell (New York and Oxford, 1993), 332.
[72] Edward Knight, The triall of truth (1580), fo. 2ᵛ; Robert Shelford, Lectures . . . concerning the ver-
tuous education of youth (1602); Edward Hake, A touchstone for this time present (1574), sig. C4–D;
Samuel Hieron, A helpe unto devotion (1608), in Workes (1628), 724. For further examples of this theme
in sermons from the late sixteenth and early seventeenth centuries, see Michael Wigmore, The way
of all flesh (1619), 13; Richard Carpenter, The conscionable Christian (1623), 2; W.P., The young-mans
guide to godlinesse (1619), sig. A5.
[73] See esp. Crowley's Epigrams (1550), discussed in J. N. King, English Reformation Literature: The
Tudor Origins of the Protestant Tradition (Princeton, 1982), esp. 343–6.

perceptions rather than reality.[74] 'How slenderly are the poor members of Christ provided for now-a-days!' exclaimed Thomas Becon, whose 1564 work, *The news out of heaven*, is a litany of complaints against the manners of the time. The number of beggars, he argued, was everywhere on the rise, covetousness was rife, and whoredom had become no longer a sin but a sport. 'O how different are our times from those of our Ancestors?' asked the cleric William Typing. 'They were not more rigidly superstitious, then we are vainely secure.'[75]

In the previous chapter, the impact of changes in building styles on sensitivity to change was highlighted. The ruins of the great religious houses where, as one seventeenth-century writer put it, 'the well fed monkes and fryers did (in the days of old) juggle and jumble', often evoked a sense of loss even in fervent Protestants, who recognized the piety behind the foundations while decrying their popish connections. Even a staunch reformer such as Laurence Chaderton, born just after the last abbey fell, thought it unfortunate that the papists could always 'cast in our teeth the great and famous hospitalitie of their nobility, and cleargie, the buylding of abbies, monasteries, and nunneries, cathedrall churches, colledges, with many other outward works; which in deede are such as do stoppe our mouthes, & put us protestants to silence'.[76] A century later John Aubrey pined for the monastic life while John Evelyn commented wistfully of his parents' house at Wotton, Surrey, that it was built 'after the antient fashion of our Ancestors . . . according to the mode of those hospitable days'; employing a common topos, he contrasted the luxury of his own time with the simple tastes of his forebears, 'who relyed on the providence & blessing of God, on their honest and industrious course of life'.[77] Robert Thoroton blamed enclosures in the Vale of Belvoir on the 'stupendous act' of the dissolution.[78] Abraham de la Pryme, the Augustan cleric and antiquary, thought it 'a pitifull thing to hear the lamentation the people in the country made for them, for there was great hospitality kept amongst them, & as it was thought more than 1,000 persons, masters & servants, lost their livings by the putting of them down'.[79]

Clerics had a vested interest in promoting charity and criticizing the lay impropriation of monastic property that had once provided alms and funded pious giving, and they were often echoed by secular allies such as Sir Henry Spelman. Thomas Westcote, who did not believe in the general decay of the world, was saddened by the 'carcases' of the monasteries, whose original 'godly purposes' were

[74] W. K. Jordan, *Philanthropy in England: 1480–1660: A Study of the Changing Pattern of English Social Aspirations* (1959); F. Heal, *Hospitality in Early Modern England* (Oxford, 1990); F. Heal and C. Holmes, *The Gentry in England and Wales, 1500–1700* (Basingstoke, 1994), 372, point out that, though Jordan's specific monetary figures for giving have long been discredited, his central point about the general increase in private support for poverty relief and education from 1560 to 1640 is still defensible.

[75] Thomas Becon, *The news out of heaven* (1564), in *Early Works of Thomas Becon*, PS 2 (Cambridge, 1843), 40–1; William Typing, *A discourse of eternitie* (Oxford, 1633), 40.

[76] Laurence Chaderton, *An excellent and godly sermon* (1580, preached in 1578), sig. C5.

[77] Anthony Powell, *John Aubrey and his Friends* (1948), 137–8; Evelyn, *Diary*, i. 5, 15.

[78] M. W. Barley and K. S. S. Train, 'Robert Thoroton', in J. Simmons (ed.), *English County Historians, First Series* (Wakefield, 1978), 22–43, at p. 31.

[79] BL MS Lans. 897 (Abraham de la Pryme's History of Hatfield, Yorkshire, *c.*1700), fo. 118ᵛ.

no longer being honoured; he did not, however, conclude that charity as such
was in decline, since a number of schools and almshouses had been founded in
their place.[80] The preacher George Benson did not share this optimism, asserting
the decay both of 'good workes' and of 'good life and conversation', meaning manners in general.[81]

Catholics frequently harked back to pre-Reformation England, and their
yearnings often ascribed deteriorations in morals or even nature itself to the
onset of Protestantism: one writer noted that common folk in Christchurch,
Hampshire, would say that 'there came fewer salmon up their river, since the masse
went downe'. The black-letter ballad 'Little John Nobody', from the time of Edward
VI, attributes a range of social ills explicitly to the Reformation:

> For bribery was never so great since born was our Lord
> And whoredome was never lesse hated sith Christ harrowed hell
> And poor men are so sore punished commonly through the world
> That it would grieve any one that good is to hear tell
> For all the homilies and good books, yet their hearts be so quell
> That if a man do amisse, with mischiefe they will him wreake
> The fashion of these new fellows it is so vile and fell
> But that I little John Nobody dare not speak.[82]

The Lancashire Catholic William Blundell the elder (d. 1638) expressed similar
sentiments in the early seventeenth century, lamenting the passage of hospitality
along with religious stability.

> The tyme hath been wee hadd one faith,
> And strode aright one ancient path,
> The thym is now that each man may
> See newe Religons coynd each day . . .
>   The tyme hath beene the prelate's dore
> Was seldome shotte against the pore,
> The tyme is now, so wives goe fine,
> They take not thought the kyne . . .[83]

[80] Henry Spelman, *De non temerandis Ecclesiis* (1613) and *The History and Fate of Sacrilege* (1698); Thomas Westcote, *View of Devonshire* (Exeter, 1845), 145–6; for a similar reaction to the fall of the monasteries, see John Weever, *Ancient funerall monuments within the united monarchie of Great Britaine, Ireland, and the islands adjacent* (1631), preface, n.p.

[81] Benson, *A sermon preached at Paules Crosse the seaventh of May MDCIX*, 44.

[82] K. Thomas, *The Perception of the Past in Early Modern England* (Creighton Lecture, 1983), 12–19; John Favour, *Antiquitie triumphing over noveltie* (1619), 8; *The Ballad of Little John Nobody. Being a Libell upon the Reformation in the time of K. Edward ye 6th* (title inserted later, probably by Samuel Pepys), in *Catalogue of the Pepys Library at Magdalene College, Cambridge: The Pepys Ballads*, ed. W. G. Day (Cambridge, 1987), facs. vol. i, pp. 19–21.

[83] *Crosby Records*, pp. 24–9; Lancs RO DDBl (Blundell of Little Crosby), Acc. 6121, Great Hodge Podge, fo. 132ʳ Latin verses on 'An expostulation or chyding of Jesus with man perishinge throughe his owne fawlte; translated out of latin verse into Englishe as foloweth by Wil. Bl'; ibid., fos. 135ᵛ–136ʳ *et seq.* for more ditties and music written by William; cf. D. R. Woolf, 'Little Crosby and the Horizons of Early Modern Historical Culture', in D. R. Kelley and D. H. Sacks (eds.), *The Historical Imagination in Early Modern Britain* (Cambridge and Washington, DC, 1997).

Nostalgia did not recognize confessional lines, and Protestants might share these or similar views depending on their attitude to the church practices of their day. Richard Carrier, a Derbyshire JP, was examined before Star Chamber in 1631 for having said 'that it was never good since there was soe much preaching'.[84] Others regretted a corruption of hierarchy. Sir William Vaughan complained in 1626 that 'Joane is as good as my lady, citizens wives of late [have] growne gallants'.[85] After the Restoration, cavaliers wistfully lamented the godly zeal of the 1640s and 1650s, not all the consequences of which had been undone. Sir Roger Twysden, the Kentish magistrate and antiquary, concluded in 1662 that, while the 'sinne of whordom' had always been commonplace, 'since the taking away the Ecclesiastique Courts by the Long Parlyament I think much more frequent than formerly'. A ballad summarizing the history of the popish plot and reign of James II ended with regret at the invasion of Dutchmen under William III and an appeal to the ever-popular memory of Queen Elizabeth:

> Ah England, that never couldst value thy peace:
> Had matters been now as in Elsabeths day,
> The Dutch had ne'r ventur'd to Fish in our Seas.[86]

Some changes for the worse, it was acknowledged, had occurred much earlier than the Reformation. The alleged introduction of sealing by the Normans (another incorrect belief as it turned out, since the Anglo-Saxons had also used seals) was blamed by William Camden, the greatest antiquarian scholar of his day, for the end of a simpler, trusting, 'plaine dealing' age when men 'used to make all their assurances of whatsoever, in a few lines, and with a few gilt crosses'.[87] The Worcestershire antiquary and loyal adherent of Rome Thomas Habington placed the end of a golden age of hospitality and goodwill not at the advent of Protestantism but as early as the Conquest, which had restricted charitable giving, and the statute of Mortmain (1279), which had confirmed this:

Nowe descendinge to thease later ages when, iniquityes aboundinge, charity grewe coulde, and the auncient Englishe, suppressed by the Conquest, weare not able as before to extend theire bounty to the church; and the Normans growinge after into one body with the Englishe, laying aside the severity of conquerors and joyninge with them in reedifyinge the churche's ruines, weare both checked and forbidden by the statute of mortmaine.[88]

Another frequent complaint throughout the period concerned a decline in martial values and in the nation's capacity to defend itself; this would be overlaid in the seventeenth and eighteenth centuries by the separate but related Tacitean trope

---

[84] *Reports of Cases in the Courts of Star Chamber and High Commission*, ed. S. R. Gardiner, Camden Soc., NS 39 (1886), 92, 98.

[85] William Vaughan, *The golden fleece* (1626), cited in M. Campbell, *The English Yeoman* (repr. 1983), 43.

[86] CKS, U47/47/01 (Twysden's JP notebook), p. 53; *Private Occurrences: or, the Transactions of the Four Last Years* (c.1689), in *The Pepys Ballads*, ed. Day, facs. vol. v, p. 101.

[87] William Camden, *Britain*, trans. P. Holland (1607), 444.

[88] Thomas Habington, *A Survey of Worcestershire*, ed. J. Amphlett, 2 vols., Worcestershire Historical Soc. (Oxford, 1895–9), ii. 12.

of luxury inducing sloth and weakness. When confronted by the modernist's claim that the invention of gunpowder marked technological improvement, champions of decline took up the gauntlet and pointed to its greater destructive capacity or to the falling-off of more traditional forms of defence. George Hakewill, John Donne, Fynes Morison, and Donald Lupton each thought artillery had made war less bloody; Samuel Daniel, on the other hand, believed it had merely made killing easier and more cold-blooded.[89] As early as the end of the fifteenth century, William Caxton the printer, lamenting this winter of chivalry, asked his knightly audience where was 'the custome and usage of noble chyvalry that was used in th[e] dayes' of the Romans, of King Arthur, and of the mythical heroes Brennus and Belinus. He inveighed against recreations such as dice and against baths, because they distracted men from more worthwhile martial pursuits, and enjoined his readers to rediscover the glories of their forefathers in history-reading.

Leave this, leave it! And read the volumes of the Holy Grail, of Lancelot, of Galahad . . . of Gawain . . . And look in the latter days at the noble acts since the conquest; as in the days of King Richard Coeur de Lion; of Edward I and III, and of his noble sons; of Sir Robert Knowles, Sir John Hawkwood, Sir John Chandos . . . Read Froissart![90]

Over a century later, despite the attempts of several successive regimes to impose compulsory archery practice and improve the quality of the musters, the situation had not changed. William Vallans was convinced that martial discipline was 'mannaged with much more honourable regard and reward' in previous centuries than in his own.[91] Even the old weapons were no longer in demand. William Somner and George Silver both observed with sadness the change in weaponry among their countrymen: longbow had given way to musket, short sword to rapier. Peacham thought that few men could even manage to handle the huge bows used four generations earlier.[92] In 1614 Samuel Rowlands noted a common belief that the age of English military glory had ended in 1544 with Henry VIII's expedition to Boulogne, an event accorded much attention in almanac chronologies.[93]

This tradition of nostalgia for recently vanished martial valour is quite distinct from another with which it is often confused, that of the 'golden age', an era in which men and women behaved with honesty, openness, and charity, and none

[89] Hakewill, *Apologie*, 260; *Sermons of John Donne*, vol. iii, no. 17, pp. 359–60: Donne's pessimistic *The first anniversarie*, on the other hand, should serve as a warning against categorizing writers as 'ancients' or 'moderns' simply according to their opinion of modern inventions; Donald Lupton, *Emblems of rarities* (1636), 91–2; Fynes Morison, *Itinerary* (1617), iii. 28; Samuel Daniel, *The civil wars* (1595–1609), ed. L. Michel (New Haven, Conn., 1958), book VI, stanzas 37–40; Ferguson, *Clio Unbound*, 391–6; id., 'Historical Thought of Samuel Daniel: A Study in Renaissance Ambivalence', *Journal of the History of Ideas*, 32 (1971), 185–202; D. R. Woolf, 'Community, Law and State: Samuel Daniel's Historical Thought Revisited', *Journal of the History of Ideas*, 49 (1988), 61–83.

[90] William Caxton, preface to *The Book of the Ordre of Chyvalry*, ed. A. T. P. Byles, EETS os 168 (1926), 121–3.

[91] William Vallans, *The honourable prentice: or, this taylor is a man* (1615), sig. A2.

[92] William Somner, *Antiquities of Canterbury* (1640), 267; George Silver, *Paradoxes of defence* (1599), *passim*; Peacham, *The truth of our times*, 189 ff.

[93] B. S. Capp, *Astrology and the Popular Press: English Almanacs, 1500–1800* (London and Boston, 1979), 218, citing Samuel Rowlands, *A fooles bolt is soone shot* (1614).

went hungry. This notion, a utopianism projected on to the past, intersects with a more specifically chivalric nostalgia from time to time, for instance in the great Elizabethan epic, Spenser's *Faerie Queene*, or, in a more popular form, in a ballad entitled *The Golden Age: Or, An Age of Plaine-dealing*. The author of this work inverts the issue, proclaiming the return of a vanished age in which lawyers were honest and literally worked for a song rather than a fee, usurers gave up charging interest, and women were universally faithful to their husbands.[94] This view of the world also looked to the past as an ideal, but to a timeless, imagined antiquity rather than to recent memory. The golden-age myth, with its obvious connections to heroic poetry, and with a pedigree dating back to Hesiod, had deeper roots in classical convention and is found much more commonly in highly educated authors. Writers in the golden-age tradition, such as the poets Nicholas Breton and Thomas Heywood, envisaged a long-term historical decline which might yet be reversed under the guidance of a beneficent ruler. Those within the nostalgic tradition tended, in contrast, to think of decay as a relatively recent phenomenon, and to see all time before recent memory as one long age of virtue and prosperity.[95] Their sense of the meeting of past and present was defined by real changes, whether environmental or political, rather than by a code of values drawn principally from classical sources.

ANCIENTS AND MODERNS

The differing views on the dynamics of world change expounded at the start of the seventeenth century by Hakewill and by exponents of the case for decline such as Godfrey Goodman were not new, but the inheritance of a long-standing humanist argument about the status of the modern in relation to antiquity. New World marvels had merely complicated rather than resolved these. While the mineral and vegetable wonders of the Americas, and the new nautical technologies used to attain them, inspired enthusiasts such as Bacon into bold assertions of the technical supremacy of his own age, they could just as easily worry others who pointed to the importation of new diseases such as syphilis.[96] It was possible to

[94] *The Golden Age: Or, An Age of Plaine-dealing*, in *The Pepys Ballads*, ed. Day, facs. vol. i, pp. 152–3. For the theme of the golden age in learned culture, see H. Levin, *The Myth of the Golden Age in the Renaissance* (Bloomington, Ind., 1969); H. Kamen, 'Golden Age, Iron Age: A Conflict of Concepts in the Renaissance', *Journal of Medieval and Renaissance Studies*, 4 (1974), 135–55; G. Parry, *The Golden Age Restor'd: The Culture of the Early Stuart Court* (Manchester, 1981).

[95] William Terilo [Nicholas Breton?], *A peece of friar Bacons brazen-heads prophesie* (1604); Thomas Heywood, *The golden age* (1611); *The silver age* (1613); *The brazen age* (1613); *The iron age* (1632). On the golden age as an elite myth, see, in addition to works already cited, F. Yates, *Astraea: The Imperial Theme in the Sixteenth Century* (London and Boston, 1975). The agrarian tradition of nostalgia, including early 'communism', is well dealt with in A. McRae, *God Speed the Plough: The Representation of Agrarian England, 1500–1660* (Cambridge, 1996), 112–31.

[96] S. Greenblatt, *Marvelous Possessions: The Wonder of the New World* (Chicago, 1991), 52–86; A. Grafton et al., *New Worlds, Ancient Texts: The Power of Tradition and the Shock of Discovery* (Cambridge, Mass., 1992), 176–93; A. W. Crosby, *The Columbian Exchange* (Westport, Conn., 1972), 122–64.

view newness as Janus-faced, holding out great benefits or offering potential additions to the book of social evils, and many people are likely to have clung to such ambivalence. Nevertheless, Hakewill and Bacon on the one side and Goodman on the other neatly capture the conflicting positions and provide two early seventeenth-century poles between which moved most subsequent discourse on decay and improvement in general, and specific discussions of the debt of modernity to antiquity.

The conflict between those who venerated the remote past and those who believed that man's felicity had increased appears most clearly in what is known, somewhat misleadingly, as the battle or *querelle* of the ancients and the moderns. The topic is sufficiently familiar to require only brief treatment here. The *querelle* was really more an ongoing series of peace talks than a sustained struggle, though it was punctuated by some notable skirmishes and by one climactic battle; it was, as one recent scholar has aptly remarked, the intellectual world's equivalent of the Hundred Years War.[97] The discussion had already been simmering throughout Europe for several decades by the time Hakewill contended with Goodman in the early seventeenth century, and it continued at that level for a few decades. Anne Conway, née Finch, who had just read Hakewill, used his *Apologie* in 1651 to explain to her father-in-law that the apparently superior achievements of the ancients were attributable to the universal language of the pre-Babel age, and 'the extraordinary length of their lives' which permitted ancient philosophers to 'observe the revolution of a sphaere whose circuit will not be finished in 300 yeer'.[98]

The struggle heated up again in the 1660s as Thomas Sprat, historian of the Royal Society, and Joseph Glanvill, opposed by Henry Stubbe and Meric Casaubon, defended the modern achievement in certain technical areas such as the development of the experimental method of modern mechanical instrumentation, while remaining conspicuously taciturn on the separate issue of the arts and letters.[99] The earl of Clarendon, in an ironically entitled essay 'Of the Reverence Due to Antiquity', asserted his belief that

there have been many books written and published within these last hundred years, in which much more useful learning is not only communicated to the world, than was known to any of those ancients, but in which the most difficult and important points which have been handled by the fathers, are more clearly stated, and more solidly illustrated, than in the original treatises and discourses of the ancients themselves.[100]

---

[97] Spadafora, *Idea of Progress in Eighteenth-Century Britain*, 23.

[98] *The Conway Letters: The Correspondence of Anne, Viscountess Conway, Henry More, and their Friends, 1642–1684*, ed. M. H. Nicolson, rev. edn. (Oxford, 1992), 37 (Anne Conway to Viscount Conway, 2 Oct. 1651).

[99] T. Sprat, *The History of the Royal Society*, ed. J. I. Cope and H. W. Jones (St Louis, Mo., 1958), 24–9; Joseph Glanvill, *Plus Ultra: or, the Progress and Advancement of Knowledge since the Days of Aristotle* (1668); M. Hunter, *Science and Society in Restoration England* (Cambridge, 1981), 148.

[100] Edward Hyde, earl of Clarendon, 'Of the Reverence due to Antiquity', *Essays Moral and Entertaining, on the Various Faculties and Passions of the Human Mind*, ed. J. S. Clarke, 2 vols. (1815), ii. 132.

The issue reached a noisy if humorous climax in the famous 'Battle of the Books' that commenced in the 1690s. This ensued when Sir William Temple, provoked by the Frenchmen Charles Perrault and Bernard de Fontenelle, penned *An Essay Upon the Ancient and Modern Learning* (1690) in defence of the ancients, defending not only their literary greatness but their achievements in science as well.[101] This in turn was attacked by the formidable young scholar William Wotton, a classicist but also a member of the Royal Society, in his *Reflections on Ancient and Modern Learning* (1694).[102] Before the dust had settled, the battle had engaged the polemical talents of some of the greatest scholars of the day, including Richard Bentley, who ranged his formidable talents against the Christ Church 'wits' and their champion, the considerably less able Charles Boyle; their immediate conflict concerned the application of modern philological criticism to ancient texts, in particular the phoney *Epistles of Phalaris* that were being hailed as an example of ancient literary supremacy. The larger controversy is now particularly memorable for having inspired Swift's *A Tale of a Tub* and its briefer appendage, *The Battle of the Books*, two wickedly funny satires, though as a friend of Temple, Swift was hardly neutral in weighing in on the side of the ancients.[103] The English battle overlapped with an even more vicious, and longer-standing, French debate, the so-called *querelle*, in which Fontenelle and Perrault had been late entrants on the side of modernity. It also embraced a separate English controversy involving the age of the earth and the capacity of reason to understand natural wonders. This was sparked by Thomas Burnet, a promising young cleric, in his *Sacred Theory of the Earth*, one of the more notorious publications of the late 1680s, and a further thorn in Temple's side for its bold defence of novelty and dismissal of the achievements of earlier ages.[104]

[101] Spadafora, *Idea of Progress in Eighteenth-Century Britain*, 25–6; R. F. Jones, *Ancients and Moderns: A Study of the Rise of the Scientific Movement in Seventeenth-Century England*, 2nd edn. (St Louis, Mo., 1961); id., 'The Background of *The Battle of the Books*', in *The Seventeenth Century: Studies in the History of English Thought and Literature from Bacon to Pope* (Stanford, 1951), 10–40; Hunter, *Science and Society in Restoration England*, 159, which distinguishes between this controversy and the earlier one involving Stubbe, Casaubon, Sprat, and Glanvill; J. M. Levine, *The Battle of the Books: History and Literature in the Augustan Age* (Ithaca, NY, 1991). Professor Levine's book is the definitive account of this episode, and though I do not concur with all of his conclusions with regard to the significance of the battle and the broader *querelle* for historiography, I have derived much benefit from his account of the debate.

[102] Wotton's position, less strident than that of some of the French moderns because it conceded literary superiority to the ancients, pleased one of his readers twenty years later. Dudley Ryder (whose diarized reactions to the French *querelle* and general preference for ancient historians such as Sallust make him out at first as an unabashed ancient), thought in 1716 that Wotton had found a 'middle way' between Temple, 'who entirely gives the preference to the ancients and Perrault and others who give the preference to moderns in everything'. *The Diary of Dudley Ryder 1715–1716*, ed. W. Matthews (1939), 263–4.

[103] Swift, *A Tale of a Tub, to which is added the Battle of the Books*, ed. A. C. Guthkelch and D. Nichol Smith (Oxford, 1920); J. W. Johnson, 'Swift's Historical Outlook', *Journal of British Studies*, 4 (1965), 52–77.

[104] Thomas Burnet, *Sacred Theory of the Earth*, 2 pts. (1684–90); 1st pub. in Latin, 1681–9, as *Telluris theoria sacra*; Levine, *Battle of the Books*, 21; Davies, *The Earth in Decay*, 68–74; Roy Porter, *The Making of Geology: Earth Science in Britain 1660–1815* (Cambridge, 1977), 40–61, 70–90.

There were those, however, who found the whole business profoundly silly. Sir Richard Steele mocked its antagonists in an imaginary feast to which 132 historical characters are invited—the sum total of all those persons ever living 'who have any competent share of fame'. At this banquet they are to be seated at three tables, arranged according to the degree of their fame, not according to the significance of their actual achievements. Fame, indeed, rather than sheer antiquity, is the mark of honour and seniority, 'for if Julius Caesar shall be judg'd more famous than Romulus and Scipio, he must have the precedence'. No churchmen, nor any 'person who has not been dead an hundred years must be offer'd to a place at any of these tables'. (As for historians, they too remain seatless, serving merely as ushers to the famous.)[105] Even Lewis Theobald, a moderate 'ancient' who eventually used Bentleyesque methods to edit Shakespeare, admitted that he expected to be laughed at for preferring a marble head of Marcus Aurelius to 'a Golden One of any of the greatest men of the last century'.[106]

The sides seem drawn clearly enough by Swift, but appearances can be deceptive. The 'moderns' Bentley and Wotton were great classicists precisely by virtue of standing at the end of three centuries of philological achievement; Temple the 'ancient' was paradoxically the author of an essay 'Of heroicke virtue' which compares the accomplishments of the Chinese, Goths, and Tartars favourably with those of the ancients, in addition to his *Introduction to the History of England*.[107] In fact, the debate turned less on the respective merits of ancients and moderns than on the proper method of their presentation. Temple favoured letting them speak for themselves, unelaborated by editorial comment, while Wotton and Bentley urged the necessity of elaborate philological notes and commentary which would update and emend errors in the textual tradition; it was this role of the modern 'critick' in the treatment of the writings of antiquity that featured so prominently in the responses of Swift and other 'ancients'.[108] Yet the controversy also drew attention to a further problem, the roots of which lay in the ambiguous meaning of the word 'ancient'. Hakewill had put his finger on this in the 1620s: 'If we will speake properly and punctually,' he had written, 'antiquity rather consists in the old age, then infancie or youth of the world.' Were the real ancients the men like Plato and Cicero who had lived in the 'youth' of the world, or were they the moderns who lived when the world was more 'ancient'?[109] In concluding *Leviathan*,

[105] *The Tatler*, 67 (13 Sept. 1709), ed. D. F. Bond, 3 vols. (Oxford, 1987), i. 462–5.
[106] Lewis Theobald, *The Censor*, 3 vols. (1717), i. 31.
[107] Temple, 'Of heroick virtue', *Miscellanea*, pt. 3, *The Works of Sir William Temple Bart.*, 2 vols. (1731–50), i. 191–232; R. Faber, *The Brave Courtier: Sir William Temple* (1983), 129–61; R. C. Steensma, '"So Ancient and Noble a Nation": Sir William Temple's History of England', *Neuphilologische Mitteilungen*, 77 (1976), 95–107.
[108] Swift, *A Tale of a Tub*, section III, 'A Digression concerning Criticks' (pp. 92–104), which mockingly recounts the 'antiquity' of criticism.
[109] Hakewill, *Apologie*, 23; William Temple, 'An essay upon the ancient and modern learning', *Miscellanea*, pt. 2, in *Works* i. 151–70; William Wotton, *Reflections on ancient and modern learning*, in *Critical Essays of the Seventeenth Century*, ed. J. Spingarn, 3rd edn., 3 vols. (Bloomington, Ind., 1968), iii. 201–26; W. von Leyden, 'Antiquity and Authority: A Paradox in the Renaissance Theory of History,' *Journal of the History of Ideas*, 19 (1958), 473–92; Jones, *Ancients and Moderns*, ch. 2. Ferguson, *Clio*

Thomas Hobbes similarly conceded that he revered men of ancient time, so long as they wrote truth or 'set us in a better way to find it out ourselves', but not antiquity itself. 'For if we will reverence the age, the present is the oldest.'[110]

This was an old conundrum, noted throughout the seventeenth century by other writers, such as Bacon, and reflected in casual comments elsewhere.[111] John Manningham had noted with regard to Elizabethan Rochester 'that it had been an auncient towne, as though it were not more auncient by continuance'.[112] The Cambridge Platonist Ralph Cudworth made a similar argument to the House of Commons in 1647, preaching on the text 'in the latter dayes knowledge shall be increased'.[113] Was not an antiquity itself merely something old that had been discovered by later generations, and valuable only by virtue of its modern discovery? Sir Thomas Browne thought that even the continent of America was an antiquity, since it had existed time out of mind but had only recently been discovered. 'Time hath endlesse rarities, and shows of all varieties; which reveals old things in heaven, makes new discoveries in earth, and even earth itself a discovery. The great antiquity *America* lay buried for a thousand years; and a large part of the earth is still in the urne unto us.'[114]

What had changed in the debate of ancients and moderns during the time that separates Hakewill and Goodman from Swift, Wotton, and Bentley was not the question of the advancement of knowledge but the social and intellectual backdrop within which that question was now heard in a different way. The immediate Battle of the Books may well have ended in a draw, yet set in the broader perspective of nearly two centuries, the 'moderns' were the eventual victors. This was not because their wits were sharper (which they were not) or their philological abilities deeper (which they most often were), but because the context in which the Augustan version of the *querelle* took place was itself much changed, to the degree that it was very difficult to deny some measure of progress unless one wished to appear hopelessly obscurantist. As we have seen in these two chapters, English minds had by then grown accustomed, however reluctantly, to the fact of change, and environmentally desensitized to effects that their great-grandparents would have regarded with greater suspicion. Antiquity remained old in 1700, but novelty was no longer new.

Unbound, 355–6; H. Baron, 'The *querelle* of Ancients and Moderns as a Problem for Renaissance Scholarship', *Journal of the History of Ideas*, 20 (1959), 3–22; Levine, *Humanism and History*, 155–77, and his 'Ancients and Moderns Reconsidered', *Eighteenth Century Studies*, 15 (1981), 72–89.

[110] Thomas Hobbes, *Leviathan*, ed. M. Oakeshott (Oxford, 1940), 467.

[111] For example in Blount, *Essays on Several Subjects*, 82; Swift, *Battle of the Books*, ed. Guthkelch and Smith, 227.

[112] *Diary of John Manningham*, 196; Hakewill, *Apologie*, 23.

[113] Ralph Cudworth, *A sermon preached before the house of Commons March 31, 1647* (Cambridge, 1647), 2.

[114] Browne, *Hydriotaphia: Urne-Buriall; or, a brief discourse of the sepulchrall urnes lately found in Norfolk*, in *The Works of Sir Thomas Browne*, ed. G. Keynes, 2nd edn., 4 vols. (1964), i. 135.

Part II

THE ANCESTRAL PAST

CHAPTER THREE

The Cultivation of Heredity

THROUGHOUT THE SIXTEENTH and seventeenth centuries, the theme of ancestry recurs again and again in literature, politics, and ordinary social discourse. Like the notion of antiquity, to which it was often related, ancestry figures prominently in the early modern perception of the past and its relationship to the present. This chapter will explore some of the shifts in early modern attitudes to ancestry; the next chapter will deal more specifically with the relation between these changing perceptions and the social circulation of historical, and especially genealogical, knowledge, with special attention to what is often called the 'pedigree craze' of the late sixteenth century, and to the shift in attitudes to the legitimacy of imagined or fabricated lineages.

Pride in one's ancestors is in some form or other a characteristic of most cultures, but it is especially important to those in which individual identity is shaped by family ties and blood relationships. In some societies, the relationship to ancestors can be felt as religious experience. Judaism, which on one view 'derives its charters of authority from genealogy', also makes regular commemoration of ancestors, or *yizkor*, a part of ritual life. Japanese law traditionally enforced ancestor-worship (*sosen sûhai*) in an ellipse constructed around the dual foci of clan-consciousness and reverence of imperial divinity (each emperor being deemed a direct descendant of the sun goddess Amaratsu Ōmikami). In both Japan and China, as well as in many African societies, ancestors have an immediacy, a 'presence' (in the form of regular commemoration services and even the omnipresent oversight of household gods) which, either through fear or love, make them part of the living present rather than dead spirits from the past to be honoured only in name; some ancestors, indeed, are undesirable and need to be dispensed with accordingly.[1]

---

[1] E. Durkheim, *The Elementary Forms of Religious Life*, trans. J. W. Swain (New York, 1965), 70, 80–6; J. Goody, *Death, Property and the Ancestors* (Stanford, 1962), 382; H. Wimberley and J. Savishinsky, 'Ancestor Memorialism: A Comparison of Jews and Japanese', in W. H. Newell (ed.), *Ancestors* (Paris and The Hague, 1976), 241–59; C. Takeda, ' "Family Religion" in Japan: *Ie* and its Religious Faith', ibid. 119–28; Richard J. Miller, 'Ancestors and Nobility in Ancient Japan', ibid. 163–76; Nobushige Hozumi, *Ancestor-Worship and Japanese Law* (1st edn., 1912; 6th edn., Tokyo, 1940); P. Beillevaire, 'Japan: A Household Society' and 'The Family: Instrument and Model of the Japanese Nation', in A. Burguière *et al.* (eds.), *A History of the Family*, trans. S. H. Tenison, 2 vols. (Cambridge, Mass., 1996), i. 523–65, ii. 242–67. For an example of similar attitudes to ancestors among the Incas, see *The Huarochirí Manuscript: A Testament of Ancient and Colonial Andean Religion*, trans. F. Salomon and G. L. Urioste (Austin, Tex., 1991), 129 (ch. 27, sect. 360). I am grateful to Sabine MacCormack for this reference.

Different visions of ancestry can occur within a single culture. Roland Lardinois has pointed to a fundamental difference in India between orthodox brahman Hinduism, which construes the next world as one of reincarnation, and a more popular Hindu religiosity that focuses on the after-life as the dwelling-place of the revered dead. Looking less far afield, to modern Calabria, Maria Minicuci discovered striking differences between two neighbouring villages' senses of the ancestral past. In one, ancestors were still deemed participants in ongoing village life who could 'come when they want to'. In the other, the sense of continuity between past and present—of ancestral *presence*—was less strong, and carried with it an indifference to the village's historical past to the degree that 'it is as if nothing had ever happened in the course of time'.[2]

THE PLACE OF THE DEAD

These examples of ancestor-consciousness bear a passing resemblance to the interventionist religious beliefs of later medieval Europe, where saints fulfilled the ameliorating function, but where close attention was also paid to the spiritual condition of one's forebears, and especially to those in purgatory.[3] The Reformation almost completely severed this connection to the familial past.[4] In sixteenth- and seventeenth-century England, unlike contemporary China or Japan, ancestors had to assume a passive role in relation to their living descendants. They were 'there', only in the sense of being symbolic objects of mild reverence and providing examples of appropriate behaviour. They never intervened to 'help' or hinder their descendants, and were thus not part of the living present. They existed, rather, as echoes of the past, their souls in heaven or hell, only occasionally appearing as ghosts, like Banquo or Hamlet's father.[5] Though the biblical phrase 'buried with his ancestors' turns up periodically, for example in Sir James Whitelocke's *Liber Famelicus*,[6] no 'cult' of ancestry on an Asiatic or African scale existed: for the English, ancestors were truly dead and part of the past.

In an important book on late medieval and sixteenth-century popular religious practice, Eamon Duffy has closely studied the chronology of a change in attitudes

---

[2] R. Lardinois, 'The World Order and the Family Institution in India', in Burguière *et al.* (eds.), *A History of the Family*, i. 566–600, at p. 599; M. Minicuci, 'Time and Memory: Two Villages in Calabria', in D. O. Hughes and T. R. Trautmann (eds.), *Time: History and Ethnologies* (Ann Arbor, 1995), 71–104, at pp. 82–3.

[3] P. Brown, *The Cult of the Saints: Its Rise and Function in Latin Christianity* (Princeton, NJ, 1983), 30, 82 on the *praesentia* or literal presence of saints at the reading of the *passio*.

[4] For the decline of purgatory and 'separation of the dead from the living' in the early German Reformation, see C. M. Koslofsky, *The Reformation of the Dead: Death and Ritual in Early Modern Germany, 1450–1700* (New York, 2000), 19–39.

[5] F. L. K. Hsu, *Under the Ancestors' Shadow: Chinese Culture and Personality* (New York, 1948), esp. pp. 154–65, on death and funeral rites. According to Hsu, ancestors actively help their descendants when they can (pp. 240–1), and 'The attitude of the dead toward the living is completely in line with that of the living toward the dead.'

[6] *Liber Famelicus of Sir James Whitelocke, a Judge of the Court of King's Bench, in the Reigns of James I and Charles I*, ed. J. Bruce, Camden Soc., os 70 (1858), 10.

towards the dead from the pre- to post-Reformation eras, comparing, for example, the quite different approaches taken within the brief compass of three years by the successive Edwardian prayer books of 1549 and 1552. In the former, the dead retain a presence, and can be spoken to directly, as in the funeral service, which stressed their community with the living. The 1552 burial rite, in contrast, utterly removed anything that resembled a prayer for the dead and focused the service instead upon exhortation of the living. Beginning at about the same time, parishes began to purge themselves—albeit slowly and with considerable reluctance in some cases—of memorial brasses and inscriptions that had further maintained the deceased's ongoing connection with the present. Post-Reformation inscriptions drop the demands of the dead for intercessionary prayer and instead historicize the deceased, commemorating their accomplishments not as good works towards their own salvation but as examples urging on the living to greater virtue in their own lives.[7] Such reduction of the dead to the realm of the past, their displacement into secular time, emphasized, like contemporary biography, the exemplary deed itself—still 'alive' in the minds of observers—rather than the state of the doer, now gone.[8] In place of invocations to pray for the deceased, inscriptions soon began to provide a historical record, listing a dead man's or woman's spouse, parentage, children, and grandchildren. From about 1600 they provide a marble or stone version of the sort of eulogizing microbiography already contained in funeral sermons, commemorating the person's virtue, piety, and achievements, teaching history, as Nigel Llewellyn has remarked, to stray visitors.[9]

ANCESTRAL RIGHTS

It has been argued by historians such as Lawrence Stone and Alan Macfarlane that English society placed relatively little emphasis on kinship, or extended family affiliations across space.[10] Stone's 'patrilineal/nonaffective' model of the English family has come under criticism, and undoubtedly admits of numerous

<hr/>

[7] Eamon Duffy, *The Stripping of the Altars: Traditional Religion in England, c.1400–c.1580* (New Haven, Conn., 1992), 333, 475, 495. P. Marshall, *Beliefs and the Dead in Reformation England* (Oxford, 2002), is of relevance here but regrettably appeared as the present volume was in press.

[8] Natalie Z. Davis, 'Ghosts, Kin, and Progeny: Some Features of Family Life in Early Modern France', in A. S. Rossi, J. Kagan, and T. K. Hareven (eds.), *The Family* (New York, 1978), 87–114, notes the importance of diaries and autobiographies in England, and of the comparable Italian *libro di ricordanze* and French *livre de raison*. The end of purgatory made an end to the debt owed to dead ancestors, but even at its strongest the cult of the dead had never been ancestor worship along Asiatic or African lines. People remembered their ancestors; they did not live under their shadow or converse with them, and French wills do not indicate a strong preference for being buried with one's ancestors.

[9] H. W. Macklin, *Macklin's Monumental Brasses*, rev. J. Page-Phillips (New York and Washington, DC, 1969), 101; N. Llewellyn, *The Art of Death: Visual Culture in the English Death Ritual, c.1500–c.1800* (1991), 133–4.

[10] But cf. F. Heal and C. Holmes, *The Gentry in England and Wales, 1500–1700* (Basingstoke, 1994), 91–6, who point out the importance of social, emotional, and financial connections among kin, and the greater emphasis on kinship in representations of familial connection among women than men, and among younger sons and cadet branches as opposed to direct primogenitural lines.

exceptions. Many aristocratic and gentry families maintained, throughout the period, a considerable level of interest in constituting, preserving, and displaying to the world lineal connections across time to the past, connections that extended back in more than one direction to embrace both broader kinship affiliations and the strict succession of heirs by primogeniture.[11] The window heraldry of the manor house built by Sir Francis Hastings at North Cadbury in the later sixteenth century, for example (much of it rearranged and altered between the seventeenth and late nineteenth centuries), provides armorial quarterings of several of Hastings's more remote relatives, in an effort to spread the tentacles of interfamilial connection, while excluding some more direct ancestors.[12] Nonetheless, it is still the case that in early modern England direct lineage was more commonly mentioned as a measure of honour and status than kin affiliation. In the course of the fourteenth and fifteenth centuries, as the traditional definition of the aristocracy as the class of fighters began to lose meaning, ideas about nobility began to crystallize around such particular criteria as the antiquity and authority of title, and even (in the case of peers) specific privileges such as a summons to advise the monarch in the parliament, or the right to trial in the House of Lords.[13]

Ancestral and family privileges were jealously guarded. Evidence of ancestral right (as distinct from an appeal to custom or long use) frequently figured in property disputes. When Sir Francis Hastings conducted a survey of the properties of his brother, the earl of Huntingdon, in 1583, he noted that a neighbouring lord of the manor was encroaching on the Hastings land by occupying a few small islands along a Somerset river bank: this Hastings could prove by showing that 'my lorde's ancestours hathe had rente for two of thiese ilandes'.[14] A long-running rivalry between the Lisle and Dudley faction and Gloucestershire's Berkeley family would culminate in a lawsuit by Robert, earl of Leicester, against Henry, the eleventh lord Berkeley, over land boundaries and hunting privileges. While the case was *sub judice*, Leicester is alleged to have engineered the theft of some critical documents from the Berkeley family muniments by persuading the hunting-mad Lord Berkeley, whom he had invited to join him on a chase at

[11] L. Stone, *The Family, Sex and Marriage in England 1500–1800* (New York and London, 1977), 124–42; A. Macfarlane, *The Origins of English Individualism: The Family, Property and Social Transition* (New York, 1979), 144–7. For criticisms and revisions see R. Houlbrooke, *The English Family 1450–1700* (1984), 14–15; D. Cressy, 'Kinship and Kin Interaction in Early Modern England', *Past and Present*, 113 (1986), 38–69; J. J. Hurwich, 'Lineage and Kin in the Sixteenth-Century Aristocracy: Some Comparative Evidence on England and Germany', in A. L. Beier, D. Cannadine, and J. M. Rosenheim (eds.), *The First Modern Society: Essays in English History in Honour of Lawrence Stone* (Cambridge, 1989), 33–64. On the place of post-Reformation funerals as community rituals see F. Heal, *Hospitality in Early Modern England* (Oxford, 1990), 374.

[12] A. J. Jewers, 'Heraldry in the Manor House of North Cadbury, with the Heraldry and Monuments in the Church', *Proceedings of the Somerset Archaeological and Natural History Society*, 36, pt. 2 (1890), 137–67. Drs Heal and Holmes have recently added other examples of the visual display of kinship connection: *The Gentry in England and Wales*, 91–6.

[13] On the development of the nobility in the fourteenth century and after, see C. Given-Wilson, *The English Nobility in the Late Middle Ages: The Fourteenth-Century Political Community* (London and New York, 1987).

[14] *Letters of Sir Francis Hastings, 1574–1609*, ed. C. Cross, Somerset Rec. Soc., 69 (1969), 29.

Kenilworth, to admit 'one Harvey an herald' (William Harvey, Clarenceux King of Arms, d. 1567) into the muniments at Berkeley Castle, on the pretext of securing information to fill in Leicester's own descent from Berkeley's ancestors.[15]

Conflicts over claims of longer or more distinguished ancestry ranged far beyond the commonplace problem, dealt with unsuccessfully by the College of Arms, of completely illegitimate pedigrees. In a case of disputed inheritance involving the earl of Devonshire, rival claimants produced a visitation by the heralds and a pedigree proved by five witnesses and a book; even this was not sufficient to settle the case, which had to be postponed to a future date.[16] In 1632 a wager over family antiquity was adjudicated by the Clarenceux King of Arms, Sir Richard St George, between two gentlemen, William Coe of Wickham St Paul and Edward Harrington of Petmarsh. Coe and Harrington had made a £6 wager over which of them was 'of the most auntient family of gentry', and left the wagered funds in the hands of Michael West, a Hedingham tapster. When St George and other heralds decided in Coe's favour, Harrington, in league with West, refused to pay, and Coe sued them both at the Court of Requests.[17]

The possession of and basis of claim to church pews was increasingly a subject of litigation from the late sixteenth century onwards. One such case in the Lancashire parish of Eccles involved a chapel of ease, connected to the parochial church, which had been built by the ancestors of Thomas Young, a local gentleman, some two centuries earlier. Young's family had traditionally reserved certain seats for household members and servants, one of whom, the ploughman John Sayer, had a regular place. But on 3 May 1629, when Sayer seated himself as usual, he was attacked by Thomas Broughton, a former sheriff of Lancashire, later described as 'being growen greater then his ancestors'. Broughton, who had seats in the lower part of the chapel, assaulted both Sayer and his master, Young, for having had the effrontery to sit in a place higher than Broughton himself; the ex-sheriff, for his part, claimed that the seat was his. A fight ensued, which resulted in a hearing before the council in Star Chamber, during which each side claimed an ancestral right to the higher seats. Sir John Finch pointed out that 'Mr Younge's ancestours and Mr Broughton's sate in one seate together, and Mr Younges ancestours sate in the higher part of the seat.' Witnesses were called to establish that Young was indeed a gentleman of good family, that Sayer was an 'honest servant', and that 'Mr Younges ancestours sate in that seate'. It was then also established both that Broughton had initiated the brawl and 'that 40 yeares since Mr Broughton's grandfather did come into the lower part of the said seat with his sonne in law, and there they sate'. Broughton's defence was that 'his ancestours have right and have sate there in the seat'. The hearing was soon diverted on to

[15] As reported by the Berkeley steward John Smyth of Nibley, in *The Berkeley Manuscripts*, ed. J. Maclean, 3 vols. (Gloucester, 1883–5), ii. 292–3. The incident is discussed in R. B. Manning, *Hunters and Poachers* (Oxford, 1993), 138.

[16] John Hawarde, *Les Reportes del cases in Camera stellata, 1593–1609*, ed. W. P. Baildon (London, 1894), 340. Hawarde does not report the final outcome in the case of Champernoun and Baker v. the earl of Devonshire, who died in 1606 without legal issue (heard 12 Nov. 1607).

[17] PRO REQ2/296/61. This is misdated 1637 in the printed index.

the issue of whether fighting was more permissible in a private chapel than in a parish church, and failed to settle the dispute, both Young and Broughton being fined £100.[18] A similar case from Hexton, Hertfordshire, in the early seventeenth century, turned on a dispute over one family's claim to seats in an old chapel, which was based on the mistaken belief that an image of St Anthony in a stained glass window was the great-grandfather of one of the disputants.[19]

The rightness or wrongness of such claims is of less importance than the fact that the disputants in such cases spoke a common language, one that associated privileged space with family inheritance, and that they mounted competing claims to direct ancestral links with the parish's long-ago elite. Depending upon the nature of the argument, such questions could also be referred to popular memory,[20] as a final example demonstrates. In 1713 Theobald Gascoigne told Sir Bridges Nightingale, in a bristling letter wherein he struggles to maintain civility, that he had 'enquired of the most ancient inhabitants now living in Needham what they can remember concerning the pew now in dispute between us'. To his own 'satisfaction' (but not, presumably, Nightingale's), Gascoigne had learned that 'the undoubted right' lay in his family and had, according to a 'cloud of witnesses' for the past sixty years. Gascoigne had also learned that Needham had once been a distinct parish and that therefore as hereditary lord of the manor he had surely inherited the right to a seat in the merged parish's church, a point demonstrable 'without searching very far into the antiquities of that famous place'. It was with some pleasure that Gascoigne records on his own letter that Nightingale refused a reply, but henceforth kept his own tenant out of Gascoigne's pew.[21]

Matters of honour overlapped with immediate and sometimes serious pecuniary concerns. Among the types of cases adjudicated by civil lawyers in the High Court of Chivalry during the seventeenth and eighteenth centuries were the claims of families to extraordinary financial concessions from educational institutions, including schools and the various colleges of both universities, whose founders

---

[18] *Reports of Cases in the Courts of Star Chamber and High Commission*, ed. S. R. Gardiner, Camden Soc., NS 39 (1886), 139–44. Laud, too, believed that such disputes were increasing in frequency, ibid. p. 244. On the growth in litigation over this issue, see R. H. Helmholz, *Roman Canon Law in Reformation England* (Cambridge, 1990), 176–7.

[19] The incident is recounted by the landlord who opposed this claim, Francis Taverner, in 'The History and Antiquities of Hexton, in the county of Hertford', BL Add. MS 6223, fos. 8–28; cf. Bodl. MS Top. gen. e. 80 (parish notes of Edward Steele, 2 vols., 1712, vol. i), fos. 131ʳ–132ᵛ, summarizing Taverner's account; *VCH, Hertfordshire*, 4 vols. and index (1902–23), ii. 352; Henry Chauncey, *The Historical Antiquities of Hertfordshire* (1700), 517–19. For a similar example from Essex in 1657, recorded by the Augustan antiquary Samuel Adamson, rector of Barnestone, see Essex RO D/Y/1/1/4 (Adamson to William Holman, 6 Mar. 1722–3).

[20] See further Chs. 8 and 10 below, on memory and oral evidence. Pedigree was one area that constituted a major exception to the general exclusion, after about 1700, of hearsay evidence, with oral information deriving from reputation and common knowledge remaining acceptable as evidence of descent (along with informal writings such as notes in bibles and almanacs, which would also later be banned in most judicial circumstances) well after it had ceased to be admissible in other causes, though by the late eighteenth century this was limited to evidence emanating from family members: R. W. Baker, *The Hearsay Rule* (1950), 98–101.

[21] Suffolk RO HA1/BB/2/6 (Gascoigne to Nightingale, n.d. 1713; Nightingale to Gascoigne, 13 May 1713).

or subsequent benefactors had provided for the admission of their heirs in perpetuity; this indeed was a privilege that only died with Victorian educational reforms.[22] Ancestry-based arguments such as this could not admit of overlap or duplication: in any dispute, one party needed to have precedence. As Henry Sacheverell wrote to a friend who was seeking a place at Corpus Christi College, Oxford, on the basis of ancestry, 'to render your claim sufficient there must be a disproof of the pretensions of others'.[23] This is well illustrated by a late sixteenth-century example, the argument between Humphrey Wickham or Wykeham of Swalcliffe, Oxfordshire, and his enemy Sir Richard Fiennes of Broughton Castle in the same shire. The immediate quarrel turned on Wickham's claim to have his son admitted to Winchester and to New College Oxford, as kindred of the founder of those bodies, the fourteenth-century bishop, William of Wykeham. There was more involved than mere ancestral pride, or even the claim to a place: Fiennes had already successfully seated his own son at Winchester in 1569 on the basis of his own claim to descent from Bishop William's sister, but he sought a judgement from the college against Wickham as a defence against the latter's claim to some of Fiennes's own land under an old entail. Both men were required to produce title deeds (in Wickham's case to show his descent from the medieval bishop's cousin, Thomas), and Wickham also produced 'an antient rolle parchment bearing date Ao 2 Ric. 2' showing expenses of Richard Wickham, then a scholar in Oxford. Fiennes's claim, in contrast, rested on the college statute books, 'where the Bishops genealogy is described and his father called John Long', a proof which Fiennes argued was not countered by the 'presumption and likelihood' in Sir Humphrey's claim.

It is interesting to note in this case that, apart from putting mutually exclusive claims to kinship with a long-dead prelate, both men were also appealing to two quite different types of record. In Fiennes's case, authority sprang from a public document recording his own direct descent from Bishop William's father, and added to by accretion over the generations. On his opponent's side, not only were the documents private rather than public, but they were also unambiguously ancient writings composed at a single point in the past. For all the moral certainty that contending parties possessed in disputes such as this over title, succession, and heritage, it was often difficult to agree as to what might constitute definitive and compelling evidence. When a committee of two civilians and a herald ruled in favour of Humphrey Wickham—despite admitting that much of his evidence was 'presumptive, conjecturall, & aequivoce'—the wardens of both colleges still refused to admit Wickham's son. He was then compelled to sue them

---

[22] G. D. Squibb, *Founders Kin: Privilege and Pedigree* (Oxford, 1972), 1–31, 135–63; no less than thirty-nine endowed schools had founders' kin privileges at the end of the seventeenth century. But many privileges, Squibb points out, were self-limiting by imposing other restrictions. No kinsman of Francis Dee, bishop of Peterborough, was ever admitted by virtue of this relationship as a fellow of St John's College Cambridge, for instance, because Dee's endowment also required an education at Merchant Taylors' School or Peterborough School: ibid. 32.

[23] Staffs. RO D1178/2, unfoliated papers (Henry Sacheverell to Edward Willson, 13 Sept. 1704).

at Chancery. A compromise worked out in 1580 admitted Wickham's immediate heirs but required the family to renounce any further claims on the basis of founders' kin; an attempt to revive the claim in the 1630s was rejected.[24]

It was very difficult to avoid basking in the glow of one's own ancestry. Elizabeth I was observed to smile when a spectator yelled 'I remember old king Henry theyght' during her coronation procession, while on her Coventry visit in 1565 the town recorder put her in mind of the great benefits that her Plantagenet ancestors had showered on the borough.[25] The redoubtable Lady Elizabeth Hatton, involved in litigation with the duchess of Richmond in 1626, reminded Charles I that there was little distance between the duchess and herself save friends and money, that her birth was not inferior to her opponent's, and that her ancestors had not been 'demeritors' in the kingdom.[26] There are times at which it seems that early modern society valued lengthy ancestry above all else. Tristram Risdon thought that the unfortunately named but long-lived Suckbitch family was worth noting, though no member of it had ever achieved 'any eminency', simply because 'it hath pleased God to continue one name amongst a thousand, to enjoy a place so many ages'.[27] But many commentators considered ancestry only one measure of a claim to honour and prestige, and it would lose its position at the head of this list by the middle of the seventeenth century. From Sir Thomas Elyot to Sir William Temple, Tudor and Stuart writers engaged in a protracted debate on the nature of virtue and honour, and whether these derived from blood or from individual education and action.[28]

Early opinion, heavily influenced by the medieval conventions of chivalry and the feudal vision of a three-ordered society that produced it, emphasized the

[24] Bodl. MS Rawl. Essex 11, fos. 191ʳ–194ᵛ; a full and near-contemporary account of this affair, including the findings of Burghley's commission, taken from an early seventeenth-century transcript, is in C. E. L[ong], 'Descent of the Family of Wickham of Swalcliffe', *Collectanea topographica et genealogica*, 2 (1835), 225–45, 368–87; T. F. Kirby, *Annals of Winchester College* (1892), 97–106; Squibb, *Founders' Kin*, 34, 37–9, 188; for problems of establishing kinship in other cases, see Squibb, pp. 71–113.

[25] J. Nichols, *The Progresses and Public Processions of Queen Elizabeth*, 3 vols. (1823), i. 58, 194 ff.; *REED: Coventry*, ed. R. W. Ingram (Toronto, 1981), 232–4.

[26] Hist. MSS Comm., *The Manuscripts of the Earl Cowper, K.G., Preserved at Melbourne Hall, Derbyshire*, 3 vols. (1888–9), i. 267 (Hatton to Charles I, 18 Apr. 1626).

[27] Tristram Risdon, *The chorographical description or survey of the county of Devon* (1811), 63.

[28] The classic account of the debate on gentility, with a bibliography of contemporary texts, is Ruth Kelso, *The Doctrine of the English Gentleman in the Sixteenth Century* (Chicago and Urbana, 1929; repr. Gloucester, Mass., 1964), 18–30; this should be read in concert with more recent studies such as J. P. Cooper, 'Ideas of Gentility in Early-Modern England', in his *Land, Men and Beliefs*, ed. G. E. Aylmer and J. S. Morrill (1983), 62–70; M. James, 'English Politics and the Concept of Honour, 1485–1642', in *Society, Politics and Culture: Studies in Early Modern England* (Cambridge, 1986), 308–415, esp. pp. 375–83; D. A. L. Morgan, 'The Individual Style of the English Gentleman', in M. Jones (ed.), *Gentry and Lesser Nobility in Late Medieval Europe* (New York, 1986), 29–35; L. Stone, *The Crisis of the Aristocracy* (Oxford, 1965), 66–71; A. Bryson, *From Courtesy to Civility: Changing Codes of Conduct in Early Modern England* (Oxford, 1998), 234–42.

importance of ancestry.[29] Some humanists, such as Erasmus, asserted that great deeds would perfect or accentuate a worthy ancestry—not that such deeds made it irrelevant. At the funeral of Lady Margaret Beaufort, Bishop Fisher divided nobility into several categories, praising the king's grandmother for her descent from Edward III 'within the .iiij degre of the same' while also drawing attention to the nobility of her manners, deeds, and marriage. James Cleland, writing in 1607, dismissed property and chattels as primary marks of nobility, especially if unaccompanied by honour, and thought those who trumpeted an 'ancient descent' without much else to offer were indeed 'nobles of bloud; but of bloud only without bones'. He did, however, explicitly avoid ruling between birth and merit, refusing 'to grinde my selfe betweene two milstones, in extolling the one above the other'. The Caroline essayist Owen Feltham presented a more straightforwardly traditional view. 'Earth hath not any thing more glorious then ancient nobility, when 'tis found with vertue', he wrote. 'What barbarous mind will not reverence that blood, which hath untainted run thorow so large a succession of generations?'[30] Often, however, other factors are added to the mix. 'A long descent of noble ancestors was not necessary to have made you great', wrote John Dryden in 1683 to the duke of Ormonde. 'But heaven threw it in as over-plus when you were born.'[31]

An increased deference to personal achievement and landed or (to a lesser degree) material wealth, as opposed to ancient lineage, is a feature of the later seventeenth century. But the more ambivalent and individualistic outlook of the post-Restoration era was less a radical repudiation of the importance of lineage than a subtle shift in the balance of opinion. In fact, there was a long tradition of thought in England which ran against placing emphasis on ancestral merit and which denied the importance of blood. A number of Tudor commentators had insisted that ancestry had little to do with individual merit. Nobility, wrote Richard Pace, 'is surely created by virtue, and not by a long and famous line of ancestors'.[32] Sir Thomas Smith, the formidable Elizabethan minister and social analyst, voiced very clearly the view that gentility emanated from prosperity, and that he who could comport himself in the manner of a gentleman could so style himself.[33]

This viewpoint was vigorously opposed by defenders of traditional gentility such as John Ferne, who allowed some scope to education or virtue while holding firm to the position that the least accomplished descendant of a great line was, flaws

[29] See e.g. William Caxton's translation of *The Book of the Ordre of Chyvalry*, ed. A. T. P. Byles, EETS os 168 (1926), 58.
[30] *Panegyric for Archduke Philip of Burgundy*, trans. Betty Radice, in *Collected Works of Erasmus*, vol. xxvii, ed. A. H. T. Levi (Toronto, 1986), 38; cf. *The Education of a Christian Prince*, trans. L. K. Born (New York, 1936), 151; *English Works of John Fisher*, ed. J. E. B. Mayor, EETS es 27 (1876), 290–3; James Cleland, *The Institution of a Young Noble Man* (Oxford, 1607), 8–9; Owen Feltham, *Resolves: divine, morall, politicall*, 2nd edn. (1628), 86.
[31] Dryden, *Contributions to Plutarch's Lives* (1683), in *Works of John Dryden* (Berkeley, 1956–), vol. xvii, ed. S. H. Monk, A. E. Wallace Maurer, and V. A. Dearing, p. 230.
[32] Richard Pace, *De Fructu Qui ex Doctrina Percipitur*, ed. and trans. F. Manley and R. Sylvester (New York, 1967), 125.
[33] Thomas Smith, *De Republica Anglorum*, ed. M. Dewar (Cambridge, 1982), 70–3; Cooper, 'Ideas of Gentility in Early-Modern England', 62–70.

and all, still noble or gentle 'not for the cause of him selfe, but for the reverend commemoracion of his ancestor'.[34] However, a potent attack on honour based strictly upon blood could also be made from a different direction, by arguing that ancestry could be as much a liability as an asset. Sin, as puritan preachers reminded their audiences, passed down from generation to generation. Any family was just as likely to have blackguards and cut-throats in its lineage as heroes and saints, and unlike the case in predominantly oral societies, these were difficult to purge from the record. The jurist Sir John Dodderidge thought that the infamy of an evil ancestor could be a blot on the reputation of descendants, just as honour due one was due the other.[35] Daniel Defoe made a similar point in the early eighteenth century: were not the crimes of a single member of certain notable families a continued blot on their reputations? 'Do we see any of the family and posterity of Guy Faux or Lieutenant Felton?' His contemporary Lewis Theobald thought any vanity in ancestry could be punctured by learning that current grandeur began in a 'drudging plebeian . . . or sordid slave'.[36] Gerrard Winstanley, from a more radical perspective, had already reminded landowners in 1649 of the curse their acquisitive progenitors had placed them under by leaving them land wrested by the sword from their fellow men:

And therefore, though you did not kill or theeve, yet you hold that cursed thing in your hand, by the power of the Sword; and so you justifie the wicked deeds of your Fathers; and that sin of your Fathers, shall be visited upon the Head of you, and your Children, to the third and fourth Generation, and longer too, till your bloody and theeving power be rooted out of the Land.[37]

Tobie Combe of Hemel Hempstead included in his diary an 'advice' to his dissolute drunkard of a son that consists largely of potted biographies of his own father and grandfather, both notorious for having brought the family low through bad financial planning, and hence cautionary tales rather than inspirational examples.[38]

A further worry among Protestants concerned the status of pre-Henrician ancestors who, regardless of their individual vices or virtues, had lived in error as Catholics. The religious changes of the mid-sixteenth to mid-seventeenth centuries, occurring at a time that did not widely recognize the legitimacy of multiple faiths,

---

[34] John Ferne, *The Blazon of Gentrie* (1586), 16, as spoken by Paridinus, the herald in this dialogue who may be taken as Ferne's spokesman. A virtually identical position was maintained four decades later by Francis Markham in *The Booke of honovr* (1625), 47.

[35] Devon RO Z19/34/2 (Dodderidge, 'A treatice concerning nobilitye according to the lawes of England'), fo. 169ʳ.

[36] Daniel Defoe, *The Compleat English Gentleman*, ed. K. B. Bülbring (1890), 31–2; Lewis Theobald, *The Censor*, 3 vols. (1717), i. 190.

[37] Gerrard Winstanley, *Selected Writings*, ed. A. Hopton (1989), 26.

[38] Herts RO D/Z16.Z1 (diary and notebook of Tobie Combe (1664–1743)), esp. fo. 14ʳ. This contrasts markedly with Meyer Fortes's definition of filial piety, based on his studies of the Tallensi during the 1930s, as 'a parent's unquestioned and inalienable right because he begot you—or in the mother's case, she bore you'. Fortes, 'Pietas in Ancestor Worship', in his *Time and Social Structure* (London and New York, 1970), 177. In England, such unconditional duty attached in most cases to parents, following the Mosaic commandment, but did not extend further back.

fostered doubts as to the state of ancestral shades as men feared their Romish ancestors might be damned. The Henrician humanist Thomas Starkey was among the first to address this complaint, in 1540, by applying Melanchthon's concept of *adiaphora* in answer to the worry that centuries of Englishmen who had acknowledged the supremacy of Rome were languishing in hell: 'I juge it not so yll and damnable, that all our forefathers, whiche have ben obedient therto this vii C yeres therfore be damned.'[39]

This attempt literally to 'grandfather' Catholic ancestors into heaven was reasonably reassuring in the conservative reformation of the 1530s and 1540s. It was probably less so later in the century, when serious doctrinal differences between the Church past and Church present had become clarified by decades of controversy, but this was also the time that ancestors were losing their quasi-sacred status. Robert Crowley, perhaps insensitive to the grief it might cause, went so far as to suggest to parliament that preachers be placed in rural areas in order to convince the common people that their fathers and grandfathers had lived in superstition, since rural folk 'wyll not be perswaded that theyr forfathers supersticion was not true fayth of Christ'. Thomas Hopkins, a Worcestershire parson, urged his parishioners to pray that God would show mercy to sincere, if misled, papists who undoubtedly would have believed the true faith were they still alive.[40] This ran against a general tendency to think well of one's progenitors. More typical was the response of a moderate Protestant like William Camden. When he was criticized for his interest in the monasteries and their superstitious founders, the antiquary urged his critics to remember that medieval men, howsoever misplaced their piety, were devout 'ancestors and Christians'.[41]

'THE ONELY SPUR TO TRUE GLORY': ANCESTRY AND DUTY

A desire to be thought worthy *of*, though not *by* their ancestors certainly figured in spurring the political and social elite on to glory. The converse of this is equally true; there existed a sense of duty to protect and conserve familial achievements, liberties, and forms of civilized life from erosion. A strong commitment to ancestral traditions and values reflects a deeply conservative society, and long before Edmund Burke spoke his famous words about a social contract between the dead, the living, and the yet unborn he had been anticipated by three centuries of early modern political and social discourse. In this regard, respect for and pride in one's personal, familial, ancestors were of far less moment than consciousness of a general duty towards the cumulative generations of forebears who were the

[39] Thomas Starkey, *An exhortation to the people* (1540?), fo. 6ᵛ. This point of view is very similar to modern Chinese villagers' belief in an underworld of eternal punishment which none of *their* ancestors could possibly merit: E. Ahern, *The Cult of the Dead in a Chinese Village* (Stanford, 1973), 221.

[40] Robert Crowley, *An informacion and peticion agaynst the oppressours of the pore Commons of this Realme. The select works of Robert Crowley, printer, archdeacon of Hereford*, ed. J. M. Cowper, EETS ES 15 (1872), 154; Thomas Hopkins, *Two godlie and profitable sermons* (1611), no. 2, p. 28.

[41] William Camden, *Britain*, trans. Philemon Holland (1610), 'To the reader'.

predecessors of a particular group or community; within this context, appeal to 'our ancestors' could provide a forceful argument against innovations in manners or in politics.

Erasmus had once advised the prince to 'love the land over which he rules just as a farmer loves the fields of his ancestors', and critics of government actions played to this feeling of proprietary responsibility.[42] Nowhere is this attitude more apparent than in the political debates of the early seventeenth century, when MPs and peers frequently fell back on an appeal to English forebears in mounting an argument in parliament, or in attempting to put a case to the Crown. In the 'addled' parliament of 1614, Sir Dudley Digges obliquely criticized the Crown's continued levying of impositions by praising the practice of the much-venerated Edward the Confessor—not, of course, the literal ancestor of any king, but an increasingly iconic figure of just kingship during the seventeenth century. Digges, who was grossly distorting details he probably took from the Tudor chronicler Richard Grafton, recounted how Edward, on seeing a pile of £20,000 of Danegeld, had been so remorseful as to command that no more be collected.[43] In 1628, as MPs gathered to discuss the recent incursions of arbitrary imprisonment, forced loans, martial law, and military billeting, such arguments became even more common. At the opening of that parliament, the Lord Keeper responded to the Speaker's remarks with fulsome allusions to the 'glorious catalogue' of Charles I's forebears, which included 'a Solomon' in James I, several Scottish Davids, and 'the blood of Harry the Great'. He urged MPs and peers to hope for the same success in parliament that their ancestors had enjoyed: 'as we are the sons of our ancestors, so we should do the deeds of our ancestors'.[44] Throughout the session, speakers on both sides of debates defended their actions as an expression of piety towards their ancestors and deference to the ancestral wisdom which had been sanctioned by centuries of custom.

This regular appeal to ancestral liberties as a kind of inheritance, passed down over the centuries, was intimately related to the defence of the 'ancient constitution', since the laws of England, whether they derived from time immemorial or from specific, time-bound precedent, were at bottom the product of ancestral wisdom and experience. Rhetorically, this was far more effective than any argument based on paper precedent: thus Sir John Eliot spoke with particular force when he claimed to act neither for himself, nor indeed for the country, 'but for the ancient glory of the ancient laws of England', since the recent infringements made his contemporaries unworthy of their forefathers' liberties. 'But this reflects on all that we call ours, those rights that made our fathers free men, and they render our posteritie less free.' Lawyers appealing to Magna Carta in the debates

---

[42] Erasmus, *The Education of a Christian Prince*, trans. Born, p. 205.

[43] *Proceedings in Parliament 1614 (House of Commons)*, ed. M. Jansson (Philadelphia, 1988), 96. Digges was fond of references to the Confessor: J. Greenberg, *The Radical Face of the Ancient Constitution: St Edward's 'Laws' in Early Modern Political Thought* (Cambridge, 2001), 32, 166.

[44] *Proceedings in Parliament, 1628*, ed. R. Johnson *et al.* 6 vols. (New Haven, 1977–83), v. 69. For the examples cited in the following paragraph, see ibid, II.57, III.114, 117, V.312.

over arbitrary imprisonment on 21 April suggested that it had been confirmed no less than thirty times since 1215. The earl of Warwick picked up on this theme and suggested that the peers ought not to question 'that which has been so often confirmed by our ancestors'. Sir Edward Coke similarly reminded the lords that their 'noble ancestors' had been parties to Magna Carta; on 26 April, however, he objected to the reference to ancestors in the propositions of the Lords for a protestation or petition on the grounds that this would leave out the bishops, who had no ancestors, only predecessors.

Such examples could be multiplied from other parliamentary sessions: those of 1628 have been selected simply because of their relative frequency and their obvious connection with the major political document of the late 1620s, the Petition of Right. They underline once more the added force that appeals to antiquity acquired when they were humanized with references to the glories, liberties, and privileges of long-dead Englishmen, however vague, general, and improbable these references were. Such arguments were not confined to political discourse (although they can be found there in particularly high density), since a claim to the approval of departed generations was not the monopoly of the social elites of court and parliament. Others made use of the appeal to ancestors in many contexts throughout the seventeenth century, and even the most radical groups of the civil war period referred to their duty to revive the liberties of their fore-bears. The Leveller and Digger attack on the 'Norman yoke' turned the arguments of 1628 on their head by arguing that the post-Conquest period amounted to nothing more than a betrayal of ancestral freedoms.[45]

The problem with arguments based on an appeal to ancestral wisdom is that, while their intent is conservative, they also lend themselves naturally to positive change or innovation, which can then be legitimized under the guise of a return to ancestral values. By the end of the seventeenth century, it was increasingly commonplace to talk not simply of stewarding the achievements of ancestors, but of improving on them. The more historically minded realized that blind obedience to the dictates of an ancestral wisdom which was the product of very different times and circumstances was an ignorant sort of piety. When visiting Doncaster in 1695, the archdeacon of York charged the clergy to 'deliver this age down to our posterity in a better condition by half than we received it from our ancestors'. Sir Josiah Child repudiated the attempts of earlier generations to restrict the price of labour, an issue about which 'we are since, with the rest of the world, grown wiser'—though when it suited his purpose he could fall back on the 'excellent example of our ancestors' as readily as any Elizabethan or Caroline MP.[46] The same increased tolerance for improvement and innovation which resulted in a more balanced and critical attitude to past customs and traditions, and tilted

[45] C. Hill, 'The Norman Yoke', in his *Puritanism and Revolution* (1958), 50–122; S. Kliger, *The Goths in England* (Cambridge, Mass., 1952), and Greenberg, *Radical Face of the Ancient Constitution*, for later seventeenth- and eighteenth-century anti-Normanism.

[46] *Diary of Abraham de la Pryme*, ed. Charles Jackson, Surtees Soc., 54 (1869–70), 58; Sir Josiah Child, *A new discourse of trade* (1693), pp. xii, 81.

the debate between ancients and moderns in favour of the latter by the end of the century, is also revealed in a more circumspect attitude towards the demands of long-dead English ancestors.

An important expression of the emergent early modern understanding of the past is the emphasis placed on tokens and symbols of lineage. These exist in many cultures, but are not always used in the same way. In his study of Australian aborigines, for example, Claude Lévi-Strauss observed that *chirunga*, totemic objects of stone or carved wood stored in sacred places, were used to bring past and present together. Held to be contemporaneous with the ancestors they represent, the *chirunga* are 'palpable traces of their presence on earth at one time', and play a significant role in regular historical rites designed to recreate the past. Clifford Geertz has made similar arguments with respect to the Balinese, who hold all imaginable people, past or present, to be present simultaneously as 'person-types' represented by tokens.[47] Western European usage of the symbols of ancestry which applies, with some significant variation, to England, was very different. Just as the English did not regard ancestors as either 'present' or, after the Reformation, spiritually interventionist, so the reminders of their existence, whether portraits, funeral monuments, or coats of arms, were intended as commemorative rather than ritually restorative. They marked a chronologically demarcated past rather than an ongoing present in which all generations were spiritually present at a single time.[48]

English ancestor-veneration was nothing new in itself: there are plenty of examples in the Middle Ages of an awareness of family lineage and a pride in its achievements, and in his study of the northern counties Mervyn James has demonstrated various ways in which the concept of lineage dominated the political and social life of magnate families into the late sixteenth century.[49] Yet no medieval expressions of family pride can adequately anticipate either the place of ancestry in common discourse during the sixteenth and seventeenth centuries, or the degree to which this became externalized and objectified in the production and defence of family genealogies and coat armours. The following chapter will examine the connection between genealogical pursuits and historical conscious-

---

[47] C. Lévi-Strauss, *The Savage Mind* (1966), 236; C. Geertz, 'Person, Time and Conduct in Bali', in *The Interpretation of Cultures* (New York, 1973); Alfred Gell, *The Anthropology of Time: Cultural Constructions of Temporal Maps and Images* (Oxford and Providence, RI, 1992), 27, 70. On the symbols required for the process of *becoming* an ancestor in East Asia, see H. Ooms, 'A Structural Analysis of Japanese Ancestral Rites and Beliefs', in Newell (ed.), *Ancestors*, 61–90, at p. 76.

[48] The pre-Reformation practice of relic-worship, however, comes closer to the totemic model in the sense that the relic's connection with a dead but heavenly saint is supposed to offer a direct connection between the possessor and the interventionist power of the saint of whom it was *literally* a part or possession; see further discussion of this point below, Ch. 6, in the context of antiquarianism.

[49] M. James, *Family, Lineage, and Civil Society* (Oxford, 1978), esp. pp. 52–63, 108–12.

ness more closely; in the context of the present discussion, however, it is necessary to note some more general features of the interest in pedigree and genealogy.

The concept of pedigree was not confined to the nobility or the gentry, or even to human beings. It was a fundamental category for the arrangement and analysis of the world throughout various social groups; thus institutions could be spoken of as having a 'pedigree' in the sense of an unbroken lineal connection to the past, as thoroughbreds and dogs are now so described. So far as it concerns people, a pedigree may be taken either as an imagined line of succession in time, each occupant of which holds a place in a chain, or, conversely, it may be understood as the tangible signifying token (document, genealogical chart, or coat of arms) of such a succession. Used in the first sense, a pedigree is a great chain of being that extends backwards into the past rather than upwards and downwards socially.[50] Men, women, clerics, offices, and even inanimate objects had a well-defined place in time, a locus in an orderly succession. Even priests, said Jerome Phillips, had a pedigree, which they derived from Adam, Melchizedek, and the patriarchs.[51] In defence of their status, Jacobean bishops referred to their offices, rather than their persons, as having pedigrees.[52] The most important form of pedigree, however, was that of family, which reached new heights in the late sixteenth and early seventeenth centuries, years of great social mobility and economic change. Family pedigrees had been much less necessary in the closed feudal aristocracy of the period up to the fourteenth century; no full-scale collection of them is extant before the fifteenth century, though individual examples survive.[53]

The study of genealogy (in essence the recovery and mapping of the lines of inheritance from which pedigrees can be drawn), is now often referred to as an 'ancillary' of history, and in the next chapter we will focus on the question how, in the seventeenth century, it got to be that way. Genealogy's relationship to historical writing was much less clear before the antiquarian scholarship of the late

---

[50] Goody, *Death, Property and the Ancestors*, 382 n. 1 and 388, makes a rigid distinction between pedigrees and genealogies: the pedigree traces lines of filiation (for example in the case of a European royal family) and 'does not serve primarily as a reference for group orientation or kinship orientation' but rather as 'a charter to office and to other rights'; the longer the pedigree, 'the more imposing and the more effective it is as a device for legitimizing both the office and the officeholder'. Genealogies, in Goody's definition, are characterized by 'shrinkage', especially in oral tradition, as generations are lopped off or 'telescoped'. This division of terms has, unfortunately, a limited applicability to England where 'pedigree' is by far the dominant term for *all* written representations of descent, whether or not they branch off and include extended kin. I have therefore opted in general to use 'pedigree' to signify both the literal record as found in family archives and recorded by heralds, and also the theoretically espoused lineage asserted by some contemporaries without reference to written documents; where I use the terms 'genealogies' or 'genealogy' it is with reference to the deliberate compilation for specifically *historical* purposes of an authentic, or at least authenticatable, family descent.

[51] Jerome Phillips, *The Fisher-Man*, a sermon preached at Southwell, Notts. (1923), 4.

[52] William Barlow, *The antiquitie and superioritie of bishops* (1606), sig. E. Since many clerics, especially in the pre-Reformation era, were younger sons of noble houses, they too bore arms: the 1531 Devonshire visitation by Thomas Benolt, Clarenceux, for example, includes the arms of the noble founders of churches and abbeys, and also those of priors and abbots: Bodl. MS Ashm. 763, art. 1, fos. 1–87ʳ.

[53] A. Wagner, *English Genealogy*, 3rd edn. (Chichester, 1973), 352.

sixteenth century, but its practice certainly increased, and the study and representation of pedigrees was perceived as having ancient, even scriptural origins. Much of the Old Testament consists in an extended series of 'begats', which in one assize sermon was referred to as the 'boast' of the Jew; a Restoration writer thought that 'the law of Moses engaged the Jews to the study of genealogy'.[54] The Elizabethan lawyer John Manningham recalled hearing 'one Clappam' (probably the puritan Henoch Clapham) preach that 'none could soundly interpret or understand the Scripture without genealogy, which he commended very highly', while the Jacobean historian John Speed supported himself for several years on the lucrative privilege of drawing up the genealogies for the Authorized Version. Perhaps the most familiar genealogy to the ordinary English Protestant, because it appeared in pictorial form on the walls of many churches, was that of Christ, tracing his descent from the stem of Jesse: three windows, since destroyed, in the Lady Chapel at Exeter Cathedral, depicted fourteen generations of Christ's descent, together with the story of his nativity and his revelation to his disciples.[55]

J. H. Plumb has observed that outbreaks of 'genealogical fever' occur when a new class is emerging, pushing its way up the social or economic ladder. Similar interest in family trees had occurred in various Continental societies, for instance among the merchant elites of Quattrocento Italy.[56] One need neither subscribe to nor reject the famous Tawney–Stone thesis about the 'rise of the gentry' in order to accept Plumb's helpful insight. Part of the process of assimilation of the upwardly mobile yeomen and merchants into the gentry, and of the gentry into the nobility, consisted in a certain amount of retroactive rank-validation. Much as the Yorkist and Tudor kings had appealed to genealogy in order to support their titles to the throne, so the *nouveaux noblesses* of Tudor and Stuart England, families such as the Howards and Russells, and later the Cecils, Sidneys, and Holleses, legitimized their new positions of wealth, power, and national stature by emphasizing in their private and public writings the length and depth of their ancestry. The early seventeenth-century antiquary George Owen Harry (d. 1614) declared that any Welsh gentleman of the 'meaner sort' ought to have in his house the written pedigree of his family, and if he could not name by memory his four great-grandfathers and their wives, he would be accounted 'out of love with himselfe'.[57]

---

[54] William Yonger, *Judah's Penance* (1617), 38; SAL MS 226 (commonplace book of Nathaniel Ellison), vol. iii, fo. 38 (p. 874), *c.*1670.

[55] *The Diary of John Manningham of the Middle Temple, 1602–1603*, ed. R. P. Sorlien (Hanover, NH, 1976), 159; BL MS Add. Egerton 2255 (Speed's tract on the genealogy of Christ, dedicated to Bishop James Montagu); for editions of the printed *Genealogies recorded in the sacred scriptures*, see STC ii. 352–4, nos. 23039 *et seq.*; Anon. (attrib. to one Lieutenant Hammond), *A Relation of a Short Survey of the Western Counties made by a lieutenant of the military company in Norwich in 1635*, ed. L. G. W. Legg, *Camden Miscellany*, 16, Camden Soc., 3rd ser., 52 (1936), 48; BL MS Sloane 3927 ('Genealogia et chronologia sacra'), fos. 1–12.

[56] J. H. Plumb, *The Death of the Past* (Boston, 1971), 31–2. For valuable insights into the interest in genealogies elsewhere, see W. L. Gundersheimer, *Ferrara: The Style of Renaissance Despotism* (Princeton, 1973), 280–3; L. Martines, *The Social World of the Florentine Humanists, 1390–1460* (1963), 57.

[57] George Owen Harry, 'The Wellspring of True Nobility', seventeenth-century transcript, in National Library of Wales MS 9853E, p. 95, cited in E. White and R. Suggett, 'Language, Literacy and Aspects of Identity in Early Modern Wales', in A. Fox and D. Woolf (eds.), *The Spoken Word* (Manchester, 2002), 52–83, at p. 58.

By the time Owen wrote, those slightly lower on the social ladder, such as the prosperous Devon yeoman Robert Furse, were already beginning to take a similar interest in their own ancestry and its preservation, for the sheer practical purpose of maintaining knowledge of land transactions and acquisitions and a command over the family's expansive holdings. For the upwardly mobile and ambitious Furse—who in vain enjoined his own children to continue the record he had begun in 1593—thoughts of tracing his ancestry back to illustrious ancestors were entirely subordinated to more basic economic and legal necessities. His book would allow his descendants always to 'be abell to make a perfytt petygree and to understonde the ryght name of your londs and your wrytynges and what you ofte to have and what you ofte to do'. Furse's lengthy history of his own family was addressed in 1593 to his heirs 'and to there sequele' in order to 'sette furthe what our progenytors have bynne of them selves and spessyally those that have bynne wythyn this seven score yeres'. As Furse points out, this is more than an idle affectation of antiquity. The real reason for the record is defensive, economic, and practical: a cautious and measured beating of the family's historical bounds.[58]

Furse was far from alone among the emergent 'middling sort' of the seventeenth century in seeking access to what had hitherto been a preoccupation of the peerage and gentry. Roger Harries, a Shrewsbury draper, presented himself to the heralds in 1584 during their visitation of Shropshire, only to be 'disclaimed' as a gentleman. This did not stop either him or his family from usurping a coat of arms. When Harries's younger son, Thomas, a lawyer and MP, rose into the baronetcy in 1622, his claim to that title would be challenged by other Shropshire gentry on the grounds that he was of low birth and known for usury and crafty dealing.[59] Denis Bond, the Dorchester puritan described by David Underdown, was, like other prosperous townsmen, eager to prove the antiquity of his family, and made copious genealogical jottings on his family and its relatives; he paid the appropriate fee in 1623 to have his pedigree registered at the heralds' visitation that year. In 1611, Thomas Fella of Hallisworth, Suffolk, an executor of the will of Robert Launce (a well-to-do yeoman of Metfield, Suffolk, who had died in that year at the age of 88), composed a 'memorable note' of Launce's family based on a book in Launce's own handwriting.[60]

Expressions of familial pride occur frequently in diaries, letters, draft genealogies, and, rather less often, in lengthier biographical tracts—these could usually be left to some admiring client or servant, as the Berkeley family left their fame

---

[58] H. J. Carpenter, 'Furse of Moreshead: A Family Record of the Sixteenth Century', *Reports and Transactions of the Devonshire Association for the Advancement of Science, Literature and Art*, 26 (1894), 168–84.

[59] G. W. Fisher, 'Sir Thomas Harris of Boreatton, Shropshire, and his Family', *Trans. Shropshire Archaeological and Natural History Society*, 2nd ser., 10 (1898), 77–92.

[60] D. Underdown, *Fire from Heaven* (New Haven, 1992), 49; Suffolk RO (Ipswich), Jc 1/15/1, 'A memorable note wherin is conteyned the names in part of the cheefest kendred of Robert Launce'; for another example, of collections from chronicles, charters, close rolls, the rolls of parliament, and other documents, with a family genealogical focus, see the 120-leaf, late sixteenth-century book by 'J. Estford', W. Sussex RO, Add. MS 2890.

to John Smyth, or as the Vere earls of Oxford were described in a family history of the early eighteenth century.[61] Yet by European standards the English were not a nation obsessed with genealogical record-keeping. Lengthy recitations of ancestry do not feature prominently in most autobiographical writings of the seventeenth century except by way of prefatory comment, and were arguably at odds with the Calvinist thrust of many of these, in which personal election rather than inherited merit was the focus. With a few notable exceptions such as Smyth's *Lives of the Berkeleys*, which integrates family muniments with materials drawn from the public records and from published history books, there is little in England to compare with the weighty, formal family chronicles of German aristocrats, such as the sixteenth-century *Zimmerische Chronik*. This is perhaps attributable to the considerably greater autonomy and sovereignty enjoyed by German nobles within their own territories.[62] But there are likewise only a few instances of the type of family business record analogous to Italian *ricordanzi* of the fifteenth and sixteenth centuries.[63] Several generations of the Catholic Blundells of Little Crosby, beginning with William the elder in the early seventeenth century, and continuing with his grandson and great-great-grandson, maintained the family genealogical and documentary 'hodge podges'.[64] The Anglican baronet Sir William Cowper (d. 1664) compiled a similar document in the mid-seventeenth century, and it was continued by his son, the second baronet, and then by his grandson, the Whig Lord Chancellor, Earl Cowper. Early in the eighteenth century, Samuel Storr produced something similar, though he went no further back in the male line than his father, a Quaker, about whose family he knew little other

---

[61] Bodl. MS Rawl. Essex 6, 'An Hystorical and Genealogical Account of the Ancient Noble Family of the Veres, earles of Oxford, their armes, wives, issues and actions'. This is in the hand of the Essex antiquary William Holman but may not have been originally written by him. Nobility were often as interested, of course, in the past lives of their titular (as opposed to familial) ancestors: one example is Thomas Gaynsford's 'The historie it selfe exemplifying the unmatchfull lives and deathes of Richard duke of Yorke and Richard earle of Warwicke', dedicated by him to Robert Rich, earl of Warwick, in BL MS Sloane 3071, art. 2.

[62] E. Bastress-Dukehart, 'Family, Property, and Feeling in Early Modern German Noble Culture: The Zimmerns of Swabia', *Sixteenth Century Journal*, 32 (2001), 1–19; Hurwich, 'Lineage and Kin in the Sixteenth-Century Aristocracy', 35, 48–59. For a case study of the role of genealogy in the early eighteenth-century French aristocracy, see H. A. Ellis, 'Genealogy, History and Aristocratic Reaction in Early Eighteenth-Century France: The Case of Henri de Boulainvilliers', *Journal of Modern History*, 58 (1986), 414–51.

[63] F. W. Kent, *Household and Lineage in Renaissance Florence* (Princeton, 1977), 99, 113, 273; C. Klapisch-Zuber, *La Maison et le nom: Stratégies et rituels dans l'Italie de la Renaissance* (Paris, 1990), 37–58, 256.

[64] Lancs RO DDBl Acc. 6121 (Blundell of Little Crosby, unfoliated boxes); *The Great Diurnal of Nicholas Blundell of Little Crosby, Lancashire*, ed. F. Tyrer and J. J. Bagley, 3 vols., Rec. Soc. of Lancashire and Cheshire (1968–72), vol. iii, p. ix. Nicholas Blundell was relatively uninterested in history, unlike his immediate ancestors. He nevertheless bestirred himself to study his family's genealogical past at the encouragement of his grandfather, William Blundell the younger or 'the Cavalier' (1620–98), who had first introduced him to the family's history. William Blundell reminded his grandson that their descent had been unbroken for several centuries—a point which must later have annoyed Nicholas, who was unable to produce a son of his own. All this, and the weight of family documents now assembled in the collection called the 'Great Hodge Podge' was enough to stimulate Nicholas into a search of family muniments going back to the twelfth century. For access to the hodge podges and other family documents on deposit in the Lancashire Record Office I am indebted to Mr Brian Whitlock Blundell.

than that it had been driven from Holderness some time after the Restoration; Samuel's grandson William would continue the volume.[65]

Most such records tended to be informal compilations rather than conscious attempts at a family history; often they were kept together with notes on children's births and deaths inscribed in a central place such as the household bible. A highly unusual family diary from the Wilbrahams of Cheshire is remarkable in that the same volume was passed on for multiple generations from 1513 to 1962 (and in fact the pages for the years after 1940 remain closed to public scrutiny). Different generations took their responsibility to preserve the diary more seriously than others, but at its minimum it is a record of births, marriages, and deaths over several centuries. This is as good an example of the character of the English attitude to ancestry as any, both because of its sense of the need to preserve the names and dates, and because there is little beyond those pieces of information to suggest that each generation lived in the shadow of the previous one; on the contrary, each new diarist clearly signalled his identity and independent authorial voice in the margin as he initiated his entries. [66]

If formal attempts to write extended family histories were relatively uncommon, the same is emphatically not true of the more casual and informal collection of materials pertaining to ancestral names and descents. As a token of his respect for William Lee, a former mayor of Oxford, Thomas Crosfield presented him with a genealogy as a new year's gift in 1631.[67] The antiquary Sir Symon Archer urged a kinsman to provide him with papers which 'will in no way pleasure you, but may much helpe me in setting forth myne own pedigree'.[68] A gentry family such as the Finches of Kent kept up a list of family marriages, descents, and alliances with other leading families from the mid-sixteenth to the mid-seventeenth centuries, while the Yorkshire recusant Thomas Meynell was prouder of the five coat armours his mother had brought into his family than of the property which had accompanied her.[69] When Robert, Lord Brooke, was killed in the English civil war, his widow was presented by an admiring cleric with a genealogy and biography of her husband, which its author intended to demonstrate Brooke's 'antiquitie, noble extraction, and eminent vertues'.[70]

---

[65] Herts. RO D/EP. F.25 (William Cowper's commonplace book, vol. i); Borthwick Inst., York, MD 112, ('Book of William Storr'). For another Quaker example see the Lancaster tradesman William Stout's reference, in his autobiography, to 'a booke with a parchent cover' in which he had put the names of his parents, siblings, and 'all their ancestors, so farr as I had certaine information; as also my father's first wife and her kindred, so farr as I had knowledge or information'. *The Autobiography of William Stout of Lancaster 1665–1752* (Manchester and New York, 1967), 67.

[66] Cheshire RO DDX 210/1 (Wilbraham family diary), *passim*.

[67] *The Diary of Thomas Crosfield*, ed. F. S. Boas (Oxford, 1935), 56–9.

[68] Nichols, *Progresses of Queen Elizabeth*, i. 58; BL MS Add. 28564, fo. 235; Philip Styles, 'Sir Simon Archer: "a lover of antiquity and of the lovers thereof"', in his *Studies in Seventeenth-Century West Midlands History* (Kineton, 1978), 1–41.

[69] BL MS Add. 34177 (Twysden papers), fo. 16; Houlbrooke, *The English Family*, 43.

[70] Bodl. MS Eng. hist. e. 240 (Thomas Spencer (vicar of Budbrooke, Warwickshire), 'The Genealogie, Life and Death of the Right honourable Robert Lord Brooke, Baron of Beauchamps Court in the Countie of Warwicke').

TOMBS AND MONUMENTS

Among the wealthy, the most visible proclamation of one's lineage, designed like genealogy to reflect the status and prosperity of the living as much as the achievements of the dead, lay in improvements to estates such as major building, and in particular the erection of funeral monuments and vaults; cheaper varieties of commemoration such as engraved brasses and wooden panels permitted the less affluent to engage in this form of public commemoration.[71] Marked graves go back to the Middle Ages, though few medieval gravestones survive. The spread of literacy at the same time as the Reformation changed the primary function of monuments from intercession on behalf of the dead to their commemoration.[72] Among the well-to-do, buildings, tombs, and other monuments were the most obvious reminder of the debt of the present generation to its ancestors: as George Meriton, the Jacobean dean of Peterborough put it, a country might be defined simply as that place 'where are many monuments of our ancient predecessors'.[73]

The most affluent, from royalty down, lavished money on grand alabaster tombs and effigies, importing foreign masters such as Pietro Torrigiano and, later, Grinling Gibbons, or patronizing a number of celebrated native practitioners. After the Restoration, the proportion of monuments ordered by heirs and survivors increased as the practice of arranging, designing, and even building one's own memorial before death, a frequent occurrence in the sixteenth century, declined.[74] Most monuments were tributes to spouses, parents, or (sometimes) grandparents. Others were erected to friends or associates, such as Lady Anne Clifford's erection of the monument in Beckington church, Somerset, to her beloved childhood tutor, the poet and historian Samuel Daniel.[75] Rare was the monument deliberately dedicated to more remote antecedents, whose lives and achievements seemed distant and shadowy, though some do occur, signifying, as Nigel Llewellyn has put it, 'seamless succession rather than individual virtue' (an important distinction to which we will return further on).[76] John Evelyn recalled the 'pious monument' erected for his grandfather, who had died when Evelyn was 7, by his grandmother, a woman of 'antient family'. When his publican father

[71] N. Llewellyn, 'Honour in Life, Death and in the Memory: Funeral Monuments in Early Modern England', *TRHS*, 6th ser., 6 (1996), 179–200; id., *Funeral Monuments in Post-Reformation England* (Cambridge, 2000); R. Houlbrooke, *Death, Religion, and the Family in England, 1480–1750* (Oxford, 1998), 343–71.
[72] R. Houlbrooke, 'Death, Church, and Family in England between the Late Fifteenth and Early Eighteenth Centuries', in id. (ed.), *Death, Ritual, and Bereavement* (London and New York, 1989), 25–42, at pp. 39–40. As Houlbrooke notes, more durable gravestones in the churchyard and slabs in the church become more common from the seventeenth century onwards, while the use of brass allowed much more detailed texts and images to be recorded.
[73] George Meriton, *The Christian mans assuring house* (1614), 5.
[74] Houlbrooke, *Death, Religion, and the Family*, 369.
[75] *DNB*, *sub* 'Clifford, Anne, Countess of Dorset, Pembroke and Montgomery'; *The Diaries of Lady Anne Clifford*, ed. D. J. H. Clifford, corrected paperback edn. (Phoenix Mill, Glos., 1992), 2.
[76] Llewellyn, *Funeral Monuments in Post-Reformation England*, 305.

died in 1679, the young Thomas Rawlinson (a future lord mayor, and father of the antiquary Richard) asked the vestry of St Dionis Backchurch, London, for permission 'to sett up and fix a Monument for his father on the piller next the pullpit on the westside'.[77] The Buckinghamshire antiquary Browne Willis thought his parents, who had died young, had accomplished enough in life that they 'needed no mausoleums or such pious helps from posterity to preserve their memory', but he felt compelled nonetheless to pay them the 'customary respect of a monument'; between 1704 and 1709 he contributed over £1,000 to the refurbishing of the Bletchley parish church in which they lay.[78] Thomas Wilbraham proudly records the erection of a monument to his grandfather in 1636, which also served to commemorate Thomas's more recently deceased son. Forty years later his successor Roger Wilbraham, one of the more forthcoming of that family's diarists, would lie awake at night wondering how he might erect 'a monument that might transmitt the memory of my d[ear] w[ife] to posterity'.[79]

If new monuments rarely looked further back than parents, English manor houses and churchyards were still filled with the memorials of more distant forebears, though the practice of individual, marked outdoor graves was rare before the seventeenth century.[80] The protection of monuments was another expression of ancestral piety, combined with a more general religious dread of disrespect to the dead that was not, however, universally shared. It was widely believed that those who desecrated tombs, like those who robbed churches, would meet with dire fates.[81] When vandals desecrated the tombs of her Yorkist ancestors in 1573, Elizabeth I lost no time in commissioning replacements; she had already expressed regret, on seeing the buildings erected by her predecessors on a trip to Cambridge in 1564, that she herself had made no similar contribution. A proclamation of 1560 prohibited the kind of destruction meted out in the early 1550s to church and other public monuments, both because 'the true understanding of divers families in this realm (who have descended of the blood of the same persons deceased) is thereby darkened', thereby damaging their knowledge of 'the true course of their inheritance', and because such iconoclasm contributed to 'the extinguishing of the honorable and good memory of sundry virtuous and noble

---

[77] Evelyn, *Diary*, i. 7; Bodl. MS Rawl. D.863, fo. 19ʳ. On the evolution of funeral monuments in this period, see, in addition to Llewellyn, *Funeral Monuments in Post-Reformation England*, K. A. Esdaile, *English Church Monuments 1510–1840* (1946); the humbler sort of churchyard memorial is dealt with by F. Burgess, *English Churchyard Memorials* (1963), esp. 219–29. Before a monument could be erected, a faculty needed to be obtained that testified to the agreement of the patron of the church: Llewellyn, 'Honour in Life, Death and in the Memory', 184.

[78] Bodl. MS Willis 2, fos. 99ʳ–102ʳ. The will of Sir Nicholas Garrard of Eastham, Essex, who died in 1728, committed the baronet's body to be buried 'amongst my Ancestors' in Langford Chancel, Norfolk, while leaving £400 for the erection there of a monument to his own grandparents and parents: Suffolk RO, HA 93/2/2502 (will of Sir Nicholas Garrard, 22 Feb. 1727/8).

[79] Cheshire RO DDX 210/1 (Wilbraham family diary), fos. 19ᵛ, 26ᵛ.

[80] On churchyard memorials see Houlbrooke, *Death, Religion, and the Family*, 360–9 and, more briefly, D. Cressy, *Birth, Marriage, and Death: Ritual, Religion, and the Life-Cycle in Tudor and Stuart England* (Oxford, 1997), 469–73.

[81] Henry Spelman, *The history and fate of sacrilege* (1698), *passim*; A. Walsham, *Providence in Early Modern England* (Oxford, 1999), 109–10.

persons deceased'. Prelates were obliged to make note of damaged monuments on any visitation, and to enforce their repair on parochial officials.[82] Part of the *casus belli* against the Irish rebels in 1599, given in an oration by the earl of Essex to his troops, was that they had 'defaced the auncient monuments of our elders'.[83] Such vandalism was not always the consequence of excess zeal; on most occasions, it was simply the result of local indifference to the ancestral monuments of the propertied. At Riblechester in Lancashire, where Roman coins, statues, and pillars were often unearthed, William Camden found that more recent funeral monuments had not fared so well: the 'country folke have so disfigured the inscriptions', he complained, 'that although I did see many, yet could I scarce read one or two of them'.[84]

The wanton destruction meted out to churches and tombs was sometimes a consequence of the official elimination of pre-Reformation church decoration, but it just as often sprang from plain old vandalism: Camden's own monument in Westminster Abbey would be defaced in this way during the civil war.[85] William Burton, explicitly linking the destruction of monuments with the spectre of innovation, excoriated those who destroyed church antiquities as 'novelists', men with no love of their heritage, a charge repeated six decades later by William Dugdale.[86] There was some reason for concern since, as later antiquaries would note, the disappearance of old buildings often led, very quickly, to the erosion of their popular memory. Most commentators, however, were more immediately concerned with the sacrilegious and irreverent aspects of such attacks. Tristram Risdon complained bitterly about the desecration of the tombs of Edward Courtenay, earl of Devonshire, and his wife in the early seventeenth century. He thought no punishment too awful for those who 'deny the dead their rest, and after death assault them in their graves'.[87] The 78-year-old John Stow told John Manningham that he had not included a number of new monuments in his *Survey of London* 'because those men have bin the defacers of the monuments of others, and soe [he] thinks them worthy to be deprived of that memory whereof they have injuriously robbed others'.[88]

---

[82] Proclamation of 19 Sept. 1560, in *Tudor Royal Proclamations*, ed. P. L. Hughes and J. F. Larkin (New Haven and London, 1969), ii. 146–8; D. M. Palliser, *The Age of Elizabeth* (1983), 368; Nichols, *Progresses of Queen Elizabeth*, i. 150, 176–8. On the eve of the civil war, the members of the Long Parliament still found time to discuss a bill for the prevention of the defacement of tombs, arms, and monuments in respect for the dead: *The Private Journals of the Long Parliament: 7 March–1 June 1642*, ed. V. F. Snow and A. S. Young (New Haven, Conn., 1987), 42; *Journals of the House of Lords*, vol. vi (1643), 201 records a similar provision a year later.

[83] 'An oration to be made by the general to the whole armie before the battel', in Richard Crompton, *The mansion of magnanimitie* (1599), sig. A4.

[84] Camden, *Britain*, 750.   [85] *DNB sub* 'Camden, William'.

[86] William Burton, *The description of Leicester Shire: containing matters of antiquitye, historye, armorye, and genealogy* (1622), 98. Dugdale decried destruction of church glass and tombs as the work of 'certain persons, delighting as may seem in novelty, for they can abide no mark of antiquitie': *The Antient usage in Bearing of such Ensigns of Honor as are commonly call'd arms* (Oxford, 1682), 40.

[87] Wood, *Life and Times*, i. 265, 277, 309; Risdon, *Description of Devon*, 72, 342; cf. below, Ch. 10.

[88] *Diary of John Manningham*, 154–5.

In 1631 John Weever published a huge edition of *Ancient funerall monuments* which he and a few associates had collected, 'of which few, or none, of any antiquity, are remaining in the said churches at this present day; such is the despight not so much of time, as of malevolent people to all antiquities, especially of this kind'. Weever contrasted the ancient respect of pagans for their ancestors' tombs with contemporary indifference and with puritan iconoclasm, which he blamed for the worst examples of desecration.[89] Much worse lay ahead. Weever would have been horrified at the depths that vandalism plumbed during the civil war, though the extent of this would be much exaggerated by royalist propaganda.[90] The Long Parliament forbade the destruction of funeral monuments while permitting attacks on images of the Trinity, Virgin, saints, and angels in two ordinances of 1643 and 1644, but the distinction was frequently lost on enthusiasts. When Philip Candler drew up a summary of the notable church monuments of Suffolk, he recorded a number of depredations, including the removal of the inscription on the marble tomb of a priest who had died in 1489; this had been 'taken away being superstitious'.[91] Abraham de la Pryme, visiting Peterborough Cathedral in 1694, was appalled at how much it had suffered in 'the late damnable wars' from roundheads who had stabled their horses within the church and 'defaced all the curious monuments therein', removing brass from gravestones and shattering funeral effigies and statues. A fervent opponent of Catholic use of images in church, Abraham de la Pryme was nonetheless sickened by a hundred years of puritan iconoclasm beginning with Elizabeth's reign, at the start of which 'Marbles which coverd the dead were digged up and put to other uses, tombs were hack'd & hewn in pieces, the images or representations of the defunct were all broken in pieces & their very dead bodys digged up'. [92] Another clergyman, Thomas Brockbank, noted that most of the monuments in Lichfield Cathedral were of post-Restoration origin. 'What monuments there were formerly I know not, but they all suffer'd in Oliver's time.'[93]

---

[89] John Weever, *Ancient funerall monuments* (1631), preface.

[90] S. Porter, *Destruction in the English Civil Wars* (1994), 64–89 and, for a gazetteer of notable casualties, 134–40; Llewellyn, *Funeral Monuments in Post-Reformation England*, 261.

[91] *Acts and Ordinances of the Interregnum*, ed. C. H. Firth and R. S. Rait, 3 vols. (1911), i. 266, 426; Bodl. MS Tanner 324 (Suffolk collections, for Coddenham), fo. 10ᵛ. It is worth noting that many of the monuments described by Candler dated back only two or three decades, suggesting that wholesale destruction of or replacement of medieval monuments, especially in a puritan county like Suffolk, may have been going on for some time.

[92] BL MS Lans. 897 (Pryme's History of Hatfield, Yorkshire, *c*.1700), fo. 154ʳ. Despite these depredations, several Anglo-Saxon tombs remained undisturbed, having also survived what Pryme called the 'covetious fury' of Henry VIII, who had pulled down the monastery to which the minster had formerly been attached: *Diary of Abraham de la Pryme*, 46. For the religious context of iconoclasm, see C. M. N. Eire, *War Against the Idols: The Reformation of Worship from Erasmus to Calvin* (Cambridge, 1986); M. Aston, *England's Iconoclasts*, i: *Laws Against Images* (Oxford, 1988).

[93] *The Diary and Letter Book of the Rev. Thomas Brockbank 1671–1709*, ed. R. Trappes-Lomax, Chetham Soc., NS 89 (1930), 54.

LITERARY MONUMENTS

By Jacobean times, monument-building in some parts of England far exceeded
house-building, according to Pevsner, though in certain counties such as Shropshire the construction of larger monuments lagged well behind the national
average.[94] Increasingly, these visual symbols also incorporated verbal records—
'chronicles' of decedents' ancestry in Latin or English.[95] This was part and parcel
of the adaptation of the laity to literacy and print, a development which reoriented
and modified older forms of commemoration, though this shift to textuality
should not be overstated: Italianate narrative pictorial reliefs or 'stories' depicting the virtuous life of a subject increased in popularity after 1600.[96] By the 1680s
the genealogical epitaphs once accepted by the heralds as independent evidence
of lineage, and the heraldic decorations on tombs that had characterized the late
Tudor and early Stuart arts of death were well on their way to being replaced by
the angelic, allegorical, and stoic figures of eighteenth-century monuments, with
epitaphs emphasizing the decedent's secular virtues, deeds, and public service rather
than his ancestry. For Lewis Theobald, tombs and monuments were less a source
for filling in gaps in family genealogy than they were the rock and marble equivalents of the historical manuscript, 'abstracts of history' from which could be
reliably gleaned 'many points in history, and the dates of occurrences'.[97]

Writing was often conceived of as a literary counterpart of monument-
building, and it provided an even more accessible medium for the expression
of ancestral piety. If one could not afford the luxury of a monument, then it
was perhaps better still to describe one's ancestors for posterity. In exile during
the interregnum, Gervase Holles was in no position to construct monuments, so
it was left to him to build a metaphorical monument in his family memoirs, 'to
pay my last duty to the ashes of my most deare father and mother and to erect
something wch may praeserve their memories and life amongst their posterity'.
Holles conceived of his genealogical studies as 'an act of piety to those that are
dead and gone, whose memories every day (more and more) threatens to a for-
gottennesse'.[98] It was a poetic topos that words were more durable than the hard-
est tombstone; Abraham Cowley would reiterate the superiority of verse to a
'pyramide of marble stone' or 'tombe cut out in brasse' in mid-century. Sir Edward
Rodney, an influential Somerset knight who wrote a family genealogy for his daughters in the 1620s, commented that 'it is ordinary to perpetuate the memories of
men by Monuments, which yet we see Time deface, and therefore I thought it

[94] Pevsner, *BE: Worcestershire* (1968), 25–7. Although churches themselves were rarely built with a
view to the monuments they contained there are some exceptions, such as Great Whitley, Worcs.,
consecrated 1735, and featuring a large monument to the first Lord Foley by Rysbrack: ibid. 29; Pevsner,
BE: Shropshire (1958), 32; Pevsner, *BE: Berkshire* (1966), 31 for the national level of building.
[95] As some contemporaries realized, the genealogical record on tombs was only as reliable as its
source of information, and could be distorted by a careless or linguistically incompetent engraver.
Llewellyn, *Funeral Monuments in Post-Reformation England*, 120–21.
[96] Ibid. 136, 223.   [97] Theobald, *The Censor*, ii. 121–2.
[98] Gervase Holles, *Memorials of the Holles family, 1493–1656*, ed. A. C. Wood, Camden Soc., 3rd ser.,
55 (1937), 8, 193.

best to keepe my selfe alive amongst you by this [parchment] monument of writing, by which being dead I may yet speak to you'.[99] Even an antiquary like John Evelyn, who was normally fascinated by the material paraphernalia of death, felt impelled to compose a 'little history' of his daughter Mary upon her demise in 1685, because her qualities merited 'a monument more durable than brasse & marble'.[100] Anne Clifford, praised in her own funeral sermon for her restoration of ancestral homes to their former glory, also assembled with the help of scholars three large volumes of materials on the families of her mother and father.[101]

Ancestry was more than a set of recent or remote forebears, a historical family: it provided part of the living individual's identity, his or her 'self', especially among the gentry and aristocracy. Many seventeenth-century memoirs and autobiographies begin with an account of the subject's immediate forebears, though they are often notably deficient as to detail, beyond noting the general fact of lengthy and worthy lineage. In the memoir of her life and family which she drew up for her children, Ann Fanshawe reported that her grandfather had originated in a small Derbyshire estate 'where the family had been some hundreds of years'; she herself had visited the parish church of Drawnfield and inspected the gravestones with family names, 'many of them very antient'. She urged her offspring not to be 'lesse in your industry to exceed, at least not shame, the excellent memory of your ancestors'.[102] After her father's death in 1624, Lady Mary Honeywood of Elmsted, Kent, felt compelled to draw up an account of his life in order to vindicate his memory against the 'envious calumnies of injurious detractors'; intending the tract for her own offspring, she pointed out that 'the glory of children are ther fathers' and reminded them of their duty to 'ancestors departed'. At the end of the century, Jonathan Priestley prefaced his own family memoirs with a similar plea. 'It would be a pleasing entertainment to some persons to know something of their ancestors, or their quality, of the condition they had lived in, and the places of their abode where they have sojourned while they have continued in this world.'[103]

The memoirs of the Restoration courtier Sir John Reresby, Bt., the ambitious son of a royalist officer, and thus of very recent affluence, provide an excellent

[99] 'On the prayse of poetry', in *Complete Works in Verse and Prose of Abraham Cowley*, ed. A. B. Grosart, 2 vols. (1881; repr. New York, 1967), i. 29; E. Rodney, 'The Genealogy of the Family of Rodney of Rodney Stoke, as Compiled in the Seventeenth Century by Sir Edward Rodney, Knt', *The Genealogist*, NS 16 (1900), 207–14, and 17 (1901), 6–11 and 100–6, quotation at vol. 16, p. 207. This was also the view of George Wither, who rated the 'pen of learned wise men' above 'marble monuments' as a preserver of fame: *A collection of emblemes, ancient and moderne* (1635), book 3, illus. viii, p. 142.

[100] Evelyn, *Diary*, iv. 429.

[101] E. Rainbowe, *A Sermon preached at the funeral of the Right Honourable Anne Countess of Pembroke, Dorset and Montgomery* (1677), 20–3 (on her building activities) and 51–2 on her historical collections.

[102] *The Memoirs of Anne, Lady Halkett, and Ann, Lady Fanshawe*, ed. John Loftis (Oxford, 1979), 103, 108.

[103] Bodl. MS Rawl. D. 102 (Lady Mary Honeywood, 'A briefe historicall narration of my Fathers life, and of certaine occurrances wch happened before & since his death: dedicated (by an obliged child) to the vindicating of his honour and reputation against ye envious calumnies of injurious detractors' (1635)), fo. 1ᵛ, p. 47; Jonathan Priestley, 'Some Memoirs Concerning the Family of the Priestleys, written . . . 1696', in *Yorkshire Diaries and Autobiographies in the Seventeenth and Eighteenth Centuries*, Surtees Soc., 77 (1883; published 1886), 18.

illustration of the impact of some modest genealogical research, mixed with family tradition, on the beginning of an autobiography. Reresby repeated what was by then a topos that one ought not to stand on 'the tombs of the dead'. He nevertheless believed that 'a good extraction doth add lustre to personal merit', and he began his autobiography with such a recitation.

A deed dated 1349 is the first that mentions the altar of Saint Leonard, the tutelar saint of Thrybergh, according to the custom of Roman rites. Tradition will have him to have been one of the family of Reresby, and conveys to us a long story concerning him, the substance of which is this: that one Leonard de Reresby, serving his prince in the holy war, was taken prisoner by the Saracens, and there detained captive nearly seven years; that his wife, according to the law of the land, was towards being married to another; that being apprehensive of this accident, by the power of prayer he was miraculously delivered and insensibly conveyed with shackles and gyves or fetters upon his limbs, and laid upon the East Hill in Thrybergh Field as the bells tolled for his wife's second marriage, which her first husband's return prevented; though he presently died as soon as brought into the church, where he desired to pay his first visit.[104]

Reresby was no scholar, but his above-cited interest in the historical context of an alleged ancestor's life, rather than in the mere fact of his own descent therefrom, signifies an important shift in genealogical thinking that we will take up in the next chapter. In reviewing the discussion to this point, it might seem that English attitudes to the place and importance of family ancestry had changed little over the course of two centuries, in the sense that one can find comments endorsing the importance of a long pedigree, or the duty to maintain the inheritance of one's forebears for posterity, just as often in 1730 as in 1530. Closer examination tells a different story. The views of mid-Tudor commentators such as Richard Pace and Sir Thomas Smith on the greater importance of intrinsic merit and individual accomplishment over birth and blood were a minority intellectual position before 1600. They were much more widely held a century later. Fundamental pieties remained in place, and the same themes—appeal to and praise of long ancestry and distaste for disregard of its monuments—can be found at both ends of our period (as well as before and after), but some important changes in attitude need to be drawn out. In the present context, among the most significant of these are a substantially greater interest among the literate in the achievements and contributions of specific, named, individual ancestors, a much-diminished inclination simply to value the continuity of descent in its own right, and a more acute sense of the reasonable chronological limits beyond which ancestral claims could not be convincingly pressed. There would also develop during the seventeenth century a much more intimate connection between the familial and the national pasts, as knowledge of the details of family ancestry both improved and became more commonplace (if inconsistently so), and genealogy itself became more generally recognized as an aid to historical writing and antiquarian scholarship rather than as an end in itself.

---

[104] *The Memoirs of Sir John Reresby of Thrybergh, Bart., M.P. for York, & c.1634–1689*, ed. J. J. Cartwright (1875), 1, 2–3.

CHAPTER FOUR

The Genealogical Imagination

THERE CAN BE little doubt that during the late sixteenth and early seventeenth centuries English men and women became interested in the histories of their own families in ways they had not been previously. The cultural assumptions and social conventions driving such interests are apparent in the various remarks quoted in the last chapter. Students of the history of historiography have been quick to point out the great strides in historical methodology which are owed to the principal architects of systematic family history, the heralds, and have rightly singled out particular famous examples, from Camden to Dugdale, for their erudition and attention to detail. They have also pointed out the degree to which accurate family history, based on documentary and physical evidence (such as monuments) was a slow process of development, with snares of error impeding the path towards a rigorous and sceptical establishment of genealogies.

This picture is too simplistic. While it is correct as to the scholarly virtues and insights of certain leading antiquaries, some but not all of whom were heralds, it overstates the collective importance of the heralds as a group. Moreover, it again assumes that the driving impulse behind the advances in historical method during the sixteenth and seventeenth centuries was a small number of highly educated individuals, while failing to allot any credit to the efforts of the very families which they were studying. To some degree this is a consequence of a rather anachronistic projection of our modern distinction between the 'professional' and the 'amateur', a division of historical labour that is virtually worthless before the late nineteenth century. It also reflects a lingering positivist notion of the gradual progress of historical knowledge, as the myths and legends accepted by a credulous Middle Ages were gradually dispelled by a heroic few. There was indeed a remarkable change in attitudes to the historicity of ancestors over the 200 or so years covered by this study. But the developments are indicative of a much wider awareness of the chronological limits of historical knowledge, of changes in the ways in which remote ancestors were regarded in relation to national history, and of a considerably broader and more energetic circulation of genealogical information. Seen in this light, certain phenomena that once looked like wrong turns, such as the wild claims to distant Trojan and biblical ancestors that are widely thought to have characterized Elizabethan genealogical practices, become instead signs of a growing public interest in the connection between families and external historical events.

OF ARMS AND THE HERALDS

Many family evidence collections were amassed and organized in the sixteenth century to be utilized by the official scrutinizers of coats of arms, the heralds, whose work for a time made them also the *de facto* licensers of ancestral claims. Heralds postdate the development of arms by nearly a century. They first appear in English records at the time of Edward I, and from then until the sixteenth century were increasingly entrusted with the conduct of tournaments in those regions of Europe where tournaments were held. The heralds acquired ambassadorial functions at the commencement of the Hundred Years War.[1] They began to develop a separate role as guardians of the tokens of lineage a little over a century later.[2] Not surprisingly, several of their number overstated the antiquity of their calling. The Elizabethan writer Gerard Legh was certainly mistaken in pushing the heraldic tradition back to the Norman Conquest, and in asserting that it was a language 'common to every Englishe man'. Others pressed it even further back: several Tudor writers believed that coats of arms were a natural and divine, not merely customary, sign of social distinction, traceable to Adam.[3] Among the Arderne family papers in the Cheshire Record Office are notes and collections (possibly by the Elizabethan haberdasher Francis Tipsley of London) that include a section on the conquerors of England since Brutus, all of whom, including Julius Caesar, are assigned spurious arms.[4] One writer drew up what amounted to a genealogy of genealogy which found arms in use by Japhet and at the siege of Troy, ending with an account of 'howe longe coote armors weire begune before the Incarnatione of our Lord Jesus Christ'.[5] Dugdale was more sceptical than others and thought hereditary arms 'of no greater antiquity then King Richard the First time'.[6]

M. T. Clanchy has plausibly suggested that the iconographic language of heraldry emerged in the Middle Ages as a graphic mode of discourse for the feudal nobility in answer to a clerical monopoly on Latin writing, though historians of heraldry such as Sir Anthony Wagner insist that armorial symbols are largely arbitrary in meaning. There is general concurrence, however, that systematic heraldry

---

[1] A. Wagner, *Heralds and Heraldry in the Middle Ages*, 2nd edn. (Oxford, 1956), 26, 34.

[2] A. Wagner, *English Genealogy*, 3rd edn. (Chichester, 1973), 355–8.

[3] Gerard Legh, *The accedens of armory* (1562), fo. 2; John Ferne, *The Blazon of Gentrie* (1586), 2; Francis Markham, *Booke of honovr or five decads of epistles of honovr* (1625), 21–2.

[4] Cheshire RO DAR/J/8 (Arderne papers), Armorial Liber F, 'A note of the names and armes of the five Conquerors of this famous Ilande called England and of the nobilitye at and since the Normans Conquest'. This begins with Brutus the Trojan, and includes invented arms of various invaders including Caesar, Hengist, Swein of Denmark, and William the Conqueror. The manuscript continues with 'The armes of all the knights and gentlemen which wer at the Seidg of Calverocke in Scotland, colected together by Francis Tipsley, citizen and haberdasher of London 1600', which second item may be by a different author from the first. Both sections of the manuscript were in the Arderne family collection at Utkinton estate library by 1758. The arms are all crudely drawn.

[5] BL MS Harl. 3504, fos. 245ʳ–246ʳ. For another contemporary attempt at explaining the origins of arms, see Bodl. MS Top. gen. d. 59, fos. 7ᵛ–8ʳ.

[6] William Dugdale, *The Baronage of England*, 2 vols. (1675–6), preface, vol. i, sig. b2ᵛ.

began at some point in the twelfth century, when arms first appear on baronial seals and in the occasional armorial roll, the oldest known example of which dates from 1254 and survives only in a 1586 copy by the Elizabethan herald Robert Glover. Heraldry began to establish its formal rules more seriously in the fifteenth century.[7] By 1500 it had more or less developed its standard system of symbolic conventions, which remained the commonly accepted code for the categorization and presentation of family honour to outsiders and onlookers long after it ceased to be of practical, battlefield value. The late Elizabethan and early Stuart years witnessed the publication of a number of popular guides to heraldry and arms, such as John Guillim's influential *Display of Heraldry* and Edmund Bolton's *Elements of Armories*, both published in 1610. These in turn spurred many other writers interested in arms to attempt similar manuals, a tradition leading up to Sylvanus Morgan's lavish Restoration contribution, *The Sphere of Gentry*.[8] The earlier entries in the heraldic genre were responding not only to curiosity about arms and their history, but to a parallel interest in the grounds for bearing them, which was supplied by the public recognition of family lineage.

The College of Arms was first chartered as the heralds' governing body by Richard III, and by the end of the fifteenth century it had acquired a major officiating function at all royal and many noble official occasions, including coronations, creations, progresses, tournaments, and even funerals. At these events they had primary responsibility for ensuring that those in attendance followed the order of precedence, and that coats of arms were correctly displayed—genealogical tableaux were a stock feature of much royal pageantry.[9] There is ample evidence of the prominence of the heralds in the funeral procession: the ultimate rite of passage, this symbolized the journey of the soul into the next life while marking its departure into a familial history visually represented by the colourful panoply of banners, arms, and crests.[10] Indeed, the absence of a herald, or subordinate pursuivant, at the funeral of a great was more noticeable than his presence; in 1560

[7] M. T. Clanchy, *From Memory to Written Record: England 1066–1307* (1979), 229–30; Wagner, *Heralds and Heraldry in the Middle Ages*, 12–40; id., *The Records and Collections of the College of Arms* (1952), 6–8.

[8] Sylvanus Morgan, *The Sphere of Gentry* (1661). Other Restoration examples include Randle Holme II's *The Academy of Armory* (1688). There are numerous unpublished efforts in this genre as well, for instance CUL MS Add. 3078, Joseph Bokenham's 300-page book on heraldry, composed in 1711, and consisting of a 'dictionary of arms' (fos. 1–254) followed by a list of 'Atchievements of the English nobility' (fos. 255–308), itself little more than a summary of arms and mottoes. Edmund Bolton's work was less widely read in the early seventeenth century than Ferne's because the former was a Catholic and not a herald; but it was admired by the elder John Anstis, Garter King of Arms in the 1720s and 1730s, who recommended Bolton as 'a very learned man' in a letter to the earl of Hertford, president of the Society of Antiquaries: Nichols, *Literary Illustrations*, iv. 133 (Anstis to Hertford, 18 Apr. 1737).

[9] A. R. Young, *Tudor and Jacobean Tournaments* (New York and London, 1987), 43–5; John N. King, *Tudor Royal Iconography* (Princeton, 1989), 46; M. James, 'Two Tudor Funerals', in *Society, Politics and Culture* (Cambridge and New York, 1986), 176–87; R. Houlbrooke, *Death, Religion, and the Family in England, 1480–1750* (Oxford, 1998), 258–61, 267–74.

[10] A. Van Gennep, *Rites of Passage*, trans. M. B. Vizedom and G. L. Caffee (1960), 146–65; J. Goody, *Death, Property and the Ancestors* (Stanford, 1962), 44, 379–415.

the London diarist Henry Machyn expressed surprise at one such burial in the Tower 'without an offeser of armes'.[11] This practice declined in the seventeenth century, though a heraldic presence at the obsequies of major public figures remained common.[12]

In the course of the sixteenth century, arms increasingly figured as domestic, ecclesiastical, and civic decorations. They were part of the ornamental culture, and by 1700 were as omnipresent as religious art had been before the Reformation, filling windows in churches once occupied by the saints, and often dominating funeral monuments.[13] Gentry homes were known to display both their own and the arms of their county's major families.[14] Herald painters, operating outside the College of Arms but under its watchful eye (rather like the relationship of apothecaries and surgeons to the College of Physicians) increasingly provided the decorative arms required by families and local communities; occasionally they even intruded on the heraldic privilege of conducting noble funerals.[15] Although the heralds were quick to assert their own superiority, there was some overlap in their numbers: Sir William Segar was both a herald and a painter, while the great Camden inherited his own skill at heraldry from his painter-stainer father (a fact notably omitted on his Westminster monument).[16] Those skilled in painting glass were frequently brought in from the Continent, beginning with Baernard Dininckhoff, a Bohemian Protestant who became a freeman of York in 1586.[17] The citizen in the urban environment, with or without his family's own arms, would at least be exposed with frequency to the heraldic devices of his corporation. In Plymouth, the townsmen paid William Stayner, whose surname denotes his craft, 1s. in 1497 to paint the town's arms on an official book. Nearly two centuries later John Somerton was paid the much greater sum of £6 for cutting

[11] *The Diary of Henry Machyn*, ed. J. G. Nichols, Camden Soc., os 42 (1848), 213, 216, 241. Henry VIII used the College of Arms in order carefully to control participation in and the order of aristocratic funerals, such as that of the sixth earl of Northumberland in 1537: G. Broce and R. M. Wunderli, 'The Funeral of Henry Percy, Sixth Earl of Northumberland', *Albion*, 22 (1990), 199–215; for early Tudor aristocratic ceremonial see F. J. Furnivall's edition of Bodl. MS Ashm. 837, art vi, *A Booke of Precedence* (1869). In the early seventeenth century noblemen began to object to the heralds' strict control over funerals, and by the end of the century their funerary role had been all but usurped by undertakers, who dealt with a much broader range of society: C. Gittings, *Death, Burial and the Individual in Early Modern England* (1984), 96, 166–87; Houlbrooke, *Death, Religion, and the Family*, 278–81.

[12] R. Houlbrooke, 'Civility and Civil Observances in the Early Modern English Funeral', in P. Burke, B. Harrison, and P. Slack (eds.), *Civil Histories: Essays Presented to Sir Keith Thomas* (Oxford, 2000), 67–85, esp. pp. 79–81.

[13] N. Llewellyn, *Funeral Monuments in Post-Reformation England* (Cambridge, 2000), 143. For the aesthetics of decoration in Renaissance England see Patricia Fumerton, *Cultural Aesthetics* (Chicago and London, 1991), 18–24.

[14] J. Broadway, *William Dugdale and the Significance of County History in Early Stuart England*, Dugdale Soc. Occasional Papers, 39 (1999), 7.

[15] Dugdale, *Life, Diary and Correspondence*, 364.

[16] Llewellyn, *Funeral Monuments in Post-Reformation England*, 185.

[17] H. Murray, 'The Heraldic Window at Fountains Hall', *Yorkshire Archaeological Journal*, 62 (1990), 171–86. For heraldic decoration of royal buildings, see *The History of the King's Works*, iii: *1485–1660*, ed. H. M. Colvin, 2 pts. (1975–82), pt. 1, 441 (index), *sub* 'Heraldic Decoration'.

Fig. 4.1. Central panel from the Clifford 'Great Picture' triptych, in Appleby Castle, Westmorland, attributed to Jan van Belkamp

both the town and the royal arms (and those of Sir Francis Drake, its most famous historical figure) into the newly rebuilt conduit outside Town Gate.[18]

Anne Clifford's famous commissioned triptych of her family features a middle panel bordered by coats of arms of her remote antecedents, and portraits of parents (the earl and countess of Cumberland), siblings, and teachers, with inscriptions (Fig. 4.1) composed by her on the advice of Sir Matthew Hale. The 'Great Picture' exemplifies the link between visual symbol and literary recollection, as does her own self-designed tomb, which offered no effigy to the world but, behind it, a wall with a further display of ancestral arms. But not everyone, male or female, had Clifford's profound interest in the details of her family history—perhaps driven in her case by her own disinheritance by her father (and a subsequent unsuccessful court action) as much as by the happier experience of

[18] R. N. Worth, *Calendar of the Plymouth Municipal Records* (Plymouth, 1893), 95, 168. A really elaborate pedigree could cost much more. That which Dugdale designed and had painted for the earl of Denbigh in 1659 cost £100. Dugdale, *Life, Diary and Correspondence*, 105.

having been taught as a child by Samuel Daniel.[19] Precisely because arms were so commonplace, one should be cautious about inferring from their presence an interest in or knowledge of either genealogy or history. The mid-century Cheshire engraver Daniel King thought that the proliferation in coats of arms was partly due to invention, and partly due to men's ignorance of their heritage:

A man sometimes purchaseth arms of the herauld, not knowing that he hath any of antiquity: or else willingly leaveth his old and ancient arms, (which commonly are very plain and simple to see to) and purchaseth new of brave and glorious colours, which in his imagination be better.

Those who had no right to arms exhibited them with impunity, he thought, and those who had the right betrayed time-honoured traditions for the sake of conspicuous display.[20]

Arms could appear in almost any form, but their function was increasingly to decorate or identify property. When Thomas Jenney, an Ipswich gentleman, died in 1619, he left his nephew a silver cup on which were engraved a number of coats of arms; this Jenney had inherited from his mother, who had in turn been given it by her father on the day of her wedding. The cup itself was the sentimental gift, the arms merely decorative and without any immediate family association.[21] In marked contrast, when Sampson Erdeswicke wanted to record the arms of Edward Threlkeld, chancellor of Hereford, 'one of my old acquayntance syns K. Edward his tyme', during a tour of Northumberland and Cumberland in 1574, he was able to take them not out of evidences but 'out of an old armchair which was his grandfathers, the back whereof I saw'.[22] Arms were also, especially in the seventeenth and eighteenth centuries, a prominent feature of the bookplates on volumes in aristocratic and gentry libraries, and were often stamped on the spine or front of bindings. One Restoration historian, Thomas Lane, asked Sir John Perceval for permission to put the latter's arms on a map in Lane's *Saracen History*, cheekily indicating that he would regard a refusal as a criticism of the book and its author.[23] Corporate and institutional coats of arms, such as those of towns or

---

[19] *The Diaries of Lady Anne Clifford*, ed. D. J. H. Clifford, corrected paperback edn. (Phoenix Mill, Glos., 1992), 98–9; *DNB*, *sub* 'Clifford, Anne, Countess of Dorset, Pembroke and Montgomery'. I am indebted to Ms Aki Beam, who is completing a doctoral thesis at McMaster University on women and ageing in early modern England, for helpful comments on Clifford and the issue of women's interest in ancestry.

[20] Daniel King, *The vale-royall of England or, the county palatine of Chester illustrated* (1656), i. 98.

[21] Will of Thomas Jenney of Ipswich, gent. (proved 25 Mar. 1620), in *Wills of the Archdeaconry of Suffolk, 1620–1624*, ed. M. E. Allen, Suffolk Rec. Soc., 31 (1989), no. 2, p. 2. Engraving arms on family plate may have provided insurance against robbery as much as it projected symbolic ancestry. Richard Brownlow noted in his account book for January 1617 paying 2*d*. for 'engraving the arms' on a basin and ewer he had bought for £23. 7*s*. 8*d*. *Records of the Cust Family: Second series, the Brownlows of Belton 1550–1779*, ed. E. Cust (1909), 54.

[22] Sampson Erdeswicke, 'Certaine verie rare observations of Cumberland, Northumberland, &c', in Anon. (ed.), *Reprints of Rare Tracts* (Newcastle, 1849), 15. For some other examples of arms in the decorative arts see Coll. Arms, *Heralds' Commemorative Exhibition 1484–1934* (1936), plates 43, 51.

[23] Hist. MSS Comm., *Report on the Manuscripts of the Earl of Egmont*, 2 vols. (1905–9), ii. 116 (Lane to Perceval, 6 June 1682).

of companies, continued to feature prominently in public or semi-public contexts, constituting an important part of the memorial culture of urban communities in particular.[24] Familial arms, in contrast, lost some of this public exposure
in the course of the seventeenth century. In particular, family arms became detached
from the military function for which they had first been developed. Many civil
war flags and banners were influenced by the more recent fashion for non-heraldic
emblems and *imprese*; they depart significantly from the battle paraphernalia of
earlier campaigns in finding very different forms of symbolism, much of it
explicit propaganda. Future conflicts evolved regimental colours which fulfil a similar role but without reference to family.[25]

THE PEDIGREE 'CRAZE'

Thomas Tusser, an Elizabethan gentleman who wrote for a rural yeoman and minor
gentry audience, enjoined his readers to consult Tusser's own pedigree 'in
Harolds booke'.[26] It was at this time that the heralds' role in sanctioning claims
to lengthy or distinguished descents—on which rested, in turn, the right to bear
particular coats of arms—peaked during the so-called late sixteenth-century
'craze' for genealogies and pedigrees.[27] This was really a brief phase of intense
pursuit of the official legitimation of lineage, within a much longer period of
genealogical interest that did not subside even when the heralds began to lose
their authority, though its motives and aims became rather different. The interest of the relatively new members of the gentry in establishing their claims to ancient
lineage through official channels drastically increased the workload for the members of the already understaffed College of Arms.

   Heraldic visitations to the counties—periodic but irregular inspections of
arms and the authority for bearing them—began in 1529–30, when Thomas
Benolt, Clarenceux King of Arms, was given the first visitation commission by
letters patent, in an effort by Henry VIII to regularize the recognition of honour.
A 1558 royal commission added the investigation of titles of honour such as
gentleman and esquire to the heralds' tasks, and this quickly involved the heralds more closely in questions of descent. These two functions, armorial and
genealogical, had an extensive overlap but were never quite the same, since many

   [24] I. W. Archer, 'The Arts and Acts of Memorialization in Early Modern London', in J. F. Merritt
(ed.), *Imagining Early Modern London: Perceptions and Portrayals of the City from Stow to Strype, 1598–1720*
(Cambridge, 2001), 89–113, esp. pp. 96–100.
   [25] A. R. Young, *The English Emblem Tradition*, iii: *Emblematic Flag Devices of the English Civil Wars,
1642–1660* (Toronto, 1995); I. Gentles, 'The Iconography of Revolution: England 1642–1649', in I. Gentles,
J. Morrill, and B. Worden (eds.), *Soldiers, Writers and Statesmen of the English Revolution* (Cambridge, 1998), 91–113, esp. p. 93.
   [26] Thomas Tusser, 'The author's life', in *Five Hundred Points of Good Husbandry* (1580; repr. Oxford,
1984), 204.
   [27] J. H. Plumb, *The Death of the Past* (Boston, 1971), 31–2; cf. M. James, *Family, Lineage and Civil
Society* (Oxford, 1974), 108–12; L. Stone, *The Crisis of the Aristocracy* (Oxford, 1965), 22–7.

families of gentle birth had no claim to arms. The visitations of counties about once every four decades continued till 1686, when Sir Henry St George, Clarenceux King of Arms (and the third generation of his family to attain high office in the college), received the last such commission from James II.[28] The Dutch-born William III would refuse to revive the practice of visitations (though the college retained its monopoly in the granting of arms), but this political decision merely reflected a declining interest in the work of the heralds and a shift in social assumptions about what constituted legitimate gentility.[29] Within half a century, the heralds had also ceased their long-standing practice of bringing actions against 'usurpers' of arms to the Court of Chivalry, a separate body also under the jurisdiction of the Earl Marshal.[30]

In the century and a half between Thomas Benolt and Henry St George, the provincial Kings of Arms and their subordinate heralds and pursuivants were charged with ensuring that every claim to antiquity was thoroughly documented, every pedigree verified by family or local muniments, every coat of arms properly recorded, and new and unique coats bestowed on suitable claimants.[31] Authorized to grant arms to any person of free birth with a minimum worth of £10 per year in land or £300 in movable goods, the heralds made nearly 4,000 grants between the accession of Elizabeth I and the outbreak of the civil war.[32] The number of such processes, like the visitations themselves, declined notice-ably in the later seventeenth century. By this time the Earl Marshal, already the honorific head of the College of Arms, had also formally become the person respons-ible, under the Crown, for issuing authority to bear arms, on recommendation of a herald, who retained oversight of the details. In twenty years as Garter King of Arms, the college's senior position below the Earl Marshal, Sir Edward Walker passed under his hand 134 grants and confirmations of arms and crests—an

---

[28] M. Maclagan, 'Genealogy and Heraldry in the Sixteenth and Seventeenth Centuries', in L. Fox (ed.), *English Historical Scholarship in the Sixteenth and Seventeenth Centuries* (1956), 31–48; Wagner, *Heralds and Heraldry in the Middle Ages*, 9–11, 76–82, 83–99 (for the controversy surrounding the powers and emoluments of Garter and Clarenceux arising in 1530); Wagner suggests (pp. 52, 106–20) that a group of medieval rolls of arms he terms 'local rolls' may in fact be direct 'ancestors' of the Tudor and Stuart visitations.

[29] Devon RO 3121 Z/Z1–2, instructions to Edward Pike of Exeter, painter-stainer, and deputy to Sir Henry St George. These instructions, which license Pike to visit the churches in Devon to 'take notice of any such arms and crests' therein in case they were usurped and to advise St George accord-ingly, offer a good example of the heralds' tendency to decentralize their activities and use local herald-painters as their agents: P. Borsay, *The English Urban Renaissance: Culture and Society in the Provincial Town 1660–1770* (Oxford, 1989), 229.

[30] J. H. Round, 'Peerage Cases in the Court of Chivalry', in his *Peerage and Pedigree: Studies in Peerage Law and Family History*, 2 vols. (1910; facs. repr. 1970), i. 69–102. The last recorded case occurred during a brief period of revival in this medieval court's activity, from 1709 to 1735: Wagner, *Records and Collections of the College of Arms*, 37.

[31] For some interesting implications of the visitations on the social context within which the novel and its antecedents arose, see M. McKeon, *The Origins of the English Novel, 1600–1740* (Baltimore, 1987), 132, 151–3; for a case study of the late visitations and the methods of the heralds, see P. Styles, 'The Heralds' Visitation of Warwickshire 1682–3', in his *Studies in Seventeenth-Century West Mid-lands History* (Kineton, 1978), 108–49. For the abatement of visitations and their overall effectiveness, see F. Heal and C. Holmes, *The Gentry in England and Wales, 1500–1700* (Basingstoke, 1994), 10.

[32] D. M. Palliser, *The Age of Elizabeth* (1983), 69–70.

average of less than seven per year, which pales in comparison with Tudor and early Stuart figures. In Warwickshire, the county of Sir William Dugdale, one of the most illustrious of heralds, the number of pedigrees recorded in 1682 was a mere 105, down from 256 at the visitation of 1619.[33]

At the proclamation of a visitation, the gentry of a given shire were given public notice to appear at a particular place and time with their appropriate authorities. Peers, who fell under the jurisdiction of the Garter King of Arms rather than the provincial kings of arms and heralds, were excluded from the general summons, and arrangements were generally made to visit them in their homes separately, a privilege that by the mid-1600s many mere gentlemen were beginning to demand.[34] A typical Tudor visitation summons, that by William Flower, Norroy King of Arms, to the gentry of Derbyshire in 1569, commanded a specified list of county men to appear at nine in the morning with their arms and 'such of theire evidence or matter of recorde as may (if neede so requyre) justifye the same'. A century later, the summons had evolved into a standard printed form, complete with blank spaces for the insertion of a recipient's name and address: in 1665 the Berkshire antiquary Hannibal Baskervile received such a summons from Elias Ashmole, then Windsor herald, ordering him to appear a few weeks hence at the New Inn in Abingdon 'with any arms & crests he bears'.[35]

At first oral testimony was often considered sufficient evidence, without reference to the detailed documentation that would later give the Elizabethan heralds their apprenticeship as antiquaries. A decade before the formal beginning of visitations, Sir Thomas Writh or Wriothesley (uncle of the more famous Henrician chancellor), together with his principal rival in the college, Benolt, granted arms to the humanist Richard Pace, apparently without written evidence, citing 'common renown', their own knowledge, and 'the report of other credible and noble persone' who had testified that Pace through his actions and other signs of virtue merited the outward marks of gentility. Dependence on oral evidence was virtually inescapable at a time when many families preserved their domestic histories mainly by memory and tradition. The methodical yeoman Robert Furse, though he enjoined his descendants to continue his record of the family's genealogy, had gathered his information both out of written 'evydenses' and 'by reporte off old awncyente men and some of my on knowlege and experyens', and he used proverbs and old sayings to elaborate on and explain the actions of his ancestors.

[33] SAL MS 455 (Walker papers), fo. 14ʳ; see e.g. a copy of the standard form under name of Henry, earl of Norwich, earl Marshal, at fo. 11ʳ; Styles, 'The Heralds' Visitation of Warwickshire', 130.

[34] Styles, 'The Heralds' Visitation of Warwickshire', 124, 145. Clergy were theoretically exempted from the visitations, though this did not prohibit them from seeking heraldic authentication of their claims to gentle pedigree. The gradual blurring of the lines between them, as the Church became a profession for gentry rather than a distinctive order, meant that they were often in practice summoned anyway. Thus no clergy appear in the entries for the Warwickshire visitation of 1619, but twenty-six were summoned there in 1682—though only three pedigrees were actually entered.

[35] Bodl. MS Ashm. 798, fo. 18ʳ ᵛ; the previous visitation, by Thomas Tonge, Norroy, had occurred in 1530; Bodl. MS Rawl. D. 859 (Baskervile papers), fo. 70ʳ; on documents pertaining to Ashmole's heraldic career, see M. Hunter (comp.), *Elias Ashmole 1617–1692: The Founder of the Ashmolean Museum and his World* (Oxford, 1983), esp. pp. 43–48; C. H. Josten, *Elias Ashmole (1617–1692)*, 5 vols. (Oxford, 1966), iii. 1013.

The Cheshire antiquary Randle Holme I (the first of four of his name who practised herald-painting in seventeenth-century Chester, and a local deputy to the
College of Arms) lists both written evidence and 'testymonye' in some of his collections.[36] Amid the assortment of arms and inscriptions in the collections of Henry
Savage, assembled between 1650 and 1677, one finds the occasional fact resting
only on verbal information. 'Sam: Gorges told me that the first seate of the family (which came in with Wm Conqueror) was at Tamworth, & after Wraxhall.'[37]
Sometimes it was simply easier to accept a claim than to be too scrupulous about
its proof. Thomas Habington, one of the more sceptical of early Stuart antiquaries,
was 'morally certayne' that the ancient Worcestershire family of Rous 'came into
England with the conqueror', though he admitted that this was not actually sustained by the surviving evidence.[38]

   This trust in oral evidence would diminish as the seventeenth century wore
on. A failure to legitimize the family lineage through a written record was to embar-
rass Anthony Wood, who lamented in later years 'that his father did not enter
three or more descents of his owne familie, which he had then been better able
to doe'.[39] A defect in the keeping of records, or a failure to register a pedigree,
was felt all the more strongly because personal memory and family 'tradition' were,
like orally based 'fame', rapidly losing pride of place to an emphasis on the
written record, which was seen as both more durable and more accurate. As early
as the start of the seventeenth century Sir William Wentworth recorded for his
son Thomas the family pedigree as related orally to Sir William by his own father,
while evincing a desire to verify this by reference to documentary sources.
Wentworth had 'herde thatt our name and progenie hath for a long tyme before
the Conquest bene of worship and reputation' but he also vaguely recalled 'that
thear are att this daie in the Lowe Cuntries records thereof in some towne, butt
I can nott as yett lerne the certaine place'.[40] In the 1620s, Sir Edward Rodney of
Rodney Stoke compiled a genealogical history for his children that reflected the
contemporary belief—itself soon to wane—that tradition and written evidence
were sources of virtually equivalent authority. Asserting the 'constant tradition'
in his family that it had first come into England with Empress Maud or Matilda
in the reign of Stephen, Rodney confessed that 'I have no evidence by mee
to provve this tradition' except a later pedigree. 'Yet', he went on to argue, 'my
want thereof will not make it false in it selfe, though it gaine the lesse credit

---

[36] PRO SP 9/1/2 (17 Feb., 9 Hen. 8 (1518)); H. J. Carpenter, 'Furse of Moreshead: A Family Record
of the Sixteenth Century', *Reports and Transactions of the Devonshire Association for the Advancement
of Science, Literature and Art*, 26 (1894), 168–84, at pp. 170, 179; BL MS Harl. 1997 (Holme pedigrees,
descent of Sir William Norres of Speke); Cheshire RO, DCH /Z/8 (1631 pedigree of Fitton and Brereton).
On the Randle Holmeses, I to IV, and the function of deputy heralds, especially in Chester, see
G. D. Squibb, 'The Deputy Heralds of Chester', *Journal of the Chester Archaeological and Historic Society*,
56 (1969), 23–36.
[37] Bristol RO, MS 36074 (88), collections of Henry Savage, fo. 73.
[38] BL MS Add. 28,564, fo. 237ᵛ (Habington to Symon Archer, 9 Nov. 1634).
[39] Wood, *Life and Times*, i. 263.
[40] *Wentworth Papers, 1597–1628*, ed. J. P. Cooper, Camden Soc., 4th ser., 12 (1973), 26.

wth others'.[41] The perceived weakness of family genealogies dependent solely on tradition and recollection is well illustrated by the experience of the Devon anti-quary Thomas Westcote, who was castigated by a minor gentleman for ignoring the man's family in Westcote's *View of Devonshire*. Duly apologetic for the oversight, Westcote asked the man to provide him with a pedigree for insertion in a future edition, 'to which he suddenly replied, (not without a smile of two, or three discreet gentlemen present) that he knew not his father . . . who died when he was a youngling, and therefore he could not possibly name his ancestry'.[42]

But it was just when documents became the rule in heraldic inspections that the whole exercise began to fall into disrepute, as the gentry's enthusiasm for official, Crown-recognized gentility abated in comparison with the desire for public acknowledgement of a status now produced as much by comportment, conspicu-ous expenditure, and civil interaction.[43] The visitations in general became more rather than less thorough in the middle decades of the seventeenth century, judg-ing by the swelling quantity of material in the archives of later Stuart heralds such as Dugdale and his much younger clerk and protégé, Gregory King. The latter may even have developed his later skills as a social statistician from his innovat-ive use of Hearth Tax returns as a means of establishing the financial status of the Warwickshire gentry prior to his visitation there in 1682.[44] Moreover, the heralds were often able to enlist the assistance of local officials such as hundred bailiffs since, for logistical reasons, visitations were often timed to coincide with Assizes,[45] a social event which the county worthies could be expected to attend, and at which the commission to conduct the visitation was read publicly.

No amount of organization and determination, however, could overcome the problem of an uncooperative clientele. Documents were often missing or simply withheld, and the very persons who should have been most concerned to pro-tect the integrity of arms, the local gentry, consistently failed to appear at the appointed times for visitations, which in any case were held too rarely to serve as a foolproof control. In areas of concentrated population such as boroughs, the heralds could hope for corporate assistance: when Camden sent two deputies to inspect arms in Leicester the town officials duly noted in advance the forth-coming visit and the heralds' authority to 'enter into all churches, castles, howses

---

[41] E. Rodney, 'The Genealogy of the Family of Rodney of Rodney Stoke, as Compiled in the Seventeenth Century by Sir Edward Rodney, Knt', *The Genealogist*, NS 16 (1900), 207–14, and 17 (1901), 6–11 and 100–6, quotation at pt. 1, vol. 16, pp. 213–14.

[42] Thomas Westcote, *View of Devonshire*, *c*.1630, (1st edn., Exeter, 1845), 449. J. Youings, 'Devon's First Local Historians', *The Devon Historian*, 1 (1970), 5–8, makes the interesting point that similarit-ies among Westcote and other Devon local historians such as Tristram Risdon can be explained by common derivation of information from an oral source, which gentry gathered at shire meetings like the Assizes.

[43] Significantly, the heralds got a new lease on life during a reintensification of genealogical activ-ity beginning with George III, as a further wave of 'new men' achieved prominence in the imperial wars against Bourbon, Revolutionary, and Napoleonic France: Wagner, *Records and Collections of the College of Arms*, 41.

[44] Styles, 'The Heralds' Visitation of Warwickshire', 109, 115.

[45] Dugdale, *Life, Diary and Correspondence*, 116–17.

and other places'.[46] Elsewhere, especially in later decades, they were not so lucky. Nearly one-third of those summoned to Dugdale's visitation of Yorkshire in 1665–6 failed to turn up.[47] When the heralds sat at the Crown Inn at Oxford in 1669, few of those who had been summoned actually appeared, preferring to attend a horse race elsewhere. On the heralds' return in 1676, Anthony Wood noted that 'even the university appeared not'. When Wood's own father was summoned to appear before the heralds in 1634, 'with his armes and pedegree and to have them entred into their books', he had refused, pleading privilege as a member of the university, though he consented to appear as a witness on behalf of a friend whose own claim to arms was under examination.[48]

By the 1660s, most gentlemen regarded visitations as a nuisance, involving expense and often inconvenient travel. When Hannibal Baskervile received his summons from Ashmole in 1665, he dutifully presented himself at Abingdon and paid the herald £37. 6s. od. to record 'the names of all my children dead and alive', and those of his father and grandfather. But to Baskervile's annoyance, Ashmole refused to accept as evidence the pedigree which the former had inherited from his father-in-law and which had already been registered by the heralds in 1629. Ashmole insisted on original documents, a practice we are apt to applaud from the vantage point of the history of scholarship, but one which was increasingly at odds with the mood of a provincial gentry grown impatient with the bother of it all.[49] A measure of the disregard into which the heralds had sunk by the eighteenth century can be found in Henry Prescott's comment on seeing the coat of arms, 'finely writ and splendidly adorn'd', of Chester's new mayor in 1718, sealed by John Vanbrugh and Peter Le Neve (Clarenceux and Norroy Kings of Arms respectively): 'solemn respect is paid to it tho little reguard is had to the Heralds'.[50] By 1714 it was possible for one of Mandeville's characters to speak of the heralds' business as simply 'contriving and finding out high and illustrious pedigrees for low and obscure people'.[51]

This tar was applied with too broad a brush, but neither was it entirely undeserved. A series of vicious internecine quarrels among the late Tudor and early Stuart heralds occurred, of which only the most famous was the controversy between Camden and Ralph Brooke at the end of the sixteenth century. These did not advance the reputation of the college, and a series of attempts to reform both it and the process of visitation proved stillborn.[52] Moreover, though several of the

[46] *Records of the Borough of Leicester*, ed. H. Stocks (Cambridge, 1923), 187.

[47] G. H. Dashwood, introduction to vol. i of *The Visitation of Norfolk in the Year 1563 taken by William Harvey, Clarenceux King of Arms*, 2 vols. (Norwich, 1878–95), 2.

[48] Wood's earliest antiquarian activities were devoted to discovering the facts about his own ancestry that his father had neglected to set down: Wood, *Life and Times*, i. 263.

[49] Bodl. MS Rawl. D. 859, fo. 71r–v.

[50] *The Diary of Henry Prescott, LL.B., deputy registrar of Chester Diocese*, ed. J. Addy, J. Harrop, and P. McNiven, 3 vols., Rec. Soc. of Lancashire and Cheshire, vols. 127, 132, 133 (Chester, 1987–1997), ii. 619.

[51] Bernard de Mandeville, *The Fable of the Bees*, ed. F. B. Kaye, 2 vols. (Oxford, 1924; Liberty Classics facs. repr., Indianapolis, 1988), ii. 31 (dialogue 1).

[52] W. Rockett, '*Britannia*, Ralph Brooke, and the Representation of Privilege in Elizabethan England', *Renaissance Quarterly*, 53 (2000), 475–99. See further below, Ch. 10.

heralds were accomplished antiquaries and meticulous scholars, many others were men of limited energy, indifferent ability, or spectacularly ill temper. Several had acquired a reputation for mendacity and corruption, others for sheer laziness. Sir Edward Bysshe, for example, one of Camden's successors as Clarenceux King of Arms, presided at the 1676 Oxford visitation, phlegmatically entering the arms of 'such that came to him' without question, and refusing to pursue absentees, making the whole visitation 'a trite thing'. A participant in Bysshe's visitation at Ilchester in Somerset (1672) complained that 'neither any of the ancients appeared at all in our county, for I was the best that appeared at Ilchester . . . and if I had not been a very young man, not above 18, I believe I should not have been there, and parted with my money for nothing!'[53]

Political difficulties help in part to explain the heralds' decline. The Court of Chivalry on which they depended for prosecuting cases of usurped arms was abolished in 1641 and never recovered its stature, despite its restoration in 1660; the feudal tenures on which the whole system had originally been built were also done away with for good in 1661; and several successive legislative attempts to put the heralds' authority on a statutory basis for the first time failed in 1661, 1664, and 1678. All of this left the college with little to do by way of penal enforcement.[54] But an even more fundamental cause of the diminution of the heralds' importance in controlling access to gentility may well have been the increasing recognition of the anachronistic impossibility of their task in the greatly changed social structure of the Restoration and Augustan period. Under the Tudors and into the early seventeenth century, upward mobility was limited and birth still predominated as the mark of status. By 1660 this situation had changed, particularly given the emergent prosperity of an urban middling sort unwilling to remain consigned to the ranks of the vulgar. Gentility was increasingly being defined according to economic status and its symbols, dress, demeanour, and property, rather than by heredity. By the latter part of the seventeenth century, merchants of substance could style themselves gentle, and were defended in this apparent pretension by social commentators such as Edward Waterhouse, doctor of laws, herald and future Anglican minister, who held 'that trades may be as gentilely managed, and as becoming free and noble persons in it, as other professions may'. (Of course there were also those, such as the conservative Edward Chamberlayne, who continued to pronounce all tradesmen ignoble.) Even in the Elizabethan and Jacobean period there had existed a sizeable minority of non-armigerous lesser gentry, and by the 1660s, many of those summoned to visitations elected simply

[53] Wood, *Life and Times*, ii. 152; William Harbin, quoted in *The Visitation of Somerset and the City of Bristol 1672 Made by Sir Edward Bysshe, Knight, Clarenceux King of Arms*, ed. G. D. Squibb, Publications of Harleian Soc., NS 11 (1992), pp. xiv–xv; Styles, 'The Heralds' Visitation of Warwickshire', 111.

[54] Dugdale, *Life, Diary and Correspondence*, 142; Styles, 'The Heralds' Visitation of Warwickshire', 131. The 1678 bill for registering with the college certificates of the burials of nobles and gentry might have passed had the Popish Plot not intervened and caused the dissolution of parliament; it was not revived subsequently. Internecine squabbling between particular heralds also cannot have helped their reputation, including frequent accusations of incompetence and negligence, and even theft of books and manuscripts.

to do without securing a coat of arms, preferring to base their claim to gentility on other things: 'I have no pedigree nor coate of armes nor ever had, nor do I pretend to any, nor am I ambitious to be blazond for any thing but honesty & loyalty', wrote William Pestell, rector of Coleorton, Leicestershire. 'I am a Master of Artes, & that makes me a gentleman & that a worshipfull one & I care not to go higher.' This was a far cry from Ferne's claim a century earlier that no one without a coat of arms could be considered a gentleman.[55]

A further reason for the waning of heraldic authority must also lie in the greater public awareness among the elite, precisely those who should most jealously have guarded the privilege of their lineage, of the details of family ancestry. This often meant not just their own pedigrees but that of the principal families in their vicinities: as George Owen Harry put it at the end of the sixteenth century, a gentleman should know both his own descent and, 'yea, and most of the gentlemen of th[a]t country wherein he dwelleth'.[56] The casual notes of gentry and town-dwellers with no particular training in or gift for heraldry steadily increase in volume through the seventeenth century, long after the demand for heraldic recognition that marked the Elizabethan and early Stuart period had petered out.[57] So do the more lengthy decorative parchment rolls bearing pedigrees that one finds in family collections of the period.[58] And what was written about with regularity was also talked about publicly, matters of descent, arms, and heraldry becoming frequent topics of conversation. When visiting Ruthin in 1717, Henry Prescott—the same man who would so casually dismiss the heralds a year later—was thoroughly entertained by an aged apothecary, descended from the Ashworth family of Rochdale, and the two men passed the time discussing the family names of Lancashire. 'Heraldry and good healths' provided Prescott and his bookseller, Joseph Hodgson, with diversion on another evening.[59]

[55] Edward Waterhouse, *The Gentlemans Monitor; or, a Sober Inspection into the Vertues, Vices, and Ordinary Means of the Rise and Decay of Men and Families* (1665), 205; A. Sharp, 'Edward Waterhouse's View of Social Change in Seventeenth-Century England', *Past and Present*, 62 (1974), 27–46; Borsay, *English Urban Renaissance*, 229; Styles, 'The Heralds' Visitation of Warwickshire', 145 (whence comes the quotation from Pestell); L. Stone and J. C. F. Stone, *An Open Elite? England 1540–1880* (Oxford, 1984), 286–9.

[56] George Owen Harry, 'The Wellspring of True Nobility', seventeenth-century transcript, in National Library of Wales MS. 9853E, p. 95, cited in E. White and R. Suggett, 'Language, Literacy and Aspects of Identity in Early Modern Wales', in A. Fox and D. Woolf (eds.), *The Spoken Word* (Manchester, 2002), 52–83 at p. 58. I am indebted to Richard Suggett for providing me with a lengthier extract from Owen's treatise.

[57] For instance, Cheshire RO DAR/I/37, times and dates of birth and death of members of the Crewe family of Utkinton, complete with the descent of Chief Justice Sir Ranulph Crewe (1558–1646), chief justice, and grandfather of Sir John Crewe, 1631–1711; Bodl. MS Don. c. 100, 'The Armes Genealogies & pedigrees of most of the families of the surname of Browne inhabiting in the sevearll shires of England. By mee Edmund Weaver 1640', pp. 1–58, including painted arms and an anonymous twentieth-century continuation (pp. 25–51); *Records of the Cust Family*, 64–70. A typical family pedigree is Lancashire RO DDF 408, 'The Paternall Genealogy of Richard Bradshaw Esq, then of the city of Chester since of Penington in com. Lanc. First drawne Aprill 1641. And transcribed Aprill 1698'. This is a four-foot-long paper roll giving references to deeds, and dates of marriage for some family members.

[58] Heal and Holmes, *Gentry in England and Wales*, 35; R. Cust, 'Catholicism, Antiquarianism and Gentry Honour: The Writings of Sir Thomas Shirley', *Midland History*, 23 (1998), 40–70, illustrated at p. 41.

[59] *Diary of Henry Prescott*, ii. 342, 587.

There is no contradiction between the occurrence of such sociable scenes as Prescott describes and the waning of heraldic authority. The heralds, quite simply, had lost their monopoly, if they had ever truly had it, on genealogical knowledge at the same time that the social status they were charged with limiting was acquiring a much more expansive definition. Honour and gentility, if not the higher status of peerage that remained the exclusive gift of the Crown, was now exactly what Thomas Smith had prophetically thought it was a century earlier, a matter of public recognition as much as blood inheritance. The visitations lost their power less because of a waning interest in genealogy than for two other reasons. First, they were no longer needed because such pursuits, even on a very casual level, had become much more commonplace among their former clients, who no longer routinely required the heralds' assistance, much less their authority. Secondly, the very centrality of genealogy itself to various forms of legitimation, including property claims, had been undermined by the existence of a growing body of alternative evidence generated by the courts. This in turn dealt much more effectively with the complexities of a changing land market during a period in which long-standing past connection to a specific property mattered less than its preservation or accumulation in the future—and the ability to demonstrate clear title, however recently and by whatever means that title might have been acquired. The advent of such devices as the strict settlement among most segments of the gentry, the greater attention to provision of estates for younger children, and the expanded role of the central courts in settling property disputes were all features of the land market in the century after the Restoration. They in turn gave rise to a vast assortment of documents that were much more powerful at law than a genealogy, however long and well supported by ancient family muniments.[60] Looked at from a different perspective, the conveyancer and the attorney were likely to be of more value than the herald in the age of entails, contingent remainders, and life interests. And the prudent landowner who had once bolstered his own sense of position through Ferne or even Camden was now obliged to confine such pursuits to leisure hours and attend routinely to the subtleties of property transactions.

The pedigree 'craze', if it can be so called, was certainly over by the Restoration. Yet genealogical interest did not subside. Indeed, what is striking is that, though facts of pedigree became rather less important in the legitimization of claims to gentility (and thus also less dependent on the independent arbitration of the heralds), genealogical knowledge more generally had increased in value as a species of cultural currency. Among nobility and gentry, as well as among the moderately prosperous and the ambitious rural and urban worthies such as Cheshire's Henry Prescott, acquiring a smattering of familiarity with personal and local family history was fast becoming desirable in its own right. Genealogical knowledge could serve those who possessed it as a conversational tool, a mark of

[60] A. W. B. Simpson, *A History of the Land Law*, 2nd edn. (Oxford, 1986), 237–41; L. Bonfield, *Marriage Settlements, 1601–40: The Adoption of the Strict Settlement* (Cambridge, 1983); S. Staves, *Married Women's Separate Property in England, 1660–1833* (Cambridge, Mass., 1990), 56–76.

connection to a local community, or simply a sign of educated status, even if their command of that knowledge was often erratic, undisciplined, or shallow.

In the late sixteenth century, genealogical knowledge among the gentry and prosperous middling sort had begun to improve, and within a hundred years it had reached a respectable mark among a specific subset, those whose familiarity with their own muniments was matched by a broader interest in English history. This did not mean that it was plain sailing for local antiquaries aspiring to write up to date county histories, for the level of interest and knowledge in any given shire was quite uneven. So was the evidence itself. Bishop Nicolson added a section 'Of Conveyances, Deeds, and other Evidences in the Hands of Private Subjects' to revised editions of his *English Historical Library*, lamenting both the destruction of private and public records in the civil war (and the loss of muniments through sequestration and forfeiture). He also noted the inconsistency with which such records had been maintained up to his own time:

Had pedigrees been carefully preserv'd in all the great families of England, I can hardly think of any better old stores of history than they might probably have afforded us, since the most notable circumstances of the life of any eminent person in the progeny, are usually recorded there with accuracy and niceness; but many of this kind we shall not meet with.[61]

The substantial archive left by the Essex antiquary William Holman provides a remarkable record of both the degree of interest and of the still somewhat shallow limits of genealogical knowledge in the first quarter of the eighteenth century. When Holman, a nonconformist who was planning a history of Essex,[62] investigated the family origins of the county's gentry, he often encountered the very ignorance and indifference that had greeted the heralds of half a century earlier. Holman had been warned. Browne Willis, a fellow antiquary, had decided to investigate Buckinghamshire families and their pedigrees, together with that shire's antiquities, in 1712. He had commenced in a systematic fashion, by sending out printed questionnaires and asking for responses—an early example of the use of a survey to collect data for historical purposes.[63] Holman asked for a copy of the form, which Willis provided, but it came attached with the disappointing

[61] William Nicolson, *The English Historical Library* (1696); cf. id., *The English, Scotch and Irish Historical Libraries* (1736), 240–7, quotation at p. 245.

[62] Holman intended to complete the labours of an earlier Essex antiquary Thomas Jekyll of Bocking: C. F. D. Sperling, 'Thomas Jekyll', *Essex Review*, 3 (1894), 254–61; Jekyll's history of Essex from Julius Caesar to James I was lost some time in the mid-eighteenth century; on Holman himself, see C. F. D. Sperling, 'William Holman', *Essex Review*, 3 (1894), 261–6. Holman, who appears periodically in the present book because of the unusually wide range of local correspondence which he left (now principally in the Essex RO), came to Halstead in 1700. His own history of Essex was never completed nor published by him, though portions exist in the Essex RO and the Bodl., e.g. Bodl. MS Rawl. Essex 8 ('The Historie of Panfield'), fos. 182ʳ–197ᵛ. See, however, below, n. 135.

[63] A questionnaire was issued in 1673 asking for information to be used in a new edition of Camden's *Britannia*: Anthony Powell, *John Aubrey and his Friends* (1948), 152.

message that 'what you have here of my Buckingham queries is what was dispersed all over the county, but I had about 27 answers in all & there being but few of them printed I am forced to send you one that was wrote upon which I pray you to excuse'. So, he told his Essex colleague, 'all I can say in the matter is that if you think any part of it for your purpose you may extract it and print such like queries, but by my fate you must [not] depend on much'.[64]

Holman was undeterred, and though he appears not to have used the printed form, opting instead for personal letters, in the end he fared much better than Willis. He received many more responses than the Buckinghamshire antiquary—then as now an individually addressed request is less easily committed to the wastebasket than a form letter. A more troublesome problem was that the people to whom he wrote sometimes did not know very much about their family background—one recalls Thomas Westcote's above-cited experience, a century earlier, with the man who wanted his family included in a history of Devon but could provide no information on them. William Coggeshall referred Holman to his uncle, Thomas Coggeshall, for some patents in 'old English' that he thought might contain the family arms. Thomas was 'an antient man above eighty years old', wrote his nephew, 'and perhaps may give some account of my grandfather; tho' I fear but little for he died before he was fifty'. On the other hand, William Coggeshall, though ignorant, was at least prepared to help Holman with his enquiries, acting as intermediary between the antiquary and a cousin, John Coggeshall, who was 'skilld in heraldry'; William Coggeshall even offered to subscribe to Holman's projected work.[65] Anthony Collins of Baddon Hall was similarly agreeable and offered to assist Holman 'either by my library, or the writings of my estate in this county . . . or by conversation with you, or by directing you to others from whence you may receive information'. This was better help than Holman would get from a gentleman whose only response was 'I have nothing of antiquity here. I can only tell you I am descended from a Lincolnshire family, and but of late in Essex'. Though he knew his own and his mother's family's arms, he had no 'antique writings' to prove them, these having been 'dispers'd I know not where' during the civil wars.[66] Dr Samuel Dale, Holman's associate (and also his most severe critic), reported a similar lack of cooperation from one Mr Man. Dale showed Man a pedigree of his family, but found that 'he knew little of his one Ancestors, wherefore I had recourse to our parish registers'. On abstracting materials from the parish records, Dale returned to Man but found him no more enthusiastic, claiming to have a seal of his father's but unwilling to hunt it out. A third visit produced nothing but a frustratingly vague promise to Dale that Man, who had 'no time' for such pursuits, would make some kind of a search in his evidences

---

[64] Buckinghamshire RO D/X.579 (Willis papers), questionnaire (1712) attached to letter to William Holman of 13 Feb. 1719/20.

[65] Essex RO D/Y/1/1/56–57 (Coggeshall to Holman, 2 Jan. 1711/12 and 16 Jan. 1711/12); D/Y/1/1/58 is a copy of John Coggeshall's letter to his cousin, including a pedigree.

[66] Essex RO D/Y/1/1/59 (Collins to Holman, 30 July 1719); D/Y/1/1/53 (M. Carter to Holman, 19 July 1715).

at the next long vacation, 'which I beleive will be long indeed!' exclaimed Dale, 'for I do not expect to get any help from him'.[67]

Mr Man's indifference put him in the minority among Holman's and Dale's correspondents and associates. The general picture that emerges from Holman's archive is of a male gentry sympathetic and even mildly interested, with limited knowledge to share, but willing at least to refer the antiquary to more knowledgeable family members. Perhaps most remarkable, however, is the success which Holman had in enquiries that he directed to women. At several points in his correspondence Holman was steered by local gentry, and even fellow antiquaries, towards wives, aunts, and sisters for reliable genealogical information. In 1723 Elizabeth Cressener searched on Holman's behalf 'over all our writings & cannot find that which you mention, & I beleve we have it not amongst what papers we have hear'. She nevertheless located and sent Holman her brother's and husband's wills, which she had read and understood—down to the details of how various parts of family property had been acquired and by whom.[68] Another female correspondent, Elizabeth Bassett Goffen or Coffyn, wrote with information on her own family and that of the Audleys, which she obtained on his behalf by asking her godmother. 'As to Madam Audeley she has not her pedigree; but what I could learn from her of it I will as well as I can acquaint you with. Her great grandfather was Chancellor Audley's god-son and his near relation, but she cannot tell whether he was his nephew or second cousin.' Her own husband's father had settled in the county from Hampshire at or about the start of Charles I's reign, but he had died soon after; this was, she added, the reason why she lacked a more 'exacte knowledg of the family'. Elizabeth was nevertheless able to describe in detail and with some technical knowledge the family coat of arms, and she had attempted to augment her own erudition by examining funeral monuments. For further information she referred Holman to her spinster daughter, who lived elsewhere.[69]

Some of Holman's more frequent male correspondents deferred to their wives, as William Ashby did when answering Holman's queries about the manor of Wennington; his wife, apparently, could provide details going back half a century on the conveyancing of the manor from the Aleyn family of Little Waltham. And for information on *them*, wrote a straight-faced Ashby, 'I will recommend you to the honourable Lady Howard, who was an Aleyn and married my Lord George Howard, the present Duke of Norfolkes uncle', who still had the pedigree.[70] Holman's experience with female informants was not unique, and there are good grounds for inferring, with due caution against over-generalization, a more acute sensitivity to genealogical detail on the part of females than males. Anne Clifford's diaries, for instance, are especially full of information. Clearly the result of

---

[67] Essex RO D/Y/1/1/97 (Dale to Holman, 11 Apr. 1712).
[68] Essex RO D/Y/1/1/95 (Cressener to Holman, n.d. 1723).
[69] Essex RO D/Y/1/1/55 (Goffen to Holman, 11 Sept. 1720); P. Morant, *The History and Antiquities of the County of Essex*, 2 vols. (London, 1768), ii. 449.
[70] Essex RO D/Y/1/1/12 (Ashby to Holman, 8 Aug. 1720). For a similar example, regarding the Somers family of Witham, see D/Y/1/1/100 (Samuel Dale to Holman, 16 May 1714).

much reading in 'old records and chronicles' concerning her forebears on the male and female sides, her knowledge, and her devotion to preserving the memory and reputation of her progenitors, were highlighted in Bishop Edward Rainbowe's sermon at her funeral in 1676.[71]

For many women, genealogical pursuits were less a matter of amassing super-fluous erudition than of constructing a personal historical domain by applying imagination and feeling to documentary and material evidence. The discovery of both the correspondence and the Elizabethan clothing of one of her female ancestors, for instance, encouraged Cassandra Willoughby to embark on a fam-ily history in which she also consulted William Dugdale's *Antiquities of Warwick-shire*, Robert Thoroton's *Antiquities of Nottinghamshire*, and Richard Baker's *Chronicle*.[72] Genealogical pursuits also provided a means for women to counter-act the anomaly in the English legal system that acknowledged them as kin for purposes of inheritance, but overlooked them in the written record of descents, which stressed the male line. Consequently, women were not infrequently the prin-cipal source of basic information about land, estates, and buildings whose histor-ies had been complicated through marriage and alienation. When the Jacobean knight Sir Edward Rodney wrote a family history for his daughters, he owed to his own mother information about the family's origins in the time of King Stephen, which she recalled from a brass plaque no longer extant by the time her son wrote. Elizabeth Pepys, who at other times accompanied her husband on visits to historic sites, took refuge from Samuel's philandering in the pursuit of her family's history and arms. The Pepyses often discussed genealogical matters, and in 1667 Samuel bought his wife a copy of Guillim's *A Display of Heraldry*, a Jacobean heraldic manual that had been reprinted in 1664.[73]

The strong interest of women in genealogy did not escape notice, especially when public display of such knowledge transgressed the rules of humility and mod-esty laid out in such books as Richard Allestree's *The Ladies Calling*.[74] Like Theobald's imagined female antiquary, those who turned erudition into conversa-tion were given short shrift by many male observers. One of Joseph Addison's mock correspondents, Sir John Enville, complains of his wife, who uses her own family's pedigree to subjugate him.

---

[71] *Diaries of Lady Anne Clifford*, e.g. pp. 154, 224; Edward Rainbowe, *A Sermon preached at the funeral of the Right Honourable Anne Countess of Pembroke, Dorset and Montgomery* (1677), comments throughout on her ability to discourse with scholars and virtuosi, her great personal knowledge, and especially her enquiry into 'the lives, fortunes, and characters of many of her ancestors for many years' (p. 38).

[72] Cassandra Willoughby, 'An Account of the Willughby's of Wollaton, taken out of the Pedigree, old Letters, and old Books of Accounts, in my Brother Sir Thomas Willoughby's study, Dec., A.D. 1702', calendared in Hist. MSS Comm., *Report on the Manuscripts of Lord Middleton* (1911), 504–609.

[73] Pepys, *Diary*, ii. 93 (2 May 1661); viii. 422 (6 Sept. 1667).

[74] Richard Allestree, *The Ladies Calling*, 2 pts. in 1 vol. (1673); M. McKeon, 'Historicizing Patriarchy: The Emergence of Gender Difference in England, 1660–1760', *Eighteenth-Century Studies*, 28 (1995), 295–322; F. A. Childs, 'Prescriptions for Manners in English Courtesy Literature, 1690–1760, and their Social Implications', D.Phil. diss., University of Oxford, 1984.

Our children have been trained up from their infancy with so many accounts of their moth-er's family, that they know the stories of all the great men and women it has produced. Their mother tells them, that such an one commanded in such a sea engagement, that their great grandfather had a horse shot under him at Edgehill, that their unkle was at the siege of Buda, and that her mother danced in a ball at court with the duke of Monmouth.

Enville is most vexed by the fact that his daughter has asked why he never tells tales about the generals and admirals in *his* family. Elsewhere, in a description of a ladies' meeting, Addison describes 'one of those female historians that upon all occasions enters into pedigrees and descents, and finds herself related, by some offshoot or other, to almost every great family in England: for which reason she jars and is out of tune very often in conversation, for the company's want of due attention and respect for her'.[75]

As William Holman would discover, the information to be provided by men was, in comparison, sometimes sketchy and incomplete. 'As to my family, unless I was to go into Hertfordshire I cannot give you the genealogy' admitted James Gray in 1716. 'What I have heard my father often speak, being young and since imploy'd my thoughts on other subjects, I have not so regarded as to give the History.'[76] Yet Gray's letter, and many others sent to Holman, betray ignorance of detail rather than lack of interest. They have the apologetic tone of men who realize they should know better. That many other families had a keener sense of both their familial history and the historical reputations of its individual mem-bers is demonstrated by antiquarian worries about causing offence through either omission or error, or simply through publishing unpleasant facts about the past. Writing in the obscurity of the rural parish of Myddle about 1700, Richard Gough expressed the concern that no man would 'blame mee for that I have declared the viciouse lives or actions of their ancestors'.[77] Camden, the very success of whose *Britannia* exposed him to criticism for statements made about the ancestors of some notables, was perhaps the first to run into this problem. The Leicestershire antiquary William Burton ducked it altogether by confining himself to the invest-igation of 'the old and ancient, whose families are now extinct'.[78] As time wore on, chorographical and genealogical writers would go out of their way to seek gentry and aristocratic input into their volumes so as to ensure accuracy and avoid

---

[75] *The Spectator*, 299 (12 Feb. 1712), ed. D. F. Bond, 5 vols. (Oxford, 1965), iii. 70–1; *The Tatler*, 157 (11 Apr. 1710), ed. D. F. Bond, 3 vols. (Oxford, 1987), ii. 381.

[76] Essex RO D/Y/1/1/acc.3921 (unsorted alphabetical correspondence, series G, Gray to Holman, 28 Nov. 1716). The interest of these women in genealogical information and other matters related to women's distinctive relationship to history are discussed at greater length in D. R. Woolf, 'A Feminine Past? Gender, Genre, and Historical Knowledge in England, 1500–1800', *American Historical Review*, 102/3 (June 1997), 645–79.

[77] Richard Gough, *The History of Myddle*, ed. D. Hey (Harmondsworth, 1981), 78. Gough, how-ever, was unsure whether his namesake, the churchwarden who had copied out the parish register a century earlier, had been his great-grandfather or his father's great-grandfather, 'for they had both the same christian name of Richard, as likewise all that were chief of our family have had for many generations': ibid. 37.

[78] William Burton, *The description of Leicestershire* (1622), 'To the Reader'; Broadway, *William Dugdale and the Significance of County History*, 13–14.

giving offence. Elliston Barrington, counsellor to the earl of Cleveland, wrote in 1715 to warn Holman that the pedigree he had done of the earl's family, the Wentworths, had omitted a small detail, the year in which Sir Roger Wentworth had died ('I thinke it was in Henry the Eighths time'), which the earl wished to have included when Holman published his history.[79] When the Essex antiquary Edward Alexander drew up, at Holman's request, pedigrees of the families in his neighbourhood of Ongar, he took care to send them back to some local gentlemen 'to be corrected by them and to make further additions', though their slow response delayed his completion of the task.[80] In 1673 Robert Thoroton, an antiquary in his own right, would urge the young Theophilus Hastings, seventh earl of Huntingdon, to box up all evidences or 'anything that may concern any marriages or other historical matter' of his family and send them to William Dugdale's home at Blith Hill in Warwickshire. Dugdale himself was the originator of the request, since he badly wanted materials to work into a text that was due at the printers in less than three weeks.[81]

The seventeenth century gradually saw limits imposed on the reasonableness of claims to extreme family antiquity, as an increasing number of provincial antiquaries unofficially did the heralds' work for them, collecting large quantities of family muniments. As local men, they had a significant advantage over heralds visiting for a short period from outside, since they had the trust of local gentry and greater familiarity with parochial history. Lack of knowledge of heraldic conventions did not stop those interested in noble descents from drawing up their own lists of the peerage without the illustrative coats of arms that are found in other private antiquarian collections.[82] The manuscript collections of antiquaries, from Francis Thynne in the late sixteenth century to Ralph Thoresby in the early

[79] Essex RO D/Y/1/1/21 (Barrington to Holman, 17 June 1715).

[80] Essex RO D/Y/1/1, loose documents (Alexander to Holman, 24 May 1722). The dispersal of family papers through cadet lines was a further impediment to, and constraint on, the construction of pedigrees. James Whitelocke, recounting his own family's history, had to refer to documents held by his cousin William: *Liber Famelicus of Sir James Whitelocke, a Judge of the Court of King's Bench, in the Reigns of James I and Charles I*, ed. J. Bruce, Camden Soc., os 70 (1858), 1–2; an undated set of genealogical notes on the Littleton family (Staffs. RO D/1178/4) indicates that its unknown author made use of the wills of his kin, having otherwise been unable to push his own pedigree back beyond 1620. The tracking of documents through dispersed kin has some parallels in the great families of Renaissance Italy: W. J. Connell, '*Libri di Famiglia* and the Family History of Florentine Patricians', in D. Radcliff-Umstead (ed.), *Italian Culture: Selected Proceedings*, 8 (1990), 279–92.

[81] Hist. MSS Comm., *Report on the Manuscripts of the Late Reginald Rawdon Hastings, Esq.*, 4 vols. (1928–47), ii. 164 (Thoroton to Huntingdon, 24 July 1673). The use of private documents by antiquaries dates back to the early Elizabethan and Jacobean efforts in this field, e.g. the various genealogical papers owned by Sir Simonds D'Ewes, including notes on Cheshire collected by Ralph Starkey: BL MS Harl. 139, fos. 13ᵛ, 60ʳ (n.d.). Walter Chetwynd made similar use of private evidences in constructing his 'Short Survey of Staffordshire' (in fact only Pirehill Hundred), unpublished till the twentieth century: Staffs. RO D.649/3, e.g. p. 69.

[82] Bodl. MS Eng. hist. e. 222, pp. 1–128, for example (written c.1580 but with early seventeenth-century additions) is a guide (with an index, at p. 123) to medieval earldoms, including creations and descents, but without coats of arms. Another contemporary example describes the most famous men in England and records their descent and honours back to Edgar Aetheling, the eleventh-century Saxon prince; this, too, is almost entirely heraldic in focus and again lacks the crucial sketches of arms used by heralds and antiquaries: Bodl. MS Tanner 183, fos. 1–79ᵛ.

eighteenth, are filled with transcriptions of royal, noble, and gentry family muniments and sketches of arms contained in private papers or inscribed on church monuments.[83] These vary widely in accuracy and erudition even within roughly the same place and time. The Suffolk collections of Henry Chitting, a member of Gray's Inn who purchased the post of Chester herald in 1618, consist largely of abbreviated transcriptions that are less reliable than those of his near contemporaries in the county, Robert Ryece or Reyce, and the writer usually known as the Anonymous Chorographer.[84]

The heralds had a good deal of competition by Chitting's time from enthusiastic local amateurs, the number of whom swelled over the course of the seventeenth century. Several major evidentiary collections of the eighteenth century were contributed by rural clerics of various persuasions, such as the nonconformist Holman. Churchmen in fact began their long commitment to local antiquities in this period, in what amounts to a substantial re-clericalization of historical writing, after a century of domination by gentry writers; this is especially noticeable in the areas of antiquarianism, local genealogy (for which Anglican ministers' role as custodians of parish registers placed them ideally), and Church history. It would of course be a gross error to assume that every parish curate shared the enthusiasm or determination of William Holman or his Yorkshire contemporary, Abraham de la Pryme. Many lacked either the time or the inclination to engage in genealogical investigation, especially if they were not native to a parish. They would have sympathized with the bored response of George Hellier of North Weald, who was reluctant to carry out a search of his parish register on Holman's behalf since, 'Being only curate of this parish, and having no real estate in it, I have had but little curiosity, and lesse opportunity.'[85]

All this being said, however, the number of collections that survive in local record offices, to say nothing of the British Library, and which formed the basis for later, nineteenth-century biographical and genealogical activities, speaks to an enormous growth in interest in the familial past since the mid-sixteenth century. This interest should be viewed as complementary to, rather than competitive with, the parallel, officially sanctioned activities of the College of Arms, since the heralds often incorporated the findings of local antiquaries into their own collections. And once

---

[83] See e.g. Roger Twysden's collections on his own and the Finch families in BL MS Add. 34,177, fo. 16; Francis Thynne's 'The hystorye, lyves, descents' of the family of Cobham, BL MS Add. 37,666, fos. 1–60 (dated 20 Dec. 1598); and the parliamentarian 'A.N.', 'A breife discourse of the pedigree of the bloud roiall from H.7 to our soveraign king Charles with their armes & effigies matches & issues, & titles of honour', Bodl. MS Eng. hist. e. 211 (dated 1641 but continued into the 1650s, and extracted, according to the author's statement at fo. iii^r, from a larger manuscript). This last includes engravings and woodcuts, taken from printed books, of contemporary worthies such as Pym, Waller, and General Lesley.

[84] D. MacCulloch, 'Henry Chitting's Suffolk Collections', *Proceedings of the Suffolk Institute of Archaeology and History*, 34, pt. 2 (1978), 103–28.

[85] Essex RO D/Y/1/1/1 (unfoliated alphabetical correspondence, vol. Hales-Husbands, Hellier to Holman, 27 Oct. 1723). On the other hand, even with this reluctance Hellier still found time to write Holman a three-page letter.

a pedigree had passed under a herald's hand, it became no longer a local or familial document, but a matter of record, to be placed into one of the college's many thick manuscript Office Books or series of rolls (many of which have since been published by the Harleian Society). These in turn would be consulted by later generations of local antiquaries, continuing the flow of genealogical information from periphery to centre and back again. To give one example, Sir Henry St George, Norroy King at Arms in the 1630s, put all of his pedigrees into a 'greate thicke booke', the contents of which were, however, largely the work of his subordinate, the Lancaster herald Nicholas Charles or Carles. In the 1640s and later, the same Black Book would in turn be mined by the likes of Roger Dodsworth, who transferred its contents into his own collections, errors and all. Conversely, one must consider the 'upward mobility' of the writings of locals like the Yorkshire antiquary Richard Gascoigne (1579–c.1661), who admitted at the start of his ambitious catalogue of baronets, knights, and gentry that 'I professe not heraldrie'. Gascoigne's book, extracted in part from a book belonging to Nicholas Charles, made its way via the collections of Augustine Vincent, Windsor herald, back into the College of Arms.[86]

The point of this is not to minimize the contribution of the heralds, who had a formal base of knowledge lacked by many local antiquaries, and who remained, despite the decline of the visitations, theoretically at the summit of genealogical activity. Nor is it to exaggerate the knowledge and individual contributions of their provincial counterparts. Rather, it is to emphasize that heraldic and genealogical materials, like other forms of the past in early modern England, were socially circulating commodities, continuously in a process of revision, not a set of static historical 'facts' intended to advance the development of scholarship. What mattered in the enhancement of genealogical knowledge was not the individual fact or document, even when enshrined by the heralds in their collections or printed in antiquarian and chorographical treatises, but rather the availability of multiple sources of information and their free transmission from one interested individual to another. This in turn is what encouraged eighteenth- and nineteenth-century researchers, all the way up to the Harleian Society, the *Victoria County Histories* and the *Dictionary of National Biography* to make use of their predecessors' collections while at the same time checking details against original documents where these survived. The cautious Samuel Dale would recognize the dialogic nature of genealogical knowledge in urging his friend Holman to balance his fervour for familial sources of information with attention to other types of document. Dale advised Holman not to 'have genealogies published as you find them', which would be simply to 'continue the errors of others' but to check them against an external source such as parish registers 'and other evidences'.[87]

---

[86] Bodl. MS Dodsw. 97, fos. 122–9, extracts by Dodsworth from St George's Black Book and from another 'booke in the Herald's office'; Coll. Arms MS Vincent 406, and other materials in vols. 400–15 inclusive, of which vol. 414 is extracted from Charles's book.

[87] Essex RO D/Y/1/1/103 (Dale to Holman, 24 Nov. 1712).

IMAGINING THE GENEALOGICAL PAST

Unfettered by the controls of heraldic authority or peer scepticism, the genealogical imagination could run comparatively freely, but less and less often did it reach back exuberantly to the dawn of time. The overwhelming majority of pedigrees found in family collections of the seventeenth century in fact stick to the evidence, reaching back only to Anglo-Norman times, and many go no further back than the sixteenth century.[88] The year 1066 would increasingly mark a distant mental horizon beyond which lay a murky but penetrable historical space. One should overstate neither the linearity nor the universality of this development. There are medieval and Tudor examples of family historians placing boundaries on their ancestral pasts. Fulk of Anjou, about 1100, admitted in his own family history that he could go only so far back, before which 'I know nothing, for I do not know where my ancestors are buried'.[89] Sampson Erdeswicke, the Staffordshire antiquary who died in 1603, looked no further back than Domesday Book in the genealogical inscription of his family's history affixed to his monument in Sandon church.[90] Conversely, many cases can be adduced from both medieval and later times of creative genealogy,[91] and it has been correctly suggested that the advent of supposedly critical antiquarian skills could serve as a scholarly buttress to fictitious claims to lengthy ancestry as much as a control. The Kentish antiquary Sir Edward Dering was dissatisfied with his grandfather's pedigree going back to the fourteenth century; he used his abilities as an Anglo-Saxonist to perch in his family tree a mythical thane, supposedly killed at Hastings.[92]

By the mid-seventeenth century, however, a family descent back to the Conquest was sufficiently prestigious to amount to the equivalent of the modern

[88] For instance, Coll. Arms MS 28/22 (Arundel Castle deposits), draft pedigree of the Blundell family back to the time of Richard II, written in the seventeenth century and continued up to 1711; Coll. Arms MS 9/26, pedigree of Plot family from 1343 to 1673; for a much shorter reach, see the genealogical notes in the commonplace book of Sir William Cowper (d. 1664, ancestor of the Georgian Lord Chancellor Earl Cowper), going back only to the descendants of William (d. 1558) and Margaret Cowper: Herts. RO D/EP.F.25 (Panshanger MSS), and continued by his own son and grandson. I base my assessment of the relatively short descents claimed in most genealogies on samplings of family collections in several record offices and local repositories, and the British Library. This is not a systematic search, but it does suggest that flagrantly mythistorical pedigrees were by 1700 increasingly the exception rather than the rule, and that the remote reaches of such pedigrees were intended to be taken rhetorically, not literally.
[89] R. Fossier, 'The Feudal Era (Eleventh–Thirteenth Century)', in A. Burguière *et al.* (eds.), *A History of the Family*, trans. S. H. Tenison, 2 vols. (Cambridge, Mass., 1996), i. 407–29, at p. 422.
[90] *DNB*, *sub* 'Erdeswicke, Sampson'.
[91] The practice of forged arms and genealogies goes back to the Middle Ages as demonstrated by both J. H. Round and more recently V. H. Galbraith and Anthony Wagner. It was used then principally for the purpose of securing title to land rather than honours, and it is therefore completely erroneous to attribute it exclusively to the Tudor 'craze', which may, however, have increased its occurrence: Wagner, *English Genealogy*, 363; V. H. Galbraith, *Studies in the Public Records* (1948), 49; Round, *Peerage and Pedigree*, ii. 262 (on the relation of early genealogy to medieval romance).
[92] Maclagan, 'Genealogy and Heraldry in the Sixteenth and Seventeenth Centuries', 31–48; Heal and Holmes, *Gentry in England and Wales*, 36–7. Anthony Grafton has offered a more general study of the scholarly talents of notorious forgers during the two centuries after the Renaissance: *Forgers and Critics: Creativity and Duplicity in Western Scholarship* (Princeton, 1990).

American 'my family came over on the *Mayflower*'. Like this, it was a broad assertion that needed little proof but did not push the envelope of credibility. In particular, it avoided the by now derisory claim of an ancient British descent going back to Arthur or Brutus the Trojan.[93] The Conquest turns up frequently throughout the period as the *terminus a quo* of family descent, though pushing lineage claims back to 1066 provided no guarantee of veracity in the pedigree thereby produced.[94] In the dedication to his *Life and Death of Sir Thomas More*, Nicholas Harpsfield praised his fellow biographer William Roper for his 'woorthye pedegree' which included 'one of the chiefest and auncient families in Kent, and one of the three chiefe gentlemen that compelled William Conquerour to agree and to confirme the auncient customes of Kent'.[95] Even in the mid-sixteenth century, John Lambert of Kirkby Malhamdale, Tudor ancestor of the Cromwellian major-general, found a descent from the Conqueror's man Radulph de Lambert adequate to his purposes, though he was obliged to rely on forged charters (which as a lawyer he may or may not have concocted himself) for its proof. His family subsequently registered this pedigree during the visitation of Yorkshire in 1612.[96] In a narrative pedigree appended to her *Life* of her husband, Margaret, duchess of Newcastle made the passing claim that the duke could 'reckon up a great many of his ancestors, even from the time of William the Conqueror'; in the end she regarded this as 'a work fitter for heralds' and pursued this genealogy no further back than the duke's grandparents.[97] In the early eighteenth century William Ashby would tell the Essex antiquary Holman that 'we have lived in the parish ever since the Norman Conquest' and that his house was 'purchased of Nicholas Breakspears who was after Pope Adrian'. Another of Holman's informants, Thomas Bridge, passed on to the antiquary a set of verses that had been in the family for years:

> From Normandy we in the Conquest came
> Five years before One thousand seventy-one
> For William the Great we gain'd immortall fame
> And help'd to seat him on the Brittish throne.
> What greater honour from Loud fame can spring?
> We made our Normand Duke a Brittish king.[98]

---

[93] The boundaries between 'incredible' and 'credible' genealogy are well explored (especially for Italy) in R. Bizzochi, *Genealogie incredibili: Scritti di storia nell' Europa moderna* (Bologna, 1995), esp. pp. 189–219; pp. 71–4 deal with England but in much less detail.

[94] J. H. Round, 'Tales of the Conquest', in his *Peerage and Pedigree*, i. 284–323.

[95] N. Harpsfield, *The Life and Death of Sir Thomas More*, ed. E. V. Hitchcock, EETS, os 186 (1932), 5.

[96] J. W. Morkill, *The Parish of Kirkby Malhamdale in the West Riding of Yorkshire* (Gloucester, 1933), 147–9; I am indebted for this latter reference to R. W. Hoyle.

[97] Margaret Cavendish, duchess of Newcastle, *The Life of William Cavendish, duke of Newcastle*, ed. C. H. Firth, 2nd edn. (London and New York, 1906), 113–19.

[98] Essex RO D/Y/1/1/12 (Ashby to Holman, 8 Aug. 1720); D/Y/1/1/46 (Bridge to Holman, n.d. 1715). Cf. Cheshire RO DAR/I/5, 'A trew and perfecte Rowle of all the Nobillitie of England as well of those that are Linially descended from the Antiant Nobillity sens the tyme of William the Conquerer . . .', a small book of arms and names of peers and their creations apparently written in 1628.

Sir John Oglander similarly pushed his own family's establishment in the Isle of Wight no further back than the Normans, and took pride in the continuation of the family name from that day to his own, though confessing that most of its representatives had been 'of better esteem the first hundred years immediately after the Conquest than they have been since'. It was not so much the absolute antiquity of the family that occasioned his pride, but the close and continuous hereditary link between the family and its geographical place.[99]

The Conquest, and the massive land distribution summarized soon after in Domesday Book, increasingly delineated the boundaries of verifiable genealogical memory in the way that the year 1189 had long been the limit of 'legal memory'. 1066 marked a kind of safe zone of travel for the genealogical imagination. Beyond it, in the Anglo-Saxon era, lay a past that was still quite clearly traversable, in the sense that historical documents for it survived, but to which it was much more difficult to establish a connection.[100] The past of Roman Britain, for which evidence was principally archaeological and textual, entailed a trip to the provinces of memory, and that to the pre-Roman past of Samothes, Albion, and Brutus a much more intellectually risky journey to what increasingly seemed a different country altogether, a foreign realm of myth and legend where one might go on occasion for an outing, but not tarry long. Historians such as Samuel Daniel, whose *Collection of the Historie of England* (1618) was the single most highly regarded survey of the medieval past through much of the seventeenth century, refused to discuss the pre-Conquest period at any length, and Daniel was reflecting a caution that was already taking hold in antiquarian and genealogical circles.[101] The number of completely invented pedigrees reaching back to Adam produced during the Elizabethan and early Stuart periods has in any case been considerably exaggerated, and their significance distorted by the frequent repetition of a few notorious examples. Even these have been entirely misunderstood as a battle between modern scepticism and a recalcitrant medieval credulity. As early as 1600, when the 'craze' was not yet over, many writers interested in the descent of their own and other families felt satisfied beginning their accounts and lists of arms with 1066. A family genealogical history, completed to commemorate the elevation in 1620 of Oliver St John of Lydiard Tregoze, Wiltshire, to the Irish peerage as Viscount Grandison of Limerick, indicates his connections to an extinct ancient family whose name he had revived in the viscountcy. Verses added on the last page, in a

---

[99] Sir John Oglander, cited in Heal and Holmes, *Gentry in England and Wales*, 20, 22. For the significance of 1066 in the lineages on funeral monuments, see Llewellyn, *Funeral Monuments in Post-Reformation England*, 302.

[100] For examples of genealogies pushed back to the Saxons, see Broadway, *William Dugdale and the Significance of County History*, 9. Dr Broadway plausibly suggests that the known existence of shires prior to the Conquest (unlike manors, most of which could not be traced back beyond Domesday Book) encouraged some families to push their inheritance further back than 1066 to establish their seniority.

[101] Samuel Daniel, *The collection of the historie of England* (1618), 1; compare an even earlier anonymous manuscript, 'The creacion of all the nobilitie from the tyme of William the Conqueror to the yeare of grace 1592', Bodl. MS Ashm. 763, fos. 113^r–139^r.

considerably later hand (though perhaps copied from an early seventeenth-
century document), push the family's history back to just before the Conquest:

> When Conquering William won by force of sword;
> Of Lydiard then was Ewyas only Lord;
> This famous Island now call'd Brittons land;
> Whose heir, to Tregoz linck't in marriage band . . .[102]

Attempts to project descents back into the Anglo-Saxon era, or further still into
the reaches of British antiquity, were less and less defensible as both historical
knowledge—and the awareness of its limits—increased towards the end of the
sixteenth century. Lord Burghley, who regularly doodled genealogies of foreign
royal houses, also financed research to prove that he was descended from Welsh
princes and a friend of King Harold. But his son Robert Cecil, who saw the political value of the foreign genealogy, shunned the vanity of his own pedigree,
having little time for 'these vain toys, nor to hear of such absurdities'.[103] Many
nonetheless continued to press such claims, either citing tampered documents or
simply asserting tradition. The Barringtons of Essex boasted of their pre-
Conquest ancestry, leading Sir Francis Barrington's friend, Lord Rich, to mutter
sarcastically that they were 'knightes before Englishe was in England'. Joan
Thynne, a widowed Wiltshire gentlewoman, was proud to announce in 1607 the
betrothal of her daughter to one Mr Whitney, 'a gentleman of a very ancient
and worshipful house', adding in a postscript that Whitney's great-grandfather
had been married to the daughter of Lord Audley, and that 'I credibly understand, that all the lands whereof Mr Whitney is now seised . . . was Whitney's lands
before the conquest of England'. Though the suitor was 'but an esquire, yet
there were eighteen knights of his name before the Conquest which were lords

---

[102] SAL MS 405, 99 folios. According to a modern note on this manuscript, the east window
at Battersea church commemorates the same event. This is a colourful MS, complete with colour
pictures of arms and of knights. The genealogy proper, however, starts with the reign of Edward VI,
perhaps signifying a cautious distinction between a documentable recent history and a grander, but
largely traditional and speculative, past. For another, less historically circumspect, St John effort at
commemoration through funereal monument, the wooden triptych at Lydiard Tregoze, see N.
Llewellyn, 'Claims to Status through Visual Codes: Heraldry in Post-Reformation Funeral Monuments', in S. Anglo (ed.), *Chivalry in the Renaissance* (London, 1990), 145–60; and Llewellyn, *Funeral
Monuments in Post-Reformation England*, 300–1.

[103] PRO SP 9/206, art. 1 (notes by both Cecils on Spanish, Portuguese, and Swedish genealogies);
SP 9/200/9 (Burghley's genealogies of French kings); Hist. MSS Comm., *Calendar of the Manuscripts
of the Most Honourable the Marquess of Salisbury . . . : preserved at Hatfield House, Hertfordshire*, 24
vols. (1883–), xvii. 595; D. M. Palliser, *The Age of Elizabeth* (1983), 83. Ministers of state continued to
sketch foreign and domestic genealogies for their own practical information late in the seventeenth
century: Sir Joseph Williamson, whose papers form PRO SP 9, inherited the Cecils' notes and added
his own: SP 9/32 (unbound papers), art. 1, fos. 256^r–361^r; Bodl. MS Perrott 6, fos. 1–108, 'The Descent
or Pedigrees of the principal Princes of Europe', dedicated by 'JB' to Burghley 1 Jan. 1584/5 and including, at fos. 44^r–69^v, a genealogical history of the kings of England from the Conquest. Bulstrode Whitelocke
recorded of his father, Sir James, that he 'knew the pedigrees of most persons of honor & quality in
the kingdom', and Bulstrode himself became a great repository for information on descents, though
he was not a herald. In 1657 he was asked by one Mr Talbot for his opinion regarding that family's
antiquity: *The Diary of Bulstrode Whitelocke 1605–1675*, ed. R. Spalding (Oxford, 1989), 66, 455.

and owners of the same lands which are now his'. The anonymous author of a set of family genealogical collections asserted that the Talbot family's nobility and antiquity derived from its descent from both Norman and old English stems.[104]

As Charles I cultivated a connection to Anglo-Saxon monarchs such as Edgar, Egbert, and Alfred (in panegyrical histories such as Robert Powell's 1634 *Life of Alfred*, or Thomas Heywood's designs for the flagship *Sovereign of the Seas*), a particularly vigorous cultivation of pre-Conquest origins developed in the 1620s and 1630s.[105] Amid a later political context in which 'English liberties' were increasingly held up against the 'Norman yoke', it is not surprising to see claims to Saxon lineage continuing well after Charles had proved himself less Alfred than Ethelred the ill-counselled. The merchant and nonconformist alderman of Restoration Newcastle, Ambrose Barnes, traced his ancestry back to the Saxons —his family having, naturally, always been gentry—while noting that its prosperity had been 'much impaired by the irruption of the Danes, Scots, and lastly the Norman conquest'. Barnes cannot have been amused by a local physician who, when asked about his family origins, replied cheekily that it was unnecessary to discuss them 'for he was sure he was descended from Adam though he could not prove his descent'.[106]

The alternative to claiming Anglo-Saxon descent was to assert a pre-Conquest Norman ancestry, depending on the suspected etymology of a family name. Gervase Markham showed considerable restraint in praising the ancient house of Vere, earls of Oxford since the eleventh century, 'which is honour almost as early as could be; for before the Conquest there is no certaintie any of Honour hereditarie in this land'.[107] But seventy years later the dean of Durham, Thomas Comber, began his autobiography in 1695 with the assertion that his family, 'as tis said' had come over with William I, who had given one de Combre the family manor 'for killing the Saxon, or Danish lord of it'.[108] Comber's profligate High Church predecessor, Denis Grenville or Granville, who had followed James II into exile in 1688, had in similar fashion traced his own ancestry back to the Norman 'Grandvilles', adding his own annotations to a genealogy drawn up by a relative in 1639, which he had inherited with the family papers. Granville's genealogy traced

[104] *Barrington family letters, 1628–1632*, ed. A. Searle, Camden Soc., 4th ser., 28 (1983), introduction, p. 1; *Two Elizabethan Women: Correspondence of Joan and Maria Thynne*, ed. A. D. Wall, Wiltshire Rec. Soc., 38 (Devizes, 1983), 38; BL MS Lans. 1165 (anonymous collection on various peerages, written *c.*1630), fo. 5ʳ.

[105] SAL MS 503, for instance, is a three-membrane roll of 2.5 metres, and gives a genealogical table of descent of Henry IV from Ethelwulf, and Rollo duke of Normandy. This was written by Sir Henry Spelman in 1632 and given by him to Henry St George, Garter King of Arms.

[106] M.R., *Memoirs of the Life of Mr Ambrose Barnes, late merchant and sometime alderman of Newcastle upon Tyne*, ed. W. H. D. Longstaffe, Surtees Soc., 50 (1867), 23. For further pre-Conquest claims, see Round, *Peerage and Pedigree*, vol. ii, *passim*; id., 'The Heneage Fiction', in his *Family Origins and Other Studies*, ed. W. Page (New York, 1930), 125–9.

[107] Gervase Markham, *Honour in his perfection* (1624), 19.

[108] *The Autobiographies and Letters of Thomas Comber*, ed. C. E. Whiting, Surtees Soc., 156–7 (1941–2), i. 1.

the ancestry of his father Sir Bevil Grenville (who had fallen in the king's service at Lansdowne in 1643, 'with the same honour hee had lived after the example of his famous and renowned auncestors') back to Rollo, the first duke of Normandy. After a few years of retirement at Corbeil, Granville happened 'accidentally' to come upon the seat of ancestors, the earls of Corbeil; this led him to make out another descent 'in a strait line by confronting my Pedigree sent me out of England with the written Antiquities and records of the towne . . . which is made beyond all dispute'. Pleased that James II personally acknowledged this descent, Granville expressed the further hope that in the event of the former king's death, his new-found descent would be worth some financial support from nobles at the court of Louis XIV.[109]

Pedigrees stretched back into remote time were a cause of labour to the heralds, of annoyance to older noble and gentle families and, increasingly, of much amusement to the literate public; but they were incomparably less difficult to discredit than more subtle attempts to adjust lines of succession or fill in gaps between two authenticated points, such as Dering's above-mentioned invention, or the herald John Philipot's ingenious rewriting of a Chancery roll in order to plug a fourteenth-century hole in the pedigree of the Finches of Sussex.[110] Both types of genealogical creativity are illustrated in the career of one of the Elizabethan age's greatest bibliophiles, John Lord Lumley, though his reputation in this regard was notorious even in the early seventeenth century. When James I was shown around Lumley Castle, near Durham, in 1603, Lumley was away. His friend the dean of Durham conducted the king around, descanting on Lumley's genealogy back to Liulph, a Saxon killed in William the Conqueror's time. This evoked a famous instance of the acerbic wit for which James would be known, 'I did na ken Adam's name was Lumley.' But Lumley—an heirless old man for whom pursuit of a great ancestry offered both solace and the prospect of an enduring reputation—was a gap-filler as well as a stretcher. He prevailed on the bishop of Durham to permit him to remove some statuary from Durham Cathedral and place them in the parish church of Chester-le-Street, together with a few bona fide effigies, since he believed (or at least wished others to believe), that they represented some of his missing medieval ancestors. As a finishing touch, Lumley even composed a Latin genealogy to accompany them. A similar inscription and

---

[109] Denis Granville, 'A Breife History of the Originall Descent of the most noble family of the Grandvilles . . . descended from the dukes of Normandy, faithfully collected out of severall auncient writings in ye Tower & elsewhere', Bodl. MS Rawl. D. 849 (Granville papers), fos. 13ʳ–16ʳ; J. H. Round, 'the Granvilles and the Monks', in his *Family Origins*, 130–69. Even satirists remarked on the choice of the Conquest as a demarcation line, for instance the humorous letter under the name 'Blank' giving the ancestry of that family, near kin to John a Styles and John a Nokes (fictitious names for parties in a legal action), 'and they, I am told, came in with the Conqueror': *The Spectator*, 563 (5 July 1714), ed. Bond, iv. 522–3.
[110] J. H. Round, 'The Origin of the Finches', *Sussex Archaeological Collections*, 70 (1929), 19–31. Philipot was fined in 1630 for permitting unwarranted quartering of arms at a funeral, and in 1639 he was charged with forging the Garter King of Arms's signature in order to acquire a coat of arms for a low-born man who had paid him a bribe: Maclagan 'Genealogy and Heraldry', 47.

nineteen coats of arms would surround his own monument in Cheam church following his death in 1609.[111]

Such inclinations as Lumley's are less an example of contemporary credulity, since they were already mocked at the time, or of a mendacious willingness to lie about one's past, than they are a testament to one salient feature of the English mind that is reflected in other spheres, such as formal history-writing, namely a profound dislike of gaps in the record. One Mr Bray of Doverdale, Worcestershire, dated his family's arrival in the parish to the mid-fourteenth century, but he was unable to trace a family tree between that time and his own day, causing the antiquary Thomas Habington to chortle that 'his petegree [is] defectyve because it hathe head and feete without a body, or towe ends without a myddle'.[112] Since as far back as Geoffrey of Monmouth, the English historical mind had abhorred a vacuum. Faced with spotty evidence and large holes in their lists of ancestors, filling in the blanks with a putative or supposititious list of forebears was less threatening to the public authenticity of a pedigree than to leave empty spaces. This is almost exactly the reverse of the genealogical tradition in non-Western cultures, especially those more heavily dependent on oral commemoration than the muniment-amassing English. In place of the kind of 'telescoping' that Evans-Pritchard and others have noted, for instance among the Nuer of the Sudan, whereby the number of generations *ab origine* is regularly kept limited to six or so, the English practice went in the opposite direction, adding and filling in rather than truncating and jettisoning sections of the familial past.[113]

Contemporary writers recognized the problem of the over-extended and unauthenticated pedigree, though some caution must be adopted in accepting their ascription of it to social climbing among the vulgar sort. A long literary tradition mocking ancestral pretensions among the poor stretches from Erasmus's *Folly* at the beginning of the sixteenth century, amused at the way 'the humblest worker' would trace his ancestry back to Brutus, Aeneas, or Arcturus, to Thomas Hardy's 'Sir' John Durbeyfield and his luckless daughter Tess in the nineteenth century.[114] But the real practitioners of this were those of much higher station, the well-off merchants, aspiring yeomanry, gentry, and newer members of the baronetage and peerage. There is a literary tradition of these, too, from Sir Roger de Coverley to Jane Austen's Sir Walter Elliot, baronet: fixation on lineage is presented in many of these fictional treatments as the last refuge of families teetering on the brink

[111] R.W., *Mount Tabor* (1639), 124–9; James, *Family, Lineage, and Civil Society*, 109; Llewellyn, *Funeral Monuments in Post-Reformation England*, 96, 305. Sir Edward Dering, generally regarded as one of the more scrupulous of early Stuart antiquaries, made miscellaneous notes on monuments not simply because of an enthusiasm for them but because he was trying to establish a reputation as an expert on them, so that his 'restorations' of the family brasses at Pluckley, many of which were false, would be publicly accepted: CKS, U350/Z24, and R. H. D'Elbroux, 'The Dering Brasses', *The Antiquaries' Journal*, 27 (1947), 11–23.
[112] Thomas Habington, *A survey of Worcestershire*, ed. J. Amphlett, Worcestershire Historical Soc., vol. v, 2 pts. (Oxford, 1893–9), i. 192.
[113] E. Evans-Pritchard, 'Nuer Time-Reckoning', *Africa*, 12 (1939), 189–216; for criticism see A. Gell, *The Anthropology of Time* (Oxford and Providence, RI, 1992), 21.
[114] Genealogy and family history would be a recurrent theme for Hardy: Tess O'Toole, *Genealogy and Fiction in Hardy: Family Lineage and Narrative Lines* (New York, 1997).

of economic ruin.[115] In the early seventeenth century Thomas Habington criticized those who 'grace or rather disgrace theyre pedegrees' with references to King
Arthur and his knights; Henry Crosse sneered at men who 'derive their pedigree
even from Cadwallader, the last king of the Britons, when in sadnes they are
not so much as sprinkled with one true drop of gentle bloud'.[116] Robert Furse
recorded in his family record that 'our progenytors and fforefatheres were at the
hedde I do mene at the begynnynge but plene and sympell men and wemen and
of smalle possessyon and habylyte'; through divine favour and their own 'wysedom and good governanse' they had improved the family's fortunes 'by lytell and
lytell', raising it to its current comfortable level of prosperity.[117]

   The Edwardian deflator of genealogical balloons John Horace Round noted the
concocted pedigree of one of the more successful new families of the sixteenth
century, the Spencers, which attempted to span an unbridgeable gap between themselves and the famous medieval De Spensers. Round placed the blame for this
not on the family itself but squarely on the College of Arms.[118] Even under Elizabeth,
the heralds themselves were already often seen as perpetuating and pandering
to mythic descents and invented ancestors rather than eliminating them. Sir
Thomas Smith had suggested as early as 1583 that the heralds would, for the right
sum, bestow 'armes newly made and invented, which the title shall beare that the
said Herauld hath perused and seen olde Registers where his auncestors in times
past had borne the same'. (John Selden would quip much later that 'the Heralds
are the best gentlemen, because they make their own pedigree'.) After one incident in which a candidate for admission to All Souls' College in 1589 produced a
flawed pedigree signed by Robert Cooke, Clarenceux King of Arms, the college
resolved that no further pedigrees would be accepted on the basis of the heralds'
words alone.[119] A hundred years later a fellow of the same college, George Clarke,
thought that little stock should be placed on heraldic pedigrees unless supported
by other evidence, 'for their way is in their Visitations (as they told me) to take
ye persons word that comes to them for ye Account of ye Family he would be,
or is of; so that for ought I can find, a man may be of kin to whom he pleases,
if he will come and enter with them'.[120] The addition of a buckle to the arms of
the Sussex Pelhams (a device long employed on the family's seals but after 1620

[115] The literary stereotype had, of course, a basis in reality. Examples of the sort of fraudulent genealogy later exploded by J. H. Round continued to occur among the nineteenth-century aristocracy. Bertrand
Russell's great-grandfather, the duke of Bedford, hired a historian to plot an elaborate descent from a
French noble who crossed the Channel with William the Conqueror; their true origins lay in a late medieval family of Dorset wine-merchants. Ray Monk, *Bertrand Russell: The Spirit of Solitude* (1996), 4.
[116] Erasmus, *The Praise of Folly*, trans. B. Radice (Harmondsworth, 1971), 131; Habington to Sir Simon
Archer, 9 Nov. 1634, BL MS 28,564, fo. 237ᵛ; Henry Crosse, *Vertues common-wealth* (1603), sig. M3ᵛ.
[117] Carpenter, 'Furse of Moreshead', 171.
[118] Round, *Studies in Peerage and Family History*, 285.
[119] Smith, *De Republica Anglorum*, 72; *Table-talk: being the discourses of John Selden, Esq.*, ed. R.
Milward, 2nd edn. (1698), 33; G. D. Squibb, *Founders Kin: Privilege and Pedigree* (Oxford, 1972), 80.
[120] Round, *Peerage and Pedigree*, ii. 317; Squibb, *Founders' Kin*, 80. By the early nineteenth century
Brasenose College would not accept pedigrees from individual officers of arms or even those produced by the College of Arms itself, unless authenticated by the opinion of a chancery lawyer or conveyancer: Squibb, *Founders' Kin*, 86.

made to symbolize a spurious connection to a fourteenth-century knight who had fought at Poitiers), was attributed by Sir Thomas Pelham to heraldic pressure that he personally found distasteful and at variance with his own knowledge of the family's arms. Writing to his cousin Sir William, who had urged him to register the family pedigree, Thomas complained that he disliked 'the altering and buying and selling of arms for gayne'.[121] Nearer the end of our period, in 1724, a writer praising the diligence of the heralds would in the same breath refer readers to Chamberlayne's *Angliae notitia* for guidelines on how to purchase a coat of arms. An essay by an unknown early Stuart antiquary on the origins of coats of arms was scathing towards the 'un-written falsityes' that family 'tradition' had produced, and on the issue of spurious pedigrees assigned to King Arthur he commented,

I would I could finde proofe of K. Arthur's armes . . . I would I were as certeine of St Georges cross, as I am that there was no St. George. Surely our auncient Heroes are much beholding to our later heralds, and itt appears no other to me but that courteous posterity, hath with reverence fancyed and bestowed armes upon their worthy ancestry.[122]

Disputing the 'pretended antiquity' of the Genevan-modelled church of Thomas Cartwright, Richard Bancroft pointed out that anyone could claim such antiquity,

The Herroldes at armes they say, can do verie much, in a mans pedigree though peradventure his Gentilitie be not of fiftie yeares standing: yet if neede require, William Conquerours time is nothing: they will fetch it from Adam.

As a genealogical narrative in the College of Arms suggests—noting with confidence that Adam 'died of the gowte'—Bancroft did not exaggerate.[123]

It is obviously difficult to know when to take such comments seriously and when as brave jest or provocative aside; and one can even forgive the pretensions of a Lumley when one recalls that technically, from the point of view of all Christians, the entire world was indeed descended from Adam. If one takes descents from extreme antiquity as a kind of trope or convention, then it becomes easier to understand their appearance, very late, and in the work of persons who clearly knew that they were not to be taken literally. The distinguished antiquary William Stukeley would draw up a pedigree of George I in the 1720s, tracing the king's

---

[121] L. F. Salzman, 'The Early Heraldry of Pelham', *Sussex Archaeological Collections*, 69 (1928), 53–70; the culprit was probably, once again, John Philipot. Visitations could be profitable to the college, even at the end of the seventeenth century: revenues from King's visitation of Herefordshire, Monmouthshire, Leicestershire, Rutland, Northamptonshire, and Warwickshire in 1682–3 came to £530, which was used to finance new building at the college: Styles, 'The Heralds' Visitation of Warwickshire', 127.

[122] Bodl. MS Top. gen. d. 59, anonymous work on arms and pedigrees, fo. 15ʳ, written *c*.1630. What Round saw as the endurance of lax standards of proof I prefer to think of as recognition that possession and granting of arms to newly gentrified families was no longer a matter over which the college had much control; in short, the genealogical-historical activities of the heralds and their role as issuers of arms had crept apart once again.

[123] *Heralds' Commemorative Exhibition, 1484–1934* p. 74. Richard Bancroft, *A survay of the pretended holy discipline* (1593), 71.

lineage back to Noah, Japhet, and Gomer without a second thought, and he added
for good measure such old chestnuts as the foundation of York by Ebrauk
and the discovery of Britain by Brutus. Stukeley showed considerably greater restraint
in researching the descent of Sir Isaac Newton prior to writing a short memoir
of the recently deceased mathematician, going back to Newton's parish of birth
to locate its registers.[124] A late Stuart provincial antiquary such as Thomas
Machell, who one might expect to disdain imagined descents, was not content
with pushing his own pedigree back to the Norman Conquest, fantasizing that
he was in fact descended from a Roman family.[125]

A problem seems to arise from the question of 'belief': while it is certain that
outright forgeries and imaginary extensions back to remote times continued to
take place, it is much less clear, especially as we move towards the eighteenth
century, that these were always intended to be taken literally. J. H. Round, who
did more than anyone else in the first part of the twentieth century to expose
fraudulent or fictitious pedigrees—many of which he took from the pages of
his literary *bête noire, Burke's Peerage*—bears a certain responsibility for this. The
examples he lists in his many publications on the subject range from subtle alterations to the record—which probably were genuine attempts to deceive for some
particular political or economic gain—to more outlandish claims to pre-Conquest
or even biblical ancestry which in many cases were intended rhetorically; and they
stretch over the entire period from the Middle Ages to his own time. Round saw
them all alike as instances of evidentiary failure, naivety, or outright malice, without making an adequate distinction among categories of error.[126]

Sincere or not, the over-zealous preening of family ancestry in the form of the
pedigree generated its own critics, of whom few proved more severe than
Gervase Holles, himself the younger son of a recently ennobled family:

There is nothing appears to me more ridiculous or more nearly allied to a vulgar spirit
then what I meet with in most gentlemen of England, namely a vayne affectation to fly
beyond the moone and to credit themselves (as they thinke) with long and fictitious pedigrees. How many have wee that will confidently tell you their sirnames flourished even in
the Saxon times, though the understanding antiquary knowes that they can have no record
to justify it and that those times had no setled sirnames at all, and very few for above two
hundred yeares after the Conquest. How many have wee in Lincolneshire that will affirme
themselves to have been gentlemen there ever since the Normans' entrance, when I knowe
there are scarse six families in the whole county that can make proofe they had one foot
of land there the 20th yeare of K. Henry the third.

[124] Bodl. MS Eng. hist. c.1029 (William Stukeley, 'A synchronical genealogy of all the monarchs
that ever reign'd in the island of Great Britain'), fos. 1ᵛ, 4ᵛ, 45ʳ. Newton himself, on being knighted,
launched an enquiry into his descent by asking for extracts from several relevant parish registers, according to Stukeley: Nichols, *Literary Illustrations*, iv. 26–7 (Stukeley to Richard Mead, 16 June 1727).
[125] Cumbria RO (Carlisle), Dean and Chapter MSS, Machell collections, vol. i. p. 563 (1698).
[126] Round, *Peerage and Pedigree*, i. 1–54 (for the nineteenth-century Bertie–Willoughby d'Eresby
case), and ii. 307–84; id., *Studies in Peerage and Family History* (Westminster, 1901), 45, for typical
examples of Round's very strong views on the 'absurd fables' that he continued to find in *Burke's
Peerage*.

Holles warned his son against confusing a contrived pedigree with genuine historical achievements, which alone could add lustre to a family, and urged him to undertake research into the family history rather than simply listing ancestors:

And this satisfaction it will give you, that you shall not only know the names, the qualities, the services and the matches of your ancestors, but in many of them their very features and dispositions (a designe I dare boldly say wch in any private family hath not hitherto beene undertaken) and whilst most others dully sleep in the ignorance of what concernes them in this kinde, or content themselves with forged, spurious and insignificant genealogies, you will be able not only to justify theis descentes of yr owne by unquestionable authority of record, *but also to set the right stamp and value upon every person, wch indeed is the true life of this part of venerable antiquity.*

It is worth remarking that Holles is not simply mounting another criticism of the vanity of ancestral pretensions among those of little present means or virtue. Rather, he is pointing out the need to place appreciation of one's ancestors within a wider historical context. Genealogy without history, Holles continued, is a 'useless carcase', and only history proper 'hath made us acquainted with our dead ancestors and out of the depth and darknes of the earth delivered us their memory and fame'.[127]

By the Restoration, criticism and scepticism had turned to mirth and satire. Samuel Butler remorselessly pilloried both the antiquary and his subject in the Cromwell-figure Colon in *Hudibras*:

> It was a question whether He
> Or's Horse were of a Family
> More Worshipful: till Antiquaries,
> (After th' had almost por'd out their eyes,)
> Did very learnedly decide
> The bus'ness on the Horse's side.[128]

Perhaps the sharpest Restoration response to the maker of a genealogy came not from an individual but an entire city. In honour of his home town, Sir Thomas Widdrington, former Speaker of the Commons, drew up a history of York, its mayors, and antiquities from archives, chronicles, and charters, even taking the trouble to give the town a pre-Roman origin. The response of an ungracious citizenry—which belies again the gentry perception of the middling sort's ancestral credulity—was sufficient to keep Widdrington from publishing the tome:

Now, sir, for the Britons you mention: we can neither derive pedigree nor wealth from them; nor can we hear of any of their descendants, unless in Wales and Cornwall . . . and we find by experience that it is not a long series, or beadroll of ancestors, and predecessors, but wealth and estate which set a value upon men and places.

---

[127] Gervase Holles, *Memorials of the Holles family, 1493–1656*, ed. A. C. Wood, Camden Soc., 3rd ser., 55 (1937), 2, emphasis mine.

[128] Samuel Butler, *Hudibras*, pt. 1, canto ii, lines 465–70, ed. J. Wilders (Oxford, 1967), 42.

The town's 'sad complaynt' about the practical uselessness of the exercise concludes with a plea for more concrete, monetary, assistance from its prominent son.[129]

In the early eighteenth century it was the turn of the pedigree-mongering squire to become a figure of ridicule, perhaps most amusingly in the literary periodicals edited by Addison and Steele. 'Of all the vanities under the sun, I confess, that of being proud of one's birth is the greatest', wrote Steele, while exploring his alter ego Isaac Bickerstaff's descent from various Staffs and Distaffs and providing a genealogy 'as a kinsman of ours has sent it me from the Herald's Office'.[130] On the other hand, Addison conceded—in contradiction to a Horatian dictum devaluing the value of ancestry—that those who have 'nothing else to distinguish them but the virtues of their fore-fathers, are to be looked upon with a degree of veneration even upon that account, and to be more respected than the common run of men who are of low and vulgar extraction'.[131]

CONCLUSION

The general tendency noted in the last two chapters, away from degree proclaimed through traditional symbols of gentility (coats of arms and lengthy descents) and towards a status maintained by an individual's achievements in the civic, religious, literary, or commercial spheres has been previously pointed out by social and economic historians. What has not been explored, however, is what this implies for the changing historical culture of the period, and in particular for the exercise of genealogy-making. These changes reflect the emergence of a national historical tradition to which individual subjects could see themselves contributing. The intense devotion to family ancestry, the early compliance with heraldic visitations, and the indiscriminate use of armorial decoration are indicative of a historical mind that saw the family as fundamentally definitive of an individual's potential to contribute to the commonwealth, and appealed to family heritage in asserting individual merit or virtue. It also reflected a period in which lineage in its own right, and, better yet, lineage connected over a long period to a particular geographic location, was a primary basis for an entitlement to privilege and deference.

[129] Thomas Widdrington (d. 1664), *Analecta Eboracensia, or some remaynes of the auncient city of Yorke. Collected by a citizen of Yorke*, ed. C. Caine (1897), p. x, from BL MS Egerton 2578. Caine's edition includes the text of the town's 'sad complaynt' (fos. 174ʳ–175ᵛ), but leaves out other parts of Widdrington's manuscript, including its list of bailiffs.

[130] *The Tatler*, 11 (5 May 1709), ed. Bond, i. 98. This is continued by Addison in no. 59 (25 Aug. 1709), ed. Bond, i. 411, where the Greenhat family claim to be related to the Bickerstaffs, descended from 'Maudlin, the left-handed wife of Nehemiah Bickerstaff, in the reign of Harry II'.

[131] *The Guardian*, 137 (18 Aug. 1713), ed. J. C. Stephens (Lexington, Ky., 1982), 455. Steele printed a petition from a stationer claiming that he and his forefathers had been sellers of books 'for time immemorial'. His ancestor, Crouchback Title-Page, 'was the first of that vocation in Britain' and stationers were so-called after that man's 'station' on Lothbury Street in London: *Spectator*, 304 (18 Feb. 1712), ed. Bond, iii. 70–1.

By the late seventeenth century this had changed. A claim to long lineage was no longer so impressive, even when it could be sustained by evidence, and the politically or socially ambitious were using other arguments. The civil war, which divided many families on religious lines, had also occasioned further significant shifts in land ownership and for a time abolished the House of Lords. Former Cavaliers seeking redress or favour after the Restoration tended to base their pleas on their recent sufferings on behalf of the Crown, without leaning very hard on the further validation of heredity. An emphasis on individual achievement in the present was, in turn, projected back on the past. Ancestors continued to be admired and commemorated, as they had been previously for their collective role in making a family great or prosperous; but there is a noticeable increase in reference to their own individual achievements, rather than the mere longevity and continuity of their line. Moreover, references to immediate and more remote forebears, in monuments and in biographies, increasingly set these achievements within the context of national history. There is a subtle but critical difference between a claim, true or false, that one's family has been 'in England since the Conquest' and a claim, true or false, that one's ancestor fought alongside William the Conqueror at Hastings. The first gives priority to place and landed interest, and secondarily to time, construed as an unbroken lineage beginning with a putative founder who has, in a sense, 'conquered' the family's particular parcel of land and established its claim to notability. The second, however, subordinates place to time. It locates the remote ancestor in a broader master narrative of English history with which readers of upper and middling status were rapidly growing more familiar during the seventeenth century. It also makes the direct line of descent recorded in a genealogy a means of proving relation to this worthy forebear, rather than an end in itself. The ancestors who came earlier, or in between, remain of little consequence so long as relation can be proved—unless they, too, are notable figures. Thomas Tickell observed that most pedigrees displayed in manor houses will list 'first in the catalogue a great statesman, or a soldier with an honourable commission', with earlier artisans or farmers shorn off.[132]

In other words, the family genealogy by 1700 was much less a pseudo-biblical series of 'begats' emphasizing continuity, and much more a bridge connecting the political present to a famous person in the historical past whose deeds had a significance beyond the family, as Gervase Holles had suggested it should be. There are indeed signs of this as early as the reign of James I, for instance in the genealogical writings of Sir Edward Rodney of Rodney Stoke, Somerset, whom we have already encountered. A reader of Camden who approached matters of remote genealogy with moderate scepticism, Rodney fell back on the use of conjecture and tradition (both approved by Camden himself), in pushing his family's pedigree back to the reign of King Stephen; but throughout this account he took pains to stress the connections between the 'worthy examples' in his lineage and the

---

[132] *The Spectator*, 612 (27 Oct. 1714), ed. Bond, v. 191–3.

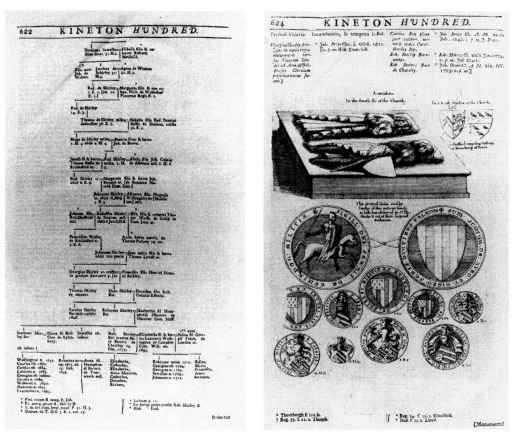

Fig. 4.2. Pedigrees in print: detail of the pedigree of the Shirley family. From Dugdale, *Antiquities of Warwickshire*, i. 622

Fig. 4.3. Arms, seals, and effigies of the Shirley family, 'as hath been observed by Sr Tho. Shirley Kt., out of their originall evidences'; Shirley was a Catholic antiquary of note. From Dugdale, *Antiquities of Warwickshire*, i. 624

political events of their own times.[133] The trend is clearer a generation later. Dugdale's *Antiquities of Warwickshire* (1656) prints pedigrees of the county's great families (Fig. 4.2), and the book is full of illustrated arms, seals and effigies (Fig. 4.3), but its focus is not strictly heraldic or even genealogical. Episodes in the lives of some famous antecedents are selected for graphic illustration that render their subjects into more than mere links in a chain (Fig. 4.4). Even Dugdale's portrait by Wenceslas Hollar in the work's frontispiece draws the viewer's attention away from its minimalist arms in the upper corners towards the foregrounded books and pens that

---

[133] Rodney, 'Genealogy of the Family of Rodney of Rodney Stoke', p. 1, pp. 208–12, pts. 2 and 3, *passim*.

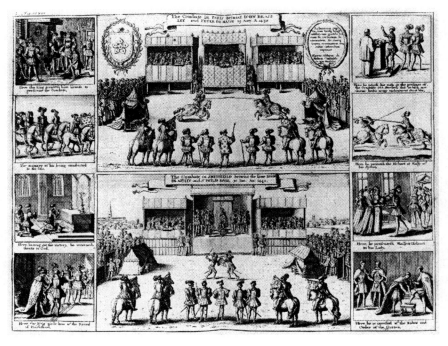

Fig. 4.4. Graphic representation of a famous ancestor: a series of engravings representing the chivalric exploits of Sir John de Astley (early fifteenth century), in Dugdale's account of the Astley family of Knightlow Hundred, Warwickshire. From Dugdale, *Antiquities of Warwickshire*, vol. i, between pp. 110 and 111

Fig. 4.5. Portrait of William Dugdale by Wenceslas Hollar; note the foregrounding of Dugdale's books and writing implements in comparison with the simple, backgrounded armorial shields. Frontispiece to volume i of Dugdale, *Antiquities of Warwickshire*

are the implements of a scholar (Fig. 4.5). By the time of Dugdale's *Baronage*, published in the 1670s, arms are eschewed by its author (soon to be promoted Garter King of Arms), who organized its two volumes around individual noble titles, which in turn were subdivided into family histories. The *Baronage*, a recent commentator has observed, amounts in places to a series of well-documented biographies of famous family members and narratives of the events in which they were actors; one of Dugdale's contemporaries confessed to having not known 'the twentyeth part' of the 'gests of his ancestors' prior to reading Dugdale's tome.[134] To put it another way, the respect owed to ancestors had, over the course of two centuries, been more or less thoroughly historicized. From being great family founders whose nobility or gentility had enabled the prosperity and privileged status of their remote descendants, ancestors had evolved into historical figures in their own right who reflected by analogy and example the deeds of their progeny, but were in no way accountable for either their successes or failures. The eighteenth century would continue to esteem heritage and honourable lineage, but only in so far as it was maintained in the present.

That ancestry mattered rather less, both socially and historiographically, by the mid-seventeenth century was to have some profound implications for the shape of historical enquiry over the next 200 years, and in particular for the antiquarianism that will concern us in the next part of this book. Genealogy continued to provide evidence of unbroken and extended lineage, and knowledge of its basics, if not always its details, had certainly become more commonplace. Yet such knowledge was also increasingly demoted to the status it has enjoyed since then of an ancillary activity, useful principally for providing evidence for more wide-ranging historical and antiquarian accounts: both William Holman and his eventual successor Philip Morant saw their local genealogical enquiries as material for a more wide-ranging history of Essex rather than a catalogue of descents.[135] To the extent that genealogical information continued to be adduced in county histories and in biographies, it was literally marginalized into notes or consigned to specialized works of reference. The ultimate result of this trend, which goes back to the late Elizabethan and Jacobean works by Ralph Brooke and Augustine Vincent, would be the Debretts and Burkes of the late eighteenth and nineteenth centuries, works solely concerned with the pedigrees of particular families and titles. But there was another reason for this that we have not yet addressed: genealogy was, by the last decades of the seventeenth century, no longer the major, or even the most important, arm of antiquarianism as a whole, which increasingly focused instead on the architectural and natural remains of the past. Unlike vanished ancestors, these remained visible and tangible in the present.

[134] Dugdale, *Baronage*, *passim*, quotation at vol. i, preface, sig. B3ʳ; Dugdale, *Life, Diary and Correspondence*, 399; F. C. Lancaster, ' "Those Flourishing Ages Past": William Dugdale and the English County Survey', Ph.D. thesis, University of Western Australia (2002), 205–6. I am indebted to Dr Lancaster for permission to read and cite his thesis.

[135] On the plans to publish Holman's history see D. R. Woolf, *Reading History in Early Modern England* (Cambridge, 2000), 248, 250.

Part III

THE TANGIBLE PAST

CHAPTER FIVE

Varieties of Antiquarianism

THERE IS A crucial difference between an all-encompassing veneration of things in general because they are old—and therefore safe and familiar, unlike new things—and the love of specific objects whose oldness makes them rare and exotic. The first, as we have seen, is a general characteristic of the sixteenth and seventeenth centuries, shared in broad terms by all levels of society. The second, however, is a much more historically specific attitude, and one which is unlikely to develop in a society that is both marginally literate and geographically insular. A society that has little exposure to things that are very new need not devise any special mental shelf or 'closet', nor any corresponding discursive space, in which to store the very old; it can keep or throw out past traditions as present needs demand.

But what happens when that same society undergoes a period of rapid cultural, technological, or economic change? Beset by newness, the initial reaction of most people will be exactly that outlined in Chapter 2: a reflexive appeal to the old ways as the standard and a counter-offensive against novelty. Yet sooner or later the fact of novelty will be undeniable, its flow a tide that cannot be stopped. When novelty becomes socially acceptable, the old can then itself be renewed, becoming as much a collectible sign of its owner's advancing knowledge of his or her world as it is an excavated token from a past era. Old things then become less familiar fellow-travellers than exciting, interesting visitors, intruders on a mental landscape progressively readjusting itself to change and innovation. Under such circumstances an 'antiquity', in the sense of an object surviving from the remote past, becomes itself a 'novelty', a 'rarity' or 'curiosity'. The formerly mundane becomes, to reapply Stephen J. Greenblatt's apt phrase, a 'marvellous possession', as exotic in its displacement from a time of origin as Chinese silk or North American beaver pelts, objects rendered more valuable because of geographical displacement. As with New World imports, an increase in traffic can then work to contain or diminish the sense of newness, as what was initially rare now becomes commonplace once more, and newer, rarer objects have to be sought to maintain the barricade between excitement and ennui. This second type of attitude to material objects from the past was beginning to develop in the sixteenth century, and it continued to take hold in the course of the seventeenth, eventually removing some aspects of antiquarianism from the realm of classical philology, where they had begun, and aligning them with natural philosophy.

Antiquarianism is a loaded word, and not only because it now has a popular pejorative connotation from which it was not entirely free even in the seventeenth
century. It is a broad term, useful in its comprehensiveness but tending to
obscure the differences between a variety of intellectual activities all of which were
connected in some way with the study of the past. It can itself be distinguished,
of course, from another grand category of writing about the past, narrative history, the concerns of which were for a long time very different, despite some early
Stuart attempts at reconciliation.[1] Once one gets beyond this distinction, the
picture is further complicated by the meaning of the words 'antiquarian' or 'antiquary' in themselves. One can distinguish within antiquarianism, for instance,
two parallel streams of activity. The first of these is the activity of the humanist
philologists, descendants of Continental and early Tudor language scholars, who
sought verbal artefacts, especially manuscripts and inscriptions, to fill in gaps
in their largely textually derived reconstructions of the past. The second is that
of the travelling antiquary, making periodic trips from place to place within a
county and in some instances throughout both kingdoms and abroad, in search
of scattered monuments, buried artefacts, and features of the landscape. The first
of these activities tends to be stationary, based in one or more major libraries,
with gaps filled in through correspondence and some judicious borrowing of material from afar. The latter is peripatetic by design, beginning with wide reading
and much the same classical education, but subordinating that to observation and
collection. The philological tradition connects the world of late medieval and early
Renaissance critical scholarship with that of eighteenth- and nineteenth-century
litterae humaniores. Although methods and knowledge improved between the time
of Lorenzo Valla and that of Richard Bentley, three centuries later, the essential
principles and goals remained the same: the establishment of accurate texts and
the elucidation of their meaning through criticism, so as better to understand the
culture that had created them.

The 'archaeological' side of antiquarianism evolved in another direction over
the same period, and the changes are more striking. Although a strong archaeological base existed in the originating works of certain key early figures, such as
the fifteenth-century Italian Flavio Biondo, the initial impulses of English antiquarianism were very different.[2] Both of the first two authors of national surveys,
Leland and Camden, were fundamentally traditional Renaissance humanists,
focused on language—Camden (Fig. 5.1) was a teacher of Greek long before he

[1] For this distinction see A. Momigliano, 'Ancient History and the Antiquarian', in his *Studies in Historiography* (1966). The negotiations between these varieties of historical interest are the subject of my earlier book, *The Idea of History in Early Stuart England* (Toronto, 1990).

[2] G. Daniel, *A Hundred and Fifty Years of Archaeology* (Cambridge, Mass., 1976), 16–25, does not give the early modern antiquaries sufficient credit. This is remedied in A. Schnapp, *The Discovery of the Past*, trans. I. Kinnes and G. Varndell (New York, 1996), 121–273; Schnapp's account is useful and informative, especially on the European side, but remains devoted to telling the conventional story of the rise of archaeology as a 'positive science'.

Fig. 5.1. Portrait of William Camden, engraved by R. White. Frontispiece to *Camden's Britannia*

became a herald. Their works certainly include descriptions of observable, tangible monuments and natural features, and Camden himself, between editions of *Britannia*, went on expeditions in search of artefacts. But the textual-philological heart of Leland's activities is unmistakable; Camden inherited this and added the close attention to genealogy that made *Britannia* among other things the greatest product of the sixteenth-century heraldic visitations.[3] This was equally a feature of most of the early Stuart 'chorographies' (a word coined simply to describe writings about a particular place since they fit under no known rubric of history proper) even though their accounts were frequently more detailed and based on greater first-hand familiarity with their counties. The most notable exception to this, Richard Carew's *Survey of Cornwall*, departed from this pattern, but in the direction of a more intense ethnography of Cornish customs and manners rather than a study of the objects of the past. Carew really belongs with the travel writers such as William Harrison rather than the antiquaries.[4]

By the end of the seventeenth century the picture was very different. Peripatetic antiquarianism had increased, and its thrust had also changed to a considerable degree. This was due in part to the influence of a Baconian-inspired agenda for the systematic observation and categorization of nature, and in part to a much more well-developed visual sense of history—a sense, not always accurate, of 'how the past looked' (for which see the next chapter). This shift in antiquarian interest is illustrated in works such as Joshua Childrey's 1661 *Britannia Baconica*, and especially by the wholesale adoption of Baconian principles by the Royal Society after the Restoration. Many of the antiquaries of the last third of the seventeenth century began to refocus their attention on the objects in their path. These included, on the one hand, man-made remains, such as ruins, megaliths (for instance Avebury, the subject of a brief burst of interest at the Royal Society in July 1663), and burial mounds, and, on the other hand, natural features such as flora and fauna; the natural and the antique overlapped in certain key areas, notably the study of fossils.[5] This archaeological tendency certainly occurred from time to time in different antiquarian works as far back as the late fifteenth century, but it becomes especially noticeable from the early 1680s, in a variety of articles in the *Philosophical Transactions of the Royal Society*.[6] Some of these antiquaries were

---

[3] W. Rockett, '*Britannia*, Ralph Brooke, and the Representation of Privilege in Elizabethan England', *Renaissance Quarterly*, 53 (2000), 475–99, esp. p. 496.

[4] J. Simmons, 'The Writing of English County History', in id. (ed.), *English County Historians: First Series* (Wakefield, 1978), 4–9. The eighteenth-century scholar Richard Gough provided a useful history of the development of antiquarianism in Britain in the preface to his *Anecdotes of British Topography: or, an historical account of what has been done for illustrating the topographical antiquities of Great Britain and Ireland* (1768), pp. i–xxxv.

[5] M. Hunter, 'The Royal Society and the Origins of British Archaeology', *Antiquity*, 65 (1971), repr. in his *Science and the Shape of Orthodoxy: Intellectual Change in Late Seventeenth-Century Britain* (1995), 67–98, 181–200; id. *John Aubrey and the Realm of Learning* (1975), 202–8; P. J. Ucko, M. Hunter, A. J. Clark, and A. David, *Avebury Reconsidered: From the 1690s to the 1990s* (1991), 10.

[6] Hunter, 'The Royal Society and the Origins of British Archaeology', 183. By the early eighteenth century, the shift in interest towards natural history is even clearer in works such as John Morton's *The natural history of Northamptonshire; with some account of the antiquities* (1712) and Thomas Robinson's

less interested than their predecessors in the niceties of textual philology, and this apparent impatience actually helped. The conclusions that they drew from direct observation, and from the comparison of objects with each other, were most acute when not distorted by unfortunate attempts to reconcile them with the literary inheritance, as is perhaps most remarkable in the case of Aubrey's unpublished *Monumenta Brittanica*. At the same time, many of them now paid less heed to the transcription of muniments and tombstones, and they lingered less often on the great families of an area and their pedigrees. In a single chapter on 'Antiquities' near the end of the *Natural History of Stafford-shire* (a transitional work that still owed more to textual sources than to direct observation), Robert Plot bluntly declared his intent 'not to meddle with the pedigrees or descents either of families or lands'.[7] This certainly reflects the reshaping of ancestral interests suggested at the end of the last chapter, and such activities, though far from being banished from antiquarian works, increasingly devolved on more specialized writings, the precursors of books such as Burke's *Peerage*.

These intellectual changes were not immediately clear. Contemporaries continued to throw about words like 'antiquary' with abandon, and we should remain attuned at all times to the interconnections that they perceived among these various approaches to the past, not least because many of the major figures had more than one historical arrow in their quiver. The most learned antiquary of the early seventeenth century, John Selden, a sedentary polymath who travelled out of London as rarely as possible, was anchored even more firmly in the philological tradition than Camden had been. Even Sir William Dugdale, widely travelled as he was, remained part of that tradition in his relative dependence on literary and documentary sources. Aubrey and his Augustan successors, such as Edward Lhwyd, William Stukeley, and John Horsley, lay closer to modern archaeological methods.[8] At the same time, however, they remained well acquainted with the evidence of manuscripts and books. Lhwyd's considerable contributions to the study of fossils in his *Lithophylactii Britannici Ichnographia* (1699) must be set against his equally impressive studies of Welsh language that built on the longer tradition of philology while adopting a comparative approach that was in turn derived from his archaeological activities.[9] Although the distinctions are there, even the most persuasive current student of Restoration antiquarianism admits that 'there was no absolute gulf between history and archaeology'.[10] One should

An essay towards a natural history of Westmorland and Cumberland. Wherein an account is given of their several mineral and surface productions, with some directions how to discover minerals by the external and adjacent strata and upper covers, & c. (1709).

[7] Robert Plot, *The Natural History of Stafford-shire* (Oxford, 1686), 392; M. Paffard, 'Robert Plot— A County Historian', *History Today*, 20 (1970), 112–17. Plot's understudy, Edward Lhwyd, similarly makes a clear distinction between antiquities and natural history in a letter to the Revd John Lloyd (22 Sept. 1695): R. T. Gunther, *Early Science in Oxford*, xiv: *Life and Letters of Edward Lhwyd* (Oxford, 1945), 285.

[8] Hunter, *John Aubrey and the Realm of Learning*, 160; R. Sweet, *The Writing of Urban Histories in Eighteenth-Century England* (Oxford, 1997), 47–64.

[9] F. Emery, *Edward Lhuyd F.R.S. 1660–1709* (Cardiff, 1971), 39–49, 53–7, 71–81.

[10] M. Hunter, *Science and Society in Restoration England* (Cambridge, 1981), 158.

therefore be careful about making too rigid a distinction among antiquarianism's branches, especially as one form of activity looks enticingly progressive and scientific as it lurches, however haltingly, towards Lyell and Darwin,[11] while the other appears a bit old-fashioned and retrograde, casting constant wistful glances towards the bookshelves, and particularly to the pressmarks denoting classical authors.

Personal preference clearly played a considerable role in defining scholarly activities. Not every form of antiquity was equally attractive to every scholar; nor was every type of antiquarian study. Some had different intellectual capacities, others different 'tastes', to borrow from Pierre Bourdieu, that directed their choice of objects for acquisition, gift, display, or study.[12] Samuel Dale of Braintree, Essex, may have been reacting against the blurring of boundaries between antiquarianism and natural history in works such as Plot's *Natural History of Oxfordshire* when, in writing to William Holman about Essex's antiquities, he specifically excluded information on the natural features of their county.[13] There were also physical and personal constraints on the integration of mineralogical, zoological, and botanical study with text-based philological antiquarianism. Here again individual inclination must not be discounted, because it reveals a wide array of preferences for one type of research over another. Just as some historians today are more at home in libraries than in local record offices, so in the past there were those who preferred to deal with books rather than artefacts, or vice versa. The Essex antiquary Thomas Cox put it best in a letter to Holman in 1717:

Perhaps considering all things I am better provided for journeys then you, because I am more healthy, & keep a good horse, but I hate journeys, & love to sit upon a contemplative cushion, & my books about me, which I have used so long that I am not willing to go out of that path.[14]

Thomas Gerard of Somerset delighted in searching through 'old rolles and bookes, churches, windowes, tombes and antient seales', though he conceded that to many readers this would 'seeme a needles labour'.[15] John Aubrey, hardly the most sedentary of Restoration antiquaries and a pioneer of the archaeological approach to the past, drew the line at hanging about in churchyards; expressing regret that he had not made a more complete study of church monuments in Wiltshire, he confessed that 'of all studies I take the least delight in this'.[16] This

[11] S. Piggott, *Ruins in a Landscape* (Edinburgh, 1976), 129.

[12] P. Bourdieu, *Distinction: A Social Critique of the Judgement of Taste*, trans. R. Nice (Cambridge, Mass., 1984), 270–83.

[13] Essex RO D/Y/1/1/129, unfoliated correspondence (Dale to Holman, n.d. (1722)). S. A. E. Mendyk's otherwise useful book, *'Speculum Britanniae': Regional Study, Antiquarianism and Science in Britain to 1700* (Toronto, 1989), over-simplifies the link between antiquarianism and science, and the assumption of their close relation is also prominent in J. M. Levine, *Humanism and History* (Ithaca, NY, 1987) and *Doctor Woodward's Shield* (Berkeley and Los Angeles, 1977; repr. Ithaca, NY, 1991).

[14] Essex RO D/Y/1/1/90 (Thomas Cox to Holman, n.d. probably 1717/18).

[15] Thomas Gerard, *The particular description of the county of Somerset*, ed. E. H. Bates, Somerset Rec. Soc., 15 (1900), 3.

[16] John Aubrey, *Wiltshire. The Topographical Collections of John Aubrey FSA*, ed. J. E. Jackson (Devizes, 1862), 17.

bespeaks a temperament rather different from those such as John Weever or John Davies of Kidwelly, who carried to the point of obsession the study of funeral monuments—another activity driven mainly by the genealogical priorities of previous decades.[17]

Ultimately, the connection between the two types of antiquarian enquiry would remain a fruitful one—the *Victoria County Histories* and the *Agrarian History of England and Wales* are prominent descendants of this seventeenth-century coupling. In combination, both remained at a much greater remove from 'history proper', the activity of narrative historians, which had expanded its scope considerably in the seventeenth century but still remained overwhelmingly concerned with the recounting of major past events.

BECOMING AN ANTIQUARY

Although 'antiquarianism' as the conscious pursuit and study of old things originated well before the early modern period, it is only then that it achieved a firm place as a part of the broader historical culture.[18] Initially the part-time occupation of a handful of scholars such as the Italian Flavio Biondo, the Frenchman Guillaume Budé, and Englishmen such as William Worcestre and John Leland,[19] it grew by the early eighteenth century into a common pastime, a leisure activity, for the gentry and aristocracy. Eventually, enthusiasm for the flotsam of centuries would involve not merely the most highly-trained scholars but gentlemen, nobles, rural parsons, and city virtuosi in the search for old coins, fossils, funeral urns, and assorted weaponry. Men felt awed, fascinated, even humbled, before

[17] Weever's *Ancient funerall monuments* (1631) is the earliest printed collection devoted entirely to the preservation of funereal antiquities from destruction; for Davies's collections see CUL MS Gg. II. 15, which was published in 1672 'from ancient sources about the time of the dissolution' under the title *Ancient rites . . . of Durham.*

[18] In addition to the standard accounts of the early antiquarian movement in England cited elsewhere in this chapter, three works that focus, in very different ways, on Continental antiquarianism have been useful: R. Weiss, *The Renaissance Discovery of Classical Antiquity*, 2nd edn. (Oxford, 1988), is the indispensable study of the early Italian antiquaries; F. Haskell, *History and its Images: Art and the Interpretation of the Past* (New Haven, 1993); L. Barkan, *Unearthing the Past: Archaeology and Aesthetics in the Making of Renaissance Culture* (New Haven, 1999). Finally, W. Muensterburger, *Collecting, an Unruly Passion: Psychological Perspectives* (Princeton, 1994), 165–224, also offers valuable insights into the impulse behind Renaissance and seventeenth-century antiquarian activity.

[19] A. Gransden, 'Antiquarian Studies in Fifteenth-Century England', *Antiquaries' Journal*, 60 (1980), 75–97, repr. in her *Legends, Traditions and History in Medieval England* (London and Rio Grande, 1992), 299–327, is the best recent survey of the pre-Leland material, neglected by McKisack in her *Medieval History in the Tudor Age* (Oxford, 1971). I entirely agree with Dr Gransden that both McKisack and Sir Thomas Kendrick (who did not neglect the fifteenth century) exaggerate the 'impact of the Renaissance'. On the other hand, I cannot concur with her belief in the continuity between medieval and early modern antiquarianism, the social and intellectual environments for which were profoundly different. There is certainly a continuity of method and purpose between the likes of Thomas Elmham or Thomas Burton of Meaux, and the better-known Rous and Worcestre, in the fifteenth century and Leland and Bale in the mid-sixteenth; but there is a discernible break in the tradition with the Elizabethan antiquaries, and a much greater fissure after the Restoration with the intrusion of Baconian science and an enormous expansion of antiquarian interest among the general public.

the surviving fragments of a vanished age, which the artefact allowed them to recapture. To put it another way, very old objects had what has been called an 'age-value' independent of their monetary worth or value as historical sources.[20] The educated orders, from which the vast majority of publishing antiquaries sprang, could even seem on occasion obsessed with the old and decayed: like Mr Fearing in *Pilgrim's Progress*, they 'love[d] much to see antient things, and to be pondering them'. Meric Casaubon, a philologist rather than an artefact-hunter, described the antiquarian sentiment rather well:

Antiquaries are so taken with the sight of old things; not as doting (as I take it) upon the bare either form or matter (though both oftentimes be very notable in old things); but because those visible superviving evidences of antiquities represent unto their minds former times, with as strong an impression, as if they were actually present, and in sight as it were: even as old men looke gladly upon those things, that they were wont to see, or have beene otherwise used unto in their younger yeares, as injoying those yeares again in some sort, in those visible and palpable remembrances.[21]

It has been suggested that nostalgia plays a role in alienating people from the social present,[22] but this may well set the cart before the horse. Given the notorious eccentricities of a variety of early modern antiquaries from Leland, who died a madman, through the ill-tempered Wood, to the idiosyncratic Thomas Hearne, it seems probable that many of those who were socially disaffected were predisposed to seek solace in the past: the various comments on declining manners mentioned in Chapter 2 are a case in point, Catholic longing for the pre-Reformation era another. The antiquarian activities of one Lancashire recusant, William Blundell of Little Crosby, which will be examined more closely in Chapter 7, were driven by his profound hatred for Protestantism.[23] The past could provide a refuge from the burdens, threats, and worries of the present.

On the other hand, the antiquarian bug was often caught very early in life, well before any mature disaffection could appear to guide it. While still a boy, his sister Elizabeth recounted, William Elstob the Augustan divine and scholar acquired such a keenness for antiquities that by the age of 11 'he was called the little Cambden'.[24] As an undergraduate, during the latter years of the civil war

---

[20] This term is adapted from an earlier usage (by Alois Riegl) by Stephen Bann, in his ' "Views of the Past": Reflections on the Treatment of Historical Objects and Museums of History', in id., *The Inventions of History: Essays on the Representation of the Past* (Manchester and New York, 1990), 122–47, at p. 125; id., 'Clio in Part: on Antiquarianism and the Historical Fragment', ibid. 100–21. However, I would not agree with either Riegl or Bann that a sense of age-value originates in the nineteenth century.

[21] John Bunyan, *Grace Abounding . . . and the Pilgrim's Progress*, ed. Roger Sharrock (1966), 347; Meric Casaubon, *A treatise of use and custome* (1638), 97.

[22] D. Lowenthal, *The Past is a Foreign Country* (Cambridge, 1985), 13; but cf. pp. 49–52 for the past as 'escape'.

[23] See D. R. Woolf, 'Little Crosby and the Horizons of Early Modern Historical Culture', in D. R. Kelley and D. H. Sacks (eds.), *The Historical Imagination in Early Modern Britain* (Cambridge, 1997), 93–132.

[24] CUL MS Add. 4481, fo. 3ʳ (Elizabeth Elstob to George Ballard, 29 Aug. 1735 (written as 1795)).

and Interregnum Anthony Wood had made occasional notes on churches, but the real turning point for him was gaining admission to the Arts End of the Bodleian in 1653, 'where the books of English historie and antiquities stand', and where he was delighted to happen upon a copy of William Burton's *Description of Leicestershire*. Three years later, he greeted the appearance of Dugdale's *Antiquities of Warwickshire* with rapturous enthusiasm as 'the best book of its kind that hitherto was made extant'. A few weeks after reading Dugdale, he undertook a more systematic survey of the monumental inscriptions and armours in various Oxford churches and college chapels, and by the following summer he was back in the Bodleian, reading the manuscript of Leland's *Collectanea*, a work still unpublished a century after its learned compiler's death. In 1658 Wood ventured further afield to collect inscriptions from rural Oxfordshire churches. When granted access to the university archives in 1660 he worked so frantically, 'least the keys should be taken away from him', that after a while he looked ill, whereupon the keeper, John Wallis, took pity on him and allowed him to take the documents home.[25] The initiation of William Stukeley two generations later was very similar. When he was 12 he obtained some specimens from a pot of Roman coins and 'began a collection & drew them out on paper, as I got them, & that gave me an inclination to antiquitys'. At the same time he developed an interest in drawing which would make him one of the most visually accurate of the early eighteenth-century antiquaries. Of his visits to Avebury, 'an antiquity altogether unknown' and then Stonehenge (a trip he took with the brothers Samuel and Roger Gale), he remarked that the latter 'surpriz'd me beyond measure'. It was to become a lifelong preoccupation.[26]

Once incubated, the antiquarian virus could rage into obsession. Bishop Francis Godwin, the Jacobean antiquary and ecclesiastical historian, enthusiastically seized on any interesting old object, manuscript, or coin that he unearthed. Writing to Camden in 1604 about an old inscription he had removed from a 'ruinous thatcht house', Godwin was barely able to contain his rapture as he hoped 'ere long to gather together so many antiquityes of thys kynd, as you will think it worth a journey to come & see them'.[27] This is the same sort of zeal shown by Wood several decades after, and by Stukeley half a century later still. But even their fixation on the past pales beside the outpourings of the Yorkshire curate Abraham de la Pryme, who had an almost pathological love of old things. Pryme virtually provides a self-parody of the antiquary, his 'zeal for old MSS., antiquitys, coins and monuments' being so great that it 'almost eats me up, so that I am sometimes almost melancholy that I cannot prosecute ye search of them so much as

---

[25] Wood, *Life and Times*, i. 326.

[26] Bodl. MS Eng. misc. e. 121, Stukeley memoirs, fos. 4ʳ, 11ʳ; in MS Top gen. e. 61, fo. 87ᵛ (vol. reversed), he notes 'three pecks' of coins, mainly from the reign of Gallienus, found in 1696. The coins found are drawn in MS Num. e. 18. For Stukeley's life and career, see S. Piggott, *William Stukeley: An Eighteenth-Century Antiquary* (Oxford, 1950; rev. edn., 1985); but cf. the important revision to Piggott's treatment of Stukeley in Ucko *et al.*, *Avebury Reconsidered*, esp. p. 54.

[27] BL MS Cotton Julius F. VI, fo. 299.

I would'.[28] Pryme got his first taste of antiquities at the age of 14, when he was taken by relatives to see the church at Beverley, where he was unable to read the monumental inscriptions; from there they went to Hull, 'where we saw most of the raritys'. The following year he visited York and was especially struck with the Minster and the royal statues contained in its chapel. Various 'reliques of famous and noble houses' were scattered about the city, but most exciting was the house of Sir Arthur Ingram, the Jacobean financier, which had a garden decorated with fountains, gardens, and statues of Roman emperors, most of which were 'much consumed by time'.[29] John Woodward—whose own preoccupations led him to mistake for Roman a sixteenth-century shield—warned against the blinding effects of antiquarian enthusiasm. 'I cannot but be somewhat surprized to find a gentleman of the great diligence and ingenuity of Mr [William] Somner taking the Roman bricks, that he observed in the walls of Canterbury, for British bricks', Woodward wrote. 'But 'tis not easie, when once a man suffers himself to grow fond of a subject, not to be over far transported, and screw things to a pitch much too high for those who are only indifferent lookers on, and not touch'd with the passion that such a writer may himself feel.'[30]

THE HISTORIC SITE

Interest steadily developed in buildings, ruined and refurbished, and in points on the map which, because they could not be moved from their original settings, had to be experienced outside the walls of the library. Travellers from Leland to Defoe visited the scenes of famous battles and political events, which themselves were becoming part of an everyday civilized idiom among the gentry. At the time that Leland was writing, in the 1540s and early 1550s, public consciousness of the 'historic site' was neither widespread nor particularly well informed: remarks on historical points emerge incidentally from travels undertaken for other purposes than antiquarian interest. By 1640, and still more half a century later, such knowledge had become relatively commonplace: one has simply to track the travels in the 1690s of Celia Fiennes, no great font of erudition, to see that trips were now being deliberately made to particular places of historical significance. In Britain and abroad, tour guides of sorts were available to show the visitor the highlights, and travellers could purchase engravings of individual sites or of town prospects with interesting features foregrounded (Fig. 5.2). Mary Wortley Montagu reported seeing in Tunis the reputed tomb of Achilles, which Alexander the Great is supposed to have run around naked, in Achilles' honour; this, she added drily, 'no doubt was a great comfort to his ghost'. The merchant James Houblon,

---

[28] *The Diary of Abraham de la Pryme, the Yorkshire Antiquary*, ed. C. Jackson, Surtees Soc., 54 (1869), 203.

[29] Wood, *Life and Times*, i. 182–243, *passim*; *Diary of Abraham de la Pryme*, 7.

[30] John Woodward, *An account of some Roman urns, and other Antiquities, lately digg'd up near Bishops-gate* (1713), 20. On Woodward's own tunnel vision see Levine, *Doctor Woodward's Shield*.

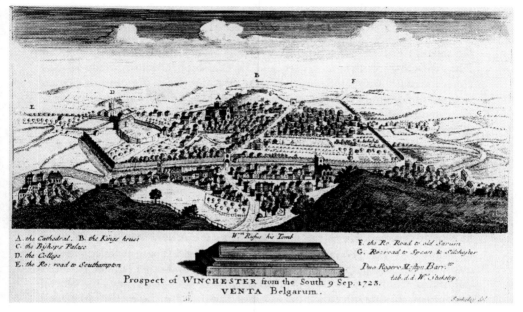

Fig. 5.2. 'Prospect of Winchester, from the south, 9 Sept. 1723'. In fact, the prospect is from the east; note the reference to major buildings and roads, and the foregrounding of William Rufus's tomb. Hants. RO Top. 343/2/3

travelling in Italy in 1699, found that 'In most great towns you will find antiquaries to shew you the curiosities of the place, and at Rome for a pistoll you may have one who will attend you all the time you are there.'[31] In the early eighteenth century the people of Woodstock built on the legend that a tree had turned to stone on the death of Henry II's mistress Rosamond, signifying her salvation. They showed travellers not only an imitation of the stone (which in fact had been at Godstow nunnery), but also a pond called 'Rosamund's Pool' in which she had bathed. This they did, said Hearne, 'for no other reason but to get money'.[32] We will return to this economic aspect of antiquarian activity, and its relation to popular memory and tradition, at various points throughout the remainder of this book.

This movement of a formerly recondite class of information into the realm of routine civility was certainly owed in part to the labours of Elizabethan antiquaries such as Camden and Stow. Their published works provided the seventeenth-century gentry, clergy and, increasingly, town-dwellers with the earliest form of tour guides to sites of interest. Stow's detailed *Survey of London* and Camden's *Britannia* were books much less important for any scholarly discovery they made

---

[31] *The Letters and Works of Lady Mary Wortley Montagu*, ed. W. Moy Thomas, rev. edn., 2 vols. (1887), i. 251; *Private Correspondence and Miscellaneous Papers of Samuel Pepys, 1679–1703*, ed. J. R. Tanner, 2 vols. (New York, 1926), i. 187.

[32] Thomas Hearne, *Gulielmi Neubrigensis historia*, 3 vols. (Oxford, 1719), cited in J. Westwood, *Albion: A Guide to Legendary Britain* (1985), 232–3.

in their own right than as guides for antiquaries of the following century.[33] In the wake of *Britannia* alone, prominent early Stuart county gentry such as Sir Edward Dering, Sir Symon Archer, and Sir Christopher Hatton would all take closer looks at the antiquities of their shires,[34] as did clerics from Bishop Francis Godwin to Edmund Gibson. A future bishop of London, Gibson would synthesize a century of post-Camden county information into the revised 1695 edition of *Britannia*, a recension of the great work that in itself reflects the trend away from the older chorography in its modest inclusion of archaeological materials.[35]

The availability of various historical and antiquarian writers in print had an even broader impact on tourists with few scholarly aspirations. The widely travelled Peter Mundy, making a recreational 'petty progress' through parts of England and Wales in 1639, during a break from his various expeditions 'in the service of and att the cost off others', had read Stow and many chronicles before he took to the road. He reveals familiarity with, if not deep knowledge of, most of the events or persons connected with particular places. These included the various Oxford colleges, 'the worcks off Kings, Queenes and other famous persons', the ruined Monmouth Castle, 'in which Henry the Fifft was borne', the funeral monuments of King John and Prince Arthur Tudor at Winchester Cathedral, and the burial site at St Albans of 'good duke Humphrey' of Gloucester, of whom Mundy had a vague notion that he 'was poisoned aboutt the tyme off the Civill Warres beetweene the Houses off Yorcke and Lancastar'. A mere decade later, in 1649, the 32-year-old John Worthington, embarked on a tour of the southern and western counties, shows a much clearer command of the history behind points of interest, undoubtedly aided by repeated references to the copy of *Britannia* which he carried with him. Worthington passed by 'the meadows & river, where Magna Charta was sworn'; he came two days later to the New Forest, 'where William the Conqueror's sons Richard & Rufus were slain', before ending up at the ancient, mysterious site of Stonehenge, for which no such connections to political history could be made.[36]

There had also been a dramatic increase in the level of 'common' knowledge of history acquired through other channels than the major authors. By the middle of the seventeenth century, many schoolboys and undergraduates were

[33] E. Moir, *The Discovery of Britain: The English Tourists* (1964), 1–57. By the early eighteenth century, the degree of public knowledge of their own county and their family histories among at least the gentry of Hertfordshire was sufficiently strong for several of them, meeting at a Sessions of the Peace in 1711, to insist that Sir Henry Chauncy honour the commitment made in the preface to his *Hertfordshire* to correct any errors in a later edition: Nichols, *Literary Illustrations*, iv. 79 (Chauncy to Robert Dale, 20 Mar. 1711).

[34] Archer referred to Hatton as 'a generall sercher of all antiquities concerning the whole kingdome, but cheifely Northamptonshire, his own country': BL MS Add. 28564, fo. 221 (Archer to Thomas Habington, 26 Dec. 1634); ibid., fo. 233 (Archer to Hatton, 22 Jan. 1638); J. Wake and G. Isham, 'Sir William Dugdale in Northamptonshire', *Northamptonshire Past and Present*, 22 (1955), 8–12.

[35] Emery, *Edward Lhuyd*, 59–61. Later, eighteenth-century editions of *Britannia* continued this trend: Hunter, 'The Royal Society and the Origins of British Archaeology', 195–6.

[36] *The Travels of Peter Mundy in Europe and Asia, 1608–1667*, ed. R. C. Temple, 5 vols. in 6 (Cambridge, 1907–36), vol. iv (Hakluyt Soc., 2nd ser., 55 (1925)), 15, 23, 25–6, 31; *The Diary and Correspondence of Dr John Worthington*, ed. J. Crossley, p. 1, Chetham Soc., os 13 (1847), 32, 34, 36.

receiving at least informal exposure to English history on top of the regular diet of Latin and Greek, so much so that incidental references to monuments and scenes of great historical significance became, by 1700, quite unremarkable. Popular media such as almanacs regularly included historical 'facts' in their pages, beginning in the late sixteenth century. Among the notable features of Newark recorded by John Percival in his travel diary of 1701 is the brief remark that 'King John here ended his life'; the ruined Kendal Castle was 'the birthplace of Catherine Parr'.[37] When the Reverend Jeremiah Milles (1717–84) made his tour of England and Wales in the 1730s he knew that Holdenby House, by then in ruins, was 'remarkable for having been the place of K. Charles the 1st's retirement'. As for Carnarvon Castle, he needed no reference to Camden or other guides for its historic significance as the birthplace of Edward II, a fact which he observed 'Every body knows'.[38]

It was not merely the leisured sons and daughters of the well-to-do who visited such scenes. Men of business, travelling on other matters than curiosity, could take the time to break their journeys with a trip to a monument or building of note. Henry Prescott, the deputy registrar of Chester diocese, a stay-at-home haunter of pubs rather than an impassioned antiquary, took note of the sites of interest that fell in his path, such as the chamber in an inn where he stopped overnight at Newtown, called 'the Kings Room from K. Charles 1st having lain in it when in [16]44 in these parts'. Sleeping in the same chamber and perhaps the same bed as the martyred monarch almost certainly appealed to this High Churchman, who regularly kept 30 January in (for him) relative sobriety, and civil war battlefields such as Edgehill and Worcester also figure prominently on his tours.[39] The travels of the Plymouth surgeon James Yonge tell a similar tale. While aboard ship he visited Rhegium, 'the place that Paul landed from Syracusa'. As he grew older and went to sea less often, he contented himself with domestic visits to places such as Westminster Abbey and Henry VII's chapel, wherein lay, he thought, 'most of the kings that have reigned in England'. Yonge's diary reminds us that awareness of the historical past was often casual and passive rather than deep and profound—as one would expect from most tourists today. Yonge noted, for instance, the chair in which all kings since William I have been crowned as 'an old thing and under it is a great stone brought out of Scotland by King James and said to be of some such ancient use'. On a subsequent trip, to Richmond, he saw 'the place the Duke of Buckingham and the Earl of Shrewsbury fought, and the latter [was] slain' (referring to a duel between the two peers on 16 January 1668), and the place where Queen Elizabeth had died. At Lansdowne in 1681 Yonge stood on the site of the 1644 civil war battle. In each case, the remarks are those

[37] Sir John Percival, *The English Travels of Sir John Percival and William Byrd II: The Percival Diary of 1701*, ed. M. R. Wenger (Columbia, Mo., 1989), 99, 135. On travel and tourism within England, see Moir, *The Discovery of Britain*, 1–57; R. W. Frantz, *The English Traveller and the Movement of Ideas, 1660–1732* (Lincoln, Nebr., 1967), 15–30.

[38] BL MS Add. 15776, fo. 22ʳ, travel notes of Jeremiah Milles, who also asserted (fo. 260ʳ) that 'Everybody knows that [William Rufus] was accidentally shot whilst he was hunting in the New Forest.'

[39] *The Diary of Henry Prescott, LL.B., deputy registrar of Chester Diocese*, ed. J. Addy, J. Harrop, and P. McNiven, 3 vols., Rec. Soc. of Lancashire and Cheshire, vols. 127, 132, 133 (Chester, 1987–97), ii. 325, 327, 440.

of a somewhat bored observer rather than an enthusiast; and at Winchester, where Yonge saw the tombstone of William Rufus, he added the disappointed qualifier 'though it's said his bones are removed' and the limp afterthought that 'Here also lies the body and monument of another king whose name I have forgotten.'[40]

We are now accustomed to praising the efforts of the giants of Tudor and Stuart antiquarianism, wishing to see in them our scholarly precursors. The names of two Williams, Camden and Dugdale, stand out among the many funeral monuments that historians of English historiography have erected to their illustrious ancestors.[41] The enormous influence of Camden and the extraordinary energy of Dugdale justify this high opinion, and similar bouquets can without fear be tossed on the graves of John Aubrey, Edward Lhwyd, or even the erratic Robert Plot. Their achievements need little by way of further encomium here. What is sometimes overlooked, however, is that their efforts were highly dependent upon voluntary contributions of epitaphs, coins, inscriptions, and muniments from interested individuals in all parts of England. Their contribution lay less in the individual nuggets of information that they uncovered than in the 'value added' in scholarly technique, combined with the capacity to keep the material they received in circulation through their correspondence and printed works.[42] The rising interest in the national past fed information into works such as *Britannia* and the Elizabethan-Jacobean county surveys, and maintained a steady readership for them. The regular re-publication of these works and the periodic addition of new ones from 1600 to 1700 in turn created even more interest in the shires and boroughs. Thus William Blundell the younger, heir to his Catholic grandfather's antiquarian interests, made sure that the latter's 1611 discovery of some Anglo-Saxon coins—which the older man had identified through reference to the 1607 edition of *Britannia*—found their way into Gibson's 1695 revision of Camden's book.[43]

By far the vast majority of individuals who were interested in antiquities never set down their researches in any systematic fashion. Still fewer actually published the results. A number left behind manuscript collections: Thomas Beckham, an East Anglian cleric who may have written the earliest chorography of Norfolk, for instance; or Thomas Stanley, an Elizabethan Cheshireman whose collection of antiquities, preserved in family papers, would be rescued and continued in the

[40] *The Journal of James Yonge* [1647–1721] *Plymouth Surgeon*, ed. F. N. L. Poynter (London, 1963), 77, 157, 173–4, 184, 193.
[41] For two recent examples see Levine, *Humanism and History*, and Mendyk, *'Speculum Britanniae'*.
[42] This aspect is highlighted in Graham Parry's recent study of seventeenth-century antiquarianism, *The Trophies of Time* (Oxford, 1995).
[43] Woolf, 'Little Crosby and the Horizons of Early Modern Historical Culture', and below, ch. 7.

early eighteenth century by the Chester bookseller Randall Minshull.[44] Walter Chetwynd, a Stafford MP and antiquary, is now known principally for having encouraged Robert Plot to publish his *Natural History of Stafford-shire*; Chetwynd's extensive collections, including the revised edition of William Burton's *Leicestershire* that he projected but never saw into print, remain in the Staffordshire Record Office.[45] Several others ended up like Saintlow Kneviton (or St Loe Kniverton), 'an ancient fellow' of Gray's Inn whose own chorography of Derbyshire has been lost but who provided information on the county to Camden and on the Inns of Court to Sir George Buck; or like the Warwickshire scholar Edward Palmer, 'a curious and diligent antiquarie' who assisted Camden with his section on Gloucestershire but who never published a word himself. Palmer has become little more than a footnote to the history of antiquarianism, a man whose collection of coins and antiquities was lost after his death, 'coming into the hands of such persons who understood them not'.[46] The same is true of his contemporary, James Strangman, self-confessed 'lover of antiquities in generall', whose Essex collections were to be useful to Morant over a century later. Beaupré Bell, at the other end of our period, left his books, medals, and manuscripts to Trinity College, Cambridge, and is principally known to us for having assisted the more famous Francis Blomefield and Thomas Hearne.[47] Of the obscure Onslow Gardyner, a mid-seventeenth-century Croydon collector who inherited the herald John Philipot's collections in 1648, virtually no information survives.[48] And an even greater number, scribbling sketches and notes in

[44] Bodl. MS Gough Norfolk 26, 'An hystoricall & chorographicall description of Norffolk', attributed to Beckham by Thomas Tanner and consisting of a short descriptive section followed by detailed notes and monumental transcriptions for each parish; Bodl. MS Gough Cheshire 1, a neatly drawn up presentation MS of Thomas Stanley's 'Antiquitys concerning Cheshire; collected from authentick records', fos. 3–242 of which are by Stanley (dated 1591,with some 1595 additions), and the balance of which was added later by Minshull.

[45] Staffs. RO D 649/4/1, printed edition of Burton interleaved with notes by Chetwynd and additions; Staffs. RO D 649/4/2, a manuscript version of the same, apparently prepared for printing, perhaps written by Chetwynd's chaplain and amanuensis, Charles King. Chetwynd inherited Burton's manuscripts from the latter's son Cassibelan, having also inherited many of Sampson Erdeswicke's earlier Staffordshire collections: see M. W. Greenslade, *The Staffordshire Historians* (Stafford, 1982), 41, 49, 54; Plot, *Natural History of Stafford-shire*, 392; J. Broadway, *William Dugdale and the Significance of County History in Early Stuart England*, Dugdale Soc. Occasional Papers, 39 (1999), 17–18; D. Williams, 'William Burton's 1642 Revised Edition of the "Description of Leicestershire"', *Leicestershire Archaeological and Historical Society Transactions*, 50 (1974–5), 30–6.

[46] George Buck, *The third universitie of England*, in Stow, *Annales*, ed. Edmund Howes (1631), 1073; Camden, *Britain*, trans. Philemon Holland (1610), 366; BL MS Cotton Otho E X, fo. 301; Anthony Wood, *Athenae Oxonienses: an exact history of all the writers and bishops who have had their education in the University of Oxford*, ed. P. Bliss, 6 vols. in 4 pts. (1813–20), ii. 28.

[47] John Nichols, *Literary Anecdotes of the Eighteenth Century; Comprising Biographical Memoirs of William Bowyer*, 9 vols. (1812), v. 278–82; McKisack, *Medieval History in the Tudor Age*, 147; *DNB*, sub 'Bell, Beaupré'.

[48] Coll. Arms, index to owners of Vincent MSS, vol. i, p. 480, by R. Yorke. Gardyner (d. after 1648) is now known simply as the individual who preserved the Philipot manuscripts and sold them to Arthur Annesley, earl of Anglesey (d. 1686), whose estate sold the MSS to the College of Arms. I am indebted to Mr Robert Yorke for allowing me access to the college's muniments and to his unpublished index of owners. The college today contains a large number of similar collections assembled by obscure individuals, such as MS Vincent 195, 'Gatherings of Shropshire, Ao 1584', a collection of church armorials with additions in seventeenth-century hands.

the privacy of their own houses and rectories, have never been recorded at all, or are known in passing, like the anonymous mid-seventeenth-century reader who annotated his copy of Stow's *Survey of London* with armorial and monumental notes, or the vicar of Caerleon, who kept notes on his church's antiquities in his own copy of Camden's *Britannia* during the 1720s.[49]

As the number of antiquaries increased between the death of Elizabeth I and the Restoration, correspondence and cooperation between them improved, both within England and, to a lesser extent, internationally. Although travel to sites of interest became easier during the seventeenth century, most antiquaries remained dependent upon friends and colleagues for information. The Worcestershire scholar Thomas Habington, a Catholic exiled to his manor after the Gunpowder Plot, drew upon an extensive list of correspondents across England to aid him in the study of his shire's antiquities. So did Warwickshire's Sir Symon Archer, who asked George Brock to come for a visit in 1635 and to bring along transcriptions of two funeral inscriptions, admonishing his friend to 'be sure not to mistake what is there engraven on the Brasse'.[50] Even Francis Bacon, who thought antiquarianism an inferior form of history, suited to lesser men, went to the modest trouble of having John Selden dig up some archival sources for his *History of Henry VII*.[51]

By 1700 few antiquaries studied in isolation, and those with even the most casual interests generally had like-minded friends or correspondents with whom to converse. One is struck repeatedly by the dogged determination of individual scholars to track down books and documents of various sorts, public and private, and also by the increasing sense among many of a responsibility to make these materials reasonably accessible to those who came suitably recommended by mutual acquaintances.[52] The centralized recording of historical manuscripts—a remote antecedent of the Historical Manuscripts Commission and National Register of Archives—began informally among the revived Society of Antiquaries in the reign of George I. It was proposed that each of its members catalogue all the materials on English history in their custody, 'fairly written on whole sheets of paper', and with a view to publication.[53] The publication of guidebooks to official records commenced even earlier owing to their practical applications, as lawyers such as Arthur Agarde and Thomas Powell produced manuals for searching archives which circulated widely in manuscript long before they reached print. Dugdale, from the somewhat different perspective of a herald, produced a local equivalent in a

[49] Bodl. shelfmark L.3.7.Art, copy of 1633 edition of Stow, later the property of Richard Rawlinson; Bodl. MS Top. gen. e. 85, p. 16, for a note of the Caerleon vicar by Thomas Martin, who visited the area in 1724.

[50] Habington, *Survey of Worcestershire*; BL MS 28564, fos. 231–2 (Archer correspondence).

[51] D. R. Woolf, 'John Selden, John Borough, and Francis Bacon's *History of King Henry the Seventh*, 1621', *Huntington Library Quarterly*, 47 (1984), 47–53.

[52] The spirit of scholarly generosity should not, of course, be overemphasized: given the polemical nature of much intellectual activity throughout the period, and divisions among the learned according to religion, political disposition, and sheer personal dislike, it is not surprising that the amicable tone of much of the correspondence is balanced in equal measure by scathing denunciations, satirical barbs and polemical attacks, the tone of which did not improve between the sixteenth and eighteenth centuries.

[53] SAL, Minute Book 1718–32, 10 Feb. 1720.

set of *Directions* for the finding of provincial records in the Tower.[54] Although
Elizabeth I had ignored pleas for a national library, her government initiated
the classification of diplomatic papers by creating the State Paper Office under
Dr Thomas Wilson, a repository that survived until it was swallowed by the Public
Record Office in the nineteenth century. Further attempts came with William Prynne
in the 1660s, and then William Petyt, who was nominated by the Lords after the
Glorious Revolution to improve the order of the Tower records. A variety of Com-
mons committees from 1703 to 1732 took pains to survey the holdings of several
government departments.[55] The labours of Thomas Rymer, Thomas Tanner,
Richard Rawlinson, William Nicolson, and other historico-bibliographical scholars in the early eighteenth century would continue this work of managing the
Crown's documentary inheritance.

The civil war wreaked havoc on particular repositories of records and documents, as it did on ecclesiastical art, though there were a few lucky escapes. The
Yorkshire antiquary Roger Dodsworth managed to transcribe many of the documents housed in St Mary's Tower, York, before it was destroyed in the siege
of 1644. Sir Thomas Fairfax, the parliamentary commander, was praised by the
royalist Dugdale as a 'preserver of antiquities' for having promised a reward to
soldiers who could retrieve any of the ancient charters blown up in the siege.[56]
Outside wartime other dangers could threaten. The Great Fire, which ruined
several booksellers and destroyed entire runs of some books, was kinder to
London's manuscript collections, but the College of Arms lost some irreplaceable materials (despite having had a full day's notice to move them).[57] Much of
Elias Ashmole's early collections was consumed in the terrible Middle Temple
fire of 1679. Most notoriously, the Cottonian Library was gutted by a 1731 fire that
destroyed many of its holdings.[58]

Despite the disasters of war, fire, flood, and sheer neglect, efforts were well under
way by the Restoration (including the labours in the Tower of the former puritan agitator Prynne) to preserve what existed and begin to take stock of it. Some
sixty years afterwards, a project was initiated to index the public records. This
did not get very far, but the correspondence it generated demonstrates both the

---

[54] Arthur Agarde, *The Repertorie of Records* (1631); William Salt Library, Stafford, 5 MS 505,
'Directions for the Search of Records, and making use of them in order to an historicall discourse of
the Antiquities of Staffordshire' (c.1680), printed as an appendix to Greenslade, *The Staffordshire
Historians*, 161–3, and probably intended by Dugdale for his nephew, John Huntback (1639–1705) of
Featherstone. For discussion of the records and attempts to make sense of them, see McKisack, *Medieval
History in the Tudor Age*, and R. B. Wernham, 'The Public Records in the Sixteenth and Seventeenth
Centuries', in L. Fox (ed.), *English Historical Scholarship in the Sixteenth and Seventeenth Centuries*
(1956), 11–48.

[55] Wernham, 'The Public Records', 26–7.

[56] Parry, *The Trophies of Time*, 222; S. Porter, *Destruction in the English Civil Wars* (Phoenix Mill
and Stroud, Glos., 1994), 64–89, for civil war depredations in general. Dodsworth died in 1654 and
left his collections to Fairfax, who deposited them in the Bodleian Library.

[57] Pepys, *Diary*, vii. 410 (16 Dec. 1666).

[58] C. H. Josten, *Elias Ashmole (1617–1692): His Autobiographical and Historical Notes, his
Correspondence, and Other Contemporary Sources Relating to his Life and Work*, 5 vols. (Oxford, 1966),
iv. 1635–7, 1643; R. F. Ovenell, *The Ashmolean Museum, 1683–1894* (Oxford, 1986), 11, 13.

difficulties faced by early users of such materials and also the degree to which cooperation could lower barriers and reduce distances. With the assistance of George Holmes, the deputy keeper of the Tower records (most famous for his work on Rymer's *Foedera*), John Baynard made copies of a number of records, in the Tower and other repositories such as the Cottonian library, for Dr John Thorpe, the leading antiquary in Rochester. The cost of transcribing ten Anglo-Saxon deeds was quoted by the Cottonian librarian to Baynard at 2s. 6d. each, and research delays were common. Baynard apologized to Thorpe that he would have been able to do more work on his transcriptions 'if Mr Chibley had not carried out the key of the place where they are kept, on Thursday last, & his clark had stayd at home to day'. The North American scholar who has experienced short opening hours and limited reprographic facilities at record offices can only sympathize.[59]

Other endeavours to improve the preservation and cataloguing of documents occurred in the eighteenth century. A committee of the House of Lords was appointed in December 1718 to undertake an inspection of the keeping of the records in the Tower, and in debate it was Bishop White Kennett who spoke most strongly about the need for serious archival management (incidentally repeating the infamous, and apocryphal, tale of Polydore Vergil shuffling off back to Rome with England's choicest manuscripts):

I will presume to say that no nation has been so happy in preserving so vast a multitude of their ancient monuments and records as our English nation has been, from the time of the Norman Conquest (as they call it) which is near 700 years. We have more original MSS and papers for our political and historical affairs, than any one nation, perhaps than all the nations in *Europe* have. And we should have had many more, if, my Lords, your noble Ancestors had frequently taken the same care that your Lordships are now taking, to examine into the state and condition of your public records, and into the strength and safety of the places, wherein they are reposited.[60]

The sheer logistics involved in making antiquarian expeditions, easily underestimated by those who follow such itineraries in the modern era of the cheap day return and the inexpensive bed and breakfast, is evident from the planning of Browne Willis for conducting a survey of his own county, Buckinghamshire. This included a list of the distances to each part of the county from his home at Whaddon, with those more than a day's ride away separated from the rest.[61] Even the early modern equivalent of a 'where to stay while doing research' listserv enquiry can be found in the Scottish historian Sir Robert Sibbald's advice to Edward Lhwyd on how to find not only accommodation but also useful guides to places of interest between the Forth and the Clyde.[62] Visitors often had to contend with local

[59] SAL MS 202 (Thorpe papers), fo. 16ʳ (Baynard to Thorpe, 14 Aug. 1725); ibid., fo. 18ʳ (same to same, 2 May 1726).
[60] SAL Misc. I (Letters and Papers), art. 15, 9 Dec. 1718; *Journals of the House of Lords*, 21 (1718–21), Anno. 1718 5 Geo., pp. 19–20. For similar measures with respect to local records see Ch. 8 below.
[61] Bodl. MS Willis 68.
[62] Bodl. MS Carte 269, fos. 131ᵛ–132ʳ, n.d. (c.1700); for Sibbald's career and importance in Scottish antiquarianism and science see R. Emerson, 'Sir Robert Sibbald, Kt, the Royal Society of Scotland and the Origins of the Scottish Enlightenment', *Annals of Science*, 45 (1988), 41–72.

antagonism towards strangers, roads of uneven quality, and public indifference. Locals were often willing to help the visiting scholar, but the assistance they could provide was sometimes limited. When the Augustan antiquary Thomas Machell visited Windermere church in 1692, he spotted some interesting coats of arms on the east window and, fearful of heights, sent the local schoolmaster up a ladder to investigate them, but he soon found that the man had 'no manner of skill in heraldry' and was thus obliged to draw them for himself from a distance.[63] Other antiquaries met with more serious resistance: Weever complained in *Ancient Funerall Monuments* in 1631 that, though he had been taken inside many churches by parish churchwardens, in some instances he had been denied sufficient opportunity to study a church's monuments or transcribe its epitaphs 'for that I wanted a warrent'.[64]

To reduce the wastage of time and money and to carry out visits more systematically, Restoration and Augustan antiquaries sometimes circulated 'Queries', heads of topics listing the questions to which answers were required, and invited responses from interested readers. Plot did this for his study of Staffordshire, while in the 1670s Thomas Machell sent a four-sheet list to the gentry of Westmorland and Cumberland, 'That the northern counties which abound in antiquities and ancient gentry, may no longer be bury'd in silence. Information is desired concerning the following queries as they lye in order.'[65] William Holman's and Browne Willis's systematic questioning of gentry in their respective shires, described earlier in Chapter 4, are further examples of the same exercise applied more narrowly to questions of descent.

Antiquaries travelling from place to place could also take advantage of third-party acquaintances, using letters of introduction from well-connected collectors such as Sloane or the Harleys to make the acquaintance of informed local scholars and interested amateurs. When Dr Cromwell Mortimer, fellow of both the College of Physicians and the Royal Society, was obliged to go to Rochester 'on account of curiousities', his colleague Sloane asked John Thorpe, another physician and the leading antiquary of early Georgian Kent, to assist Mortimer in his enquiries.[66] Established and self-sufficient scholars also used such letters of introduction in their capacity as patrons of the less fortunate but intellectually deserving. In 1695 Samuel Pepys provided a letter of introduction to Dr Thomas Smith, keeper of the Cottonian library, on behalf of a 23-year-old draper's

[63] *Antiquary on Horseback*, ed. J. M. Ewbank, Cumberland and Westmorland Antiquarian and Archaeological Soc., ES 19 (1963), 114. Machell, a fellow of Queen's College Oxford and former chaplain to Charles II, left an extensive unfinished history of Westmorland in six volumes in the Cumbria RO (Carlisle): Dean and Chapter Library, Machell MSS; see H. Prince, 'Towards an Account of Thomas Machell', typescript volume in Cumbria RO; and J. Rogan and E. Birley, 'Thomas Machell the Antiquary', *Transactions of the Cumberland and Westmorland Antiquarian and Archaeological Society*, NS 55 (1955), 132–53.

[64] Weever, *Ancient Funerall Monuments*, 'To the Reader', quoted in Parry, *Trophies of Time*, 206.

[65] Prince, 'Towards an Account of Thomas Machell'; Rogan and Birley, 'Thomas Machell the Antiquary'; R. Porter, *The Making of Geology: Earth Science in Britain 1660–1815* (Cambridge, 1977), 18–19, 37; Gunther, *Early Science in Oxford*, xiv. pp. 17–18.

[66] SAL MS 202 (Thorpe papers), fo. 212[r] (Sloane to Thorpe, 29 July 1730).

apprentice from Coventry, whose sole desire was 'a curiosity only to see the inside of Sir John Cotton's library' with its vast collection of manuscripts. Despite his humble background, books were not 'wholly strangers' to this young man, none other than the future palaeographer, librarian, and Anglo-Saxon scholar, Humfrey Wanley.[67] Years later, when Wanley had established himself as librarian to the Harleys, he was not above commenting on the less fortunate status of others such as Alban Thomas, one-time assistant to Edward Lhwyd, the keeper of the Ashmolean. In contrast to Lhwyd, who had succeeded his own superior Robert Plot (whom he despised) in 1690, Thomas was passed over on Lhwyd's death in 1709 for another junior, David Parry, and soon found himself out of a job altogether. He wrote to Rochester's Thorpe asking if he knew of 'any place whereby I could get my livelihood, and if possible with some gentleman that has any curiosity in naturall things'. Thomas expressed a strong wish to acquire some work with Sloane, whom he knew to be a friend of Thorpe's.[68] Even in the rarified world of antiquarian scholarship, it helped to be 'networked'.

A measure of the social interaction among scholars between the time of the great Renaissance patronage connections and the modern era of the international scholarly conference can be found in documents like the *album amicorum*, a kind of Renaissance 'guest book' of autographs, and in correspondence. Camden's frequent exchanges of books, papers, and miscellaneous information with a constellation of celebrated Continental scholars made the English study of the past anything but insular, and his extensive list of correspondents was inherited by younger men such as Cotton, Selden, Ussher, and Edward Pococke, who began to add oriental books, manuscripts, and antiquities to the list of subjects they studied.[69] In the twelve years between June 1720 and September 1732, William Stukeley's *album amicorum* was signed by a Who's Who of English intellectual life that included Newton, Halley, Wren, William Whiston, the earl of Pembroke (Stukeley's principal patron), Godfrey Kneller, Hans Sloane, Roger and Samuel Gale, Humfrey Wanley, and Ralph Thoresby.[70] That it is less cosmopolitan a collection of names than one finds in Camden's circle a century or so earlier should not be taken as a sign of closed borders so much as an index of the powerful growth of the domestic scholarly community and the stronger interconnections of antiquarianism and natural philosophy. A well-established European republic of letters still lay very much at the disposal of English antiquaries, collectors, and

---

[67] *Private Correspondence of Samuel Pepys*, i. 104.

[68] SAL MS 202 (Thorpe papers), fo. 230ʳ (Thomas to Thorpe, 25 July 1709). Thorpe in fact offered the impoverished Thomas some work, documented in subsequent letters (fos. 232–4); Wanley, *Diary*, i. 9.

[69] BL MS Add. 36294 (Camden's letterbook); Bodl. MS Selden Supra 108–9 (Selden correspondence); *Gulielmi Camdeni et illustrium virorum ad G. Camdenum epistolae*, ed. T. Smith (1691). For international scholarship and communication involving Cotton, Camden, Selden, and other early Stuart antiquaries see K. Sharpe, *Sir Robert Cotton 1586–1631: History and Politics in Early Modern England* (Oxford, 1979), and Woolf, *Idea of History in Early Stuart England*, 204–10. For the sociability underpinning this 'republic of letters', in particular late Renaissance notions of virtue and friendship, see P. N. Miller, *Peiresc's Europe: Learning and Virtue in the Seventeenth Century* (New Haven, Conn., 2000), 49–75.

[70] Bodl. MS Eng. misc. d. 459, unfoliated.

virtuosi. This republic would survive even the gradual decline of Latin as its lingua franca, a change that (ironically in the ultra-classicizing Augustan age) lent Latin language works an exotic and recondite image that they would not have possessed a century earlier.[71] The doors of English antiquarian collectors, who increasingly had some personal exposure to the great wealth of European treasure-houses, lay open to visiting European scholars. In addition to the various refugees from persecution who sought shelter in England, a steady stream of occasional visitors runs from the Dutch geographer Abraham Ortelius in the 1570s (who first encouraged Camden in his plans for a national historical topography) to the French-born orientalist and traveller Sir John Chardin, who held the Royal Society captive to his tales of the ruins of Nineveh in 1680, and enlisted the aid of its members in publishing his works in England.[72]

Within a generation after the Restoration the community of antiquarian interest, overlapping with the mathematical, zoological, and botanical communities, had expanded to include printers, booksellers, and readers in the production of knowledge. Readers interested in antiquarian and philological scholarship supported expensive projects such as the 1695 re-edition of *Britannia* through advance subscription or outright donations. On the recommendation of its dean, Thomas Comber, the chapter of Durham Cathedral voted the nonjuring bishop George Hickes £20 in 1698 to support the publication of his Anglo-Saxon grammar.[73] As the cost steadily rose of producing increasingly elaborate volumes on antiquities, history, and natural history, illustrated with expensive engravings, prospective authors distributed proposals in advance of publication to secure the cooperation of worried booksellers.[74] They were not always successful in this regard. Lhwyd complained that the thrifty undertakers of the 1695 *Britannia* expected him to produce his thorough revisions of the Welsh sections using only materials available in Oxford.[75] When George Fleming, a Lancashire cleric, received in 1699 proposals for a natural history of the county by Dr Charles Leigh, he sought Thomas Tanner's opinion as to the project's worth. 'I must desire your oppinion of the work, and whether it's worth my purchase or no. For we poor country clarks cannot as Fellows of College open our purses for every book that's printed.' Philip

---

[71] John Anstis, who confessed that he did not write or read in Latin more than once a year, nevertheless considered a manuscript written in that language 'the masterpiece of my collections, & that it may be without having anything extraordinary in it'. Essex RO D/Y/1/1/2 (Holman correspondence, unfoliated, John Anstis to Revd William Holman, n.d. 1720). Anstis's statement on his rare use of Latin must, however, be taken carefully since as a herald he would in fact have had to read, though not write, it with some frequency.

[72] Evelyn, *Diary*, iv. 212–14, 369.

[73] *Camden's Britannia* (1695), ed. E. Gibson; G. Walters, and F. Emery, 'Edward Lhuyd, Edmund Gibson, and the Printing of Camden's *Britannia*, 1695', *The Library*, 5th ser., 32 (1977), 109–37; Levine, *Humanism and History*, 174–7; *Autobiography and Letters of Thomas Comber*, ed. C. E. Whiting, Surtees Soc., 156–7 (1941–2), i. 35; Mendyk, 'Speculum Britanniae', 212–15.

[74] Publishing by subscription is covered in greater detail in my book, *Reading History in Early Modern England* (Cambridge, 2000), ch. 6.

[75] Ovenell, *The Ashmolean Museum*, 80; Walters and Emery, 'Edward Lhuyd, Edmund Gibson and the Printing of *Britannia*'.

Kinder attempted to raise support for his projected history of Derbyshire by dedicating a 'prolusion' or prospectus of his 'future historie' to the nobility, gentry, and commons of the shire. This document described the methods to be used in the history and expressed the need for 'some good clarke' to copy documents in the Tower and elsewhere—'or', a hopeful Kinder added, 'if I have advance I will doe it my selfe'.[76] The involvement of local, county, and national connections in getting work published demonstrates that even if the great aristocratic Maecenases of the Tudor and early Stuart era had not been shoved aside, there were now all sorts of opportunities available for a kind of 'micropatronage' by the general public.

The early institutional embodiments of all this activity were creations of common interest rather than engines of scholarship in their own right. Already by the 1580s there were enough interested scholars in London, with connections to the provinces and, more important, abroad, to found the first Society of Antiquaries. This met, with interruptions, till 1614, when the scholars were given to believe, Spelman tells us, that James I 'misliked' their activities.[77] While a great deal of what the antiquaries had to talk about pertained to the Romano-British past, they by no means neglected the Middle Ages, as indicated in their discourses. These remained unpublished until Thomas Hearne edited them early in the eighteenth century as a kind of testament to the ancestry of his own activities.[78] The Elizabethan discourses had little direct influence on those without access to copies, but they did at least provide a temporary outlet for what was then still a small number of scholars. When the society ceased to meet, the Cottonian library took its place as a centre for the exchange of information and a major repository of manuscripts, until Charles I had it locked up in the 1630s. After the civil war, a reopened Cottonian library remained, and a string of Sir Robert's successors in the baronetcy maintained the collection until 1702, when Sir John Cotton, the fourth baronet, donated it to the nation. By that time, there were other bodies as well, such as the Royal Society and Gresham College, whose members' interests clearly overlapped with those of the antiquaries. It is thus almost as an afterthought that in 1718, a little more than a century after its Jacobean dissolution, and a few years after it had commenced informal gatherings on the

[76] Bodl. MS Tanner 21, fo. 5ʳ (Fleming to Tanner, 12 Nov. 1699); Bodl. MS Ashm. 788 (Kinder, prolusion to *Historie of Darby-shire*), fos. 191ᵛ–204, esp. 199ᵛ. Kinder was unsuccessful, and the work was not published until the nineteenth century.

[77] L. Van Norden, 'The Elizabethan College of Antiquaries' (Ph.D. thesis, University of California at Los Angeles, 1946); ead., 'Sir Henry Spelman on the Chronology of the Elizabethan College of Antiquaries', *Huntington Library Quarterly*, 13 (1949–50), 131–60. The extent of antiquarianism can be demonstrated by a list of the re-founders of the Society of Antiquaries, SAL, Misc. I, Letters and Papers 1707–40, art. 2; and by a list and bibliography of the members of the Elizabethan society (art. 3), including antiquaries of the intervening century, perhaps assembled to provide the society with an unbroken descent and suggesting its continuous existence, rather like the Apostolic Church.

[78] BL MSS Stowe 1045–6; MS Cotton Faustina E. V; Coll. Arms, MS Vincent 106 (Augustine Vincent's commonplace book), unfoliated, esp. 27 Nov. 1590, 'What is the Antiquitye & exposicion of the woord sterlingorn or sterling'; Thomas Hearne, *A Collection of Curious Discourses*, ed. J. Ayloffe, rev. edn., 2 vols. (1771).

Elizabethan model, the Society of Antiquaries was reconstituted in London, where it remains today.[79]

The eighteenth century was, of course, the classical era for the foundation of clubs and intellectual and charitable societies, so it was perhaps inevitable that London did not retain a monopoly on associations of scholars and virtuosi. The Society of Dilettanti, founded in 1734, was based in London but focused on the salvation of classical and especially Greek antiquities, sponsoring artistic and antiquarian expeditions to Ionia throughout the middle and later years of the eighteenth century.[80] In the provinces, 'gentlemen's clubs' would begin to form which, because they took an interest in antiquarian and historical matters, are the recognizable ancestors of modern local historical associations. The first of these appeared at Spalding in 1709 and was followed by a second at Peterborough in the 1720s.[81]

It is very tempting to see such interests in a whiggish light as pioneering the free and open discussion of historical matters; it should at all times be recalled that early modern antiquarianism possessed in spades the conservative and anti-innovative inclinations noted above in Chapter 2. This attitude, perhaps natural in minds firmly fixed on the past, is nowhere clearer than in the uniformly establishment and Anglican membership of the revived Society of Antiquaries, whose members expelled one of their number, Joseph Hall, following his censure by the House of Lords for heterodoxy in 1720.[82] Yet Stuart Piggott's judgement that the society was founded at the start of a long period of Georgian decline in the practice of antiquarianism, a period of renewed foundation myths and 'fantastic' philological speculation, which the society itself 'did little to arrest', seems unduly harsh. It is easy to dismiss as derivative, naive, and amateur the efforts of eighteenth-century enthusiasts driven by excitement rather than learning into publishing works of less value than those earlier achievements of Camden, Dugdale, and Lhwyd. But that is once again to fall into the trap of viewing the matter from the modern scholar's perspective: in fact, the circulation of antiquarian knowledge, right or wrong, promoted a yearning to understand the past that continued to develop between the time of George I and that of Victoria.[83]

[79] Levine, *Humanism and History*, 73–106; J. Evans, *A History of the Society of Antiquaries* (Oxford, 1956).

[80] W. H. Stiebing, Jr, *Uncovering the Past: A History of Archaeology* (Oxford and New York, 1993), 121.

[81] SAL, Minute Book 1718–32, p. 70 (14 Nov. 1722) for Peterborough; for Spalding see SAL Misc. 2 (Letters and Papers 1718–36), art. 18 (3 Mar. 1730); Nichols, *Literary Anecdotes*, vi. 1–162.

[82] SAL, Minute Book 1718–32, p. 31 (28 Feb. 1720). Hall's book, *A Sober Reply to Mr Higgs's Merry Arguments* (1720), had allegedly ridiculed the doctrine of the Trinity and was burned by the hangman; Hall's name was ordered to be expunged from the society's book. For the religious context of historical debates at this time see J. A. I. Champion, *The Pillars of Priestcraft Shaken: The Church of England and its Enemies, 1660–1730* (Cambridge, 1992), 25–98.

[83] S. Piggott, 'Antiquarian Thought in the Sixteenth and Seventeenth Centuries', in his *Ruins in a Landscape*, 21. This early essay of Piggott's, first published in the 1950s, remains a useful survey, but is less sympathetic to the eighteenth-century achievement than his later essays in the same volume, and subsequent monographs such as *Ancient Britons and the Antiquarian Imagination: Ideas from the Renaissance to the Regency* (1989).

FROM CLOSET TO MUSEUM

The urge to collect was powerful, and its force increased in the seventeenth century, together with the level of disposable wealth allotted to its pursuit by the social elite. This eventually included well-off merchants and tradesmen, professionals, and civil servants in addition to the traditional land-owning classes. It should immediately be pointed out of course that only a portion of the collecting activity that occurred in the 1600s pertained to antiquities. A typical closet, such as that of the lawyer Sir Edward Coke, who died in 1634, or the merchant Daniel Thomas, who died exactly seventy years later, might include a variety of bric-a-brac arranged in no particular order, and with the oldest objects granted no special place of honour. Coke's collection included books, manuscripts, and coins. Thomas's was even more variegated, reflecting both his occupation and the increasingly close alliance by 1700 between antiquarian interests and a taste for the instruments of modern technology. It comprised several hundred books, some maps, two model churches, a sailing compass, three telescopes, and some fishing tackle, while elsewhere in his house he had collected nearly a hundred pictures, a Noah's ark, and numerous weapons.[84] Nevertheless, it is clear that for some collectors, such as the second earl of Clarendon, whose tidily arranged cabinet of imperial medals was catalogued in 1700, the remnants of other times exuded an especially powerful attraction.[85]

Public interest in the visible traces of the past grew slowly but steadily in Elizabeth I's reign, and more quickly from about 1600, especially in London. London came to dominate the country commercially and culturally in the course of the seventeenth century, a time of increasing consumption during which various forms of leisure activity were increasingly concentrated in the capital. By 1700 London had attracted many collectors and their treasures; the same was true, to a lesser degree, of larger towns such as Bristol, and of England's two universities and their environs.[86] A trip to the galleries and museums of London was to the provincial visitor the equivalent of the visits to European collections made by wealthier youths on the Grand Tour. Some, like Evelyn, were constant travellers to and from the metropolis; others, like the Worcestershire squire Henry Townshend, came on occasion to see such wonders as the Egyptian mummy which arrived on a trading

---

[84] P. Earle, *The Making of the English Middle Class: Business, Society and Family Life in London, 1660–1730* (1989), 296. For Coke's antiquities, coins, books, etc., partially listed, see Hist. MSS Comm., *Report on Manuscripts in Various Collections*, 8 vols. (1901–14), iv. 323.

[85] Bodl. MS Smith 23, pp. 1–6, list of Clarendon's medals compiled c.1700 by Thomas Smith.

[86] On London's importance, see M. Kitch, 'Capital and Kingdom: Migration to Late Stuart London', in A. L. Beier and R. Finlay (eds.), *London 1500–1700* (1986), 224–5; Earle, *Making of the English Middle Class*, ch. 1. On life and leisure activity outside, see S. McIntyre, 'Bath: The Rise of a Resort Town, 1660–1800', in *Country Towns in Pre-Industrial England* (Leicester, 1981), 197–249; A. MacInnes, 'The Emergence of a Leisure Town: Shrewsbury 1660–1760', *Past and Present*, 120 (1988), 53–87, and *The English Town 1660–1760* (1980); D. H. Sacks, *Trade, Society and Politics in Bristol 1500–1640* (1985); Robert Tittler, *The Reformation and the Towns in England: Politics and Political Culture, c.1540–1640* (Oxford, 1998), 275–304.

vessel in 1662, 'preserved in and with her coffin entire 2500 years at least from any putrefaction'.[87]

The process whereby great collections of antiquities and *naturalia* were assembled in Britain and on the Continent has become much clearer over the past twenty years owing to detailed documentary research into the acquisition of items by individual collectors or the purchase or inheritance of whole collections by wealthier and more expansionist rivals.[88] Many smaller collections simply remained in the family at the death of their owner: when Sir Nicholas Bacon, Bt., composed his will in 1666, he left his son Edmund all his 'pictures, auncient coynes & medalls', though the pictures were to remain in the house of his widow until her death.[89] The general tendency was for smaller cabinets of marvels, manuscripts, and books to be gobbled up by bigger ones, sometimes as direct bequests from one scholar to another, but just as often through passage to uninterested or cash-hungry heirs who quickly placed them on the market. When the recorder of Kendal, Thomas Brawthwaite, died in 1674, he left his small collection of 'ancient medals and Roman antiquities' from the Roman camp at Ambleside to the provost of Queen's College, Oxford; a similar collection belonging to the Gloucestershire antiquary Timothy Nourse went on his death in 1699 to the Bodleian 'in thankful remembrance of the obligations I have to that famous university'.[90] John Bargrave, prebendary of Canterbury, gave his collection of medals and other antiquities to the cathedral library, while saving his engravings of 'the ancient ruines, statues, fountains' and other antiquities of Italy for his nephews.[91] When Lord Melfort fled to France in the wake of the Glorious Revolution, his personal collection of

---

[87] *The Diary of Henry Townshend of Elmley Lovett, 1640–1663*, ed. J. W. Willis Bund, 2 pts., Worcestershire Hist. Soc. (1915–20), pt. 1, 85. For other examples of early interest in Egyptology, see the travel notes of the mathematician John Greaves (in the Middle East in 1637–38), Bodl. MS Savile 49, esp. vol. iii, fo. 13ᵛ, and vol. iv, fo. 10; and an undated inventory of Egyptian antiquities in England drawn up by William Stukeley in the mid-eighteenth century, SAL MS 264, fo. 73ʳ⁻ᵛ.

[88] O. Impey and A. MacGregor (eds.), *The Origins of Museums: The Cabinet of Curiosities in Sixteenth- and Seventeenth-Century Europe* (Oxford, 1985), esp. A. MacGregor, 'The Cabinet of Curiosities in Seventeenth-Century Britain' (pp. 147–58), J. D. Hunt, '*Curiosities* to Adorn *Cabinets and Gardens*' (pp. 193–203), and M. Hunter, 'The Cabinet Institutionalized: The Royal Society's "Repository" and its Background' (pp. 159–68); P. Findlen, 'The Museum: Its Classical Etymology and Renaissance Genealogy', *Journal of the History of Collections*, 1 (1989), 59–78, and the same author's *Possessing Nature: Museums, Collecting, and Scientific Culture in Early Modern Italy* (Berkeley and Los Angeles, 1994); K. Pomian, *Collectors and Curiosities: Paris and Venice, 1500–1800*, trans. E. Wiles-Portier (Cambridge, 1990), 34–44; Muensterberger, *Collecting*, 183–203 (esp. on the German *Wunderkammer*); A. MacGregor, 'Collectors and Collections of Rarities', in A. MacGregor (ed.)., *Tradescant's Rarities: Essays on the Foundation of the Ashmolean Museum* (Oxford, 1983), 70–97; Sharpe, *Sir Robert Cotton*, chs. 1–3; P. C. D. Brears, 'Ralph Thoresby: A Museum Visitor in Stuart England', *Journal of the History of Collections*, 2 (1989), 213–24.

[89] Bodl. MS Tanner 312, fo. 27ᵛ, will of Sir Nicholas Bacon, Bt. (20 Feb. 1665/6).

[90] *The 'Boke off Recorde' of the Burgh of Kirkbie Kendall*, ed. R. S. Ferguson, Cumberland and Westmorland Antiquarian and Archaeological Soc., ES VII (1892), 245; Hearne, *Remarks and Collections*, i. 3.

[91] CKS, PRC 32/54/481, will of John Bargrave, DD, prebendary of Canterbury Cathedral, 29 April 1676 (proved 28 May 1680), now reproduced in David Sturdy and Martin Henig, *The Gentle Traveller: John Bargrave, Canon of Canterbury and his Collection* (Canterbury, 1985); a recent study of Bargrave as a collector is S. Bann, *Under the Sign: John Bargrave as Collector, Traveler, and Witness* (Ann Arbor, Mich., 1994).

relics, pictures, and 'rare pieces of antiquity', valued at £1,000, was seized and exhibited at Castle Tavern in Paternoster Row.[92]

Larger collections were concentrated in the hands of wealthy professionals such as the Augustan physicians John Woodward and Sir Hans Sloane.[93] The latter inherited the coins, medals, and *naturalia* of the London virtuoso William Charleton alias Courten in 1702, and purchased the botanical collections of James Petiver. Together with the libraries of political figures from Sir Robert Cotton to Sir Robert Harley, these collections gravitated into London, where they formed the basis for the British Museum in the middle of the eighteenth century.[94] Oxford was not far behind, and would develop the second greatest collection of books and manuscripts in the kingdom, in large measure owing to the early influence of powerful men such as Sir Thomas Bodley himself and Archbishop Laud. The latter was responsible, among other things, for the acquisition of the Greek manuscripts belonging to the Venetian Giacomo Barocci, imported into England by the stationer Henry Fetherstone, and deposited with Laud (then bishop of London and the university's chancellor), who in turn encouraged the earl of Pembroke to buy them and donate them to the Bodleian.[95]

It was through such munificence that the university also became the home to many natural specimens, inventions, and antiquarian curiosities. The extensive botanical and zoological collections of the former royal gardener and client of the duke of Buckingham, John Tradescant, who had presented a stuffed dodo to the Oxford anatomy school in 1634, passed to his son in 1637.[96] After the younger John Tradescant died heirless in 1662, the Tradescant collections became the subject of a bitter Chancery suit between the latter's widow, Hester, and the astrologer, antiquary, and, for a time, Windsor herald Elias Ashmole. Chancery ruled in Ashmole's favour, but Hester was allowed to keep the closet of rarities for a few years, until she was found drowned in her own pond, possibly a suicide. Ashmole, meanwhile, had been negotiating with Oxford University for a 'room' that soon became a building, and in 1683 he was finally able to deposit the collections in the new Ashmolean Museum, under the initial curatorship of Robert Plot. There the Tradescant rarities joined the equally famous remnants of an earlier collection, the Arundel marbles, and were soon augmented by further

---

[92] Devon RO Z19/40/3 (Portledge Library, Lapthorne-Coffin correspondence, vol. ii, Lapthorne to Coffin, 14 Feb. 1691).

[93] MacGregor, 'Cabinet of Curiosities', in *Origins of Museums*, 157; G. R. de Beer, *Sir Hans Sloane and the British Museum* (1953), 108–34; W. E. Houghton Jr., 'The English Virtuoso in the Seventeenth Century', *Journal of the History of Ideas*, 3 (1942), 51–73 and 190–219. Haskell, *History and its Images*, 20, speculates that the medical training of many early numismatists may have been partly responsible for the relatively high standard of technical achievement in that branch of historical study.

[94] On the foundation of the museum, its various purposes, and the social limits on its 'public' access see A. Goldgar, 'The British Museum and the Virtual Representation of Culture in the Eighteenth Century', *Albion*, 32 (2000), 195–231.

[95] F. Madan et al., *A Summary Catalogue of Western Manuscripts in the Bodleian Library at Oxford*, 7 vols. (Oxford, 1895–1953), vol. ii, pt. 1, p. 3. Pembroke also added a Javanese manuscript which, according to Laud, no one in England could read.

[96] M. Allan, *The Tradescants: Their Plants, Gardens and Museum, 1570–1662* (1964).

bequests such as the manuscripts of Ashmole's father-in-law, Dugdale, and by donations from the likes of Martin Lister and John Woodward.[97]

Techniques of preservation and systematic cataloguing were in their early and rather carefree stages. Woodward, who had previously acquired catalogues of several European collections, dictated a catalogue of his own cabinet (consisting of minerals, fossils, and his famous iron shield) from his sick-bed in 1725, with regrettably misleading results.[98] But attempts were made to publicize acquisitions. The opening of the Ashmolean on 24 May 1683 was heralded, Anthony Wood tells us, by the beadles visiting each college and hall to inform the doctors and masters. Individuals might even publicize their own collections. The Tradescant catalogue was published in 1656, and in 1664 Robert Hubert, alias Forges, would publish an exhibition catalogue of foreign rarities, principally natural, that would eventually be purchased by the Royal Society. These included: an Egyptian mummy 'adorned with hieroglyphicks, that shew both the antiquity, and eminent nobility of the person, whose corpse it is'; a giant's thigh bone found in Syria; 'a peece of old worme-eaten barke of a tree in stone'; 'a rose of Jericho, that is an hundred years old'; and various other curiosities, several of which were of interest simply for having been previously owned by such notables as the Emperor Ferdinand III, and King Charles I. There are lesser examples, such as James Petiver, who issued a series of catalogues of his principally botanical collection between 1695 and 1703, the contents of which would eventually be purchased by Sloane.[99]

The strict security measures that surround most museums today were not practised then, and it is not surprising that many of the most valuable exhibits could go astray. In 1691 the new keeper of the Ashmolean, Edward Lhwyd, wrote to the collector William Charleton to report that the museum had been robbed of eighteen valuable items, including several coins, pieces of amber, a small picture of John Aubrey in water colour by Samuel Cooper, and a picture of Archbishop Richard Bancroft set in an ivory box. (Lhwyd's book-keeping was imprecise, and

---

[97] *Diary of Thomas Crosfield*, ed. F. S. Boas (1935), 71, 135 n.; Josten, *Elias Ashmole*, i. 143–4, iii. 853–4, and iv. 1646, 1816; Evelyn, *Diary*, iii. 199; Porter, *Making of Geology*, 21–2; M. E. Jahn, 'The Old Ashmolean Museum and the Lhwyd Collections', *Journal of the Society for the Bibliography of Natural History*, 4 (1962–8), 244–8; M. Welch, 'The Foundation of the Ashmolean Museum', in MacGregor (ed.), *Tradescant's Rarities*, 59–69; R. F. Ovenell, *The Ashmolean Museum 1683–1894* (Oxford, 1986), 1–17 and *passim*; M. Hunter, *Elias Ashmole 1617–1692* (Oxford, 1983), 1–27; Piggott, *Ruins in a Landscape*, 102, 106–7; M. Swann, *Curiosities and Texts: The Culture of Collecting in Early Modern England* (Philadelphia, 2001), 27–38.

[98] Having dictated part of this to his amanuensis Joseph Polden, the incomplete work, discontinued on his recovery and journey abroad, was miscopied by John Hindle, 'who not being a master of Latin, I fear it is very wrongly and ill wrote'. CUL MS Add. 7570, fo. 1ʳ, dated 31 July 1727.

[99] Wood, quoted in M. Welch, 'The Ashmolean as Described by its Earliest Visitors', in MacGregor (ed.), *Tradescant's Rarities*, 59–69; [R. Hubert alias Forges], *A Catalogue of Many natural rarities, with great industry, cost, and thirty years travel in foraign countries . . . and dayly to be seen, at the place called the musick house, at the Miter, near the West end of Paul's church* (1664), 1–2, 37, 47; J. Petiver, *Musaei Petiveriani* (1695–1703). Woodward's own catalogue was published upon his death in 1728: C. Bateman and J. Cooper, *A Catalogue of the Library, Antiquities, &c. of the Late Learned Dr. Woodward* (1728).

this proved an underestimate of the losses.) They had disappeared between 17 and 22 September—but Lhwyd could narrow it down no further. Lhwyd described the person whom he suspected, a recent visitor to the museum, as 'a forreign gent. supposed by his speech to be a German . . . betweene forty & fifty years of age, a pretty corpulent man with a red full face, a long periwig, a shite coat pretty much worn'. The keeper noted that one Mr Alexander, of Gerard Street, was a person 'suspected of sometimes receiving such commodities'. Lhwyd asked Charleton to make enquiries of a prominent informant, none other than Godfrey Kneller, who in turn put him in touch with one Dr Pragestus at the Latin coffee house in Ave Maria Lane, who 'knows all outlandishmen'. This antiquarian all-points bulletin apparently yielded results, as within a day the keeper had traced the mysterious stranger, now established as a Dutchman, to the Abingdon Road, but the objects were never recovered; only Ashmole's own illness and imminent death saved Lhwyd from the founder's fury.[100]

MANUSCRIPTS AND RARE BOOKS

Ancient and medieval manuscripts held a fascination for collectors throughout the early modern period. Sir John Strangeways, a leading Somerset gentleman, was fond of showing off the old Saxon deed to his manor of Chiselborough.[101] Even a century and a half after the advent of print, the handwritten document retained a privileged status, reflected in the fact that poets, antiquaries, and historians continued to present their works to patrons and friends in that form. The virtuoso Francis Kynaston indulged his antiquarian interests near the end of the masque *Corona minervae* by having the audience of royal and noble children receive gifts of books, one of which, labelled *Manuscripti*, is inscribed

> Amongst so many bookes tis not oreslip't
> That you have here a Manuscript.
> You well may see by what you doe finde in't
> 'Twas done by hand and never yet in Print.[102]

Collectors were remarkably willing in the face of limited security to share their manuscripts. 'I desire you to send the Antiquitys of Oxford in manuscript by the bearer and you will oblige', wrote Robert Clavering, in Lambeth, to Dr John Thorpe, then attending a Royal Society meeting.[103] As Aubrey would put

---

[100] BL MS Sloane 3692 (Charleton papers), fos. 288ʳ, 291ʳ (Lhwyd to Charleton, 25 and 26 Sept. 1691), transcribed in Ovenell, *The Ashmolean Museum*, 64–5; Josten, *Elias Ashmole*, iv. 1883–6.

[101] Thomas Gerard, *The Particular Description of the County of Somerset*, ed. E. H. Harbin, Somerset Rec. Soc., 15 (1900), 136.

[102] T. Kelly, *Early Public Libraries* (London, 1966), 43, citing Aubrey, *Natural History of Wiltshire*, ed. J. Britton (1847), 78–9; Francis Kynaston, *Corona Minervae* (1635), sig. Dᵛ.

[103] SAL MS 202 (Thorpe papers), fo. 87ʳ (Robert Clavering to Dr John Thorpe, 29 Aug. 1713).

it, in his grandfather's days the manuscripts had flown like 'butterflies'.[104] Certainly they were routinely passed back and forth for criticism and comment, while books changed hands from private libraries with increasing frequency, and scholars watched for the publication of lists giving the contents of personal collections put up for sale after the death of their owners.[105] The letterbooks of historians, antiquaries, and virtuosi from Camden to Rawlinson are full of references to manuscripts and rare books, together with stones, coins, and other marvels, committed with a surprising readiness to the 'common carrier', or to tradesmen willing to take letters or parcels.[106] Yet even by 1700, when the conditions of transportation had improved considerably, some antiquaries remained wary of transporting their treasures. Thomas Hearne noted the damage inflicted on books transported carelessly over even short distances, and the topographer Thomas Cox of Bromfield, Essex, frequently complained of the unreliability of the post. His fear of the 'uncertainty' of it provided him with an excuse not to return the manuscripts and books he had borrowed from William Holman in Halstead, some miles away, and not to lend out others of his own.[107] Given the obvious and indisputable influence of print on knowledge of the past, it is easy to overlook the fact that many contemporary or recent works on antiquarianism and history circulated initially in manuscript.[108] The existence of a large number of copies of early works such as Sampson Erdeswicke's *Staffordshire*, not published for well over a century after it was written, or the works of various Devon antiquaries such as Thomas Westcote and Tristram Risdon, bears this out.[109]

[104] B. Gutfleisch and J. Menzhausen, '"How a Kunstkammer should be Formed". Gabriel Kaltemarckt's Advice to Christian I of Saxony on the Formation of an Art Collection, 1587', *Journal of the History of Collections*, 1 (1989), 3–32.

[105] Thomas Comber, dean of Durham, for example, kept a lending list in an interleaved almanac: among the books he borrowed from Sir Richard Graham, the sheriff of Yorkshire, were John Selden's *Titles of Honor* (1614), Richard Blome's popular chorography *Britannia* (1673), and an edition of the *Corpus Juris Civilis*; Graham in turn had the use of Comber's copy of Eusebius among other works: *Autobiography and Letters of Thomas Comber*, i. 76–7.

[106] Elias Ashmole, for instance, casually recorded, next to some extracts he had made from the French *Journal des Savants*, a note of the coins he had borrowed from his friend, William Petty: Bodl. MS Ashm. 826, fos. 64^r–67^v. BL MS Sloane 3962 (Charleton papers), fo. 264^r (Colerane to Charleton, 29 Mar. 1695) confirms that shipping large quantities of coins and medals was still a difficult and expensive process. Thomas Tanner observed that the celebrations at harvest time kept tradesmen such as weavers off the roads and delayed the arrival of letters: Bodl. MS Rawl. Essex 6, fo. 134^r (Tanner to William Holman, 24 Oct. 1718).

[107] Hearne, *Remarks and Collections*, v. 82; Essex RO D/Y/1/1/86, 87 (Thomas Cox to William Holman, 5 May and 14 Dec. 1716). Cf. the example of one Mr Seager, who borrowed the papers of Arthur Collins and apparently insisted on a fee for returning them: D/Y/1/1/62 (Collins to Holman, 8 Aug. 1715).

[108] On 'scribal publication' and the circulation of manuscripts see three excellent studies: H. Love, *Scribal Publication in Seventeenth-Century England* (Oxford, 1993); A. F. Marotti, *Manuscript, Print, and the English Renaissance Lyric* (Ithaca and London, 1995); and H. R. Woudhuysen, *Sir Philip Sidney and the Circulation of Manuscripts, 1558–1640* (Oxford, 1996), the range of which is considerably broader than its title suggests.

[109] Devon RO Z19/18/13a–b, a two-volume eighteenth-century copy of William Pole's *Survey of Devonshire* (1st pub. 1791), made in 1730 by the Revd George Harbin from an earlier copy by John Anstis, itself taken from the original; West Country Studies Library, Exeter, Acc. 110714, 'A view of Devonshire by Thomas Westcote' (late seventeenth-century transcript) and Acc. 106085–6, a two-volume copy of Westcote's work; West Country Studies Lib., Acc. 110715, Tristram Risdon's 'The

There is no doubt that subsequent scholarship owes a great deal to the major mid-Tudor collectors of earlier manuscripts, Leland, Bale, and Parker, as well as to their early Stuart successors, Ussher, Selden, and especially Cotton; it is almost certainly the case that the major editorial achievements of the later seventeenth and early eighteenth centuries, authoritatively depicted by D. C. Douglas long ago,[110] could not have occurred without the labours of earlier generations. A welling feeling of admiration stirs within us as we imagine them heroically saving priceless treasures from monastic ruins, as did Leland and Bale, or creating great collections, as did Parker and Cotton. Many modern bibliographers and editors know better, having scented some very soft clay at the feet of these scholarly idols. Their use of techniques of conservation and cataloguing, wherein manuscripts were frequently rearranged or interfered with to produce what to their minds were neater and more useful volumes, offer us less an Olympian summit of antiquarianism than a chamber of codicological horrors.

Parker, a less intellectually gifted scholar than Leland, offers perhaps the best (or worst) example. Queen Elizabeth's first archbishop of Canterbury and a former Master of Corpus Christi College, Cambridge, Parker has been much revered as a pioneering manuscript collector who, in the words of his Augustan biographer John Strype, was 'one of the greatest Antiquarians of the Age'. And at one level he remains a man to whom the scholarly community (which Strype revealingly called simply 'the world') owed a heavy debt 'for retrieving many antient authors, Saxon and British, as well as Norman'. Yet as editors have recognized from the time of Frederic Madden to that of Richard Vaughan (both of whom edited Matthew Paris from Parker's copy), the great patron of Anglo-Saxon and medieval learning in Elizabethan England was a fit heir to the tradition of codicological interference already exemplified by John Bale. Parker saw his manuscripts, many of which were acquired under licence from Lord Burghley, as an arsenal of weapons in the fight to place the Church on a more secure historical footing. He also played ducks and drakes with the integrity of individual manuscripts, taking a leaf out here, inserting one there, and crayoning through pages. R. I. Page, without succumbing to the harsh judgement of a Madden (who would most likely have had Parker ejected from his own library and his reader's ticket publicly burned), has carefully documented a number of examples of Parker's intrusions, some of which were made for purely aesthetic reasons. A tidy man, Parker habitually removed 'superfluous' opening or closing leaves, or added new ones; when time had left only part of a text extant at the start or

---

corographicall description of the county of Devon with the city & county of Exeter', dated 1616 but probably a later copy; and Acc. 4877, 'Notitia Devoniae', another copy of Risdon, with additions from Hooker's description of Exeter, purchased by an owner at Oxford in 1658 according to a note on the back page; and Acc. 43200, a late seventeenth-century transcript, probably made by John White (who certainly paginated it), in 1697. On Risdon, Hooker, and Westcote see J. Youings, 'Devon's First Local Historians', *The Devon Historian*, 1 (1970), 5–8.

[110] D. C. Douglas, *English Scholars 1660–1730*, 2nd edn. (1951) remains the best account of medieval scholarship from Dugdale to Hearne and Madox.

conclusion of a manuscript, a comparable intellectual orderliness dictated that he excise or erase the balance of that text in order to have a proper opening or conclusion to the entire manuscript. When the Anglo-Saxon Gospel book now known as CCCC MS 197B was sent out to be bound with other, paper manuscripts of smaller size, it was deliberately and substantially cropped to produce a new volume of uniform size, with the effect of destroying much of the margins of the text and spoiling a good deal of the illumination; this, too, can be laid at Parker's door.[111] The conflict between aesthetics and scholarship revealed by Parker's activities has parallels in attitudes to ruins and artefacts we shall explore more fully in Chapter 6.

Great libraries such as that which Humfrey Wanley would assemble for the Harleys did not rest on manuscripts alone. By the late seventeenth century, the manuscript had a new competitor for the hearts and purses of bibliophiles in the 'rare book'. As early as the opening of the Bodleian Library, in 1602, its founder fought off an attempt by his librarian, Thomas James, to separate books from manuscripts by arguing that some of the printed books were 'not muche lesse to be respected, then som of your rarer manuscripts'. A century later, incunabula in particular were regularly being separated from later printed books: the Cambridge University Library assigned a special stall, near the fossils and medals, 'where all the old books are put which were first printed'.[112]

Printing, a novelty in the early sixteenth century, had become so much an accepted medium after a century or more of use that the old book itself became, for the first time, an antiquity.[113] The mid-seventeenth-century antiquary Sir Symon Archer recalled his excitement when reading, as a boy, 'a very ancient history booke printed when printing first came into England'.[114] In 1678 John Evelyn, charged with purchasing the Arundel library for the Royal Society, bought several printed books and seven hundred manuscripts, noting that the printed books were 'of the oldest impressions' and were therefore 'not the lesse valuable' than the manuscripts. Five years later Evelyn was equally impressed by the collection of a Scottish antiquary which included not only 'divers Roman antiquities' but also a selection from the press of the great fifteenth-century printer Aldus Manutius; in 1699 he praised the library of the bibliophile Lord Spencer (later earl of Sunderland), which included several volumes 'printed at the first invention of that wonderfull art'.

[111] R. I. Page, *Matthew Parker and his Books* (Kalamazoo, Mich., 1993), 46–58 and plate 33; T. Graham, 'Matthew Parker and the Conservation of Manuscripts: The Case of CUL MS Ii.2.4', *Transactions of the Cambridge Bibliographical Society*, 10/5 (1995), 630–41. I thank Dr Mildred Budny for drawing these two studies to my attention, and for a valuable discussion of Parker's 'conservation' techniques.

[112] *Letters of Sir Thomas Bodley to Thomas James*, ed. G. K. Wheeler (Oxford, 1926), 25 f., 28. James fought a long battle on this point, but the principle of separating books from manuscripts was only established under his successor, John Rous; BL MS Add. 15776, fo. 40^r, travel notes of Jeremiah Milles, c.1735.

[113] For early attempts to establish the history of printing, and the copyright disputes that underlay this, see the account in A. Johns, *The Nature of the Book: Print and Knowledge in the Making* (Chicago, 1998), 324–79.

[114] Dugdale, *Life, Diary and Correspondence*, 272; P. Styles, 'Sir Simon Archer', in his *Studies in Seventeenth-Century West Midlands History* (Kineton, 1978), 9.

Among the many objects of interest sent to Abraham de la Pryme by his helpful parishioners was a Caxton translation of an unnamed work, published by Wynkyn de Worde in 1495. Thomas Brockbank asked a friend to lend him 'any thing of antiquity', particularly books dealing with the apostolic church, and even offered to pay for a private carrier to transport the item both ways.[115] Browne Willis, early in the eighteenth century, thought any book from before the Reformation 'old' and used printed material from that era together with manuscript episcopal registers to research his *Notitia Ecclesiastica*.[116] One of Thomas Baker's two copies of the *Polychronicon* was, he noted, among the oldest works printed by Caxton (1482) and was 'so scarce & dear that it cost me what I am asham'd to owne'.[117] The Society of Antiquaries, whose members' interests included specimens of the more recent past as well as the Roman and medieval artefacts of which they are more famous students, discussed at one of their meetings 'an old book printed by Winkyn de Worde'. Stukeley, one of its leading members, produced for another meeting 'the drawings of a very old pack of cards' from the cover of 'a very old printed book'.[118] The Royal Society was similarly interested in the early history of printing, in particular the technological 'progress of this invention' during its first years.[119] So vigorous had the market for old books grown by the later seventeenth century that the occasional book appeared with a colophon deliberately fabricated by its printer to create a false impression of antiquity.[120]

The Harleian library, in contrast to that of Sir Robert Cotton a century earlier, had a good collection of incunabula (many acquired from the earl of Sunderland's library at his death in 1722) once again thanks to the acumen and interests of Wanley, whose diary is full of items such as the 'very fine Tully printed by the old Aldus', which he hoped to acquire from Jonah Bowyer the bookseller in 1720. Palaeographer though Wanley may have been, he loved the early book nearly as much as the manuscript, as did his employer Edward Harley. So did Wanley's friend John Bagford. A regular supplier of rare books to the Harleian

---

[115] Evelyn, *Diary*, iv. 144–5, 330, v. 322; *Diary of Abraham de la Pryme*, 177; *The Diary and Letter Book of the Rev. Thomas Brockbank 1671–1709*, ed. R. Trappes-Lomax, Chetham Soc., NS 89 (1930), 177. For an early eighteenth-century list of works printed by Caxton and other old printed works, see SAL MS 264, fos. 110ʳ–111ᵛ, 118ʳ.

[116] Bodl. MS Willis 13, fo. 1c, recto. The growth in private collections is further testified by the publication of price lists for the cost of binding: such lists came out, for instance, in 1646, 1669, and 1695. See, for instance, the broadsheet *A generall note of the prices for binding all sortes of bookes* (Wing G. 504).

[117] F. Korsten, *The Library of Thomas Baker* (Cambridge, 1990), 6.

[118] SAL, Minute Book 1718–32, p. 73, discussed 28 Nov. 1722; ibid., p. 36 (9 Nov. 1720) for Stukeley's contribution, given him by Thomas Rawlinson. Other recent documents that the society studied included almanacs, parish records, prints, and pictures, and a 1655 letter patent of Oliver Cromwell (ibid., p. 63).

[119] [Humfrey Wanley], 'Some Observations concerning the Invention and Progress of Printing, to the Year 1465', *Philosophical Transactions of the Royal Society*, 288 (Nov.–Dec. 1703), 1507–16; the authorship is established as Wanley's in an editorial note in *Bodl. Lib. Rec.*, 6/6 (Sept. 1961), 634–5.

[120] Johns, *Nature of the Book*, 330.

library, and to the collections of Hans Sloane and John Moore, Bagford shared Wanley's low social origins. A London shoemaker turned book-dealer, he had a keen personal interest in the history of printing, and he possessed a collection of curious writing implements, such as a Chinese pen, that had attracted Wanley's attention as early as 1696.[121] Bagford's interests were taken up in the 1720s and 1730s by the likes of John Lewis, a Kentish cleric who would write the first biography of Caxton (but who thought Bagford 'a weak, inaccurate, and injudicious man [who] had not learning and knowledge enough for what he undertook'), and by Lewis's friend Joseph Ames, whose own labours led to his *Typographical Antiquities* in 1749.[122]

From being a curious innovation two centuries earlier, the early printed book had itself become an antiquity, though, as with buildings and artefacts, aesthetics and age bestowed different sorts of value. As Bagford's friend, the Cambridge bibliophile Thomas Baker, noted on his copy of the Jacobus Rubeus Venetian edition of Ovid's *Opera* (1474), 'this book, tho' very beautifull, yet has the marks of great antiquity', by which Baker meant its lack of pagination and the presence of some by then archaic typographical features. Baker would similarly comment on the disjunction between the contents of some books, now irrelevant to his age, and their value as prizes. Of the second Caxton edition of Vincent of Beauvais's *Mirror of the World* (1489), Baker noted 'It was then valued for the matter it contains, is now valuable for the print, & is yet a present for a Lord.'[123]

ANTIQUARIAN AND VIRTUOSO

Closely related to the spread of antiquarianism was the emerging idea of the gentleman as 'virtuoso'.[124] Beginning in the late Elizabethan period, antiquaries and interested noblemen such as the earl of Arundel and Lord Lumley, and scholars such as John Dee, assembled cabinets of marvels and curiosities to adjoin and adorn their libraries, symbolizing the connections between the worlds of nature, art, and learning. These often served more than scholarly interest, becoming pieces of furniture or decoration. The size of such collections became an index of honour and intellectual sophistication. At the time of his premature death in 1612 the young Prince Henry (whose royal father had already bestowed on him the

---

[121] Wanley, *Letters*, 25 (Wanley to Bagford, 15 Mar. 1696); for Wanley's evaluation of Bagford's collection, ibid. 244–7 (Wanley to Hans Sloane, 6 May 1707); Wanley, 'An Account of Mr. Bagford's Collections for his History of Printing', *Philosophical Transactions of the Royal Society*, 310 (Apr.–June 1707), 2407–10.

[122] Wanley, *Diary*, i. 15–16; M. M. Gatch, 'John Bagford, Bookseller and Antiquary', *British Library Journal*, 12 (1986), 150–71; Nichols, *Literary Illustrations*, iv. 157–97 (Ames–Lewis correspondence), esp. p. 173 for Lewis's dismissive comment about Bagford. On Bagford, Ames, *et al.*, see Johns, *Nature of the Book*, 347, 349, 352, 364–5.

[123] Korsten, *Library of Thomas Baker*, 3, 8.

[124] Bann, *Under the Sign*, 1–3; the classic account of virtuoso activity remains Houghton, 'English Virtuoso'.

former Lumley library) had assembled a 'cabinet-room' filled with a collection of paintings and 'medalls or antient coins of gold' worth £3,000.[125]

The distinction between the virtuoso and the antiquary is difficult to draw with any precision, and many collectors fit both labels. They shared, for a time, an interest in the *display* of artefacts and curiosities. The whole point of a cabinet of marvels or *monstra* is that they are a 'show' (*monstrare*), without significance if not seen, or even touched. The genuine virtuoso had much in common with the antiquary, frequently including an appetite for objects such as coins and medals; he was not always possessed of the historical sense which so many of the earliest antiquaries, especially those in the philological textual tradition (always much less dependent on communication by 'showing') reveal. It is especially hard to distinguish them before 1640, since many antiquaries had a wide range of interests. The separating islands of knowledge, observed John Selden (a philologist but no virtuoso), remained an archipelago that could still be bridged, each outcrop visible from another once it had been conquered.[126] William Camden's correspondence and various published works demonstrate a curiosity spanning classical literature, Roman antiquities, the history of the English language, old proverbs, emblems, and inscriptions. His contemporary Francis Thynne made notes on alchemy, drew Hermetic diagrams, and studied the writings of Ramon Lull. Nor did Thynne see these activities as being distinct from his antiquarian and historical investigations: his alchemical writings can be found in the same collection of notes which contains his biographical research into English kings for corrections to Holinshed's *Chronicles*; he also composed a tract for Lord Burghley on the origins of letters and communications.[127] John Dee, who is usually thought of primarily in connection with hermeticism and magic, was among the first Elizabethans to suggest the foundation of a national library.[128] The common element was 'curiosity' itself (in the sense of a quality of mind, rather than of a particular object), which through much of this period furnished the standard of appreciation for both nature and art, as the 'sublime' would come to do for a later age.[129]

---

[125] *The Letters of John Chamberlain*, ed. N. E. McClure, 2 vols. (Philadelphia, 1939), i. 391–3 (Chamberlain to Carleton, 19 Nov. 1612). Veterano, the aged protagonist of Shakeley Marmion's *The Antiquary*, extols the virtues of such antiquities as 'the registers, the chronicles of the age they were made in', proclaiming that they 'speak the truth of history better than a hundred of your printed commentaries': Shakerley Marmion, *The Antiquary*, Act II (no scene or line divisions), in *The Dramatic Works of Shakerley Marmion*, ed. J. Maidment and W. H. Logan (Edinburgh and London, 1875), 228.

[126] John Selden, *Titles of Honor*, 2nd edn. (1631), epistle dedicatory. The contrasts between European intellectuals of the age of Selden and his contemporary, Peiresc, and those of the later seventeenth century, as well as the greater weight acquired by science in between, are well treated in Miller, *Peiresc's Europe*, 148–51.

[127] Camden, *Remaines of a greater worke, concerning Britaine . . .* (1605), *passim*; BL MS Add. 11,388, fos. 39–44; Francis Thynne, 'Homo animal sociale', written for Burghley in 1578, BL MS Lans. 27, fos. 70–5, art. 36; D. Carlson, 'The Writings and Manuscript Collections of the Elizabethan Alchemist, Antiquary, and Herald Francis Thynne', *Huntington Library Quarterly*, 52 (1989), 203–72, esp. pp. 208–15.

[128] W. H. Sherman, *John Dee: the Politics of Reading and Writing in the English Renaissance* (Amherst, Mass., 1995), 37, 119.

[129] K. Whitaker, 'The Culture of Curiosity', in N. Jardine, J. A. Secord, and E. C. Spary (eds.), *Cultures of Natural History* (Cambridge, 1996), 75–90, at p. 76.

In the later seventeenth century this situation began to change, as collecting activities attracted a larger segment of the educated population. While many antiquaries (in defiance of the increasingly pejorative sense that word carried) acquired artefacts with some sense of the historical context within which they had been created, the virtuoso often collected 'curiosities' indiscriminately, with little attention to the contexts of time and space. To some virtuosi it did not matter even whether an object was especially old, so long as it was rare, unusual, and exhibitable. The German traveller Thomas Platter, who visited England at the end of the sixteenth century, had even then noted the number of people in London who had collections of curiosities—none of which, however, was especially 'ancient' or even historical. He was especially impressed with the collections of one wealthy citizen, which included African charms, Asiatic clothing, several 'heathen idols' and an Indian stone axe, which had come to him as a sponsor of commercial activity in the far east. Travelling abroad in the 1640s, the young John Evelyn saw several public and private galleries containing medals, gems, portraits, and richly bound books displayed together with old coins, fossils, and other genuine antiquities.[130] Francis Molle, on tour in Venice with his pupil Robert Clayton, wrote to Lady Clayton in 1698 that 'the curiosities and antiquities will take up some time befor all cane be seen', while young Clayton himself, though mildly interested in items like the sword of Scanderbeg and an engine which could light 500 matches at once, exuded an unmistakable air of boredom with the various items on display in St Mark's.[131]

Antiquarian interests had been the object of satire for some time, with John Donne, John Earle, and Shakerley Marmion all providing caricatures in the early Stuart period, and further mock-definitions appearing after the Restoration.[132] One of the Reverend George Plaxton's correspondents referred to an antiquary as 'a remover of Cornavian rubbish'.[133] Joseph Addison made fun of antiquaries in a satirical dissertation on the cat-call (a cheap metal whistle then popular), for which he consulted many antiquaries and a fellow of the Royal Society, who expressed various opinions as to its antiquity and origins.[134] But the antiquaries were not alone in being targeted. By the last quarter of the century, the generality and uselessness of virtuoso knowledge, treated so seriously by Kynaston, Peacham, and the Arundel circle in the 1630s, was also being satirized in the person of Sir Nicholas Gimcrack, the title character of Shadwell's *The Virtuoso* (1676), 'a rare mechanic philosopher' modelled on members of the Royal Society such as Boyle. For Gimcrack,

[130] Evelyn, *Diary*, i. 74, 77, 82; M. Hunter, 'John Evelyn in the 1650s: A Virtuoso in Quest of a Role', in Hunter, *Science and the Shape of Orthodoxy*, 67–98. For the early development of Continental numismatic interests, see Haskell, *History and its Images*, 13–79.

[131] Bodl. MS Eng. lett. c. 309 (Clayton papers), fo. 55ʳ (Molle to Lady Clayton, 9 Apr. 1698); ibid., fo. 51ᵛ (Robert Clayton to his uncle Sir Robert Clayton, 17/27 Feb., 1697/8).

[132] *Sermons of John Donne*, ed. G. R. Potter and E. Simpson, 10 vols. (Berkeley and Los Angeles, 1953–62), vol. i, no. 5, p. 246; John Earle, *Micro-cosmographie*, 6th edn. (1633), 246; Marmion, *The Antiquary*, cited above; *A new dictionary of the canting crew* (1690); cf. James Puckle, *The club: or a dialogue between father and son* (1711), 10–11.

[133] Staffs RO D593/K/1/1/7 (F[rancis] Skrimsher of Forton to G. Plaxton, 29 Sept. 1716).

[134] *The Spectator*, 361 (24 Apr. 1712), ed. D. F. Bond, 5 vols. (Oxford, 1965), iii. 351.

knowledge, not application, is the sole end, and 'so it be knowledge, 'tis no matter of what'. Swift would follow up with the Grand Academy of Lagado in *Gulliver's Travels*.[135]

Yet by Shadwell's time, and certainly by Swift's, the stereotype no longer precisely fitted the reality. There are signs as early as the Restoration of a willingness to separate the natural from the artificial, and the antiquity from the modern curiosity, rather as a division between manuscripts and printed books was already being made in libraries: Gimcrack's activities are all 'inventions' and experiments rather than book learning or antiquarian collection, quite unlike the collection of Marmion's Veterano, three decades earlier.[136] Sir Nicholas's fictitious will, published by Addison in the *Tatler*, would include everything from a female skeleton and a humming-bird's nest to a box of butterflies. While it mentions an Egyptian mummy, it is notably devoid of the usual sorts of antiquities: coins, Roman bricks, and manuscripts.[137] The satirized virtuoso in Judith Drake's *An Essay in Defence of the Female Sex* (once attributed to Mary Astell), is similarly a collector of seashells, not of Caesars.[138]

The antiquaries of the last quarter of the seventeenth century were, however, beginning to fall into distinct (if by no means mutually exclusive) sets. One group fixed their eyes more squarely on the past, where antiquarianism had begun a century or so earlier. There was a revival in medieval studies, as practised by Madox, Hickes, and Wharton among others, of the sort of manuscript- and text-based scholarship then being brought to a higher pitch in the realm of classical philology by the likes of Richard Bentley. Meanwhile, some exponents of the new natural philosophy were abandoning virtuosity in the other direction, calling for an orderly and discriminating inventory of knowledge of the natural world under various categories, and repudiating the cult of rarity in order to make knowledge not exotic, but comprehensive, familiar, and taxonomically organized.[139]

---

[135] Thomas Shadwell, *The Virtuoso*, II. ii. 303, and III. iii. 26–27, ed. M. H. Nicolson and D. S. Rodes (1966), 43, 69. For the ambivalent relations of the newer scientific community to the virtuosi, see Hunter, *Science and Society in Restoration England*, 66–72.

[136] Marmion, *The Antiquary*, edn. cit.; Houghton, 'English Virtuoso', suggests that Marmion's antiquary is in fact a virtuoso, though his chattels are predominantly *ancient* rarities like the 'urn that did contain the ashes of the emperors'. This is not mistaken, but it does suggest that the terminological confusion was then (at mid-century) at its most pronounced.

[137] *The Tatler*, 216 (26 Aug. 1710), ed. D. F. Bond, 3 vols. (Oxford, 1987), iii. 133–5; cf. Lady Gimcrack's fictitious letter to Bickerstaff in *Tatler*, 221 (7 Sept. 1710), ed. Bond, iii. 153–5. On the other hand, Lewis Theobald's satire on 'useless antiquaries' also included a mock will, of Sir Tristram Littlewit, who had mathematical instruments and air pumps with his coins, medals, and broken statues: Lewis Theobald, in *The Censor*, 91, 3 vols. (1717), iii. 206–13.

[138] Judith Drake, *An Essay in Defence of the Female Sex* (1696), 102–4. For a mid-eighteenth-century example of antiquarian satire, see A. Shell, 'The Antiquarian Satirized: John Clubbe and the Antiquities of Wheatfield', in A. Hunt, G. Mandelbrote, and A. Shell, *The Book Trade and its Customers 1450–1900: Historical Essays for Robin Myers* (Winchester, England and New Castle, Del., 1997), 223–45.

[139] Thomas Sprat, the great apologist for the society, was critical of the virtuoso cabinets while advocating the society's museum; a call for comprehensiveness comes out of the botanist Nehemiah Grew's 1681 catalogue of the society's collections: Hunter, 'The Cabinet Institutionalized', 163–4.

Krzysztof Pomian has usefully described the later seventeenth century as a transitional period during which institutional mechanisms such as journals and societies brought the era of 'curiosity' in Europe to a close.[140] So far as England is concerned, this reminds us that the interests of Augustan antiquarianism and Augustan science, so often closely associated, were never quite the same. Rather, they were two plots of knowledge with a common waste in between, an uncultivated patch that was beginning to shrink as enclosing fences first went up and then moved progressively forwards from both directions.

COMMON GROUND: FOSSILS AND THE AGE OF THE WORLD

The connections between virtuoso and antiquarian interests are, therefore, most obvious in the century between John Caius, early Elizabethan student of dogs, medicine, and the antiquity of Cambridge, and John Aubrey, biographer, antiquary, student of archaeology, and early folklorist. Aubrey may well have been the last of the great seventeenth-century antiquaries to work effectively in several fields, but his *Naturall Historie of Wiltshire* has been identified by Professor Hunter as the first work to depart from the older county chorographies by abandoning the place-by-place itinerary used since Leland in favour of a description and arrangement of natural and artificial objects according to type.[141]

The overlap is less apparent as we move from the Restoration to the Georgian era, though some topics by their very nature continued to demand the attention of antiquary and naturalist alike, Edward Lhwyd's interest in fossils, plants, runic inscriptions, and linguistics being an excellent example—his pursuit of these in the field occasioned a four-year break from his post as Keeper of the Ashmolean between 1697 and 1701.[142] Fossils, long seen not as the remains of once living organisms but as oddly shaped natural stones 'resembling' living molluscs and other animals, eventually came to be recognized as clues to species that might have existed before the Flood. Assertions of their organic origins caught on slowly in the seventeenth century, as writers such as Robert Hooke, John Ray, and John Woodward in varying degrees rejected the 'stone' theories still advanced by others such as Athanasius Kircher.[143] The London apothecary John Conyers's discovery of some fossil 'ivory' near a flint spearhead in 1690 led him first to think that they were the bones of a unicorn, then an elephant; a friend's explanation of the bones as coming from a Roman elephant slain by a heroic Briton during

[140] Pomian, *Collectors and Curiosities*, 64.
[141] Hunter, *John Aubrey and the Realm of Learning*, 192.
[142] Ovenell, *The Ashmolean Museum*, 90.
[143] Porter, *Making of Geology*, 21–5, 46–53; R. W. Purcell and S. J. Gould, *Finders and Keepers* (New York and London, 1992), 81–94; M. J. S. Rudwick, *The Meaning of Fossils: Episodes in the History of Paleontology*, 2nd edn. (Chicago and London, 1985), 39–42, 49–63, an incisive treatment that scrupulously avoids judging early treatments by the standards of modern knowledge; cf. his more recent essay, 'Minerals, Strata and Fossils', in N. Jardine, J. A. Secord, and E. C. Spary (eds.), *Cultures of Natural History* (Cambridge, 1996), 266–86, principally on the eighteenth century.

Claudius's invasion was certainly easier to accept at the time than the suggestion that it might be a now extinct animal such as a mammoth.[144]

The fossil provided a subject of correspondence and discussion among both antiquaries and virtuosi beginning with the naturalist Conrad Gesner's publication of his *De Rerum fossilium, lapidum et gemmarum maxime, figuris et similitudinibus liber* (1565), complete with woodcut illustrations.[145] Early works emphasized their magical or medicinal qualities and were firmly cast in the philological tradition whereby they were 'explained' in terms of categories generated by the ancients such as Aristotle and Pliny. Interest mounted over the next two centuries, since, quite aside from the classificatory problems they created, there arose from them serious difficulties for the received view of the age of the world and the biblical account of its origins. These difficulties became more intractable when the organic nature of the fossils was finally realized and had to be reconciled with the Flood. Could there once have been other species on earth, not saved on the Ark? This problem followed close on the heels of a bigger quandary, raised by the discovery of the New World nearly two centuries before the birth of Abraham de la Pryme. That northern curate's own version of the Flood and its effects on land formation, written in the wake of Thomas Burnet's *Theory of the Earth*, and similar works by Woodward, William Whiston, and Robert Hooke was contained in a now lost manuscript entitled 'A new system of the Creation of the earth', which he summarized in an unpublished history of his Yorkshire parish of Hatfield. Pryme doubted that all fossils could have been left in the time since the Flood, scattered as they were over a wide geographic area; such massy bodies belonged at the bottom of the sea but had somehow been 'forced over land, over hills and mountains many hundreds of miles together'. With all the confidence of youth, Pryme resolved to 'frame another system of the Noachian Deluge contrary to all others which is most certainly the truth & solves all these things very easily'. His explanation, by no means the silliest advanced in the decade, held that 'the sayd old world was almost wholly absorp'd, swallowed up, & coverd by the seas that we now have & that this earth of our's riss then out of the bottome of the Antidiluvian sea in its room, just as we see any islands swallowed up, & others thrust up in their stead'.[146]

More than any other unearthed antiquity, fossils, together with non-fossilized animal remains, such as skeletons and mollusc shells, provided the link for scientifically inclined antiquaries of the later seventeenth century, men such as Aubrey and Robert Plot, between the study of nature in all its forms and the study of the remote past. Large skeletons and 'teeth' had long been adduced as evidence by

---

[144] W. H. Stiebing Jr., *Uncovering the Past: A History of Archaeology* (Oxford and New York, 1993), 35; J. Redwood, *Reason, Ridicule and Religion: The Age of Enlightenment in England, 1660–1750* (1976), 116–32.

[145] Rudwick, *The Meaning of Fossils*, 1–48; many similar examples can be found in Lhwyd's correspondence in Gunther, *Early Science in Oxford*, vol. xiv.

[146] In other words, the parts formerly at the bottom of the sea rose, bringing with them shells and other submarine life; single shells Pryme explained as indicative of the fact that a few years before the Flood parts of the earth began rising and falling: BL MS Lans. 897 (A. de la Pryme, 'History of Hatfield', *c.*1700), fo. 186ʳ ᵛ; Porter, *Making of Geology*, 80.

those who wished to assert the physical superiority of the ancients over modern men, though George Hakewill, who did not subscribe to that theory, was sceptical of such evidence, suggesting that it might have been manufactured artificially. Richard Verstegan reported several instances in the early seventeenth century of Dutch labourers unearthing old seashells and animal bones while digging wells or excavating waterways; these he took as evidence for his belief that Holland had been entirely submerged in the period before the Great Flood.[147] The fish bones dug up by Sir Robert Cotton at Conington in the early seventeenth century were still the subject of correspondence in 1658 when Dugdale, who was then at work on his *History of Imbanking and Drayning* (published in 1662) sent a specimen of these to Thomas Browne, to elicit that learned doctor's opinion as to the animal's size.[148] At the end of the century the antiquary Richard Richardson, in company with better-known practising zoologists such as Edward Lhwyd and his inveterate enemy John Woodward, made fossils a major part of his correspondence with like-minded scholars.[149] The London parson William Stonestreet, another friend of Lhwyd, collected fossils, Roman coins, and an enormous variety of shells.[150]

By the last decades of the seventeenth century the world of knowledge had become so large that few men could visit, let alone feel at home in, all its parts. Anthony Wood took chemistry lessons from a Strasbourg Rosicrucian, but his interests were much more narrowly focused on the past than were those of his associates, Aubrey, Ashmole, and Evelyn. Wood admitted that his brief flirtation with alchemy merely made him anxious to return to his beloved antiquities, and to his music.[151] Evelyn in turn, though more catholic in interest—he delighted in curiosities such as a 'toade included in amber'—was less so than Ashmole, at whose astrological preoccupations Evelyn sneered. Lhwyd's contempt for Plot, his former superior at the Ashmolean, can be seen in the design of the *Archaeologia Britannica*, which eschews Plot's error-prone attempts to reconcile natural history and antiquarianism.[152] Specialization began to occur, though the age of the polymath did not truly end for another century. It would be wrong to regard this as an absolute division rather than as a trend, since examples continue to occur through the late seventeenth and into the eighteenth centuries of individuals, such

[147] George Hakewill, *An Apologie of the Power and Providence of God in the Government of the World* (1627), 193–5; Richard Verstegan, *A Restitution of decayed intelligence* (1605), 104–8.
[148] *Works of Sir Thomas Browne*, ed. G. L. Keynes, 2nd edn., 4 vols. (Chicago, 1964), iv. 309 (Dugdale to Browne, 17 Nov. 1658).
[149] Bodl. MS Radcliffe Trust *c*.1 (letters from various correspondents to Richard Richardson, mainly from the 1690s), esp. fos. 38–9; Gunther, *Early Science in Oxford*, vol. xiv, *passim*; Leigh, *Natural History of Lancashire*, 114–30, for fossils and petrified shells found in the north-west; G. L. Davies, *The Earth in Decay: A History of British Geomorphology 1578–1878* (1969), 74–84.
[150] *The Diary of Ralph Thoresby*, ed. J. Hunter, 2 vols. (1830), i. 343. I owe the reference to Stonestreet to Anita McConnell.
[151] Wood, *Life and Times*, i. 475. Wood noted, incidentally, that the only member of his 'chemistry class' who obstinately refused to take notes was the 'prating and troublesome' young man, John Locke; Evelyn, *Diary*, iv. 138.
[152] Ovenell, *The Ashmolean Museum*, 30–63 (Plot) and 64–107 (Lhwyd).

as Woodward or Sloane, whose interests spanned antiquarianism, natural philosophy, philology, and history. We remember Edmond Halley principally for his
assistance to Newton, and for the comet that bears his name, but a this-worldly
marvel such as Stonehenge also captured his attention, together with historical
problems such as the chronology of Caesar's invasion of Britain.[153]

CONCLUSION

This survey of the growth and development of antiquarianism from the early sixteenth to the early eighteenth centuries has been thematic rather than chronological. It may therefore be useful to summarize some of the main points before
we proceed further, in particular to highlight the significant changes that
occurred during these two centuries. Although antiquaries at both ends of the
period would all profess an interest in, even a devotion to, the past, there are some
critical differences between preoccupations and practices at the time of Leland
and those at the time of Stukeley. The first and most obvious is the wider range
of activities deemed 'antiquarian' at the end of the seventeenth century. These
now included not only the older forms of philological scholarship (still very much
a part of polite learning, as the Battle of the Books demonstrates), but also a much
greater orientation to material remnants of various sorts, natural as well as man-
made. A second change lies in the much closer connection between antiquarianism, especially its archaeological side, and other intellectual movements not
specifically focused on the past, in particular natural philosophy.

  At the beginning of this chapter I distinguished two grand streams of antiquarianism, which might be summarized respectively as the philological and the
archaeological. The increasing weight attached to the latter was not necessarily
at the expense of the former—antiquarian activity was not a finite pie in which
greater attention to one mode of apprehending the past implied a diminution of
the other. Moreover, both sorts were practised from the beginning to the end of
the period, albeit in different combinations. So long as one recognizes that they
are abstractions admitting of many exceptions and anomalies, it is in fact possible to identify three distinct but overlapping phases of antiquarian practice during the longer period from 1530 to 1730. The first of these, the period beginning
with Leland and running up to the mid-seventeenth century, where we find Cotton,
Spelman, and Selden, was dominated by humanist philological study. This paid
close attention to aspects of language and orthography, and to the preservation
and restoration of ancient and (towards the end of this phase), medieval texts.
Peripatetic observation of the sort illustrated by Leland's *Itinerary* and by
fifteenth-century precursors such as William Worcestre certainly occurred, but
it occupied at best a supporting role. During the second phase, beginning with

---

[153] Royal Society, *The Philosophical Transactions and Collections, to the End of the Year 1700*, ed.
J. Lowthorp, 3rd edn., 3 vols. (1722), iii. 412–14.

Camden's *Britannia* and continuing through the works of Dugdale and Plot, antiquaries combined philological work with an increasing emphasis on local antiquities (with an initial emphasis on the genealogical and heraldic that declined after the Restoration). Travel, observation, and illustration were featured much more prominently during this phase, but the objects observed and depicted (including coins, urns, funeral monuments, and buildings) continued to be explained, by and large, against a backdrop provided by literary and especially classical texts. The third phase harks back to Bacon's directives on observation, induction, and classification, but it really begins in earnest with the collecting activities of Elias Ashmole and especially the archaeological and naturalist writings of John Aubrey. It reached maturity in the early eighteenth century with the likes of Edward Lhwyd and, in the next generation, William Stukeley. Much of the antiquarian activity in this phase also combined textual knowledge with observation, but it did so in a very different way that severely reduced emphasis on the heraldic and genealogical in favour of the material and especially the natural. Methodologically, one also now finds a much greater attention being given to the comparative relationship among and classification of similar objects, in the manner of natural history, rather than the explication of individual objects by reference either to their location and its history, or to categories and explanations provided by texts.

Any periodization such as this is at best a crude tool, admitting of numerous exceptions, not least given the propensity of some individuals to fit into more than one category, and the fact that one can find both the philological and archaeological species of the larger antiquarian genus flourishing at the end of seventeenth century. There is certainly no basis for asserting the dominance of fieldwork-based, archaeological antiquarianism at the same time that major philological advances in the editing of classical and medieval texts and the publication of documents were continuing to occur, not least in the sub-fields of palaeography, diplomatic, and sigillography. D. C. Douglas's Thomas Madox and Thomas Hearne are thus as much full citizens of the Augustan and early Georgian intellectual community as Stuart Piggott's Stukeley and Michael Hunter's Aubrey. So, for that matter, is Joseph M. Levine's John Woodward,[154] whose own inability to escape classical categories offers a telling warning against overstating the achievements of induction and comparison at this stage in the history of scholarship. Nevertheless, the differing approaches to the remnants of the past are recognizably distinct and should be acknowledged. Their overlapping goes some way towards explaining the ambiguous and complicated usage of terms like antiquary and virtuoso among contemporaries.

As useful as this categorical analysis may be, it is deficient in one respect, since it once again privileges an elite pantheon of scholars (of whichever sort) while overlooking the social environment within which they operated. A further major change in English historical culture lies in the degree to which the study of the

---

[154] Levine, *Dr. Woodward's Shield*, esp. pp. 151–80.

antiquarian past, once the activity of a tiny minority among the well-educated (itself a small fraction of the general population), had become a social activity of considerable prominence. As we have seen, there were local enthusiasts for antiquities in the time of Camden and the Elizabethan chorographers as well as in that of Dugdale. But even allowing for greater archival survival rates in the early eighteenth century, the volume of informal antiquarian writing is notably greater in 1700 than a century earlier. So, too, is the frequency of reference to antiquarian activity both serious and casual, from the meetings of the revived Society of Antiquaries to the most undisciplined youth on the Grand Tour: what remained a focused intellectual activity for some was a form of leisure and polite discussion for a great many more. This should not be surprising, in light of the considerably increased opportunities for travel, the enormous increase in printed historical works of various kinds, and the much improved institutional framework for study of, and conversation about, the past, including public and private libraries, museums, coffee-houses, and clubs. Moreover, beyond this 'non-expert' educated elite, there stands an overlooked but critically important element in the circulation of knowledge of the past, the participation of ordinary, uneducated people in what will here be called an 'archaeological economy'. The workings of this provide the subject of Chapter 7. Before we can get to this topic, however, we need to pause in order to explore another important feature of antiquarianism, its relationship to the development of a 'visual' sense of the past. This in turn bears on another thread altogether, the relations between oral and written communication, and popular and elite culture, taken up in the final part of this book.

CHAPTER SIX

Seeing the Past

> The pleasure of [antiquities] is best knowne to such as have seene them abroad
> in France, Spaine, and Italy, where the gardens and galleries of great men are
> beautified and set forth to admiration with these kinds of ornaments. And
> indeed the possession of such rarities, by reason of their dead costlinesse, doth
> properly belong to princes, or rather to princely minds.
>
> (Henry Peacham, The Compleat Gentleman[1])

IN THE LAST chapter I offered a number of explanations for the emergence of
antiquarianism in the mid-sixteenth century and its impressive growth in the seventeenth, emphasizing the growth of networks of information that underlay the
works of the major antiquaries, and the types of collecting activity that they, and
many others, undertook. In Chapter 7 the collection of and trade in artefacts will
be examined more closely, with special attention to interchange between learned
and popular culture. In the present chapter, I wish to explore a variety of ways
in which the physical remains of the past (manuscripts, old books, and non-
literary artefacts) and modern commemorative replicas of that past (statuary, painting, landscape design) created, for the first time in England, a visual culture of
'pastness'.[2]

Much has been written about the transition in early modern times from an
oral/aural culture to one based on visual experience. Perhaps most influential in
this regard have been the works of Walter J. Ong SJ,[3] whose arguments, subsequently exploited by advocates of the 'printing revolution' thesis, apply largely
to one aspect of cultural life, the representation of knowledge in book form.[4] There

---

[1] Henry Peacham, *The Compleat Gentleman*, 3rd edn. (1634), 104.

[2] Stephen Bann, dealing with a somewhat later period, usefully theorizes about the development,
aided by antiquarianism, of a 'view of the past', that is a way of visually perceiving past objects, especially monuments and artefacts: S. Bann, ' "Views of the Past": Reflections on the Treatment of Historical
Objects and Museums of History', in id., *The Inventions of History: Essays on the Representation of the
Past* (Manchester and New York, 1990), 122–47. A visual culture of pastness, however, includes not
merely the actual act of seeing, but the development of mental images of historical figures from the
past who, unlike physical artefacts, no longer exist.

[3] W. J. Ong SJ, *Ramus, Rhetoric and the Decay of Dialogue* (Cambridge, Mass., 1958); id., *The Presence
of the Word: Some Prolegomena for Cultural and Religious History* (New York, 1967), 3, 35, 75; id., *Rhetoric,
Romance and Technology: Studies in the Interaction of Expression and Culture* (Ithaca and London, 1971),
esp. ch. 2, 'Oral Residue in Tudor Prose Style', and ch. 6, 'Ramist Classroom Procedure and the Nature
of Reality'; id., *Orality and Literacy: The Technologizing of the Word* (London and New York, 1982).

[4] E. L. Eisenstein, *The Printing Press as an Agent of Change* (Cambridge, 1979); but cf. the important revisions to this thesis, and the notion of 'print culture' generally, in A. Johns, *The Nature of the
Book* (Chicago, 1998).

is little reason to quarrel with Ong's findings concerning the increasing 'spatial-ization' of knowledge in the form of charts and tables, or of the reduction of pre-viously oral conveyance of learning to the printed page. But when one scrutinizes Ong's thesis closely, or Elizabeth L. Eisenstein's related arguments about the spread of print culture, one almost immediately runs into difficulties of periodization. For a start, the culture of the Middle Ages can be argued to have been as much oriented to the eye as the ear, given the priority it placed on visual symbols such as heraldry and representations of holiness such as images and religious paint-ing; its learned culture can especially be demonstrated as focused on the visible text or document, as Michael Clanchy and Brian Stock have argued in different ways.[5] Conversely, while Protestantism repudiated much of this in the name of Scripture, on the face of it another visual medium, its godlier practitioners also placed a greater emphasis on the sermon, an oral form. In the second place, recent scholarship has emphasized the continuing interdependence of oral, written, and printed modes of discourse during the early modern era, though there can be little doubt that the advance of both writing and print had serious implications for the 'remembered past' (see Part IV, below).[6] Unless one was either blind or deaf, both were used in the Middle Ages, the Renaissance, and subsequently.[7] That does not mean that each sense was always employed in the same way: time-telling, previously dictated by the bell, became attuned to the face of the clock and watch during the seventeenth century. But it does mean that we ought to be very cautious about mistaking shifts in modes of perception within a few areas for a general and comprehensive cultural shift.

To assert that no seismic cultural shift from hearing to seeing occurred is not to abdicate responsibility for identifying more subtle perceptual changes that can be detected in certain areas. Attitudes to physical remains of the past (including textual examples such as manuscripts and old books, here treated as visible and tangible objects of value independent of any information contained in their texts) are among these. What I wish to assert in this chapter can be summarized in two points. First, that *within* the sphere of visual perception, there was a trend in early modern England away from an unconscious acceptance of an environ-ment of past survivals, as part of 'every-day life', towards a more conscious

---

[5] M. T. Clanchy, *From Memory to Written Record: England 1066–1307* (1979), 202–30; B. Stock, *The Implications of Literacy* (Princeton, NJ, 1983), 12–87.

[6] See e.g. D. F. McKenzie, 'Speech-Manuscript-Print', in D. Oliphant and R. Bradford (eds.), *New Directions in Textual Studies* (Austin, Tex., 1990), 87–109; R. Scribner, 'Oral Culture and the Diffusion of Reformation Ideas', *History of European Ideas*, 5 (1984), 237–56; R. Finnegan, *Literacy and Orality: Studies in the Technology of Communication* (Oxford, 1988), esp. pp. 5–14; J. Goody, *The Interface between the Written and the Oral* (Cambridge, 1987), *passim*. We might do better to adopt the division favoured by art historians between visual and verbal culture, which fits the movement away from symbolism towards the text much better, and explains such phenomena as the decline of funeral effigies in favour of inscription-bearing gravestones. I am grateful to Irving and Marilyn Lavin for many discussions of these issues.

[7] D. R. Woolf, 'Speech, Text and Time: The Sense of Hearing and the Sense of the Past in Renaissance England', *Albion*, 18 (1986), 159–93; M. McKeon, *The Origins of the English Novel 1600–1740* (Baltimore, 1987), 33–45; M. Elsky, *Authorizing Words: Speech, Writing, and Print in the English Renaissance* (Ithaca and London, 1989), 69.

recognition of objects from the past as being out of place—or more accurately out of time. The second point, which is a corollary of the first, is that there had developed by 1700 a distinctively visual aspect to the sense of the past. If often wildly inaccurate from the perspective of modern scholarship, this nonetheless induced those who read and wrote about history, or who visited historic sites, to think more carefully about what people living in earlier times may have looked like, and imaginatively to reconstruct the appearance of famous scenes from history. John Evelyn captures both of these developments in advising Samuel Pepys, during the 1660s, to adorn his library with 'pictures of men illustrious for their parts and erudition', worthies, statesmen, and captains, while elsewhere stressing the need for painters themselves to be 'good historians, and generally skill'd in the best antiquities'.[8]

This realization could lead in a number of directions, and not necessarily in favour of maintaining or preserving the past (the recycling of old buildings has been mentioned in this regard), but it did involve coming to grips more thoroughly than had ever been done before with the difference between past and present, and it involved making decisions that were often based as much on tides in aesthetic taste as on a scholarly devotion to accurate representations of history. It is thus less accurate to say that a visual culture emerged from an oral one than to say that relations between the two modes of perception were altered, while visual contemplation of images and physical remnants was itself displaced from the sacred on to the exotic or historical.

ANTIQUITIES AND THE FEAR OF POPERY

There were some serious political and religious constraints on the pursuit of antiquarian knowledge, especially in the Elizabethan and early Stuart decades. The political constraints were occasional and transparent, including all the many well-known instances of royal censorship, from James I's closure of the Elizabethan Society of Antiquaries, to the arrest of John Selden and the seizure of Sir Robert Cotton's library after the tumultuous parliamentary session of 1629. The impact of religious beliefs and sensibilities on the study of the remains of the past (and of the influence of those remains themselves on perception) has been rather less well studied.[9] When Thomas Fuller published his *The Holy State* in 1642, he included a character of 'the true Church Antiquary', a man devoted to describing the practices of the primitive Church and the decline of morals and customs since that

[8] W. E. Houghton, 'The English Virtuoso in the Seventeenth Century', *Journal of the History of Ideas*, 3 (1942), 51–73, 190–219, at p. 209; Evelyn, preface to R. Fréart, *An Idea of the Perfection of Painting* (1668), in *The Miscellaneous Works of John Evelyn*, ed. W. Upcott (1825), 561.
[9] M. Aston, 'English Ruins and English History: The Dissolution and the Sense of the Past', *Journal of the Warburg and Courtauld Institutes*, 36 (1973), 232–55; A. B. Ferguson, *Clio Unbound: Perception of the Social and Cultural Past in Renaissance England* (Durham, NC, 1979). The seventeenth century has been much less well served, but see now J. A. I. Champion, *The Pillars of Priestcraft Shaken: The Church of England and its Enemies, 1660–1730* (Cambridge, 1992), 25–98.

time. He also warned his fellow antiquaries against the seductive power of the lost culture of monastic England, and he acknowledged that study of pre- and post-Norman antiquities led, almost inevitably, to a romanticization of medieval Catholic civilization. Fuller was right to worry about falling in the way of such temptation. Thirteen years later, after a decade of puritan iconoclasm, in his own *Church-History of Britain*, Fuller would bestow praise on the monastic orders for their great learning and traditions of hospitality, both of which had been lost at the Reformation.[10]

There was always a danger that fondness for antiquities, especially those from the Middle Ages, would attract the derision of satirists, but in the early decades of antiquarian interest, during and immediately after the Reformation, and again in the religiously turbulent 1630s to 1650s, enthusiasts had to worry about the more serious charge of supporting popery. While it is true that the reformers of the English Church, especially the more puritanical, wanted a return to a remote, apostolic past in the form of a 'primitive Church', it is also the case that they repudiated much of the previous millennium of history in as radical a fashion as has ever occurred. Hostility to the artefacts of the Catholic past expressed itself in periodic bursts of iconoclasm, both official and spontaneous, and also in a lingering suspicion of anyone who appeared over-fond of the 'relicks' of bygone times. Thus Hugh Latimer blamed the decaying condition of sixteenth-century Worcester on the town's reliance on an old image popularly called 'Our Lady of Worcester', which when it was removed and stripped down in 1538, turned out to be the statue of a bishop.[11] Individual antiquaries often fell under suspicion. Camden, certainly no closet papist, avowed his Protestant beliefs periodically in his published and unpublished writings, while John Stow, who may well have had Catholic sympathies, was brought before the council under suspicion of popery and had many of his books and papers seized in 1569.[12]

Undisputed Catholics among the antiquaries there certainly were. Without difficulty one can rattle off the names of William Claxton, John Lord Lumley, Humphrey Llwyd (Lumley's brother-in-law), John Caius, Henry Ferrers, Nicholas Roscarrock, William Howard of Naworth, Thomas Habington, Richard Verstegan (alias Rowlands), Robert Hare, William Blundell the elder, and Edmund Bolton, from the period before 1640. The prominence of Catholics after 1640 is somewhat less obvious, though one can still identify a number such as

---

[10] Thomas Fuller, *The Holy State* (1642), and *Church History of Britain* (1655), both discussed in G. Parry, *The Trophies of Time: English Antiquaries of the Seventeenth Century* (Oxford, 1995), 268–73.

[11] *Works of Hugh Latimer*, ed. G. E. Corrie, 2 vols., PS 27–8 (Cambridge, 1844–5), ii. 403.

[12] William Camden, *Annales rerum Anglicarum et Hibernicarum regnante Elizabetha*, 2 pts. (1615–27), pt. 1, pp. 166, 326–7; *Gulielmi Camdeni et illustrium virorum ad G. Camdenum epistolae*, ed. Thomas Smith (1691), 246–8 (Camden to James Ussher, 10 July 1618); BL MS Lans. 11, fos. 4ʳ, 7–8, an inventory of the thirty-eight books seized from Stow in 1569, including only four historical works but many Catholic books; J. Wilson, 'A Catalogue of the "Unlawful" Books found in John Stow's Study on 21 February 1568/9', *Recusant History*, 20 (1990), 1–30; Aston, 'English Ruins and English History'. B. L. Beer, *Tudor England Observed: The World of John Stow* (1998), 6–8, suggests that the popish tendencies of which Stow was accused may have faded later in his career as he became accustomed to the Elizabethan settlement.

John Theyer (a convert to Rome in the middle of the civil war), William Clifford, Christopher Towneley, Charles Eyston, Henry Keepe, Ralph Sheldon, Cuthbert Constable, and William Blundell the younger.

The connection between Catholicism and antiquarianism was therefore not an imaginary one, but its explanation is not very clear. Certainly some antiquaries, like the Blundells of Little Crosby, Lancashire allowed their religious views very strongly to guide their antiquarian activities. Others did so much less. Sir Thomas Shirley took his Catholicism very seriously, but it did not prove an obstacle to collaboration with Protestants such as Sir Christopher Hatton, Sir William Dugdale, and Sir Edward Dering, as well as with fellow Catholics such as Thomas Habington.[13] The sole major gesture towards his religion of Shirley's contemporary Edmund Bolton was the adoption of 'Maria' as his middle name. Nearer the end of the seventeenth century Henry Keepe converted to Rome at the succession of James II for careerist rather than antiquarian reasons, changing his name to Charles Taylour in the process. While there is, therefore, no high degree of correlation between antiquarianism and Catholicism, this would not have soothed contemporary worries, especially in the first century after the break with Rome. Nor would it have provided much solace to Protestant antiquaries such as William Lambarde. They were often torn between their appreciation for medieval artefacts (including the decaying corpses of the monasteries), and the religious beliefs which so strongly convinced them that these were the spoils of superstition, brought low by vengeful providence.

From the 1530s, various governments and puritan writers regularly warned against the dangers attached to the images which survived from the age of superstition. The saints and their shrines were attacked in 1535, the religious houses dissolved over the next five years, and many of their monuments and images destroyed or removed. Royal injunctions in 1538 commanded the removal of certain parish images from public places; further measures under Edward VI extended these proscriptions, which were in any case generally exceeded by over-zealous local reformers who took removal to mean destruction. The more prudent parishioners, sensing the continued instability of the religious settlement, simply hid them away and were able to fetch them back under Mary.[14] Monumental crosses were only officially condemned in 1644, but they had suffered from unofficial vandalism long before: Cheapside Cross, erected by Edward I in 1290 in memory of Queen Eleanor and rebuilt in the 1480s, was attacked and restored on at least six occasions up to May, 1643, when Wenceslas Hollar engraved the scene of its final destruction by a mob of 'furious and zealous people'.[15]

---

[13] D. R. Woolf, 'Little Crosby and the Horizons of Early Modern Historical Culture', in D. R. Kelley and D. H. Sacks (eds.), *The Historical Imagination in Early Modern Britain* (Cambridge, 1997), 93–132; R. Cust, 'Catholicism, Antiquarianism and Gentry Honour: The Writings of Sir Thomas Shirley', *Midland History*, 23 (1998), 40–70, at p. 43.

[14] E. Duffy, *The Stripping of the Altars* (New Haven, 1993), 543–55.

[15] *Cheapsides Triumphs*, in *The Pepys Ballads*, ed. H. E. Rollins, 8 vols. (Cambridge, Mass., 1929), ii, no. 55, p. 47; Dugdale, *Life, Diary and Correspondence*, 50.

Although the most severe incidents of iconoclasm tended to occur in spurts, during periods of pronounced anti-popery or puritan fervour, English men and women were regularly reminded of the sin of idolatry and enjoined to purify their parishes of visual images in obedience to a God who was to be heard rather than seen. Edward Dering's *Catechism for householders* (which also roundly condemned the old chivalric hero Guy of Warwick and Robin Hood as reminders of the priestly past) warned readers of the dangers of images, while certain days such as Ash Wednesday and, later, 5 November, became the occasion for destructive rituals of purification by local iconoclasts. The most severe iconoclasm was over by the Restoration, but examples continued to occur, such as Thomas Robinson, the eighteenth-century Avebury Baptist who boasted that he had 'killed' forty stones of that town's famous monument, or the owner of the conventual ground of the former Croyland Abbey, who dug up the stone coffins of the abbots and sold them for hog troughs.[16]

Untold damage was inflicted on the stained glass windows in churches and cathedrals during the Reformation, despite the official teaching of the episcopate that innocent decoration of holy places did not constitute idolatry. As in the case of funeral monuments, there was little that authorities could do by way of preventing independent and unexpected acts of iconoclasm by conscientious individuals. When the single-minded Salisbury puritan Henry Sherfield could no longer stand a painted window portraying God as an aged astronomer, he smashed it to bits, in defiance of episcopal authority; the £500 fine inflicted on him by the court of Star Chamber (unpaid at Sherfield's death) could not bring back the window.[17] Much more widespread destruction would occur during the civil wars and interregnum. William Dowsing, Richard Culmer (the destroyer in 1644 of 'proud Becket's glassy bones', a large window at Canterbury Cathedral), and other officially sanctioned iconoclasts wreaked vengeance on offending buildings, glazing, pictures, crosses, funeral monuments and inscriptions, and ornamentation throughout the kingdom's churches.[18] Half a century later antiquaries such as Edward Steele, observing the ruins of one Norfolk church (Diss) defaced of its brasses and inscriptions, commented that 'these are the dismal remains of that confusion reigning in the unnatural Civill war, which yet we see the sad effects of'. The work of the iconoclasts was thorough and unforgiving, and not only scriptural idolatry was targeted. The stained glass windows smashed at Peterborough Cathedral in the civil war had been principally images of kings rather than biblical figures. Thomas Ford similarly excoriated 'the giddy zeal of the times which

---

[16] SAL Antiquaries MS 265, fo. 53ᵛ, 'Notorious Destroyers of Antiquitys'; SAL, Minute Book 1718–32, p. 152, minuted 24 Mar. 1724/5.

[17] P. Slack, 'Religious Protest and Urban Authority: The Case of Henry Sherfield, Iconoclast, 1633', *Studies in Church History*, 9 (1972), 295–302.

[18] Richard Culmer, *Cathedrall News from Canterbury* (1644), 19–24; S. Porter, *Destruction in the English Civil Wars* (Phoenix Mill and Stroud, Glos., 1994), 130–2; M. Briggs, *Goths and Vandals: A Study of the Destruction, Neglect, and Preservation of Historical Buildings in England* (1952), 64; J. G. Cheshire, 'William Dowsing's Destructions in Cambridgeshire', *Trans. Cambridge and Huntingdonshire Archaeological Society*, 3 (1909–14), 77–91.

destroyed so many ancient monuments' while celebrating the survival into the 1690s of Queen's Cross near Northampton.[19] It is important to note that there was no sense of period involved in these attacks: images were condemned primarily because they were images, not specifically because they were medieval; the windows with 'scripture stories' that were painted and placed in Christ Church in the 1630s were broken for being 'diabolical and popish' barely a decade later, no distinction being made between them and similar windows of medieval date.[20]

Much the same suspicion could adhere to more modern representations of famous persons in a non-religious context. Beginning in the earliest stages of the Reformation, there are signs of a much broader antipathy to imagery *of any kind*, not merely the manifestly popish, an antipathy that Professor Collinson has usefully called 'iconophobia'. Even something as innocuous as a gallery of contemporary portraits, the only means of preserving the likeness of notables for their family, friends, and posterity, might lead the most godly down the slippery slope back into idolatry.[21] In 1550 Christopher Hales wrote to his friend Rudolph Gualter to request portraits of Gualter himself, Zwingli, Pellican, Bullinger, and Théodore de Bèze, because he wanted to surround himself with the likenesses of the great reformers, many of whom were dead. But he had to write to Bullinger himself to assure him that these portraits were simply for ornamentation, not for worship. In a subsequent letter to Gualter, who had similar scruples, Hales defended the painting of images purely for decoration and remembrance. Who, he enquired, bows to the statue on the south tower of Zurich Cathedral, which was then believed to be a likeness of Charlemagne? The sin of idolatry was in any case in the eye of the beholder, not in the subject of the image. 'Who lays it to the charge of the Romans of old, that we have their resemblances engraved upon numerous medals?' Hales asked. 'Who blames Luther, Bucer, Philip, Oecolampadius and very many others yet living, because their likenesses are everywhere to be met with?' Such reproductions were tokens of respect, intended to preserve a man's image for posterity, not blasphemous baubles, and Hales's attitude proved to be that of the majority during an era in which the portrait, woodcut,

---

[19] Bodl. MS Top. gen. e. 79, fo. 248^v, Edward Steele's parish notes, vol. i (1712); CUL MS Mm. 6.50 (Covel transcripts), fos. 204–5 (Thomas Ford to John Covel, n.d.); J. Phillips, *The Reformation of Images: Destruction of Art in England, 1535–1660* (Berkeley and Los Angeles, 1973), for an older account of iconoclasm based largely on theological literature, and less thorough on actual instances than M. Aston, *England's Iconoclasts*, i: *Laws against Images* (Oxford, 1988), 65, 74–84, or Duffy, *Stripping of the Altars*, 379–423. Cf. J. Morrill, 'William Dowsing, the Bureaucratic Puritan', in J. Morrill, P. Slack, and D. Woolf (eds.), *Public Duty and Private Conscience in Seventeenth-Century England* (Oxford, 1993), 173–203; C. M. N. Eire, *War against the Idols: The Reformation of Worship from Erasmus to Calvin* (Cambridge, 1986).

[20] *The Travels of Peter Mundy in Europe and Asia, 1608–1667*, ed. R. C. Temple, 5 vols. in 6 (Cambridge, 1907–36), vol. iv (Hakluyt Society, 2nd ser., 55 (1925)), 27.

[21] On 'iconophobia' versus iconoclasm, see P. Collinson, *The Birthpangs of Protestant England: Religious and Cultural Change in the Sixteenth and Seventeenth Centuries* (New York, 1988), 117; T. Watt, *Cheap Print and Popular Piety, 1550–1640* (Cambridge, 1991), 134–9. Cf. N. Llewellyn, *Funeral Monuments in Post-Reformation England* (Cambridge, 2000), 217–71, for a discussion of the contemporary literature on visual experience.

and engraving frequently provided graphic representations of personalities and episodes from the past.[22]

Nearly two centuries after Hales, William Stukeley would regard it as 'too evid-ent to need any illustration, how proper engravings are, to preserve the memory of innumerable antiquitys, & how much better *idea* they convey to the mind than written descriptions'.[23] In between, during the Elizabethan and Stuart periods, the use of paintings, tapestries, and wall hangings, including woodcuts and engrav-ings snipped from books, had become commonplace, further contributing to a visual sense of the past and the propagation of images of famous personalities, biblical and historical.[24] Towns, their livery companies, and parishes memorial-ized their worthies and benefactors in portraits, along with coats of arms and prominently posted lists or tables.[25] In private homes, wills and probate invent-ories speak of quilts, tapestries, and other forms of hanging depicting stories or characters from the Old Testament, such as the 'great Cownterpointe of Nabingodonosor' that Lord Wharton of Healaugh possessed at his death in 1568, or the many hangings of Noah, Judith and Holofernes, David and Jezabel in the earl of Leicester's furnishings at Kenilworth twenty years later.[26] Over the following century and a half, that tendency to graphic visualization of scenes and persons would increasingly embrace secular subjects, and places in addition to persons. At the same time, it also spread to media much less durable than tapestries, but even more public, such as playing cards and tickets to county feasts, featuring pictures of historical personalities, Saxons in kilts, and images of famous build-ings.[27] By the eighteenth century, urban histories and guidebooks increasingly included plans, prospects, and illustrations of particular historic buildings, in

[22] *Original Letters Relative to the English Reformation*, ed. H. Robinson, 2 vols., PS 37–8 (Cam-bridge, 1846–7), i. 186, 190–3. The continued use of saints' names for churches was a similarly innoc-ent act of veneration, and was defended by Richard Hooker: *Of the Laws of Ecclesiastical Polity*, V, 13.3, in *The Folger Library Edition of the Works of Richard Hooker*, ed. W. Speed Hill, 7 vols. in 8 pts. (Cambridge, MA, 1977–98), ii. 55.

[23] SAL, Misc. I (letters and papers 1707–42), art. 12, MS note by Stukeley for a preface to an edi-tion of copperplates. Stukeley attempted an inventory of images of English kings and queens, prin-cipally of the fifteenth and sixteenth centuries, some time in the early eighteenth century. SAL MS 265 (antiquaries' commonplace book), p. 3.

[24] Visual decoration was by no means universal. Marjorie Keniston McIntosh contends that visual arts were unimportant for most denizens of the parishes in the liberty of Havering, the wall paintings of the pre-Reformation period having been whitewashed by Elizabeth's reign. In contrast, funeral monuments were a subject of interest and a source of family status, and a dozen brasses still survive in Hornchurch parish church from 1500–1620. M. K. McIntosh, *A Community Transformed: The Manor and Liberty of Havering, 1500–1620* (Cambridge, 1991), 273.

[25] I. W. Archer, 'The Arts and Acts of Memorialization in Early Modern London', in J. F. Merritt (ed.), *Imagining Early Modern London: Perceptions and Portrayals of the City from Stow to Strype, 1598–1720* (Cambridge, 2001), 89–113; Robert Tittler is engaged on a study of civic portraiture in provincial English towns; I am grateful to him for discussion of the topic.

[26] *Yorkshire Probate Inventories, 1542–1689*, ed. P. C. D. Brears, Yorkshire Archaeological Soc., Record ser., 134 (1972), 25; J. O. Halliwell, *Ancient Inventories of Furniture, Pictures, Tapestry, Plate &c* (1854), 115 ff.

[27] J. R. S. Whiting, *A Handful of History* (Totowa, NJ, 1978); N. E. Key, 'The Localism of the County Feast in Late Stuart Political Culture', *Huntington Library Quarterly*, 58 (1996), 211–37, at p. 224.

addition to coins and arms, all amounting to a 'visual check-list', as one recent author has remarked, of a city's past.[28]

ANTIQUITIES AND RELICS

One reason that artefacts from the past initially aroused suspicion is that they bore a superficial resemblance to relics, those detached body parts (and some-times associated bits of clothing or property), associated with the now discred-ited cult of the saints.[29] Most late medieval churches contained shrines with such items, such as the knife and boots of St Thomas Becket kept at Bury St Edmunds together with the coals used to burn St Lawrence; or the Virgin's milk and finger of St Peter at Our Lady of Walsingham.[30] Although the high tide of interest in boots and fingers had already passed, and popular piety had refocused on the images of saints rather than their relics, the latter did not escape the attention of early reformers, who strove to extinguish such popular occasions as Relic Sunday, which was celebrated in London on 6 July in 1536.[31] Archbishop Cranmer inveighed against beliefs such as that 'men, women and children, should wear a friar's coat to deliver them from agues or pestilence'. Hugh Latimer commented on how the people of western England came 'by flocks' to venerate relics such as the blood of Hales, which he dedicated some effort to exposing. An inventory of the pieces of holy cross, bones of Mary Magdalen and the other saints, removed from Reading Abbey in 1538 filled four sheets of paper, as John London remarked to Thomas Cromwell.[32]

Because of the endurance of recusancy in most parts of England, and espe-cially in the north, the practice of relic-worship actually continued long after its official condemnation.[33] The puritan Sir Francis Hastings, examining the priest William Hanse in 1582, enquired as to the meaning of a 'certeyne relick' he wore; the reply was that it was 'a drop of his brother's bloud that was hanged

---

[28] R. Sweet, *The Writing of Urban Histories in Eighteenth-Century England* (Oxford, 1997), 134–41.

[29] For background see P. Brown, *The Cult of the Saints: Its Rise and Function in Latin Christianity* (Princeton, 1983), 78, 88–94; W. Muensterberger, *Collecting, An Unruly Passion: Psychological Per-spectives* (Princeton, 1994), 58–66; K. Pomian, *Collectors and Curiosities: Paris and Venice, 1500–1800*, trans. E. Wiles-Portier (Cambridge, 1990), 16–17.

[30] Phillips, *The Reformation of Images*, 24–7.

[31] Charles Wriothesley, *A Chronicle of England during the Reigns of the Tudors*, 2 vols., Camden Soc., NS 11, 20 (1875–7), i. 51; Duffy, *Stripping of the Altars*, 167, 396.

[32] Thomas Cranmer, *An homily or sermon of good works annexed unto faith*, in *Miscellaneous Writings and Letters of Thomas Cranmer*, vol. ii of *The Works of Thomas Cranmer*, ed. J. E. Cox, 2 vols., PS 15–16 (Cambridge, 1844–6), ii. 147–8; *Works of Hugh Latimer*, ii. 364, 407; Bodl. MS Tanner 343, fo. 19ʳ (London to Cromwell, 18 Sept. 1538).

[33] On relics and religion during the Reformation, see R. Whiting, *The Blind Devotion of the People: Popular Religion and the English Reformation* (Cambridge, 1989), 55–8, 72–4; Duffy, *Stripping of the Altars*, 384–5, 406–7, 414–15; on the medicinal and sacred functions of relics in the medieval Church and their endurance after the Reformation, see K. Thomas, *Religion and the Decline of Magic* (1971; Peregrine edn., 1978), 29 ff., 60, 83. As Thomas points out, even some Protestants were reluctant to give up on relics; some were being kept at York Minster at the end of the seventeenth century.

for the Catholike religion'.[34] Even after such remains were no longer believed to hold medicinal or magical powers, it was difficult to break the habit of treating them with reverence or dread rather than dealing with them as inanimate objects. Mid-seventeenth-century Glastonbury, legendary resting place of Joseph of Arimathaea, still had its peculiar ancient thorn tree, which inexplicably flourished in midwinter. Some asserted that it regularly bloomed overnight on Christmas Eve, and country people for miles around referred to it as 'the Holy Thorn'; this is certainly a residue of the medieval belief in the flourishing of vegetation on the graves of the sanctified.[35]

Human bones, dug up regularly on the Salisbury plain throughout the period, often ended up as pseudo-relics, that is, as objects for contemplation, devoid of any specific saintly or magical association, but still capable of exciting an interest that must have irritated the godly. When a cadaver was discovered beneath the aisle of a parish church in Buckinghamshire in 1619, it was in such perfect condition that the bones were kept on display 'to bee showne to strangers as reliques of admiration'; local gentlemen dismembered the rest of the body and took the pieces home. At Hatfield Chase in the mid-seventeenth century, the breaking of a church wall so that the end of an altar rail could be anchored in it produced a young child's coat and shoe, which Abraham de la Pryme, writing a history of the parish some years later, thought 'some reliques in times of Popery that some of the religious had hid there'. This sort of thing revolted James I, who thought the proper place for relics was under the earth or in charnel houses, not on public display like condemned men's quarters.[36]

Certain sites, particularly ancient churches, retained an interest for travellers, including Protestants, for the alleged relics in their care: what had once drawn the pious pilgrim could now attract the curious traveller. Glastonbury had so many relics in its vaults that one early Stuart traveller spoke of having 'weary'd my selfe with tossing and tumbling over their Saints bones'; in the Isle of Thanet, the same man had been shown various relics imported by Augustine of Canterbury, including a piece of Christ's coat and 'Arons rod that budded, which you may beleeve if you be at leisure'. At Winchester Cathedral in the 1630s visitors could

[34] *The Letters of Sir Francis Hastings, 1574–1609*, ed. C. Cross, Somerset Rec. Soc., 69 (Frome, 1969), 25.

[35] Brown, *Cult of the Saints*, 76.

[36] John Weever, *Ancient Funerall Monuments* (1631), 6, 30; BL MS Lans. 897, fo. 127^{r-v} (Warburton collections, Pryme's unfinished history of Hatfield); James I, *A Premonition to all Most Mightie Monarches* (1609), in *Works of James VI and I*, ed. C. H. McIlwain, 2nd edn. (New York, 1965), 124. Funeral monuments were much studied in the seventeenth century, though the most successful works dealt with the tombs of royalty and nobility: see for instance William Camden, *Reges, reginae, nobiles, et alii in ecclesia collegiata B. Petri Westmonasterii sepulti* (1600); Henry Keepe, *Monumenta Westmonasteriensa; or, an Historical Account of . . . the Abbey-Church of Westminster* (1682); Jodocus Crull, *The Antiquities of St Peters; or, the Abbey-church of Westminster*, 3rd edn., 2 vols. (1722). As so often, a cautionary note to enthusiasm about their value as a historical source is provided by Joseph Addison, who remarked that as 'registers of existence' they contained only dates of birth and death for a person, 'The whole history of his life, being comprehended in those two circumstances that are common to all mankind'. *The Spectator*, 26 (30 Mar. 1711), ed. D. F. Bond, 5 vols. (Oxford, 1965), i. 109.

see chests containing the bones of Anglo-Saxon kings and bishops. In 1642, at
the start of the civil war, Sir William Waller's troops looted the cathedral and
scattered the bones, much to the horror of John Evelyn; they were gathered and
stored in new boxes at the Restoration.[37]

The same object could simultaneously be a timeless focus of religious reverence and a historical object arousing the intellectual curiosity of those who repudiated such veneration. Sacred artefacts in great numbers awaited the virtuoso
on tour in Catholic Europe, especially France and Italy, and it was not without
reason that Protestant parents feared the influence of popish trinkets and treasures on their travelling offspring, since these were a part of any visit to the great
cathedrals of Catholic Europe. Evelyn, visiting St Denys on his Grand Tour in
1643 was shown the sepulchres of a number of Frankish kings and several relics,
including 'a pretended naile of the Crucifix'. Like any good Protestant he waxed
indignant and sceptical of the claims made for this relic, as also of the crown of
thorns he saw in Louis IX's chapel.[38]

The Lancashire Catholic Nicholas Blundell (grandson of the younger William
referred to above) was a meticulous record-keeper generally more interested in
his estate and his greyhounds than in historical matters. He nevertheless made
occasional visits to booksellers and the odd trip to sites of interest, especially tombs,
while in London. He viewed Ralph Thoresby's collection of antiquities on a trip
to Leeds in July 1720, 'which are very well worth seeing' but of which he notes
nothing particular, rather like the bored tourist who bolts through the National
Gallery or the Louvre between lunch and teatime just to say he's been.[39] Very
little interest in historic sites emerges from his account of a trip to Catholic Flanders,
though much concern with relics and reliquaries, which he helped to buy and
sell the way Protestant antiquaries would barter for coins or manuscripts. Yet for
Blundell, unlike many of his Protestant contemporaries who treated foreign
relics with derision, these remained fundamentally sacred objects, not antiquarian collectibles. He kissed 'the blood of Christ' at the Chapel of the Holy Blood,
Bruges, on his visit there in March 1715, and visited other shrines in Antwerp
and Liège. When visiting the church at Leigh, he and a friend 'saw there some
remarkable bones of persons as were dead'. In addition to the pyx and chalice
that his great-great-grandfather, William Blundell the elder, had made from the
Anglo-Saxon coins discovered in a burial site on the family property, Nicholas
Blundell owned and 'constantly wore' a silver heart-shaped reliquary, and the only

---

[37] Anon. (attrib. Lt. Hammond), *A Relation of a Short Survey of the Western Counties, made by a
lieutenant of the military company in Norwich in 1635*, ed. L. G. Wickham Legg, in *Camden Miscellany*,
16, Camden Soc., 3rd ser., 52 (1936), 21, 46–7, 78; Evelyn, *Diary*, iv. 472.

[38] Evelyn, *Diary*, i. 58, 65. An unknown English traveller in Italy in the early 1660s was more amused
than offended by the spectacle of locals kissing the shrine of St Anthony: Hants. RO 19M 59/5, p. 25,
anonymous travel diary, c.1664 and companion volume of inscriptions, 19M 59/6, p. 12.

[39] Blundell spent 2s. 3d. on a trip to the Tower in May 1703, noted in his disbursement book; he
made another visit there with his wife and another female tourist in Aug. 1717 to see the armoury:
The great diurnal of Nicholas Blundell of Little Crosby, ed. F. Tyrer, 3 vols. Rec. Soc. of Lancashire and
Cheshire (1968–72), i. 315, ii. 206, iii. 17.

book mentioned in the inventory of his goods at his death in 1737 was a collection of lives of the saints.[40]

By the late seventeenth century, however, the popular veneration of relics had been largely extinguished, and iconoclastic zeal was held in some circles a greater evil than recalcitrant popery. Most Protestants could safely adopt an attitude of benign amusement to popular Catholicism, so long as it was kept outside the church and off the throne. With this relaxation of the fear of religious infection came a greater degree of detachment towards the objects of the past—though as late as 1711 Edward, Lord Harley was told by his friend and tutor William Stratford that excessive love for antiquities might still make a person superstitious.[41] The relic could safely be removed from grave or shrine and transferred to the closet. The discovery in 1682 of a sealed glass coffin in a garden at Rumford, Essex, became well known over the ensuing decade, partly because the bones within were those of an infant. Abraham de la Pryme, who learned of its existence in 1695, was unable to discern from his informants whether this was the body of 'the onely child of some great king or queen, or the reliques of some little martyr layed up there in the times of popery'.[42] In 1700 John Jackson, on tour in Italy, collected a number of relics for his uncle, Samuel Pepys. 'I have not only a stock of holy-door mortar, but Agnus Dei's, pieces of the rock of Gaieta that cleft at our Saviour's Crucifixion, etc.', Jackson proudly reported, 'enough to enable me to sett-up for the curing of all distempers at my return to England.'[43]

It is possible that the official abolition of relic-worship in the 1530s helped to nurture, rather than to deter, an interest in antiquity. The antiquarian artefact filled the empty space left by the relic, by providing an object of interest for people in the present which could be more safely examined, fondled, cherished, and displayed, even if it were no longer venerated. As Baudrillard has observed, the antique object shares with the relic a tendency to 'reorganize the world' in a manner that purely functional objects do not.[44] The deliberate excavation of objects given the secular sanctity of antiquity provided an opportunity for a non-superstitious version of the 'pious archaeology' represented by the earlier, pre-Reformation discovery of a new relic. By the same token, the expedition to visit a historic site offered a journey to see an object of antiquity in a fixed location,

---

[40] Blundell, *Great diurnal*, ii. 19–20, 163, 175, 201, 203, iii. 46, 239. The elder Blundell's coins and what he did with them are discussed in Ch. 7 below.

[41] Hist. MSS Comm., *The Manuscripts of His Grace the Duke of Portland, Preserved at Welbeck Abbey*, 10 vols. (1891–9), vii. 36 (Stratford to Harley, 28 June 1711).

[42] *The Diary of Abraham de la Pryme, the Yorkshire Antiquary*, ed. C. Jackson, Surtees Soc., 54 (1870), 100; for another example of a lead coffin containing an ivory staff and a silver coin, see Camden's manuscript 'suplement' to the 1610 translation of *Britannia*, Bodl. MS Smith 19, p. 69, written late in 1622 or early in 1623.

[43] Pepys himself sarcastically urged his nephew to see the pope's tiara and kiss his toe: *The Private Correspondence and Miscellaneous Papers of Samuel Pepys*, ed. J. R. Tanner, i. 304, 321.

[44] J. Baudrillard, *The System of Objects*, trans. J. Benedict (London and New York, 1996), 79. This is a useful suggestion, though one that sets up too sharp a polarity between antiquity and functionalism. This is perhaps appropriate today, but the boundaries were more blurred in the early modern era, as we shall see below in discussing the circulation of antiquarian objects.

thereby replicating the 'therapy of distance' involved in the saintly pilgrimage.[45] In the case of some Catholic antiquaries, especially in the first half-century or so following the Reformation, the discovery of an antiquity can have offered something like that quality of *praesantia*, a bridge to the remote past, that the relic had done. This was surely how William Blundell I saw his coins, found on ecclesiastical land, and connected in his mind with holy Saxon kings such as Alfred and Edmund, but the sense of awe emerges even from an Elizabethan Protestant such as George Owen, in his 'Dialogue of the government of Wales'. In this the Welsh native Demetus tells the visiting Italian civilian Bartholus how 'wee allso of Penbrookeshyre reserve as a treasore the bones of that famous prynce Edmund earle of Richmond' (the father of Henry VII). A 'treasore' is not the same as a relic, but Demetus's statement implies a quality of reverence not far removed from William Blundell and his treasure trove.

In fact, the very word 'relic' remained part of the language while losing its specifically religious connotations. John Philipot could refer casually in the mid-seventeenth century to 'some reliques yet remaining of a [Roman] camp' in Kent, while John Milton, certainly no friend to popery, wrote eloquently on Shakespeare's 'honor'd bones' and 'hallowed relics'.[46] Aubrey tells us that the first duke of Buckingham had dug for antiquities on Salisbury plain in the 1620s but had found only a silver-tipped bugle-horn, which 'his Grace kept in his closet as a great Relique'. Superstitions would continue to surround the discovery of antiquities well into the eighteenth century, and probably later, but these did not necessarily derive from a strong Catholic presence in an area. 'Even the present inhabitants of Littlemore [near Glastonbury] talk often of relicks being dug up at the Minchery,' smiled the sceptical Thomas Hearne in the 1720s, 'but then few of them know that it belong'd to nunns.'[47]

Was the antiquity, then, simply the relic desacralized? Antiquarianism came in to England just as the relic was on its way out, but we must not suppose from this coincidence that the one was simply a convenient secular replacement for the other. Despite the superficial similarity of the activities of relic-worship and antiquarian collection, a straightforward ascription of antiquarian interest to the same impulses that venerated pieces of bone and hair seems problematic. First of all, such a theory does not explain equally fervent antiquarian movements across Catholic and Protestant Europe, all of which produced *Wunderkammern* consisting

---

[45] Both phrases are Peter Brown's: *The Cult of the Saints*, 90, 92.

[46] George Owen, 'Dialogue of the government of Wales' (written 1594), in *The description of Penbrookeshire*, ed. H. Owen, 3 vols. (1892–1906), iii. 38; John Philipot, *Villare Cantianum: or Kent surveyed and illustrated*, ed. Thomas Philipot (1659), 238; John Milton, 'On Shakespeare', *Complete Poems and Major Prose*, ed. M. Y. Hughes (New York, 1957), 63, lines 1–3; *A Relation of a Short Survey of the Western Counties*, 18.

[47] M. Hunter, *John Aubrey and the Realm of Learning* (1975), 160; [Charles Eyston], *The History and Antiquities of Glastonbury*, ed. Thomas Hearne (Oxford, 1722), preface, p. xxiii. An anonymous Welsh antiquary at the beginning of the eighteenth century expressed fascination with the 'incombustible linnen' in which ancient Britons had supposedly wrapped their dead before burning 'to preserve their bones and ashes': Anon., 'The Description of Wales', Bodl. MS Gough Wales 5 (written c.1700 and added to by later authors), fo. 2ᵛ.

of natural marvels housed together with coins, medals, and other trophies of time. Secondly, the medieval relic and the post-Reformation antiquity performed different cultural functions. The relic, valued for sacred, medicinal, and prophylactic qualities, connected its owner or worshipper with the original object or person to whom it had putatively belonged, and by extension with God and eternity: it was fundamentally timeless rather than historical.[48] In contrast, while the antiquity often had some intrinsic monetary value—jewels, weapons, and coins could be sold—it typically had little practical use, and it connected its collector not with eternity but with temporality, mutability, and social change. This very temporality invited imaginative reflection on the social and political world within which it had been created, and thereby offered a much greater stimulus to thought about the past, even if that thought very often fell wide of the truth.

Sir Thomas More provides an early example of a way of looking at such objects quite remote from that of the later Tudor or Stuart antiquary. More recalled how he had once, thirty years earlier, been standing in Barking Abbey when a number of relics, including a piece of wood in the shape of a cross, fell from an image which was being moved into a new tabernacle; he observed that no one could tell how long the image had been there, but guessed that 'iiii. or v c. yere ago that ymage was hyden whan the abbey was burned by infydels and those relyques hyden therin'. Yet it did not concern him that the origins of or circumstances of the relics were unknown; it did not even matter that they might be recent fakes, since it 'nothyng hurted the soules of them that mysse take it'.[49] The relic was, for More and virtually every orthodox Tudor Catholic, a sacralized object whose significance could be divorced from specific times and places. A later antiquary might, if he were Catholic, take the same attitude, but would also have been much more interested in discovering where the object came from, why it was made, to whom it belonged, and what functions it had served in past times.

Ultimately, the growth of an antiquarian culture was furthered less by the similarity between antiquities and saintly relics than by the cosmic correspondences and resemblances evoked by certain types of antiquities, particularly natural ones such as fossils. As late as the eighteenth century, objects such as these could be assumed, for instance, to have prophylactic or medical powers of the sort that Keith Thomas has described. Isabella Swinburn, a Northumberland Catholic, importuned her son William to locate for her a specimen of 'a ston about Cackston . . . that is very like an Ougly oyster shell and is cald the devels claw' because this was believed to be an effective cure for gallstones.[50] Fundamental assumptions about the cosmos, about the manner in which things fit together in the natural, occult, and divine spheres, rendered the study of primitive and medieval

---

[48] As Peter Brown has remarked, the late antique and medieval *passio*, or account of the passion of a saint, is similarly ahistorical, breaching 'the paper-thin wall between the past and the present'. *The Cult of the Saints*, 81.

[49] Thomas More, *Dialogue Concerning Heresies*, in *Complete Works of St Thomas More*, 15 vols. (New Haven, Conn., 1963–97), vol. vi. pt. 1, pp. 222–3.

[50] Northumberland RO ZSW 510/0 (Isabella Swinburn to Sir William Swinburn, Bt., n.d., c.1706–16).

antiquities acceptable in the same way that study of nature itself became desirable, as an expression of reverence for God and his creation. Gallstones, animal bones, amber, and other artefacts were valued primarily for the system of natural correspondences that they were believed to illustrate. The late Renaissance fervour for such items had, in turn, as much to do with the continuing influence of Pythagorean and Neoplatonic cosmology as it did with a growing 'scientific' interest in natural history, even if it would ultimately survive the displacement of these conceptual frameworks by Newtonianism.[51]

THE VISUAL REPRESENTATION OF HISTORY

The lack of an English tradition of narrative history painting is one of the unsolved mysteries in the history of Western art. Explanations linking greater English individualism to the comparative wealth of portraiture, courtly, familial, and civic, and the rarity of history-painting to Protestant hostility towards images are not wholly persuasive. In truth, England had never developed the habit of representing the sequential past visually, even prior to the Reformation, stained glass windows filled with Bible stories being the notable, non-secular exception; paintings of historical episodes are virtually unknown. Sienese, Venetian, and Florentine artists were busy decorating civic buildings and noble *palazzi* with a profusion of images drawing on both sacred and secular history (and even more commonly mixing the two),[52] but there is no corresponding English tradition. Where Italian examples such as Paolo Uccello's *Battle of San Romano* and Raphael's rendition of the Academy depict respectively a real episode from recent history and an idealized meeting of ancient philosophers, there are no corresponding Tudor paintings of the Wars of the Roses, or Stuart renditions of the execution of Anne Boleyn. Even in the seventeenth century, when exceptions occur such as Sir James Thornhill's series of story panels for the dome of the rebuilt St Paul's, they remain on biblical rather than profane subjects.[53] All this is in contrast to the more frequent pictorial representation of history in the printed media, for instance the inclusion of portraits of authors and of kings in history books, or the depiction of historical scenes in Foxe's Book of Martyrs, which relied on graphic representations of trials, torments, and burnings to convey its author's message to those who could not read. When Richard Verstegan published his *Restitution of Decayed Intelligence* in 1605, a pioneering study of the Anglo-Saxon heritage, he too included woodcuts of episodes such as the imagined landing of the first

[51] Houghton, 'English Virtuoso,'; Lawrence Stone, *The Crisis of the Aristocracy, 1558–1641* (Oxford, 1965), 715–22.

[52] M. Baxandall, *Painting and Experience in Fifteenth-Century Italy*, 2nd edn. (Oxford, 1988), 45 ff., is an incisive introduction to the place of paintings in the cognitive field of Renaissance Italians.

[53] Thus Dudley Ryder, who visited the dome in the company of Thornhill in 1716, when the dome was built but 'the history part . . . not begun yet', approved the choice of story sequences deleting the account of St Paul escaping Rome by being let down in a basket because this was a 'trifling' story, unworthy of its serious topic. *The Diary of Dudley Ryder 1715–1716*, ed. W. Matthews (1939), 307.

Fig. 6.1. The arrival of the Anglo-Saxons in Britain. Illustrated in Richard Verstegan, *A Restitution of Decayed Intelligence* (1605), 117

Anglo-Saxons—here garbed in sixteenth-century clothing (Fig. 6.1).[54] The most popular history of england of the first half of the eighteenth century, by Paul de Rapin-Thoyras, featured simple scene illustrations at the head of several chapters, though these compare poorly with the work's numerous portraits, many of them researched and engraved by the antiquary George Vertue.[55]

Richard Steele commented in 1712 on the distinctive English orientation towards the portrait rather than the continuous narrative, contrasting English art

[54] On the later development of a visual culture of English history in the early nineteenth century, see esp. R. Mitchell, *Picturing the Past: English History in Text and Image 1830–1870* (Oxford, 2000); on the influence of Romanticism in engendering a sense of the picturesque, the several works of Stephen Bann, though they emphasize the French rather than English experience, are helpful, in particular *The Clothing of Clio* (Cambridge, 1984) and *Romanticism and the Rise of History* (New York, 1995).

[55] Paul de Rapin-Thoyras, *The History of England, as well Ecclesiastical as Civil,* trans. N. Tindal, 15 vols. (1728–32); M. Myrone, 'Graphic Antiquarianism in Eighteenth-Century Britain: The Career and Reputation of George Vertue (1684–1756)', in M. Myrone and L. Peltz (eds.), *Producing the Past: Aspects of Antiquarian Culture and Practice 1700–1850* (Aldershot, 1999), 35–54.

with Italian 'history-painting', an observation repeated later in the eighteenth century by Sir Joshua Reynolds, who sharply distinguished between the history painter, who 'paints man in general' and the portrait artist, who paints 'a particular man'.[56] Steele's contemporary Jonathan Richardson did not allow the lack of English history painting to stop him prescribing rules for the artist desiring to represent the past in colour. These are worth repeating for their close comparison of the visual licence and creativity of the artist with the exact precision of the writing historian. 'He that paints a history well, must be able to write it; he must be thoroughly inform'd of all things relating to it, and conceive it clearly, and nobly in his mind, or he can never express it upon the canvas', Richardson argues. 'A painter of this class must possess all the good qualities requisite to an historian.' But knowledge of events would not in itself be sufficient; the history painter must grasp the culture of the age, 'he must moreover know the forms of the arms, the habits, customs, buildings, &c. of the age, and countrey, in which the thing was transacted, more exactly than the other needs to know 'em.' Indeed, the artist's calling is higher than the historian's—there are clear echoes here of Sir Philip Sidney's comparison of poetry and history a century and a half previously. 'And as his business is not to write the history of a few years, or of one age, or countrey, but of all ages, and all nations, as occasion offers, he must have a proportionable fund of ancient, and modern learning of all kinds.' In short, the history painter must have the qualities of a good historian 'and something more', the talents of a good poet. As to strict representation of historical reality, there is a small zone for invention. 'A painter is allow'd sometimes to depart even from natural, and historical truth.' Yet Richardson was writing in a different age than Sidney's, one in which history, not poetry, now ruled the intellectual waves, and in which accuracy and fidelity were steadily contrasted to fiction and deception. In the final analysis, he reins in his artist's ability to embroider historical truth: 'But these liberties must be taken with great caution and judgment; for in the main, historical and natural truth must be observed, the story may be embellish'd, or something of it par'd away, but still so as it may be immediately known ... History must not be corrupted, and turn'd into Fable or Romance.'[57]

Richardson's extensive thoughts on the subject should be read as a prescription on the theory of art, conceived universally and with the benefits of the Grand Tour in mind, rather than as a comment on domestic history painting. With some notable Augustan exceptions such as William Kent's scenes from the reign of Henry V, painted episodes from the British past were still relatively uncommon in England. So it would remain till the 1760s, when artists such as Robert

[56] *The Spectator*, 555 (6 Dec. 1712), ed. Bond, iv. 496; Joshua Reynolds, *Seven Discourses Delivered in the Royal Academy by the President* (1778), 103 (for the 'sufficiently general' appeal of classical and scriptural subjects across Europe), 110, 138 (for a comparison of the purposes of history painting and portrait painting).

[57] *Historienmalerei*, ed. T. W. Gaehtgens and U. Fleckner (Berlin, 1996), which reference I owe to the kindness of Irving Lavin. This includes the quoted extract from Jonathan Richardson, *An Essay on the Theory of Painting* (1725), and from Reynolds, *Discourses on Art* (1769–90).

Edge Pine and John Hamilton Mortimer began a tradition of historical painting that would mature slightly later with the American émigré Benjamin West.[58] A broader tradition of narrative painting, and a much-expanded use of narrative illustration in history books, would follow in the early nineteenth century.[59] Although portraits of kings, nobles, and other famous personages could be found throughout the kingdom, depiction of non-contemporary historical scenes and persons lagged well behind the Continent,[60] where English visitors could peruse them in palaces, closets, churches, and museums. In 1679, for instance, James Bonnell would describe for John Strype a way of cheaply decorating a room with 'Cronologie & historie, according to a model I have seen abroad', wherein a wall was divided into a number of sequential squares, 'each square being assigned to a year, or 10 years, or a century (as we see caus, or design a more particular or general history) & the most remarkable passages of that time being painted theron, by frequent looking, the pictures will mind us of the history, & the plat in which it lyes (which will not be difficult to remember, the order being so distinct) will tell us the year'.[61] George II's German queen, Caroline, decorated her closet at Kensington Palace with Kent's scenes from the French wars of Henry V, along with various Holbein portraits, as a means of familiarizing herself with the history of her adopted country, but similar examples elsewhere are hard to find for a further generation.[62]

Despite the paucity of narrative painting, the homes of royalty, the aristocracy, and the gentry were not devoid of visual representations of famous people, historical or legendary, apart from their direct ancestors. Heroic figures such as the Nine Worthies, pagan, Hebrew, and Christian, decorated the beams in the hall of a house at Great Binnal in Astley Abbots, Shropshire, built in 1611.[63] Highly skilled foreign painters such as the Fleming Theodore Bernardi, who decorated Chichester Cathedral with a series of kings of England and bishops of Chichester, added to a late medieval tradition of domestic wall painting which survived the Reformation. William Harrison commented in the 1570s on the inclusion of 'divers histories, or herbs, beasts, knots and suchlike' on wall hangings.[64] When the furnishings at Belton House (the Lincolnshire seat of the Brownlow baronets) were surveyed in 1688 the hall alone included 'eight and twentie pictures of Kings and

---

[58] A. U. Abrams, *The Valiant Hero: Benjamin West and Grand-Style History Painting* (Washington, DC, 1985), 45–71, 186–9; P. Cannon-Brookes (ed.), *The Painted Word: British History Painting: 1750–1830* (Woodbridge, 1991), 9–22; R. Strong, *And When Did You Last See Your Father? The Victorian Painter and British History* (1978) provides an excellent account of the eighteenth-century background, though its understanding of the related historical writing is dated. For later depictions of ancient British history, see especially S. Smiles, *The Image of Antiquity: Ancient Britain and the Romantic Imagination* (New Haven and London, 1994).

[59] D. Irwin, *Neoclassicism* (1997), 129 ff.; Mitchell, *Picturing the Past*, 15 and *passim*.

[60] P. F. Brown, *Venetian Narrative Painting in the Age of Carpaccio* (New Haven and London, 1988); L. Andrews, *Story and Space in Renaissance Art: The Rebirth of Continuous Narrative* (Cambridge, 1995), esp. pp. 95–112 on 'Space and Narrative'. I owe this latter reference to Marilyn Lavin.

[61] CUL MS Mm. 6.49 (Strype letters), item 3 (Bonnell to Strype 14 Jan. 1679/80).

[62] Strong, *And When Did You Last See Your Father?*, 15.

[63] Pevsner, *BE: Shropshire* (1958), 63.

[64] William Harrison, *The Description of England*, ed. G. Edelen (Ithaca, NY, 1968), 197; F. W. Reader, 'Tudor Domestic Wall-Paintings', pt. 1, *Archaeological Journal*, 92 (1935), 243–86, at p. 249; for the Bernardi paintings see id., pt. 2, *Archaeological Journal*, 93 (1936), 220–62, at p. 228.

Queens'.[65] The palace at Sheen or Richmond built by Henry VII at the very end of the fifteenth century was destroyed under the Commonwealth. Few ruins remain, but it is known that between the windows were representations of some famous rulers of England including Brutus, Hengist, Arthur, William Rufus, Richard I, and Henry VII himself. A visitor to Kensington House at the end of Queen Anne's reign would have found the queen's dressing room decorated with a kaleidoscope of the classical, biblical, and English pasts. The queen's closet, as befitted a place devoted to study and reflection, featured a head of Erasmus by Holbein and various images of biblical history, such as the meeting of Jacob and Esau. The royal gallery was similarly furnished with Titian's Tarquin and Lucretia, Tintoretto's Esther and Ahasuerus, and various Van Dyck Stuart portraits. In the store room were pictures of more historical personages and the rare historical scene, such as the landing of Charles II in 1660, early portraits of Henry VII and his older son Prince Arthur, a head of Julius Caesar and—in a decidedly antiquarian mood—a Van Alst scene of five Turks taking an inscription from Aristotle's tomb amid ruins.[66]

The visual historical image was not confined to the painting, owing to the relative ease with which woodcut and copperplate engravings could be made. In another context, Tessa Watt's recent book on the popular religious literature of the later sixteenth century has demonstrated how woodcuts and other images either printed as separates or removed from books, large and small, were used to decorate humbler homes. Some of these images may well have been historical as well as religious, even if the owner did not necessarily know what they signified, or care to make a distinction between the sacred and the historical. By the end of the seventeenth century, aided by new and cheaper reproductive techniques, local artists were busily selling historical and topographical prints and engravings, many of which had been produced a century earlier. Antiquaries were, from the 1660s, paying much closer attention to matters of size, shape, and orientation in rendering precise drawings of the objects they studied, and the historical art of the middle and later eighteenth century was in turn often informed by earlier antiquarian illustration. The re-founded Society of Antiquaries made both the preservation *and* the circulation of antiquities in engraved form its principal mission:

whereas our own country abounds with valuable reliques of former ages, now in the custody of private gentlemen, or lying in obscurity; & more are daily discoverd either by chance or by the diligence of such as tread in the commendable footsteps of those who revivd the spirit of this kind of learning among us, in the last century.[67]

---

[65] *Records of the Cust Family: Second Series, the Brownlows of Belton 1550–1779* (London, 1909) 160.

[66] These were called pictures in the contemporary descriptions, but Colvin suggests that they were probably sculptured figures. *The History of the King's Works*, iii: 1485–1660, ed. H. M. Colvin, 2 pts. (1975–82), pt. 2, p. 227; Bodl. MS Douce 74, list of pictures at Kensington, c.1710.

[67] SAL Minute Book 1718–32, pp. 2–3; SAL Misc. I, Letters and Papers 1707–40, art. 6, the original plan for the restored society. In its first few years, the minute book shows the society making a concerted effort to acquire portraits of English kings. Those of Edward III, Elizabeth of York, and Henry VII were purchased in 1718 for a guinea (£1. 1s. 0d.), 12s. 6d., and £1. 0s. 4d. respectively; prints of the Vertue engraving of Richard II's portrait were ordered to be sold at 2s. 6d. apiece as a revenue-generating measure: ibid. 7 May 1718 and 4 Feb. 1719. For the development of draughting techniques for antiquities, especially larger ones such as the megaliths, see P. J. Ucko, M. Hunter, A. J. Clark, and A. David, *Avebury Reconsidered: From the 1690s to the 1990s* (1991), 63–70.

At its revival in 1717, the society made George Vertue both a fellow and its official engraver; over the next four decades he would publish eighty-six plates ranging from maps and views to individual artefacts.[68] Prints of objects like the horn presented by 'Ulphus' prince of Deira to the church of York, owned by Samuel Gale (who presented a learned discourse on the object to the society in 1718) circulated at a cost of 1s.[69] Old maps and plans were sold in similar fashion. Gale's fellow antiquary William Stukeley saw 'an old ground plot' of Exeter, drawn during Elizabeth's reign, at the shop of a goldsmith who had made a plate of it.[70] While walking around the Chester walls in 1717, Henry Prescott spied a picture 'supplying the busienes of a window, in a sordid house, keeping out the weather'. He enquired after it and paid 1s. for an unidentified figure, dressed as a 'knight or soveraign of the Garter' and drawn in colour. He took it to be a representation of Queen Elizabeth. There is no evidence as to what the former owner, to whom it principally represented protection from the weather (and who had clearly displayed the image to the outside rather than inside of his dwelling), thought it might have been.[71]

The representation of historical personages in the form of statues and busts also increased during the Restoration and early eighteenth century, the Augustan taste for depicting its magnates as Roman citizens being complemented by the placing of statuary from recent history in public places. The Guildhall in Exeter, for instance, had statues of General Monck and of Princess Henrietta Maria, daughter of Charles I, while the bishop of Winchester commissioned Grinling Gibbons to make a new marble statue of Thomas Wolsey for a niche at the college that the cardinal had founded, Christ Church.[72] University colleges were also the site of many figures, at first of medieval founders and later, as tastes veered towards classicism, of Roman and contemporary figures: until it was replaced in 1709 by a figure of Queen Anne, the pseudo-Gothic niche in the third stage of University College's gatehouse, for instance, contained the figure of King Alfred, long credited with the establishment of both the college and the university, and whose arms continue to adorn the building.[73] When the East Range of Oriel College was

[68] Myrone, 'Graphic Antiquarianism', 39.

[69] SAL Minute Book 1718–32, pp. 11, 18. For a list of such engravings up to 1722, including such famous images as the funeral effigy of Richard II, Waltham Cross, and the horn of Ulphus, see SAL MS Stukeley III/289. The Vertue engraving of the horn is reproduced in Myrone and Peltz, *Producing the Past*, 34.

[70] SAL MS Stukeley IV/i/336 (Stukeley to earl of Pembroke, Aug. 1723).

[71] *The Diary of Henry Prescott, LL.B., deputy registrar of Chester Diocese*, ed. J. Addy, J. Harrop, and P. McNiven, 3 vols., Rec. Soc. of Lancashire and Cheshire, vols. 127, 132, 133 (Chester, 1987–97), ii. 594 (17 Sept. 1717).

[72] SAL MS Stukeley IV/i/336 (Stukeley to earl of Pembroke, Aug. 1723) for the Exeter statuary. Unfortunately, Gibbons's statue, when executed, looked the wrong way for the niche in which it was intended to stand. Hist. MSS. Comm., *Portland*, vii. 38, 249 (Stratford to Edward Harley, 7 July 1711 and 28 Feb. 1718/19).

[73] Royal Commission on Historical Monuments, *An Inventory of the Historical Monuments in the City of Oxford* (London, 1939), 116. Alfred, along with fifteenth-century statuary of King Arthur, Cnut, Edward the Confessor, Emperor Constantine, Edgar, Ethelbert, and Oswald, was also among the historical figures moved from the old library windows to the chapel windows at All Souls in 1750: ibid. 18.

constructed between 1637 and 1642, before the high tide of Palladianism, it was given two niches with pseudo-Gothic canopies, featuring statues of Edward II, that college's putative founder, and James I.[74] This sort of juxtaposition of figures separated widely in time was not at all unusual, and continued into the more anachronistically sensitive Restoration. The new library at Queen's College, built in the early 1690s, featured figures of moderns such as Charles I, Queen Henrietta Maria, and Charles II's Secretary of State Sir Joseph Williamson along-side Edward III and Queen Philippa, the founder.[75] Statues of kings adorned both churches and palaces, especially royal buildings: the reliefs in the Inner Court at Nonsuch, Samuel Pepys noted in 1665, were 'filled with figures of stories'.[76] Oxford and Cambridge colleges also had other rarities with historical connections on display, such as New College's carved chest showing scenes from the battle of Courtrai.[77]

In addition to the routine armorial display, funeral effigies, and pictorial narratives of the creation that adorned most parish churches, travellers to the larger and older churches or surviving castles could see more remarkable images and objects of interest, including pictures of long-dead kings, churchmen, and mag-nates. A visitor to the chapel of St Thomas Becket at Christ Church Cathedral, for instance, would see painted on its windows the images of King Edward IV and his children, juxtaposed with the story of Christ's martyrdom. Exeter Cathedral's entrance and sedilia featured several freestone statues of historical figures, including Edward the Confessor, Leofric, the see's first bishop, 'receiving his congee desleere in an humble posture on his knee'. Near the effigy of Walter Stapleton, the see's murdered medieval bishop, was depicted in stone the failed escape attempt of the bishop's brother after avenging the death.[78] Tourists stopping by St Gregory's in Suffolk were shown the bust of another murdered fourteenth-century prelate, Simon Sudbury, though in the 1720s this was vandalized.[79] Worshippers at Chichester Cathedral at the end of the seventeenth century could see on the south side of the church pictures of many past kings of England, pre-Conquest monarchs being featured on the east wall and rulers from William I to William III on the west.[80]

---

[74] Ibid. 93.

[75] Ibid. 99 and plate 52. The use of classical figures for decoration at such classically oriented insti-tutions of course pre-dated the more widespread aristocratic classicism of the latter part of the cen-tury, as busts and portraits of ancients served as iconic encouragements to scholarship: the Roman imperial busts over Sir Robert Cotton's predominantly medieval and Tudor collections are one famous instance. Another is the marble monument, acquired by Merton College for its chapel in 1621–2, fea-turing figures of Ptolemy, Euclid, Tacitus, and St John Chrysostom: ibid. 81 and plate 143.

[76] Pepys, *Diary*, ii. 199.

[77] Royal Commission on Historical Monuments, *Inventory of the Historical Monuments in the City of Oxford*, p. xxviii.

[78] *Relation of a Short Survey of the Western Counties*, 12, 74–6.

[79] Suffolk RO (Ipswich) HD 1538/79 (unfoliated church notes by Francis Blomefield, 1723–6).

[80] *Diary and Letter Book of the Rev. Thomas Brockbank 1671–1709*, ed. R. Trappes-Lomax, Chetham Soc., NS 89 (1930), 91.

BETTER (LOOKING) HOMES AND GARDENS

Beginning in the seventeenth century, remnants of the past increasingly decorated the outdoor and indoor living space of the wealthy.[81] Lord William Howard of Naworth, whose daughter married Sir Robert Cotton's son, took time out from the management of his northern estates to study the nearby Hadrian's Wall, to draw inscriptions and Roman coins, and to decorate his garden with excavated Roman altars. Place House, the Wriothesley home at Titchfield, had a sumptuous gallery, open to visitors in the 1630s, 'beautify'd with many neat curious pictures, of kings, queens, princes, and noble persons, both deceas'd and living'.[82] William Stukeley's detailed description of his tour through Wilton in 1723 depicts a neoclassical house, strewn with graphic and plastic icons of ancient virtue and medieval valour: paintings, busts, and statuary of the royal family, ancient Romans such as Scipio and Marcus Aurelius, and, at the end of one passage, a fully armoured, larger-than-life statue of a medieval ancestor. Separate galleys bore pictures of other forebears, and images of Richard II, as well as pictorial extracts from Sidney's *Arcadia*. But most spectacular of all was the view from inside out: the twelve vistas cut through the woods, each opening on to 'some remarkable object' of history, whether Salisbury Cathedral, a Roman road, or the Greek urns that adorned the garden. And the visitor could stroll on 'Sidney's walk' where the Elizabethan poet composed his work, and wander into the oldest part of the house, a 'famous old armour' dating to Edgar's time.[83]

The physical appearance or beauty of an object or an old building was often of greater concern to collectors and tourists than the information it might provide to those of scholarly inclinations. It was only in the late nineteenth century that the great archaeologist Pitt-Rivers urged students to study the commonplace and ugly together with the rare and beautiful.[84] In the three preceding centuries, the balance of opinion fell squarely on the side of beauty, with apologies needed for an interest in the poorly made or damaged.[85] Many members of the public who expected to find splendour and beauty in a celebrated artefact were disappointed—rather like modern visitors to the Louvre who find the real Mona Lisa an anti-climax. This was certainly Sir William Brereton's reaction on seeing St Peter's chair at York Minster in 1635, 'an old, little, decayed chaire, and famous

---

[81] G. Worsley, *Classical Architecture in Britain: The Heroic Age* (New Haven and London, 1995), esp. pp. 198–221, for garden buildings; Smiles, *Image of Antiquity*, 194–217, for the use of prehistoric remains in gardens at the end of the eighteenth century.

[82] *Relation of a Short Survey of the Western Counties*, 43; *DNB*, *sub* 'Howard, Lord William'; Camden, *Britain*, trans. P. Holland (1610), 642.

[83] SAL MS Stukeley IV/i/333 (copied in SAL MS 264, fos. 77ʳ–79ʳ), Stukeley to Dr [Richard] Mead, n.d. 1723. The close connection between the cabinet and the garden is brought out in J. D. Hunt, 'Curiosities to Adorn *Cabinets* and *Gardens*', in O. Impey and A. MacGregor (eds.), *The Origins of Museums: The Cabinet of Curiosities in Sixteenth- and Seventeenth-Century Europe* (Oxford, 1985), 193.

[84] G. Daniel and C. Renfrew, *The Idea of Prehistory*, 2nd edn. (1988), 65.

[85] For an early seventeenth-century discussion of this, see P. N. Miller, *Peiresc's Europe: Learning and Virtue in the Seventeenth Century* (New Haven, Conn., 2000), 142.

for nothing butt the antiquitie thereof'.[86] To Henry Oxinden, who attended his cousin's wedding at Leeds Abbey in 1640, its most noteworthy feature was its great antiquity, which in this case was accentuated by the visual appeal of grounds and gardens.[87] When the acerbic Thomas Nashe visited the ruins of Burgh Castle near Yarmouth, which had been described earlier in *Britannia*, he revealed little of Camden's sensitivity to fallen grandeur. 'Nothing of that castle, save tartered ragged walles nowe remaines, framed foure square, and overgrowne with briars and bushes, in the stubbing up of which, erstwhiles they digge uppe Romane coynes, and booies and anchors.'[88] Thomas Martin of Palgrave thought Cardiff Castle 'very ruinous' in 1724, though conceding it also looked 'very noble'; but Llandaff church he simply found 'wofully dilapidated'.[89]

Old buildings and walls did not all seem rustic and romantic, even to antiquaries with a profound devotion to the past. For the vast majority of observers the truly magnificent medieval structure was not that which showed its age but that which, through careful (and often expensive) refurbishment retained its original freshness. The Winchester lawyer and historian John Trussell penned a poetic 'Complaint of the Castell of Winchester' in the 1630s in which the decaying medieval structure, still used for much of the shire's judicial process, despairs at its own 'growing infamy' and calls upon town authorities to restore it to its medieval grandeur.[90] The inhabitants of Ambleside, near Lake Windermere, lived near the 'dead carcasse', as Sir Daniel Fleming had it, 'of an ancient city, with great ruines of walls and many heapes of rubbish'; he valued a 'good old house' like Sackbridge not because of its great age but because it 'of late hath been much beautified and amended'. John Percival's diary is full of distaste for buildings fallen into decay, such as the gargantuan Audley End, which 'for want of repair would fall to the ground of it Self' (and would in fact be partly pulled down and rebuilt by Vanbrugh about 1718). Wholesale destruction of medieval buildings and their replacement by modish Palladianism marked much of the construction of the later seventeenth century. Even an antiquary such as Samuel Gale, because an admirer of Roman above medieval antiquities, thought the rebuilding of Stanwick Park, Yorkshire, by Sir Hugh Smithson a splendid contribution,

[86] 'Journal of Sir William Brereton, 1635', *North Country Diaries: Second Series*, ed. J. C. Hodgson, Surtees Soc., 124 (1914), 3.

[87] *The Oxinden Letters*, ed. D. Gardiner (1933), 165.

[88] Thomas Nashe, *Nashes Lenten Stuffe*, in *Works of Thomas Nashe*, ed. R. B. McKerrow, 5 vols. (1904–10), iii. 205. Castles were already falling into decay by the early Tudor period with the end of baronial warfare. A systematic campaign of demolition by the Long Parliament during and after the civil war, which continued after the Restoration, resulted in more ruins and sometimes in the complete razing of these edifices to the ground. M. W. Thompson, *The Decline of the Castle* (Cambridge, 1987), 138–57.

[89] Bodl. MS Top. gen. e. 85 (Thomas Martin's 'Some Remarks and Observations') is an account of a tour from Eton to Oxford, and is full of observations of ruined or desecrated churches.

[90] John Trussell, 'The Complaint of the Castell of Winchester' (c.1630), Bodl. MS Top. Hants. c. 5, pp. 91–2. These comments may not have been well received locally. Trussell, who had been mayor in 1625, was in trouble with justices of the peace in 1632 for 'very unsemlie speeches and uncivile behaviour' and his ability to practise as an attorney was suspended temporarily: Hants. RO W/K1/11/1.

replacing a medieval mansion house with a Roman palazzo; it was doubly appropriate in Gale's view because the place was once 'a station of that brave people, it being neare the great Via Militaris'.[91] Symbols of the past such as Roman statuary, which increasingly figured in the landscape gardening and interior design of the seventeenth and eighteenth centuries, were marks of taste as much as indices of historical interest, their proper display requiring adequate space. Jeremiah Milles, future president of the Society of Antiquaries, admired the earl of Pomfret's collection at Easton, near Towcester, but thought it 'a great pity my Lord does not furnish his house, or some grand room in it, with so many good statues as he has; they now loose half their beauty, by being crowded so close together'; this was in contrast to the 'handsome room' at Althorp in which the duke of Marlborough maintained both his library and busts of the twelve Caesars.[92]

A few decades earlier, John Evelyn had been of much the same sentiments as Gale and Milles, favouring outright replacement of decayed medieval buildings rather than attempts at modernization and preservation. Evelyn thought the ducal palace at Norwich 'an old wretched building', better demolished and rebuilt elsewhere. When he visited Nonsuch Palace in 1666 he marvelled that the plaster statuary had endured so well since Henry VIII's time. But he wanted the pieces removed to a gallery, or at least to 'some dry place' for preservation. Some time later he was asked by their owner, Henry Howard, to find a new home for the Arundel marbles which had passed into his custody. Evelyn was shocked to discover the marbles 'miserably neglected, & scattred up & downe about the Gardens & other places of Arundell-house'. Fearing that the corrosive air of London would ruin them he advised Howard to bestow them on Oxford University, where they remain today in the Ashmolean. At Arundel House the marbles lay about in much the same neglected state from which the earl of Arundel's agents had removed them in the 1620s. Historically, this was not an entirely inappropriate way to keep them: outdoors, open to nature and providing inconspicuous decoration for the pleasure of domestic visitors rather than artificially displayed in—or displaced to—a public museum.[93] But to Evelyn, as to many others who were scholars at home

[91] 'Sir Daniel Fleming's Description of Cumberland, Westmorland and Furness, 1671', pp. 10, 25, in *Fleming–Senhouse Papers*, ed. Edward Hughes, Cumberland Rec. Soc., 2 (1962), 10; Percival, *The English Travels of Sir John Percival and William Byrd II: The Percival Diary of 1701*, ed. M. R. Wenger (Columbia, Mo., 1989), 78; Bodl. MS Top. gen. c. 66 (Samuel Gale collections), fos. 29–30. Two miles from Stanwick, noted Gale, lay Ashe, the seat of Sir Conyers Darcy, which peculiarly juxtaposed a stuccoed hall, decorated with the busts of Roman emperors, in front of 'a large mount on which is erected a noble Gothick Temple' (ibid., fo. 30ᵛ). On the beautification of public buildings in the Augustan era see P. Borsay, *The English Urban Renaissance: Culture and Society in the Provincial Town 1660–1770* (Oxford, 1989), 111.
[92] BL MS Add. 15776 (Jeremiah Milles's travels in England, 1735–43), fos. 17ʳ, 21ʳ.
[93] Evelyn, *Diary*, iii. 427, 495, 534; this would seem to anticipate the distinction between *in situ* exhibition of fragments in a facsimile 'reality' such as a reconstructed town or house, and the 'in context' exhibit which isolates the artefact from its refabricated surroundings but envelops it with labels and other sources of textual information: one aims at a realistic 'feel', the other at the representation of knowledge arising from and relating to the object. See B. Kirshenblatt-Gimblett, 'Objects of Ethnography', in I. Karp and S. D. Lavine (eds.), *Exhibiting Cultures: The Poetics and Politics of Museum Display* (Washington, DC, 1991), 386–443, esp. pp. 388–90; S. Greenblatt, 'Resonance and Wonder', in Karp and Lavine (eds.), *Exhibiting Cultures*, 42–56, repr. in Greenblatt, *Learning to Curse: Essays in Early Modern Culture* (New York, 1990), 170 ff.

but spectators while abroad, classical aesthetics and the requirements of conservation combined to outweigh strict fidelity to history, and to leave so magnificent a set of marbles in this 'natural' setting was neither practical nor desirable. A sense of taste and his dislike of Gothicism as 'heavy, dark, melancholy and monkish piles' overruled any possible fetish for a sublime, ruined historicity.[94] As Evelyn would remark to Thomas Browne, he had been drawn to an interest in landscape by 'the many defects which I encounter'd in Bookes and in Gardens, wherein neither words nor cost had bin wanting, but judgement very much'.[95]

Evelyn also appears to have had a strong sense that gardens and cabinets of antiquities should be connected, an impression developed during his travels through Europe in the 1640s. As early as 1634, Henry Peacham, one of the earl of Arundel's retainers, had pronounced that antiquities could be kept in both 'gardens and galleries', and Italianate influences on early seventeenth-century collectors like Arundel created, for a time, a disposition towards the display of exclusively classical busts and fragments indoors and out, such as the marbles Arundel had been permitted to import in 1613.[96] In the eighteenth century, however, the legitimacy of a decorative, and often entirely manufactured, pastness that drew eclectically on a wider variety of period styles became well established. Writing to the earl of Manchester in 1707, Sir John Vanbrugh expressed the hope that the mansion he was building to replace the Tudor house at Kimbolton Castle, Huntingdonshire, could be given 'something of the castle air' without a real castle's roughness; the use of old stone to this effect would save money and 'make a very noble and masculine show'.[97] When the long-lived Stourton family sold its Wiltshire estate to the Hoare family of London bankers in 1714, the medieval house —a 'gothique building' as Aubrey had once termed it—was almost immediately pulled down and replaced by a modern dwelling on a nearby site. Renamed Stourhead by Henry Hoare the elder, it passed in 1725 to his son and namesake, who would spend much of the next sixty years building its magnificent gardens. Stourhead was fashioned into a 'paradise', as Hoare called it, which synthesized the classical and the Gothic, including the transplanted and reconstructed Bristol Cross.[98] The plan called for a Temple of Ceres or Flora in the north, containing

---

[94] Evelyn, *Account of Architects and Architecture* (1723), quoted in Worsley, *Classical Architecture in Britain*, 179. Evelyn appears to have been among the first Englishmen to use the term Gothic with great frequency, though inconsistently, to describe architecture ranging from ancient to that 'betwixt ancient and modern': E. S. De Beer, 'Gothic: Origin and Diffusion of the Term: The Idea of Style in Architecture', *Journal of the Warburg and Courtauld Institutes*, 11 (1948), 149–62, at p. 155 and n. 2.

[95] *Works of Sir Thomas Browne*, ed. G. Keynes, 4 vols. (1964), iv. 274 (Evelyn to Browne, 28 Jan. 1659/60); cf. *Travels of Peter Mundy*, iv. 46.

[96] Peacham, *The Compleat Gentleman*, 3rd edn. (1634), 'Of Antiquities' (a chapter not included in the 1st edn. of 1622), 109–24; Hunt, '*Curiosities* to Adorn *Cabinets and Gardens*', 195, 201; M. Vickers, 'Greek and Roman Antiquities in the Seventeenth Century', in Impey and MacGregor (eds.), *Origins of Museums*, 223–44.

[97] *The Complete Works of Sir John Vanbrugh*, iv: *The Letters*, ed. G. Webb (1928), 14 (Vanbrugh to earl of Manchester, 18 July 1707); also quoted in Worsley, *Classical Architecture in Britain*, 189.

[98] P. Thompson, 'The Survival and Revival of Gothic Architecture', *Apollo*, 76 (May 1962), 283–7, at p. 284; N. Boulting, 'The Law's Delays: Conservationist Legislation in the British Isles', in J. Fawcett (ed.), *The Future of the Past* (1976), 9–33.

imitation seats, altars, and busts whose designs were lifted directly from the pages of antiquarian authors such as Montfaucon: a pantheon, statues of Neptune and Apollo, and a grotto with nymphs. At the western end came a silent shift to the medieval with what Hoare saw as the 'scheme which will Crown or Top all', Alfred's Tower. This was an edifice erected as a testament to the value of peace, in the wake of the Seven Years War, and it bore a memorial inscription to King Alfred, in modern English rather than Anglo-Saxon.[99]

To be sure, more than aesthetic concerns or attitudes to the sanctity of the past were involved in building and decorating: taste and intellect overlap with the exigencies of comfort and convenience. Though as a rule age and antiquity were normally equated with authority and quality, the converse of this has previously been noted in the present work. The old also represented decay, and the limitations and requirements of everyday life required that the outworn or broken be dispatched, destroyed, and replaced, or at least mended. In the context of the massive rebuilding which took place across England beginning in the late sixteenth century, one's relative enthusiasm for the past might shape a decision to build anew or to renovate and improve an existing structure. The Cecils chose the former, building Theobalds and later Hatfield; the earl of Leicester simply modernized his ancient castle at Kenilworth so that it might be suitable to receive the queen, a tactic emulated by the Sidneys at Penshurst early in the seventeenth century. The Percy earls of Northumberland, whose nobility was much older than that of the Sidneys and Cecils, undertook minimal changes to their 'auncient castle'. As a result Charles I refused the earl's offer of hospitality in 1639, choosing instead the comforts of a more fully restored nearby abbey.[100] Edward Pytts bought a ruined castle at Kyre, Worcestershire, in 1586, and within a decade had transformed it. By the 1610s, however, he had embarked on a completely new structure in an even more lavish style. As Bishop Fisher had once pointed out in a different context, old walls do not a building make.[101]

The kind of Romantic admiration for decaying structures that is more generally associated with the later eighteenth and early nineteenth centuries, and with the displacement of classical taste by the sublimely natural or artificially Gothic,

---

[99] K. Woodbridge, *Landscape and Antiquity: Aspects of English Culture at Stourhead 1718 to 1838* (Oxford, 1970), 51–70; id., *The Stourhead Landscape* (1986), 25–7, 58, 60; J. Turner, 'The Structure of Henry Hoare's Stourhead', *The Art Bulletin*, 61/1 (Mar. 1979), 68–77; National Trust, *Stourhead* (1986); M. McCarthy, *The Origins of the Gothic Revival* (New Haven and London, 1987), 31; G. Worsley, *Classical Architecture in Britain: The Heroic Age* (New Haven and London, 1995), 109. I am indebted to Barbara Paca for pointing out to me the case of Stourhead. Another invented Alfredian monument, 'Alfred's Hall' at Lord Bathurst's park at Cirencester, was built in the 1720s and resembled ruins 'Imbrowned with Age' within twenty years: S. Piggott, *Ruins in a Landscape* (Edinburgh, 1976), 119.

[100] W. G. Hoskins, 'Rebuilding of Rural England, 1570–1640', *Past and Present*, 4 (1953), 44–59; J. Summerson, *Architecture in Britain, 1530 to 1830* (London and Baltimore, 1953); D. E. Wayne, *Penshurst: The Semiotics of Place and the Poetics of History* (Madison, Wis., 1984); 'Journal of John Aston', in *Six North Country Diaries*, ed. J. C. Hodgson, Surtees Soc., 118 (1910), 13.

[101] M. Airs, *The Making of the English Country House 1500–1640* (London, 1975), 14; John Fisher, *Treatyse concernynge . . . the seven penytencyall psalmes*, in *English Works of John Fisher*, pt. 1, ed. J. E. B. Mayor, EETS, ES 27 (1876), 151.

can be found in the Tudor and Stuart periods in a less pronounced form.[102] It remained a perquisite of those who did not have to live in such buildings on a daily basis. Even an antiquary such as John Stow, who deplored the demographic expansion of London and the changes it had caused, did not value ruins for their own sake. Stow praised those who restored or even outrightly replaced decaying buildings, such as the merchant-tailor Richard May, who left £300 for the refurbishing of Bakewell Hall, a medieval centre for cloth trade. In 1588, after ten months, the medieval structure was gutted and 'the foundation of a new, strong, and beautiful storehouse' had been laid. The real heritage lay in the historic purpose of the building, not in its crumbling mortar, and many thought the restoration of a building to its original purpose the best form of reverence for its antiquity.[103]

James Yonge's reaction on seeing the ruins of Westminster and London after the Great Fire of 1667 reveal feeling for the lost buildings, but also a strong sense of the need to press on with reconstruction in a modern way:

What sorrow possessed my soul and heart when I saw that once glorious city lie in ruins and ashes, divers of the heaps of rubble yet smoking. It's not to be exprest how dismal it lookt, nor how unconcerned most people that past by were at it—that city that was once the glory of this isle, if not the world, now made a ruinous heap, a filthy, inaccessible place.

As fervent a lover of antiquities as Stukeley spoke with great approval of how the citizens of Exeter had 'demolished' several old religious and aristocratic houses, turning them into streets of new houses 'full of numerous familys, thriving inhabitants instead of indolent and useless monks'.[104] William Cowper, the future chancellor, wrote to his first wife Judith of his disappointment on seeing the house of one Mr Atkins, which the Cowpers had contemplated purchasing, 'the most dismal I ever saw, dark, low and old-fashioned', a problem not improved by the old furniture. 'If I should attempt to live in it, without rebuilding, I should dye of the spleen.'[105]

Among the most thoughtful considerations of this issue is a letter from John Vanbrugh to the duchess of Marlborough (with whom he was already beginning to fall out) concerning the building of Blenheim and the landscaping of its grounds. Convinced that the planned demolition of the old Woodstock Manor

---

[102] H. M. Colvin, 'The Origins of the Gothic Revival', in *Il neogotico in Gran Bretagna: problemi attuali di scienza e di cultura* (Rome, 1978), 3–18; Piggott, *Ruins in a Landscape*, 118–29; on the continuity of Gothic tastes in architecture, see G. Worsley, 'The Origins of the Gothic Revival: A Reappraisal', *TRHS*, 6th ser., 3 (1993), 105–50, and id., *Classical Architecture in Britain*, 175–95.

[103] Stow, *Survey of London*, 258–9. When St Peter's church, Ipswich, was rebuilt in the seventeenth century, the plans included restoring an ancient, but obstructed, passage, and a concurrent installation of an altar rail in front of the chancel so as to force traffic along the new route: Bodl. MS Tanner 310 (Suffolk collections), fo. 2ʳ, undated.

[104] *The Journal of James Yonge [1647–1721] Plymouth Surgeon*, ed. F. N. L. Poynter (1963), 107; SAL MS Stukeley IV/i/336 (Stukeley to earl of Pembroke, Aug. 1723).

[105] Herts. RO D/EP. F81 (unfoliated letters of William and Judith Cowper, 13 Sept. 1702). On the development of notions of comfort, in so far as they affected domestic building, see J. E. Crowley, *The Invention of Comfort: Sensibilities and Design in Early Modern Britain and Early America* (Baltimore, 2000). I am grateful to my former colleague Jack Crowley for allowing me to read this book prior to publication.

in its entirety would be an aesthetic as well as a historical loss, he made a compelling case for the preservation of ruins that did *not* specifically depend on an emotive sympathy but drew rather on an imaginative understanding of the actual history which the meanest dwelling had witnessed:

> There is perhaps no one thing, which the most polite part of mankind have more universally agreed in; than the vallue they have ever set upon the remains of distant times; nor amongst the severall kinds of those antiquitys, are there any so much regarded, as those of buildings: Some for their magnificence, or curious workmanship; and others; as they move more lively and pleasing reflections (than history without their aid can do) on the persons who have inhabited them; on the remarkable things which have been transacted in them, or the extraordinary occasions of erecting them.

Future travellers, Vanbrugh continues, will be told that Blenheim is a historic site—Marlborough's favourite dwelling, erected by the bounty of the queen for the duke's great services to the country. So, in turn, should Woodstock Manor be preserved because though it is not a monument to the prowess of Henry II, 'one of the bravest and most warlike of the English kings', it is nevertheless famous as the 'scene of his affections', namely his dalliance with Rosamond. Vanbrugh perhaps calculated, wrongly, that this domestic and romantic episode from the past would appeal to the duchess as a woman. Rosamond's death, allegedly at the hands of Eleanor of Aquitaine, was long associated in both chronicles and oral tradition with the maze or bower at Woodstock. What were believed to be remnants of this could be seen from Stow's time to Vanbrugh's. Most important, the architect asks, among the multitude of visitors who daily watched the erection of this monument to the memory of the battle of Blenheim, 'Are there any that do not run eagerly to see what ancient remains are to be found of Rosamonds Bower?'[106]

Herein lies an early example of an issue that has divided the curators of art and artefacts down to the present, with greater urgency after the development of a more systematic preservationist programme in many countries during the nineteenth century.[107] To what degree does historicity inhere in an object, be it artefact, book, or building, that is preserved in its received state, however decrepit? Is it legitimate to restore an object to its pristine form, at the cost of adding modern ingredients and removing it from its original setting, or ought it to be kept in a state of decay, wormholes and all? If an old wooden house is rebuilt, plank by plank, over a period of time, at what point does it cease to remain the original building, however much it may *look* like it? Modernity has clearly opted to employ all the tools at its disposal to cleanse, restore, and beautify antique treasures with minimal intrusion, but our early modern predecessors had yet to develop such sophisticated

---

[106] Vanbrugh then gilds the lily by offering further, aesthetic, reasons for not removing the structure, in case 'the historicall argument stands in need of assistance', specifically that its destruction will leave 'an irregular, ragged ungovernable hill': *Complete Works of Sir John Vanbrugh*, ed. Webb, iv. 29–30. (11 June 1709). He was unsuccessful in defending the house, which was gone by the time Hearne visited it in 1719, after Vanbrugh's loss of favour with the duchess of Marlborough.

[107] C. Dellheim, *The Face of the Past: The Preservation of the Medieval Inheritance in Victorian England* (Cambridge, 1982), 77–130.

conservation techniques.[108] Wholesale replacement, especially of objects that were required to be functional and not simply decorative, often offered the path of least resistance. Thus without any murmur of discontent or sentiment did the civic leaders of Reading sell their old armour in 1624 and order new to be bought in its place.[109] We have seen several other contexts in which, when push came to shove, the old lost its aura and was quickly jettisoned in the interest of practicality.

Between destruction and recycling on the one hand and careful restoration on the other lies the third course of leaving the ruin as a ruin for its own exemplary and inspirational sake. That proto-Romantic attitude, too, can already be seen developing in the later seventeenth century.[110] How different from both the fastidious Evelyn's views of architecture, and Vanbrugh's attempt at castle emulation through recycled brick, is Anthony Wood's veneration of ruins in their unaltered state. Wood had little interest in tampering with them in the name of restoration. In this he anticipates John Ruskin's 1849 opinion that old buildings are not ours to touch but 'belong partly to those who built them, and partly to all the generations of mankind who are to follow us'. On seeing Eynsham Abbey in 1657 Wood was 'strucken with a veneration of the stately, yet much lamented, ruins of the abbey there, built before the Norman Conquest'; he spent 'some time with a melancholy delight in taking a prospect of the ruins of that place'.[111] Abraham de la Pryme similarly described the remains of Thornton monastery in Lincolnshire, of which little more than the gatehouse remained in 1696, as 'the finest place that ever I saw in my life'. In recounting what was likely an imaginary visit to the remains of a castle, Richard Steele remarked in *The Guardian* that 'the ruins of the several turrets and strong-holds, gave my imagination more pleasant exercise than the most magnificent structure could do, as I look upon the honourable wounds of a defaced soldier with more veneration than the most exact proportion of a beautiful woman'. Even in the late seventeenth century theirs was clearly a minority position, the majority opting for taste, order, and beauty above age, like John Percival on his travels, or like Bishop Burnet, who was impressed with a third-century Greek manuscript because though it was of less antiquity than some of those in the royal collection at St James, 'yet this has been better preserved and is much more entire'.[112] This was the dominant view well into the

[108] D. Lowenthal, *The Past is a Foreign Country* (Cambridge, 1985), 385–96; M. Hunter, 'The Preconditions of Preservation: A Historical Perspective', in D. Lowenthal and M. Binney (eds.), *Our Past Before Us: Why Do We Save It?* (1981), 22–32; H. Prince, 'Revival, Restoration, Preservation: Changing Views About Antique Landscape Features', ibid. 33–49.

[109] *Reading Records: Diary of the Corporation, 1431–1654*, ed. J. M. Guilding, 4 vols. (1892–96), ii. 175.

[110] Prince, 'Revival, Restoration, Preservation', 33, for a useful distinction between three different types of conservation: revival (making new buildings look old by introducing period features); restoration (making old buildings serve new purposes by replacing outmoded or visually unpleasing parts); and preservation (keeping old buildings in good repair but with minimal replacement of structures).

[111] Wood, *Life and Times*, i. 228–9, 455; J. Ruskin, *Seven Lamps of Architecture* (1849), quoted in Prince, 'Revival, Restoration, Preservation', 45.

[112] *Diary of Abraham de la Pryme*, 131–2; *The Guardian*, 50 (7 May 1713), ed. J. C. Stephens (Lexington, Ky., 1982), 196; Percival, *The English Travels of Sir John Percival and William Byrd II*, passim; Gilbert Burnet, *Dr Burnet's Travels* (Amsterdam, 1687), 43.

eighteenth century. Indeed, we have seen the same questions arise on the textual side of antiquarianism, in the exactly contemporary discussions by 'ancients' and 'moderns' of the proper treatment of texts—whether Homer and Livy were best left on their own or ought instead to have the restorative tools of modern philology applied in order to enhance appreciation and understanding.

APPEARANCES AND REALITIES

The preference for neatness and order over ruin and decay overlaps with intellectual predispositions for or against the medieval and 'Gothic' as opposed to the classical and Roman. It is not identical with that distinction, since both classical and medieval artefacts could be possessed and displayed in various states of repair, and since, too, both could be replicated in the sort of grand artificiality achieved at Stourhead. But in the dissenting opinions of landscapers, antiquaries, and the proud owners of seventeenth-century *Wunderkammern* and gardens alike, we can also see an early conflict in the long campaign between devotion to the ancient and celebration of the medieval. That is a campaign more analogous to trench warfare than to open battle. It is marked by the slow advances and retreats of classicism, from Jones's first experiments with Palladianism and the decline of vernacular architecture, through the Baroque of Wren, Hawksmoor, and Vanbrugh, the neo-Palladianism of Kent and Paine, and the Gothic revival of Strawberry Hill.[113] It is also marked by a frequent desire for verisimilar artificiality that conflicted with historical preservation as supported throughout the eighteenth century by the Society of Antiquaries. The Gothic revival would itself see the destruction of much genuine medieval architecture, especially cathedrals, so that restored (that is, new) 'medieval' buildings, could be erected in their place, with further damage to be rendered by improvers such as James Wyatt and, a generation or so later, G. G. Scott.[114] And it is a campaign in which many of the participants, like Henry Hoare, found themselves in an antique no man's land. When the Society of Antiquaries set up shop once more in Anne's reign, with a devotion to particularly British antiquities, the students of Roman artefacts dominated the early membership. When interests appeared to be veering a bit too near the Gothic, a number of them formed a special subgroup, the Society of Roman Knights, whose members called each other by a mixture of Celtic and Roman titles, and devoted themselves to collecting and publishing Roman remains exclusively. But the group did not last long.[115] As it had been in the time of Camden a century or more earlier, the separation

---

[113] Briggs, *Goths and Vandals*, 31–49, 79–117; McCarthy, *Origins of the Gothic Revival*, 63–115.

[114] J. Fawcett, 'A Restoration Tragedy: Cathedrals in the Eighteenth and Nineteenth Centuries', in Fawcett (ed.), *The Future of the Past*, 75–115.

[115] For the Society of Roman Knights see J. M. Levine, *The Battle of the Books: History and Literature in the Augustan Age* (Ithaca, NY, 1991), 388–9; Piggott, *William Stukeley: An Eighteenth-Century Antiquary*, 2nd edn. (New York, 1985), 53–5. For the influence of antiquarianism on Gothic architecture and the close ties between eighteenth-century architects and members of the Society of Antiquaries, see McCarthy, *Origins of the Gothic Revival*, 17–26.

of study by chronological period was problematic. Camden had found himself, in beginning with Roman remains in the *Britannia*, inexorably drawn towards the post-classical past that overlaid them like a palimpsest, and his willingness to embrace the medieval as well as the classical comes across in his *Remains*. So, too, his greatest Augustan successor, Stukeley—Chyndonax to his fellow knights —would find no incompatibility between his membership in the maverick Roman Knights and the secretaryship of the society as a whole.[116]

Preferences for classical order over both pre-Roman roughness and medieval ruin also played a significant, and not altogether helpful, role in the ability to identify and set a period to the physical remains of the past, great and small. The origins of that most famous of prehistoric monuments, Stonehenge, perplexed many a scholar from Camden, who thought it a 'huge and monstrous peece of worke',[117] to Inigo Jones and John Aubrey, and beyond to Stukeley and the eighteenth century. Single-sheet prints of it were circulating among the literati as early as the Restoration, and engravings of it turn up in a number of Augustan antiquarian works (Fig. 6.2). [118] To the ordinary traveller it was an indecipherable enigma, most often comfortably ascribed to one or other of the ancient British monarchs listed in Geoffrey of Monmouth; popular tradition, repeated in Geoffrey and elsewhere, believed that Merlin had moved the stones from Ireland to their current site.[119] One English traveller was confident in his information that it had been founded by Aurelius, 'a Brittish king above 1000. yeeres since' to commemorate the Saxon massacre of his nobility. Many others were less sure of their information.[120] The Reverend Thomas Brockbank, who visited Stonehenge in 1695, was fairly

[116] Nichols, *Literary Illustrations*, iv, 497 (Samuel Gale ('Cunobelin') to Stukeley ('Chyndonax'), 1 Aug. 1727). Cf. Roger Gale's comment on the noticeable Roman theme to his visit to Chester with Stukeley in 1725. 'We got hither last Saturday at 11 in the morning, and before dinner the Doctor had disinterred a most magnificent Roman Gate . . . and indeed every thing is so much Roman, that we are to have a Roman salmon for dinner to-day.' Nichols, *Literary Illustrations*, iv. 487 (Roger Gale to Samuel Gale, 3 Aug. 1725).

[117] Convinced that the 'rudnes and deformity' of the structure ruled out its having been erected in Romano-British times, 'when architecture was come to the topp of perfection', he was nevertheless sceptical of the 'doting impiety' that the stones had been fetched by magic from Ireland, since 'the like stones for greatnes and graine are found at Avely [i.e. Avebury] and elsewher': Camden, *Britain*, 251–4; Camden, 'A Suplement of the Topographicall description of Britain published MDCX . . .', Bodl. MS Smith 19, p. 45. I am grateful to Mr M. Kauffmann of the Bodleian Library for permission to consult this Select Manuscript.

[118] Dr Thomas Browne collected such a print, through his son, in 1678: *Works of Sir Thomas Browne*, iv. 81–2 (Browne to Edward Browne, 8 May 1678).

[119] On the Galfridian account of the origins of Stonehenge and its variants see L.V. Grinsell, 'The Legendary History and Folklore of Stonehenge', *Folklore*, 87 (1976), 5–20; L. Spence, *Minor Traditions of British Mythology* (New York, 1972), 138–9.

[120] Camden, *Britain*, 251; T. D. Kendrick, *British Antiquity* (1950; repr. 1970), 133–67; Inigo Jones, *The most notable antiquity of great Britain, vulgarly called Stone-heng on Salisbury plain. restored by Inigo Jones Esquire* (1655; Scolar Press facs. edn., Menston, Yorks., 1972); Evelyn, *Diary*, iii. 116; John Aubrey, *Monumenta Britannica, or a miscellanie of British antiquities* (comp. 1665–93), ed. J. Fowles (Sherborne, Dorset, 1980), 74–102; Hunter, *John Aubrey and the Realm of Learning*, 148–208; G. Daniel, 'Edward Lhwyd: Antiquary and Archaeologist', *Welsh History Review*, 3 (1967), 345–59. James I was interested in Stonehenge, and the monument's association with past monarchs was perhaps enhanced in the Restoration because Charles II had rested there in his flight from the battle of Worcester in 1651, and retained an interest in both it and Avebury: Parry, *Trophies of Time*, 286.

Fig. 6.2. Stonehenge, engraved by Johannes Kip. From *Camden's Britannia*, 95–6

typical in being thoroughly confused by the tangled knot of oral and written explanations of the monument which he encountered:

Some will needs have y^m to be made by Art, (but y^s I can scarce credit), and say they were set here in memory of some great Battle; Others y^t this was a place of worship, some sort of a Temple; and all agree in nothing but y^t ye can give no certain account of them.[121]

[121] *Relation of a Short Survey of the Western Counties*, 65; *Diary and Letter Book of the Rev. Thomas Brockbank*, 88.

Inigo Jones's essay on Stonehenge, which would vex readers from Samuel Gale to the twentieth century, can be seen less as an amusing and wildly erroneous speculation, than as a logical and resourceful attempt to make sense of a mysterious monument within the limits of a highly truncated concept of world time, and with a gaze set firmly on the Graeco-Roman artistic heritage, reinforced by a New World understanding of ancient Britons as primitives. Jones, the early importer of Palladianism, saw Stonehenge as first and foremost a piece of classical architecture, and idealized it accordingly (Fig. 6.3). Since to his mind the Druidic Britons had no knowledge of architecture, the earliest date at which it could have been erected was some time after the Roman conquest. He proceeded from there to present a well-reasoned argument for the monument as a Roman temple. He did not see that it was the remnant of an age far more remote, because he had no concept of such a remote period.[122] Other writers disagreed with Jones as to the monument's original purpose and its time of building, but with little more success. Walter Charleton ascribed it to the Danes; Aylett Sammes, following a theory advanced by the Huguenot scholar Samuel Bochart (1591–1667), thought it Phoenician. John Aubrey, with a greater faith in the native ingenuity of the ancient Britons, made it a pre-Roman Druid temple. (He was in any case less impressed by Stonehenge than by the Avebury monolith, the name of which resembled his own, and which 'does as much exceed in greatness the so renowned Stoneheng, as a Cathedral doeth a parish church').[123] William Stukeley, a few decades later, was familiar with Aubrey's unprinted writings on both Stonehenge and Avebury; he defended the earlier antiquary's estimate of the purpose of the former with great erudition, but dated the work to about 460 BC. As late as 1860 it could still seriously be argued that the monument was post-Roman.[124] Only Edmond Halley, among the early students of this most perplexing of monuments, seems to have guessed that it was much, much older. His explanation baffled Thomas Hearne, who remarked that 'Dr Halley hath a strange, odd notion that Stonehenge is as old, at least almost as old, as Noah's Floud.'[125] Amid this flurry

[122] Jones, *Stonehenge restored*, 3, 72–5.

[123] Walter Charleton, *Chorea Gigantum, or the Most Famous Antiquity of Great-Britain, Vulgarly Called Stone-heng* (1663); Aylett Sammes, *Britannia Antiqua illustrata* (1676), 395–402; Aubrey, *Wiltshire*, 315, 320; Hunter, *John Aubrey and the Realm of Learning*, 158; Ucko et al., *Avebury Reconsidered*, 10–35.

[124] William Stukeley, *Stonehenge, a Temple Restored to the British Druids* (1740) and *Abury: a Temple of the British Druids* (1743); S. Piggott, *William Stukeley: an Eighteenth-Century Antiquary* (Oxford, 1950; rev. edn., 1985); id., 'Antiquarian Thought in the Sixteenth and Seventeenth Centuries', in L. Fox (ed.), *English Historical Scholarship in the Sixteenth and Seventeenth Centuries* (1956), 108; Parry, *Trophies of Time*, 312 ff. on Sammes and Bochart; R. J. C. Atkinson, *Stonehenge* (1956), 94, 181–204; A. Schnapp, *The Discovery of the Past*, trans. I. Kinnes and G. Varndell (New York, 1996), 212–19. J. M. Levine, *Dr. Woodward's Shield: History, Science, and Satire in Augustan England* (Berkeley, 1977), 73–4, 313, contains an excellent discussion of the problems facing seventeenth-century students of Stonehenge and the equally mysterious monument at Avebury. For a critique of Piggott's influential evaluation of Stukeley (and in particular his contrast of Stukeley's accurate, 'fieldwork' phase of the 1720s with a later period when his observations were vitiated by a passionate interest in Druid religion and culture, with which in fact he had been familiar much earlier), see Ucko et al., *Avebury Reconsidered*, 53–4, 74–98, 244.

[125] Hearne, *Remarks and Collections*, vii. 350.

Fig. 6.3. Stonehenge drawn as present reality and past ideal. This series of early eighteenth-century engravings presents two views of Stonehenge (top left and right), compared with Inigo Jones's classicized representation of an idealized Stonehenge as constructed by the Romans, to whom Jones attributed it. Most significant, however, are the four European megaliths depicted in the middle panels, a mark of the increasing inclination at the end of the seventeenth century to group and compare similar objects and monuments. From Bernard de Montfaucon, *The Supplement to Antiquity Explained and Represented in Sculpture*, trans. D. Humphries, 5 vols. in 2 (1725), vol. v, book VII, p. 567.

of opinions the former puritan preacher turned wit, Robert Gay, may be pardoned for letting fly *A Fool's Bolt*, his own half-serious exploration of the subject (with a notable attack on 'Out-I-Go Jones').[126]

[126] Robert Gay, *A Fool's Bolt Soon Shott at Stonage*, written in the 1660s and read by Aubrey in manuscript, but published first by Hearne as an appendix to his edition of *Peter Langtoft's Chronicle* (Oxford, 1725). This is reproduced, and attributed to Gay (on the basis of a manuscript note by Aubrey) by Rodney Legg, in his *Stonehenge Antiquaries* (Sherborne, Dorset, 1986), 17–51. Gay's remark about Jones is at p. 29 of Hearne's edition and p. 43 of Legg's.

The disagreement of England's greatest scholars could be frustrating to those with tidy minds, fond of periodizing. Samuel Gale, whose taste for classical order led him to denounce the 'uniform structure' of Stonehenge, was nevertheless drawn into speculation on its origins. 'The learned are still in suspense about its original', noted Gale after visiting the site in 1705, 'and the very stones with which it is built have not a little contributed to the obscurity, since there are no quarries in this country that produce such a sort of stone'. Gale's own inability to find a wholly satisfactory time slot for the structure, to fix it as *either* Roman *or* Druid, was clearly an irritation to him. Unlike the equally classically minded Jones, Gale saw the very untidiness of Stonehenge as an argument against Roman origins, since the Romans, as famous architects, would scarcely have erected such a monstrosity. As for Jones's argument that the upright stones were of the Tuscan order of columns, Gale could only add that ''tis so far from being any order, that it has neither proportion in any particular or the least symmetry but a barbarous, unhewn composition altogether different from [and] below the Roman genius'. But he was equally unhappy with Aubrey's theory that it had been a Druid temple and with various other explanations: a tomb to the memory of Boadicea, or Uther Pendragon, or Constantine; or, even less likely, a Danish fortress.[127]

It would take the fuller development of a science of stratigraphy before an accurate system for the dating of land formations and of the artefacts buried beneath them would be possible, though scholars such as Stukeley, methodically noting the depth at which objects were buried as well as the type of soil in which they were found, were making a good start in this direction.[128] Correct dating of structures as ancient as Stonehenge would wait longer still.[129] Yet as early as the Restoration some scholars, such as Plot and especially Aubrey, realized that the key to a full understanding of landscape features and antiquities alike lay in closer attention to natural history, and especially to the geology of the areas in which they were located or discovered, coupled with a firm grasp of the chronology of floods and other 'great mutations' which affected the quality of soil. Others, such as Sir Thomas Browne, remained pessimistic. Fixed on the marvellous qualities of antiquities, on their beauty or their hoary repulsiveness—their own sense of 'wonder' overwhelming the object's potential historical 'resonance', they were unable to see them, as some of their contemporaries did, in a colder light as part of a past which was susceptible to reconstruction. In Browne's view, even the improved

---

[127] Samuel Gale, 'Tour through parts of England' (written 1705), Bodl. MS Top. gen. c. 66, fos. 40^r, 43^{r-v}.

[128] SAL MS Stukeley IV/i/296, here referring to a Roman silver plate dug up 6 June 1729 in Risley Park, Derbyshire, within a mile of Dale Abbey; for another example, at the ruins of Roman Vernumetum, see MS Stukeley IV/ii/309.

[129] Stukeley produced a model of Stonehenge that he had made, in wood, and some sketches, 'whence he demonstrated the true form thereof' to members of the Society of Antiquaries in 1722: SAL, Minute Book 1718–32, p. 56 (7 Feb. 1722). On stratigraphy and related developments, see S. J. Toulmin and J. Goodfield, *The Discovery of Time* (1965), 198; C. C. Albritton, Jr., *The Abyss of Time: Changing Conceptions of the Earth's Antiquity after the Sixteenth Century* (San Francisco, Calif., 1981; repr. Los Angeles and New York, 1986), 106–11; R. Porter, *The Making of Geology: Earth Science in Britain, 1660–1815* (Cambridge, 1977); G. Daniel, *A Hundred and Fifty Years of Archaeology* (Cambridge, Mass., 1976), 13–28.

state of knowledge that existed concerning English and foreign archaeology was insufficient to prevent confusion surrounding 'subterraneous discoverie'. As he remarked to Dugdale in 1660, the body of a man buried five years earlier in the horned hide of an ox might, 'when the memorie heereof is past', confuse its future discoverers, '& what conjectures may arise thereof, it is not easie to conjecture'.[130]

To fault these writers for a seeming inability to divine the meaning of such objects is to misunderstand the mental context within which they were studied. There had yet to evolve any notion of a 'prehistoric' era (except in the limited sense of 'a time before histories were written').[131] The most obvious division among types of human being that was available was that between the savage and the civilized, and this division was not a specifically historical one. It is often commented that the discovery of indigenous populations in the New World gave European authors a sense of the 'ascent' of man.[132] Exposure to alien societies, represented in graphic form since the drawings of John White (engraved by Theodore de Bry in the late sixteenth century), and textually in the literature of the Spanish Conquest, did provide support for the idea that civilizations could advance, and stimulated a healthy sense of cultural relativism. Yet it in no way engendered an understanding of biological evolution, or even a very clear concept of technological development. Indeed, rather the opposite was the case: Europeans could conceive of the division between savage and civilized man as cutting across national boundaries at a specific time rather than separating primitive 'man', taken as a species, from his successors. They therefore tended to view savage races, such as the pre-Roman Britons, or Roanoke Indians, as less fortunate heathen cousins, bereft of the benefits of Christianity and civil government. They did not see in them the surviving examples of a remote and primitive way of life that had at one time been common to all humankind.[133] A time-scheme of 6,000 years simply did not allow for an evolutionary concept of prehistory. Without this, it was also impossible to establish an accurate chronology for the dating of archaeological discoveries.

The boundary between ancient and medieval was still murky, all the more so when artefacts could be dated with no certainty; it was too easy to reach an opinion based on their physical appearance and then find negative or positive evidence to support it in a number of sources: the stream of correspondence directed

---

[130] *Letters of Sir Thomas Browne, Works*, iv. 325 (Browne to Dugdale, Oct. 1660); A. C. Howell, 'Sir Thomas Browne and Seventeenth-Century Scientific Thought', *Studies in Philology*, 22 (1925), 61–80. I borrow the very useful distinction between 'resonance' ('the power of the object displayed to reach out beyond its formal boundaries to a larger world, to evoke in the viewer the complex, dynamic forces from which it has emerged') and 'wonder' ('the power of the object displayed to stop the viewer in his tracks, to convey an arresting sense of uniqueness') from Stephen Greenblatt's essay, 'Resonance and Wonder', in id., *Learning to Curse*, 161–83.

[131] Daniel and Renfrew, *Idea of Prehistory*, 9–14.

[132] M. T. Hodgen, *Early Anthropology in the Sixteenth and Seventeenth Centuries* (Philadelphia, 1964), 354–85; Ferguson, in his otherwise admirable *Clio Unbound*, makes rather too much of accounts of cultural 'progress' as progenitors of later evolutionary theory.

[133] On the problem of integrating the Americas into British history see D. Armitage, 'The New World and British Historical Thought from Richard Hakluyt to William Robertson', in K. O. Kupperman (ed.), *America in European Consciousness 1475–1750* (Chapel Hill, NC, 1995), 52–75.

at Cambridge's John Covel concerning a 'jewish pot' is a minor, and Stonehenge a major, example of the conjectures that could be made when scholars stood on ground less familiar than Roman Britain.[134] This was all the more true because classical antiquity, as Professor Levine has reminded us, remained the mark against which medieval culture and its artefacts were measured even by their most devoted students. The tesselated pavements uncovered by a 'country farmer' named George Hannes at Stonesfield, near Woodstock, in January 1712 illustrate this well. The pavements became the subject of much local and, eventually, national discussion as their fame reached London, home of the Royal Society and the Society of Antiquaries. Abroad, they were included by Bernard de Montfaucon in his mammoth ten-volume study of ancient monuments and artistic images, *L'Antiquité expliquée*. Opinions flew back and forth as to whether these were early Roman, Romano-British, Anglo-Saxon, Danish, or Norman: the young Thomas Hearne, initially convinced that they were post-Norman, was eventually persuaded of their antiquity, since they were 'far better than could have been done in the Saxon or Danish times, or indeed since'.[135] Visitors came from afar to see the beautiful mosaic that most thought to represent either Bacchus or Apollo; fees were charged for viewing. All the attention did the pavements no good. A dispute between the landlord on whose property they had been found and the sitting tenant as to who should reap the financial benefits (coupled with protests by locals who refused to pay for the privilege) brought them near to ruin.[136] As we shall see in the next chapter, the economic and social interactions between scholars and local populations, an under-studied topic, form an essential part of the story of English antiquarianism.

CONCLUSION

An accurate mental picture of the past, an instinctive recognition of blatant historical anachronism, and a sympathetic, sentimental response to the remnants of

[134] CUL Mm. 6.50 (Covel transcripts), fos. 180, 186 (Charles Ellis to Covel, 26 Aug. 1696; Isaac Abendana to Covel, 9 Oct. 1696, interpreting the Hebrew inscription for Covel). Found in an old mote in Norfolk in the 1690s, the pot came to Covel as Master of Christ's College, which owned the land; it was later purchased by the earl of Oxford.
[135] Hearne, *Remarks and Collections*, iii. 296–8, 400–1 and *passim*; ibid. v. 81–2; Bernard Montfaucon, *L'Antiquité expliquée et représentée en figures*, 5 vols. (Paris, 1719), followed by five further volumes of a *Supplément* (1724); English edition, *Antiquity explained, and represented in sculpture*, trans. D. Humphreys, 5 vols. + 2-vol. supplement (1721–5). On the influence of this book see F. Haskell and N. Penny, *Taste and the Antique: The Lure of Classical Sculpture 1500–1900* (New Haven, 1981), 43–5.
[136] Montfaucon, *Antiquity explained*, trans. Humphreys, i. 152–3; John Pointer, *An account of a Roman pavement lately found at Stonesfield* (Oxford, 1713); M. V. Taylor, 'The Roman Tesselated Pavement at Stonesfield, Oxon', *Oxoniensia*, 6 (1941), 3–8; *VCH, Oxfordshire* (1933), i. 315, and especially J. M. Levine, *Humanism and History: Origins of Modern English Historiography* (Ithaca, NY, 1987), 107–22, 256. For a similar discovery by some workmen pulling down old houses in Bishopsgate, London, in 1707, see John Woodward, *An account of some Roman urns, and other Antiquities, lately digg'd up near Bishops-gate* (1713); for the pavement at Littlecote Park, see SAL, Minute Book 1718–32, 238.

past times: all are commonly associated with the later eighteenth and early nine-teenth centuries, and in particular with Romanticism. Certainly the later period produced a much richer tradition of pictorial historical representation than can be found in early modern times. But the two centuries following the dissolution of the monasteries (the most prominent and visible link to a vanishing medi-eval past) were nonetheless critical in developing a visual sense of the past that cannot be found in England before the mid-sixteenth century. There were lim-its to this, to be sure. Among these may be included the constraining association between images and artefacts on the one hand and superstition and Catholic survivalism or recidivism on the other; the ambivalent attitude to oldness and newness discussed in a previous chapter; and the peculiar refusal of English art to evolve its own grand tradition of narrative painting, in contrast to the wealth of portraiture. But the period was important, also, in the development of aes-thetic principles against which to judge surviving ancient and medieval survivals, and many a plan to restore, refurbish, or recycle signifies a prior decision, often reached after reading and reflection, either to let the remnants of the past alone or to adapt them in various ways to present circumstances.

To put a sharp point on all this, it can be said that English men and women in 1500 were only dimly conscious, if at all, of the fact that the people, scenes, buildings, and material culture of previous centuries would have looked differ-ent from those to which they were accustomed. Their educated descendants in 1700 for the most part understood this very well, even if they could not agree on preferences for one style or another, or (as in the case of Stonehenge) were unable accurately to situate an object temporally. This grasp of the visual dimension of the past was informed and nurtured by observation, graphic representation, and even dramatic recreation. But, to return to a point made at the outset of the chapter, it would be a serious mistake to assume that increased orientation to the visual necessitated a concomitant weakening of the oral aspects of the percep-tion of the past. The continued association of particular places and monuments with legends was reiterated often simultaneously in text and tradition (such as Rosamond's bower as described above by Vanbrugh). The discussion of the past conversationally among the educated also bespeaks the vigorous endurance of an oral and aural side to English historical culture. This came into conflict with the visual in a number of ways, and especially with the increasingly authoritative status of the written document. The tensions between the oral and the written have social as well as intellectual aspects, and these must be taken up within the broader context of relations between elite and popular culture.

CHAPTER SEVEN

The Archaeological Economy

MUCH OF THE discussion in the previous two chapters has turned on the activity of collection. Werner Muensterburger has proposed a plausible psychological explanation for the instinct to collect, linking it to a deeply felt wish to be able to use objects as substitutes for absent people, and sometimes to have the collection of objects supplant human contact. Collectibles, he suggests, are 'strictly speaking, implements that are meant to enhance or restore a narcissistically injured person's sense of self'. The standard contemporary characterization of the early modern antiquary or the virtuoso lends support to this notion; the satires of Earle, Marmion, and Shadwell represent the seventeenth-century collector as an obsessive, disengaged from his own social world, and seeking refuge from an alienating present in rare or exotic man-made and natural objects.[1]

The urge to collect is also, however, an urge to own,[2] to remove a fragment of the past, or a marvel of nature, from the public arena and into the privacy of the closet. The spirit of inquisitiveness which seems so laudable in Renaissance antiquaries and virtuosi alike, a spirit that labelled these objects 'curiosities' in the first place, is thus met in equal measure by an equally powerful instinct towards *acquisitiveness*, wherein one's sense of identity and status is reinforced by the power to mark personal territory with objects that are unique or unusual, exquisitely beautiful, or remarkably old.[3]

Humfrey Wanley's relentless efforts at manuscript acquisition are well documented in his diaries and letters, but it is worth noting that, for all his success at building a library for the Harleys, he still felt aggrieved to be always the keeper

---

[1] W. Muensterburger, *Collecting, an Unruly Passion: Psychological Perspectives* (Princeton, 1994), 25, 234; for a similar argument see B. Hillier, 'Why Do We Collect Antiques?', in D. Lowenthal and M. Binney (eds.), *Our Past Before Us: Why Do We Save It?* (1981), 70–82; G. Kubler, *The Shape of Time: Remarks on the History of Things* (New Haven and London, 1962), 80; and M. Rheims, *The Strange Life of Objects: 35 Centuries of Art Collecting and Collectors*, trans. D. Pryce-Jones (New York, 1961). Jean Baudrillard goes even further in asserting that the antique responds to an even deeper-rooted psychological need for 'definitive or fully realized being' by serving as a channel back to an irretrievable, womb-like origin. 'The tense of the mythological object is the perfect: it is that which occurs in the present as having occurred in a former time, hence that which is founded upon itself, that which is "authentic"': J. Baudrillard, *The System of Objects*, trans. J. Benedict (London and New York, 1996), 75.

[2] This point is argued persuasively in Lowenthal, *The Past is a Foreign Country*, 43.

[3] K. C. P. Smith and M. J. Apter, 'Collecting Antiques: A Psychological Interpretation', *Antique Collector*, 48/7 (1977), 64–6, who apply psychoanalysis to the question, 'Why is it nice to *own* beautiful things rather than just see them around?'

of someone else's collections. Admitting his inability to get up to the universities more than once in a while, he told one correspondent in 1715 that 'I have begun to think of making a little Collection of *my own*; of which *I may be the Master, and which I may* consequently consult at my own leasure without controul.'[4] Wanley could in fact have access to nearly any manuscript he wanted, either through his position with the Harleys or his network of connections; but treasures so acquired were not his property. Antiquarian treasures were commodities as much as historical artefacts, and this chapter will examine their circulation as economic objects, not only among elite collectors, but across the entire social spectrum.

Manuscripts and printed books were what preoccupied Wanley, a librarian and palaeographer, but they were not, of course, the only form of antiquity sought by the early modern collector. As interest grew in the more archaeological side of antiquarianism, non-literary desiderata, such as coins, urns, marbles, busts, and medieval weaponry assumed a greater prominence in the collections of scholars and virtuosi. These objects were available in expanding quantities as the period wore on, but they reached the hands of their eventual owners by a rather more complex route. Unlike the book or manuscript, the non-literary antiquity turned up not primarily in church roods and gentry attics, but under the spades and pickaxes of the labouring orders, who have not generally had much of a presence in histories of scholarship, for the understandable reason that they left no direct literary evidence, beyond scattered references by third parties, to any substantive involvement in scholarly activity.

The present chapter will address this issue by focusing on the antiquity as a matter for negotiation between collectors and scholars of similar status, but also between the learned and their social inferiors. This will serve as a reminder that the artefact, as a subject of scholarship, is constructed as such by the scholar. Before that happens, and before it passes into the library, museum, or closet, it remains simply a material thing, and things have a social life of their own.[5] As Stephen Greenblatt has usefully put it, 'cultural artifacts do not stay still . . . they are bound up with personal and institutional conflicts, negotiations, and appropriations'. The event of discovery itself can be illustrated many times over, and tells us much about social as well as intellectual relations. The more complicated process whereby an object ceases to be *merely* an object and becomes an artefact to be restored to the present through integration into the world of learning, is somewhat more difficult to document in detail, but we will end this chapter with a detailed analysis of an especially rich example from the early seventeenth century.[6]

---

[4] Wanley, *Letters*, 314 (Wanley to Bateman, June 1715), my italics.
[5] A. Appadurai, 'Introduction: Commodities and the Politics of Value', in id. (ed.), *The Social Life of Things: Commodities in Cultural Perspective* (Cambridge, 1986), 3–63; Kubler, *The Shape of Time*, passim.
[6] S. J. Greenblatt, 'Resonance and Wonder', in his *Learning to Curse: Essays in Early Modern Culture* (New York, 1990), 161–83, at p. 161.

FINDERS AND KEEPERS

Antiquaries travelling to sites of interest often found local inhabitants willing to share curiosities that had come into their possession. The prosperous and educated were keen to display choice muniments and books from their collections, along with whatever minor marvel had been turned up in their garden or had been purchased abroad. Tenants and labourers, less in love with the past for its own sake, were eager to make a profit from revealing the sources of these ancient trinkets that their social superiors so loved to collect. When Abraham de la Pryme took up a curacy in his native Yorkshire parish, the local gentry flocked to provide him with information for his antiquarian writings—no doubt hoping to be mentioned therein. They kept Pryme busier than he cared to be. In a short time the young minister found himself 'so exceeding busy in old deeds and charters, which the gentlemen are pleased to send me in on every side, that I cannot take time to think or write of anything else'. Among his willing helpers was a local JP, Thomas Yarborough; shortly before his death, this aged gentleman sent Pryme a manuscript of his lives of the earls of Warenne for use in any writing on the parish or county antiquities that the young curate might attempt.[7]

Information about antiquities had to be treated with caution, regardless of the social status of the informant: it was not the common folk but the local gentry who boasted in the 1680s that they had 'humbugged' Robert Plot in his search for information about the natural history and antiquities of Staffordshire.[8] Over the course of the century, however, visiting scholars grew more critical of claims advanced about local antiquities, especially those uttered by humbler folk; truth increasingly came stamped with a coat of arms. On the other hand, even when an antiquary proved sceptical about the identification of an object, he was perfectly content to use informants of any social status as a divining rod to locate it. Some objects were simply known to be about. They had appeared so frequently and over so many generations that they had been absorbed into 'folk memory'.[9] As we will see in some detail further on, scholars in the archaeological tradition of antiquarianism such as Aubrey, who also had an acute interest in popular lore, could not fail to heed such information as it presented itself.

Common knowledge of local terrain could similarly remove the need for a single informant. One such 'report of the people' told Bishop Francis Godwin where to 'bestowe some mony in diggyng' for artefacts in the early seventeenth

---

[7] Pryme made similar use of the collections of Nathaniel Johnston (1627–1705), a Yorkshire physician who spent thirty years collecting materials for the history of that county: a draft history of Strafforth and Tickhill Wapentakes, called 'Antiquities of Warwickshire', contains a section on Doncaster annotated by Pryme: Bodl. MS Top. Yorks. c. 34, fos. 32–135; Hist. MSS Comm., *Sixth Report* (1877), appendix, p. 462; *The Diary of Abraham de la Pryme, the Yorkshire Antiquary*, ed. Charles Jackson, Surtees Soc., 54 (1870), 171. Pryme was writing a history of the town of Hatfield, Yorks., which was cut short by his own premature death in 1704.

[8] *DNB, sub* 'Plot, Robert'.

[9] Walter Johnson, *Folk-memory; or, The Continuity of British archaeology* (Oxford, 1908), 105.

century.[10] When a farmer named Thomas Smith was repairing a fence on his land in the small village of Roxby in 1699, he unearthed a Roman pavement. Uninterested in it, he left it exposed for local schoolboys to desecrate. Abraham de la Pryme, then living in Hull, heard of the discovery and went with two friends to dig up the stones, which he sent to Thomas Gale, the dean of York. Pryme's account of his 'dig' is worth repeating since it provides a good illustration of the methods used by these early archaeologists:

Haveing got a spade, a shovel, and a besom, we fell to work, and with a great deal of labour, bared about yard and a half squair; in bareing of which we cast up many pieces of Roman tyle, ye bone of ye hinde legg of an ox or cow, broken in two, and many pieces of lime and sand, or plaster, painted red and yellow, which had been ye cornish either of some altar, or some part of ye building that was there, whatever it was . . .

Then, haveing swept ye space aforesayd, that we had bared, very clean, ye pavement look'd exceeding beautifull and pretty, and one would not imagine that such mean stones could make such pretty work.[11]

Direct excavation on the basis of common information such as Godwin or Pryme described was not unheard of in the sixteenth and seventeenth centuries, but it became considerably more frequent after the civil war. Among major discoveries, over a dozen tesselated pavements were uncovered in southern England between 1667 and 1739, according to a list compiled by Stukeley.[12] Such deliberate digs were plainly social events and occasions for camaraderie, and antiquaries often made discoveries themselves, especially when picking their ground carefully. While digging in his garden at Grantham, Stukeley and some friends found 'a pot full of silver coin'.[13] In many cases there were middlemen, as someone other than the initial discoverer was responsible for saving the item and eventually bringing it to an antiquary's attention. On their trip to Cumberland in 1599, Camden and Cotton encountered John Senhouse, a worthy who had decorated his house and garden with altars, statues, and inscription-bearing stones dug out of his grounds. Camden was thankful that the collector was 'well learned' and a lover of ancient literature, since he 'with great diligence preserves such inscriptions as these which by other ignorant people in those parts are presently broke to pieces, and turn'd to other uses, to the great damage of these studies' (Fig. 7.1). [14]

---

[10]   BL MS Cotton Jul. F.VI, fo. 299.

[11]   *Diary of Abraham de la Pryme*, 212. For other Roman pavements and their locations see the list in SAL MS 265, fo. 13[r]. A Roman stone with picture of Apollo, dug up in 1648, had by 1720 become a 'corner-stone' in Salisbury Hall, former home of the Talbots: Charles Leigh, *Natural History of Lancashire, Cheshire and the Peak* (Oxford, 1720), bk. III, pp. 9, 82 (and 1766 MS note in Lancs. RO copy, at p. 82).

[12]   SAL MS 264, fo. 39[r]; cf. ibid., fos. 101[r]–103[r], 'An account of Roman pavements', in particular that found at Wells in 1737.

[13]   Bodl. MS Eng. misc. e. 121 (Stukeley memoirs), fo. 28[r], 7 Oct. 1726.

[14]   *Camden's Britannia*, ed. E. Gibson (1695), 824–6. Gibson's translation of Camden's Latin, rendered in the 1610 Philemon Holland edition quite differently, is instructive: Holland's more neutral 'unskillful and unlettered' here becomes the more value-laden 'ignorant', a mark of the hardened attitude towards the vulgar discoverers of such objects.

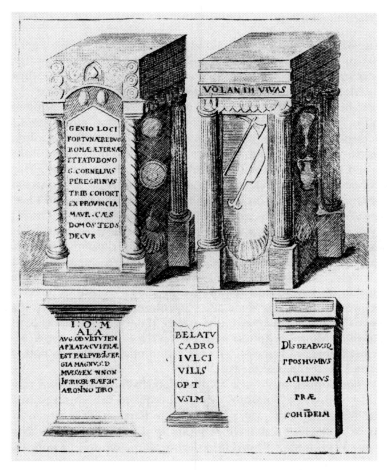

Fig. 7.1. Roman remains excavated from the ground of John Senhouse, Netherhall, Cumberland, and shown to Robert Cotton in 1599, from whose drawing the engraving is derived. From *Camden's Britannia*, 824–6

Antiquities were often turned up by ploughboys and shepherds with little interest in and less knowledge of their meaning, but were 'saved' from the rubbish heap by some interested local worthy. Thomas Braithwaite reported seeing an equestrian statue, 'found by a man plowinge' in Lancashire.[15] The leaden urns uncovered in 1602 by two Carmarthenshire shepherds, which contained a large quantity of silver coins of great antiquity, were still being marvelled at by antiquaries a century later; a gold chain found near Harlech castle in 1692 was popularly supposed to have been worn 'by some Cambrian prince or nobleman'.[16]

[15] BL MS Cotton Julius F. VI, fo. 302 (Braithwaite to [Camden?], 18 Jan. 1605). Cf. MS Cotton Julius F. VI, fo. 316, for a similar report by Henry Savile to Camden (26 Aug., no year).

[16] Bodl. MS Gough Wales 5 (Anon., 'The Description of Wales', c.1700), fos. 5ᵛ, 14ʳ, 19ʳ, 21ᵛ.

Thomas Sprat, the historian of the Royal Society (who was making a point about the need for 'labour' at the foundations of new knowledge rather than about antiquities as such) would comment on the circumstantial manner in which coins and medals had been found and the 'rarities of antiquity . . . restor'd'.[17]

An excellent example of this 'rescue' process at work is the skeleton found at Corbridge, Northumberland, which included a 'thighbone' of some two yards in length; the whole body was estimated in reports at seven yards. According to one account, it was discovered by some boys who, unaware of its value, broke it into pieces 'and squander'd them abroad before it was publicly known'. The earl of Derwentwater, hearing of this, managed to collect many of the fragments but would willingly have paid hundreds of pounds to have it whole. All the earl's horses and all the earl's men could not put this together again, but parts of it were put on display in 1695, and the Royal Society reported the discovery in its *Philosophical Transactions*. John Horsley speculated, thirty years later, that the bones had actually been 'the teeth & bones of oxen and other creatures sacrificed here at some pagan temple'. Abraham de la Pryme, who was sent details of the Corbridge giant shortly after its discovery, seized on the 'huge and monstrous bones' as grist for his own theories of the Flood and repopulation. He believed that it and the 'thousands' of similar finds were evidence of 'those wicked Antideluvian giants mentioned by Moses'. Scriptural authority for the existence of giants, as we will see further below in Chapter 9, gave them continued standing in both popular and learned perceptions of the past.[18]

Mysterious stones, man-made or natural, including fossils, often turned up. 'Long Harry' Savile, a Yorkshire antiquary, acquired two engraved stones uncovered by a ploughman, which he sent on to Camden for inclusion in a new edition of *Britannia*.[19] Labourers working at the bottom of the 'Picts wall' (Hadrian's Wall) west of Newcastle in the late 1660s discovered a stone three feet in length, complete with inscription. Word soon reached Dr Davenport, chaplain to the bishop of Durham, who rode out to examine it and then sent drawings to William Dugdale.[20] In 1693 the Ashmolean's Lhwyd heard of a 'large stone chest (for so they called it)' of three or four tons in weight, which he conjectured had been the coffin of some long-dead prince.[21] After a prodigious storm on 14 July 1687, near Odstock and Botenham in Wiltshire, a large hailstone was found

[17] Thomas Sprat, *The History of the Royal Society*, ed. J. I. Cope and H. W. Jones (St Louis, Mo., 1958), 436.

[18] Northumberland RO ZAN M13/D19 (notebook of Revd John Horsley), p. 213; BL MS Lans. 897 (Abraham de la Pryme's history of Hatfield, c.1700), fos. 188ᵛ–189ʳ. A similar case is that of the fossilized skeleton discovered about 1718 at the rectory of Elston near Newark, Notts., near a quarry, which was reputed to be human but that Stukeley believed to be the bones of an animal: SAL MS Stukeley IV/1/331A (Stukeley to unknown recipient, 7 Feb. 1718/19).

[19] BL MS Cotton Jul. F.VI, fo. 316 (Savile to Camden, 26 Aug., no year); cf. the inscriptions sent by Reginald Bainbrigg, the schoolmaster of Appleby, 27 Mar. 1600, ibid., fos. 337–47.

[20] Bodl. MS Ashm. 826, fo. 37ʳ (Davenport to Dugdale, 31 May 1670); Davenport also sent Dugdale (24 June 1672), fo. 39ʳ, the inscriptions from two stones found near monastic ruins in Cumberland.

[21] Bodl. MS Aubrey 5, fos. 34–5 (Lhwyd to Aubrey, n.d., 1693, interleaved copy in Aubrey's hand in Aubrey's *An Interpretation of Villare Anglicanum*).

with a heart-shaped stone inside. According to Lord Coleraine, it was 'pickt up by a little boy att Botenham, & put into his hatt from whence itt was taken by one of my servants after hee had tryed to break itt'. The servant then passed it to the estate steward, 'who sent itt to mee; & thus you have the descent or pedigree of this stone, but I want physicall skill to give you itts genealogy'.[22] In each of these cases an object became an antiquity only because it had been uncovered and then assessed by a humanistically trained scholar, but the importance of the finders' contribution is not the less important for that.

By the later seventeenth century, the number of travellers, virtuosi, and antiquaries had increased sufficiently for enterprising locals to profit from discoveries that normally would have done little to excite them. Anthony Wood gave a 'poore man digging in the ruins' of Osney Abbey 8d. for a leaden impression of the seal of the anti-pope John XXIII which had been found there a year earlier. Sometimes the love of curiosities and artefacts rubbed off on those without the time or means to devote to such pursuits. Dugdale wrote to Sir Symon Archer in 1635 to commend the letter bearer as a man with 'a great inclinacion to the love of armes and antiquities'. Unfortunately, the man lacked both 'meanes and learninge', so Dugdale suggested that Lady Archer employ him in her garden.[23] Thomas Ford of Christ Church wrote to John Covel at Cambridge recommending the bearer, one Cole, a man of 'settled business' who wanted to make a map of Cambridge and its vicinity; he might, wrote Ford, 'be also usefull in graving college plate, seals, &c, he being curious in medals & having a collection of his own'.[24] The landlord of the Bull, a tavern in Caerleon, can scarcely have had the time or the education necessary for Latin epigraphy, but early Georgian travellers who stopped there would still be shown his piece of inscribed Roman brick, part of a large find made in the area in 1723.[25]

When he made his travels around England in the reign of Henry VIII, John Leland had principally been interested in salvaging the manuscript inheritance of the Middle Ages, with the aim of improving classical learning rather than studying medieval culture, which nevertheless features prominently in his *Itinerary*. Consequently, Leland had recorded the artefacts found by local people without making much effort to acquire them. An early sixteenth-century Kentish hermit showed Leland many 'antiquates' from a nearby cave where men had 'sowt and digged for treasure', while a Bristol brewer displayed a parchment from the tomb of Robert of Gloucester, unearthed in the 1540s.[26] This situation had changed dramatically by the time, at the end of our period, that the *Itinerary* was first edited and published by Hearne. In the intervening period of a century and three

---

[22] BL MS Sloane 3962 (Charleton papers), fos. 225ʳ–226ʳ (Henry Lord Coleraine to Charleton, n.d. (1687)).
[23] Wood, *Life and Times*, i. 241; BL MS Add. 28564, fo. 199 (Dugdale to Archer, 16 Nov. 1635); repr. in Dugdale, *Life, Diary and Correspondence*, 152.
[24] CUL MS Mm. 6.50 (Covel letters), fo. 243.
[25] Bodl. MS Top. gen. e. 85, p. 13, 'Remarks and Observations' by Thomas Martin.
[26] *Leland's Itinerary*, iv. 62, v. 88.

quarters, the antiquity had become a commodity, its now routine transformation from thing to artefact the end result of what amounted to an 'archaeological economy'. This is simply another form of the social circulation of the past, specifically the process of location, trade, presentation, bequest, and purchase that could take an object from its place of rest via the cottage, kitchen, or alehouse, thence to the parlour, closet, and library, before it eventually wound up in the museum.

After its discovery and recognition, a number of fates awaited the antiquity. Some objects became gifts, entering the cultural exchange system of the elite and even circulating among friends, kinsfolk, patrons and clients, husbands and wives, kings and courtiers. A gold helmet turned up by an Ancaster ploughman in the early sixteenth century became a present for Catherine of Aragon. In 1590 Dean Alexander Nowell, brother of one of the early Elizabethan antiquaries, Laurence, sent the queen's solicitor Thomas Egerton an unspecified 'poore tooken, for the antiquitie rather then for the value of the same'. Jonson's Volpone receives as a gift a piece of plate 'huge, brassy and antique', while the expatriate Catholic antiquary Richard Verstegan sent Sir Robert Cotton the petrified tongue of a fish. When a papal pardon was unearthed at the ruins of Eynsham Abbey in the late 1630s, it was sent to the earl of Derby as lord of the manor. Some Roman medals found in Cambridgeshire in the early eighteenth century were immediately conveyed to St John's College, which owned the land in which they had been buried.[27] A picture, set in gold, and ascribed to King Alfred, 'who, 'tis said wore it about his neck', was found in Somersetshire some time in the seventeenth century; only in 1718 did it reach the hands of Dr George Clark for deposit in the Bodleian.[28]

Antiquities were often provided by one collector to another less fortunately situated. John Locke, who collected coins in the 1680s, received some foreign specimens through the courtesy of a friend. Henry Lord Coleraine, the Wiltshire coin and medal collector, relied on his friend William Charleton, alias Courten, to keep him informed about new finds and to do much of his buying for him—Coleraine lamented the fact that most chapmen were not willing to trade in such a 'dead stock only fitt for learned & monyed persons'.[29] Henry Prescott, the Chester diocesan official who preferred books to work, coins and seals to books, and liquor to coins, was extremely proud of his own collection (which even attracted visitors from as far afield as the University of Edinburgh), and occasionally gave up a cherished item as a gift, or by way of exchange for something even more exotic. Even more frequently he found himself in receipt of such a gift. Having met a friend at a pub who had just arrived, hot and sweaty, from Warrington, Prescott was delighted to be given a 'gold Augustus and silver Aurelius', particularly because

[27] *Leland's Itinerary*, i. 28; *Egerton Papers*, ed. J. P. Collier, Camden Soc., os, 12 (1840), 136; Richard Verstegan, *Letters and Despatches*, ed. A. Petti, Catholic Rec. Soc., 52 (1959), 266; Wood, *Life and Times*, i. 255; Samuel Dale, 'Iter Cantabrigiensis' (written c.1731), Essex RO T/A 489 (microfilm of CUL MS 3466), fo. 16ᵛ.
[28] Bodl. MS Ballard 20 (Charlett letters) (Clark to Dr Arthur Charlett, 17 Nov. 1718).
[29] Bodl. MS Locke f. 4 (Locke's journals, volume iv), p. 99 (6 May 1680); BL MS Sloane 3962 (Charleton papers), fo. 254ʳ (Coleraine to Charleton, 14 Dec. 1694).

the former was a coin he had coveted for nearly thirty years, since seeing a speci-men found on the lands of another friend near Kendal.[30]

THE VARIETIES OF ARCHAEOLOGICAL FINDS

From the late sixteenth century through the seventeenth century, funeral urns and other burial items became highly valued artefacts. In 1576 some workers dig-ging clay at Spitalfields in London discovered several 'earthen pots, called *urnae*'. These eventually came to the attention of Stow, who had a substantial collection of urns, including one complete with ashes and bones. Harrison records the recov-ery of some funeral urns from a well at Little Massingham, Norfolk, in 1578, which he compared to the eleventh-century excavations by Eadmer—who had destroyed the vessels which he found and melted down the coins inside them for use in his church. Antiquaries soon recognized that the discovery of such treasures could assist them in locating the sites of ancient settlements; as Dr John Woodward advised Christopher Wren, one could discover 'the ancient bounds and extent of the City, by attending to the places where sepulchral urns are digd up'.[31] The human bones, armour, and Roman coins excavated from a Norfolk park and given to its owner, Sir Nicholas L'Estrange, were, naturally enough, conjectured by William Stukeley and others 'to have been bureyed there after a battle'.[32] A similar explana-tion was offered for the tumuli at 'Julaberry's Grave' in Chilham after a deliber-ate programme of archaeological excavation, at the instance of Lord Weymouth, turned up an assortment of animal and human bones. In this instance close atten-tion to the levels at which the objects were found, and in what sorts of earth, supported the notion that 'it must have been the work of part of an army'.[33]

Interest in funeral urns grew steadily, and by the mid-seventeenth century they were among the most sought-after of artefacts, partly because of the immediacy of their connection with the past, and partly because they answered a natural human instinct which became more acute periodically, the fear of death.[34] Thomas

[30] *The Diary of Henry Prescott, LL.B., deputy registrar of Chester Diocese*, ed. J. Addy, J. Harrop, and P. McNiven, 3 vols., Rec. Soc. of Lancashire and Cheshire, vols. 127, 132, 133 (Chester, 1987–97), ii. 354, 502, 586.

[31] Bodl. MS Rawl. D. 400, fo. 55ᵛ (Woodward to Thomas Hearne, n.d.). Edward Steele similarly held in 1713 that the variety of urns (as well as medals and coins) regularly turned up at Sandy, Bedfordshire 'undoubtedly intitles it an auncient Roman station'. Bodl. MS Top. gen. e. 80 (Steele's parish notes, vol. ii), fo. 257ʳ.

[32] SAL MS Stukeley IV/i/331B (Stukeley to unknown recipient, 7 Feb. 1719).

[33] Nichols, *Literary Illustrations*, iv. 97 (H. Finch to John Battely, 14 May 1702). A bricklayer dig-ging a cellar at what remained of the old church of St Mary's the Lesser at Wallingford in the late seventeenth or early eighteenth centuries dug through a large heap of bones that came to the atten-tion of Richard Skinner. Bodl MS Top Berks d. 28, Richard Skinner's 'Antiquities of Wallingford' (1720), nineteenth-century transcript, p. 61.

[34] Urns also featured in seventeenth-century funeral monuments; used to contain human entrails, they were associated with the practice of 'secondary' burials for those remains. See Nigel Llewellyn, *Funeral Monuments in Post-Reformation England* (Cambridge, 2000), 44.

Browne's moving *Urn-burial*, which fell into the classicizing trap of ascribing to Romans what were in fact Saxon artefacts, is the most famous mid-Stuart expression of the kinds of sentiment evoked by such objects, but it was hardly unique.[35] When the Royal Society devoted its first full meeting of October 1685 to the study of 'an urn full of bones' dug up by highway repairmen in Camberwell, Surrey, its members were driven at least as much by a psychological fascination with the relics of anonymous, long-dead humans as they were by more rational, scientific, and historical concerns.[36] The contents of such vessels proved even more captivating. Joshua Childrey thought that the black earth found in an earthen pot near Foy in Cornwall was likely 'the ashes . . . of some ancient Roman'. Wood was impressed by the nearly perfect human heart dug up in a leaden container at Oxford in 1644; fifteen years later a local gardener told him of another such discovery.[37] As early as 1520, a leaden coffin which its discoverers supposed to contain the remains of a medieval duke was unearthed in Cornwall; this information was handed down verbally over the years until it was recorded about 1600 by Richard Carew, but by this time the identity of the duke had been lost.[38]

Weapons and the paraphernalia of battle were often discovered, especially axes and arrowheads from remote antiquity, and swords and shields from more recent centuries, the latter generally lying on or near the surface of one-time battlefields.[39] The unearthing of brass horse harnesses and armour in mid-Tudor Camelford (or Gaffelford) in Cornwall reinforced, if it did not create, the belief of inhabitants that a great battle had been fought there.[40] Ancient stone weapons were for some time held to be natural formations rather than man-made. Although English antiquaries such as Dugdale and Plot, exposed to the ethnographic evidence of native American weaponry, eventually saw them as man-made, a tradition continued for some time that they were the work of fairies.[41] Cornish

---

[35] Cf. the correspondence between Dugdale and Browne on the subject: *Works of Sir Thomas Browne*, ed. G. L. Keynes, 2nd edn., 4 vols. (1964), iv. 302–5 (Browne to Dugdale, 27 Oct. 1658); ibid. iv. 305–6 (Dugdale to Browne, 9 Nov. 1658). Roman artefacts on exhibit in London caused John Woodward, for instance, to wax reflective about the merits of the Revolution settlement: 'They best know how to set a just value upon the present happy settlement who are vers'd in our history, and duly appriz'd what England suffered of old from the descent of the Romans, and afterwards of the Saxons, and Danes: from the frequent wars of Scotland, and our own intestine divisions during the heptarchy, the barons, and the late civil wars.' Woodward, *An account of some Roman urns, and other Antiquities, lately digg'd up near Bishops-gate* (London, 1713), 11 (written in the form of a letter to Sir Christopher Wren dated 23 June 1707).

[36] Evelyn, *Diary*, iv. 483.

[37] John Stow, *The Survey of London*, ed. H. B. Wheatley (1912; repr., 1980), 152; William Harrison, *The Description of England*, ed. G. Edelen (Ithaca, NY, 1968), 212; Joshua Childrey, *Britannia Baconica* (1661), 24–5; Wood, *Life and Times*, i. 112. Wood reports several incidents of the discovery of leaden coffins at or near Oxford in the seventeenth century: ibid. i. 255.

[38] Richard Carew, *The Survey of Cornwall* (1602), fo. 111ᵛ.

[39] R. T. Gunther, *Early Science in Oxford*, xiv: *Life and Letters of Edward Lhwyd* (Oxford, 1945), 202–3, for brass daggers found in Wales and described by Lhwyd; see ibid. 258 for a bronze axe; see Dugdale, *Life, Diary and Correspondence*, 413, for an iron spearhead uncovered in a supposed battlefield mass grave.

[40] Camden, *Britain*, trans. P. Holland (1610), 194.

[41] S. Piggott, *Ruins in a Landscape: Essays in Antiquarianism* (Edinburgh, 1976), 138.

tin-miners uncovered a trove of brass spearheads, axes and swords, wrapped in linen, in the mid-sixteenth century.[42] The sword of Odard or Hudard, whose descendants called themselves Dutton, Sir Peter Leycester noted in 1665, remained in the custody of Lady Eleanor Kilmorey.[43] Shortly before he died, the Yorkshire antiquary Abraham de la Pryme told Sir Hans Sloane something he had himself heard from Edward Canby, a Hatfield gentleman, that 'about 50 years ago under a great tree in this parish' had been found an old, shaped knife with a haft of 'a very hard black sort of wood', perhaps ebony. The blade had mouldered away and been replaced with a new one, on which was engraved the verse:

> Ever since No's Flood was I lefte,
> My old blades consumed, but this is ye Heft.[44]

Ironwork such as anchors and forges, and less durable domestic items such as crockery from more recent times could also appear. When Nicholas Blundell and his wife visited Francis Ferrers of Astley he showed them 'a place in his ground where 'tis supposed there formerly stood a small castle and in takeing up the foundation (for that was all as was left of it) he found a large mugg-bottle which I suppose held about three gallons', and several other pieces of crockery and tiles; the dates of these did not apparently interest either Blundell or his host. At Ribchester in 1722 Blundell would see 'two remarkable stones for antiquity', one of which was believed to be part of a Roman altar, and he stood on Anchor Hill 'where tis supposed there had ben [an] ancor smiths shops, becaus some times ancors & peeces of ancors are found; one who was with me shewed me where he or his workmen a few years since found neare halfe a bushell of small ship nailes some yards deep in the said ancor hill'.[45] In 1688 Henry Keepe, a recent convert to Rome, would publish a little work on the discovery of what appeared to be a crucifix belonging to Edward the Confessor.[46]

THE USES OF COINS AND MEDALS

Benedict Leonard Calvert, a pupil of Thomas Hearne, was not interested in the bric-a-brac of war nor, it would seem, in much else from the Middle Ages. He passed up the chance to acquire a trumpet, spur, sword, and battle axe dug up in Windsor Forest by a clergyman, items then on sale as part of a larger collection in London, because his attentions were fixed elsewhere, on purchasing the

[42] Camden, *Britain*, 188.
[43] Cheshire RO DDX 180 (Peter Leycester, 'A short view of Greate Brettaine and Ierland ffrom the beginning', written 1670), fo. 64ᵛ.
[44] BL MS Sloane 4025, fos. 206ʳ–211ᵛ (Pryme to Sloane, 19 Nov. 1701).
[45] *The Great Diurnal of Nicholas Blundell of Little Crosby, Lancashire*, ed. F. Tyrer, 3 vols., Rec. Soc. of Lancashire and Cheshire (1968–72), iii. 53–4, 76.
[46] Henry Keepe (alias Charles Taylour), *A true and perfect narrative of the strange and unexpected finding of the Crucifix and Gold Chain of that pious prince S. Edward, the King and Confessor, which was found after 620 years' interment* (1688).

Roman coins in the same collection.[47] Coins, especially of the Romano-British period, were by far the most frequently discovered and most vendible of all anti-quarian objects; they were rivalled in popularity by commemorative medals, which could be of either antique or modern origin. A casual collector who had a pass-ing interest in rather than a consuming obsession with antiquities was much more likely to have a number of coins or medals in his closet than the more exotic artefacts valued by the likes of Ashmole or Evelyn. Coins were also, in many ways, another point of overlap between varieties of scholarly interest: often found in the ground like bones, weapons, and fossils, they nevertheless had a primar-ily literary and historical utility through their images and inscriptions that long outweighed any significance attached to the place of their finding. The most wide-ranging English manual on numismatics, Evelyn's *Numismata*, illustrates the fundamental historical preoccupations well in its view of coins and especially medals (his principal subject) as useful in so far as they 'relate to the confirmation of some remarkable matter of fact, discover the genius of the age, and link the his-tory of divers notorious passages of the latter centuries and revolutions'. Coins and medals were 'the most lasting . . . and vocal monuments of antiquity' and were 'not only an ornament, but an useful and necessary appendage to a library'. This historical focus is found in most of the other numismatic manuals of the time, though there are glimmers of a broader interest in the coins themselves, and the reasons for their production, in passing comments such as Evelyn's reflections on their metallurgy, and on 'the time when the several metals came into use . . . I am inclined to think, that the hard and more vulgar iron and copper, as most useful for the field abroad, and house within might be of the elder date.' But Evelyn's work also reflects the breadth of virtuoso interest, with attention to the proper arrangement of medals in a cabinet or library, and a lengthy digression on physi-ognomy inspired by the heads of various numismata. [48]

Coins had been turned up periodically through the Middle Ages, but in the sixteenth century such discoveries either became more commonplace or were at least much more frequently recorded. In the 1540s, Leland heard of late medieval discoveries from old men, who were recalling them from many years earlier, such as a pauper in Folkestone, who happened upon 'a boote almost ful of antiquites of pure silver and gold' and gave it to the town's lord, Lord Clinton.[49] Nearly two centuries later this was still the case. John Horsley, visiting Bath in 1728, wrote home to a friend that he had bought several of the coins which were there 'thrown up every day'.[50] Perhaps because coins had a more obvious value to their immediate discoverers than most artefacts, they made a greater impact—at least

[47] B. Steiner, 'Benedict Leonard Calvert', *Maryland Historical Magazine*, 3 (1908), 191–227, 283–341; A. E. Yentsch, *A Chesapeake Family and their Slaves* (Cambridge, 1994), 76–7. I owe this last refer-ence to my former colleague, Jack Crowley.

[48] John Evelyn, *Numismata, a discourse of medals* (1697), sig. A3v, pp. 1, 13, 292 ff.

[49] *Leland's Itinerary*, i. 28, 31, 186, iii. 101, 103, 111, iv. 20, 60, 62, 64, 85, 166–7.

[50] Northumberland RO, ZAN M13/D19 (unfoliated correspondence, Horsley to Robert Cay, 20 July 1728).

initially—on the local mind. This was especially true when the money turned up in large quantities, as it did on the sites of former Romano-British towns, such as Lincoln. The swineherds of Bedfordshire often found Roman coins, which the inhabitants of nearby Dunstable referred to as 'madning money', a local corruption of the ancient Roman camp of Magioninium or Magintum; in Binchester, Durham, however, such coins apparently had no such explicit popular association with the area's Roman past but were colloquially known as 'Binchester pennies'.[51] At Brough, near Newark, a place whose inhabitants believed that the nearby Foss Road had been built by William the Conqueror, Roman coins were known as 'Brough pennies'.[52] The common people at Great Chesterford, Essex, referred to the ancient Roman encampment there as the Burrough—the land on which was believed to be unusually fertile—and the coins frequently turned up there were called Burrough money.[53] A Wroxcester schoolmaster regularly dispatched his pupils out to gather 'dinders', as they termed Roman money, after rainfalls; he melted the silver ones into a tankard.[54] Littleborough on Trent, as John Jackson noted from his reading of the *Antonine Itineraries*, was:

a litle town but very antient; that the Romans held it there are many things which cause a beleif. For the military way went here, & the tract of the walls yet appear to be seen, thre [*sic*] is so great plenty of Roman coynes in the neighbouring fields, that they are often rooted up by the very swine: whence it is that they are commonly called swinepennies.[55]

Discoveries of old coins probably seem more numerous from the sixteenth century on because the classically educated were beginning to take a keen interest in them for reasons that were not merely intellectual. As early as the 1560s, the future Lord Burghley had a tract drawn up for his use on the value of various ancient coins, drawn in part from the French philologist Guillaume Budé.[56] Not everyone who was interested in coinage would have read the early Renaissance classics of numismatics, such as Budé's *De Asse*, and, as interest increased in the seventeenth century, profundity of understanding among the majority of collectors did not keep pace. But gentlemen and nobles had begun by 1,600 to consider an ability to value coins, including those which were not current, a worthwhile skill. Late Renaissance European intellectuals such as Nicolas-Claude Fabri de Peiresc even pointed to the contemporary, practical application that recondite knowledge of ancient coins produced, in an age when the value of modern

---

[51] Camden, *Britain*, 105, 243, 402, 450, 511, 738, 769.

[52] SAL MS Stukeley III/317, Stukeley's account of his visit to the Foss Road.

[53] Essex RO D/Y/1/acc. A3921A (uncatalogued William Holman correspondence) (B. Powell to Holman, 10 June and 27 July 1722).

[54] SAL, Minute Book 1718–32, p. 159, as reported by Stukeley, 12 May 1725. For commonplace discoveries in the north-west, see Leigh, *Natural History of Lancashire, Cheshire and the Peaks in Derbyshire*, book III, p. 13, who describes subterranean tunnels in which Roman coins were found.

[55] CUL MS Dd.II.62 (John Jackson, commonplace book, 1663–94), fos. 68ᵛ–69.

[56] SAL MS 116, fos. 1–24ᵛ, anonymous treatise on coinage. This is attributed to Sir Thomas Smith in a pencil note and is dedicated to Sir William Cecil, who may in fact have been most interested in matters such as the payment of soldiers in coin during Roman times.

specie was shifting with disturbing frequency.[57] As early as the middle years of Elizabeth's reign, William Harrison had already devoted two chapters of his *Description of England* to coins and other antiquities and spoke of 'the pains that I have taken to gather great numbers of them together'; these allowed him to 'set down the lively portraitures of every emperor engraven in the same', and several kings since Edward the Confessor, though he professed complete ignorance of Anglo-Saxon coins.[58] Harrison's comment points again to the fundamentally literary and historical interest in coins that characterizes the first two-thirds of our period: the individual coin was valued for its ability to shed light on particular episodes of the past, or simply taken as a wondrous memento of long-passed events. There was as yet little attention paid to its location and depth, or to what this could reveal about such matters as ancient settlement practices.

By the early seventeenth century, knowledge of coins was rapidly becoming an indispensable part of the study of history proper, though at first coins were employed mainly as a decoration in history books rather than as a source, even for particular facts. Perhaps the earliest historical work in England actually to examine the coins of an entire period systematically as a supplement to textual evidence was Edmund Bolton's 1624 biography of *Nero Caesar*.[59] Various late Tudor and early Stuart manuals on gentility frequently recommend a correct knowledge of ancient currency as a necessary prerequisite for understanding the past. George Hakewill referred to knowledge of ancient coins (together with weights and measures) as a necessary 'appendix' of history; without it, 'marveilous great mistake and confusion in histories' was inevitable, and he praised the efforts of those such as Budé, Rudolf Agricola, and Edward Brerewood (the linguist and astronomer of Gresham College), who had devoted their energies to this end.[60] By 1700, when the older Renaissance *ars historica* had been transformed into a manual on the collection and study of various types of historical source, the authors of such works routinely included sections on numismatics in their books, or published such works separately.[61] Their more active readers in turn annotated such books with their

---

[57] P. N. Miller, *Peiresc's Europe: Learning and Virtue in the Seventeenth Century* (New Haven, Conn., 2000), 78; A. Schnapp, *The Discovery of the Past*, trans. I. Kinnes and G. Varndell (New York, 1996), 132–8.

[58] Harrison, *Description of England*, 292–301.

[59] Edmund Bolton, *Nero Caesar, or Monarchie Depraved* (1624), discussed in D. R. Woolf, *The Idea of History in Early Stuart England* (Toronto, 1990), 194–5.

[60] George Hakewill, *An apologie of the power and providence of God* (1627), 236; Edward Brerewood, *De ponderibus . . .* (1614); Justus Lipsius, *Iusti Lipsi tractatus ad historiam Romanam cognoscendam apprimè utiles* (Cambridge, 1592), sig. E2ᵛ, which contains four chapters on coins.

[61] Examples include Bernardo Davanzati, *A discourse upon coins* (1696); Louis Jobert, *The Knowledge of Medals*, trans. Roger Gale (1697), 171–83; Rice Vaughan, *A Discourse of Coins and Coinage* (1675); John Arbuthnot, *Tables of ancient coins, weights and measures* (1727); William Nicolson, *Of the medals and coins of Scotland* (1700); id., *The English Historical Library, pt. 3: Giving an Account of Our Records, Law-books and Coins* (1699), 247–315, and *The English, Scotch and Irish Historical Libraries* (1736), 248–67; Obadiah Walker, *The Greek and Roman History Illustrated by Coins and Medals* (1692) and Hist. MSS Comm., *Report on the Manuscripts of the Marquess of Downshire*, 6 vols. (1924–95), vol. i, pt. 1, 173 (for Walker's licence to print); Evelyn, *Numismata*; Joseph Addison, *Dialogues upon the Usefulness of Ancient Medals* (1726), and comments by Addison in *The Guardian*, 96 (1 July 1713), ed. J. C. Stephens

own finds—as we have seen they did with other antiquities such as parochial monuments—or drew up manuscript treatises on their own and other coins.[62]

The relatively narrow view of the uses of coins endured for some time following the Restoration, though one does see a marked increase in attention to the details of inscriptions as opposed to sheer fascination with their age or beauty. Joseph Addison would have a character observe that 'a cabinet of medals is a body of history' and that coinage itself was 'a kind of printing, before the art was invented'. Coins were of great use to the historian because they 'tell their story much quicker' than books, and were more reliable, since 'a coin is in no danger of having its characters altered by copiers and transcribers'.[63] As Evelyn advised Pepys in 1689, it was among medals he would 'meet legislators, Solon, Lycurgus, Numma...'.[64] The less well educated bookseller John Dunton would put it even more bombastically in advising young students to look beyond the printed page for their knowledge of the past, adding medals to a list of those objects—maps, monuments, bas-reliefs—that 'mightily strengthen and confirm history'.[65] William Blundell the younger thought that the coin was the ideal object for introducing illiterates to history. Writing to an absent Catholic friend on whose land a tenant had just unearthed a trove of Roman coins bearing the image of Vespasian and symbols such as 'SPQR' and the Roman eagle, Blundell enthused

(Lexington, Ky., 1982), 344. An interleaved copy (Bodl. MS Willis 113) of Stephen Martin Leake's *Nummi Britannici Historia: or an historical account of English money* (London, 1626 [misprint for 1726]) is full of jottings and notes on the coins by Browne Willis, for whose gold and silver coins, given to the Bodleian, see I. Philip, *The Bodleian Library in the Seventeenth and Eighteenth Centuries* (Oxford, 1983), 83. Three widely read European manuals by Charles Patin include *De numismata antiqua Augusto et Platonis* (Basle, 1675); *Imperatorum romanorum numismata ex aere, mediae et minimae formae* (Paris, 1697); and *Histoire des médailles* (Paris, 1695).

[62] Some examples: a list of Anglo-Saxon and English coins composed by Patrick Young, royal librarian, covering the period from the British era up to the accession of Richard II and arranged by year in Latin annals with added English notes (Bodl. MS Smith 22, pp. 91–4); a manuscript treatise on the history of coins, focusing on Roman, British, and Saxon pieces, and possibly by William Stukeley, is in Norwich RO, MS 11292, and copied in the SAL Stukeley MSS (which copy is used here); cf. Bodl. MS Num. f. 10 for another seventeenth-century example, an eighty-five-leaf anonymous list of Roman imperial coins, arranged chronologically; CUL MS Gg. 6.9, art. 2, fos. 136–78, an alphabetical catalogue of Greek coins, apparently intended for publication. The virtuoso William Charleton kept detailed notes of the value of coins and medals in 1667, and of his expenditures on these and other curiosities: BL MS Sloane 3988 (1667), fos. 6ᵛ–7ʳ, and Sloane 3879, fos. 1–19, 'Numismata Imperatoria secundum varios raritatis gradus per Ezechielum Spanhemium'; MS Sloane 3961 (c.1690); Staffs. RO D 649/5/2, 'Numismata antiqua pnes Walt[er] Chetwynd', a collection of early Roman imperial coins with Walter Chetwynd's description of the images on each coin.

[63] Addison, quoted in M. McKeon, *The Origins of the English Novel 1600–1740* (Baltimore, 1987), 43. As McKeon points out, the growing preference for physical antiquities over literary sources 'reflects not a flight from the abstraction of script and print but a heightened commitment to it, to the sort of authoritative and "objective" knowledge that can be gained only from the study of that which time cannot efface'.

[64] Evelyn saw medals as an essential, not only in seeing images of the past but in understanding points of history such as weights and measures: HRC Pforzheimer MS 35.I (Evelyn to Pepys, 26 Aug. 1689), transcribed in *The Carl H. Pforzheimer Library: English Literature 1475–1700*, 3 vols. (New York, 1940), iii. 1216 ff.

[65] John Dunton, *The-Young-Student's Library, containing extracts and abridgments of the most valuable books printed in England, and in the foreign journals, from the year sixty-five to this time* (1692), p. vi.

about the tangible history lesson that coins could provide the poorer sort. 'Thus, sir, you may see that your learned Worships poore tenants [neigbours, interlined], without the trouble of Livie, Tacitus, Sueton, or any other of thos crabbed companions, are as conversant with the noble old heroes as your self.'[66] As historical interest broadened beyond the classical past to include the Middle Ages, increasing numbers of gentry began to add Anglo-Saxon and post-Conquest coins to their collections,[67] side by side with the Roman coinage that by 1700 was almost commonplace; once again the antiquaries printed images of the most interesting (Fig. 7.2), and issued textbooks on their historical interpretation. John Stow, whose lack of formal classical education gave him a greater interest in post-Roman antiquities than most of his contemporaries, made a study of Saxon coins part of his *Survey of London* in the 1590s. In 1607 an inhabitant of Higham, Leicestershire, discovered 250 pieces of silver under a paving stone. The antiquary William Burton, who lived in the same parish, arrived the following day, and identified and distinguished these as coming partly from the reign of the emperor Trajan and partly from the reign of Henry III.[68] Sir Thomas Browne boasted to his 14-year-old son Thomas that he had acquired '60 coynes of King Stephen' found in a gravesite before Christmas 1661, and had bought sixty Roman coins to go along with them two months later.[69]

Coins and medals are sometimes spoken of in the same breath by contemporary collectors, who were wont to confuse the two—a gold taler of Sigismund III, known to have belonged to the early Stuart diplomat Sir Thomas Roe, was long mistakenly held to have been a medal minted in his honour.[70] But the two pieces are not the same, and this difference was already recognized in the seventeenth century. The collectable coin was an archaic form of previously current money (hence a mundane object attractive for its antiquity); the medal, in contrast, was a decorative token minted primarily for commemorating a person or event, exotic at its time of origin as well as its time of rediscovery. To put it another way, the marvellous aspect of the medal was inherent and connected with the event or person it commemorated, rather than bestowed by its antiquity. Consequently modern medals could be as fervently sought after by collectors as ancient ones. In the later seventeenth century the ancient or medieval coin was to be rivalled, and perhaps even eclipsed, as a feature of virtuoso closets, by the contemporary medal commemorating recent events or personages. Although as shrewd a collector as Richard Rawlinson considered these to be 'historical medals' much like

[66] Lancs RO DDBl Acc. 6121, Great Hodge Podge, fo. 85ᵛ (William Blundell to James Scarisbrick, 29 Apr. 1655); repr. in Blundell, *Cavalier's Note Book*, 280, with modernized spelling.

[67] For a list of cabinets of English coins seen by Stukeley from 1720 to 1730, see SAL MS 264, fo. 41ʳ.

[68] Stow, *Survey of London*, 48; William Burton, *The description of Leicester Shire: containing matters of antiquitye, historye, armorye, and genealogy* (1622), 131–3.

[69] *Works of Sir Thomas Browne*, iv. 8 (Browne to Thomas Browne the younger, 22 Apr. 1661); cf. Browne, *Hydriotaphia*, in *Works*, i. 104–5.

[70] The piece was presented to the Ashmolean Museum in 1668 by Lady Roe, where it remains: M. Strachan, *Sir Thomas Roe 1581–1644* (1989), 209–10.

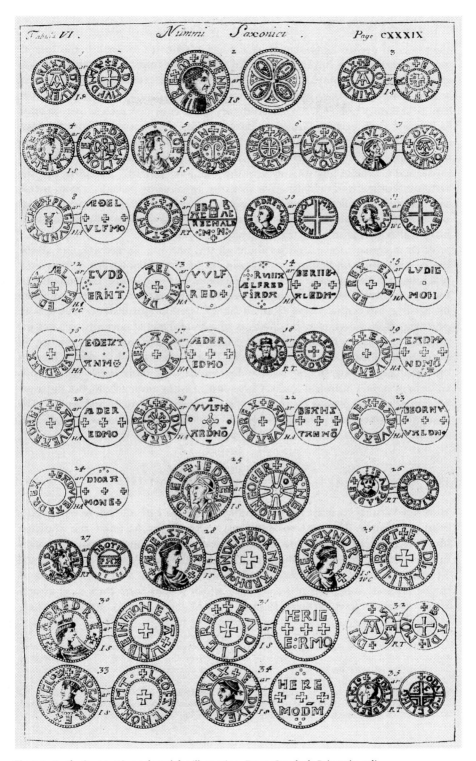

Fig. 7.2. Anglo-Saxon coins, selected for illustration. From *Camden's Britannia*, cxli

their ancient predecessors, they were actually an attempt by English and foreign governments to turn the enthusiasm for collectables into a money-making and image-enhancing venture, one that literally engraved events into the historical record. This was a more lucrative form of public celebration than the observation of statutory holidays. An extraordinary number of new medals were minted in England in the early eighteenth century. Rawlinson's list of those from the reign of Anne alone includes those issued to mark her coronation, the Queen's Bounty to the clergy in 1704, military victories at Blenheim, Ramillies, Malplaquet, Saragossa, and Gibraltar, and the union of the kingdoms in 1707.[71] Paradoxically, the virtuoso treatment of medals, often arranged by country, period, or even metal, more accurately reflects Baconian principles of systematic collection and categorization than did the more atomized epigraphic analysis of individual coins for historical evidence on particular points of fact.

What is perhaps most striking about all this numismatic activity, and all the books advocating the importance of coins to historical knowledge, is how little real impact it continued to have on mainstream historiography. The activities of the antiquary and narrative historian were no longer as distinct as they had been in the sixteenth century. Many individuals—Clarendon for instance—were both practising historians and keen collectors of coin and medal portraits; yet, despite this, the number of histories published before 1700 that made extensive use of numismatic illustrations is small indeed. That would change in the eighteenth century, culminating in the fashion for interleaving with lavish illustrations editions of certain historical works, Clarendon's *History* among them, but the overwhelming urge to possess far outstripped the desire to evaluate and learn.[72] The desire to move beyond political history and treat the coin, like bones, urns, sherds, and fossils, as a clue to past social life, lagged even further behind.

THE MONEY MARKET: TRADE IN COINS AND MEDALS

Humfrey Wanley's acquisition of manuscripts for the earls of Oxford has already been mentioned. He used similarly aggressive tactics to build the Harleian library's collection of coins and medals, including the maintenance of an enormous network of agents and would-be friends of the earl. A medal dealer named Kennedy indicated to Wanley that he could furnish, at cost, some additions to the Harleys' collection of medals, for which joiners were then busy assembling 'cards' or trays. Wanley learned from William Slyford, Browne Willis's

---

[71] Bodl. MS Rawl. N. 9, fos. 1–4, lists a total of twenty-seven medals for Anne's reign. For a contemporary satire of such medals, in particular one celebrating the victory of Marlborough at Guelderland, that casts doubt on the reliability of the 'trusty medal's word' as a source for history, see Bodl. MS Smith 23, p. 109.

[72] F. Haskell, *History and its Images: Art and the Interpretation of the Past* (New Haven and London, 1993), 70–1, for Clarendon, and for the general comment on the lack of impact of images on mainstream historiography, a theme already well treated by Momigliano and others.

amanuensis, that the Buckinghamshire antiquary was prepared to part with his collections in 1720.[73] Four years later, in 1724, another Wanley contact, the goldsmith Joseph Barret, offered to buy the coin collection of the late Dr Arthur Charlett, Master of University College and Wanley's earliest patron, and sell to Harley whichever coins he wanted. As an inducement to make the deal, Barret also gave Wanley, as a present for the earl, a free copy of a newly published heraldic book.[74]

Wanley appears to have had considerable latitude in deciding what to buy and for how much, though almost as often materials were left for Oxford to inspect, after which Wanley was allowed to negotiate their purchase, sometimes unsuccessfully. When Thomas Great, a Colchester apothecary, brought in some coins and other antiquities from Essex for Wanley and his employer to inspect, Wanley failed to reach a decision for about eighteen months. After a visit from Mr Great on 16 November 1720, Wanley promised him a speedy answer, which was still not forthcoming. But six months later, on 19 May, Great returned, still without an answer, and pressed Wanley more firmly. The next day he returned in a vexed mood, and asked, not unreasonably after this delay, for what Wanley called 'an exorbitant price for his things'. Wanley, continuing to stall, told him to return on Monday when Oxford, who was by now uninterested in these coins, would give him a gratuity. When Great returned on Monday to remove his coins (but leaving some tiles and other fragments), the earl was out and Wanley recorded 'I could not give him the gratuity', whereupon, to Wanley's amazement, Great felt himself ill used.[75]

The market for old coins—for Roman imperial specie in particular—was sufficiently brisk and volatile by the end of the seventeenth century that it would be possible for two collectors to arrange a sale of a gold coin on the spot over a drink; Henry Prescott made some of his finest acquisitions, including a gold Nero, in pubs.[76] But where money is involved, greed will surely follow—perhaps all the more so when the item being sold is also money. Despite the above-mentioned confidence invested by commentators such as Addison in the reliability of numismata as a 'body of history', a growing quantity of bogus coins and medals was on the market throughout Europe. The greatest northern English antiquary of the early eighteenth century, John Horsley, was also the outstanding English epigrapher of his day, a man who really was more interested in the inscriptions

[73] Wanley, *Diary*, i. 75, ii. 261; for some of his earlier essays into the coin market, Wanley, *Letters*, 38, 39 (Wanley to Sir Henry Puckering, June 1696, and to unknown correspondent, July 1696). Ancient coins could sometimes acquire the status of 'medals' purely because of their antiquity, as Addison satirically noted in his mock autobiography of a shilling which 'being now of great credit and antiquity . . . was rather looked upon as a medal than an ordinary coin': *The Tatler*, 249 (11 Nov. 1710), ed. D. F. Bond, 3 vols. (Oxford, 1987), iii. 269–73, at p. 272.

[74] Wanley, *Diary*, ii. 275.   [75] Ibid. i. 108.

[76] *Diary of Henry Prescott*, ii. 330, 341. In 1717 the Sussex barrister Timothy Burrell left his 'curious collection of gold coins' to his infant granddaughter. R. W. Blencowe, 'Extracts from the Journal and Account-Book of Timothy Burrell, Esq . . . from 1683 to 1714', *Sussex Archaeological Collections*, 3 (1850), 117–72, at p. 172. On the market for archaeological antiquities today, which has continued unabated since the seventeenth century, see W. H. Stiebing Jr., *Uncovering the Past: a History of Archaeology* (Oxford and New York, 1993), 278.

on coins than in their monetary worth. He would lament in his *Britannia Romana*, publication of which he did not live to see, 'the high prices of curious Roman coins' which he perceived as directly connected to the manufacture of 'a great many forgeries contrived very artfully'.[77] This should have come as no great surprise, for a great deal of money was at stake, in both senses. Medal-makers such as Alexandre Bassiano and Juan Cavino had become famous in the 1570s for having established a lucrative business engraving legitimate imitations of Greek and Roman coins and medals, just as there was already a small but growing market for replicas of ancient bronze statues. Jonathan Swift would compare them to 'some fellows' whom he ran across in 1708, 'that could make Medals faster than the Padua Brothers, onely they dealt altogether in modern ones; and equally struck them upon the high Road'.[78]

Genuine ancient coins or medals, as opposed to acknowledged modern imitations, were expensive. Depending on its metal content, a Roman imperial coin purchased from an Italian dealer could cost anything from 5 to 40 scudi, with most gold specimens at the upper end of that range. Richard Rawlinson, easily among the best-informed collectors in the reign of George I, kept a close accounting of his purchases of coins and medals, many of which were purchased abroad, and regularly purged his collection of duplicates or inferior specimens.[79] Not everyone was so discriminating. John Evelyn was among the numerous writers on numismatics who warned 'beginning' collectors of the perils of counterfeit medals, suggesting that fraudulent artefacts were quite widespread—he suggested that the thrifty beginner avoid buying single coins haphazardly but look instead for complete collections on auction. The French numismatist Louis Jobert likewise complained of the 'fraud and avarice of the selling merchants'.[80] Wanley refused the offer of some coins from the Hungarian émigré artist, James Bogdani, partly because his employer, the earl of Oxford, did not like buying coins in 'little parcels', and partly because the vendor had already left for inspection some phoney specimens.[81] Collectors were also well aware of the existence of coins and medals that had been forged—like some texts—during the Middle Ages. A 'cart-load' of gold imperial medals near Bonn, some of great weight, aroused suspicions that because of the 'rude manner of their sculpture' they had been 'counterfeited 4 or 500 years ago'; but they were still on the market some years later,

---

[77] John Horsley, *Britannia romana, or, The Roman antiquities of Britain* (1732), 293, cited in J. M. Levine, *The Battle of the Books: History and Literature in the Augustan Age* (Ithaca, NY, 1991), 394.

[78] F. Haskell and N. Penny, *Taste and the Antique: The Lure of Classical Sculpture 1500–1900* (New Haven, 1981), 93–116. *The Correspondence of Jonathan Swift*, ed. H. Williams, 5 vols. (Oxford, 1963–5), i. 140–1 (Swift to earl of Pembroke, 13 June 1709), referring to a visit by the medal-makers in the previous year.

[79] Bodl. MS Rawl. N. 3, fos. 1–39 list of prices of Roman imperial and Greek coins recorded by Richard Rawlinson; cf. his 'Notizie delli prezzi delle Medaglie antiche ben conservate' in Bodl. MS Rawl. N. 11, fos. 1–3ʳ, moneys paid and received for coins and medals by Rawlinson (13 Dec. 1720 to Apr. 1726); some of these were resold in 1733.

[80] Evelyn, *Numismata*, 198–9; Jobert, *The Knowledge of Medals*, 171–83.

[81] Wanley, *Diary*, i. 22. For rumours of coins planted to impress tourists see Thomas Hearne, *Discourse concerning the Stonesfield tesselated pavement* (1728), 109.

giving rise to much correspondence as to their origins. Evelyn thought English 'countrey-people, day-labourers and such as dig about old foundations' sufficiently simple that 'one would little suspect [they] should deceive us', but noted the higher degree of subtlety practised abroad 'where even those seemingly plain and boorish people have now and then imposed upon the less wary medallist'.[82]

These fears of sharp practice by dealers may have been exaggerated, but that there were gullible collectors is beyond doubt. In practice an intimate acquaintance with the details of numismatics eluded most enthusiasts. The ordinary gentleman or citizen who had purchased or inherited a small collection of coins or medals could not be expected to have the knowledge of Camden or Evelyn, much less of Ezechial Spanheim, the greatest European numismatist of the late seventeenth century, though he might very well know of their books.[83] Nor did most collectors, more interested in the coins for their curiosity and show-and-tell worth than for any historical evidence they might offer, care to develop such skills, to the annoyance of more devoted antiquaries.[84] Typical of the manic, spare-no-expense enthusiasm of the budding collector is a letter from Brian Fairfax to the Rochester antiquary Dr John Thorpe. 'Hearing there are severall gold coyns found near Sittingbourne if they are Roman or English,' effused Fairfax, 'I shoud think my self oblig'd to you could you commission anybody to procure some for me if anyway curious'; he declared his willingness to repay Thorpe, sight unseen, 'whatever is the expense'. When Abraham de la Pryme visited one parishioner, a Mrs Anderson, in the 1690s, she 'ran and fetched me down several old coins to look at'. These were arranged indiscriminately and included a rose noble, 'one of those that Raymond Lully is sayd to have made [by] chymistry', a silver medal commemorating the restoration of Charles II, and a few Anglo-Saxon coins, 'one which was a Danish one'. Their owner was less interested in deciphering the historical meaning of the coins, or even in querying her learned curate about them, than in recounting to Pryme stories of vast troves of old coins found in nearby underground caves, graves, and hills.[85] And lest we think that the traffic in antiquities was invariably up the social ladder, let us note the example of Henry Whitfield, a minor gentry collector of St Albans and Rickmansworth, whose passion for

---

[82] Nichols, *Literary Illustrations*, iv. 95–6; Evelyn, *Numismata*, 209. Lady Mary Wortley Montagu, who had embarked on a collection of medals in 1717, expressed disdain towards Greek antiquaries. 'Their trade is only to sell . . . One of them shewing me the figure of a Pallas, with a victory in her hand on a reverse, assured me it was the Virgin holding a crucifix. The same man offered me the head of a Socrates on a sardonyx; and, to enhance the value, gave him the title of Saint Augustine.' *The Letters and Works of Lady Mary Wortley Montagu*, ed. W. Moy Thomas, rev. edn., 2 vols. (1887), i. 205.

[83] Spanheim (1629–1710) was the author of the *Dissertatio de praestantia et usu numismatum antiquorum*, first published at Rome in 1664 and republished by subscription in a revised, two-volume Latin edition by Richard Smith between 1706 and 1717. On Spanheim, Jacob Spon, and the European pioneers of numismatics see Schnapp, *Discovery of the Past*, 182–5.

[84] Nor did every heir to a collection care to preserve it. The third earl of Bridgewater, John Egerton, specified that his coins and books were to 'remaine as heire-loomes to my family' in his 1687 will, though by 1701 he had grown confident enough in his son's development of an interest to add a codicil giving them outright to him: Herts. RO AH 1188 (will and codicil of earl of Bridgewater).

[85] SAL MS 202 (Thorpe papers), fo. 105 (Fairfax to Thorpe, 27 Aug., no year); *Diary of Abraham de la Pryme*, 104–5.

coins was extinguished by his greater love of expensive cheeses. Whitfield's
memorandum book for 1729 shows him selling, for £42 payable in instalments,
his own Roman coins, tiles, and urns, and pawning a gold piece of Henry V to
his poulterer.[86]

In the process of finding, as opposed to purchasing, numismata, classical texts
such as the *Antonine Itinerary* provided a guide as to the likely whereabouts
of former Roman settlements and garrisons. By the early eighteenth century, the
older authorities had been joined by modern works, both cheaper vade mecum
books like Joshua Childrey's *Britannia Baconica* and more lavish productions
like Robert Castell's *Villas of the Ancients*. Place names provided another clue,
towns with 'caster' or 'cester' as suffixes being favoured destinations for antiquaries
because of their Roman connections. But this sort of information could only get
the prospector so far. As with other types of antiquity, the cooperation of local
labourers and farmers proved invaluable to antiquaries in search of a quick find,
by narrowing down the area that had to be searched. Leland encountered a 'scantly
lettered' man (which probably meant a gentleman with poor Latin) who thought
he had seen 'Pont. Max.' on a coin. John Norden, pursuing some coins at the
ruins of St Albans, which he had found mentioned in *Britannia*, tracked them
down by asking the locals for directions, who informed him of 'some fragmentes
of the scituation of some decayed buildings, where sundry peeces of Romish coyne
have beene taken up'. A conversation with shepherds directed Evelyn to one such
site in 1658.[87]

As with other antiquities, the common folk could take advantage of the
appetites of collectors to make a profit—one recalls Sir Thomas Fairfax's promise to be 'generous' to any soldier who could rescue documents displaced by
his siege of York in the first civil war.[88] Many locals were engaged in the sale of
coins and medals throughout the seventeenth and early eighteenth centuries. An
Odington butcher found several Roman coins, including one featuring Romulus
and Remus, in the 1640s, and promptly sold them to a scholar at Corpus Christi
College, Oxford. A Yorkshire ploughman turned up an urn 'full of all Roman
coins, amongst which was several of gold' about 1680, but was unwise enough to
sell them for only a pound to the Darfield goldsmith, a decision which his
brother, who knew better, still rued nearly two decades later, since they were 'worth
above 3 times as much as he gave for them'. In 1699 a labourer named John Mizred,
digging for the foundations of a new house, turned up several round pieces of
brass, believed to be Roman ornaments for horses and then a Roman brass medal;
he brought these to the attention of John Philips, who, 'taking a more peculiar
care in opening the ground', found a larger number of bones and man-made artefacts. In 1698 Abraham de la Pryme bought several Roman imperial coins for a

[86] Herts. RO 79872 (unfoliated MS), memorandum book of Henry Whitfield.
[87] *Leland's Itinerary*, iii. 101; John Norden, *Speculi Britanniae pars: the discription of Hertfordshire* (1598), 23–4; Evelyn, *Diary*, iii. 221.
[88] See above and G. Parry, *The Trophies of Time: English Antiquarians of the Seventeenth Century* (Oxford, 1995), 222.

few shillings each which had been dug up at Boroughbridge; at the same place, a ploughman had discovered a gold plate 'which the *country clown* sold for five shillings to a Scotchman, who, coming over the field, chanced to see it, who sold it again for fifty pounds'.[89] Even Stukeley, by no means the most condescending Augustan, noted how 'a countryman digging a ditch to divide a pasture, found an urn . . . conteining about £30 weight of copper Roman coyn: which the fellow sold for 6d per £'.[90] Stukeley congratulated himself on buying several coins from an Ilchester gardener who had turned them up while digging at the town's south-west wall, and 'chanced not to have lost'.[91]

It is easy to share in the mixture of frustration and amusement of the learned at the ignorance of those who parted with valuable artefacts for a pittance. It is worth remembering, however, that the vendors may have had similar difficulty comprehending the stupidity of gentlemen willing to pay hard currency for rather impractical chunks of brick and metal. And not all labouring purveyors of antiquities were quite as ignorant as their clients liked to pretend. Some, in fact, knew perfectly well that these objects were worth looking out for, and which gentry in the neighbourhood were worth cultivating. On a spring morning in 1723 a Chelmsford bricklayer named Michael Saward, who had recently completed work on the Braintree Dissenters' meeting house, called on Dr Samuel Dale of Braintree. They were not strangers. Saward had previously been asked by Dale to obtain for him some Roman bricks found at nearby Moulsham, and on this particular occasion he proved an almost bottomless source of information about local antiquities:

He among other discourses affirmed that some Roman town had been there, for which he alledged not only the the [sic] pavement to which those bricks belong, but likewise the finding of foundations in divers of the feilds near my Lord ffitz-waters house, one of which still retains the name of Shop-row. And he likewise told me that ancient coins were frequently found particularly in his own orchard.[92]

Like Dale's bricklayer, the gardeners of Georgian Dorchester, another former Roman encampment where coins turned up with regularity, had a standing order, according to one of their number, to take any and all medals and coins that they should dislodge from the soil to Dr Archer, a local physician.[93] The owner of a house at the ruins of Glastonbury Abbey pulled down an ancient mantelpiece to sell it, but after the stones had lain in the street for a while, no chapman being

[89] Wood, *Life and Times*, i. 266; Nichols, *Literary Illustrations*, iv. 98 (J. Philips to J. Batteley, 23 Aug. 1703); BL MS Lans. 897 (Pryme's History of Hatfield), fo. 7ᵛ, and *Diary of Abraham de la Pryme*, 108, 186 (my emphasis).

[90] The coins, found in Wold, Gloucestershire (midway between Stow and Broadwell), were 'sent to Dr Mead' and identified as from the reigns of Constans and Constantine: undated note by Stukeley, SAL MS 265 (antiquaries' commonplace book), p. 1.

[91] SAL MS Stukeley IV/1/335, and III/315/2 (1723). Ilchester was an especially productive place for those interested in Roman diggings at the start of the eighteenth century.

[92] Essex RO D/Y/1/1/135 (Samuel Dale to William Holman, 7 Mar. 1722/3); cf. ibid., art. 139 (same to same, 11 Apr. 1724).

[93] BL MS Add. 15776 (travel account of Jeremiah Milles, n.d. [c.1735]), fo. 109ᵛ.

willing to pay the 10 groats he asked, the owner's daughter had a workman turn it into a new set of stairs. This construction produced the unexpected bonus of eighty or so gold coins from the reign of Richard II, which she and the mason split between them.[94] Jonathan Swift was unable to persuade a 'Fellow' in Leicester to give up his three Anglo-Saxon coins 'which the Owner values as I did My Alexander Seal, and with equall Judgment'. Hearne noted the visit to the Bodleian coin collection of one Sanford, a man who 'makes it his business to pick up such curiosities, & to sell them afterwards, being a person of no skill in history or any other parts of learning, as having not been bred up to it'.[95] John Evelyn resented paying extra for such objects to middlemen, mainly goldsmiths and braziers. He thought that 'countery people and labourers' ought to be encouraged to bring their finds directly to the learned, as was the case in Italy, rather than disposing of them on the next market day to unscrupulous tradesmen. (There is no evidence that Evelyn believed the labouring discoverers themselves deserved more money.[96])

Familiarity breeds contempt, dependence perhaps even more so. The social bias against the discoverers of antiquities, only barely noticeable from Leland to the civil war, is palpable by the later seventeenth century. In addition to accusations of greed, charges of barbarism and vulgarity were lobbed at common folk by their superiors. Wanley, who had escaped his own low social origins through his enthusiasm for antiquities, linked what he saw as a monstrous increase of deism, profanity, and vice to 'the barbarous ignorance observable among the common people, especially those of the poorer sort'. Ralph Thoresby wrote in similar vein when informing Sir Hans Sloane of an incident near Leeds. 'Some time ago here was dug up a statue to the full proportion of a Roman officer, with an inscription, both which perished thro, the brutish ignorance & covetousnesse of the laborers.' In a 'superstitious conceit', Thoresby noted, they had burned the 'knight' in hopes of 'finding some hid treasure.' But after, 'in anger at their disappointment, [they] broke him to peices, of which only the head is now forthcoming'. Two inscriptions also found there 'fell into a more intelligent hand', in this case the artificial hand of a local gentleman named John Robinson, whose fingers had been burnt off in childhood through the carelessness of a servant.[97]

A remarkable example of how such artefacts could circulate, and of the growing social distance of the scholar from his popular supplier, comes from the late 1690s, when some medals were found in Wallingford. According to Thomas Ford, writing about the discovery,

[94] Bristol RO MS 36074 (88), notes by Henry Savage, 1677, concerning the Porter's Lodge at Glastonbury thirty years earlier.

[95] *Correspondence of Jonathan Swift*, i. 140 (Swift to earl of Pembroke, 13 June 1709); Hearne, *Remarks and Collections*, i. 40.

[96] Evelyn, *Numismata*, 199. Cf. Stukeley's notice of a Druid artefact found in a Northamptonshire wood, SAL MS Stukeley IV/i/332B.

[97] CUL Mm. 6.50 (Covel letters), fo. 255 (Wanley to Covel, 18 Apr. 1702); BL MS Sloane 4025 new numbering, fo. 289r (Thoresby to Sloane, 23 Nov. 1702).

'Tis suspected there were gold & pure silver peices amongst them, tho' concealed by the greedy discoverers. A great part of them they sent to London to be refined for the silver; some few were distributed to such country fellows as came to gaze & wonder at such strange money; the rest are ingrossed by an ironmonger in Wallingford who having heard how valuable single & particular medals are, sets extravagant rates on them, imagining all to be such.

Ford himself had heard of these only at Christmas 1699, while visiting relations in the area, but by that point only a handful were still there. Ford's lament for the fate of this discovery echoes the 'greedy ignorant countryman' motif common to such accounts by 1700. 'Tis pitty', Ford remarks, 'so many excellent monuments of antiquity should be so lost or that some curious person was not at the discovery who might have redeemed many valuable pieces from the crucible & settled many controverted points of history by their most certain testimony.'[98]

Exotic objects decline in both intellectual appeal and economic value in inverse proportion to their supply. At some sites, the discovery of old coins soon became routine. Camden found that an 'infinite deale' of old coins was 'daily gotten out of the ground' at Colchester, and in 1673 Richard Blome recounted the frequency of such discoveries in the vicinity of Burgh Castle, near Yarmouth, and elsewhere.[99] By the mid-seventeenth century, the novelty had arguably worn off, and the coin become a much more commonplace curiosity—Wood was given a few as a casual gift in 1657 when he visited his old schoolmaster, David Thomas, at Dorchester, near Oxford, which both archaeological evidence and local tradition suggested had been the location of a Roman garrison. At Ilchester, again a former Roman military centre, Thomas Gerard reported that coins and medals 'have bin and almost daylie yet are digged up'; a local gentleman had gathered up several and sent them to him.[100] Fresh discoveries remained local news. Samuel Dale of Braintree wrote to William Holman in 1728, enclosing copies of the inscriptions on two medals dug up by a gardener a week earlier; while this was not a major find, one can still catch a breath of excitement about Dale's description. Henry Hare, Lord Coleraine, corresponded frequently with William Charleton on numismatic matters and at one point directed him to inspect and perhaps purchase for him the ancient medals being sold by a tailor named Bradford.[101]

Although coins and medals could still arouse enthusiasm if they were rare specimens, the attention of many antiquaries and collectors had shifted by the

[98] CUL MS Mm. 6.50 (Covel letters), fo. 229 (Ford to Covel, 29 Jan. 1699/1700).

[99] Camden, *Britain*, 450; Richard Blome, *Britannia* (1673), 176, 217. Medals and coins were still surfacing almost daily at Burgh Castle over a century later, according to Sir John Percival, *The English Travels of Sir John Percival and William Byrd II: The Percival Diary of 1701*, ed. M. R. Wenger (Columbia, Mo., 1989), 56.

[100] Wood, *Life and Times*, i. 223, 226; Thomas Gerard, *The particular description of Somerset* (written 1633; 1st edn., 1900), 204.

[101] Essex RO D/Y/1/1, unsorted bundles (Samuel Dale to William Holman, 30 Apr. 1728); BL MS Sloane 3962 (Charleton papers), fos. 270ʳ, 274ʳ–275ᵛ (Coleraine to Charleton, 2 Nov. 1699; Charleton to Coleraine, 7 Dec. 1699).

middle of the seventeenth century to rarities of an even more curious nature. Krzysztof Pomian's analysis of several hundred Parisian collections of the eighteenth century demonstrates a movement of attention away from medals and towards natural rarities such as shells.[102] This waning of interest occurred, paradoxically, just as rules for numismatics were being formalized, both in mammoth scholarly works such as Spanheim's *Dissertationes de praestantia et usu numismatum antiquorum* and in more accessible manuals by Evelyn, Addison, and other more learned enthusiasts. As the coin became an accepted and even standard historical source, it lost some of the mystique it had previously enjoyed. A buried treasure was evolving into simply one among the antiquary's kit of tools, just as had happened to genealogical enthusiasm over much the same period: method and systematization often follow undisciplined enthusiasm at a short but safe distance.

Some scholars, indeed, were waking up to the fact that the information on coins was not necessarily reliable, since they were minted by emperors trying to magnify their power and achievements. Hearne, who personally enjoyed collecting coins, nevertheless believed that their use as a historical source had become quite limited, and complained in 1705 that, despite the frequency at which they were discovered, none of 'good note' was ever dug up. Even some major collections began to look less impressive to later generations.[103] By 1757 Oxford's Francis Wise could dismiss one of the more spectacular numismatic treasures of the previous century, the Laudian collection at the Bodleian, as *passé*. 'The collection of coins is numerous, and considerable enough for the time when it was purchased by Archbishop Laud, 120 years ago,' Wise advised the librarian of Lambeth Palace, Andrew Coltee Ducarel, 'but in truth is but a mean stock, if compared with some modern collections.'[104]

OBJECT INTO ANTIQUITY: THE ANGLO-SAXON COINS
OF LITTLE CROSBY

Did any of this really matter? We have seen numerous examples of the manner in which ancient objects, wrested by accident from the ground, made their way

[102] K. Pomian, *Collectors and Curiosities: Paris and Venice, 1500–1800*, trans. E. Wiles-Portier (Cambridge, 1990), 121–38. Pomian notes that objects of natural history were also more likely to be collected by social groups outside the most wealthy Parisian elite.

[103] Hearne, *Remarks and Collections*, i. 6; but cf. Hearne's greater interest in some other coins, ibid. i. 165, 168. At its meeting of 3 Jan. 1722, the Society of Antiquaries decided that it was high time to construct a complete description of all coins relating to Great Britain from earliest times to their own, to be called *Metallurgica Britannica*: various collections were assigned to different members, with Roger Gale designated to do Roman coins, Samuel Gale Danish ones, and George Holmes, the deputy keeper of the Tower records, the Saxon coins belonging to a lawyer named Hill. SAL, Minute Book 1718–32, p. 53.

[104] Nichols, *Literary Illustrations*, iv. 451 (Wise to Ducarel, 10 Mar. 1757). This did not prevent Wise (a frequent donor of coins in his own right) from issuing a catalogue, the *Nummorum antiqvorum scriniis Bodleianis reconditorum catalogus cum commentario tabulis aeneis et appendice* (Oxford, 1750) 'only to promote the study of Medals among our youth, by giveing them a system of the science'.

into the hands of the learned. But what happened to them once they got there? Regrettably, we know all too little, beyond the many acknowledgements (and those to the local gentry rather than their bricklayers and ploughmen) printed in works such as *Britannia*, about what, in practice, such objects were used for and how knowledge added value to them. To shed some light on this question, we need much better records of many of the finds than has hitherto come to light. For the present, however, it is possible to offer one very well documented instance of a significant discovery, in this case of Anglo-Saxon coins, to illustrate the relevance of the archaeological economy to actual scholarship. It is all the more interesting in that its description was the work not of a major university-educated scholar such as Camden or Dugdale, but of precisely the sort of minor gentry antiquary whose awareness of history was being awakened in the sixteenth and seventeenth centuries.

On the morning of Monday, 8 April 1611, it was particularly wet and muddy at Little Crosby, a predominantly Catholic village of about forty households within the parish of Sefton in the West Derby Hundred of Lancashire, a few miles north of Liverpool. Thomas Ryse (the 14-year-old son of John Ryse, a local tenant farmer), was taking the cattle of his father's landlord, William Blundell the elder (1560–1638), from the hall to graze in a nearby field. His path took him directly across a ditch which marked one end of a section of demesne land known locally as the 'Harkirke', where a day earlier an old man from the village had been buried in a makeshift cemetery hastily created by Blundell to accommodate the local Catholic deceased.[105] What caught young Thomas's eye on this morning was the glint of something unusual, a number of silver coins lying on the sandy soil at the edge of the ditch, where they had been dislodged by the recent burial.

Perplexed at his find, the boy picked up a coin and took it back to the Hall, where he showed it to the other servants; none could explain the strange letters on the coin. Nevertheless, there was much discussion. No doubt someone even wondered aloud what the piece would be worth, though it would now have to be given up to the lord of Little Crosby; turned up on his property, it could not simply be sold to a traveller. Eventually the servants were joined by their master, William Blundell, who had overheard the discussions. 'I comminge into the kitchen amongst them whoe were lookinge and musing at them', he tells us, 'I presentlie tooke the coine and laide it uppe.' Blundell, whom we have already encountered (together with his grandson and great-great-grandson) on several occasions in this book, was the literate product of Continental seminaries. He had a variety of books on history and antiquities in his personal library, or available from nearby

---

[105] 'Harkirke', the name of the spot at which the coins were found, is an old English name, from *All hāra Cyrice*, handed down by tradition from a time when a 'grey and hoary' church, long vanished, had stood on the spot; it appears in local records from as early as 1275. A complete account of this episode, in the context of many of the other themes raised in this book, may be found in my essay, 'Little Crosby and the Horizons of Early Modern Historical Culture', in D. R. Kelley and D. H. Sacks (eds.), *The Historical Imagination in Early Modern Britain* (Cambridge, 1997), 93–132. Cf. M. Sena, 'William Blundell and the Networks of Catholic Dissent in Post-Reformation England', in A. Shepard and P. Withington (eds.), *Communities in Early Modern England* (Manchester, 2000), 54–75.

acquaintances; he had even consulted, if he did not actually own, as heretical a tome as John Foxe's fervently anti-Catholic *Acts and Monuments*.[106] He was passingly familiar with old coinage from reading Camden, and he even knew some Old English from reading Asser's *Life of Alfred* and Bede's *Ecclesiastical History*. Blundell realized intuitively that the prized object was a very old coin indeed, probably—though this required some research on his part—dating from the pre-Conquest period. Since the discovery had occurred on land he had set aside for the clandestine burial of his co-religionists, they appeared to be a reward for neighbourly piety and steadfast faith in the face of continued persecution.

Blundell had the boy Thomas lead him to the precise spot where he had found the mysterious money. With them went a servant, Edward Denton, and Blundell's son Nicholas, then a young man.[107] They were joined at the site a few minutes later by William's brother Richard Blundell, a priest who had been a long-time chaplain to the Houghtons, a Catholic family of nearby Lea Hall. Before very long, they had found several more coins but, the hour being late, the party returned to the hall for dinner, only to come back to the cemetery in the mid-afternoon. Perhaps eager to gather as many of the coins as he could, Blundell now took most of his family along, including his wife and his widowed mother Anne, whom it 'pleased' to visit the site of the discovery. They were to be rather disappointed, finding only a few more coins. Nevertheless, at the end of the day, Blundell had in his hands a minor hoard of 'about 4 score, none bigger than a groat or smaller than 2 pence', and several more unidentifiable fragments.[108]

Blundell immediately set himself the task of trying to identify his coins, which he did with reference to books that will be discussed further on. The hoard is now known to have been deposited by the Danes within a few years of their retreat to Northumbria in AD 910, and numismatists have identified in it the coinage of kings Alfred the Great, Edward the Elder, and Cnut of Northumbria. In many cases, Blundell's assessment of the individual pieces was not far off. He even recognized varieties of the ecclesiastical coinage of York and East Anglia, though he and most local inhabitants mistakenly called these 'the money of Sainte Peter', thinking them coins especially minted for Peter's pence. He was more thoroughly stumped by some foreign coins that bore 'strange and to me unknowen inscriptions'. Blundell set down at least two accounts of his find, each of which contains his pen and ink drawings of thirty-five of them. The first of these is a lengthy

---

[106] Lancs RO DDBl Acc. 6121, unfoliated notebook, from which this account of the find is drawn. The works cited are in this version of Blundell's narrative, together with the verbal descriptions of coins, but are absent from the roll version from which it was apparently copied, Lancs RO DDBl 24/12. Both versions were drafted by Blundell himself.

[107] Nicholas would predecease his father in 1631, leaving his son, the younger William, then aged 11, as the older William's heir.

[108] PRO E 159/469 (entries of estreats into Exchequer); *Crosby Records*, 34–40. In 1624 the Harkirke was set upon and nearly destroyed by agents of the sheriff of Lancashire. Blundell's tenants put up some show of resistance, and he was eventually fined £2,000 by Star Chamber, in the Easter term of 1629: PRO STAC 9/1/2; F. Tyrer, 'A Star Chamber Case: Assheton v. Blundell 1624–31', *Trans. Historic Society of Lancashire and Cheshire*, 118 (1966 [1967]), 19–37.

two-membrane roll of the sort that often contained deeds, surveys, and family pedigrees.[109] The second is contained in a small duodecimo paper notebook of twenty-seven leaves, bound in a medieval missal, in which he tells his story of the establishment of the cemetery and the circumstances of the initial coin find and subsequent treasure hunt. This version features one less coin than the roll, but it includes something that the roll lacks, detailed verbal descriptions of the coins together with references to several medieval and modern historical works. He had the coins engraved on copperplate, printed, and circulated (Fig. 7.3).[110] Then, keeping the thirty-five most interesting coins for himself, he turned the remainder into a pyx (Fig. 7.4) and chalice which remained in later centuries at Little Crosby's Catholic church.[111]

What to the servants were objects of mild curiosity and potential economic benefit were to the leisured Blundell a physical link to local, national, and providential pasts he had until then been able to commune with only textually, but of which he had a higher than average awareness. To put it another way, the past played its part in the mental horizons of all the denizens of Little Crosby, but only Blundell had the scholarly knowledge—the historical 'literacy', one might say—to connect its deposits to a specific moment in history. His notebook takes the bare depiction of the coins in the roll account and dresses it in the trappings of historical scholarship; for him they served as so many tiny, circular windows through which he could peer into the past to construct little mini-narratives of various kings' reigns, while obliquely commenting on the present. In contrast to the purely decorative use to which the historian John Speed was, at the very same time, putting a number of coins in his *Historie of Great Britain*,[112] Blundell's coins figure prominently in his account for their historical information. He endeavoured, for instance, to explain the name Cudberht on the reverse of one of Alfred's coins, though he could 'fynde written no espetiall cause or reason why this kinge

<hr/>

[109] Lancs RO DDBl 24/12; *Crosby Records*, 42, 63.
[110] Lancs RO DDBl Acc. 6121 includes the copperplate, which was sent by William's great-great-grandson, Nicholas (the early eighteenth-century diarist) to London through a Liverpool printer named John Aldridge, who had several prints made 'of the money found in the Harkerk': *Great Diurnal of Nicholas Blundell*, i. 86 (12 June 1705). William Blundell the younger had already printed up to 200 copies in 1676: *Crosby Records*, p. xv. Images of the coins were obtained from a manuscript in Corpus Christi College, Oxford, by the publishers of Sir John Spelman's *Aelfredi Magni Anglorum Regis invictissimi vita tribus libris comprehensa* (Oxford, 1678), sig. c2ʳ⁻ᵛ and table 3: 'Nummi in hac tabula descripti reperti sunt Aprilis 8. anno 1611. in loco *Harkirke* [in black letter] dicto in paroecia Septhoniae Comitatu Lancastriae; & habentur tum manu descripti in Bibliotheca C.C.C. Oxon. tum aere incisi & excusi.' The MS referred to by Spelman is CCC Oxon MS 255, fos. 82–3, and is an inferior copy made by a later draughtsman, in the judgement of R. H. M. Dolley, 'A Further Note on the Harkirke Find', *Numismatic Chronicle*, 6th ser., 15 (1955), 189–93, for which reference I am grateful to Mr Brian Whitlock Blundell. A further copy (illustrated here) is in BL MS Harl. 1437, fos. 128ᵛ–129.
[111] The reasons for the donation of the coins back to the church in this fashion may have to do with Blundell's awareness of the laws of treasure trove, which mandated this for trove found on (in this case former) ecclesiastical land: Woolf, 'Little Crosby', 105–6. The chalice was stolen in the nineteenth century; the pyx remains in the sacristy of Little Crosby church, bearing the inscription 'This was made of silver found in the burial place/W.Bl.'.
[112] *Original Letters of Eminent Literary Men of the Sixteenth, Seventeenth and Eighteenth Centuries*, ed. H. Ellis, Camden Soc., os 23 (1843), 108–13; Woolf, *Idea of History in Early Stuart England*, 68.

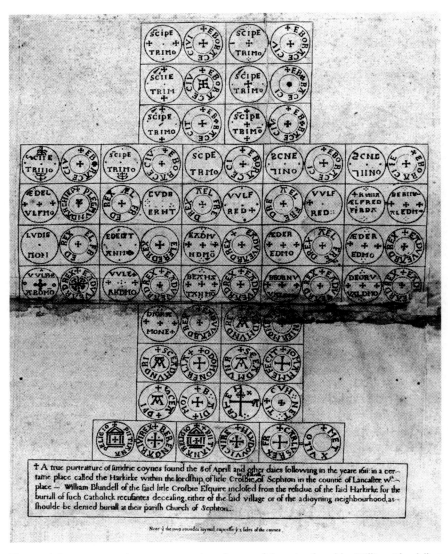

Fig. 7.3. A later seventeenth-century engraving of some of the coins found by William Blundell at the 'Harkirke' in Little Crosby, Lancs., 8 April 1611. Their arrangement in the form of a cross in this print irritated Humfrey Wanley, who identified thirty-two of the coins as Saxon and three as foreign. Wanley commented in his account of the manuscript in the Harleian catalogue that its author had 'more superstition than learning'. BL MS Harl. 1437, fos. 128ᵛ–129

shoulde set him in his coyne'. Mindful of the vision of St Cuthbert of Lindisfarne (mentioned in Bede), who is supposed to have appeared to Alfred in a vision during his darkest hour, Blundell used his imagination to bridge the gap between coin and book: 'I thinke it moste lyke and probable that K. Aelfred caused the coine so to be made in memorie of the fore said miracle.' In this vision, Cuthbert had reassured Alfred that the English were suffering 'by the swoorde of ye Danes'

Fig. 7.4. William Blundell's pyx, the product of some of the Anglo-Saxon coins discovered on his land in 1611. Blundell, a Catholic, 'restored' these to the Church by melting them down for the pyx. Photo by John Daley, *Crosby Herald*

for their sins, but that the Lord would not suffer their extinction 'in respecte of so manie saintes that had been of yt nation'.[113]

The 'living' past of the disgorged artefacts was now being mediated through and explained by the historical past, the unattainable realm of dead kings and chroniclers. Although the works to which Blundell refers in the notebook are a mixture of medieval and modern, antiquarian and historical, he was reading them for other than the conventional exemplary or commemorative value. He was instead using them as props, aids to guide his historical imagination, in thinking about how and why the coins were made, by whom, and, perhaps, how they came to be buried where they were. The exercise began with a 'more dilligent revewe' of the coins' condition and their inscriptions, but soon ran up against Blundell's own rather limited linguistic ability: several of the coins were not English but Danish, and by his own admission he was unable to 'perfectly imitate and expresse' the 'strange characters' on many of them. To proceed further he needed outside help,

---

[113] The story of King Alfred, complete with persecution by Danes, flight, and hunger, had particular appeal to the long-suffering Blundell, who saw in him an ancient model for faith in dire circumstances: *Crosby Records*, 50–1. Similar sentiments colour his account of Edward the Martyr: ibid. 59.

which was provided by his books. If Blundell was successful in identifying most of the individual coins, however, he conspicuously failed to fit them into the broader picture of Anglo-Danish history, instead reducing them to biographical mini-narratives of each depicted king's reign. Without the critical tools to generalize about life and events in the tenth-century north, he fell back on the genre he knew best, the formal history.

We know from Blundell's own account that his reading was wide and that he was better than usually acquainted with some of the major medieval and modern authors of the past.[114] By 1611, printed editions existed of many of the medieval historians. Various works by William of Malmesbury and Roger of Hoveden (or Howden) had been available in Latin for little over a decade in the collection of chroniclers published by Sir Henry Savile, while Bede, the most admired Anglo-Saxon historian, had been translated into English by the Catholic propagandist Thomas Stapleton in 1565, copies of his history having been known even earlier in private libraries.[115] Blundell's familiarity with Bede, a northerner and a monk, is not surprising. The chronicles of Malmesbury and Hoveden were a bit more out of the way.[116] His source for Edward the Confessor's payment of Peter's pence is given as a life of the Confessor by 'Alred'. This is without doubt Ailred or Ethelred of Rievaulx (c.1109–66) whose life of Edward was compiled for the translation of the king's body in 1163.[117] Acquaintance with this, and with Asser's life of Alfred, published by Archbishop Parker in a Latin and Anglo-Saxon edition in 1574, bespeaks a particular concern with the Anglo-Saxon era, one that contrasts with the usual Protestant veneration of the Wessex king as a kind of proto-Protestant prince ruling free of papal tyranny, as exemplified two decades later in Robert Powell's 1634 comparison of Alfred with Charles I.[118]

Blundell's veneration of Alfred as a pious lawgiver is clear. The king was 'of such pietie and devotion as Florent. Westmon. and others write that hee daylie heard masse, and in the night season unknowen to all his servants, hee frequented churches to here service. He wrote and promulgated most christian lawes.' Alfred alone among England's kings, notes Blundell (from Foxe's *Acts and*

[114] For the medieval historians, the indispensable work is A. Gransden, *Historical Writing in England*, 2 vols. (Ithaca, NY, 1974–82).

[115] E. Leedham-Green, *Books in Cambridge Inventories*, 2 vols. (Cambridge, 1986) lists four Tudor copies of Bede's *Ecclesiastical History*.

[116] The *Rerum Anglicarum Scriptores post Bedam*, ed. H. Savile (Frankfurt, 1601), included, in addition to Malmesbury and Hoveden, the *Chronicon Ethelwerdi*, a few other late Saxon/early Norman historical works, and the pseudo-Ingulf of Croyland, which was actually written in the fifteenth century.

[117] It was printed in a mutilated form in John Capgrave's *Nova legenda Angliae* (1516), and in a publication by Surius at Cologne in the late sixteenth century. Blundell must have used the Capgrave volume, since the full text was first accurately printed by Roger Twysden in *Historiae anglicanae scriptores X* (1652).

[118] Robert Powell, *The Life of Alfred* (1634); Ælfric of Eynsham's writings, published by Archbishop Parker's circle of Anglo-Saxon scholars as *A Testimonie of Antiquitie* (1566), is another example of the Protestant attempt to find ancient roots for the reformed Church in the Anglo-Saxon era. Asser was also published in Camden's edition of chronicles, *Anglia, Normannica ... a veteribus scripta* (Frankfurt, 1603).

Monuments of all places!) 'tooke his crowne and unction of the pope'.[119] The reference to 'Florent. Westmon.' is in itself of interest. There is no chronicler called 'Florence of Westminster'; Blundell probably meant to write 'Florent. Wigorn.', in reference to the twelfth-century Worcester chronicle which was then (and until recent times) ascribed to one Florence, a monk of Worcester. Alternatively, he may have intended the *Flores Historiarum*, a work now attributed to Matthew Paris (continuing Roger of Wendover) but then thought to be by the non-existent 'Matthew of Westminster'. Both works begin with Creation and include the reign of Alfred, and both were in print by the end of the sixteenth century.[120] But Blundell's confused reference suggests that he had conflated the two books, and thereby helps to identify the *precise* edition he used: not the first, 1592 edition of Florence which was edited by the northern Catholic antiquary Lord William Howard of Naworth, but rather the version of this appended to an edition of the *Flores Historiarum* published at Frankfurt in 1601.[121]

Higden's *Polychronicon* and Polydore Vergil are other obvious sources—Blundell was looking up 'authorities', not doing 'research' in the modern sense, and so did not discriminate among his books as to 'primary' and 'secondary'. The *Polychronicon*, in the late fourteenth-century English of Trevisa, was one of the best known potboilers of the later Middle Ages, printed by Caxton in 1482 and republished several times in the early Tudor decades. Vergil's *Anglica Historia*, though notoriously unpopular among its English critics for its doubt of Arthurian and other British myths (and its author's initial papal employment), would no doubt appeal to a stubborn Catholic.

Blundell resorted to books even more recent than Vergil's as well, since they could provide a guide to the contents of the older, less easily consulted medieval histories. It comes as no surprise to find John Stow among the authors consulted. By 1611, just four years before the second-last edition of Stow's *Annales* was to appear, his series of chronicles had become for most Englishmen the easiest point of access to their own history. More up-to-date than the earlier chronicles of Thomas Lanquet, Edward Hall, and Richard Grafton, and less bulky than the enormous and expensive Holinshed, Stow's *Summaries*, *Chronicles*, and *Annales* are frequently to be found in early seventeenth-century book lists.[122] Francis Godwin's book of bishops is a somewhat more peculiar choice, given that its account (which earned the author his own episcopal see) demonstrates the succession of archbishops and bishops free of papal suzerainty and under royal authority. But it,

---

[119] Lancs RO DDBl Acc. 6121; *Crosby Records*, 52. Blundell also relies here on Richard Verstegan's *Restitution of Decayed Intelligence* (1605).

[120] Gransden, *Historical Writing in England*, i. 143–4; R. Vaughan, *Matthew Paris* (Cambridge, 1958), 94.

[121] Florence of Worcester, *Chronicon ex chronicis, ab initio mundi usque ad annum MCXVII*, ed. William Howard of Naworth (1592); *Flores historiarum per Matthaeum Westmonasteriensem collecti . . . Et Chronicon ex chronicis, ab initio mundi usque ad annum Domini MCXVIII, deductum auctore Florentio Wigorniensi* (Frankfurt, 1601), 459–696.

[122] For the popularity of particular historical works, see my earlier book, *Reading History in Early Modern England* (Cambridge, 2000).

too, was often to be found in Stuart libraries, and its pre-Tudor emphasis lent it special relevance to Blundell's fixation on the Middle Ages. His grandson William the younger (1620–98) would make use of the same work in his own notes on bishoprics a few decades later.[123] But the most important book here, medieval or modern, is Camden's, for its examples and discussions of ancient and medieval coinage. Blundell himself was obviously able to read Latin, since he refers specifically to pages in the 1594 edition of *Britannia* (Philemon Holland's 1610 English translation having apparently not yet found its way to Little Crosby).[124]

Blundell's own synthesis of his reading from Camden with his own and his neighbours' knowledge, is evident from his treatment of the Northumbrian king, St Oswald, martyred at the hands of Penda, king of Mercia, in 642 (and more often associated with Whitchurch in Shropshire, near the site of his death). Blundell transcribed from Camden some verses inscribed on the porch of Winwick church, about thirty miles from Little Crosby:

> Hic locus, Oswalde, quondam placuit tibi valde
> Northanhumbrorum fueras Rex, nuncque Polorum
> Regna tenes, loco passus Marcelde vocato.[125]

Rather than rest here, Blundell—who unlike Camden was eager to believe stories of Oswald's miraculous deeds—embellished his account with reference to oral tradition.

See Cambden, pag. 981, in ye impression at London of ye yeare 1594. Moreo[ver], a Catholique gentleman and frend of myne whoe had dwelte heretofore nere to the saide place, beinge moved by my letter to certifie me what hee knewe thereof, writethe that the people thereaboute have yet in there mouthes (it may be by tradition) yt K. Oswalde being greevouslie wounded in a battell not farre from yt place, vowed yt if hee might wendequicke (or whicke according to there speache) hee wolde there builde a Churche, wherupon (as they saye) it was then called Wendwhicke, now Winwicke.

Moreover on yt syde of Newton parke wch is towards Winwick not eight roods (as I rem[em]ber saith this gentleman) from the pale, there is a little well walled with stone within, which ye people call St. Oswald's well, and neare therunto there was an olde tree standinge in my tyme which had (as the people say) a picture standinge in it, the place shewinge when I lived there yt it might fitlie be used for such a purpose, and further (as I remember saithe hee) I have hearde it there reported that there had bine a great pilgremage to yt place. And thus I have thought good to take or rather seeke occasion here to write of ye place of this blessed K. and martir his death, because ye same is by wronge information saide in a late pious booke to have bine at Osestree.[126]

---

[123] Lancs RO DDBl Acc. 6121 'Great Hodge Podge', fo. 93ʳ.   [124] *Crosby Records*, 55.

[125] 'This happy place did holy Oswald love | Who once Northumbria rul'd, now reigns above, | And from Marcelde did to Heaven remove.' *Camden's Britannia* (1695), col. 790; *Britannia* [Latin version] (1607), 612.

[126] *Crosby Records*, 56 and note. There is more on Oswald's miracles (which Camden regards as 'ridiculous' invention of medieval historians), and on his death see *Britannia* (1607), 452, and *Camden's Britannia* (1695), col. 854.

Blundell's antiquarian exercise was not the end of the matter; the information about the coins had one more, important, journey to take. Eight decades later, near the end of his own life, Blundell's grandson and namesake would send information about the coins, and a copy of the engraving, to Edmund Gibson, editor of the revised *Britannia* of 1695, thereby putting back into the changing text of that book something comparable to that which his grandfather had taken out.[127] The recurring interest in Blundell's coins over the course of the seventeenth century illustrates precisely how casual discoveries such as this were interpreted by those with the intellectual tools to make sense of them. It thus neatly encapsulates the circulatory nature of historical knowledge, and some of the social, religious, and geographic factors that imposed limits on scholarly enquiry. It also, incidentally, signals again the problem of the relationship between written authority and oral tradition to be raised at greater length in Chapter 10.

CONCLUSION

In bestowing praise on the great scholars of the Augustan age it is easy to overlook the fact that their achievements, and those of their Tudor and early Stuart predecessors, would not have been possible had interest in the more portable remains of the past not been both widespread and steady, and had the antiquity not come to be both socially and economically a circulated commodity. Without these early modern antiquarian transactions, there could have been no nineteenth- and twentieth-century volumes of *Antiquarian Transactions*.

The medievalist Patrick J. Geary has pointed out that 'The right to speak the past also implied control over that which gave access to the past—the "relics" by which the past continued to live into the present. How these tangible or written relics of the past were preserved, who preserved them, and who could therefore make them to disappear were thus fundamental aspects of power and authority.'[128] This chapter has demonstrated a similar process of appropriation at work in the physical past. The objects that survive in today's museums, whether urns, or axes, fossils or coins, got there because someone over the past four centuries found them, someone else bought them, and others still studied and collected them. The process of selection that has filtered out the interesting from the ordinary, the genuine from the fake, was a scholarly process, practised by gentlemen. It would be going much too far to say that antiquarianism practised a kind of enclosure movement on the physical past, stealing antiquities from helpless poor folk in order to decorate their closets and gardens. We have seen that most of

---

[127] In the 1695 edition of *Camden's Britannia*, ed. Gibson, col. 801, an addition by Gibson refers to the coins as having been found on 8 Apr. 1611 by Blundell 'in a place call'd Harkirke', and mentions their having been printed in a 'copper-plate'; it then goes on to acknowledge the assistance of the younger William Blundell, 'to whom we are indebted for some particulars belonging to those parts'.

[128] P. J. Geary, *Phantoms of Remembrance: Memory and Oblivion at the end of the First Millennium* (Princeton, 1994), 7.

the common discoverers of antiquities were happy enough to make the coin or urn an item of exchange, and it is one that can hardly have weighed heavily on people faced with genuine economic problems—among them *real* enclosures. There has not been a flood of requests for the return of British antiquities now housed in the cavern on Great Russell Street to their local environments, in sharp contrast to the heatedly contested rights to artefacts once removed from foreign countries such as the Elgin marbles, or to more recent litigation to restore lost works of art to Holocaust survivors and their descendants.

Nevertheless, though it has the appearance of symbiosis, the archaeological economy was not a system of equal trading partners. The acquisitors had wealth and rank on their side, and they also had the fount of learning (however superficial in some cases) that added value to inert objects, making bits of stone and metal into trophies. They also, increasingly as the seventeenth century wore on, saw themselves as the custodians and speakers of scholarly truth, and many drew disparaging contrasts between themselves and the suppliers of their treasures. The literary embodiment of this can be found a century later still in Sir Walter Scott's *The Antiquary*, whose central figure, Jonathan Oldbuck, happily sends off interesting stones, unearthed by his gardener, to friends and to 'various antiquarian societies', while in the next breath declaiming against 'fools, boors, and idiots [who] have ploughed up the land, and, like beasts and ignorant savages' injured an ancient ditch; he is much happier when his suppliers are of similar social station, eagerly accepting from his nephew an ancient urn.[129] Oldbuck's snobbery towards his tenants and servants as finders of antiquities manifests itself in another way, too, as a rejection of the spoken past that they have committed to memory, of the tales with which they regale him, though his scepticism is inconsistent. This estrangement of elite from popular beliefs, of the written and printed from the remembered and spoken (from the sort of local knowledge that told William Blundell of a long-vanished Saxon church) offers another example of historical culture responding to a widening social and economic gap, this time in the context not of tangible objects but of memories, popular beliefs, and oral traditions.

[129] Walter Scott, *The Antiquary* (Edinburgh, 1886), 37, 284.

Part IV

THE PAST REMEMBERED

CHAPTER EIGHT

Ways of Remembering

MUCH HAS BEEN written about the classical and Renaissance 'arts of memory', those systems inherited from ancient writings such as the pseudo-Christian *Rhetorica ad Herennium* and revived in the later Middle Ages by sages such as Ramon Lull, whence they later figured prominently in the work of English magi such as John Dee and Robert Fludd.[1] Studies by Paolo Rossi and the late Frances Yates demonstrated some interesting implications of the artificial memory of the Renaissance for the development of later philosophical and scientific interests. Jonathan D. Spence has shown how 'place memory' could be put to practical pedagogical use in his study of the Jesuit Matteo Ricci's mission to China. Most recently, William E. Engel has provided a richly suggestive connection between the mnemonic processes at work in literary and iconographic representation and the seventeenth century's melancholic preoccupation with death and wider questions of temporality.[2] For the long centuries leading up to the Renaissance, Mary Carruthers has offered the most thorough analysis of the roles of memory in elite culture.[3] Yet as Carruthers herself points out, there is a danger that in dwelling on the more exotic aspects of memory—imaginary theatres, artificial methods, and Lullist schemes—we may turn the whole subject into something unnecessarily complex and esoteric. For every historical instance of occult or artificial memory it is possible to find dozens of examples of and statements concerning its practical, everyday use.[4]

[1] Aristotle, *De Memoria et Reminiscentia*, in Richard Sorabji, *Aristotle on Memory* (1972), 47–62; Quintilian, *Institutio Oratoria*, XI, ii. 1–51, trans. H. E. Butler, 4 vols. (London and New York, 1922), iv. 211; Cicero, *De Oratore*, I. iv. 16, II. lxxxvi. 351–5 (for the story of Simonides and the invention of artificial memory), trans. E. W. Sutton and H. Rackham, 2 vols. (London and Cambridge, Mass., 1942), i. 13, 465; Augustine, *Confessions*, trans. W. Watts (1631), 2 vols. (London and Cambridge, Mass., 1972; repr. 1960–1), X. viii. 12–X. xxi. 30; H. Blum, *Die antike Mnemotechnik* (Hildesheim and New York, 1969), 70–9; H. Caplan, *Of Eloquence: Studies in Ancient and Mediaeval Rhetoric*, ed. A. King and H. North (Ithaca and London, 1970), 196–246.

[2] P. Rossi, *Clavis universalis: Arti mnemoniche e logica combinatoria de Lullo a Leibniz* (Milan, 1960); F. A. Yates, *The Art of Memory* (1966), 320–89; J. D. Spence, *The Memory Palace of Matteo Ricci* (New York, 1984); W. E. Engel, *Mapping Mortality: The Persistence of Memory and Melancholy in Early Modern England* (Amherst, Mass., 1995). The psychological aspects of mnemonic devices are reviewed in F. S. Bellezza, 'Mnemonic Devices and Memory Schemas', in M. A. McDaniel and M. Pressley (eds.), *Imagery and Related Mnemonic Processes* (New York, Berlin, and Heidelberg, 1987), 34–55.

[3] M. J. Carruthers, *The Book of Memory: A Study of Memory in Medieval Culture* (Cambridge, 1990).

[4] Carruthers's book itself remains confined to educated uses of memory, though ranging far beyond Yatesian *artes mnemonicae*; compare P. J. Geary, *Phantoms of Remembrance: Memory and Oblivion at the end of the First Millennium* (Princeton, 1994), 9. The everyday uses of memory during the period are explored at greater length in my article, 'Memory and Historical Culture in Early Modern England', *Journal of the Canadian Historical Association*, NS 2 (1991), 283–308, though I would now wish to modify the conclusions of that essay.

Because memory was so important to social and religious life, and because the artificial means of replicating it were as yet confined to a small segment of society, it was given much more attention in schooling than has been true in more recent times. Much of the curriculum offered by tutors and grammar schools concentrated on matter to be learned by rote, or by practice, so that pupils could get their subjects 'without book'. Humanist educators such as Vives stressed the improvement of mnemonic abilities through exercise. One could not always read or write, but one could always remember:

> How shal the Marchant safely kepe
> his recknings from decay
> If his remembrance shuld him fayle,
> though writing beare great sway.[5]

The institutional expression of this emphasis on the need to memorize can be found in educational manuals, in tracts offering techniques for improving the memory, and in the work of tutors whose tasks included nurturing their pupils' mnemonic capacity.[6] Henry King believed that such instruction was necessary because of the failings of the untaught memory, and early seventeenth-century London even had schools for the improvement of the 'arts memorative'.[7] A century later, Augustan law students such as Dudley Ryder continued to use artificial mnemonic systems to enhance their retention of their rising mountains of statutes and reports.[8]

Memory enabled man to fulfil his duties by providing his powers of judgement with the relevant information; it stored examples and patterns from the past so that the mind could reflect and make appropriate judgements in the present. George Puttenham thought memories 'serve as a glasse to looke upon and behold the events of time, and more exactly to skan the trueth of every case that shall happen in the affaires of man'. The Jacobean political theorist Edward Forset, who was much given to extended analogies between the human body and the common weal, made memory into the archivist for its sovereign, reason:

The soveraigne is well stored with remembrancers, nothing passeth from him, or setleth in him but by record; All his seates of judgement entereth and preserveth the proceedings in causes; and to forge, corrupt, or embezill the Recordes (whereof any good government

---

[5] *Vives' Introduction to Wisdom*, ed. M. L. Tobriner (New York, 1968), 103; Gulielmus Gratalorus, *The castel of memorie*, trans. William Fulwod (1562), translator's epistle dedicatory (hereafter cited as Fulwod, *Castel of memorie*). Fulwod echoes Plato's fears that writing would erode memory in his warning to 'Take heede lesse the writinge of thinges doe not hurte your memorye': ibid., sig. G^v. The expression 'without book' was sufficiently common by 1600 as to be proverbial: M. P. Tilley, *Dictionary of the Proverbs in England* (Ann Arbor, 1950), p. 59, no. B532.

[6] W. J. Ong, SJ, *Rhetoric, Romance and Technology: Studies in the Interaction of Expression and Culture* (Ithaca, NY, and London, 1971), ch. 6.

[7] Henry King, *Two sermons preached at Whitehall* (1627), no. 1, pp. 5–6; George Buck, *The third universitie of England*, in John Stow, *Annales*, ed. Edmund Howes (1631), facing pp. 1063, 1087.

[8] An 'artificial memory system', of which we have no details, allowed Ryder, who regularly complains in his diary of a bad memory, to repeat cases studied as he walked through the streets. *The Diary of Dudley Ryder 1715–1716*, ed. W. Matthews (1939), 93, 115.

hath a tender and strict regard) what is it else, than as if the memorie should be cleane taken from the mind, to the which it is unseperable.

Continuing the metaphor, John Fletcher deemed memory the 'store-house of the minde', a register for the recording of 'Mens Glories, or their Crimes'.[9] The Jacobean author of a manual on memory adopted Forset's image of the archive but, perhaps cognizant of the growing importance of local and family records, he refers to a multiplicity of such repositories rather than one, pluralizing the analogy to include many towers rather than the Tower in which the official records of king and parliament were held, 'So usefull so delightfull, that to it we walke as to some castle or tower of antiquity to view the records and registers of forepassed ages and accidents there hung up as monuments to our view.' Memory was the 'great *Custus Recordorum*, whereof every man is a keeper', the mental equivalent of a local *custos rotulorum* or urban recorder.[10]

WRITING AND MEMORY

Humans function because they have the capacity to recall facts and repeat actions that they have learned at various stages in their lives. Even the electronic revolution has been unable to remove the need for humans to remember.[11] It has, however, greatly reduced the range of things they *must* remember by providing artificial means for recording and retrieving huge quantities of data. In this capacity, the computer has merely extended the effects of literacy, for one of the prime functions of writing is to fix the past, to objectify it independent of the powers of human memory. As Mary, Countess Cowper would write in 1715, her own recording of events on a monthly basis, complete with missing dates of events

[9] George Puttenham, *The Arte of English Poesie*, ed. G. D. Willcock and A. Walker (Cambridge, 1936), III. xxiii (p. 264); Edward Forset, *A comparative discourse of the bodies natural and politique* (1606), 20; John Fletcher, *The historie of the perfect-cursed-blessed man* (1628), 13.

[10] Anon., *A helpe to memorie and discourse* (1621), 4.

[11] Writings on memory by psychologists, psychoanalysts, and philosophers have become, like the literature on time, enormous in quantity, particularly since the advent of the modern study of memory beginning with Hermann Ebbinghaus in the 1880s: H. Ebbinghaus, *Memory: A Contribution to Experimental Psychology*, trans. H. A. Ruger and C. E. Bussenius (New York, 1964). A useful selection of pre-Ebbinghaus discussions may be found in D. J. Herrmann and R. Chaffin (eds.), *Memory in Historical Perspective* (New York and Berlin, 1988). In formulating the argument for this chapter I have found the following especially helpful: A. D. Baddeley, *The Psychology of Memory* (New York, 1976), chs. 1, 9, 10; I. M. L. Hunter, *Memory* (1957); P. Brockelman, 'Of Memory and Things Past', *International Philosophical Quarterly*, 15 (1975), 309–25; D. A. Norman, *Learning and Memory* (San Francisco, 1982); D. Bartram and P. Smith, 'Everyday Memory for Everyday Places', in J. E. Harris and P. E. Morris (eds.), *Everyday Memory, Actions and Absent-Mindedness* (1984), 35–52; V. H. Gregg, *Introduction to Human Memory* (1986), esp. chs. 1 and 2, on auditory and visual memory respectively. F. C. Bartlett's classic text *Remembering: A Study in Experimental and Social Psychology*, 2nd edn. (Cambridge, 1967), is still of use, while helpful comments on forgetting are to be found in Freud's *The Psychopathology of Everyday Life*, trans. A. A. Brill (New York, 1914), *passim*. A useful recent guide to the neurobiology of memory is contained in M. S. Gazzaniga, *The Mind's Past* (Berkeley and Los Angeles, 1998), 123–48.

taken 'out of my head' was intended principally as 'a help to my own memory hereafter', that is, as a fallback against further forgetting.[12] Plato's ancient fears about the advent of writing and its impact on memory, expressed in his *Phaedrus*, were realized in such practices, as Erasmus anticipated they might be at the beginning of the sixteenth century:

I have never approved of youths writing down every word they hear, for this practice leads them to neglect the cultivation of memory, allowing for the fact that some may want to make a few brief notes of certain things, but that only until such a time as the memory has been strengthened and they no longer desire the prop of the written word.[13]

By 1500, however, it had already been long accepted that writing, despite its relative social rarity, was an acceptable, even a desirable, substitute for sheer reliance on memory, and that it marked an improvement over earlier methods of record-keeping. Contemporaries even had access to a medieval myth which explained the development of writing as one of the benefits of the Norman Conquest: Richard Fitz Neal's twelfth-century *Dialogue of the Exchequer* (misattributed in the sixteenth century to Gervase of Tilbury) presented Tudor and Stuart readers with the legend that William the Conqueror had brought the English from the uncertainty of reliance on memory to the use of written law.[14]

Throughout the sixteenth and into the seventeenth century the argument was frequently put that writing had, if not superseded, at least improved and extended the limits of memory. 'Every writing is said to be a faithfull keeper of the remembrance of things that are committed unto it', wrote Samuel Bird, the lecturer of Ipswich. One could turn to things written down after many years and find them as they had been written, 'where as, if we trusted our memories with them, we should not finde the like fidelity in them'.[15] Edmund Plowden, whose study of the law began at the age of 20 in 1539, resolved early on to commit to writing anything important which he heard at the courts or in moots, 'not trusting slypper memorye, which often deceiveth his master'. His younger contemporary and admirer, Sir Edward Coke, pointed out that nothing was ever very secure in the memory: 'It is therefore necessarie that memorable things should be committed to writing (the witnesse of times, the light and the life of truth) and not wholy betaken to slipperie memorie, which seldome yeeldeth a certaine reckoning.' In repeating this well-known Ciceronian definition of history but equating it with writing in general, Coke also admitted a distrust of the unaided

---

[12] *Diary of Mary, Countess Cowper*, ed. S. Cowper (London, 1864), 49.

[13] Erasmus, *De ratione studii*, in *Collected Works*, vols. xxiii and xxiv: *Literary and Educational Writings*, ed. C. R. Thompson (Toronto, 1978), ii. 691; Plato, *Phaedrus*, 275a; J. Goody and I. Watt, 'The Consequences of Literacy', *Comparative Studies in Society and History*, 5 (1963), 304–45, repr. in J. Goody (ed.), *Literacy in Traditional Societies* (Cambridge, 1968), 27–68. The topos of writing's corrosion of memory was extended in the seventeenth and eighteenth centuries to its ill effects on the powers of eloquent speech: N. Hudson, *Writing and European Thought, 1600–1830* (Cambridge, 1994), 108–10.

[14] M. T. Clanchy, *From Memory to Written Record: England 1066–1307* (Cambridge, Mass., 1979), 12–13, makes the point that literacy predated the Conquest, a fact which would not have been lost on sixteenth-century Saxonists such as William Lambarde.

[15] *The Lectures of Samuel Bird of Ipswich* (Cambridge, 1598), 125.

memory. 'I like not of those that make memory their storehouse'.[16] Thomas Gataker saw memory and writing as comparable, but he too stopped short of conceiving of memory as simply a mental 'table booke to register acts passed'. Unlike a real book it was 'not able to comprehend all that is to be recorded therein; when new things of note come to be imprinted in it, the old are wip't out'.[17] Thomas Fuller urged readers to divide their learning 'betwixt thy memory and thy note-books', commonplace books in particular being superior containers from which matter could be memorized more easily and pressed into service as needed.[18]

The relationship between memory and writing was fluid and dynamic. Most commentators perceived writing and memory as ranked extensions of each other —with writing very much the servant not the master—rather than as mutually exclusive or contradictory techniques of preserving knowledge. Coke's strong preference for writing over memory, uttered right at the beginning of the seventeenth century, is exceptional, and it came from a lawyer and future judge whose working life often turned on squaring documentary record with testimonial recollection. The practices of a Jacobean stenographer such as John Willis, who could maintain an interest both in the teaching of note-taking and in the promotion of memory-training, were probably more typical.[19] But Coke's distrust of unaided memory and his silent conflation of writing for history as the *lux veritatis* were harbingers of things to come. Within a century, the traditional master–servant relationship between memory and writing respectively would be modified significantly both by increased literacy and by the advancing ubiquity of the printed word.

MNEMONIC SCHEMES

It is difficult for us in the modern industrialized West, accustomed to near-universal literacy achieved at an early age, to get inside the minds of people for whom reading, and still more writing, were signs of social privilege. We have

---

[16] 'The prologe of the auctor', in Edmund Plowden, *Les comentaries, ou les reportes de Edmund Plowden un apprentice de le comen ley* (1571), n.p.; Coke, *Les reports de Edward Coke* (1600), 'The preface to the reader', no sig. For the place of memory in English legal culture see R. J. Ross, 'The Memorial Culture of Early Modern English Lawyers: Memory as Keyword, Shelter, and Identity, 1560–1640', *Yale Journal of Law and the Humanities*, 10 (1998), 220–326.

[17] Thomas Gataker, *An anniversarie memoriall of Englands delivery from the Spanish invasion* (1626), preface. Gataker's statement suggests that contemporaries acknowledged the existence of what modern psychologists call the 'recency effect', whereby, as Fulwod put it, 'new or wonderfull things' impress themselves on the memory at the expense of those already stored.

[18] Thomas Fuller, *The Holy State and the Profane State*, cited in P. Beal, 'Notions in Garrison: The Seventeenth-Century Commonplace Book', in W. Speed Hill (ed.), *New Ways of Looking at Old Texts* (Binghamton, NY, 1993), 131–47, at p. 131.

[19] John Willis, *Mnemonica, sive reminiscendi ars . . . in tres libros digesta* (1618); a revised translation of the third book was published in 1621 as *The art of memory, so far forth as it dependeth upon places and idea's*, but Willis remains known principally for works on stenography, including his popular handbook *The art of stenographie, teaching by plaine and certaine rules, the way of compendious writing*, at least twelve editions of which appeared before 1640. For a later tract along similar lines, see Henry Herdman, *Ars mnemonica. The art of memory made plaine* (1651).

many more facts and details to recall than did they, but we also have far more sophisticated aids to help us recall them, and do not have to encumber our memories.[20] A sixteenth-century person of any level of education was obliged to depend on memory for a far greater proportion of his personal knowledge, because it could not, as the current expression goes, always be found 'at his fingertips'. For the poorer sort of tradesman who might well be illiterate and innumerate, memory—his own and that of witnesses—was often the sole record of financial transactions.[21] The early eighteenth-century law student Dudley Ryder was impressed by the great retention of his cousin's tenant, an 'honest, cheerful man . . . of very good sense and sagacity' who, though illiterate, could keep account of his getting and spending by memory alone.[22] Memory similarly allowed easier recall of literary texts even for those who could read them directly. John Foxe gives us one example of an illiterate of prodigious memory, in the Wiltshire farmer John Maundrell, who 'when he came into any companie that could read, his booke was alwaies readie, having a very good memory', and who could recite most places in the New Testament. John Manningham was impressed in 1603 when his 62-year-old cousin 'repeated *memoriter* almost the first booke of Virg[ils] Aeniads', a feat followed the next day by a rehearsal of most of the second book, '630 verses without missing one word'.[23] Abraham de la Pryme was equally taken with a half-hour sermon given completely from memory, though the minister in question made use of a book to record the names of those who felt themselves unworthy to take the sacrament, in order to recall them the following Sunday.[24]

Then as now, the easiest things to remember without recourse to writing were actions repeated on a regular basis, or those facts of which knowledge was required daily. Even here, a record of some sort was often helpful: Gervase Markham had both the literate and illiterate female in mind when he suggested that the housewife should simultaneously remember and record 'either by score or writing' the number of strikes of hemp and flax she has broken in a single day.[25] Remembering other things, particularly details of history—the past as experienced by other

[20]   We continue, however, to associate historical events metonymically with particular places or characteristics. 'Canossa' instantly sums up to any historian the humiliation of the emperor before Pope Gregory VII. Those born before 1958 will 'remember' the assassination of John F. Kennedy even if they were nowhere near Dallas in November 1963, because the event and its aftermath have been reduced to a series of metonymical code-phrases ('lone gunman', 'Dealy Plaza', 'grassy knoll', 'Texas Book Depository', and even the name of the city itself). In such ways, our private memories intermesh with and interpret the 'objective' history that we read.

[21]   C. Muldrew, *The Economy of Obligation: The Culture of Credit and Social Relations in Early Modern England* (New York, 1998), 62–5.

[22]   *Diary of Dudley Ryder*, 165–6.

[23]   John Foxe, *Acts and Monuments* (1610 edn.), p. 1719; *Diary of John Manningham*, ed. R. P. Sorlien (Hanover, NH, 1976), 202.

[24]   *The Diary of Abraham de la Pryme, the Yorkshire Antiquary*, ed. C. Jackson, Surtees Soc., 54 (1870), 17.

[25]   Gervase Markham, *The English Housewife*, ed. M. Best (Toronto, 1986), p. 158; this reference illustrates that a basic numeracy involving marks rather than numbers could exist without literacy; for another example see Muldrew, *Economy of Obligation*, 63. On numeracy itself see K. Thomas, 'Numeracy in Early Modern England', *TRHS*, 5th ser., 37 (1987), 103–32.

people than oneself—is always more difficult. Still, various strategies could be used to reduce a variety of information to memory, including the use of images and emblems.[26] One method was to convert scriptural text into metre, which is why many ancient and medieval writings, especially narratives, were composed in verse rather than prose. Versification of the Bible was a common practice in schools,[27] since Scripture was the text most in need of memorization; an Elizabethan case in the Court of Requests involved two men in a wager over their 'remembrance' of how the Psalms began.[28] Published aids to scriptural recollection such as John Lloyd's *A Good Help to Weak Memories* (1671) turned the Bible's historical books into distychs combined with a verse chronology.[29] Versification was also used for the memorization of profane knowledge. Thomas Tusser ensured that the reader, or hearer, of his *Five Hundred Points of Good Husbandry* would be able to recall them by presenting them in the form of doggerel, while Richard Verstegan thought that many early English legal documents were written in metre 'belyke to bee kept the better in memorie'.[30]

'Homonymy', the deliberate linking of homonyms in the reader's mind (a sort of constructive punning) was a widespread technique inherited from medieval grammarians and given new life by such Renaissance educators as Guarino da Verona.[31] Later, during the Reformation, theologians and polemicists such as the martyrologist John Foxe continued to present controversial issues in what one author has called 'a quotation-reply manner that resembles debate according to commonplace'. The student would thereby be armed with an easily memorized *copia* (abundance) of phrases, examples, and arguments with which he could engage in oral or written controversy.[32] Another strategy employed by writers anxious

---

[26] Engel, *Mapping Mortality*, 54–5.

[27] The Henrician scholar John Shepery (*c*.1509–42) drew up a mnemonic verse summary of the New Testament, which would be published in 1586 by Laurence Humphrey in his *Summa et synopsis Novi Testamenti* (Oxford, 1586); Roger Ascham noted the importance of the typical school exercise of versifying the Bible for memorization in a letter to George Day, bishop of Chichester: J. Binns, *Intellectual Culture in Elizabethan and Jacobean England: The Latin Writings of the Age* (Leeds, 1990), 13, 83.

[28] PRO REQ2/106.58 (28 Jan. 1595/6, Pilkington v. Hansland). The issue was cleared up by reference to the Bible, but the defendant refused to pay the wager, occasioning the suit.

[29] John Lloyd, *A Good Help to Weak Memories: or, the Contents of Every Chapter in the Bible in Alphabetical Dysticks* (1671).

[30] Thomas Tusser, *Five hundred points of good husbandry*, ed. G. Grigson (Oxford, 1984); Richard Verstegan, *A restitution of decayed intelligence* (London and Antwerp, 1605), 146. Fulwod, *The castel of memorie*, sig. Fviii^v, also recommends the use of verse.

[31] A. Grafton and L. Jardine, *From Humanism to the Humanities* (Cambridge, Mass., 1986), 12; eid., ' "Studied for Action": How Gabriel Harvey Read his Livy', *Past and Present*, 129 (1990), 30–78.

[32] J. G. Rechtien, 'John Foxe's Comprehensive Collection of Commonplaces: A Renaissance Memory System for Students and Theologians', *Sixteenth-Century Journal*, 9 (1978), 83–9. On the importance of perceptual 'grids' or schemata see Bartlett, *Remembering*, 301; Hunter, *Memory*, 143 ff. As Bartlett has pointed out, the oral discourse of a pre-literate or semi-literate society is most likely to be heavily weighted towards the memories of the collective community than of the individual. Students of epic poetry and the mnemonic techniques used by bards in ancient Greece and in some pre-literate societies of today have come to similar conclusions in explaining the extraordinary mnemonic capacities through the repetition of formulae. A. B. Lord, *The Singer of Tales* (Cambridge, Mass., 1960); E. Havelock, *Preface to Plato* (Oxford, 1963); J. Goody and I. Watt, 'The Consequences of Literacy', *Comparative Studies in Society and History*, 5 (1963), 304–45, repr. in J. Goody (ed.), *Literacy*

to have their texts committed to memory was to group memorable things into subsets or categories, associated with numbers. Thus Tudor history and literature had its Seven Ages of Man, Four Empires, Nine Worthies of the World, Seven Champions of Christendom, Seven Wise Masters of Rome, and so on. The advent of printing merely added to the ways in which such mental categories circulated, rather than removing their necessity, at least in the short term.[33] With little more prescience than any tradesman selling the public on his new mouse-trap, William Caxton correctly predicted that printing would render much memorization unnecessary. He nevertheless listed the Nine Worthies (sub-grouped into three pagans, three Jews, and three Christians), starting with Hector of Troy, 'of whome thystorye is comen bothe in balade and in prose' at the start of his edition of the tale of King Arthur.[34]

Clusterings of individual names or related facts around a number, though often deriving from tradition and from the long-standing belief in the significance of numerical relationships, seem sometimes to have been designed for no other purpose than to aid their memorization; consequently, they tended to proliferate as writers added new mnemonics to old. The Caroline miscellanist Donald Lupton listed, in addition to the more well-known numerical associations, several others, such as 'the eight times that Rome hath beene taken' and 'the twelve peeres of France'. Lupton's same-named predecessor, Thomas Lupton, first published his own immensely popular book of *A Thousand Notable Things* in 1579. Reprinted fourteen times by 1700, this was doubtless so successful because of its author's willingness to reduce all knowledge to some form of enumerated sub-group. It had several imitators, such as Walter Owsold's *The varietie of memorable and worthy matters* (1605), which listed sixteen numerical categories: four parts of the world, four monarchies, six ages, seven wonders, seven wise men of Greece, ten sibyls, twelve Apostles, ten persecutions, eight times Rome was taken, seven electors of Germany, three crowns of the emperor, twelve peers and eight *parlements* of France, seven Saxon kingdoms, five orders of chivalry, and thirteen Swiss cantons.[35]

<hr/>

in *Traditional Societies* (Cambridge, 1968), 27–68; R. Scholes and R. Kellogg, *The Nature of Narrative* (New York, 1966), 28 and, more recently, M. McKeon, *The Origins of the English Novel 1600–1740* (Baltimore, 1987), 33–45; M. E. Hobart and Z. S. Schiffman, *Information Ages: Literacy, Numeracy, and the Computer Revolution* (Baltimore, 1998).

[33] Numerical groupings survive today, of course—for instance, the 'top twenty' of a record list, or the 'one hundred recipes for rhubarb'. But they are now much less often used for mnemonic purposes.

[34] *The Prologues and Epilogues of William Caxton*, ed. W. J. B. Crotch, EETS os 176 (1928), 92–5. The Nine Worthies were Hector, Alexander, Julius Caesar, Joshua, David, Judas Maccabeus, Arthur, Charlemagne, and Godfrey of Boulogne. They appear in visual form in pageants such as that which took place at Chester on 1 August 1620: *REED: Chester*, ed. L. M. Clopper (Toronto, 1979), 339, in which case they were accompanied by nine corresponding female Worthies. The fundamental paradigm for such groupings was the biblical mnemonic which drew a correspondence between the twelve tribes of Israel and the twelve Apostles.

[35] Donald Lupton, *Emblemes of rarities* (1636), 373; Thomas Lupton, *A thousand notable things* (1579, *et seq.*); Walter Owsold, *The varietie of memorable and worthy matters* (1605). That such numerical associations were quite commonplace is suggested by the frequency with which they occur in casual comments: Gabriel Harvey, for example, lists Ramus, Melanchthon, Sebastian Fox-Morcillo, and Cornelius Valerius of Louvain together as 'fower wurthi men of famus memori': *Letter-book of Gabriel*

Many early modern readers followed the example of such works in their own private jottings and notes. In the unpublished chronology and world description which he drew up, apparently for his own use, in 1644, George Turner appended a list of 'other remembrances' which included the dates of great events in London, and memorable facts about the Roman emperors, such as Marcus Aurelius, 'the first emp[eror] that used the diadem and costly aparell'.[36] In 1632 Hannibal Baskervile scrawled a list of 'famous soldiers' in his commonplace book, marking off those such as Gustavus Adolphus who had recently died.[37] During the 1660s one anonymous author penned a lengthy set of mnemonic verses in Latin and English, covering such subjects as the difference between allegorical and literal interpretations of the Bible, the main heads of the civil law, the names of the saints who had converted the various parts of Britain, and the names of the popes.[38] As a young man, the future historian and bishop White Kennett kept a notebook of witty sayings of famous people, headed 'Mem.' (Memoranda), and intended for repetition and reuse in either oral or written social intercourse.[39] As part of his project to reform education, John Locke recognized the crucial importance of the commonplace book as an organizer of knowledge and experience into mnemonically easy bites of information, once again fulfilling the Platonic prediction, as his commentator Jean Le Clerc remarked:

In all sorts of learning, and especially in the study of languages, the memory is the Treasury or Store-house . . . But lest the memory should be oppressed, or over-burthened by too many things, order and method are to be called to its assistance.[40]

Such mnemonic aids were not necessarily effective promoters of an 'accurate' historical consciousness, sensitive to change: precisely because they are designed for easy memorization, they 'flatten' time, making characters such as Alexander, Caesar, and Charlemagne rough contemporaries in a past that is timeless, dateless, and only vaguely distinguishable from the present. And their proliferation, paradoxically, may ultimately have led to a greater reliance upon written lists in order to preserve them, if the jottings in seventeenth-century commonplace books are any indication.

Harvey, ed. E. J. Long Scott, Camden Soc., NS 33 (1884), p. 10. Such simple systems remained popular in England long after the seventeenth century, and survive today in the oral culture of schoolchildren. The popular manual by Richard Grey, *Memoria Technica, or Method of Artificial Memory*, was first published in 1730 and reissued twenty-three times by the late nineteenth century.

[36] Bodl. MS Rawl. D. 203, fos. 156^r–158^v.

[37] Bodl. MS Rawl. D. 859, fo. 86^v. Such notes did not necessarily enhance accuracy; in Baskervile's case, he failed to mark Count Tilly as dead (though he had predeceased Gustavus) and noted Edward, Viscount Conway (who had died in 1631) as still being president of the privy council.

[38] Bodl. MS Rawl. D. 962 ('Mnemonica historica de moribus ecclesiasticae Romanae', and 'Versus mnemonici de historia ecclesiastica'), fos. 1–25^v, 46^r–57^r, 84^r.

[39] BL MS Lans. 937 (Kennett memoranda), fos. 60^r, 76^v.

[40] Bodl. MS Vet. A4, e. 895, Le Clerc's comment on Locke's *A New Method of Making Commonplace-books* (London, 1706) with additions by Le Clerc on the same subject; Beal, 'Notions in Garrison', 140–3; A. Moss, *Printed Commonplace-Books and the Structuring of Renaissance Thought* (Oxford, 1996), 278–80.

MEMORY AND HISTORY

The effect of reading and writing, magnified by print, was not to make memory superfluous, as Plato and Erasmus had feared, but to expand the possible series within which a datum could easily be situated. Important printed books such as the Geneva Bible of 1560, which imposed a numerical 'grid' on Scripture (the division into numbered chapters and verses) were, far from working against memory, designed in a manner which would aid in the recall of their contents, *ad res* if not *ad verbum*. The primarily metaphorical, analogical orientation of early Renaissance historical thought, in which exempla had meaning only in so far as they reflected on contemporary actions or mores, was the product of a cast of mind still driven primarily by the demands of the spoken word and by the ability of memory randomly to recombine these exempla into an ever-expanding number of contexts. Writing, especially as mass-disseminated through print, permitted the addition of different sorts of sequences of data about the past. The proliferation of charts denoting family history, such as genealogical trees, that show family relationships both across generations and within a generation, permitted a multi-dimensional representation of the past in a way that a memorized genealogy can achieve only with great difficulty.[41] The antiquarian chorographies, with their organization around geography as opposed to narrative, the lengthy prose romances of the late sixteenth and seventeenth centuries, and the narrative political history (that did not rely, unlike the chronicle that preceded it, on the metonymical index of the year) were all originated in the era of print culture and expanding literacy.[42]

We ought not to be surprised by the possibility that the shapes in which history came were determined in part by the expansion of mnemonic capacity enabled by reading, writing, and printing. Memory had long been explicitly linked to the writing and reproduction of the historical past. In his prologue to Ranulf Higden's *Polychronicon*, the first historical work to be printed in England, William Caxton explained the commemorative purpose of history as being analogous to the memory, and wisdom, of old men. It is a passage worth quoting at length, since it both neatly sums up one prominent late medieval line of thought about the purpose of history-reading and at the same time touches on history's merits as an extender of the memorable:

Therfore the counseylles of Auncyent and whyte heeryd men in whome olde age hath engendryd wysedom ben gretely preysed of yonger men. And yet hystoryes soo moche more excelle them. As the dyuturnyte or length of tyme includeth moo ensamples of thynges and laudable actes than thage of one man may suffyse to see.

---

[41] On the medieval use of grids and numerological mnemonics see Carruthers, *Book of Memory*, 80–1, 129–30, 144.

[42] The experience of England, which did not develop these genres until after the advent of print, is thus very different from that of Continental Europe and especially Italy, where, for instance, humanist historiography pre-dates print by several decades.

Historyes ought not only to be iuged moost proffytable to yonge men whiche by the lecture redyng [and] understandyng made them semblable [and] equal to men of greter age and to old men to whome longe lyf hath mynystred experymentes of dyverse thynges . . .

History, in Caxton's view, could excel human memory because it could reach back past the limits of living men's lives. Better still, it could sum up the memories of all ages, their *experientia*, and convey these in concise form to the young. Thus, says Caxton, history more than memory is 'a perpetuel conservatryce of thoos thynges that have be doone before this presente tyme', in addition to its role as a daily 'wytnesse' of present deeds great and wicked. So far, all this appears to mean is that history, like any form of writing, is preferable to the natural human memory as a recorder of past events. But Caxton went further, arguing for the *specific* superiority of history to *all* other forms of recalling the past, including monuments, statues, and other artefacts, on the grounds that only history can *use* time rather than be consumed by her. 'But the vertu of hystorye *dyffused* [and] *spredd* by the unyversal worlde hath tyme which consumeth all other thynges as conservatryce and kepar of her werke.'[43] Here, at the very dawn of the age of print in England, we have a clear statement of the proper place of history as the most trustworthy custodian of a culture's past. Without knowing it, Caxton had anticipated both the supremacy of written history in the hierarchy of modes of knowing the past, and the significance of the press, the mechanism by which history would over the ensuing three centuries 'spredd' itself like a blanket across the national sense of the past.

Right from the beginning of its career in England, therefore, history as a *printed* genre was conceived of as an artificial mnemonic, the *vita memoriae* of Cicero's formulation. Humanist authors from Erasmus to Bacon and beyond picked up on this theme. Brian Melbancke, virtually paraphrasing Caxton, urged youthful readers to 'turne over the volumes of auncient histories: for so you being yong without experience, your knowledge shall stretche further then your fathers remembraunce', while the continental pedagogue J. T. Freigius, whose *Historiae synopsis* was among those *artes historicae* read by early seventeenth-century scholars, defined history simply as *memoria rerum in hoc mundo gestarum*.[44] It is not necessary to add further examples of this familiar view. Yet we should avoid leaping to the assumption that the advent of print or the increasing availability of historical works in the later sixteenth century somehow eliminated the connection between the past and unaided memory. Because knowledge of the past

[43] William Caxton, prologue to Higden's *Polychronicon* (1482), *Prologues and Epilogues of William Caxton*, ed. Crotch, 64–6, my emphasis. Caxton's formulation of the relationship between memory and history is not remarkably different from that outlined by Pierre Nora, a leading modern student of collective memory in France. Nora argues that history is the problematic reconstruction of events or things which no longer exist; memory is 'a living tie to an eternal present'. P. Nora, in *Les Lieux de mémoire*, ed. P. Nora, 3 vols. (1984–92), vol. i, p. xix; idem, 'Between Memory and History: Les Lieux de Mémoire', *Representations*, 26 (1989), 7–25. For a different view, see E. Tonkin, *Narrating our Pasts: The Social Construction of Oral History* (Cambridge, 1992), 118–21.
[44] Brian Melbancke, *Philotimus* (1583), sig. Mii; J. T. Freigius, *Historiae synopsis* (Basle, 1580).

was so useful a subject in daily discourse—increasingly so as the period wore on and historical knowledge became a mark of civility—it was all the more essential that the educated citizen be able to recall, both from reading and conversation, a wide variety of details. What was remembered about the past could find its way into the history books; and what was there found by others at any later time could be appropriated and reused in speech or correspondence. Many a tale ran to and fro between speech and writing, or print, often several times. In May 1660 Samuel Pepys noted having been told a story taken from a translation of a 'novel' by Paul Scarron. His source, Dr Timothy Clarke, had read the tale, memorized its most significant features, and was now in the process of transmitting it to his associates. Pepys himself found the tale 'an exceeding pretty story and worth my getting without book when I can get the book'. In this instance, the printed work remained simply the source for a subject of oral discourse.[45]

Tudor and early Stuart antiquaries often relied on memories—both their own and others'—in compiling their materials. Like John Leland three decades earlier, William Lambarde talked to the learned as well as the illiterate and relied on what the former had read and committed to memory. He based his *Perambulation of Kent* on material 'as either faithfull information by worde, or credible hystorie in writing, hath hitherto ministred unto me'.[46] And for all their devotion to texts and careful note-taking, and their awareness of the failings of memory, antiquaries relied on it when reference to a written or printed original proved difficult. Camden himself apologized for 'some escapes of memorie, for who doth so comprehend particularities, in the treasury of his memory, that he can utter them at his pleasure?'[47] The erudite antiquary of Devon, Sir William Pole (d. 1635), was praised by his younger friend and disciple Tristram Risdon for his incredible memory rather than for the careful transcriptions of documents and inscriptions which have made Pole so useful to modern genealogists. 'Such a gift had he of rare memory, that he would have recited upon a sudden, the descents of most eminent families,' Risdon wrote in awe, 'from whose lamp I have received light in these my labours.'[48] Anthony Wood prided himself on a strong memory, particularly for music, which permitted him to sing or play on the violin any tune 'upon hearing it once or twice'. His powers of recall for more remote events were notoriously less accurate. A voluminous note-taker, he was unable to remember the name of the schoolmaster who had taught him at the age of 8,

[45] Fulwod, *The castel of memorie*, epistle dedicatory; Pepys, *Diary*, i. 135, 266.

[46] William Lambarde, *The Perambulation of Kent*, 2nd edn. (1596), 30.

[47] William Camden, *Britain*, trans. Philemon Holland (1610), 'To the reader'. Leland had relied on his memory often: *Leland's Itinerary*, iii. 10; *Joannis Lelandi antiquarii de rebus britannicis collectanea*, ed. Thomas Hearne, rev. edn., 6 vols. (1770), ii. 427.

[48] Tristram Risdon, *The chorographicall description or survey of Devon*, written c.1635 (1811), 29. Conversely, the writings of some antiquaries might be more incomprehensible than their oral information. Arthur Crew, a near-deaf Wiltshire antiquary who died in 1663 had, according to Anthony Wood, 'a great skill and knowledge in heraldry and matters relating to English families'. His deafness, however, insulated him from discourse with other scholars to such a degree that his enormous collections and writings were destroyed at his death by his heir, who could not understand them: Wood, *Life and Times*, i. 476.

but he nevertheless relied on memory, both his own and that of others, in compiling his biographical accounts of Oxford men—with erratic results. The mistakes involved in such recollection were often quite trivial, and Thomas Fuller lashed out against Peter Heylyn in the 1650s after the latter had challenged the accuracy of Fuller's *Church-history of Great Britain*, in the writing of which he had relied in places on memory without rechecking his sources. 'As for memory-mistakes,' Fuller protested, 'they are so far from overthrowing the credit of any book, as a speck (not paring-deep) in the rind of an apple is from proving of the same rotten to the core.'[49]

By the end of the seventeenth century, most scholars were increasingly reluctant to make assertions they had not double-checked for themselves at the source, or at least asked a friend to verify for them. When John Woodward wrote to Thomas Hearne to describe some Roman road fragments which he had seen, and which resembled others in Somerset, he added a marginal warning to his correspondent. 'That was 4 or 5 years ago: and being unwilling to rely upon my memory too far, I got Mr Hutchinson, a very intelligent gentleman, to ride thither this morning, and take a review of this way.'[50] The enormous correspondence among Augustan antiquaries, and the almost obsessive sense of detail in the citation of sources (complete with the routine addition of the footnote to the pages of scholarly texts) are an indication that the willingness of historical writers to trust in their recollection of events and facts without reference to a document had significantly diminished over the previous century. This may well be a praiseworthy improvement in scholarly method, and one that reduced inaccuracy, to all of which the modern scholar can say 'Amen'. But it was also an instance of the writer removing himself from the world of *viva voce* knowledge, from details of history now deemed more suited to the alehouse or the village pump than to the coffee-house or club, and unworthy of the library.

COLLECTIVE AND SOCIAL MEMORY

Social memory is currently a subject of much interest to scholars of all periods, ancient through modern. The founder of modern sociological studies of memory was Maurice Halbwachs (1877–1945). In a number of works, especially *La Mémoire collective*, Halbwachs argued that the collective memories—the plural is important—that inhere in societies are rarely inherited genetically or racially but instead are progressively determined and revised by social conventions. The use of the definite article in the English translation of his work has allowed Halbwachs's views to be misunderstood, however: he never claimed that there was a single, monolithic collective memory shared by society, but rather a number of competing and overlapping collective memories. In Halbwachs's judgement

---

[49] Wood, *Life and Times*, i. 48, 173, 178; Thomas Fuller, *The appeal of injured innocence* (1659), 4.
[50] Bodl. MS Rawl. D. 400, fo. 52ʳ.

it was history, rather than memory, which was socially unitary,[51] an important distinction on which the argument of this chapter will build. As a recent commentator has put it, Halbwachs's position might be reduced to the following proposition: 'Collective memory is made up of a multiplicity of group memories, while history unifies the past into one. Collective memory is oral, history written.'[52]

This opposition of memory and history fits neatly with another dichotomy, that between history based on oral versus written sources. Both are problematic. Since, as will become clear, I believe Halbwachs to have been more right than wrong on the relation between national history and what may be called local or 'community' memory, it is necessary to pay some attention both to his errors and to the criticisms made against him. Part of the difficulty with Halbwachs's treatment inheres in the very memory/history division itself, with its assumption that 'history' is immutable and permanent and 'memory' (like the spoken word) ephemeral. Geary has pointed out, in his recent study of medieval memory and its relation to writing, that institutions and archivists engage in their own forms of selection and suppression of materials, jettisoning what appears trivial or unimportant. In the Middle Ages the 'knowledge' of Carolingian and Merovingian periods was systematically pre-shaped for subsequent scholars in a deliberate pruning of sources carried out by eleventh-century archivists.[53] Writing is permanent only as long as its media are permitted to exist, and only in so far as the classification of those media enables access to them.

A second problem derives from Halbwachs's choice of the epithet 'collective' for the memories of a group, family, or organization. Even taken as a plural, this is ill defined and overly homogeneous in terms of such intervening factors as class, gender, age, and ideology, all of which can break down any 'collective', and it again carries with it a presumption that 'collective memory was a natural, nonpurposeful creation of a group while history was an intentional, political, and manipulative process'.[54] More recent authors, outside the French tradition, such as Paul Connerton, James Fentress, and Chris Wickham, have largely abandoned

[51] M. Halbwachs, *The Collective Memory*, trans. F. J. Ditter Jr. and V. Y. Ditter (New York, 1980), 83; id., *Les Cadres sociaux de la mémoire* (Paris, 1925). For more recent views, which revise but in many ways deepen Halbwachs's stark division of memory from history proper, see P. Nora, 'Mémoire Collective', in J. Le Goff, R. Chartier, and J. Revel (eds.), *La Nouvelle Histoire* (Paris, 1978), 398–400. Useful brief introductions to the subject are provided by N. Wachtel, 'Memory and History: An Introduction', *History and Anthropology*, 2 (1986), 207–24; P. H. Hutton, 'Collective Memory and Collective Mentalities: The Halbwachs–Ariès Connection', *Historical Reflections / Réflexions Historiques*, 15 (1988), 311–22; id., *History as an Art of Memory* (Hanover, NH, 1993), 73–88; D. Lowenthal, *The Past is a Foreign Country* (Cambridge, 1985), 194–214; K. M. Baker, 'Memory and Practice: Politics and the Representation of the Past in Eighteenth-Century France', *Representations*, 11 (Summer 1985), 134–64, at p. 156. Most recently, Wulf Kansteiner has challenged several of the assumptions and methods of current studies of (modern) collective memory: 'Finding Meaning in Memory: A Methodological Critique of Collective Memory Studies', *History and Theory*, 41 (2002), 179–97.

[52] Geary, *Phantoms of Remembrance*, 11.

[53] Halbwachs, *The Collective Memory*, 80; Geary, *Phantoms of Remembrance*, 11.

[54] Geary, *Phantoms of Remembrance*, 11 and 107 ff. This process occurs today as archives decide what to keep and what to shred or incinerate, the quantity of information being generated having grown exponentially over the past few decades alone.

Halbwachs's concept of a 'collective' memory in favour of the more flexible phrase 'social memory'.[55] Since Halbwachs assumed too great a cohesion within the collective memories of distinct social groups, while also setting up an over-rigid opposition between history and memory, this is in some ways a justifiable departure. His representation of history as a unified 'ocean fed by the many partial histories' of nations and as a false 'universal memory' of the human species (false in a formal sense because 'there *is* no universal memory') is an exaggerated caricature of the process of historical synthesis. It is not, however, altogether unhelpful in understanding history's changing relation to memory during the seventeenth century.[56]

For all the problems with his particular formulation of collective memory, the reaction against Halbwachs is now in some danger of tossing the historical baby out with the theoretical bathwater. It is possible to agree with more recent authors that 'social' rather than 'collective' is the proper term for memories of the past that apply to groups beyond the individual (and especially for the semi-official memory of an entire nation). It is similarly reasonable to endorse Geary's blurring of the division between oral and written, without jettisoning the useful parts of Halbwachs's theories, especially those on the relation between written history and memory. For there is compelling evidence from the early modern period that contemporary authors were indeed erecting a hierarchy of knowledge that privileged the written over the oral so far as the *authority* of accounts of the past were concerned. At the same time, a pluralistic congeries of discrete community memories defined by place, custom, tradition, and ritual was gradually being both assaulted and scavenged from, its useful parts being appropriated and rearranged along the chronological axis beloved of humanist historiography and its readers. In this process, the local past was often submerged into a 'national' past contained in history-writing and the civilized discourse that arose therefrom, whence it eventually fed back, principally via print media, into the local.[57]

The birth of a distinctively *English* 'sense of the past' and of a modern national tradition of great events, deeds, and traditions captured in historians from David Hume through T. B. Macaulay, down to Sir Arthur Bryant and Winston Churchill in recent times can be traced to the sixteenth and seventeenth centuries. Its origins, however, lie less in the direct intellectual influence of historians such as Camden, Bacon, and Clarendon, considerable though that was, than in a much

[55] Lowenthal, *The Past is a Foreign Country*, 211. Cf. the brief treatment of 'social memory' in P. Connerton, *How Societies Remember* (Cambridge, 1989), 6–40, and the more extensive treatment in J. Fentress and C. Wickham, *Social Memory* (Oxford, 1992). In addition to the above, I have found the following works, principally anthropological, helpful: J. Goody, *The Interface between the Written and the Oral* (Cambridge, 1987), 167–90; A. Collard, 'Investigating "Social Memory" in a Greek Context', in E. Tonkin, M. McDonald, and M. Chapman (eds.), *History and Ethnicity* (London and New York, 1989), 89–103, at p. 91; D. Nugent, 'Anthropology, Handmaiden of History? An Answer from the Field', *Critique of Anthropology*, 5/2 (Sept. 1985), 71–86, with material on memory in the Mexican context.

[56] Halbwachs, *Collective Memory*, 84, my emphasis.

[57] By 'national past' I intend a national understanding of the course of history, not an understanding of *national* history only. The sense of the past that emerges in the later seventeenth century embraces English, Scottish, or Irish history, the pasts of other countries, and classical and biblical history.

broader cultural change. This involved the modification of the relationship between the memories of individuals, the memories of the local or institutional communities to which those individuals belonged, and the memory of society at large, which was itself increasingly authorized by the collective fount of literary historiography.[58] The process by which this occurred was slow and uneven, and it was much subtler than any overt act of cultural conquest or class conflict. Through it the hegemony of 'History', with a capital 'h', was established by its being read and spoken of among persons whose ancestors would scarcely have been interested in such matters a century or more earlier. 'Social' memory could be and was expressed orally like community or individual memories, just as those could be written down, and were, in an ever-increasing number of texts and documents. But in so far as it became a major constituent of social memory, history also had one crucial advantage over both the local oral tradition and the local written document, namely a privileged access to the means of (re-)production, the printing press.[59] The consequence of this would be an increasingly homogenized and chronologically rigorous (even if ideologically fragmented and contentious) national sense of the past that would prove to be much more than the sum of its component parts, and incompatible with many of them.

THE CHANNELS OF COMMUNITY MEMORY

Every individual in Tudor and Stuart England, of whatever social degree, had memories of the past as lived experience, rather than as inscribed object. The principal difference separating the fully literate person from his non-literate contemporaries was the greater variety of channels open to the former for selecting from those experiences and funnelling them into permanent records such as autobiographies and diaries. There is no reason to suppose that early modern individuals did not recall their own pasts in the way we do, through associating different types of experience, the personal with the social, the local with the national, or that they did not place present events in perspective through the process of associating and comparing them with those in their own memories. Thomas Crosfield marked the significance of the birth of the Prince of Wales in 1630 with

[58] My usage thus coheres, at least in broad terms, to the sort of national memory that David Cressy has documented in the Protestant calendar from Elizabethan times to the late seventeenth century, and that Linda Colley has similarly pursued for the eighteenth, when the 'nation' was by then a political amalgamation of two peoples, following the union of England and Scotland in 1707: D. Cressy, *Bonfires and Bells: National Memory and the Protestant Calendar in Elizabethan and Stuart England* (Berkeley and London, 1989); Linda Colley, *Britons: Forging the Nation 1707–1837* (New Haven and London, 1992); cf. H. Weinbrot, *Britannia's Issue: The Rise of British Literature from Dryden to Ossian* (Cambridge, 1993). I have opted for the term 'social' both because I believe social status to have been an important constituent of memory and because the term is consistent with the usage among recent scholars such as Connerton, Fentress, and Wickham.

[59] B. Anderson, *Imagined Communities: Reflections on the Origin and Spread of Nationalism*, rev. edn. (1991), 37–46, makes a somewhat similar argument about the impact of printing, especially in vernacular languages, on early modern nationalism.

the remark that no heir to the throne had been born in England since Edward VI, over ninety years earlier, not a detail he would have troubled to look up somewhere. When guns were fired at Berwick to greet James I on his journey south in 1603, one observer reported having 'heard it credibly reported, that a better peale or ordinance was never in any souldiers memorie (and there are some olde King Harrie's lads in Barwick, I can tell you) discharged in that place'. The community memory referred to here dated back at least sixty years, and its perceived accuracy actually served to underline the significance of the event in recent times, for no man could 'remember Barwick honoured with the approach of so powerfull a Maister'.[60]

Minor details of local life such as the weather, and periodic crises such as floods, bulked large in community consciousness. The Lancaster tradesman William Stout thought the only thing worth recording in his autobiography under the year 1683, when he had been an 18-year-old apprentice, was 'the longest and sharpest frost with snow that had been in the memory of any man then living'. A storm which blew up on 30 August 1658, a few days before Cromwell's death, demolished the 'minster' at Ripon (later Ripon Cathedral); known half a century later as 'Oliver's Storm', it would be mis-remembered as having occurred on the very day of the Protector's demise.[61] Samuel Heathcote of Hackney felt confident in observing of the severe storm of 26–27 November 1703, that destroyed considerable property and killed several people, that 'No man liveing could pretend to have seen such a storm before'.[62] Joseph Bufton, an Essex weaver, had made a similar comment about the tide that had occasioned a severe flood in 1690.[63] The meteorological diaries that begin to appear in the mid-seventeenth century provide further examples. The Reverend Samuel Say of Lowestoft, Suffolk, who kept such a diary for several decades in the early eighteenth century, deemed the winter of 1708/9 to be 'one of the most remarkable winters for cold, that had been upward of 58 years'. It had been preceded by 'the coldest summer, spring & harvest, upon the whole, of any in 47'. These recollections came largely from local informants, but over thirty years later Say would be able to turn to his own notes to observe the similarity between the severe winter of 1708/9 and that of 1739/40, which 'began on the very same day, & with the same winds'.[64] A matter once the subject of local memory had now been systematized into a written record, illustrating Nora's observation that 'modern memory is, above all, archival'.[65]

[60] *Diary of Thomas Crosfield*, ed. F. S. Boas (Oxford, 1935), 43; John Nichols, *Progresses, Processions and Magnificent Festivities of King James the First*, 4 vols. (1828), i. 63.

[61] *The Autobiography of William Stout of Lancaster 1665–1752*, ed. J. D. Marshall (Manchester and New York, 1967), 80 (and p. 181, for similar comments regarding the flood of October 1720); *The Remembrances of Elizabeth Freke 1671–1714*, ed. R. Anselment, Camden Soc., 5th ser., 18 (2001), 243; Evelyn, *Diary*, v. 2.

[62] Hants. RO, Winchester, 63M 84/235 (unfoliated diary of Samuel Heathcote, 27 Nov. 1703).

[63] Essex RO T/A 156 (diary of Joseph Bufton of Coggeshall), vol. iii, unfoliated (8 Dec. 1690).

[64] Bodl. MS Top. Suffolk e. 1, fos. 11ʳ, 16ʳ, 17ʳ, 20ʳ–21ʳ.

[65] Nora, 'Between Memory and History', 13.

TIME BEYOND MEMORY OF MAN

Changes in land usage and in the physical environment also figured in the community memory. Anthony Curwen of Carlisle, reflecting on the decline of Shrove Tuesday recreations, noted early in the seventeenth century that many old men and women remembered when the now subdivided commons 'was one contynuse ground'; in his own youth there had been 'no hinderance to the football play', nor to running horses and dancing'. In the parish of Sutton Benger, Wiltshire, was a gravelly field called 'Barret's', which was sown annually with barley. According to John Aubrey, the field was so fertile that it 'never lay fallow in the memory of the oldest man's grandfather there'.[66] Buildings, too, provided reminders of their builders, or at least of their recent inhabitants. The funeral procession of Sir Arthur Darcy in 1561 began at a house where once, noted Henry Machyn, 'lyved old Clarenshus master Benolt the kyng at a[rms in the] tyme of kyng Henne viijt'. As late as 1570 William Lambarde, discussing Henry VII's architectural improvements to the palace of Eltham, discovered that these were 'not yet fully out of memorie'.[67] When an argument erupted in 1679 over the age of a chapel at Kentish Town, and whether or not it had ever been properly consecrated, the vicar of St Pancras parish, Randolph Yearwood, used local memory to establish that 'there was a small chappell in Kentish-Towne aforesaid above 100 yeares since, which was in the year 1633 demolished, rebuilt, enlarg'd and (as some say) consecrated'.[68]

As the last example suggests, memory was often exploited in legal disputes less to establish a positive fact such as a precise date at which an event occurred than as a kind of negative resource. If no man living could recall a situation different than that which existed, it could be taken that things had always been that way. The Hamlyn family of Cleeve, Somerset, brought an action against the abbot of Cleeve in 1506 for blocking a highway which 'hath ben there usyd by the tyme that no man can remember the contrary'.[69] Petitioners for licences for alehouses commonly fell back on the argument from past practice, claiming that their community had always had such establishments in the past. The parishioners of Boxley in Kent used this tactic in 1602 to get a recently suppressed alehouse restored 'as the same house of long tyme evyn tyme out of memory of man hath byn used'. The inhabitants of nearby High Halden made a similar case seven years later, this time to have a house erected where one did not exist, arguing that there had always been one 'in the tyme of any mans memorye'.[70]

---

[66] *REED: Cumberland, Westmorland, Gloucestershire*, ed. A. Douglas and P. Greenfield (Toronto, 1986), 158 n.; *Wiltshire. The Topographical Collections of John Aubrey, F.S.A.*, ed. J. E. Jackson (Devizes, 1862), 293.

[67] *The Diary of Henry Machyn*, ed. J. G. Nichols, Camden Soc., os 42 (1848), 255; Lambarde, *Perambulation of Kent*, 524.

[68] Bodl. MS Tanner 142, fo. 27^r, 24 June 1679: the immediate issue of this dispute concerned whether or not the landlord, Robert Hewytt, would support the chapel as a proper vicarage.

[69] *Proceedings of the Court of Star Chamber in the Reigns of Henry VII and Henry VIII*, ed. G. Bradford, Somerset Rec. Soc., 27 (1911), 65. For similar legal appeals to time out of mind in 1516 and 1528, see ibid. 73, 95.

[70] *Records of Maidstone* (Maidstone, 1926), 250.

In the face of inconsistent and incomplete records, the community memory was very frequently to be found in the recollections of the aged. Old people were, in Keith Thomas's words, 'the repositories of local history and custom, of pedigree and descent'.[71] They were more than repositories, however, since they, unlike documents, could literally speak the past, retell manorial or parochial history, and transmit proverbial wisdom. The aged guided rituals such as annual perambulations as they impressed parochial boundaries on the memories of their juniors.[72] Old people were often consulted in court cases to establish past practice and custom in contexts ranging from election franchises to boundary disputes to the payment of tithes: the testimony of Eastbourne fisherman James Hutchin, for instance, was used in 1622 to establish the customs governing local tithe payment 'by the space of thirty yeares last past, and tyme out of mynde for ought that hee hath heard or knowne to the contrary'.[73] The lore that generally passed orally from father to son remained of greater use than the inaccessible writings of gentlemen, the Tudor agrarian writer Fitzherbert pointed out. Even the advent of print did not change this in his view, since the wise gentleman farmer would read Fitzherbert's book aloud to his servants regularly, thereby returning orally derived wisdom to its spoken origins.[74] Over a century later a member of the Royal Society, experimenting with the effect of wind on cherry blossoms, was much in debt to 'an old experienced Country-man' for predicting, on the basis of years of experience, that a 'blasty noon' would follow a sultry morning.[75]

The very old could also serve, for their juniors, the function of talking history books. The octogenarian John Stow, who lived from the year of the Amicable Grant to that of the Gunpowder Plot, could recount seven critical decades of recent English history for the young John Manningham, probably in a manner far more captivating than his own published *Chronicles* and *Annales*. Ambrose Barnes, a late seventeenth-century alderman of Newcastle, was a veritable fount of information on the century's major events, according to his biographer. 'He was furnisht for all manner of conversation in history. He entertained men to admiration by reciting the times, places, occasions and precise actions, as if he had seen them.'[76] Unlike written histories from the period, we can only guess at the ideological spin on such oral recitations of the past, and the younger hearers of such information would have their own beliefs and experiences with which

[71] K. Thomas, 'Age and Authority in Early Modern England', *Proceedings of the British Academy*, 62 (1976), 1–46, esp. pp. 210, 234; J. T. Rosenthal, *Old Age in Late Medieval England* (Philadelphia, 1996), 10–11; A. Fox, 'Remembering the Past in Early Modern England: Oral and Written Tradition', *TRHS*, 6th ser., 9 (1999), 233–56; id., *Oral and Literate Culture in England 1500–1700* (Oxford, 2000), 264–5, 275–9; A. Wood, *The Politics of Social Conflict: The Peak Country 1520–1770* (Cambridge, 1999), 165–7.
[72] Fox, *Oral and Literate Culture*, 268–71.
[73] W. Sussex RO, Ep. II/5/12, fo. 37ʳ (24 Apr. 1622). The proof 'by public voice and fame' had a long tradition in tithe disputes and other cases before the medieval church courts: C. Donahue Jr., 'Proof by Witnesses in the Church Courts of Medieval England: An Imperfect Reception of the Learned Law', in M. S. Arnold *et al.* (eds.), *On the Laws and Customs of England* (Chapel Hill, NC, 1981), 90–126.
[74] A. Fitzherbert, *The book of husbandry*, ed. W. W. Skeat. English Dialect Soc., 37 (1882), 91.
[75] *Philosophical Transactions of the Royal Society*, ii (1667), 424.
[76] M. R., *Memoirs of the Life of Mr Ambrose Barnes*, Surtees Soc., 50 (1866), 151.

to reinterpret what they heard. The aged had an intimate connection to the medium-term past since what for the young was history was for them memory.

Aged persons were often called upon to give evidence in property cases, or to serve as jurymen or witnesses. In 1673 the Norfolk JP Henry Goodhead took depositions from several ancients to resolve the issue of a right of way through a messuage attached to the rectory in Attlebridge. Robert Wallys, 'aged fourscore & eight yeares or thereabouts', could recall back seventy years 'and beleiveth that the said messuage is an antient messuage, & built before the memory of any man alive'; another old man, Nicholas Carr of Norwich, deposed to having known the previous owner of the land over forty years earlier.[77] The manipulation of juries by replacing the elderly with younger men, whose memories stretched less far back, suggests that the recollections of the old were taken seriously in this legal context. Robert Higgyn and fourteen other copyholders of the manor of Charlton in Hampshire launched an action in Chancery against their bailiff, William Legg, and an associate for procuring a false verdict as to the customs of the manor. The principal charge against the bailiff was that he had empanelled the youngest men in the lordship, so as to acquire the right to make a new survey for the earl of Worcester, the manor's new lord.[78] When the Yorkshire cleric Thomas Comber undertook a view of his two livings at Stongrave and Thornton in 1685, he drew up glebe terriers only 'after I had strictly enquired of old men, & had jury's to view the glebes, and titheable lands'.[79] Such testimony could even be used by mutual agreement—though without the additional support of oath-swearing—to avoid recourse to the courts. In 1611 Edward Paston suggested to his kinsman Sir Edmund that they resolve their own tithe dispute informally, through the unsworn testimony of 'honest Credibble men' without taking it to law. A dozen years later, Edward would instruct his bailiff to 'speake to diverse of the ancient tennantes' in order to help a surveyor map the boundaries of the Paston family property.[80] A controversy about the boundaries of Palace Green in front of Durham Cathedral, and whether part of it called 'the broken wall' could be shut by ecclesiastical authority, was the subject of an inquisition in 1736, at which several aged deponents, ranging from a shoemaker to a physician, testified that in their memory the bishop had indeed closed the gate from time to time. Seventy-six-year-old Richard Turner, an illiterate shoemaker, deposed that 'he was born in Durham and has lived there all his time, & yt he has known ye Palace Green at Durham, & a place there called ye broken Wall'. He added that at the upper end of a passage leading from the broken wall 'there was a Door which was used

---

[77] Bodl. MS Tanner 312, fos. 55ʳ–59ʳ.

[78] PRO C1/1359/37, Higgyn et al. v. Legg and Robert Robson, n.d. (but c.1553–5 since addressed to Lord Chancellor Gardiner).

[79] *The Autobiography and Letters of Thomas Comber*, ed. C. E. Whiting, 2 vols., Surtees Soc., 156–7 (1941–2), i. 16.

[80] *The Correspondence of Lady Katherine Paston 1603–1627*, ed. R. Hughey, Norfolk Rec. Soc., XIV (1941), 41, 60 (Edward Paston to Sir Edmund Paston, 25 July 1611; same to Lady Katherine Paston, 26 May 1623). In another instance (ibid. 45), witnesses proved an adequate remedy for the lack of a written contract.

to be shutt up & fastened every night by somebody belonging to the Castle at Durham'.[81]

It is not necessary to add further examples to this already lengthy list. Lest, however, we slip into a romantic nostalgia for a time when the words of elders were heeded and written documents less essential to proving a case, it should be observed that gathering useful information from old witnesses was not always easy. Nor, when accomplished, was it invariably definitive. Apart from the frequent difficulty of getting aged and infirm witnesses to travel in order to testify (a problem in part addressed by the use of written depositions),[82] there was a more serious concern with the *credibility* of the old.[83] For many observers the length of a witness's recollections was undermined by his or her age, not so much because of outright mendacity and exaggeration as because of the likelihood of such memories being distorted by the passing of years. In particular, the old were believed to have a great capacity for recalling remote bits of knowledge from their childhood, but only a limited ability to retrieve more recent information. 'Ancient men', remarked a Renaissance writer on memory, William Fulwod in 1562, '. . . will orderly recyte feates from the beginninge of their age; but present thinges they eyther doe not remember, or els doe confounde them in uttering.' Old age was forgetful partly because of failing health, but also because the aged mind was 'overthrowen with the multitude of thynges'. Richard Steele said virtually the same a century and a half later: 'We that are very old, are better able to remember things which befel us in our distant youth, than the passages of later days.'[84] There is something poignant in the last weeks of 86-year-old Anne Clifford in 1676, confined to her chamber at Brougham, near Penrith, her days marked by remembrances of things and persons long past, and personal anniversaries reaching back to her young womanhood.[85]

The failing memory of the old was a trope going back at least as far as Aristotle, and it has been empirically studied in the past century.[86] So far as practical matters such as testimony are concerned, distrust of aged memories grew

[81] The deposition concluded with 'the mark of Richard Turner'. For this and other depositions in the case, see Durham University Library, Cosin MS V.iii. 26 (historical notes on Durham Castle), unfoliated. I owe this reference to the courtesy of Dr A. I. Doyle of the Durham University Library.

[82] For example, the rector of Hayes, Middlesex, asked to be excused from the clerical visitation of 1680 on the grounds that a long trip would 'by reason of age' be unpleasant: Bodl. MS Tanner 125, fo. 103[r] (Michael Selby to Archbishop Sancroft, 13 Sept. 1680).

[83] On the issue of credibility see S. Shapin, *A Social History of Truth: Civility and Science in Seventeenth-Century England* (Chicago, 1994), 93, and elsewhere, which does not, however, consider age as one of the factors in conferring trust. On the legal context of witness credibility see B. J. Shapiro, *A Culture of Fact: England, 1550–1720* (Ithaca, NY, 2000), 14–33.

[84] Fulwod, *The castel of memorie*, sigs. Bvii[v], Hvii; *The Tatler*, 181 (6 June 1710) ed. D. F. Bond, 3 vols. (Oxford, 1987), ii. 484. Thomas Sprat declared that memory was strongest in children, but judgement in men (the male noun probably being intentional): *The History of the Royal Society*, ed. J. I. Cope and H. W. Jones (St Louis, Mo., 1958), 330.

[85] *The Diaries of Lady Anne Clifford*, ed. D. J. H. Clifford, corrected paperback edn. (Phoenix Mill, Glos., 1992), 229–68, *passim*.

[86] Aristotle, *De Memoria et Reminiscentia*, in Sorabji, *Aristotle on Memory*, 60. For a summary of recent findings on specific deficits of memory among the old, emphasizing that only some aspects of memory are age-related, see D. Burke, 'Memory and Ageing', in M. Gruneberg and P. Morris (eds.), *Aspects of Memory*, i: *The Practical Aspects*, 2nd edn. (London and New York, 1992), 124–46.

during the sixteenth and seventeenth centuries, as records of the past prolifer-
ated and became more widely available through libraries and private archives, though
even at the end of the period both sources were often used. Sir Josiah Child, investigating the relationship between trade and prices at the end of the seventeenth
century, was 'assured by many antient men whom I have queried' that land prices
had multiplied sevenfold since 1621. He was certainly not opposed in principle
to listening to the memories of the aged. He urged any landowners wanting
confirmation of this economic claim to consult their stewards, who might be old
enough to know; if they were not, they would at least be able to consult the records
kept by their employer's father or grandfather fifty years earlier. Yet while Child
used the memories of other men as a resource, he plainly preferred both the
reliability of writing, and 'do-it-yourself' research without intermediary; accordingly, he urged his landowning readers 'not to depend upon their memories alone'
but to examine their estate accounts.[87] It was increasingly difficult to grant oral
recollection the same solidity as a written document.

RECORD-KEEPING

The bias towards the written was not new by Child's time. It was the culmina-
tion of several centuries during which the density of written materials had
steadily increased. There had long been matters for which orally related recollection was inadequate: where one needed a precise date to an event, or the source
of a claim to title or liberty, as opposed to a consensus about an ongoing practice in the recent past, then writing rather than human memory was essential.
Medieval towns had already turned to more formal record-keeping rather than
trusting in the power of prescriptive or undocumentable customary rights.[88] A
protracted dispute between the corporation of Bristol and the abbot of St
Augustine's, which dragged on from 1491 to 1496, involved the abbey's jurisdiction over the manor on which it stood. The townsmen claimed that 'of the tyme
whereof no mynde is' they had been free to grind their corn at town mills, instead
of having to use abbey mills, in spite of the abbey's claim, based on the same
argument, that it had been seised of the manor all that time. In contesting the
town's claims, the abbot used precisely the same language to assert for his house
the abbey's prescriptive rights to take views of frankpledge in the manor, and to
grant sanctuary to vagabonds. One by-product of the dispute, which was decided
by Archbishop Morton largely on the basis of aged witnesses' oral testimony, was
the initiation of the 'Great White Book' as a written custumal, to protect the town
in the event of future disputes.[89]

---

[87] Josiah Child, *A new discourse of trade* (1693), 47, 69.
[88] R. Tittler, *The Reformation and the Towns in England: Politics and Political Culture, c.1540–1640*
(Oxford, 1998), 211–20, 223–4; R. Sweet, *The Writing of Urban Histories in Eighteenth-Century England*
(Oxford, 1997), 75–80.
[89] *The Great White Book of Bristol*, ed. E. Ralph, Bristol Rec. Soc., 32 (1979), 25–8, 34, 53.

Citizens in other towns would create similar collections during the sixteenth century, for instance John Vowell, alias Hooker, whose researches in the documents of the city of Exeter provided him with the skills he would later use in revising Holinshed's *Chronicles*.[90] In Great Yarmouth, about 1580, Thomas Damet, an alderman and future MP, compiled a 'book of charters', combining the town's rolls and other writings with transcripts from records in the Tower stretching back to Edward III, with the end of having a permanent record of the town's rights to the herring fishery. A little over a decade later, Damet went on to write 'A Book of the Foundacion and Antiquitye of the saide towne and of diverse Specialle matters concerning the same'. Parts of this in turn found their way into print in Thomas Nashe's more literary treatment of the borough's history in his *Lenten Stuffe*, and were eventually included in Henry Manship's longer *History of Great Yarmouth*, written twenty years later.[91] The construction of an urban memory through record-keeping thus provides a context for the development of antiquarian methods no less important than the ancestral preoccupations of gentry.

Claude Lévi-Strauss has observed that respect for archives is common among literate societies, and England was certainly no exception in this regard.[92] But the greater reliance on written communication represented a shift in emphasis rather than the complete supplanting of one medium by another, much less a victory of 'new' writing over 'old' speech. So far as the law was concerned, both viva voce and written evidence were admissible, depending on a variety of factors such as the established procedure of the court involved, the type of action, and the circumstances of the offence or issue that gave rise to the cause. Towns and manors had kept records going since the twelfth century or earlier, just as central government had placed a greater emphasis on record-keeping among administrative and judicial departments beginning with the Norman Conquest.[93] The increasing burden of paper in the Court of Chancery alone obliged the Crown, early in James I's reign, to consider establishing a separate office simply to ensure that written depositions from witnesses 'upon which the whole cause dependeth shold be safely and carefully kept'.[94] In keeping with Continental city-states such

[90] Tittler, *The Reformation and the Towns*, 290; for another example, see *The 'Boke off Recorde' of Kirkbie Kendall*, ed. R. S. Ferguson, Cumberland and Westmorland Antiquarian and Archaeological Soc., ES VII (Kendal, 1892).

[91] P. Rutledge, 'Thomas Damet and the Historiography of Great Yarmouth', *Norfolk Archaeology*, 33, pt. ii (1963), 119–30, and 34, pt. iii (1968), 332–4. Thomas Damet, *A Booke of the Foundacion and Antiquitye of the Towne of Greate Yermouthe*, ed. C. J. Palmer (Great Yarmouth, 1847), 34–7, for 'sondrye contencions and questions' about the liberties of the town in the 1570s, which probably played a part in Damet's researches. His editor, Palmer, attributed the work to Henry Manship the elder, father of the antiquary Henry Manship the younger (d. 1625), who would later write his own history of the town; Damet is correctly identified as the author by Rutledge. I owe these references to Damet to Robert Tittler. On the impact of the Reformation on collective memory in the towns, cf. R. Tittler, 'Reformation, Civic Culture and Collective Memory in English Provincial Towns', *Urban History*, 24 (1997), 283–300.

[92] C. Lévi-Strauss, *The Savage Mind* (Chicago, 1966), 239–44.

[93] Clanchy, *From Memory to Written Record*, *passim*.

[94] Bodl. MS Tanner 91, fos. 148–9; this is undated but internal references place it about 1617, just after the death of Lord Chancellor Ellesmere.

as Venice, English central government had also taken various precautions against the loss or fabrication of civic and parochial records, beginning with the 1538 injunctions regulating the maintenance of parish registers. A bill for safekeeping the records of the Peace at one 'local place in every county' was introduced by Sir Dudley Digges during the Addled Parliament of 1614, and got as far as a second reading before it died with the abrupt end of the session.[95]

This last point about the safeguarding of documents alerts us to an important qualification: while contemporaries were beginning both to extend the sovereignty of the written document into domains unimagined by medieval clerks, and also to take more care in their maintenance, they remained well aware that the written record carried with it problems of its own in matters of trust and authenticity. Systems of record-keeping were not foolproof, nor did the document speak to every matter at stake. Although legal records of various sorts had an authoritative status that distinguished them from other documents, generally by virtue of having been notarized or filed in a court of some jurisdiction, they were often difficult to locate; typically they were kept uncatalogued and in a common place such as a chest in the parish church or town hall, together with other muniments of lesser legal import.

During the sixteenth century, in response both to a growing quantity of litigation and to the enormous weight of regulatory responsibility being piled by statute on the shoulders of civic, parochial, and county officials, greater efforts were made to remedy such problems. In London, a tradition of record-keeping and muniment management going back to Andrew Horn in the fourteenth century was accelerated by internal and external disputes. Officials such as Robert Smith, a merchant tailor who held a succession of City posts over nearly half a century, made transcripts, calendars, and indexes of important documents to ensure the maintenance of the written record. They did so at least in part to preserve the knowledge of aged corporate officials such as William Dummer (the long-serving Comptroller of the Chamber), whose 'corporate' memories would soon be lost.[96] Outside London, limited judicial and financial record-keeping can be traced as far back as thirteenth-century tax, guild, and court rolls, but this, too, received a stronger impetus after the Reformation. Robert Tittler has noted the construction of muniment rooms in provincial town halls during the sixteenth century, Exeter's late Elizabethan renovations to its guildhall being a good example. A few records were even sporadically printed to aid in their accessibility, a trend that would continue as antiquaries included verbatim transcripts in local histories of the seventeenth and eighteenth

---

[95] *Proceedings in Parliament 1614 (House of Commons)*, ed. M. Jansson, Memoirs of the American Philosophical Society, 172 (Philadelphia, 1988), 274, 330, 335, 396. Many of these had to be reissued repeatedly, suggesting a lack of success in enforcing them. For the repeated measures taken by the Venetian government against record-tampering and forgery, see D. Queller, *The Venetian Patriciate* (Urbana and Chicago, 1986), 206.

[96] P. Cain, 'Robert Smith and the Reform of the Archives of the City of London, 1580–1623', *The London Journal*, 13/1 (1987–8), 3–16.

centuries.[97] Rural parishes similarly began to pay more attention to maintaining a common chest or press for their most important documents.

Even then, there is a casualness, when compared with modern archival methods, that may make us overlook the degree to which the situation was much improved from medieval practices. In London and in provincial towns, documents were borrowed and sent from place to place with a freedom that would make a modern archivist swoon. Arthur Agarde, the Exchequer official and Elizabethan antiquary, had noted in the late sixteenth century that the major enemies of records were fire, water, rats and mice, misplacing, and 'plain taking of them away'.[98] John Smyth's command over the papers of the Berkeley family, to whom he was steward, is well known, and he recorded his own labours in recovering 'more then 300 peices of evidence . . . from many corners' to the Berkeley muniments; but he was unable to tell whether they had been 'soe scattered by falshood or forgetfullnes'.[99]

The situation in the towns was comparable to that of Crown and family muniments. Reading, which kept its charter, borough correspondence, and other crucial documents in an 'old booke' in its 'greate chest', regularly dispatched them by messenger, and in 1644 gave its Elizabethan charter to Sir Thomas Maynwaring 'to carry home to peruse'. Three years later it lent one Mr Starkey a charter from Henry VIII 'and three paper or parchment old writinges' to assist him in searching some other records in the Tower. The recovery of missing documents was often due to sheer luck: a decree in Exchequer that had gone astray from the great chest came to light in 1641 when George Wooldridge acknowledged that it was in his possession.[100] A civic official in Plymouth during the 1580s recorded in the town's White Book the recovery of a number of important documents testifying to its antiquity, which had long been absent in private hands. 'The copye of certeyn auncyent wrytynges remaynyng wth Thomas Smyth, which came to his handes by reason of Alice his wiffe daughter to Mr Bulle' was now safely back in town custody, 'approvyng playnlie that Sutton Pryors wch is nowe called the burghe of Plymouth was a maior Towne [that is, an incorporated town with a mayor] long before Kyng Henry the Sixt is tyme'.[101] In March 1690 Edward Pratt of Woodbridge, Suffolk, found himself unable to resolve a technical question regarding the election franchise in Aldeburgh (or Aldborough), in the same county. At issue was the matter whether 'out setters' who were freemen

---

[97] G. H. Martin, 'The Origins of Borough Records', *Journal of the Society of Archivists*, 2 (1961), 147–53; id., 'The Publication of Borough Records', *Archives*, 7 (1965–66), 199–206; R. Tittler, *Architecture and Power: The Town Hall and the English Urban Community c.1500–1640* (Oxford, 1991), 12, 41–2, 89.

[98] R. B. Wernham, 'The Public Records in the Sixteenth and Seventeenth Centuries', in L. Fox (ed.), *English Historical Scholarship in the Sixteenth and Seventeenth Centuries* (London and New York, 1956), 11–48, at p. 27.

[99] John Smyth of Nibley, *The Berkeley Manuscripts*, ed. J. Maclean, 3 vols. (Gloucester, 1883–5), ii. 293.

[100] *Reading Records: Diary of the Corporation, 1431–1654*, ed. J. M. Guilding, 4 vols. (1892–96), ii. 130, iv. 101, 235, 322, 386.

[101] R. N. Worth, *Calendar of the Plymouth Municipal Records* (Plymouth, 1893), 56–8.

but not of the corporation were entitled to vote for Members of Parliament. Pratt was unable immediately to secure the town records, which might have helped, because they were then being held by an old man dwelling twelve miles distant. Instead, he tried to determine the answer from local recollections of past electoral practice. In this case, such testimony did not prove sufficient, and Pratt was eventually obliged to spend a day 'searching for many howers amongst thousands of wrightings and papers'. But the written record was no better, for though he was able to turn up the corporation's charter from the reign of Edward VI, and though he scrupulously 'researched to the bottome of their old chests', Pratt was unable to find an election return pre-dating the Edwardian charter.[102]

Some towns were cognizant of the problem of stray documents and made concerted efforts to remedy it. Tenterden, which, perhaps significantly, was also one of the boroughs to maintain a town chronicle through much of the period,[103] made persistent attempts from the beginning of the sixteenth century to keep its records in one location. In 1604 the town purchased a press and ordered that henceforth all records of the borough and hundred of Tenterden be kept therein—with the notable exception of the town's charters and custumals, which were to remain in the custody of the mayor. Four keys only were made for the press, to be held by the mayor, the jurat who was mayor-elect, the town clerk, and the town chamberlain. The system appears not to have been taken seriously however—rather fortunately for the town as it turned out. In 1661 the council hall was destroyed in a fire and all the records kept therein 'lately burnt and consumed'. But a 1672 order mandated regular inspection and renewed centralization (again in a chest with controlled keys) of all documents that had slipped back into private hands over the years, suggesting that the 1604 measure had been frequently ignored. And by 1683, when a full-scale inspection of the documents occurred, none of the new keys could be traced, obliging the mayor and jurats to break into the chest in order to find out what was inside.[104] The experience of Great Yarmouth was somewhat similar. There, Henry Manship, following on the heels of his older contemporary and enemy Thomas Damet, was also concerned with the town's record-keeping. Frequently in trouble with town authorities (on one occasion being dismissed from a post for calling Damet and his fellow MP dunces and sheep), Manship discovered in 1612 that the 'hutch' which he had been granted permission to search for records was missing several important 'charters, evidences, and writings . . . in custody of sondry persons'. He then formed

---

[102] West Sussex RO, Ac. 454 (Shillinglee MSS, Letters 892–911, Pratt to Sir Edward Turnour, 18 Mar. 1689/90 and 17 Nov. 1691). For the franchise, see *The House of Commons 1660–1690*, ed. B. D. Henning, 3 vols. (1983), i. 394–6. I am indebted to the county archivist of West Sussex for correspondence on this case.

[103] Tenterden's chronicle was initiated in the seventeenth century and is contained in a borough custumal (CKS Te/C1, fos. 136ᵛ–139). It begins with 'The names of the Bayleifs of the towne and hundred of Tenterden from the beginning of the liberty begun in the twenty and seaventh yeares of the reigne of Kinge Henry the sixte'.

[104] CKS Te/C1, fo. 113ᵛ; CKS Te/S2 (minute book of the corporation of Tenterden, 1641–1762), fos. 565, 627.

a committee of aldermen and common councillors to retrieve, describe, and reclassify the borough's records, some of which appear to have been in Damet's hands. The final result was a catalogue of Yarmouth's archives, and Manship's own descriptive history of the borough. But as late as 1619, when he was writing that history, Manship still deplored the neglect of records that had allowed many 'worthy things' to be 'wholly buried in the grave of oblivion', and he still had to borrow documents from the custody of individual common councillors and citizens.[105]

It is important to remember that records were not 'curiosities', quaint pieces of the past acquired and maintained primarily for their connection to history, much less so as to benefit modern historians. They were first and foremost a vehicle of community memory, subject to continuous if irregular use rather than 'discovery', and thus existing in a social world that was always very much of the present. This made them, as tangible objects, very different in significance and status from the kinds of antiquity described in earlier chapters. The maintenance and provenance of records was also not a matter for leisured pastime or scholarly curiosity. During the reign of Mary, the churchwardens of Sherston Magna, Wiltshire, brought an action in Chancery against one of their parishioners, Thomas Hayes, who to avoid paying a parish rate levied for repair of the church had made off with the 'grete legger boke' in which was entered each parishioner's due. Hayes contended the rate itself to have been improperly raised (despite evidence that it had been collected by this manner from time immemorial). He further insisted that no local custom or law made the missing book, which he had by this time possessed for twelve years, a document of record rather than a private writing.[106] Careless custodianship of the book of assessment at Sevenoaks led to its loss, and with it the 21s. 2d. in uncollected sums due to the poor, resulting in a 1602 judgement against the culprit.[107] When Sir Thomas Harris, rising son of a Shrewsbury draper, had his promotion into the baronetage challenged in the 1620s, he was accused of having wrongfully obtained certificates of descent from the heralds; but he was able to counter that his opponents had used a legal delay in the Earl Marshall's proceedings to suborn Shrewsbury's town clerk into lending them critical deeds and court rolls with which they tampered.[108]

Roger B. Manning has recently offered an even more compelling example of such transactions in two studies of the land-management practices of Sir Robert Cotton and his son in the first half of the seventeenth century. Cotton is much

---

[105] H. Manship, 'Inventory of Deeds and Documents, Made by Henry Manship, Town Clerk in 1612', in H. Harrod (ed.), *Repertory of Deeds and Documents Relating to the Borough of Great Yarmouth in the County of Norfolk* (Great Yarmouth, 1855), 1–3; H. Manship, *The History of Great Yarmouth*, ed. C. J. Palmer (1854), pp. ii–v, 107, 109; R. Tittler, 'Henry Manship: Constructing the Civic Memory in Great Yarmouth', in id., *Townspeople and Nation: English Urban Experiences, 1540–1640* (Stanford, Calif., 2001), 121–39.

[106] PRO C1/1363/9–11 (petition to Lord Chancellor Gardiner, n.d., 1553–5).

[107] L. A. Knafla, *Kent at Law 1602. The County Jurisdiction: Assizes and Sessions of the Peace* (1994), nos. 240, 641.

[108] *CSPD 1619–1623*, 472; *CSPD 1623–1625*, 65, 77, 95, 97, 118, 125, 401, 506; G. W. Fisher, 'Sir Thomas Harris of Boreatton, Shropshire, and his Family', *Trans. Shropshire Archaeological and Natural History Society*, 2nd ser., 10 (1898), 77–92.

celebrated among historians for his guardianship of countless historical manuscripts, and for his rather more modest contributions to historical scholarship
and to parliamentary antiquarianism.[109] Yet, as Manning points out, Cotton had
little choice but to develop a close acquaintance with living documents, especially
legal ones. Sir Robert was a landlord with a reputation for sharp practice: it was
not simply the service of the kingdom that was aided by his interest in records.
To him, the rolls and parchments of his estates were evidence useful in ratchet-
ing up entry fines, converting arable land to pasture, and enclosing common lands.
In the midst of a lawsuit between his own tenants and those of a neighbouring
manor regarding a common waste, he found a formidable opponent in one Robert
Castle. A former estate steward known for his pro-tenurial sympathies, and a man
who himself knew his way around manorial records, Castle had laid his hands
illicitly on some of Cotton's oldest documents and was prepared to use them against
him. For Cotton, therefore, his own researches were as much a matter of legal
defence as of aggressive estate management. This was not the only incident of its
kind in Cotton's career; about 1618 he complained to Lord Chancellor Bacon that
the copyholders on his wife's estate at Round in Northamptonshire had schemed
to defraud him of the heriots owed him, and that they had advanced their plot
by stealing and hiding virtually all the relevant surveys, court rolls, 'and other
writings and evidences'. Cotton's manorial troubles demonstrate that tenants were
not always at the mercy of a written word employed by their masters.[110] Indeed,
in other instances landlords and tenants alike pursued the safety of a codifying
document through the mechanism of a contrived suit to a central court such as
Chancery: the tenants of Slindon in Sussex pursued such a course in collusion
with their landlord, Anthony Kempe, in 1568.[111] As Andy Wood has recently
observed, many tenants were keenly aware of the impact of the written word
on custom and of the need to channel it to their own ends. Groups such as the
miners of the Peak District managed the transformation of ambiguous and contested oral custom into documents such as *The Liberties and customs of the miners*,
which was printed in 1645.[112]

It would be interesting to know how much removal or concealment of records
went on among both tenants and landlords. But this was not the biggest problem

---

[109] For Cotton's scholarly activities see K. Sharpe, *Sir Robert Cotton 1586–1631* (Oxford, 1979). A
somewhat different picture emerges from the various essays in a special issue of *The British Library
Journal*, 18/1 (Spring 1992), in particular J. P. Carley, 'The Royal Library as a Source for Sir Robert
Cotton's Collection: A Preliminary List of Acquisitions', 52–73.

[110] R. B. Manning, 'Antiquarianism and the Seigneurial Reaction: Sir Robert and Sir Thomas Cotton
and their Tenants', *Historical Research*, 58 (1990), 277–88. A partial edition of the Chancery documents pertaining to the case are in R. B. Manning, 'Sir Robert Cotton, Antiquarianism and Estate
Administration: A Chancery Decree of 1627', *British Library Journal*, 18/1 (1992), 88–96. For further
examples of antiquarian record research motivated by fiscal conservatism see Manning, *Hunters and
Poachers*, 80–1 (William Noy) and 216 (the third earl of Cumberland). I am indebted to Roger Manning
for correspondence on this matter.

[111] M. Zell, 'Fixing the Custom of the Manor: Slindon, West Sussex, 1568', *Sussex Archaeological
Collections*, 122 (1984) 101–6.

[112] A. Wood, 'Custom and the Social Organization of Writing in Early Modern England', *TRHS*,
6th ser., 9 (1999), 257–69, esp. pp. 266; id., *Politics of Social Conflict*, 150–62.

with the written record. Much worse than outright theft, careless loss, or shoddy maintenance was the spectre of the corrupt or bogus document, which contributed to residual suspicion of the supplanting of oral culture by written.[113] A missing piece of evidence frustrates a search and forces reliance on other types of evidence, including prescriptive claims and oral testimony; a forged or illicitly emended one can wreak havoc. The vulnerability of evidences of pedigree to alteration in matters of ancestry has been discussed in earlier chapters. In fact, virtually any sort of document was vulnerable to such corruption. The forger has been with us as long as there have been documents, and the majority of his progeny do not belong to the grand European tradition of textual duplicity recently described by Anthony Grafton.[114] A long catalogue of interference with charters and seals stretches back to the twelfth century at least, though only forgery of those relating to the Crown was treated criminally (and indeed, as treason, like counterfeiting) until the mid-sixteenth century.[115] These were the perquisite of neither landlords nor tenants, rich or poor. As central equity courts such as Exchequer and Chancery were increasingly called to balance the oral memory of past usage with the evidence of documents, so the documents themselves increasingly fell prey to tampering either during or in anticipation of disputes.[116]

Such efforts were often pedestrian and easily exposed. William Hackney's grant to himself of 40 marks a year for life in a forged document signed 'Mary the Quene' was one such clumsy fake, which earned its author condemnation for treason.[117] A minor rogues' gallery of forgers and document tamperers is preserved in court actions that turned on, or were in some instances launched to sort out, the messes created. In a family quarrel in 1557, John Cooke of Lincolnshire brought an action in Star Chamber against a priest named William Samphall, a widow named Agnes Cooke, and one John Poynton, accusing them of uttering a forged will supposedly by the plaintiff's great-grandfather. An attorney was brought before Star Chamber in 1597 for having erased the record of a debt once it had been paid. He was grudgingly excused, since there was clearly no malice or fraud intended, but, as John Hawarde noted, the court thought 'it is not a good thing to be allowed, since the Records are sacred things, and cannot be altered without the Judge in Court'.[118] Many other cases were more malign, and the problem was

---

[113] A. Fox, 'Custom, Memory and the Authority of Writing', in P. Griffiths, A. Fox, and S. Hindle (eds.), *The Experience of Authority in Early Modern England* (London and New York, 1996), 89–116, at p. 90; Fox, *Oral and Literate Culture*, 281–98.

[114] A. Grafton, *Forgers and Critics: Creativity and Duplicity in Western Scholarship* (Princeton, 1990).

[115] N. Ramsay, 'Forgery and the Rise of the London Scriveners' Company', in R. Myers and M. Harris (eds.), *Fakes and Frauds: Varieties of Deception in Print and Manuscript* (Winchester and Detroit, 1989), 99–109; for late medieval instances of minor offences, generally punished with little worse than the pillory, see p. 103. Two clerics were pilloried in Fleet Street for 'a very notorious forgery' in 1716: *Diary of Dudley Ryder*, 284.

[116] Fox, *Oral and Literate Culture*, 288.

[117] In 1536 Henry VIII extended the 1352 treason statute's coverage to include forgery of the royal signet or sign manual; this was reinforced by parliament in 1553 in order to deal with Hackney's case: Ramsay, 'Forgery and the Scriveners' Company', 101.

[118] PRO STAC 4/6/19 (Cooke v. Cooke); John Hawarde, *Les Reportes del cases in Camera stellata, 1593–1609*, ed. W. P. Baildon (1894), 89.

serious enough by the late seventeenth century to prompt Sir Christopher Wren
to invent a 'Diplographical Instrument' that could prevent forgery by making exact
duplicates of legal documents—a machine that was itself soon stolen.[119]

Document-tampering could involve outright invention or simple misdating,
and there is no way of knowing how many desperate litigants, their fortunes dependent upon some missing or non-existent record, were driven to a successful bit
of creative penmanship. Mid-Tudor legislators enacted a statute 'agaynst the forging of evidences and wrytinges' in 1563 on the grounds that such practices 'hathe
of late tyme been verye muche more practised, used and put in use . . . then in
tymes passed'.[120] The true extent of such practices is ultimately unknowable: we
have only the failures and suspected failures. Moreover, the boundary between
acceptable and intolerable interference in the written record was less hard and
fast than the legislation implied. In the case of simple redating—an offence for
which modern historians, misled by such tricks, would gladly apply the rack to
their perpetrators—the courts could be surprisingly tolerant. In 1594 a plaintiff
tried unsuccessfully to prove that a will had been forged and that some related
leases had been antedated. The ruling was that the leases were good despite the
obvious antedating, 'for a man may antedate a deed if it be not to any man's prejudice or to defeat any man's right'. Similarly, publishing a forged deed in ignorance of its character was not deemed culpable; this was in keeping with the practice
of the Scriveners' Company, which from the late fourteenth century permitted
antedating of deeds and closed letters so long as the date was not '*far* distant'. In
1596 one Mr Sute, a former servant to Lord Treasurer Burghley, obtained a copy
of a court roll bearing the words *habere sibi secundum consuetudinem manerii* ('to
have to himself according to the custom of the manor') and copied it, changing
the phrase to *habere sibi et heredibus secundum consuetudinem manerii* ('to have
to himself and his heirs according to the custom of the manor'). To give the corrupt document the look of authenticity, he hung it in a fire and smoke-dried it.[121]
After a man named Blage apprenticed his son to another named Allen, he
charged that Allen had changed the amount due to him from £100 to 100 marks
after the bond had been entered in the scrivener's book and sealed, for the sole
purpose of voiding the document. When, following Allen's 'ill usage' of the apprentice, Blage Sr. had demanded that the bond be produced, Allen at first refused;
he consented only after being imprisoned by the aldermen. Allen was then
released from the terms because the bond was indeed voided by having been altered

---

[119] A. Johns, 'History, Science, and the History of the Book: The Making of Natural Philosophy in
Early Modern England', *Publishing History*, 30 (1991), 5–30, at p. 10. Samuel Hartlib appears to have
developed a means of duplicating documents in the 1650s, while methods for the counterfeiting of
seals, and for proofing letters against opening by the wrong hands, were developed under the aus-
pices of Sir Samuel Morland in the early 1660s: A. Marshall, *Intelligence and Espionage in the Reign
of Charles II* (Cambridge, 1994), 86–7.

[120] 5 Eliz. c. 14, cited in Fox, *Oral and Literate Culture*, 274.

[121] Hawarde, *Les Reportes*, 3, 64; Ramsay, 'Forgery and the Scriveners' Company', 104. Cf. a case
of 10 Oct. 37–38 Eliz (1595), Hawarde, *Les Reportes*, 22, involving deeds to lands in the estate of Sir
Thomas Gresham, made to appear to be deeds of twenty-one years earlier.

after its sealing. Blage, who was himself a barrister of the Inner Temple, was examined by the Star Chamber, as were the scrivener and several others. Allen
responded by filing a cross-bill against Blage for perjury and was himself discharged
(over the dissenting voices of Chief Justice Popham of King's Bench, and of Sir
Thomas Egerton, the Lord Keeper), the majority of judges agreeing that there was
no evidence as to who had changed the words nor even certainty as to when it
had been done.[122]

In the main the record system worked, and English law had functioned with
it for several centuries. But contemporaries can scarcely be blamed for feeling that
the written document was not beyond reproach, and in cases of enclosure or other
types of property dispute it simply did not exist, rights and practices having been
maintained entirely by custom: hence the willingness to fall back on oral testimony of past practice 'before the memory of man living' where it was available.
The second earl of Essex was no lawyer, nor was he possessed of good judgement
in many matters, but he cannot have been alone in expressing resentment at what
he perceived, as early as the 1590s, as a discounting of oral testimony in favour
of written evidence.[123] We will have occasion to return to the theme of the comparative reliability of oral and written evidence about the historical past in the
remainder of this book.

COMMUNITY MEMORY, SOCIAL MEMORY, AND HISTORY

Individuals of much the same age, who have lived through the same events, may
have strikingly different perceptions of the way in which those events took place,
and assign different values to them, as an incident from the early years of
Elizabeth I's reign testifies. The religious settlement of 1559 stopped short of the
Edwardian reformation, particularly that which had been promulgated in the prayer
book of 1552, yet most ecclesiastical authorities proved anxious to see their own
version of the Reformation as a continuation of the movement interrupted by
Mary Tudor's reign.[124] In 1567, confronting several Londoners charged before High
Commission with holding their own conventicles, the dean of Westminster,
Gabriel Goodman, pointed out that ecclesiastical authorities were not papists:
'No, we hold the reformation that was in King Edward's days.' William White,
speaking for the accused, found this unacceptable, both because he did not
accept the similarity between the Elizabethan liturgy and the Edwardian, and because
he perceived even King Edward's time as having been too close to popery.[125]

---

[122] Allen was, however, fined for filing a false bill, unsupported by evidence, in his cross-suit for
perjury. Blage v. Allen, 1600, in Hawarde, *Les Reportes*, 118–19.

[123] Hawarde, *Les Reportes*, 30. Essex claimed to be repeating a remark by a medieval judge, and
was thus aware that the conflict between oral and written evidence was an old issue.

[124] Even some ordinary citizens felt that way: Camden, in his brief autobiography, commented on
how fortunate he felt to have been born in Edward's reign, and claimed adherence to the Edwardian
version of Protestantism.

[125] *Remains of Edmund Grindal*, ed. W. Nicholson, PS 19 (Cambridge, 1843), 213.

The long-lived antipathy of English Protestants for the age of popery, and espe-cially for its last, Marian, episode, cannot be attributed solely to government propaganda, cheap works of Protestant piety such as those discussed by Tessa Watt,[126] the Protestant calendar described by David Cressy and Ronald Hutton,[127] or even such tradition-making juggernauts as Foxe's *Acts and Monuments*, undeniably important as these were. To create an ongoing social memory of the horrors of popery, such feelings had to be maintained across generations, the message of print reinforced by individual instruction itself shaped by perceptions of the past. Elizabethan and Jacobean youth were informed by their elders, just as children are now, of the 'correct' attitude to take towards episodes in the relatively recent past, rather as a child today might ask his or her parents who was on the right side in the Second World War. The messages were reinforced indirectly through other means. Physical remains such as ruins provided visible connections to the past at the same time that they signified a discontinuity or rupture between that past and the present. The abbeys demolished at the dissolution and the castles pulled down in the civil wars are material examples of *lieux de mémoire*, in Pierre Nora's phraseology, reminders of a past either nostalgically regretted or deliber-ately repudiated; they would resonate differently depending on the beholder's political and religious inclinations.[128] The same can be said for the successive pub-lic texts that enacted or summarized sharp religious or secular change, from the several Tudor prayer books to seventeenth-century political documents such as the death warrant of Charles I or the Declaration of Rights.

What is memory for one generation's members becomes history in their retelling of it for their juniors and successors, and almost inevitably a history bent or spun in a particular direction. It was with such a purpose in mind that the puritan Sir Francis Hastings instructed the young earl of Essex in 1588, inform-ing the latter how fortunate he was to have been born 'in a time wherin the dark-ness of popery and superstition is expelled'.[129] A hundred years later, the same situation applied, in a more multi-partisan manner, as Restoration political atti-tudes and allegiances were formed by conflicting memories, both personal and second-hand, of the civil wars. It was common for royalist or moderately parlia-mentarian writers to refer to the two decades prior to the Restoration by such phrases as the late 'broken' times, or what Thomas Sprat, writing in the 1660s, called 'the late times of civil war, and confusion'.[130] Precisely where the normal passage of history had ended and the implied fracture, or temporal confusion, had occurred, would depend on one's political point of view. A royalist sym-pathizer such as John Evelyn or Anthony Wood, the former a young man and the latter a child during the first civil war, would view the whole period from the

---

[126] T. Watt, *Cheap Print and Popular Piety, 1550–1640* (Cambridge, 1991).

[127] Cressy, *Bonfires and Bells*; R. Hutton, *The Rise and Fall of Merry England: The Ritual Year, 1400–1700* (Oxford and New York, 1994).

[128] Nora, *Les Lieux de mémoire*, cited above, and id., 'Between Memory and History', 18–20.

[129] *Letters of Sir Francis Hastings, 1574–1609*, ed. C. Cross, Somerset Rec. Soc., 69 (1969), 39 (Hastings to Essex, 9 Sept. 1588).

[130] Thomas Sprat, *The History of the Royal Society*, ed. J. I. Cope and H. W. Jones (St Louis, Mo., 1958), 152.

calling of the Long Parliament to the Restoration as one huge disaster. A Presbyterian such as Denzil Holles and even a moderate cavalier such as Clarendon would have a somewhat different view, while republicans such as James Harrington, Algernon Sidney, or Edmund Ludlow would see even the events of 1649 to 1653 as a natural development, ruined only by Oliver's progressive turning back towards monarchy. Again, such memories seeped over generational boundaries as the recollections of participants in events shaped and filled the memories of their juniors. Much of the curate Abraham de la Pryme's distaste for 'the abominable wickedness of them times' derived not from personal knowledge (he was born in 1671) but from the interviews he had with veterans of the civil wars, royalist and roundhead, such as an aged former Cromwellian trooper who declared to Pryme that 'clergymen in his great master's days were no more esteem'd of than pedlars'.[131] His younger contemporary Thomas Sheridan held similarly Tory views derived from the memories of other people; he claimed to have repeatedly heard 'the memory of Cromwell . . . celebrated like that of a saint' and that of Charles I ridiculed 'and his murder justifyed even from the pulpit'.[132]

Cataclysms such as the civil wars directly affected large areas of the countryside and many towns which suffered siege or occupation. Consequently they would feature prominently in any old person's memories of the 1640s, though what was remembered is not always the expected: Mark Stoyle has noted, for instance, the tendency of royalist veterans to recall in later years minor skirmishes rather than the fixed battles celebrated by historians.[133] Moreover, the same vividness of memory might not hold for the events that preceded the wars. To the ordinary participants, or even the neutral onlookers and victims, short-term causes manifested principally in local events would assume greater significance than the longer-term political, religious, or economic influences identified by a Lucy Hutchinson or a James Harrington. It is hard to weigh the importance to a copyholder or urban artisan of the Petition of Right, or the scandals of James I's court, in attempting to make sense for himself of the events that unfolded from 1640 to 1660. He would very likely recall immediate, proximate developments, and especially religious change, which affected a broad cross-section of seventeenth-century society. The advent of Laudianism in a puritan parish, or a growth in local recusancy, or a decline in the enforcement of morals, for instance, would figure more prominently in many individuals' understanding of the causes of the war than news from the centre, notwithstanding that such news and rumours from London and abroad certainly circulated to the provinces.[134]

---

[131] *Diary of Abraham de la Pryme*, 84.

[132] *The Intelligencer*, 6 (18 June 1728), ed. J. Woolley (Oxford, 1992), 88.

[133] M. Stoyle, 'Memories of the Maimed: The Testimony of Charles I's Former Soldiers, 1660–1730', unpublished typescript. I am indebted to Mark Stoyle for allowing me to read this essay.

[134] See especially F. J. Levy, 'How Information Spread among the Gentry, 1550–1640', *Journal of British Studies*, 21 (1982), 11–34; A. J. Bellany, 'The Poisoning of Legitimacy? Court Scandal, News Culture and Politics in England', Ph.D. diss., Princeton University, 1995; Dr Bellany's published study, *The Politics of Court Scandal in Early Modern England: News Culture and the Overbury Affair, 1603–1666* (Cambridge and New York, 2002) appeared as the present work went to press.

The wider dissemination of news and the regularization of its flow beginning in the mid-seventeenth century would change this in some important respects: it created a public sphere of the present, and it pre-narrativized civil war events for readers as they unfolded, thereby facilitating the spread of political thinking among the army rank and file.[135] Even then, however, country labourers, craftsmen, and even some yeomen and minor gentry in the more remote parts of the kingdom would not necessarily have the same opportunity to observe and make sense of events at the centre as their urban counterparts.[136] It would be a mistake to judge them uniformly according to the standard of the highly articulate and perceptive London turner Nehemiah Wallington, and even he confessed to mystification as to the reasons why England was engaged in conflict with its former godly allies, the Scots. Unable to construct from his understanding of the recent past or his reading of newsbooks an explanation for this strange revolution in affairs, Wallington fell back on the ever-serviceable explanation through Providence.

And another warr did begin in goeing against Scotland in 1650 which I know not how to call it for brother did goe to warr against brother and so in 1653 we went to warr against our naighbor nation Holland for I know not what that much blood hath bine spilt upon land and sea. These warrs I cannot find any warrant for them, yet I am assured that all these seven yeers windings & turnnings and over turnings God is a doeing of grate things . . .[137]

This does not mean that the poorer sort of subjects, especially in the provinces, were without awareness of the past. Theirs may simply have been different. As Eric Hobsbawm has suggested for more recent times, those at the bottom end of society do not always have the same sense of events they have lived through as do elites, even when these events might seem to concern them. Modern oral historians have, for instance, been surprised to find that elderly workers' memories give the General Strike of 1926 relatively low prominence.[138] Within a local setting in early modern England, the further down the social scale one looks the

---

[135] D. R. Woolf, 'News, History and the Construction of the Present in early Modern England', in B. Dooley and S. Baron (eds.), *The Politics of Information in Early Modern Europe* (London and New York, 2001), 80–118. On the political implications of news in the period there is a growing literature, including: C. J. Sommerville, *The News Revolution in England: Cultural Dynamics of Daily Information* (New York, 1996); J. Raymond, *The Invention of the Newspaper: English Newsbooks, 1641–1649* (Oxford, 1996); Marshall, *Intelligence and Espionage in the Reign of Charles II*, 30, 60; S. C. A. Pincus, *Protestantism and Patriotism: Ideologies and the Making of English Foreign Policy, 1650–1668* (Cambridge, 1996), 276–88. I have also found helpful (though it does not adequately discuss the seventeenth century) the work on which many of these draw, J. Habermas, *The Structural Transformation of the Public Sphere: An Inquiry into a Category of Bourgeois Society*, trans. T. Burger with F. Lawrence (1st pub. 1962; Cambridge, Mass., 1989), 16, 21–2, 254 n.

[136] Levy, 'How Information Spread among the Gentry'; A. Fletcher, *The Outbreak of the English Civil War* (1981; repr. 1985), p. xxix: Fletcher's remark that 'no one outside London could hope to achieve more than a partial and incomplete view of the political process that led to civil war' primarily concerns the literate gentry, but this would clearly apply *a fortiori* to their poorer tenants and neighbours.

[137] Folger MS V.a.436 (Wallington's writing book, 1654), 177; P. Seaver, *Wallington's World: A Puritan Artisan in Seventeenth-Century London* (1985).

[138] Hobsbawm refers to this aspect of the popular memory as the 'Fabrice syndrome', after the hero of Stendhal's *Charterhouse of Parma*: E. J. Hobsbawm, introduction to *The Invention of Tradition*, ed. E. Hobsbawm and T. Ranger (Cambridge, 1983), 13.

less likely one is to find popular impressions of the recent or more remote past which are merely simplified reflections of the historical thought of the gentry and aristocracy.[139] Popular beliefs, village customs, and oral traditions concerning the manor are apt to occupy far more mental space—far more *memory*—than remote matters of state or foreign affairs, even among local educated worthies. In 1697, when Abraham de la Pryme returned to his native south Yorkshire fens, he was greeted with a five-year-old tale that was bandied about the parish as if it involved the death of a king. 'This day I heard for a certain truth, and there are many that will give their oaths upon it,' Pryme scribbled in his diary, 'that Tho[mas] Hill, fowler for Mr Ramsden, did shoot thirty-two pair of duck and teel at one shot in the Levels, in 1692–3.'[140] This purely local occurrence, trivial as it may seem, had as much significance in the community memory as any national event unfolding in distant London or in the war against France, its authenticity apparently worth swearing to.

Pryme's experience underlines the validity of Jan Vansina's comment, occasioned by the study of African tradition, that 'there is no such thing as a general "human memory"'. Children have different memories from adults, and, in most cultures, men from women, since *what* is remembered depends entirely on *how* information is encoded and catalogued.[141] This distinction can be extended from mere biological distinctions of age and sex to different societies, in which memory may play a more or less important role. Within a society such as that of early modern England, it is possible to distinguish various types of memory, since the ability to remember is not simply an innate human capacity, common to the species, but a variable determined by external circumstance, by factors such as class, social status, and gender, and by a community's overall construction of what is to be remembered. There is also no guarantee that individual members of the same social group will have the same memories, and some of the legal conflicts cited above suggest strongly that they did not. In this regard, Halbwachs's 'collective' memory again appears to be a useful tool, but one in need of sharpening.

Those persons who were privileged with the knowledge of how to read, a number that rose throughout the seventeenth century, had a key which allowed them to pass back and forth easily between their personal experiences and those of others living and dead.[142] The higher one moved up the social ladder, the greater the possible overlap between personal memory and memories of either the community or of society as a whole. The latter were contained principally in an ever-growing quantity of histories and other written or printed documents given official or at least orthodox status by the Crown, the Church, or simply the scholarly

---

[139] Halbwachs, *Les Cadres sociaux de la mémoire*, 301–26.

[140] *The Diary of Abraham de la Pryme*, 165.

[141] J. Vansina, 'Memory and Oral Tradition', in J. Miller (ed.), *The African Past Speaks* (Folkestone, England and Hamden, Conn., 1980), 264.

[142] The classic evaluation of literacy is D. Cressy, *Literacy and the Social Order: Reading and Writing in Tudor and Stuart England* (Cambridge, 1980). Cressy's estimates, based on ability to sign, have been challenged from various quarters. K. Thomas, 'The Meaning of Literacy', in G. Baumann (ed.), *The Written Word: Literacy in Transition* (Oxford, 1986), 97–131; cf. Fox, *Oral and Literate Culture*, 19–50.

community. At the lower levels of society, the ability to read and write gradually separated the population into those members of what is usually called the 'middling sort' who were able to gain access to the national past directly and 'interactively' (through reading and perhaps generating written texts or documents which over time have become part of the national heritage), and their own educational inferiors, whose participation was largely passive, through much more limited and selective reading, and even vicariously passive, through hearing others read or witnessing dramatized or ritualized versions of the past.

Not every variety of community memory could continue to thrive. Rural elites were able to maintain a distinctively local historical sense through such rituals as the feast sermons of the late Stuart period, even in the age of nascent 'British' identity.[143] The continued flourishing of provincial history-writing in the eighteenth century, principally in the hands of the clergy and gentry, is another manifestation of the ways in which the intervention of local worthies helped to preserve elements of community memory.[144] At the same time, countervailing forces also increased. Centralization of official commemoration—decisions on who was buried where, what statues were erected, and whose face or what image was engraved in books or on medals—continued to ensure the steady expansion of a highly selective national memory outside the boundaries of history books.[145] Today the historic monuments of England most commonly marketed to the tourist trade are either those in London (Nelson's Column, Poet's Corner, and the Tower) or those erected in localities to persons of national fame (Shakespeare's Birthplace). We speak now of the 'National' Heritage.[146]

---

[143] N. E. Key, 'The Localism of the County Feast in Late Stuart Political Culture', *Huntington Library Quarterly*, 58 (1996), 211–37. Newton Key's article attempts to strike a balance between the 'county community' school of Stuart historiography and its critics; it indirectly supplies some chiaroscuro to Linda Colley's account of common national interests in *Britons*. A further revision to Colley can be found in C. Kidd, *British Identities before Nationalism: Ethnicity and Nationhood in the Atlantic World 1600–1800* (Cambridge, 1999).

[144] Sweet, *The Writing of Urban Histories in Eighteenth-Century England*; J. Barry, 'Provincial Town Culture, 1640–1780: Urbane or Civic?', in J. H. Pittock and A. Wear (eds.), *Interpretation and Cultural History* (1991), 198–234.

[145] The modern eradication of the local and particular by the national and social is compellingly illustrated in an experiment conducted by the American historian Michael Frisch on students during the 1970s and 1980s. M. Frisch, 'American History and the Structures of Collective Memory: A Modest Exercise in Empirical Iconography', *Journal of American History*, 75 (1988–89), 1130–55. A useful analogy is provided by the selection of periods of American history for commemoration by Congress, which Barry Schwartz suggests chose to emphasize a few early figures of military and foundational significance (Washington and Jefferson for instance) and, for the post-US civil war period, many more persons whose fame lay principally in office-holding, thereby celebrating the republic's peaceful submission to government institutions. B. Schwartz, 'The Social Context of Commemoration: A Study in Collective Memory', *Social Forces*, 61 (1982), 374–402.

[146] There is no space here for an extended discussion of the later development of nationalism and of its relation to historical consciousness, but this has been well treated elsewhere; in addition to Colley, *Britons*, and Anderson, *Imagined Communities*, see G. Newman, *The Rise of English Nationalism: A Cultural History 1740–1830* (New York, 1987), which undervalues the sixteenth- and seventeenth-century background; and A. Hastings, *The Construction of Nationhood: Ethnicity, Religion and Nationalism* (Cambridge, 1997), which does not. Most recently, see R. Mitchell, *Picturing the Past: English History in Text and Image 1830–1870* (Oxford, 2000).

Over the course of the sixteenth and seventeenth centuries local culture was able to maintain its remembered past, though with difficulty. It had a much tougher time making itself heard, much less valued, in the annals of what in the eighteenth century became 'British History'. The establishment of this was closely related to the proliferation of the printed word. While the continued importance of scribal communication cannot be doubted,[147] the press proved to be a powerful engine in the creation and dissemination of a national master-narrative that largely excluded both the remembered and the local. Print accomplished this in ways that writing alone could not have done, just as, in the past fifty years, radio, film, television, and now the internet have in turn eroded literate activities and knowledge throughout much of the industrialized world. Local communities had operated comfortably with both documentary evidence and oral testimonial memory as complementary means of preserving and recovering their own past, since the late medieval period, even if the balance had been shifting in favour of the document. Print was not so easily accommodated. It could make its influence felt even where literacy remained low and it had a homogenizing effect on language and thought that mere writing could not achieve. As Adrian Hastings has recently observed, 'the effect of a relatively small increase in the number of books in a community which has, hitherto, had none or very few is far greater than people in a world used to a surfeit of books can easily realise, and it extends far beyond the literate'.[148]

The act of writing requires only a writer. It can take place in virtually any setting and reflect the most local, particular, and individual recollection of the past, from a parish register to a private diary; it does not even entail the existence of a reader beyond the author. The multiplicity and relative durability of print permits it to presume thousands of readers scattered across space and into the future. Print also requires concentrations of capital and a distribution network, both of which would be partially established by the middle of the sixteenth century and more or less fully in place by the early eighteenth.[149] Owing to improved distribution, and to publishing devices such as subscription or serialization for more expensive books, printed historical works emanating from London and the universities had a relatively easy arterial route into provincial towns and parishes, many of which were also developing libraries by the later seventeenth century.[150] The route back to the centre was much less easily travelled. Local documents, even less than local oral lore, do not as a matter of course leave their immediate surroundings; even less often are they absorbed into the national past. A resurgent neoclassical political history in the two centuries separating Clarendon from Macaulay would see to it that the documentary evidence so valued by Tudor heralds and antiquaries remained just that—documents applicable strictly to the

---

[147] H. Love, *Scribal Publication in Seventeenth-Century England* (Oxford, 1993).

[148] Hastings, *Construction of Nationhood*, 23.

[149] See the definitive treatment of the establishment of printing and publication networks in England in A. Johns, *The Nature of the Book: Print and Knowledge in the Making* (Chicago, 1998).

[150] D. R. Woolf, *Reading History in Early Modern England* (Cambridge, 2000), chs. 4 and 6.

local or familial past.[151] When such material appeared in print at all it was within the context of relatively small-run antiquarian works, subscription to which was often predominantly within a particular county; and these works themselves now had diminishing space for matters deriving from individual or community memories rather than from written sources.[152] In contrast, centrally printed newspapers, along with history books in various sizes and formats, brought with them homogenized and formalized versions of the recent or remote pasts respectively. These were absorbed into local culture through booksellers and local book-owners, and their contents repeated through conversation. In this sense, hearing remained a kind of proximate or vicarious literacy, and the printed past fed back into the oral discourse of provincial communities. As Adam Fox has written, there was already an appreciation by the mid-1600s that its inhabitants lived in 'a world defined and governed by texts'.[153]

In such a way did the neatly contained, printed past, sanctioned by the elite and preserved in its own histories, law-books, and proclamations, establish its cultural supremacy. This is true in spite of the scholarly argument over facts and sources that print enabled, and in spite of widespread ideological differences (religious, political, or simply intellectual) of interpretation. Both were endemic to literate communication about the past, and both featured routinely in published historical writing after 1640.[154] We should not confuse either arguments of fact or ideological disagreements about the moral or political significance of a historical event, however pronounced and even bitter these might be, with a much more profound incoherence between types of historical consciousness. Whether the Norman Conquest, Magna Carta, the civil war, or the Glorious Revolution were deemed good or bad, they were still accepted as major watersheds in the chronologically cast educated vision of history, and thereby established as major headings on an agenda for historical discourse in ensuing centuries. Discussions of the character, actions, and significance of William I, Henry VIII, or Cromwell

---

[151] Restoration and Augustan narrative historiography has been poorly served in comparison with the Tudor and early Stuart era, or the period from Hume onwards; that deficit is now remedied in part by P. Hicks, *Neoclassical History and English Culture from Clarendon to Hume* (New York and London, 1996); cf. L. Okie, *Augustan Historical Writing: Histories of England in the English Enlightenment* (Lanham, Md., 1991).

[152] The marginalization of the local that began in the sixteenth century would continue until very recently. It is only in the last few decades that historians have begun to restore local sources, once the preserve of provincial antiquarian societies, to the scholarly centre, making them again the foundation for generalizations about national history, both political and social. In a sense, historians of the past thirty years have reintegrated multiple community pasts into the national past and thereby begun to reverse the general trend of the past four centuries. This trend has not been without criticism from proponents of a basic curriculum in history that concentrates on the political and national, and tells the familiar story of the rise of Britain to greatness.

[153] Fox, *Oral and Literate Culture*, 298.

[154] On the genesis of multiple historical perspectives in the seventeenth century, see my earlier book, *The Idea of History in Early Stuart England: Erudition, Ideology and the 'Light of Truth' from the Accession of James I to the Civil War* (Toronto, 1990), ch. 8. For later seventeenth-century controversies, see J. A. I. Champion, *The Pillars of Priestcraft Shaken: The Church of England and its Enemies, 1660–1730* (Cambridge, 1992), chs. 2 and 3.

may vary widely in their conclusions, but they remain discourse about rulers and national affairs.

The process whereby a social memory that is more than the sum of its parts swallows up the community streams which feed it is one of co-option, not of ruthless oppression. It is not very helpfully viewed through Marxist-Bakhtinian lenses which would construe it as a straightforward triumph of an elite culture of education and capitalism over a suppressed popular culture of labour and artisanship. Antonio Gramsci's concept of hegemony may be more useful in explaining how villagers and townsmen were able to hang on to a significant portion of their beliefs about the past, even in the face of mounting antiquarian scepticism and the rising tide of printed historical material.[155] Just as innkeepers, bricklayers, and ploughmen had adapted themselves to antiquarian acquisitiveness by becoming active participants in the 'archaeological economy', so they were able to accommodate the parallel interests of historians in recounting their memories of the historical past. That being said, full literacy mattered, since with education and the ability to write as well as read came the potential to add to the pool of historical literature as well as to read or hear it. To put it another way, even if they were fortunate enough to acquire the necessary literate skills to gain 'read-only' access to the social memory, most people below the level of the gentry were excluded from making an active contribution to it, at least prior to the mass literacy of the nineteenth century.[156] At the same time, the historical memories of their betters, the linear, periodized, and chronological vision of the past created by a tiny percentage of the population, steadily encroached on local memory and threatened to 'overwrite' the shared heritage of their immediate community.[157]

CONCLUSION

This chapter has explored several different aspects of memory in early modern English culture, so it may be helpful to restate the main points, which bear on the argument of the remainder of the book. Memory taken as a mental faculty was an indispensable feature of human social existence, as it had been

---

[155] T. J. Jackson Lears, 'The Concept of Cultural Hegemony: Problems and Possibilities', *American Historical Review*, 90 (1985), 567–93; J. Joll, *Antonio Gramsci* (1977), 128–33; T. Nemeth, *Gramsci's Philosophy: A Critical Study* (Sussex and New Jersey, 1980), 142–4; W. L. Adamson, *Hegemony and Revolution: A Study of Antonio Gramsci's Political and Cultural Theory* (Berkeley, 1980), 170–4.

[156] Of the effects of nineteenth-century literacy David Vincent has commented, 'However dense and fascinating they might be, the memories of elderly relatives and neighbours were ultimately confined by place and period. To the listeners who now had the chance to become readers, the chief attraction of written history was its sheer otherness . . . At the same time, those who gained the confidence to wield a pen had the opportunity to become producers as well as consumers of history.' D. Vincent, *Literacy and Popular Culture: England 1750–1914* (Cambridge, 1989), 187.

[157] On the concept of overwriting in memory, defined as 'the erasure of information in store by the entry of new information that possesses similar sensory characteristics', see J. M. Gardiner and V. H. Gregg, 'When Auditory Memory is Not Overwritten', *Journal of Verbal Learning and Verbal Behaviour*, 18 (1979), 705–19, at p. 707; Lowenthal, *The Past is a Foreign Country*, 206–10.

during antiquity and the Middle Ages, and as it remains in somewhat different ways today. The growth in literacy and the proliferation of written records represented both a boon and a threat to memory of which Renaissance commentators were acutely conscious. By the end of the seventeenth century, there were fewer contexts in which unaided memory alone could be deemed definitive of truth, though it retained authority in local disputes about custom and traditional practices for which no documentary alternative was available. A far greater reliance on documents and attention to their proper preservation can be observed, even if the documents themselves were not immune to falsification.

With respect to the sense of the past, relations between the remembered and the written evolved in a direction that over the longer term would prove homogenizing and centrifugal. The tendency to locate historical authenticity in the written document was complemented by the parallel emergence in learned culture of what amounted to a national historical master-narrative. This was predominantly disseminated in print and underpinned by a national calendar of celebrations as well as by monuments and historic sites, either old or new. These phenomena would have an impact on the maintenance of local memories, whether oral or written. Neither the speed nor the scope of this should be overstated: local memory may have been modified and even marginalized by print and writing, but it was certainly not obliterated. As the next two chapters illustrate, there also remained opportunities for exchanges between the spoken and the written, and for interaction between 'popular' perceptions of the past and antiquarian scholarship, though these were now hedged in with scepticism and often outright disapproval.

Maurice Halbwachs certainly erred in equating written history with a monolithic and unitary vision of the past, and in identifying collective memories with both orality and a plurality of views. Notwithstanding such oversimplifications, there is much in Halbwachs, and in more recent studies of social memory, that is useful in understanding how a national narrative of history, the central elements of which commanded broad acceptance, had crystallized by about 1700, and how that narrative interacted with local memory. 'History', Halbwachs wrote in one of the more compelling passages of his last book, 'resembles a crowded cemetery, where room must constantly be made for new tombstones.'[158] In seventeenth-century England, amid accelerating change and unpredictable breaks with the past, room was made, and in various corners of the cemetery. It was made in the world of ritual, as national holidays intruded themselves on local consciousness, and many traditional celebrations gave way to the anniversaries examined by Professors Cressy and Hutton.[159] It was scooped out, too, in popular perceptions of the past, as the episodes and personalities remembered would

---

[158] Halbwachs, *Collective Memory*, 52.

[159] Cressy, *Bonfires and Bells*; Hutton, *Rise and Fall of Merry England*. Ritual was used by civic authorities in the Augustan era to create a certain type of popular memory in the form of the celebration of events such as royal visits, to which public monuments were often created in commemoration: P. Borsay, *The English Urban Renaissance: Culture and Society in the Provincial Town 1660–1770* (Oxford, 1989), 241.

increasingly be derived from national rather than local tradition. The chivalric hero Guy of Warwick by no means disappeared from the popular imagination, or even from printed literature, but he yielded pride of place as a historical figure to Guy Fawkes. The straw figures burned on 5 November are an invented tradition that have arguably no more firm connection with historical reality than the Dane-slaying warrior of ballad and legend. What makes Guy Fawkes more prominent in English consciousness than Guy of Warwick is not just the gunpowder plotter's historicity but also his identification with a powerful public mythology of the divine preservation of English Protestantism from popery. This in turn is a significant component of a national historical memory which was certainly experienced locally but which transcended specifically local beliefs about the past.[160] The nature of these beliefs forms a subject in its own right, as does the process whereby they came to be purged from history and exiled to the realm of romance, legend, and vulgar error.

---

[160] D. Cressy, 'The Fifth of November Remembered', in R. Porter (ed.), *Myths of the English* (Cambridge, 1992), 68–90. Later ages found non-religious uses for Guy and his day (first so-called in the early nineteenth century) as an occasion for social protest and misrule, leaving even the association with the original plot far behind; such events were clearly inspired by local conflicts as much as by national politics, but Guy himself was by that time a national, not a local, legend.

CHAPTER NINE

Popular Beliefs about the Past

AMONG THE POPULAR beliefs that one is likely to find in any society there is usually a significant component concerning the past. A curiosity as to one's own origins and the origins of one's material surroundings is not the exclusive prerogative of literate societies, and still less of the educated elite in those societies. Oral traditions form a large part of the popular discourse about the past in sixteenth- and seventeenth-century communities, urban and rural. The character and range of these traditions, the changing attitudes of those who recorded them to both the speakers and the speech, and their eventual decline as a historical source, offer a special set of questions, to be addressed in the next chapter. Although the subject matter makes some overlap inevitable, the principal aim of the present chapter is more descriptive than explanatory: it will illustrate a variety of popular beliefs about the past conveyed in various forms from the end of the Middle Ages to the early eighteenth century. The word 'popular' is here taken to mean 'widely held' within a broad cross-section of society. This cross-section generally included the middling and poorer elements of a community, but it might (especially in a local setting) embrace members of an educated elite that was, nevertheless, increasingly disposed to be critical of 'vulgar error'.

PROBLEMS IN THE STUDY OF POPULAR BELIEFS

Although incidental references to popular beliefs about the past occur quite commonly, the most illuminating modern study of the subject is relatively brief.[1] The subject of popular beliefs in general is fraught with difficulties. What sorts of belief count as 'popular'? Where can they be found? If a belief finds its way into the written mythology of the elite, does it cease to be popular? To what degree

---

[1] K. Thomas, *The Perception of the Past in Early Modern England* (Creighton Lecture, 1983). The existence, even by 1700, of a rigid division between elite and popular (or 'learned' and 'unlearned') cultures now appears an untenable oversimplification, given the ample evidence of transference of beliefs and practices up and down the social ladder throughout the period in oral discourse, artefacts, and cheap print media: for some of the problems involved in studying 'popular' literature, see T. Watt, *Cheap Print and Popular Piety, 1550–1640* (Cambridge, 1991), 14, 144, 212–14. For more general treatments of the relations between popular and elite culture in the context of a centralizing state, see G. Lottes, 'Popular Culture and the Early Modern State in 16th Century Germany', in S. L. Kaplan (ed.), *Understanding Popular Culture: Europe from the Middle Ages to the Nineteenth Century* (Berlin, New York, and Amsterdam, 1984), 147–88; T. Harris, 'Problematising Popular Culture', in id. (ed.), *Popular Culture in England, c.1500–1850* (1995), 1–27.

can popular beliefs current today be traced back to more remote periods? Can the literary media such as ballads and chapbooks that contain familiar stories and songs really be deemed 'popular'?

Transmission poses a particular set of problems. Because the reliable evidence derives overwhelmingly from the communication of such beliefs to contemporary literate recorders, the issue arises whether the local informants who passed them on to travellers and local worthies actually said what they are alleged to have said. This question was largely ignored in folkloric studies conducted during the nineteenth and early twentieth centuries. The authors of these chose simply to preserve, describe, and categorize tales, fables, and traditions that survived up to their own time, generally without much attention to their specific context, the reasons why they might have been preserved, or the social, religious, and moral functions that they served. The focus has principally been on tracing their direct descent back to a particular time, with priority given to oral transmission.[2] As Kenneth H. Jackson observed several decades ago, students of folklore (often still working under the influence of James Frazer's classic, *The Golden Bough*) have also overlooked the fact that in highly industrialized countries such as England, the purely oral folktale has for some time been 'all but extinct'. What survive are anecdotes, jokes, and sayings rather than full-fledged tales. Furthermore, folklorists, in contrast to historians of print culture, have tended to discount the enormous impact of cheap print on oral communication.[3]

[2] J. Simpson, 'The Local Legend: A Product of Popular Culture', *Rural History*, 2 (1991), 25–35, esp. p. 32. There are many collections on modern folklore, some of which do contain material on beliefs about the past. Henry Bett's *English Myths and Traditions* (1952), is one example, together with its earlier companion, *English Legends* (London and New York, 1950). It would seem best right at the outset to point out the problems involved in using modern folklore collections as sources for early modern beliefs. The literature on folk tales is vast and informative: the best place to begin is with G. Cocchiara, *Storia del folklore in Europa* (Turin, 1971), trans. J. N. McDaniel as *The History of Folklore in Europe* (Philadelphia, 1981). For England (and Wales and Scotland) a useful summary of the principal tales and their variants may be found in K. M. Briggs, *A Dictionary of British Folk-Tales in the English Language*, 2 pts. in 4 vols. (1971), and numerous other works by this author. Like most of its nineteenth- and twentieth-century sources, Briggs's compilation is concerned with the current form of the tale, not its historical roots. Many of the surviving tales which it cites can indeed be found in the sixteenth and seventeenth centuries, though in simpler form; many others, however, are of later origin. There is also, particularly in the historical traditions of vol. iiB, a greater sense of time and place—a more fully worked out sense of chronology—than can be found in most of the traditions recorded by antiquaries and others between 1500 and 1700. I have therefore felt free to draw upon the findings of Briggs and modern folklorists, but have not normally discussed a specific tale or legend unless it has a documentable early modern source. An additional problem, most notable in Bett's account but endemic to nearly the entire folkloric approach, are the naive, almost romantic, assumptions that those popular traditions which exist today necessarily date far back in time, and that the pressures of social memory ensure their preservation unchanged over centuries. An example of a popular but more critical approach, that recognizes the impact that excavation and antiquarian investigation may have had in actually creating or seriously distorting popular beliefs, is the reference book by J. Westwood, *Albion: A Guide to Legendary Britain* (1985). This covers some of the same material included here. Its usefulness is restricted by inconsistent documentation and, as with Bett and Briggs, a complete absence of attention to the social context in which such beliefs emerge, survive, and become both transmittable and mutable.

[3] K. H. Jackson, *The International Popular Tale and Early Welsh Tradition* (Cardiff, 1961), 3, 29. John Aubrey was among the first to notice the decline of the folk tale; for his views see Ch. 10 below.

The subset of popular beliefs pertaining specifically to the past can be found in virtually any context, from urban rituals and ceremonies that mark observation of the calendar to writings on such subjects as agriculture and medicine. They include jocular or ribald anecdotes (frequently attached to the name of a famous person) concerning the origins of certain customs.[4] One can also find cautionary tales involving the downfall of the greedy or the criminal, high or low (not unlike the *Mirror for Magistrates* or Beard's *Theatre of Gods Judgment*, but frequently with a derisive, humorous aspect lacking in those fundamentally serious works). Since the vast majority of those of which we are aware come from written sources, the extent to which they were shared by the illiterate remains open to serious question. Even if we accept that our literate informants (travellers, antiquaries, vicars, and local worthies) were reporting tales truthfully as they heard them, there remains the possibility that any story may have been scrambled or distorted in the telling by something so simple as differing language or dialect, by the listener's misunderstanding of the facial or bodily gestures of the teller, or by a failure to grasp the purpose that an explanation might serve in a local community. The sense of an absence of chronology, and of a past conceived of and related according to location rather than date, arises from many of the beliefs related below. This may derive in part from a bias in our learned sources, but it also conforms to the place-oriented character of local memory, custom, and prescription.[5]

But distortion can come from several points along the line of transmission. If the educated tended to record what they wished to hear, there is the corresponding likelihood that some of their humble informants were willing to tailor responses to the occasion, improvising details on the spot even if the general outlines of a story remained more widely accepted.[6] Divining the depth of actual popular *belief* in a tale, for instance, about the origins of a local well or the builder of a medieval church is a problem for which such sources as these will give us little help. As Paul Veyne has noted in a different context, the word ' "believe" means so many things'. In the present discussion, the word 'believe' should be taken in the sense of 'professed to believe' or 'signified assent to the statement that . . .'.[7] The fact that most of these stories have come to us through the mediation of a

[4] See, for instance, the seventeenth-century account of the origins of the beadle's cry 'Hang out your lanterns and candle-light', which ascribes this to the literal-mindedness of one Master Hobson who, in the mid-sixteenth century, responded to the formerly used cry of 'Hang out your lantern' by putting out an empty lantern: Briggs, *Dictionary of British Folk-Tales*, A.II, p. 169.
[5] E. P. Thompson, *Customs in Common* (New York, 1993), 98; B. Bushaway, *By Rite: Custom Ceremony and Community in England 1700–1880* (1982).
[6] Recent Africanist writing on oral literature similarly warns that much of it is performative and inventive, rather than strictly recitative and remembered verbatim. See especially the comments of Ruth Finnegan, *Oral Literature in Africa* (Oxford, 1970), 14–15; ead., 'Transmission in Oral and Written Traditions: Some General Comments', in her *Literacy and Orality: Studies in the Technology of Communication* (Oxford, 1988), 139–74. Cf. the introduction to A. Fox and D. Woolf (eds.), *The Spoken Word: Oral Culture in Britain, 1500–1850* (Manchester, 2002), 1–51.
[7] P. Veyne, *Did the Greeks Believe in their Myths? An Essay in the Constitutive Imagination*, trans. P. Wissing (Chicago and London, 1988), 1, 5–16, 27–57. My formulation of 'belief' thus follows closely that in S. Shapin, *A Social History of Truth* (Chicago, 1994), p. xxiii.

learned informant necessitates further caution. John Van Maanen has warned, from the perspective of anthropological fieldwork, that 'The difference between what was said and what was heard or meant can often be very great.'[8] We cannot rule out the possibility, indeed the likelihood, that many of the gentry and clergy who recorded contemporary beliefs about the past may have misunderstood what they were told, or that they may even have been told things that their own inform-ants thought they might wish to hear: stories, no less than old coins, were a kind of cultural currency. The degree to which the informants themselves *literally* believed in the stories they told is unmeasurable, but it may be observed that degrees of belief between absolute acceptance and firm rejection are possible, depending upon both the 'believer' and the subject: a child and a parent may not believe in Santa Claus or the Tooth Fairy in the same way, though both discuss the subject, and the child itself will have a different level of belief in Santa than in the reality of more observable persons and objects. Similarly, the socially superior remained notably ambivalent towards popular culture, rather than unequivocally hostile, even at the end of our period. A decision to record or transmit a particular oral report or to collect a ballad may signal partial belief as much as the half-doubt of learned scepticism. At the very least, we should acknowledge that a willing-ness to convey information, and even to profess a wish to believe it, is not incompatible with an inclination on the part of the learned to put some distance between themselves and the sources of that information—thereby simultaneously registering an affiliation with their own social and cultural peers, and with the considerably smaller scholarly community. It was, in short, possible for both parties in this cultural dialogue to eat the cake of popular belief and have doubts about it too.

There is considerable, if qualified, support in recent historiography for the notion that elite and popular cultures began to grow apart between the late sixteenth and early eighteenth centuries; it has been a recurring theme of this book that historical knowledge became sensitive to social stratification during this period in ways that it had not been previously. This, too, is a matter of degrees, and not absolutes. One cannot deny that many popular beliefs were fostered, nurtured, revised, and passed down, in either oral or written form, as a result of intercourse between various segments and levels of society. Certain types of belief retained currency at all levels of society long after others had been marginalized as the errors of the vulgar and ignorant. Moreover, other factors than literacy or social status could intrude to encourage the creation and dissemination of some sorts of belief within particular segments of society. Geography was one such influ-ence. Urban tales are often distinguishable from rural ones in content and volatility (the speed at which they are spread and their geographical range). Even within a rural context, differing local agrarian economies—David Underdown's 'chalk' and 'cheese'—will give rise to social arrangements that are more or less conducive to the exchange of traditional tales and stories. These are more easily

---

[8] J. Van Maanen, *Tales of the Field* (Chicago, 1988), 70.

communicated in areas where populations labour in close proximity, or at least have regular meeting places such as the common field, the mill or the alehouse, than in less densely populated pastoral communities in which larger meetings might be confined to church functions, tithing days, and leet court sessions.[9]

This is also true further up the social ladder. The nation's aristocratic, gentry, clerical, and commercial elites did not form a monolithic social block, any more than did their subordinates. There existed notable divisions between laity and clergy, between gentry and aristocracy, and between all of these and the so-called 'middling sort'. In the eighteenth century, outwardly an era of greater political and economic stability than the seventeenth, these fissures continued to be cross-cut with divisions over religion and, increasingly, party. Here again, geography played a significant role in determining the contours of both experience and attitude. The landowner who has spent little time outside his own manor or shire may be more apt to listen to and share in local beliefs and traditions than his more sophisticated London-going cousin.

Locality, in fact, was a potent force behind the creation of new historical traditions and the preservation of some older ones throughout the sixteenth and seventeenth centuries, even at a time of increasing cultural pressure from the centre.[10] The Reformation effected a major adjustment in the division of the calendar year, removing many of the sacred rituals that had been the hallmark of civic and parochial life, while adding newer annual celebrations of historical events, such as accession days.[11] Other practices survived intact, at least for a while, such as the Ascensiontide ritual of beating the bounds. This established and annually proclaimed to the contiguous world the frontiers of a parish, for economic as well as symbolic reasons.[12] The perambulation asserted parochial control over those things that lay within, and defended parishioners against incurring, in the absence of precise surveys, responsibility for foreign paupers, or for the repair of

---

[9] D. Underdown, *Revel, Riot and Rebellion* (Oxford, 1985).

[10] For the role of locality and its relation to national history in Habsburg Spain, see R. L. Kagan, 'Clio and the Crown: Writing History in Habsburg Spain', in R. L. Kagan and G. Parker, *Spain, Europe and the Atlantic World: Essays in Honour of John H. Elliott* (Cambridge, 1995), 73–99. The significance of place in early modern Italy is well studied in D. Cosgrove, 'Power and Place in the Venetian Territories', in J. A. Agnew and J. S. Duncan (eds.), *The Power of Place: Bringing Together Geographical and Sociological Imaginations* (Boston, 1989), 104–23; E. Muir and R. F. E. Weissman, 'Social and Symbolic Places in Renaissance Venice and Florence', ibid. 81–103.

[11] D. Cressy, *Bonfires and Bells: National Memory and the Protestant Calendar in Elizabethan and Stuart England* (Berkeley and London, 1989); R. Hutton, *The Rise and Fall of Merry England: The Ritual Year, 1400–1700* (Oxford and New York, 1994).

[12] The link adumbrated in earlier chapters between antiquarianism and a strong sense of local space is thus not coincidental, and is explicitly developed for Spain in Kagan, 'Clio and the Crown', 84–5. The earliest county chorography, by William Lambarde, was entitled *The Perambulation of Kent* (1576; 2nd edn. 1596). Elizabethan and early Stuart contributions to the genre were invariably called either descriptions or, more commonly, 'surveys', the works of John Norden in the 1590s, for instance, being the work of a professional surveyor. Only in the mid-seventeenth century, with massive tomes such as Dugdale's *Antiquities of Warwickshire Illustrated* (1656), did the close connection of the genre with its roots in local documents, and in ceremonies of spatial definition, become less prominent. The previous usage continued, however, in the 'natural history' genre of authors such as Robert Plot and Charles Leigh.

buildings, roads, and bridges that had not traditionally fallen to their charge.[13] Since it conserved the boundaries of a space that had been defined time out of mind, it was also a repetitive rite of communication between the young, the aged, and the dead, the present and the past, paying heed to the biblical injunction 'Do not move the ancient boundary-stone which your forefathers set up' (Prov. 22: 28).

That the seventeenth century produced county and estate maps in greater numbers than previously was similarly a consequence of a need to ensure the accurate preservation of familial and parochial boundaries beyond a living generation, a need all the more pressing in the face of a volatile land market and of cataclysmic events like the civil war, which caused the destruction of many traditional landmarks.[14] Such was the explanation for one rector's codification of his Essex parish's boundaries at the end of the century. 'In the time of the long Rebellion the landmarcks of our parish were cut downe, and it would be difficult for posterity to find out the proper precincts which our parish are incompassed withal', wrote Robert Poole of Belchamp Otten, who was himself adding a perambulation to the parochial accounts in his keeping 'that this may be a memorial to posterity' and thereby prevent future litigation.[15] Local communities sometimes had long-standing ceremonies that were intimately tied to their sense of identity and tradition, beyond routine institutional practices such as manorial courts or vestry meetings. In early modern times the village of Dunmow held an annual ceremony whereby a couple who could take an oath that they had not quarrelled for three years and a day would be solemnly presented with a side of bacon (the Dunmow 'flitch'). This occurred at a particular place, namely 'the two great stones lying near the church door within the said mannor' and the ritual appears to have been sporadic rather than continuous.[16] Durability and continuity were often illusory. At Barnstaple the traveller Peter Mundy saw a large stone 'made uppe in the manner off a tombe, 3 foot high', which according to a few letters on it had been a tombstone 'aboutt 200 yeares since, itt serving now as I was told to pay or tender mony theron uppon tills, bonds, etts.; allsoe to seale writings, covenantts, etts'. In fact, this was really the 'town stone', erected that very year; it still had the names of three merchants on its rim, which Mundy mistook for a funeral inscription.[17]

[13] A. Fox, *Oral and Literate Culture in England 1500–1700* (Oxford, 2000), 268–70.

[14] P. D. A. Harvey, 'English Estate Maps: Their Early History and their Use as Historical Evidence', in D. Buisseret (ed.), *Rural Images: Estate Maps in the Old and New World* (Chicago, 1996), 27–61.

[15] Essex RO D/DU 441/96 (Belchamp Otten parish accounts, 1700–1), pp. 22–3.

[16] Essex RO D/DCm Z19, fo. 42 (oath of 27 June 1701); Wanley, *Letters*, 393 (Wanley to William Holman, 30 Mar. 1719), on the subject of the Dunmow ritual. On the oath, which apparently dated to Norman times, see Philip Morant, *The History and Antiquities of the County of Essex*, 2 vols. (1763–68), ii. 429; the last incident of receiving the flitch in Morant's time was 20 June 1751. The ritual in fact appears to have been sporadic before then: originally connected to the priory of Dunmow it was then adopted by the Court Baron after the priory's dissolution. For its revival in the nineteenth century, when it was the subject of a novel by W. H. Ainsworth, see R. Mitchell, *Picturing the Past: English History in Text and Image 1830–1870* (Oxford, 2000), 98.

[17] *The Travels of Peter Mundy in Europe and Asia 1608–1667*, vol. iv, ed. R. C. Temple, Hakluyt Soc., 2nd ser., 55 (1925), 2–3.

In addition to geography and social status, gender was an important (and under-studied) influence on the creation and spread of stories about the past.[18] It is significant, for instance, that the tales told by male informants to learned listeners who were also predominantly male often involve notions of masculinity. They recall great deeds, chivalric or military settings and the frequent presence of a pivotal hero or rogue, whether a community figure or a character appropriated from learned culture, like Arthur or Hercules. Where we know the sex of inform-ants to have been female (a detail not often specified by travellers), domestic themes of love, courtship or seduction, birth, family, and death are more prominent, some-thing that appears to be a feature of some non-Western cultures as well. This conforms with the discussion above concerning the prominence of women as repositories of genealogical knowledge. It also fits with Susan Amussen's sugges-tions about the ways in which gender differences overlay social disparities within local communities. The apparent lack of interest of women in tales of violence may reflect an ambivalent attitude to a popular culture that was highly misogy-nistic and often physically abusive to females, while at the same time they bought into another aspect of that culture by retailing accounts of courtship and mar-riage that were remarkably conventional in their values.[19]

Ghost stories offer a good example of a type of belief frequently associated prin-cipally with women at all social levels, not merely the village 'old wife'. Joseph Addison was only exaggerating a widespread perception among male literati when he wrote of having heard, one winter's night, 'several young girls of the neigh-bourhood sitting about the fire with my land-lady's daughters, and telling stor-ies of spirits and apparitions'. While sitting and pretending to read, Addison overheard 'several dreadful stories of ghosts as pale as ashes that had stood at the feet of a bed, or walked over a church-yard by moon-light . . . with many other old womens fables of the like nature'.[20] Ghost stories often had familial associ-ations and were as frequently passed down among the gentry as among their

---

[18] There is significant support for the existence of a gender division in folkloric culture outside England, especially in parts of India. J. B. Flueckiger notes the dominance of a female world-view, complete with diminution of martial and heroic aspects, in certain oral genres such as the central Indian *candaini* which have increasingly attracted female performers: *Gender and Genre in the Folklore of Middle India* (Ithaca, NY and London, 1996), 148–50. Cf. V. N. Rao, 'A Ramayana of their Own: Women's Oral Tradition in Telagu', in P. Richman (ed.) *Many Ramayanas: The Diversity of a Narrative Tradition in South Asia* (Berkeley and Los Angeles, 1991), 114–36; A. K. Ramanujan, 'Two Problems of Kannada Folklore', in S. H. Blackburn and A. K. Ramanajan (eds.), *Another Harmony: New Essays on the Folklore of India* (Berkeley, Los Angeles and London, 1986), 41–75. With regard to England this issue is addressed in my article, 'A Feminine Past? Gender, Genre and Historical Knowledge in England, 1500–1800', *American Historical Review*, 102 (1997), 645–79.

[19] S. D. Amussen, 'The Gendering of Popular Culture in Early Modern England', in Harris, *Popular Culture in England*, 48–68; S. H. Mendelson and P. Crawford, *Women in Early Modern England, 1550–1720* (Oxford, 1998), 59; G. Bennett, 'Tales my Mother Told Me: The Relevance of Oral History', in T. Buckland and J. Wood (eds.), *Aspects of British Calendar Customs* (Sheffield, 1993), 96–103, for female emphasis on the calendar and repeated rituals.

[20] Joseph Addison in *The Spectator*, 12 (14 Mar. 1711), ed. D. F. Bond, 5 vols. (Oxford, 1965), i. 53. The stories that amused one of Addison's admirers, the future judge Dudley Ryder, told by his grand-mother, may also have concerned ghosts: *The Diary of Dudley Ryder 1715–1716*, ed. W. Matthews (1939), 37.

inferiors. When staying with Lady Honora O'Brien in Ireland in 1650, Ann Fanshawe was warned by her hostess, whose cousin had recently died, that it was

the custome of this place that when any dye of the family, there is the shape of a woman appears in this window every night untill they be dead. This woman was many ages agoe got with child by the owner of this place, and he in his garden murdered her and flung her into the river under your window.[21]

Such tales, or at least the telling of them, maintained their popularity among segments of the clergy and gentry long after the end of the seventeenth century, as readers of Washington Irving and Emily Brontë will know, despite the increasing scepticism of the most highly educated and the official hostility of the Church. In the case just cited, Lady O'Brien took the well-known Irish folk myth of the banshee and made it more 'real' for her non-Irish guest by attaching it specifically to her own house and family, and to a subject both women could comprehend, the not uncommon ordeal of a young woman impregnated by her master.[22]

RELIGION AND POPULAR BELIEF

The impact of religious change on popular belief was undeniably profound yet highly complicated and uneven. Many popular beliefs had a religious aspect that defied external events such as the Reformation. The citizens of late Tudor Halifax claimed that their town was originally named Horton and that its modern name derived from the 'hali-fex' (holy hair) of a murdered virgin. Many believed that Halifax was also the burial place of the head of John the Baptist, a tradition acknowledged and perpetuated by town authorities in the borough's corporate seal.[23] Such stories often had Catholic, or even magical, overtones which offended more puritanical sensibilities from the mid-sixteenth century on. George Owen, the late Elizabethan lord of the manor of Kemes, Pembrokeshire, was struck how 'all the inhabitantes, both younge and old' affirmed that the parish of Whitchurch had been free of adders for generations; a similar belief existed in the parish of St David and was ascribed to that familiar nemesis of serpents, St Patrick.[24] A succession of antiquaries, from John Leland at the beginning of the

---

[21] *The Memoirs of Anne, Lady Halkett, and Ann, Lady Fanshawe*, ed. J. Loftis (Oxford, 1979), 125.

[22] At Huddington House in Worcestershire, seat of the Wintour or Winter family, there has been since the early seventeenth century a superstition about 'Lady Wintour's walk', in front of the house, haunted by the ghost of Gertrude, wife of Robert Winter of Huddington (one of three brothers executed after the Gunpowder Plot). The house had been used to collect arms and horses for the intended rising in 1605 of Worcestershire Catholics. Gertrude had watched for messengers and instantly knew all was lost when she saw them; her spectre has since then haunted the walk: *The Chronicle of the English Augustinian Canonesses Regular of the Lateran, at St Monica's in Louvain*, ed. Dom A. Hamilton, 2 vols. (Edinburgh, 1904–6), i. 182–4.

[23] William Camden, *Britain*, trans. P. Holland (1610), 692; *The Place-names of the West Riding of Yorkshire*, English Place-Name Soc., vol. 32, p. 3 (Cambridge, 1961), 104.

[24] George Owen of Kemes, *The Description of Penbrokeshire*, ed. H. Owen, 2 vols. in 4, Cymmrodorion Record Series (1892–1936), i. 250 and n. The falchion or short sword of Sir John Conyers (d. 1396) of Sockburn, Durham, was believed in the early seventeenth century to have been used by this knight to kill a 'monstrous venomd & poisond wiverne Ask or worme': Weston, *Albion*, 341–2.

sixteenth century to John Aubrey at the end of the seventeenth, repeat the story of the salt wells at Droitwich, Worcestershire, which had supposedly dried up in the Middle Ages and been saved through the intercession of a thirteenth-century saint (Richard de la Wiche, bishop of Chichester, 1244–53).[25] The clerical sensibilities of one fellow of the Royal Society, Bishop William Nicolson, were offended by the superstitions of borderers, 'who are much better acquainted with, and do more firmly believe, their old legendary stories of fairies and witches, then the articles of their Creed'.[26] Though he disapproved of such tales, Nicolson at least attempted to explain their origins; he suspected that they derived from pagan myths going back to the Danish invasions, and suggested parallels between the oral traditions and the legends mentioned in runic inscriptions.

Conversely, religious doctrine might be rendered more accessible to a popular audience through the dramatization of biblical episodes, which for contemporaries were more familiar historical landmarks than the Norman Conquest or Magna Carta. The records of early drama are full of such performances, and despite the increasing orientation of English religion to written and printed media at the expense of more traditional forms, there is ample evidence that they survived as part of a broad-based culture. The division of sacred from 'civil' history, so tidily laid out in the early seventeenth-century *artes historicae*, was little more than a taxonomical literary convention among historians, and not even universally accepted there. Outside the boundaries of history books, in the worlds of the oral, the theatrical, and the visual, it could not prevent the intermingling of episodes from the Bible with those from classical, medieval, or recent history.[27] Ballads well illustrate this mix. One printed by Henry Gosson tells the biblical tale of the judgement of Solomon, with the king and the two 'harlots', depicted in seventeenth-century clothing, looking on as a swordsman dangles the disputed infant below his blade. Another ballad recounts the story of Jonah and the whale, depicted in an ocean-going vessel worthy of Drake, and ending with a general call for repentance.[28] Preachers, too, would commonly appeal to a wide variety of episodes from

[25] John Aubrey, *Remains of Gentilisme and Judaisme*, ed. James Britten (1881), 33, 71, 203; Underdown, *Revel, Riot and Rebellion*, 259. Wells abounded with historical, legendary, and pseudomagical associations: according to those who lived near Fotheringay Castle in the early eighteenth century, a nearby well made drumlike noises 'as a presage of some strange event, or alteration, which will happen in the kingdom', having recently done so at the death of George I. BL MS Add. 15776 (travel notes of Jeremiah Milles, *c.*1735–43), fo. 83ʳ.

[26] Royal Society, *The Philosophical Transactions and Collections, to the End of the Year 1700*, ed. J. Lowthorp, 3rd edn., 3 vols. (1722), iii. 433–4.

[27] *Dramatic Records of Sir Henry Herbert, Master of Revels 1623–1673*, ed. J. Q. Adams, 2nd edn. (New York, 1964), 47; Richard Carew recorded the 'Guary miracle', a Cornish interlude, in his *Survey of Cornwall* (1602), fos. 71ʳ–72ʳ; for this and similar biblical re-enactments up to 1600, see I. Lancashire, *Dramatic Texts and Records of Britain: A Chronological Topography to 1558* (Cambridge, 1984), 8, 76, 280.

[28] *The Pepys Ballads*, ed. W. G. Day, 5 vols. (Cambridge, 1987), facs. vol. i, pp. 28–9, 30. Subsequent ballads in this and the next chapter will be taken from this modern facsimile edition published as a set within a larger *Catalogue of the Pepys Library*. Other citations will be to the older, similarly entitled collection by H. E. Rollins, *The Pepys Ballads*, 8 vols. (Cambridge, Mass., 1929–32). To avoid confusion, references to the former source will always contain the phrase 'facsimile volume'; references to the latter will be to *Pepys Ballads*, ed. Rollins.

the past for the purpose of example. In his notes for a homily on rebellion, Archbishop Cranmer listed Old Testament subversives such as Dathan and Absalom side by side with the architects of more recent 'tumults in England', Jack Cade and Jack Straw. Even if he regarded all of these names as being equally historical, Cranmer would have understood the temporal distance between them. But to an ordinary churchgoer, listening to such examples, the nuances of time and place would very likely be lost, and the illustrative material would blur together into a vague and fuzzy but very real past.[29]

Print provided an important vehicle for the dissemination of religious ideas.[30] Perhaps no book published in the sixteenth century had a greater impact on historical consciousness than John Foxe's *Acts and Monuments*. Published in several editions, copies of it were made available after 1570 in all cathedrals within the province of Canterbury, and it can also be found in many parochial collections. It was filled with woodcuts of martyrs and their persecutors,[31] and provided an enormous fount of stories of Protestant and medieval victims of papist tyranny. It would indeed be difficult to overestimate the role of the 'Book of Martyrs' in creating a Protestant vision of national history, and its message long outlasted the Reformation to reach into the nineteenth and twentieth centuries.[32] It is also the example *par excellence* of an expensive, learned work of historical research and writing, based on both documentary and oral sources, and exercising a potent influence on popular consciousness of the nation's past; it accomplished this through a skilful mix of truth and fiction, underpinned by illustrations that consistently suppressed historical differences of period and even of individuals (Fig. 9.1). As Alexandra Walsham has recently demonstrated, Foxe and other religious writers created a reformed counterpart of the late medieval cautionary tale. The *Acts and Monuments* in particular supplied a 'corpus of protestant legend and folklore' as compelling and robust as the Catholic saints' tales that it displaced. Religion, perhaps more than other matters, provided an arena for the continued circulation

[29] Notes for a homily against rebellion, printed in *Miscellaneous Writings and Letters of Thomas Cranmer*, vol. ii of *Works of Thomas Cranmer*, ed. J. E. Cox, 2 vols., PS 15–16 (Cambridge, 1844–6), ii. 188–9.

[30] Watt, *Cheap Print and Popular Piety*; I. Green, *Print and Protestantism in Early Modern England* (Oxford, 2000).

[31] M. Aston and E. Ingram, 'The Iconography of the *Acts and Monuments*', in D. Loades (ed.), *John Foxe and the English Reformation* (Aldershot, 1997), 66–142; R. S. Luborsky, 'The Illustrations: Their Pattern and Plan', in D. Loades (ed.), *John Foxe: An Historical Perspective* (Aldershot, 1999), 67–84.

[32] Study of Foxe's book and its impact has increased dramatically in recent years. Much of this writing, most notably by Patrick Collinson and Thomas Freeman, has usefully explored Foxe's own reliance on verbal information as well as documents, and his willingness constructively to embroider on hard kernels of fact. The projected critical edition of his work will be indispensable in re-evaluating his sources and his influence. In the meantime see the following: P. Collinson, 'Truth and Legend: The Veracity of John Foxe's Book of Martyrs', in A. C. Duke and C. A. Tamse (eds.), *Clio's Mirror: Historiography in Britain and the Netherlands* (Zutphen, 1985), 31–54; P. Collinson, 'Truth, Lies, and Fiction in Sixteenth Century Protestant Historiography', in D. R. Kelley and D. H. Sacks (eds.), *The Historical Imagination in Early Modern Britain* (Cambridge, 1997); T. Freeman, 'Fate, Faction and Fiction in Foxe's Book of Martyrs', *Historical Journal*, 43 (2000), 601–23. On Foxe's later influence, see E. Nicholson, 'Eighteenth-Century Foxe: Evidence for the Impact of the *Acts and Monuments* in the Long Eighteenth Century', in Loades (ed.), *John Foxe and the English Reformation*, 143–77.

The defcription of the horrible burning of Iohn Badby, and
How hee was ufed at his death.

Fig. 9.1. The martyrdom of John Badby, 1410, from Foxe, *Acts and Monuments*, i. 681. Foxe's wood-cuts, which represent figures from the past as more or less contemporary, provided non-literate read-ers with vivid, graphic images linked to his stories; the same woodcut was often used for several different figures and their martyrdoms

of historical knowledge between writing, print, and orality, and in more than one direction. This ironically flew in the face of a Protestant equation of the oral with Catholicism and its 'unwritten verities' and 'uncertaine tradition'.[33]

ARCHITECTURE, LANDSCAPE, AND HISTORY

As we have seen in earlier chapters, little stimulated awareness of the past so much as its visual remains, natural or man-made. Very old man-made structures (buildings, bridges, tombs, and monuments) which dominated the urban envir-onment and broke up the rural horizon conditioned people's memories and their sense of change. They also acted as focal points for local traditions and legends, lightning rods which inspired the popular imagination. Almost every parish and

[33] A. Walsham, *Providence in Early Modern England* (Oxford, 1999), *passim*, esp. pp. 96–104; id., 'Reformed Folklore? Cautionary Tales and Oral Tradition in Early Modern England', in Fox and Woolf (eds.), *The Spoken Word*, 173–95.

town had either a ruined building or some feature of the landscape which had acquired historical associations for its populace, even when they did not fully grasp its significance. Around such inescapable reminders of earlier times, communities could and did weave an invented past. The local explanation for a stone bridge near South Petherton (Somerset) at the start of the eighteenth century was that it had been built to replace a wooden one after two children had drowned underneath, their effigies carved on a stone at the foot of the new bridge to commemorate the sad event.[34] The town of Oakham in Rutland had a tradition that any nobleman, upon entering it, had to forfeit a horseshoe or pay a fine, the 'evidence' for this consisting in a number of shoes nailed to the shire hall door in the later seventeenth century. In the parish of Ecclesfield or Eccleston, near Doncaster, there was a church of such great age that by the end of the seventeenth century it had inspired a local proverb. When anyone in the vicinity wished to impress someone with the great age of something he or she would say 'it is as old as Eccleston church'.[35] Even obviously recent structures could inspire stories about events from a period long before. A Jersey antiquary recorded a 'fabulous report' that a chapel built within the past century had actually been erected in memory of a Norman gentleman who had 'killed a dragon which had done much hurt to the island'.[36]

By the early eighteenth century, characters from Galfridian history such as Lud and Belinus, once accepted by antiquaries as genuine but since demoted to the status of legend, had found new life in popular tradition, joining genuine historical figures as the builders or early occupants of churches, castles, and other structures. The Gloucester historian Abel Wantner, writing at the beginning of George I's reign, noted that the local church of St Mary the Virgin 'was built (if you please to believe antiquity carried on by tradition) by the renowned Lucius, the first Christian king in the world'. A murky figure who was not completely dismissed by historians until the nineteenth century, Lucius had apparently placed a bishop and preachers there on his conversion, an event commemorated in a monument within the church. At Brill church, near Ludgershall in Buckinghamshire, Browne Willis would note in 1712 the tradition that 'King Lud was killed in the parish on a spot of ground called Ludsland'. At Ellesborough, in the same shire, the remains of a castle on a round hill had inspired the belief that King Belinus had lived there; a large hill nearby was known as Belinesbury Hill.[37]

[34] SAL MS Stukeley III/315/3, for the story as recounted to Stukeley in 1723.

[35] Richard Blome, *Britannia* (1673), 191; *The Diary of Abraham de la Pryme*, ed. C. Jackson, Surtees Soc., 54 (1869–70), 112. On proverbs and the transmission of oral lore, see J. Obelkevich, 'Proverbs and Social History', in *The Social History of Language*, ed. P. Burke and R. Porter (Cambridge, 1987), 43–72; D. F. Bond, 'English Legal Proverbs', *Proceedings of the Modern Language Association*, 51 (1936), 921–35; Fox, *Oral and Literate Culture in England*, ch. 2 *passim*.

[36] Bodl. MS Gough Islands 2 (D. Messervy, 'Historical Collections concerning Jersey', *c*.1680), fo. 5r; for other dragon-slayers see Simpson, 'The Local Legend', 33.

[37] Bodl. MS Top. Glouc. c. 3 (Abel Wantner, 'History of Gloucester'), fos. 50r, 93r; Bodl. MS Willis 13 (Browne Willis, notes on archdeaconry of Buckingham churches, 1712), fos. 71r, 136v. Lud was the eponymous builder of Ludgate, where his image and that of other kings had been erected in 1260. According to Stow, these 'had their heads smitten off, and were otherwise defaced by such as judged every image to be an idol', but were repaired by Mary; new images adorned a rebuilt gate from 1586: John Stow, *The Survey of London*, ed. H. Wheatley (1912), 37.

Ruins often led to traditions of vanished ancient cities and lost greatness, in which mythical or legendary figures jostled for status with more recent, documentable kings and benefactors. The town of Windsor, William Harrison noted, was 'builded in time past by King Arthur, or before him by Arviragus, as it is thought, and repaired by Edward the third, who erected also a notable college there'. Over a century later the inhabitants of one small Denbighshire parish firmly believed that theirs had once been a university town.[38] Inhabitants of Ilchester informed William Stukeley in 1723 that their town's suburbs once extended much further south, and that it had formerly held sixteen parish churches and several now vanished gates. They also shared with several other towns, Stukeley observed, a tradition that the older, larger city had been 'set on fire by matches' in the time of King John.[39] A Devon tradition ascribed an old church to King Athelstan, while a similar tradition in Gloucestershire attributed another to Edward the Confessor. The inhabitants of Beckermet, Cumberland, referred to the nearby mount and ruined castle as Caernarvon and ascribed it to the Britons; the place in Ipswich known as Broom-Hills in the early eighteenth century had been called, a generation earlier, Castle Hills because of a belief in the existence of a post-Conquest castle, all traces of which had disappeared.[40]

Local features of the landscape, because often associated with particular persons or events, often necessitated the spinning of aetiological legends. The village of Sevenoaks was, as might be expected, named after its seven large oaks, and traditions about these long outlasted the trees themselves.[41] A field in the parish of Eastdown, Devon, in the mid-seventeenth century was dominated by a circle of stones taller than a man. Since the field was known as Madock's Down, the local population surmised that the monument was 'in memory of one Madocke there vanquished; for no man will think that they were there set in vain'.[42] In this case the legend, which may have been of relatively recent origin, served the purpose of 'explaining' the monument. While such stories often performed this kind of toponymical function, they are also indicative of an element common to many popular beliefs about the past, namely their pre-eminent concern with conflicts

[38] William Harrison, *The Description of England*, ed. G. Edelen (Ithaca, NY, 1968), 226; Bodl. MS Top. gen. e. 85 (Thomas Martin of Palgrave, 'Some Remarks and Observations taken in a Journey from Eton ... to Oxford ... 1724'), p. 72 (parish of Llanrhaiadr). The adoption of famous figures as founders or benefactors had a long history going well back into the Middle Ages. S. Reynolds, 'The Forged Charters of Barnstaple', *English Historical Review*, 84 (1969), 699–720, documents the construction of bogus charters in the fourteenth and fifteenth centuries so that town officials could claim their immemorial liberties from King Athelstan. As early as 1340, they appealed to Edward III to confirm these liberties. In the eighteenth century Barnstaple was commonly cited as a paragon of Anglo-Saxon freedom because of the association with Athelstan.
[39] SAL MS Stukeley III/315/2.
[40] Thomas Westcote, *View of Devonshire* (written c.1630, 1st edn., Exeter, 1845), 112; Bodl. MS Top. Glouc. c. 3 (Wantner, 'History of Gloucester'), fo. 147ᵛ; Blome, *Britannia*, 71; SAL MS 91 (John Denton of Cardew, 'The Antiquitys of Cumberland', late seventeenth-century copy of MSS in Cumbria RO), fos. 11–12 for Beckermet; John Kirby, *The Suffolk Traveller* (Ipswich, 1735), a copy with manuscript additions in Suffolk RO HD 1538/66, at p. 5.
[41] BL MS Add. 15776 (travel notes of Jeremiah Milles), fo. 177ʳ.
[42] Tristram Risdon, *The Chorographical Description or Survey of Devon* (1811), 345.

and with men of extraordinary physical abilities, a preoccupation with extremes that both endowed the past with meaning and made it more easily memorable within a predominantly oral context.

The level of interest in such geographic features, like the discovery of antiquities, almost inevitably outstripped the ability to understand them historically, especially at a time when objects were almost invariably situated within a knowledge field defined by literary texts and circumscribed by the finite chronology of a few millennia.[43] It was hard to be sceptical when a geological feature had already acquired spurious historical associations. The various cromlechs given the name 'Arthur's Stone' by locals of sixteenth-century Wales and western England provide one example.[44] Near the bogs of Northumberland were heaps of stones known as 'lowes' which, one observer noted, 'the inhabitants believe were monuments of some that were slain in old time'.[45] Barrows were variously seen as Roman, Saxon, or Viking burial sites, though they originated for the most part in the neolithic era.[46] The 'dene-holes' (or 'Dane-holes') found mainly in Kent and Essex were widely believed to be hiding places from Danish invaders of the ninth and tenth centuries (and may in fact have been used as such), but they originated in the Iron Age as did the similar 'Pict-holes' noted by Camden in the north.[47] Thomas Hearne's observation of what appeared to be 'Danish barrows' in the vicinity of Woodstock led him to conclude that 'this plainly shews how much the Danes were in these parts, & that divers battles happen'd at each place'.[48]

More recent events, too, could endow a structure with historical significance. A long medieval tradition of 'political canonization', often associated with the graves or shrines of 'royal saints' or with victims of authority such as the early fifteenth-century Archbishop Scrope, had successors in the sixteenth century.[49]

[43] Such traditions often survived even Victorian scholars' efforts to dissipate popular error; see Philippa Levine, *The Amateur and the Professional: Antiquaries, Historians and Archaeologists in Victorian England, 1838–1886* (Cambridge, 1986).

[44] Owen, *The description of Penbrokshire*, editor's list of Welsh Arthur stones; cf. a note in *Archaeologia Cambrensis*, 4th ser., iii (1872) 269–70; v (1874), 88–90. For a Cumberland 'King Arthurs Round Table' *c.*1675, see Edmund Sandford, *A cursory relation of all the antiquities and familyes in Cumberland*, ed. R. S. Ferguson, Cumberland and Westmorland Antiquarian and Archaeological Society, tract ser., no. 4 (Kendal, 1890), 37.

[45] BL MS Sloane 3987 (notes by William Charleton alias Courten on Welsh and English antiquities, 1663), fo. 494.

[46] S. Piggott, *Ancient Britons and the Antiquarian Imagination* (New York, 1989), 120–2.

[47] Camden, *Britain*, 440, 766; W. Johnson, *Folk-memory; or, The continuity of British archaeology* (Oxford, 1908), 71, 234–62. For more on topography and the memory of historical enemies such as the Danes, see further below in this chapter.

[48] Hearne, *Remarks and Collections*, v. 402–3. The absence of ancient monuments could be of equal significance: William Lambarde expressed a common opinion of Kentishmen that the weald had been a barren wilderness until relatively recent times since one could not find there 'any one monument of great antiquitie'. *Perambulation of Kent*, 211.

[49] D. W. Rollason, 'The Cults of Murdered Royal Saints in Anglo-Saxon England', *Anglo-Saxon England*, 11 (1983), 1–22; S. J. Ridyard, *The Royal Saints of Anglo-Saxon England* (Cambridge, 1988); J. W. McKenna, 'Popular Canonization as Political Propaganda: The Cult of Archbishop Scrope', *Speculum*, 45 (1970), 605–23; id., 'Piety and Propaganda: The Cult of King Henry VI', in B. Rowland (ed.), *Chaucer and Middle English Studies in Honour of Rossell Hope Robbins* (1974), 72–88.

The death of Cardinal Wolsey in 1530 near the scene of Richard III's demise two generations earlier almost immediately created a popular tag for his burial place in Leicester Abbey.[50] In the seventeenth and eighteenth centuries events such as the Reformation, the Catholic resistance, and the civil war, would be added to the fount of older, medieval traditions. This would also mark a shift, noted in the last chapter in the context of memory, in the focus of such beliefs away from the local and parochial, or the mythical and legendary, towards the national and putatively historical, or at the very least an attempt to integrate popular traditions within the chronology of national history. The 'priest-holes' used for the concealment of proscribed Jesuits and other missionaries were themselves responsible for a large supply of popular traditions that have survived into this century, for instance the stories about the taking of gunpowder plotter Everard Digby. Even Oliver Cromwell was supposed to have been hidden at various times when his life was endangered: a dark hole at the gable end of Cromwell House, Mortlake, was known until the house was demolished in 1860 as 'Old Noll's hole'.[51]

London itself spawned a number of popular beliefs which, because of the city's status as the capital and a political centre, crystallized around genuinely historical figures rather earlier than was the case in the provinces. These beliefs were also less likely to survive in purely oral form, undisturbed by the influence of written history, because of the city's higher literacy rates and long-standing collection of records. In London, more than in any other place, a wide assortment of tales had sprung up concerning men and sometimes women ('Shore's wife', for instance) who figured in the mythology both of the city itself and also of its sub-communities, such as the guilds and livery companies. Many of these had monuments either officially or traditionally associated with their names. Sir William Walworth, the fourteenth-century mayor who slew Wat Tyler, turns up again and again in mayoral processions, up to the end of the eighteenth century, especially those involving the Fishmongers. It is not difficult to see how the reputation of such a character could be inflated and embellished over time. On 16 June 1562 a fishmonger named William Paris paid for Walworth's tomb to be 'nuwe frest and gyld, and ys armes gyllt, with the pyctur all in aleblaster lyung in ys armur gyltt'. The London diarist Henry Machyn noted this 'goodly remembrans for alle men of honor and worshype', remarking that Walworth had been twice mayor and had 'kyld Jake Cade in Smythfeld a-for the kynge', thereby conflating Wat Tyler with his fifteenth-century Kentish successor.[52]

With the notable exception of figures such as Caesar or Alexander the Great (the subject of numerous late medieval romances), who had crept into the

---

[50] On 4 December 1530 Eustace Chapuys wrote to Emperor Charles V that 'The cardinal [Wolsey] of York died on St Andrew's Day about 40 miles from here, at a place where the last king Richard was defeated and killed. Both lie buried in the same church, which the people begin already to call "the tyrants' grave"': *CSP Spanish, 1529–30*, p. 833. For a traditional version of Wolsey's father being a butcher, see John Kirby, *The Suffolk Traveller* (Ipswich, 1735), copy with MS additions in Suffolk RO (Ipswich) HD 1538/66, p. 11.

[51] A. Fea, *Secret Chambers and Hiding-places* (1901), 60, 225.

[52] *The Diary of Henry Machyn*, ed. J. G. Nichols, Camden Soc., os 42 (1848), 285, 390 n.

family of received traditions, popular beliefs about the past include fewer of the classical elements which were a preoccupation of most antiquaries. The occasional character from ancient mythology could be found attached to a particular location, such as 'Hercules' promontory', an outcrop near the river Torridge in Devon that the Greek hero had reputedly visited.[53] Romano-British figures such as Lucius, Constantine (supposedly the son of a British princess), Coel, and especially Arthur were more likely to be cited in connection with a specific site than were Romans themselves, Caesar being a notable exception; this was so despite the abundance of Roman coinage, but it is consistent with the tendency noted above in Chapter 7 whereby Roman coins were given local names like 'Brough pennies'. A ruined castle at Queen Camel near Yeovil, Somerset, was known locally as 'King Arthur's Palace' throughout the sixteenth and seventeenth centuries.[54] Glastonbury, fast becoming an Arthurian tourist trap at the end of the seventeenth century, inspired similar beliefs about such famous features as its perpetually blooming thorn. William Stukeley noted that its townsmen claimed King Arthur was buried under its great tower, under which they believed was a subterranean arched passage leading to the River Torr. In this case the old habit of recycling building materials proved unfortunately short-sighted:

The townspeople brought the stone of the vaults underneath to build a sorry mercat house contributing to the destruction of the sacred fabric & to their own, not discerning the benefit accruing from the great concourse of strangers purposely to see those sacred remains, which was the greatest trade of the town.[55]

A round trench with an exit at either end, which the Restoration scholar Sir Daniel Fleming attributed to the Romans, was thought by the country folk of western Westmorland 'to have been one of King Arthur's Round Tables'.[56]

TOWNS AND TRADITIONS

The more urban the community, the likelier it was that an episode from the past, whether real or fictional, would find a variety of channels of expression. In Chester throughout this period a feast called the sheriff's calves' head breakfast was held

[53] Westcote, *View of Devonshire*, 312; Aylett Sammes, *Britannia Antiqua Illustrata* (1676), 57.
[54] *Leland's Itinerary*, i. 151; Blome, *Britannia*, 199.   [55] SAL MS Stukeley III/315/1.
[56] 'Sir Daniel Fleming's Description of Cumberland, Westmorland and Furness, 1671', pp. 26, 34, in *Fleming–Senhouse Papers*, ed. E. Hughes, Cumberland County Council Record Series, 2 (Carlisle, 1962). Richard Blome thought the structure Roman, but the abundance of similar nearby trenches, ruins, and coins persuaded locals that it was a place used for tilts and tournaments by Arthur's knights: *Britannia* (1673), 238. Arthurian round tables occur in various places, but most commonly in the southwest and the Welsh marches. A well-known example could be found in the 1630s at Winchester Castle, surviving its destruction in 1646 and subsequent rebuilding: Anon. (attrib. Lieutenant Hammond) *A Relation of a Short Survey of the Western Counties made by a lieutenant of the military company in Norwich in 1635*, ed. L. G. W. Legg, *Camden Miscellany*, 16, Camden Soc., 3rd ser., 52 (1936), 51. For a Denbighshire Arthur's table, disputed by an anonymous antiquary who believed that such local traditions were 'little to be trusted', see Bodl. MS Gough Wales 5 ('The Description of Wales', written c.1700), fo. 12r.

annually on 'Black Monday', commemorating a storm on Easter Monday 1360, in which many of Edward III's troops had been slain outside Paris.[57] Bristol was supposedly founded by Brennus, a legend supported in the sixteenth century by town records and civic rituals; Colchester was allegedly named after Coel, while both Canterbury and Winchester owed their existence to Rudhudibras. Visitors to Bath in the eighteenth century were informed that it had been founded by the Galfridian figure King Bladud, and the town's late Tudor town hall included statues of both King Edgar and King Coel.[58] Many figures of urban historical legend were of more recent vintage, such as Guy of Warwick, the bastard offspring of chivalric literature and popular tradition. Guy's origins lay in the highly popular Anglo-Norman romance of *Gui de Warewic*. He had never been associated primarily with the culture of the court and had appealed to the provincial nobility and gentry of the later Middle Ages; consequently he was indelibly associated with Warwick itself.[59] Both Guy and his Southampton cousin, Bevis, were so well known by the fourteenth century that the author of the *Speculum Vitae*, a didactic poem of that period, felt obliged to warn readers that his work did not deal in such secular matters.[60] Other characters were of even later, early modern origin and reflect more urban and mercantile values. The early fifteenth-century London mayor Richard Whittington acquired added legendary reputation in the sixteenth century in numerous accounts, including the story of his famous cat.[61] Among the departures from chivalric heroes (as even a poor boy made good such as Guy of Warwick was sometimes supposed to have been) were Thomas Deloney's 'histories' of Jack of Newbury and Thomas of Reading. Aimed at successful and aspiring Elizabethan clothiers, these were essentially compilations of

[57] A. R. Wright, *British Calendar Customs*, ed. T. E. Lones, 3 vols. (1936–40), i. 113; *REED: Chester*, ed. L. M. Clopper (Toronto, 1979), 322–3.

[58] David Harris Sacks, 'Celebrating Authority in Bristol, 1475–1640', in S. Zimmerman and R. F. E. Weissman (eds.), *Urban Life in the Renaissance* (Newark, London, and Toronto, 1989), 187–223; Harrison, *Description of England*, 288; *A Relation of a Short Survey of the Western Counties*, 11, 43; P. Borsay, *The English Urban Renaissance: Culture and Society in the Provincial Town 1660–1770* (Oxford, 1989), 242; R. Tittler, *Architecture and Power: The Town Hall and the English Urban Community c.1500–1640* (Oxford, 1991), 151–2. For other references to Bath and Bladud see *The Travels of Peter Mundy*, iv. 7; Robert Gay, *A Fool's Bolt Soon Shott at Stonage*, repr. in R. Legg, *Stonehenge Antiquaries* (Sherborne, Dorset, 1986), 23; Thomas Guidott, *A Discourse of Bathe, and the Hot Waters There* (1676), 55, where Bladud and the British history in general are dismissed as 'at best, uncertain'. By 1801 Bladud's story was being dismissed as 'puerile and absurd' by Richard Warner, though a few decades earlier the architect and author John Wood had endorsed it: R. Sweet, *The Writing of Urban Histories in Eighteenth-Century England* (Oxford, 1997), 115, 126.

[59] *The Romance of Guy of Warwick*, ed. J. Zupitza, 2 vols., EETS es 25–6 (1875–6).

[60] P. R. Coss, 'Aspects of Cultural Diffusion in Medieval England: The Early Romances, Local Society and Robin Hood', *Past and Present*, 108 (1985), 35–79, at p. 53; *Speculum Vitae*, quoted in E. Duffy, *The Stripping of the Altars* (New Haven, 1992), 69, who points out that in fact many prosperous households and guilds did mix such secular works with saints' lives and religious literature.

[61] e.g. Thomas Heywood, *The Famous and Remarkable History of Sir Richard Whittington* (1656). Joseph P. Ward notes changing attitudes to mercantile profit-making in variant versions of the Whittington story: 'Dick Whittington and the Limits of Commemoration in Early Modern London', paper presented at North American Conference on British Studies (Toronto, 2001). I am grateful to Prof. Ward for providing me with a copy of this paper.

material found in a variety of sources. The characters reappear in miscellanies throughout the seventeenth century.[62]

Having found their way into popular ritual and tradition, many of these pseudo-historical figures remained in circulation for a very long time, though resonating differently for successive generations. Warwick nurtured its association with the fictional Guy into the eighteenth century: Dugdale's Augustan editor, William Thomas, irritated the 'gentlemen of Warwick' by evincing a much greater scepticism towards Guy's historicity than had Dugdale himself three generations previously (perhaps worse, he also doubted the local belief in Warwick's Roman origins).[63] Guy continued to pop up with cheery resilience, as if he were a genuine historical figure, in nineteenth-century school texts such as Richmal Mangnall's *Historical and Miscellaneous Questions*. By then, however, he had been transformed into a national symbol of resistance to French aggression.[64] Two fourteenth-century towers at Warwick Castle were and still are known as Caesar's Tower and Guy's Tower respectively, and nearby Guys Cliffe marked the site of a chapel in which the hero was believed to have spent his last years as a hermit (Fig. 9.2).[65] When Henry Prescott visited it in 1711 he noted that the chapel was supposedly named after St Margaret and that it had 'a Gigantic figure in Relieve of Stone, of the Famous Guy, and 2 Figures rudely and of later time painted of Colbron and Amarant' (Fig. 9.3). At Gosford Gate in the rival county town of Coventry during the early sixteenth century, there hung a bone of the giant boar supposedly slain by Guy. Perhaps because he was mainly Warwick's hero, Coventry had also evolved its own dragon-killer in St Margaret.[66] It also, more famously, had the

---

[62] BL MS Sloane 3890, collections of John Collet, fo. 58, extracted in *Anecdotes and Traditions Illustrative of Early English History and Literature*, ed. W. J. Thoms, Camden Soc., os 5 (1839), for an incidental discussion of Jack and his 100 looms. Briggs, *Dictionary of British Folk-Tales*, B.II, pp. 370–5; I. W. Archer, *The Pursuit of Stability: Social Relations in Elizabethan London* (Cambridge, 1991), 51 n. For nursery rhymes on historical figures, many of no earlier than seventeenth-century origin, see J. O. Halliwell-Phillipps, *The Nursery Rhymes of England, obtained Principally from Oral Tradition*, 3rd edn (1843; repr. Detroit, 1969), 18–25.

[63] William Dugdale, *Antiquities of Warwickshire Illustrated*, rev. edn., ed. William Thomas, 2 vols. (1730), i. 374–5; the fact that it is 'gentlemen', his own social peers, who objected to Thomas's line illustrates the fact that localism could easily trump gentility where attitudes to pseudo-historical figures were concerned.

[64] Richmal Mangnall, *Historical and Miscellaneous Questions* (1st pub. 1800); ed. J. Lawrence (New York, 1869), 97.

[65] Dugdale, *Antiquities of Warwickshire*, ed. Thomas, i. 273–4.

[66] Blome, *Britannia*, 40, 230–1; C. Phythian-Adams, *Desolation of a City: Coventry and the Urban Crisis of the Late Middle Ages* (Cambridge, 1979), 173; M. W. Thompson, *The Decline of the Castle* (Cambridge, 1987), 75–7; *The Diary of Henry Prescott, LL.B., deputy registrar of Chester Diocese*, ed. J. Addy, J. Harrop, and P. McNiven, 3 vols., Rec. Soc. of Lancashire and Cheshire, vols. 127, 132, 133 (Chester, 1987–97), ii. 327; there is also a promontory known as Guy's Cliff near Pateley Bridge in the West Riding of Yorkshire. Stukeley and several friends, visiting Warwick early in the eighteenth century, were shown the sword 'and other gigantic reliques of Guy the famous earl of Warwick & of his victorys'. At Coventry he saw Lady Godiva in the window painted glass, noting that 'there is still the image of a fellow looking out of a window, who they say was struck blind for attempting to look at her': 'Iter Oxoniense', Bodl. MS Top. gen. e. 61, fo. 74[v] (vol. reversed). More recent historical events could rival and even expunge older traditions: by the late seventeenth century Newbury, for example, was already beginning to evolve traditions about the battles fought there in the civil war.

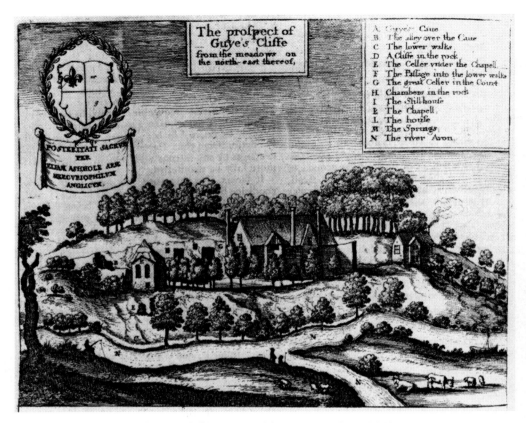

The prospect of
Guye's Cliffe
from the meadows on
the north-east thereof,

A. Guye's Cave
B. The alley over the Cave
C. The lower walks
D. A Cliffe in the rock
E. The Celler vnder the Chapell
F. The Passage into the lower walks
G. The great Celler in the Court
H. Chambers in the rock
I. The Still house
K. The Chapell,
L. The house,
M. The Springs,
N. The river Avon.

Fig. 9.2. 'Prospect of Guye's Cliffe'. From Dugdale, *Antiquities of Warwickshire*, i. 274

historical Lady Godiva or Godgifu; a character mentioned in thirteenth-century chronicles, she had taken her famous naked ride to induce her husband Leofric to release the town from taxes. The south window erected at Trinity church in the late Middle Ages and still extant in the late seventeenth century featured a picture of Godiva and her husband over the words 'I Luriche for the Love of thee | Doe make Coventre Tol-free'. A procession in honour of Godiva ran annually from 1678 to 1887.[67]

Despite their toponyms, figures such as Guy were often relatively easily transported to other communities, even outside the shire. The romance versions of their exploits tended to be less rigidly fixed to a single place and emphasized their travels and national or international adventures. Accordingly, Winchester, too, laid claim to Guy, and an account of his slaying the Danish giant Colbrand can be found in the writings of local antiquaries such as John Trussell:

[67] William Dugdale, *The Antiquities of Coventry, illustrated from records, leidger-books, manuscripts, charters, evidences, tombes and armes* (Coventry, 1765), 2 (an anonymously edited set of extracts from Dugdale's larger *Antiquities of Warwickshire*); *DNB*, *sub* 'Godiva or Godgifu'.

The Statue of
the sometime
famous Guy
standing here
wth in the Cha,
pell of S Mary
Magdalen .

Fig. 9.3. 'The statue of the sometime famous Guy', from Dugdale, *Antiquities of Warwickshire*, i. 274.
Dugdale declined to reject stories of Guy outright; his eighteenth-century editor, William Thomas,
was notably more sceptical

In a single combatt in a meddowe grownd att this day called Hide-meade under an other
ground called Denmarck mead lying on the north side of the cittie of Winchester, [Guy]
did vanquish the great gyant Colbrond, by whose name a watch tower opposite to the
place of fight in the wall of the cittie, and where the picture of a great & littell man cutt
in stone remayneth att this day, called Colbronds chayer.[68]

[68] Hants. RO W/K1/11/1 (John Trussell's 'The Origin of Cytties', dated 6 Apr. 1644), fos. 17, 21^v, 50^r.
For another description of this fight, see the commonplace book with 'Observations of Warwickshire'
in BL MS Stowe 1048, fo. 2^r. Even in the late Middle Ages Guy and Colbrand were not strictly local
figures. The king's bridge, or landing stage, at Westminster Palace was refurbished for Prince
Arthur's marriage to Catherine of Aragon in 1501, including repair of the figures of Guy of Warwick
and Colbrand the Dane that surmounted the posts on either side of it. *History of the King's Works*,
iii: *1485–1660* ed. H. M. Colvin, 2 pts. (1975–82), pt. 2, p. 287.

Trussell derived his version of this episode of Winchester's past from a manuscript given him by the warden of Winchester college, though 'where he had yt hee knew not'. In this version the story has clear affiliations with the Bible, 'little' Guy and 'giant' Colbrand being domesticated Davids and Goliaths. Trussell's chronology of more remote times places mytho-historical figures such as Ebrauk, Arthur, and Guy firmly within a time-scheme derived from Scripture and from classical antiquaries such as Varro. This attempt by learned culture to reduce figures of popular legend to the order of history stands in marked contrast to the treatment given Guy in at least one ballad, which tilts quixotically against historical chronology without altogether eschewing it, truncating history to place Guy, King Athelstan, and the Crusades all within two or so centuries of Christ:

> Two hundred twenty years and odd,
> after our Saviour Christ his birth,
> When King Athelstan wore the Crown,
> I lived here upon the earth.[69]

PRINT AND POPULAR BELIEF: HISTORY BY ALMANAC, BALLAD, AND CHAPBOOK

One of the effects of the circulation of historical knowledge between speech and printed text was to drive locally based historical beliefs increasingly from the centre to the periphery, as a national historical tradition began to solidify in the seventeenth and early eighteenth centuries, out of the nebula of traditions, chivalric romances, chronicles, and biblical history. That national tradition was, by 1700, represented in a large number of printed histories ranging from the scholarly folio to abridgements and epitomes aimed at the middling sort, as well as poems and history plays.[70] Shadows of that tradition can also increasingly be found in the chapbooks and almanacs written by the educated for their peers and inferiors, as well as in the ballad, which remained more closely linked to the spoken word. The decline and virtual extinction before 1640 of the chronicle—a more inclusive form of historical record which had plenty of room for the misplaced anecdote, the local tale, and other apparently trivial pieces of information—was partially offset by the readiness of late seventeenth- and eighteenth-century travellers and collectors of antiquarian information to include such stories in their works.[71]

---

[69] Hants. RO W/K1/11/1 (Trussell), fo. 50ᵛ; *A Pleasant Song of the Valiant Deeds of Chivalry*, in *The Pepys Ballads*, ed. W. G. Day, 5 vols. (Cambridge, 1947), facs. vol. i, pp. 522–3.

[70] On the increase in genres and formats of historical literature in the late seventeenth and early eighteenth centuries, see my *Reading History in Early Modern England* (Cambridge, 2000), esp. chs. 5 and 6.

[71] One early eighteenth-century Cambridgeshire antiquary breaks from his account of Silverley, a depopulated community remarkable only for its church steeple, to record a 'memorable story' about another steeple, elsewhere, that had once collapsed on a poor man's cottage, but did not harm his infant daughter, left alone in the house, who was protected by pieces of the belfry falling on the house ahead of the stones. CUL MS Add. 3853 (anonymous early eighteenth-century Cambridgeshire

A highly utilitarian, if prosaic, approach to the digesting of history into popular form was taken by the compilers of almanacs. From the late sixteenth century, these began to include historical tables or watered-down 'chronologies'; by the eighteenth century, as Linda Colley has suggested, these were so plentiful that for the majority of Britons they were the most accessible form of history lesson.[72] The popular 'writing tables' put out by Francis or Frank Adams, an Elizabethan bookbinder working near London Bridge, provide the names of English kings and their regnal periods (numbers of years, months, and days) beginning with William the Conqueror. But only rarely are details about those monarchs included, and these invariably revolve around something done by a king *to* or *for* London and its citizens, or sometimes simply during that king's reign. Henry III, for instance, is primarily noteworthy for having granted London's citizens the right of free passage without toll throughout the kingdom. His father, King John, is memorable because 'in the yeere 1209, the stone bridge over the Thames a London was finished'. Just because the author and readers of this almanac were Londoners did not automatically make them more conscious of events of national importance. In fact, Adams's tables only mention a few of these events briefly, mainly rebellions interspersed with accounts of miracles and prodigies, and the work is remarkably free of the moral and political judgements on kings such as Edward II, Richard II, and Richard III that dominate both the Tudor chronicle and the humanist histories that succeeded it.[73]

From the late sixteenth to the mid-eighteenth centuries, beliefs about the past increasingly worked their way from oral into written or printed form, only to double back into speech as the writers, readers, and hearers of stories, anecdotes, ballads, and legends conversed about the books they read. Perhaps the most often studied vehicle for beliefs about the past is the ballad. Beginning with the Child and Roxburgh collections of the nineteenth century, and continuing with the prolific scholarship of Hyder Edward Rollins and others in the twentieth, a vast number of medieval and early modern ballads have been reprinted. The collections of Samuel Pepys—who managed an interest in popular literature without ever abandoning a Restoration gentleman's taste for history books and the occasional French romance—have recently been thoroughly catalogued and published in facsmile.[74] The ballad, together with its increasingly popular late seventeenth-century prose rival,

collections, vol. ii), fo. 24ʳ. On the more inclusive character of chronicles see A. Patterson, *Reading Holinshed's Chronicles* (Chicago, 1994). The anecdote survived to appear again in nineteenth-century history textbooks, in particular those aimed at children: Mitchell, *Picturing the Past*, 76.

[72] L. Colley, *Britons: Forging the Nation, 1707–1837* (New Haven, 1992), 22. I cannot, however, agree with Prof. Colley's suggestion that the almanacs were 'the only history lessons the majority of Britons received'. In addition to ballads and other popular forms, the wealth of history books and articles in periodicals indicates a much broader informational base from which eighteenth-century Britons could learn; sermons, for instance, continued to refer to episodes from history.

[73] Frank Adams, *Writing Tables* (1578): BL Catalogue no. 124.b.28., no page, no sig. (other editions up to 1628 listed in *STC*, vol. ii, pp. 478–9).

[74] Francis James Child, *English and Scottish Popular Ballads*, 5 vols. in 10 pts. (Boston, 1898), of which vol. iii (pts. 5 and 6) is devoted to Robin Hood ballads and historical ballads; *The Roxburghe Ballads*, 9 vols. (New York, 1966); *The Pepys Ballads*, ed. Rollins. Other useful sources include: H. E. Rollins,

the chapbook, exemplifies the workings of the relationship between oral and printed culture and how, in the sixteenth and early seventeenth centuries, the history familiar to the middling and poorer sort was not yet distinct from the national history consumed by the aristocracy and gentry.[75] An early example is provided by *The Song of the Lady Bessy*, an account of a conspiracy by Elizabeth of York and Sir William Stanley to bring in Henry VII and depose Richard III. This tale, as C. L. Kingsford noted long ago, contains a mixture of truth and fiction which scarcely serves to distinguish it from a humanist account such as Sir Thomas More's *Richard III*, and it was probably initially composed by someone who knew some of the details of the events described. Despite its aristocratic origins, it was transmitted exclusively viva voce for three generations; the first known written version dates from Elizabeth I's reign. Once written down, however, it was repeatedly copied up to the reign of Charles II, and in this form it could feed back into and influence the original oral tradition from which it derived.[76]

Precisely because balladeers were still writing for an oral audience, and had hopes that their lyrics would be added to a variety of songs sung to well-known tunes, they searched for memorable subjects and employed highly graphic, colourful language. War and sex were favoured topics, and those historical figures occur most frequently who were well known from chronicles or oral tradition to have had military or romantic exploits—the inclusion of both in some of these was perhaps an attempt to appeal to both sexes—or to have been victims of persecution. Henry V, Shore's Wife, the duchess of Suffolk, Anne Askew, and Henry VIII all enjoyed a second life in Tudor ballad literature. They were joined in the seventeenth century and after by notorious highwaymen and celebrated war heroes —the printed ballad 'Fight on my Brave Boys' (1702/3), which commemorated the 1702 death of the tarpaulin Admiral John Benbow at Jamaica, remained in oral tradition into the middle of the twentieth century.[77] The ill fortunes of royal

Analytical Index to the Ballad Entries (1557–1709) of the Register of the Company of Stationers of London (repr. Hatboro, Pa., 1967); *Catalogue of the Pepys Library at Magdalene College, Cambridge*, ii: *Ballads*, ed. H. Weinstein (Cambridge, 1992). Other collections include R. Brimley Johnson (ed.), *Popular British Ballads, Ancient and Modern*, 4 vols. (1894), of which the first two volumes contain material for the sixteenth to the eighteenth centuries; *Merry Songs and Ballads Printed to the Year 1800*, ed. J. S. Farmer, 5 vols. (New York, 1964), consists mainly of reprints from literary sources, few of which are on historical or pseudo-historical subjects. For the printing history of ballads in this period, the following are indispensable: C. Blagden, 'Notes on the Ballad Market in the Second Half of the Seventeenth Century', *Studies in Bibliography*, 6 (1954), 161–80; L. Shepard, *History of Street Literature* (1973).

[75] Chapbooks, unlike ballads, have until recently attracted less attention. An extract of Pepys's collection of chapbooks may be found in *Samuel Pepys' Penny Merriments*, ed. R. Thompson (New York, 1977). This should be used in light of the comments by Margaret Spufford in her *Small Books and Pleasant Histories: Popular Fiction and its Readership in Seventeenth-Century England* (1981), 5 n.; Spufford's monograph remains the fullest treatment of the chapbooks.

[76] BL MS Royal 18 B. ii; C. L. Kingsford, *English Historical Literature in the Fifteenth Century* (Oxford, 1913), 252. For other instances of this throughout Britain see Fox and Woolf (eds.), *The Spoken Word, passim*.

[77] C. H. Firth, 'The Ballad History of the Reigns of Henry VII and Henry VIII', *TRHS*, 3rd ser., 2 (1908), 21–50; id., 'The Ballad History of the Reigns of the Later Tudors', *TRHS*, 3rd ser., 3 (1909), 51–124; id., 'The Ballad History of the Reign of James I', *TRHS*, 3rd ser., 5 (1911), 21–61; R. Palmer, *A Ballad History of England* (1979), 39.

mistresses who fell foul of power, like Rosamond, of luckless harlots like Jane Shore, and of ruthless consorts like Rosamond's supposed poisoner, Eleanor of Aquitaine, were a frequent subject of ballads, and a further testament to the special durability of the cautionary tale. Their ballad fates can be contrasted to the more rounded and sympathetic treatment they received at the hands of elite dramatists from Thomas Heywood and Samuel Daniel to Nicholas Rowe.[78] The very popularity of Edward III and Henry V as chivalric heroes in the three centuries following their respective deaths gave them a high profile in chronicles, poems and, eventually, plays. But because these genres influenced and were in turn influenced by popular 'brut', their selection of heroes and events often tended to percolate back down into ballads, almanacs and, eventually, chapbooks.[79] In the more confined spaces of these media, writers and performers tended to emphasize static episodes rather than complete historical processes; it was easier to create a story around one nuclear fact derived from printed or written sources than to retell the complete original narrative in abridged form. Thus in a ballad such as *The Battle of Agincourt in France*, which circulated widely early in the seventeenth century, an incidental event such as the 'tun of tennis balles' sent by the French king to insult Henry V assumes a prominence and importance that it lacked in the original chronicle sources.[80]

Not all ballads were episodic, or even focused on one famous individual. There is a small subgenre of ballads that attempt to reduce longer periods of history into a single sheet, to be committed to memory and sung. A Restoration example is *The Wandring Jews Chronicle*, which features woodcut portraits of the series of monarchs from William the Conqueror to King Charles I and 'Queen Mary' (Henrietta Maria), with Henry V inexplicably missing in the middle, and no sign of Charles II at the end—though the text includes him as then reigning.

---

[78] See, for instance, a ribald 1707 rendition of the tale *Of King Edward and Jane Shore*, in *Merry Songs and Ballads*, ed. Farmer, iv. 100–6; compare this with the more judgemental *The Wofull Lamentation of Mistris Shore . . . who for her Wanton Life Came to a Miserable End*, in *The Pepys Ballads*, ed. Day, facs. vol. i. p. 486; *A Lamentable Tall [sic] of Queen Elenor*, ibid. ii. 141. The same subject received a theatrical treatment in Nicholas Rowe's neo-Shakespearean *The Tragedy of Jane Shore*, produced at Drury Lane in 1713/14 and published later that year: *Diary of Dudley Ryder*, ed. Matthews, p. 143.

[79] Edward III and Henry V appeared at least as commonly in versifications of history further up the social scale, figuring for example in historical poems by Charles Aleyn and Thomas May in the early seventeenth century, and in political verse of the Restoration: see e.g. Nahum Tate, 'Old England' (printed 1685), in *Poems on Affairs of State*, ed. G. de F. Lord, 8 vols. (1963–75), iii. 183–206.

[80] For this ballad see *Pepys Ballads*, ed. Rollins, vol. i, no. 2 and *The Pepys Ballads*, ed. Day, facs. vol. i, pp. 90–1; cf. the somewhat later 'King Henry Fifth's Conquest of France', the oral version of which Child speculated derived from print: *English and Scottish Popular Ballads*, pt. 6, p. 321. Child also notes (pt. 2, p. 323 n.) a tradition, likely derived from this ballad and current in the Derbyshire Peaks during the nineteenth century, that Henry V would not recruit widows' sons or married men for the French campaign. The tennis-ball story appears in some, but not all, the early fifteenth-century chronicles: the *Liber Metricus* of Thomas Elmham and Capgrave's *Life of Henry V* which follows it both mention the incident, as would late versions of the vernacular translations of the *Brut* and *Polychronicon*. The 'official' Latin biography of Henry by the humanist Tito Livio Frulovisi does not, though his early Tudor translator (in Bodl. MS Bodley 966) does: on the sources for the tale see *The First English Life of King Henry the Fifth*, ed. C. L. Kingsford (Oxford, 1911), pp. xliii, 15.

The author uses the literary device of the legendary ageless Jew who must live from Christ's crucifixion to his Second Coming. Far from 'wandering', he is constantly present at court, allowing him to bear witness to all of English history, here boiled down into convenient doggerel:

> To the seventh Henry then I was
> A Servant, as it came to pass,
>   to serve him at his need:
> And while I did in Court remain,
> I saw in the eighth Henry's Reign
>   full many great men bleed . . .
> In Scotland born, in England Nurst
> Was Pious Princely Charles the first,
>   who had to Wife Queen Mary;
> But by the rage of Rebels hate,
> Murther'd and Martyr'd at his Gate,
>   this good King did miscarry.

Despite the easily memorized chronology of kings—a tactic used in textbooks of a much later time—the purpose of the ballad is not the grave and serious business of learning one's history. It is rather closer to straightforward entertainment, without much in the way of moral or political lesson, apart from its generally royalist sympathies. Sung to an older tune going back to Prince Charles's return from Spain in the 1620s, the ballad bills itself as 'The Old Historian, | His Brief Declaration, | Made in a Mad Fashion, | Of each Coronation, | That pass'd in this Nation, | Since Williams Invasion, | For no great occasion, | But meer Recreation, | To put off Vexation'.[81]

Crime, conspiracy, and treason too, became popular topics from the late sixteenth century on, and would remain so into the eighteenth century. A ballad first recorded about 1630, but certainly of older origin, describes the sorry end of one Banister, who betrayed his master, the duke of Buckingham, to Richard III. Its written version may have been inspired by such recent events as the assassination of the latter-day duke of Buckingham by a disgruntled junior officer in 1628.[82] The key point here is not that this pertains to a real historical episode, rather than a myth or folk tale, but that the balladeer was more concerned about peripheral characters and their fates than about the main event, which is pushed away from centre-stage. Throughout a great deal of Tudor and Stuart ballad literature, the 'important' figures, kings and nobles, figure only as textual guests. They make cameo appearances that provide a slender connection between history as the historians told it and history as ordinary readers or listeners liked to remember it. Didactic messages about loyalty, obedience, and the fate of the over-ambitious

[81] *The Wandring Jews Chronicle*, in *The Pepys Ballads*, ed. Day, facs. vol. i, pp. 482–3.
[82] *A most sorrowfull song, setting forth the end of Banister*, in *The Pepys Ballads*, ed. Rollins, vol. ii, no. 68. Banister is mentioned briefly in Edward Hall, *Hall's Chronicle*, ed. H. Ellis (1809), 395.

were more palatable if applied to secondary figures, and even in an elite compilation such as the *Mirror for Magistrates*, the focus is on nobility rather than
monarchs, with rare exceptions, such as the unfortunate Henry VI.[83]

This, in turn, helps to explain the prominence in ballads, chapbooks, and jestbooks of interchangeable kings who encounter artisans, apprentices, and merchants, and fall under some form of obligation (food, drink, shelter, or merely
good company) to them, as well as those which focus on characters caught up
in the conflicts of their superiors, such as the recurrent figure of Shore's Wife.[84]
To us—and probably also to the gentry and nobility who increasingly provided
the audience of 'politic' historians from Francis Bacon to Gilbert Burnet—such
tales seem fanciful, even naive. They appear to reduce historical reality to the level
of fable. But for the reader of ballads and chapbooks, or for the illiterate who
simply picked up such tales by ear and retold or sang them, the presence of such
everyday characters rendered the tale far more vivid than any scholarly, chronologically accurate account would have done. So did the recounting of the story
in such a way as to emphasize themes of violence and hospitality, poverty and
honesty, while appealing to varying combinations of commonplace emotions such
as grief, fear, joy, and sexual interest.[85] It is surely this that makes their reception
of this history crucially different from that of a Samuel Pepys, who certainly read
ballads and chapbooks, but who also enjoyed privileged access to the very different accounts available from learned historical or antiquarian texts. How historical reality is construed very much depends not only on the form or genre in
which it is represented, but also on the social realities that define the world of
the individual reader or listener in the present.

GIANTS, NATIVE AND FOREIGN

Memories of giants and other monstrous beings in the remote past endured in
tradition and folklore from the early modern to the modern eras, though it is
difficult to date many of the survivals, and folkloric studies generally provide

---

[83] P. Budra, *A Mirror for Magistrates and the De Casibus Tradition* (Toronto, 2000), 14–38.

[84] See, for instance, the ballad *The Shepheard and the King, and of Gillian the Shepheards Wife*, fea-
turing King Alfred, in *The Pepys Ballads*, ed. Day, facs. vol. i, pp. 76–7; the chapbooks 'King Henry
VIII and a Cobler' and 'Henry VIII and the Abbot of Reading', both collected by Pepys, in *Samuel
Pepys' Penny Merriments*, ed. Thompson, 24–32; 'Of King Louis of France and the Husbandman', from
Tales and quicke answeres, very mery, and pleasant to rede (1535?), in *A Hundred Merry Tales and Other
English Jestbooks of the Fifteenth and Sixteenth Centuries*, ed. P. M. Zall (Lincoln, Nebr., 1963), 260–1,
which is immediately followed by another similar tale involving 'the forenamed king'. Other such
'jestes' are often even less specific, involving variously 'a king of England' out hunting and, in an earlier jestbook, 'the most noble and fortunate prince, King Edward of England', likely Edward III but
unspecified: ibid. 122, 284. Such tales continued to be attached to later kings, including Charles I, into
the eighteenth century: Briggs, *Dictionary of British Folk-Tales*, B.II, p. 22.

[85] This may provide us with part of the explanation for a fact noticed by Margaret Spufford, *Small
Books and Pleasant Histories*, 219, that the chapbook literature of the late seventeenth century contains remarkably little reference to such a central event as the Wars of the Roses.

little chronological help. Among the educated classes belief in the existence of real, historical giants began to fade from about 1580. William Harrison was notably suspicious in his contribution to Holinshed's *Chronicles*, allowing for the likelihood of men with superior stature but taking the legends of a race of giants in early Britain as 'not altogether credible'. This scepticism had deepened considerably a century later, under the impact of increasing historical knowledge, antiquarian discoveries, and the post-Reformation hostility to superstition.[86] John Locke, for example, would record references to them in his reading but was more interested in the origins of belief in giants than in the monsters themselves.[87] As early as the 1590s, Edmund Spenser's characters Ireneus and Eudoxus, discussing old Irish burial mounds and stone monuments, dismiss the idea that these were made by giants and ascribe them to pre-Christian burial customs.[88] Spenser's attitude was probably driven as much by his pronounced distaste for things Gaelic as by historical insight. In the following century, however, antiquaries and virtuosi would come to share in what amounted to an alternative explanation for fossils, artefacts, and burial sites, which the great majority of the population still attributed to giants. A century after Spenser, the author of an important manuscript collection of highland rites and customs admired precisely the same Celtic culture that the Elizabethan poet had despised, but preferred natural explanations for phenomena such as the Scottish 'giants' finger-stones' (large stones with holes through the centre).[89]

Those legends that could be checked against some external source inevitably fell prey to learned scrutiny first, and although in time antiquaries developed an entrenched scepticism towards most forms of local tradition, their initial targets were figures of pseudo-classical, biblical, or medieval legend such as Brutus the Trojan, Samothes, and (more problematically) Gomer, grandson of Noah. Simpler still to dismiss, because foreign and contemporary sources did not mention them, were putative ancient visits by real historical figures such as Hannibal and Alexander the Great. The normally circumspect Camden, who reserved judgement on the issue of Brutus, was uncharacteristically adamant that Hannibal and

---

[86] William Harrison, 'The Description of Britaine', in R. Holinshed, *The First and Second Volumes of Chronicles* (1587), 8–12.

[87] Bodl. MS Locke c. 33 (John Locke's notes on reading, 1676–90), fos. 21ᵛ, 36ᵛ, where Locke notes 'gigantum historia sunt fabula'; Thomas Molyneux, 'An essay concerning giants', *Philosophical Transactions*, 22 (1700), 489; A. Schnapper, 'Persistance des géants', *Annales ESC*, 41 (1986), 177–200, is helpful though it deals primarily with elite discussions of giants; W. Stephens Jr., '*De historia gigantum*: Theological Anthropology before Rabelais', *Traditio*, 40 (1984), 43–89, is a useful overview of Renaissance literary treatments, further developed in his book *Giants in Those Days: Folklore, Ancient History, and Nationalism* (Lincoln, Nebr., 1989), esp. pp. 64–72. For medieval treatments of giants, especially in Galfridian legend, see J. J. Cohen, *Of Giants: Sex, Monsters, and the Middle Ages* (Minneapolis, 1999), 29–71.

[88] Spenser, *View of Present the State of Ireland* (*c.*1596), in *Ireland under Elizabeth and James the First*, ed. H. Morley (London and New York, 1890), 117–18.

[89] Bodl. MS Carte 269, fo. 12ʳ, an annotated copy by Edward Lhwyd of a work attributed to the Revd James Kirkwood, and now printed in *A Collection of Highland Rites and Customes*, ed. J. L. Campbell (Cambridge and Totowa, NJ, 1975), 46.

Alexander had never set foot in Britain.[90] The early efforts of seventeenth-century antiquaries to set a period to the building of Stonehenge, described above in Chapter 6, represented both a wish to set that monument within the chronological past of European history, and to escape from the Galfridian tradition that they had been erected by Irish giants and transported by magic to Salisbury plain.[91]

Figures deriving exclusively from oral tradition could not be as easily verified, and following the rule that it is impossible to prove a negative they were not refutable in the same way as better-known historical or legendary personages. Many of these were nameless men or women remembered solely for some great deed or for an existing monument to their memory. A great number were quasi-supernatural—the giants of Beanstalk fairy tale—but several village stories involve human giants, such as the chapbook hero Tom Hickathrift, the giant-killer of the Isle of Ely.[92] These were abnormally large men (or, inversely, tiny ones such as Tom Thumb) who provided a ready explanation for any out-of-the-ordinary natural phenomenon. They frequently figured in processions, entries, and certain other sorts of local ritual, as ludic figures of aberrant nature, as symbols of misrule, and, sometimes, as examples of men of humble origin achieving fame and prosperity.[93]

Despite the opening up of what might be called a 'credulity gap' in the early seventeenth century, giants continued for some time to occupy space in the mental worlds of both the educated and the illiterate, as the appeal of Rabelais' Gargantua illustrates.[94] The reduction in human stature since biblical times was often mentioned as evidence of the general decline of the world, and many classical sources also mention men and women of exceptional girth and height, all of which further contributed to interest in the gigantic.[95] The Bible provided the major bridge

[90] William Camden, *Britain*, trans. P. Holland (1610), 32; on the treatment of these legends by antiquaries see T. D. Kendrick, *British Antiquity* (1950), chs. 6, 7; M. McKisack, *Medieval History in the Tudor Age* (Oxford, 1971), ch. 5. Brutus had a longer afterlife in elite circles, especially among the Welsh, than the advent of scholarly scepticism towards him suggests. During a parliamentary debate in April 1614, on repealing the longstanding Henrician discretionary right to amend Welsh law without parliamentary consent, the MP for Cardiff Matthew Davies reminded the House of Commons that the ancient Britons derived from Brutus and the Welsh in particular from his third son, Kamber. From this came 'Kambria, Wales', which was 'not conquered by the Romans, Danes, Normans'. *Proceedings in Parliament 1614 (House of Commons)*, ed. M. Jansson, Memoirs of the American Philosophical Society, 172 (Philadelphia, 1988), 97–8 (18 Apr. 1614).

[91] Gay, *A Fool's Bolt Soon Shott at Stonage*, in Legg, *Stonehenge Antiquaries*, 19–20; L. V. Grinsell, 'The Legendary History and Folklore of Stonehenge', *Folklore*, 87 (1976), 5–20.

[92] Briggs, *Dictionary of British Folk-Tales*, A.I, pp. 529–31; Spufford, *Small Books and Pleasant Histories*, 247–8.

[93] K. Park and L. J. Daston, 'Unnatural Conceptions: The Study of Monsters in Sixteenth- and Seventeenth-Century France and England', *Past and Present*, 92 (1981), 20–54, deals with living giants among contemporary 'monsters'. For giants in the context of popular drama, see M. Bristol, *Carnival and Theatre: Plebeian Culture and the Structure of Authority in Renaissance England* (1986), passim. The successful pauper retained his jocular, roguish reputation in the eyes of the elite, in picaresque novels, for example: thus Dick Whittington, one of several London heroes, was ridiculed by Steele in *The Tatler*, where Lemuel Ledger offers to provide detailed historical information on the mayor, his only daughter, and his cat: *The Tatler*, 78 (8 Oct. 1709), ed. D. F. Bond, 3 vols. (Oxford, 1987), i. 531.

[94] Stephens, *Giants in Those Days*.

[95] Harrison, 'Description of Britaine', 8–12; Stephens, *Giants in Those Days*, 72–92.

between learned and popular culture since it recorded the existence of giants. Many
domestic giants, such as Goemagot or Gogmagog, represent attempts to explain
features of the Anglo-Welsh landscape in a language that blended scriptural history with characters and stories recorded in medieval writers such as Geoffrey of
Monmouth, Gerald of Wales, and William of Newburgh.

The Elizabethan necromancer and astrologer Simon Forman exemplifies
the overlap between popular and learned culture on this subject, an overlap that
would diminish but not disappear in the course of the seventeenth century. One
of Forman's manuscripts notes that Adam and Eve had four gigantic children,
while his 'Bocke of giantes and huge and monstrose formes', assembled in 1610,
records the genealogies of Gog and Magog (the Galfridian Gogmagog split into
two so as to align it with the name's biblical origins).[96] Still another manuscript
provides a genealogical and biographical catalogue of all the giants who lived in
Britain and elsewhere after the Flood, along with their dimensions. But Forman
went beyond his literary sources to link the biblical and pseudo-biblical giants to
popular rumours that had arisen around various discoveries of large bones in
England and elsewhere, from the body of a man forty-six cubits long discovered
after the explosion of a Cretan volcano, to the 'tooth' in his possession that had
been discovered in the Isle of Thanet about 1596 'with a mighti battell ax by him'.
In 1603 Forman had seen with his own eyes another such tooth 'that did way
8 pound naught' leaning against a doctor's house in Cambridge.[97]

Beliefs about giants were frequently reinforced by accidental discoveries such
as those reported by Forman, whose notes have a late seventeenth-century counterpart in John Aubrey's remarks on gigantism and monstrosity.[98] In 1668 the body
of a 'giant of 10 foot long' was dug up in Cornwall, the news of this being relayed
to various antiquaries. In the 1680s a similar discovery of 'a body of extraordinary size', buried in close proximity to some brass daggers, occurred in Beddgelert,
near Snowdon.[99] In 1725 Hans Sloane was informed by John Colbatch that, in
digging for the foundations of St Martin's church, a huge coffin had recently been
found, and within it a ten-foot skeleton. The bones were eventually sent to a surgeon, but 'for want of due care the coffin was broke to pieces' and the bones fell
apart. 'To prevent the destroying any more such pieces of antiquity', Sloane informed
the Royal Society, clumsy middlemen ought to be cut out of the process. 'When

[96] Bodl. MS Ashm. 244 ('The Bocke of giantes and huge and monstrose formes gathered by Simon Forman anno 1610'), fos. 187[r], 192[r]–199[r].
[97] Bodl. MS Ashm. 802, fos. 19[r]–48[r], 59[r v].
[98] John Aubrey, *The Natural History of Wiltshire*, ed. J. Britton, Wiltshire Topographical Soc. (1847), 69–72.
[99] Joshua Childrey, *Britannia Baconica: or, The natural rarities of England, Scotland, & Wales* (1661), 25; Wood, *Life and Times*, ii. 141; Bodl. MS Gough Wales 5 (Anon., 'The Description of Wales', written c.1688), fo. 19[v]. As Kenneth H. Jackson points out in *The International Popular Tale*, 40, it was only in the eighteenth century that Beddgelert became associated with the much older story of Llywelyn and his hound 'Gelert' that reached Wales in the fourteenth century, probably from Asia. This involved the master slaying his faithful dog by mistake, thinking it had killed his infant son, only to discover that Gelert had saved the baby from a wolf, whereupon Llywelyn raised a grave in the dog's honour. A natural formation in Snowdonia National Park is sometimes referred to as Gelert's grave.

the digging for the ffoundation of the Portico was ordered, the Commissioners gave directions that if any curiosities were found they should give me notice and deliver them into my hands.' A few more days of digging produced another coffin, with a skeleton, bell-glass, and spearhead, the last 'much eaten away with rust'.[100]

The general attitude of the new science of Restoration and Augustan England towards giant discoveries was, rather like the attitude to popular beliefs in general, one of pragmatism. The objects themselves had to be explained, preferably in naturalistic terms, without accepting the local explanations. 'Tis observable, that allmost allways upon finding those large bones', one of Sloane's correspondents observed, '. . . the finders of 'em, esteemed them the bones of Gyants.' He himself preferred to think many of them had been elephants or hippopotami, a common explanation at the end of the seventeenth century.[101] Similar discoveries were a frequent topic of conversation among members of the revived Society of Antiquaries,[102] while at a Royal Society meeting in 1697 Robert Hooke read an account 'of a great skeleton supposed to be of an elephant dugg out of the side of a sandy hill in Germany', to which it was added that similar recent discoveries had been made near Newcastle, in Essex, and in a new lead mine in Derbyshire.[103]

Foreign travellers such as Thomas Platter were regaled with stories of British giants, though it is difficult to tell from their remarks whether these were entirely popular inventions or simply the 'Samotheans' and other pre-British beings, like Gogmagog.[104] This giant had evolved in the Middle Ages from the conflation of ancient giant legends with the biblical character prince Gog of Magog (Ezek. 38–9) and the two nations Gog and Magog which were to lead the forces of Satan at Armageddon (Rev. 20: 8). The past existence of these sorts of giants was still being seriously upheld in many chronicles of the early seventeenth century, and they figured prominently in sixteenth-century civic processionals and plays, for example the midsummer pageants at Coventry and Chester.[105] Two medieval figures

[100] BL MS Sloane 4025, fo. 76ʳ (communication by Hans Sloane to the Royal Society, 21 Oct. 1725).
[101] BL MS Sloane 4025, fo. 159ʳ (John Lufkin to Hans Sloane, n.d. March 1702 (date obscured by tear in MS)); for another example see R. T. Gunther, *Early Science in Oxford*, xiv: *Life and Letters of Edward Lhwyd* (Oxford, 1945), 200–1.
[102] Samuel Gale reported to the Society of Antiquaries' meeting of 12 June 1718 the discovery at Chippenham, Cambridgeshire, of a 'large skeleton' in chains and fetters: SAL, Minute Book 1718–32, p. 13. A 'tooth, skull and bones', found in a grave were taken by Charles Leigh to be 'only the Lusus Naturae, in Sparr and other indurated bodies, which unquestionably at the first were all fluid, and capable of any impression'. Charles Leigh, *The Natural History of Lancashire, Cheshire and the Peaks in Derbyshire* (Oxford 1720), book III, p. 41.
[103] Thomas Sprat, *The History of the Royal Society*, ed. J. I. Cope and H. W. Jones (St Louis, Mo., 1958), 199; BL MS Sloane 3341 (minute book of the Royal Society, 1696–7), fo. 3ʳ.
[104] *Thomas Platter's Travels in England, 1599*, ed. and trans. C. Williams (1937), 183.
[105] 'Gogmagog' was virtually a byword for giants: the Gogmagog hills near Cambridge were the scenes of recreations and games which university authorities repeatedly tried to suppress. Sixteenth-century Newcastle had an effigy of a giant named Hogmagog, used in its pageants, to the upkeep of which money was regularly contributed by the town officials: *REED: Cambridge*, ed. A. H. Nelson, 2 vols. (Toronto, 1989), 270–2, 276–7; *REED: Newcastle upon Tyne*, ed. J. J. Anderson (Toronto, 1982), 26–7, 33, 36, and *passim*. In 1564 two painters were retained for life by the mayor of Chester, Sir Laurence

at the Guildhall in London, known as Hercules and Samson in the early sixteenth century, had been renamed Gogmagog and Corineus by Elizabeth's reign; they were re-carved by Richard Sanderson in 1708 (Fig. 9.4), after the gutting of the Guildhall in the Great Fire, only to be destroyed in the Blitz of 1940. Two quarter-jacks (figures striking the quarter-hour on a clock), also named Gog and Magog, were erected outside St Dunstan's church, London, in 1671.[106]

Smith, to paint the annual midsummer Chester giants, at a cost of 40s. per year: BL MS Harl. 1968 (Holme collections), fo. 38^{r-v}. For an overview of the relation between the Galfridian and biblical traditions of Goemagot/Gog and Magog see L. Spence, *Minor Traditions of British Mythology* (New York, 1972), 59.

[106] Stow, *Survey of London*, 243; *The Guardian*, 173 (29 Sept. 1713), ed. J. C. Stephens (Lexington, Ky., 1982), 564; Cohen, *Of Giants*, 29; Spence, *Minor Traditions of British Mythology*, 60–1, citing Anon., *The Gigantick History of the Giants in the Guildhall* (1740); C. F. C. Beeson, *English Church Clocks*

Fig. 9.4. Corineus (*a*) and Gogmagog (*b*), re-carved by Richard Sanderson in 1708, but destroyed in the Second World War, at the Guildhall, London

1280–1850: History and Classification, Antiquarian Horological Soc. (Chichester, Sussex, 1971), 111; R. N. Worth, *Calendar of the Plymouth Municipal Records* (Plymouth, 1893), 112 records 8*d.* paid to William Hawkins, baker, in 1541–2 'for cuttyng of Gogmagog the pycture of the Gyaunt at hawe'. The career of the Chester Giants roughly reflects changes in religious sensibilities in the town: this midsummer pageant endured from 1497 (and perhaps earlier) till 1599, when Henry Hardware, Chester's puritan mayor, suppressed them. Revived four years later, they were again suspended during the interregnum, restored once more in 1661, and finally abolished in 1678: Thomas Sharp, *A Dissertation on the Pageants or Dramatic Mysteries Anciently Performed at Coventry* (1825), ed. A. C. Cawley (Totowa, NJ, 1973), 200–6. On Christmas eve in Chester there was an 'old order, & custome' whereby the mayor, sheriffs, aldermen, and forty common councillors rode through the city in triumph, whereupon the Recorder would speak on the antiquity of the city, which was 'founded by Gyants': *REED: Chester*, ed. Clopper, p. 415. For Coventry examples, see *REED: Coventry*, ed. R. W. Ingram (Toronto, 1981), 667 *sub* 'giants'.

TRADITIONS OF RESISTANCE

While many popular perceptions of the past were, from the point of view of the ruling powers, innocuous enough, others threatened to be subversive. As David Underdown has recently pointed out, the common people 'had their own version of that "ancient constitution" to which their superiors in Parliament were so constantly appealing, a version based on elements such as traditional rights, usage and custom'. When Charles I tried to revive the forest laws in 1634, a member of the Essex Grand Jury charged with enforcing them asked to see a copy of the original forest charter.[107] Conversely, the historical liberties to which seventeenth-century MPs appealed had little immediate significance to the ordinary Englishman more concerned about the price of grain, relations with neighbouring clergy and landowners, or the security of his own livelihood. For him, immemorial custom and prescriptive right had much more local and specific significance. This disengagement from the high political debates of the period would be eroded in the 1640s and 1650s, first under the encouragement of gentry leaders willing to use instruments such as 'popular' petitions and the clamour of the crowd in pursuit of their own political goals, and subsequently as more democratically minded groups such as the Levellers and Diggers attempted to shift the discussion away from the liberties of the propertied to the rights of all free men.[108] Even before the civil war, statements at odds with official and semi-official views of the past might emanate from local populations with little clear understanding of the terms of the Petition of Right, much less of Magna Carta. The Mowbray deed, for instance, was a mid-fourteenth-century document used by tenants of the manor of Epworth to argue that the then lord, Sir John de Mowbray, had perpetually barred his successors from 'improving' the commons at their expense. The deed was preserved in a chest, to which the freeholders held keys, in the parish church at Haxey, Lincolnshire. According to one visitor, the chest itself stood under a window 'wherein was the portraicture of Mowbray set in ancient glass, holding in his hand a writing which was commonly reputed to be an emblem of the deed'.[109]

Among the forms of popular belief that involved the past, Keith Thomas has demonstrated how substantial was the fear among the ruling orders of ancient political prophecies, especially when these were revived in times of national

---

[107] Underdown, *Revel, Riot and Rebellion*, 125.

[108] The 'Norman yoke', often cited as an example of popular resistance to an aristocratic and subsequently capitalist regime whose control over property dated from the Conquest was in origins a learned rather than a plebeian tradition, and scarcely 'popular' in the sense applied to most of the beliefs related here, though in the writings of Gerrard Winstanley and later radicals it would penetrate somewhat further down the social scale. The sources used by Christopher Hill in his celebrated essay on this subject are uniformly those of literate culture: C. Hill, 'The Norman Yoke', in his *Puritanism and Revolution* (1958: repr. 1986), 58–125.

[109] Daniel Noddel, cited in C. Holmes, 'Drainers and Fenmen: The Problem of Popular Political Consciousness in the Seventeenth Century', in A. Fletcher and J. Stevenson (eds.), *Order and Disorder in Early Modern England* (Cambridge, 1985), 192.

crisis.[110] Political songs, many of which dated from as early as the thirteenth century, provide another example. Though many songs and ballads about the past appear unthreateningly loyal and obedient, and even condemn rebels such as Jack Straw and Wat Tyler, others are less unequivocally friendly to authority, or run against prevailing political winds. A number of sympathetic ballads appeared after the fall of Thomas Cromwell in 1540 and again after the Northern Rebellion in 1569. Two of the latter celebrate the exploits of the 'good noble erle of Northumberland' and his companion the earl of Westmorland, including the former's betrayal and execution.[111] Similarly ambivalent ballads appeared after the failure of the Essex rebellion in 1601, stopping short of outright condemnation of its leader, a 'valiant knight of chivalry'.[112]

   It would be going much too far to suggest the existence of a historical counter-culture among the populace, a unified vision of the past antagonistic to that hierarchical, orderly one represented by chroniclers and university-educated historians. There are nevertheless many indications that the printed histories of the period (most of which, up to 1640, were uniformly pro-monarchist) do not reflect the sum total of historical opinion. A traditional rhyme current in Westmorland at the end of the seventeenth century specifically attacked Henry VIII for greed:

> Henricus Octavus
> Took more than he gave us.[113]

An oral tradition at Glastonbury had it that the surviving stone kitchen had been built because 'the king of England sent word to the ritch abbott that hee purposed to come and sett fire off his kitchin', meaning that there would be much feasting. The abbot knew the king's meaning but played a joke by taking him literally and building the kitchen of stone, not timber so the king could not burn it. By the time Peter Mundy heard this tale, in 1639, it was generally attached to Henry VIII (undoubtedly because of his association with the dissolution of the local abbey); the kitchen was now being used to store turf. At the end of the

---

[110] K. Thomas, *Religion and the Decline of Magic* (1971; repr. 1978), ch. 13 *passim*; S. L. Jansen, *Political Protest and Prophecy under Henry VIII* (Woodbridge, Suffolk and Rochester, NY, 1991).

[111] 'Thomas Cromwell', 'The Rising in the North' and 'Northumberland betrayed by Douglas', in Child, *English and Scottish Popular Ballads*, pt. 6, pp. 377, 404, 411; Firth, 'The Ballad History of the Reigns of the Later Tudors', 82–8.

[112] *Roxburghe Ballads*, i. 571, also cited in Firth, 'Ballad History of the Later Tudors', 116.

[113] *Antiquary on Horseback*, ed. J. M. Ewbank, Cumberland and Westmorland Archaeological and Antiquarian Soc., ES 19 (1963), 65. This popular reputation of Henry VIII for rapacity, as opposed to the generosity for which he was famous among historians, may be contrasted to verses about his father, Henry VII, which associate him with charity, open-handedness, and social justice, once again the opposite image from the avaricious figure found in historians since Francis Bacon. Since Henry VIII closed the monasteries, symbols for many of hospitality and charity, while his father had been a loyal adherent of Rome, this inversion of their usual characterization may well have appealed especially to recusants. William Blundell the younger was informed by a fellow Catholic, Sir Vivian Molyneux, of two verses written over the gate of the Savoy at London, 'King Henry the Seventh, to his worship and honour, | Builded this hospital, poor people to succour.' Blundell, *Cavalier's Note Book*, 192.

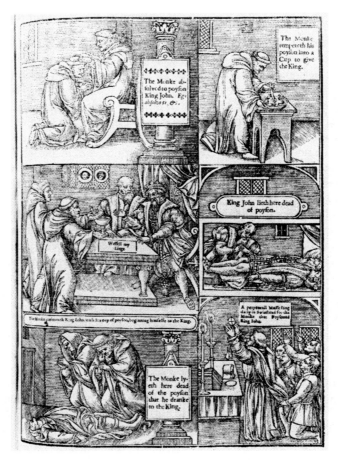

Fig. 9.5. A graphic representation of a historical episode: the poisoning of King John, the victim of monkish conspiracy. From Foxe, *Acts and Monuments*, vol. i, facing p. 332

seventeenth century it was still common in Yorkshire to hear mutterings about King Henry 'and his greedy courtiers'.[114] King John was another subject of such libels. A ballad in the Pepys collection, based on a well-known international popular tale, relates how the king, jealous of the 'abbot' of Canterbury's wealth, poses him three questions, failure to answer which will result in the churchman's decapitation. It begins, again, with a negative view of that king, and not one that makes any reference to the Protestant historiographical treatment of John as an early opponent of Rome and victim of monastic assassination (Fig. 9.5).

[114] *The Travels of Peter Mundy in Europe and Asia 1608–1667*, vol. iv, ed. R. C. Temple, Hakluyt Soc., 2nd ser., 55 (1925), 4; BL MS Lans. 897 (Pryme's History of Hatfield), fo. 121ʳ, comment by author on local complaints of the ruin of the monasteries and decline of hospitality.

Ile tell you a story, a story anon
Of a noble Prince: his name was King John
for he was a Prince, and a Prince of great might
He held up great wrongs, he put down great Right.
Derry down, down hey derry down.

Despite this opening, the ballad boasts the imprimatur of Roger L'Estrange, Surveyor of the Press, perhaps because in the end, having been tricked by the abbot's shepherd who has taken his master's place, the king is amused, pays the impostor, pardons the abbot, and calls himself 'Good K. John'.[115]

Just as the popular vision of the past liked to bring kings down to the level of tinkers and weavers, so it also often elevated brigands and outlaws. Alan Macfarlane has argued that pre-industrial England had relatively little history of banditry, though his own example of the Smorthwaites, a family of Restoration thieves, survived in oral tradition from the late seventeenth to the mid-twentieth centuries.[116] Throughout the later Middle Ages ballads circulated widely concerning heroic rebels such as Hereward the Wake (a shadowy figure first mentioned in the Peterborough recension of the *Anglo-Saxon Chronicle*) and Fulk Fitzwarin, opponents respectively of William I and John. Hereward in particular had strong associations in the fenlands, the location of much resistance to agrarian improvement in the seventeenth century. Extant written tales of the most famous of all bandits, Robin Hood, date back to *The Gest of Robyn Hode* at the end of the fourteenth century, and first surfaced in print in the early sixteenth century.[117] The researches of Maurice Keen, J. C. Holt, J. G. Bellamy, and P. R. Coss have established the importance of this and other romances, ballads, and gests in the courtly and provincial cultures of the later Middle Ages.[118] Throughout the

[115] *The Pepys Ballads*, ed. Day, facs. vol. ii, p. 128; Child, *English and Scottish Popular Ballads*, pt. 2, p. 413, version B. On the many versions of this story within and outside England see Jackson, *The International Popular Tale*, 15–16.

[116] A. Macfarlane with S. Harrison, *The Justice and the Mare's Ale* (Cambridge, 1981), 163–72.

[117] *Here begynneth a lytell geste of Robin Hode* (STC 13689, n.d., but before 1519), repr. in *Robin Hood: A Collection of all the Ancient Poems, Songs, and Ballads, now Extant*, ed. J. Ritson, 2 vols. (1795), i. 1–80.

[118] The modern literature on Robin Hood is considerable: M. Keen, 'Robin Hood—Peasant or Gentleman?', *Past and Present*, 19 (1960), 7–15, and his *The Outlaws of Medieval Legend* (1961), 11–52; R. H. Hilton, 'The Origin of the Robin Hood Myth', *Past and Present*, 14 (1958), 30–44; J. C. Holt 'The Ballads of Robin Hood', *Past and Present*, 18 (1960), 89–107, and *Robin Hood*, 2nd edn. (1989), 159–99; J. G. Bellamy, *Robin Hood: An Historical Enquiry* (Bloomington, Ind., 1984); P. R. Coss, 'Aspects of Cultural Diffusion in Medieval England: The Early Romances, Local Society and Robin Hood', *Past and Present*, 108 (1985), 35–79. There has been considerable recent interest in Robin Hood, for instance Stephen Knight, *Robin Hood: A Complete Study of the English Outlaw* (Oxford, 1994); id. (ed.), *Robin Hood: An Anthology of Scholarship and Criticism* (Cambridge, 1999). Essays from a 1997 conference at the University of Rochester have been published in T. Hahn (ed.), *Robin Hood in Popular Culture: Violence, Transgression, and Justice* (Cambridge, 2000): see esp. R. B. Dobson, 'Robin Hood: The Genesis of a Popular Hero', ibid. 61–77. Sean Field has suggested, in a perceptive essay which appeared as this volume went to press, that early sixteenth-century versions of Robin, which repeatedly mention his piety, represent a conservative position on religious issues that is consistent with aspects of Henrician religious reform, but also with anti-monasticism: S. Field, 'Devotion, Discontent, and the Henrician Reformation: The Evidence of the Robin Hood Stories', *Journal of British Studies*, 41 (2002), 6–22.

336 The Past Remembered

sixteenth century Robin Hood remained a frequent character in ballads, pageants, and plays; he was a figure popular in aristocratic circles, even though criticism of him went as far back as the fifteenth-century Scottish chronicles in which
he first appears. A young Henry VIII repeatedly disported himself with his
courtiers as Robin and his outlaws.[119] Although the number of dramatizations of
his tale diminished after 1600—thus coinciding with Professor Hutton's 'fall' of
merry England—they still occurred with some regularity. Restoration chapbook
versions such as *Robin Hood's Garland* (1656) were reprinted and read well into
the nineteenth century.[120] The plays seen by the Lancashire squire Nicholas
Blundell on his trip to London in 1717 thus included both Shakespeare's *Titus
Andronicus* at Drury Lane and a farce called 'Robin Hudd & Little John', acted
at Bartholomew Fair.[121] Robin featured prominently in May games and morris-
dancing, and at various times during the sixteenth and seventeenth centuries was
the target of hostility from reformers. This antagonism and the rituals themselves
were by no means confined to Robin's traditional Nottinghamshire home. The
churchwardens' accounts for Croscombe parish in Somerset in 1537 record
expenses for 'Maid Maryan's Kyrtle', while at Melton Mowbray in 1564, town officials
received 14s. as 'Robin Hood's money'.[122]

Robin's name also surfaced periodically as a byword for transgression of the
laws protecting the propertied. As such, he was by the sixteenth century as much
a part of the vocabulary of the elite (many of whom must have read ballads concerning him), as of their inferiors. Chief Justice Ranulph Crewe waxed indignant
at the pardon of a condemned horse-thief because the man had robbed up and
down the countryside 'like Robin Hood and his men'. Various oral traditions

---

[119] C. Hill, 'Robin Hood', in Knight (ed.), *Robin Hood: An Anthology*, 285–95; Field, 'Devotion,
Discontent, and the Henrician Reformation', 22, citing *Hall's Chronicle*, ed. Ellis (1809), 513, 582.

[120] *Robin Hoods Garland* (1663) and in general the extensive list of titles in Wing, vol. iii,
R1624A–R1644A. For other seventeenth-century examples, see e.g. BL MS Add. 71158, a late seventeenth-century octavo collection of twenty-one Robin Hood ballads of varying lengths (often concerning Robin and a 'Queen Catherine' or 'King Henry', or conversely featuring farmers or
tradesmen). An extensive assortment of Robin ballads appear in *The Pepys Ballads*, ed. Day, facs. vol.
i, pp. 78–9, vol. ii, pp. 99–123 (where Robin's ballads precede several on real historical figures in a
section Pepys entitles 'History True & Fabulous'). M. A. Nelson, *The Robin Hood Tradition in the
English Renaissance* (Salzburg, 1973), chs. 3 and 4, notes that Robin's only appearance in early Stuart
drama is in Ben Jonson's *The Sad Shepherd*, first printed in 1641. Child, *English and Scottish Popular
Ballads*, pt. 6, reprints over thirty Robin Hood ballads from the late Middle Ages to the early nineteenth century, as does *Ancient Poems, Ballads, and Songs of the Peasantry of England*, ed. J. H. Dixon,
Percy Soc., 17 (1846).

[121] *The Great Diurnal of Nicholas Blundell of Little Crosby, Lancashire*, ed. F. Tyrer and J. J. Bagley,
3 vols., Rec. Soc. of Lancashire and Cheshire (1968–72), ii. 207; Ronald Hutton, *The Rise and Fall of
Merry England: The Ritual Year, 1400–1700* (Oxford and New York, 1994), 31–3, 100, 114.

[122] Wright, *British Calendar Customs*, ii. 240–2; Lancashire, *Dramatic Texts and Records of Britain*,
provides a list of pre-1600 Robin Hood references and their sources: see esp. pp. 14, 27, 63, 65, 77–8,
81, 88, 107, 280. Instances of suggested or actual censorship or suppression of Robin Hood celebrations occurred in 1510 at Exeter, where the city council forbade Robin Hood plays except on dedication days (Lancashire, *Dramatic Texts*, 135); in 1535 when they aroused the hostility of Richard
Morison (ibid. 65); in 1580 at Burnley, Lancs. (ibid. 91), in 1589 (ibid. 75 and 148, for two alleged cases
of priests taking part in a morris involving Robin). Robin Hood plays were also staged in private
houses, such as that of John Thynne at Longleat, Wiltshire about 1562 (ibid. 223).

associated aspects of the Devon landscape with a folk-hero called Symm, whom the antiquary Thomas Westcote thought 'another Robin Hood'.[123] Robin's popularity as a historical figure is further borne out by the number of places which from the sixteenth century to modern times have carried his name, such as Robin Hood's Hill overlooking Gloucester, visited by William Stukeley in the 1720s.[124]

Yet the very conception of Robin Hood and his men in the early modern era suggests that the Robin Hood legend more often than not sanctioned social hierarchy (albeit while condemning abuses such as greed, corruption, or a lack of charity) rather than challenging it directly. In the hands of Renaissance dramatists and pageant-makers the original yeomen of the medieval ballads were raised in dignity to the status of gentlemen or nobles fallen on hard times or wronged of their rightful superior position. One seventeenth-century version focuses on 'Robin Hoods birth, breeding, valour, and marriage' (and, for good measure, confidently records him as the great-nephew of Sir Guy of Warwick).[125] They thus became mirror images of the poor boy who achieves wealth and nobility through his wits or deeds, joining the social elite rather than overcoming it.[126] At the same time, Robin remained a respected figure within the violent 'hunting culture' of the minor gentry and many members of the aristocracy, the same group that celebrated the old ballad *Chevy Chase* (first printed in the mid-sixteenth century) as a testament to traditional hunting rights.[127] By the eighteenth century various antiquaries were claiming to have identified a historical Robin Hood among the medieval aristocracy. The great Stukeley even presented his colleagues in the Society of Antiquaries with a genealogy of 'the famous outlaw, pretended earl of Huntingdon' in 1721, dating Robin's death to 1247 and tracing his ancestry back to Syward, earl of Northumberland at the time of the Norman Conquest. In the following year the society discussed the remains of an old ballad of Robin Hood that had been removed from the cover of a book.[128] The wish to locate Robin at a specific point in history was not uncommon. William Jackson of Yarmouth,

---

[123] Hist. MSS Comm., *The Manuscripts of the Earl Cowper, K.G., Preserved at Melbourne Hall, Derbyshire*, 3 vols. (1888–9), i. 282; Westcote, *View of Devonshire*, 95. A few decades earlier, John Lyly had grumbled that the English were more inclined to talk of Robin Hood 'then to shoot in his bowe': *Euphues and his England*, in *Complete Works of John Lyly*, ed. R. W. Bond, 3 vols. (Oxford, 1902), ii. 200.

[124] SAL MS Stukeley IV/i/294; for contemporary reference to Robin Hood Bay near Hackness, Yorkshire, see *Leland's Itinerary*, i. 51; *Diary of Lady Margaret Hoby 1599–1605*, ed. D. M. Meads (Boston, 1930), 205. A recent edition of the *Bartholomew Gazeteer of Places in Britain* (1986), which is not exhaustive, lists Robin or Robin Hood locations in Staffordshire, Lancashire, West Yorkshire, North Yorkshire (Robin Hood's Bay), as well as streams such as Robin's Brook (near Coggeshall, Essex). Many of these are attributable no earlier than the sixteenth century and bespeak the influence of printed accounts of Robin Hood's career such as the broadside *A ballett of Robyn Hod* (1562) and the earlier *A Gest of Robyn Hode* (1510).

[125] *Robin Hood: A Collection*, ed. Ritson, ii. 1–11, at p. 3.

[126] This is the position of Keen, *Outlaws*, 145–73, 178; but cf. Holt, *Robin Hood*, who points out that the term yeoman in the medieval literature may refer to a household servant of gentle status.

[127] R. B. Manning, *Hunters and Poachers* (Oxford, 1993), 21, 49, 168.

[128] SAL MS 264, fo. 15ʳ; SAL Minute Book, 1718–32, pp. 44, 63; the genealogy in question was lent out to a gentleman later that year but subsequently returned, and is now SAL Antiquaries MS 67: J. Evans, *A History of the Society of Antiquaries* (Oxford, 1956), 65.

the town's customs-master, placed Robin Hood within the 1265 baronial crisis of the reign of Henry III, and saw him as the ancestor of the Devereux earls of Essex. Jackson recounted Robin Hood's death in a nunnery seven miles from Wakefield, wherein was a grave with 'a stone with some obsolete letters not to be read and now to be seene called Robin Hood's grave and formerly an arbour of trees and wood'.[129]

Not all such figures were as easily historicized or rendered socially harmless. Richard Bolton, an early eighteenth-century Staffordshire antiquary, reported a Tutbury tradition whereby an entrenchment in Watling Street was called 'Knaves-castle', in the middle of which was once a 'round hill (but it is now excavated)'. According to one tradition, it had been used for a Watch, the area being infested by robbers, to which travellers were obliged to contribute. But another version of the story also existed, more disturbing in its implications. According to this 'the robbers themselves harboured here and therefore it was called Knaves-castle', the memory of brigands being thereby lent public recognition.[130] A century earlier, John Weever had recorded a story 'as it hath gone by tradition from father to sonne' of a local hero buried at Tilney, Norfolk, who 'upon a time (no man knowes how long since)' had led the commoners in revolt against an unjust landlord.[131] A ballad included by Dugdale in his *History of Imbanking and Draining* (1662) included the 'libellous song' entitled *The Powtes Complaint*, inciting fenland residents to band together in the name of their 'ancient water nurses' and of 'good old Captain Flood':

> This noble Captain yet was never known to fail us,
> But did the conquest get of all that did assail us;
> His furious rage none could assuage; but, to the world's great wonder,
> He bears down banks, and breaks their cranks and whirlygigs asunder.[132]

The two stones, fourteen feet apart, in Weston graveyard, Hertfordshire, were supposed by local 'swains' to be the grave of Jack o' Legs, the 'Weston Giant' who, apart from his prodigious size, was a local thief with a generous heart. According to Nathaniel Salmon, who recorded the story in 1728, Jack 'plundered the rich to feed the poor' until he was captured, blinded, and hanged by his long-time foes, the bakers of nearby Baldock. 'To follow such a story', Salmon concluded, 'is almost as wise as to confute it.' His considered opinion recalls the contemporaneous attempts to gentrify and historicize Robin Hood. Salmon thought it likely that Jack of Weston was based on the real, historical deeds of the twelfth-century figure 'Richard Strongbow' (Richard de Clare, earl of Pembroke), sometime lord of the manor of Weston until exiled by King Stephen. Pembroke's achievements had, Salmon deduced, been 'told by nursery fires, till they were thus happily

---

[129] CUL MS Oo.VI.15 (William Jackson, 'The pedigree of Robert earle fferrers and derby commonly called Robin Hood'), fos. 64ʳ–65ᵛ.

[130] Bodl. MS Top. Staffs. e. 2 (Richard Bolton, 'A View of Staffordshire' 1707–21), p. 200.

[131] John Weever, *Ancient Funerall Monuments within the United Monarchie of Great Britain, Ireland, and the Islands Adjacent* (1631), preface and pp. 225, 312, 646, 866.

[132] *The Powtes Complaint*, in William Dugdale, *History of Imbanking and Draining* (1662), 391.

improved'. Locals had apparently also displayed a giant's 'thigh-bone' in the first half of the seventeenth century, which they kept in the parish chest and eventually sold to the elder John Tradescant.[133]

ALTERNATIVE VISIONS OF THE RECENT PAST

As these last examples suggest, local beliefs, especially when contained in oral forms like traditions and ballads, or uttered in spur-of-the-moment declarations, were not subject to the same canons of order and hierarchy as written history. In most instances, they might be dismissed as vulgar, or subjected to Robin Hood-style domestication, but their utterance or even reprinting did not generally occasion more explicitly hostile reactions. In contrast, authorities were acutely sensitive to potentially seditious views of the more recent past, which have consequently found a place in the criminal records. A Suffolk petticoat-maker found himself before an Essex JP in 1577 for having unwisely declared to his fellows at dinner that 'It was never merry in England sithence the scriptures were so commonly preached and talked upon among such persons as they were.'[134] William Francis, a smith of Hatfield Broad Oak, found himself convicted at assizes in 1587 for claiming that Edward VI was still alive having been spirited 'in a red mantell into Germany in a ship called the Harry', a piece of lead having been buried in his place, as a witness put it, 'wher they used to burye kings'.[135] A similar claim by a Londoner pretending to be Edward was prosecuted in 1578, while in the following year a Colchester yeoman had his ears nailed to the pillory for accusing the earls of Leicester and Warwick of making away with Edward.[136]

A number of sedition cases from the Elizabethan era, often involving Catholic or at least religiously conservative nostalgia, tie economic hardship in the present to changes in religious regimes of a few years earlier. Nicholas Blundell's grandfather, William Blundell the younger, a former royalist officer who lived well into his grandson's adult life, passed on to Nicholas 'a Contry song remembring the harmeless mirth of Lancashyre in peaseable tymes', that he had written during the civil war.[137] William's own grandfather, William Blundell 'the Recusant', whose resistance to Protestantism repeatedly had him in trouble with authority, was also the author of verses that lament the lost values of pre-Reformation England:

[133] Nathaniel Salmon, *The History of Hertfordshire* (1728), 184.

[134] F. B. Emmison, *Elizabethan Life: Disorder* (Chelmsford, 1970), 47. Recreation rather than politics or social commentary were clearly on the mind of William Barnes, cordwainer, as he asserted to a friend during the interregnum that 'in former tymes when the booke of common prayer was read the people did usually goe out of the church to play at football and to the alehouse and their continued till they were drunke and it were no matter if they were hanged'. Essex RO D/B 3/3/149/7 (Malden borough records, undated).

[135] J. S. Cockburn, *Calendar of Assize Records, Elizabeth I*, 5 vols. (1975–80), iii (Essex indictments), 294, no. 1728.

[136] Ibid. iii. 175, 191, nos. 1004, 1094. In a 1586 case (ibid. iii. 287, no. 1683), the vicar of Wivenhoe was alleged to have asserted not only that he was Henry VIII's son but that Elizabeth was his *full* sister.

[137] *Great Diurnal of Nicholas Blundell*, i. 322 (appendix H).

> The tyme hath been wee hadd one faith,
> And strode aright one ancient path,
> The thym is now that each man may
> See newe Religons coynd each day . . .
>   The tyme hath beene the prelate's dore
> Was seldome shotte against the pore,
> The tyme is now, so wives goe fine,
> They take not thought the kyne . . .[138]

In 1581 David Brown, an East Tilbury husbandman, was convicted at Essex assizes for saying that 'yt was a mery worlde when the servyce was use in the latten tunge and nowe we are in an evill waye and going to the devill', while declaring his support for an anticipated invasion by the exiled earl of Westmorland. Steven Slater, a Smithfield weaver and disgruntled ex-soldier, allegedly proclaimed aloud that 'Kinge Phillipp was a father to Ingland and did better love an Inglyshe man then the Quenes Majestie did, for that he woulde geve them meete, drynck and clothe', for which he was acquitted.[139] A long ballad was circulated, though not written, by Thomas Hale, a gentleman of Walthamstow, in 1594, in which it was lamented:

> The monuments and life of sayntes are brent and torne by vyolence,
> Some shredd the holye sacraments. O Christe, they wonderous pacyence.
> The memorye of Christe his deathe is rootinge owte apace,
> The Joyes above the paynes beneath in fewe mens harts have place.[140]

The seventeenth century produced its share of seditious allusions to the past, with political as well as religious allegiance playing a part. One of many libels on the death of the earl of Salisbury blackened his memory with unmistakably hostile historical comparisons to Richard III and Judas. In 1626 one William Wrapshall is reported to have remarked of Charles I 'The King had need look to himself. His grandfather was hanged on a pear tree. His grandmother was beheaded . . . His elder brother 'twas thought he was poisoned. His sister she is driven out of her country. There is a curse laid upon him or the kingdom.'[141] These sorts of remarks were signs of strained relations between Crown and realm at various junctures, and the outbreak of the civil war could turn them positively regicidal. In May 1645 a London spinster was sought by parliament for referring

---

[138] *Crosby Records: A Chapter of Lancashire Recusancy*, ed. T. Gibson, Chetham Soc., NS 12 (1887), 24–9; Lancs. RO, DDBl 6121 (Blundell papers, Great Hodge Podge), fo. 132ʳ Latin verses on 'An expostulation or chyding of Jesus with man perishinge throughe his owne fawlte; translated out of latin verse into Englishe as foloweth by Wil. Bl.'.

[139] Cockburn, *Calendar of Assize Records*, iii. 213, no. 1233 (20 Jan. 1581); ibid. iii. 272, no. 1592 (July 1585). Similar utterances could also be made from the other religious extreme, for instance by the cleric charged in 1582 (ibid. iii. 235, no. 1369) with a criticism of the Book of Common Prayer.

[140] Ibid. iii. 426, no. 2576.

[141] P. Croft, 'The Reputation of Robert Cecil: Libels, Political Opinion and Popular Awareness in the Early Seventeenth Century', *TRHS* 6th ser., 1 (1991), 43–69, at p. 55; A. J. Bellany, 'The Poisoning of Legitimacy? Court Scandal, News Culture and Politics in England' (Ph.D. diss., Princeton University, 1995), 552–3, from which I derive this latter reference.

to the king as a 'stuttering fool' and asking (recalling the assassin of the duke of Buckingham), 'Is there never a Felton yett living?' A mere four years later such a remark would scarcely have offended the victorious parliamentary regime.[142] In October 1682 the Bath attorney Edward Whitaker was tried for having spoken, two years earlier, 'seditious and scandalous words' to the effect that 'there was talk of a war and rebellion in the late times, but he knew of none; 'tis true, there was a warr by the parliament and people in defence of their just liberties; and that the late king was putt to death by a judiciall processe and not murd'red.'[143] Tags from history could be revived and used as insults in the present: the constables of several places in Lancashire were ordered to detain a carpenter and a husbandman of Penwortham in 1722 for instigating a riot in which they had also shouted, with reference to the government and allusion to the 1650s, 'Down with the Rump.'[144]

There was of course no really effective means of censoring parish discourse, notwithstanding various Tudor attempts to deter treason in speech as well as in deed. Words once spoken, songs once sung, could be punished only after the fact, and unlike offensive books they could not be publicly burned by the hangman.[145] The ballad-singers persecuted as vagrants by Elizabethan and Stuart governments were distrusted not only for their lack of local ties but also for their irresponsible, uncensored songs.[146] Ballads, libels, songs, and oral traditions answered to no man: they constituted a kind of 'masterless history'. An oral reference to riot, brigandage, and rebellion that did not condemn these unequivocally could scarcely be more welcome to England's ruling orders than a printed history advocating the same, and it was vastly more difficult to control.

Other popular beliefs, while not socially or politically subversive, nevertheless challenged what amounted to an authoritative view of recent English history under the Tudors and early Stuarts. Sir George Buck, whose dogged attempt to rescue the character of Richard III from a century of Tudor vilification was published

---

[142] *Middlesex County Records*, ed. J. C. Jeaffreson, 4 vols. (1886–92; repr. 1974–5), iii. 93. This example is also used by Bellany, 'Poisoning of Legitimacy', 676, who points to the reconstruction of Felton as a 'patriotic hero'.

[143] Narcissus Luttrell, *A Brief Historical Relation of State Affairs from Sept. 1678 to April 1714*, 6 vols. (Oxford 1857), i. 233.

[144] Lancs. RO QSP 1191/13 (order to constables).

[145] Oral treason, and even sedition, had become very difficult to establish at law by the late seventeenth century, if not earlier. Even in the heated atmosphere of 1685, a case at Middlesex Sessions against one Thomas Child for 'speaking treasonable words' against James II fizzled for lack of convincing testimony. In 1668 a yeoman was acquitted of sedition for saying 'Soldiers were better paid in the days of Oliver': *Middlesex County Records*, ed. Jeaffreson, iv. 2–3, 284–5.

[146] Register of Passports for Vagrants, in *Poverty in Early-Stuart Salisbury*, ed. P. Slack, Wiltshire Rec. Soc., 31 (Devizes, 1975), 46, 49. Similarly offensive were claims that authorities were in some way interfering with ancient privileges. In July 1621 Star Chamber tried several people involved in a stage play at Kendal. This featured landlords in hell and a character who asserted that the landlords wanted all men reduced to tenants at will and to remove their 'ancient liberties': *REED: Cumberland, Westmorland, Gloucestershire*, ed. Audrey Douglas and Peter Greenfield (Toronto, 1986), 191 ff. Cf. R. Suggett, 'Vagabonds and Minstrels in Sixteenth-Century Wales', in Fox and Woolf (eds.), *The Spoken Word*, 138–72.

only several years after his death, and even then in a much diluted form, based his case not only on scrupulous scholarship in the written and printed sources, but also on oral traditions. Much of his information came verbatim from the octogenarian John Stow, who had himself spoken in the mid-sixteenth century with old men who recalled Richard in a favourable light.[147] The comparatively rare occurrence in antiquarian writings of memories at odds with elite beliefs about the order of things does not prove that they were not more widespread. Given the strong emphasis on social inversion in various expressions of popular culture, written, spoken, and performed, as well as fears of ancient popular prophecy, there is good reason to infer the contrary. Indeed, it may only establish that the antiquaries were themselves performing the function of unofficial censors by leaving such troublesome material out of their accounts. This filtration process, which we shall explore more fully in the next chapter, was most pronounced after the interregnum, when memories of very recent events were especially sensitive, their topicality often shunting aside older, medieval traditions. It can be seen at work in the writings of Abraham de la Pryme, whose close ties to the countryside gave him an insatiable love of local lore. Pryme exemplifies the dilemma of the educated observer, unwilling fully to endorse the popular beliefs that suffuse his local environment but that conflict with learned historical knowledge, yet equally unable to repudiate them categorically. He consistently edited, censored, and suppressed oral information from his diary for a variety of reasons, omitting, for instance, several stories about the Cromwellian preacher Hugh Peter: 'tho' they were very memorable, yet, because the[y] relate to such a rogue, they are not worthy of setting down'.[148]

THE LANDSCAPE OF ANCIENT CONFLICT

While relatively little ballad and broadside literature reflects a keen awareness of late medieval conflicts such as the fifteenth-century struggle between Lancaster and York, more ancient disturbances had a higher profile in popular consciousness, having become associated over time with specific places. Unusual geological formations, including caves, gave rise to tales of tunnels and underground sanctuaries, such as the hidden vault Henry Savage recorded running between Glastonbury Abbey and the nearby George Inn.[149] A cave cut into the soft red

[147] George Buck, *The History of King Richard the Third*, ed. A. N. Kincaid (Gloucester, 1979), pp. cxvii–cxxiv, 162, 298; C. L. Kingsford, *English Historical Literature in the Fifteenth Century* (Oxford, 1913), 270. The sixteenth-century battle between Anglo-Welsh adherents to Arthurian legend and those historians, beginning with Polydore Vergil, who denied the truth of such myths was in some measure a disagreement about the relative importance of oral and written sources for the ancient history of Britain.
[148] *Diary of Abraham de la Pryme*, 50–1.
[149] Bristol RO MS 36074 (88), p. 147, notes of Henry Savage, 6 June 1677. Subterranean cavities were also explored by archaeologically minded antiquaries such as William Stukeley and Roger Gale, who crept 'upon all-four up to the ancles in mire for several hundred yards' to explore Pool's Hole at Buxton Wells: Nichols, *Literary Illustrations*, iv. 487 (Roger Gale to Samuel Gale, 3 Aug. 1725).

rock of Nesscliff Hill, Shropshire had a natural partition, leading locals to believe that 'one Kynaston', a robber, lived in one part while using the other for his horse.[150] About 1675, the aged Cumberland antiquary Edmund Sandford noted having been told by another local gentleman of a 'stranger gentleman' staying many years earlier at an inn, having come to see the local antiquities. The stranger had sought guidance to the burial place of Sir Hugh Cesario, a 'knight errant' figure who had 'lived in disert place in a rocke', near a place where there were three vaults. An expedition with this visiting antiquary (whom Sandford's nineteenth-century editor speculated might have been the great Camden himself) turned up 'the great Long Shank bones and other bones of a man and a broad Sword besides fonde then by the Church wardens'. The kind of antiquarian discoveries discussed earlier in this book could thus do as much to reinforce popular beliefs about the past as to discredit them.[151] A 1685 broadsheet described an underground house filled with coins and medals, unearthed near Cirencester, and thought to be left over from the Roman occupation. Though it cited the authority of an unnamed 'gentleman who is a famous antiquary', the story is almost certainly a complete fabrication, synthesizing popular traditions about caves and buried palaces filled with sleeping warriors with prophetic beliefs about the return of long-dead emperors awaiting the final battle with Antichrist, and medieval chroniclers' reports of marvellous tombs lit by ever-burning lamps.[152]

The most commonplace references to ancient conflicts associated with the landscape begin with memories and recollections of invading hosts, more often than not of foreign origin. One example, from the northern counties, is provided by memory of the Picts, undoubtedly reinforced and magnified by more recent Scottish cross-border incursions and brigandage. In Cumberland in the late seventeenth century, country people commonly referred to caves and vaults as 'Pict-holes', completely unaffected by the equally erroneous insistence of antiquaries that these neolithic remains were evidence of Roman encampments.[153] The Picts were an old enemy, memories of whom were not improved by conflation with their medieval and modern successors, the Scots. Local tradition tended to conflate many

---

[150] Bodl. MS Gough Wales 5 (Anon., 'Description of Wales'), fo. 19ᵛ; Bodl. MS Top. gen. e. 85 (Thomas Martin of Palgrave, 'Some Remarks and Observations taken in a Journey', 1724), p. 92. This explanation exasperated Martin, a natural sceptic, who sneered: 'How his horse got up, or how we may credit any other part of the story, I know not.' For similar 'fabulous stories' involving a cave said to have been inhabited by an old woman, see Martin, 'Some Remarks', 67.

[151] Sandford, A cursory relation of all the antiquities and familyes in Cumberland, 37. Sandford himself speaks of having visited other monuments six decades earlier.

[152] Anon., A Strange and Wonderful Discovery Newly Made of Houses Underground (1685), printed by William Budden (Wing S.5844), emphasis in original. The story's authenticity was discredited by Stuart Piggott, 'Background to a Broadsheet: What Happened at Colton's Field in 1685?', in id., Ruins in a Landscape: Essays in Antiquarianism (Edinburgh, 1976).

[153] Fleming–Senhouse Papers, ed. E. Hughes, Cumberland County Council Record Series, 2 (Carlisle, 1962), 43; for another example see SAL MS 265, fo. 45ᵛ, where the caves of Hawthornden, six miles south-west of Edinburgh, are said to have been the home of the ancient Pictish kings. Houses, too, occasionally had hidden rooms for which elaborate explanations were created. When a 'secret' chamber was discovered at New Hall in Boreham, Essex, it was soon put about that this had been 'Cardinal Woolseys contrivance to lay treasonable transactions in, or of that sort, and no doubt riches . . .': Essex RO D/Y/1/Acc. A3921A (Nicholas Jekyll to William Holman, 23 Feb. 1724/5).

centuries of depredation—Lesley's civil war troops with those of Robert the Bruce
and his minion the Black Douglas, for instance—and sometimes even blamed the
Scots for damages they had not inflicted. The ballad of *The Battle of Otterburn*
commemorates local border conflicts rather than national Anglo-Scottish campaigns, and echoes of these days could be heard well into the eighteenth century.[154]
Noting the remains of an old castle in his manuscript survey of Northumberland parishes about 1730, George Mark observed that, while the original castle
had apparently been used by the Scots as a fortification before their great defeat
at Flodden (1513), it had been ruined in the civil wars by Cromwell's army, 'tho'
the inhabitants, who seldom fail to lay the blame of most of their ills on the Scots,
tell us an antient story of it'. According to this tale, James IV, in order to take
the castle after a long siege, had shot an arrow with a paper attached in which
he had promised to reward any man who shot the arrow back with news of the
condition of the besieged; a sentinel's treacherous compliance resulted in the taking of the castle. It is interesting to note that, though Mark steadfastly believed
the destruction of the castle to have occurred within the past eighty years, and
not at the hands of the Scots, he had very little difficulty accepting much of what
he heard. 'This is the tradition in relation to the destruction of this castle, which
tho' not true in every particular, yet perhaps, as most traditions have, has some
foundation in truth.'[155]

Elsewhere it was the historically earlier depredations of the Normans that were
most often recalled. Various families evolved complicated traditions involving
resistance to the Conquest. In Lancashire, the Pilkington family of Pilkington,
and the Traffords of Old Trafford, both families whose documentable lineage,
J. H. Round pointed out, could not be carried back further than the twelfth century, claimed to have an ancestor who, pursued by Norman troops, disguised himself as a thresher and hid in a barn. The Elizabethan antiquaries Arthur Agarde
and Joseph Holland, and the mid-seventeenth century cleric and biographer Thomas
Fuller, encountered two versions of the story in the 1590s and 1640s respectively.
Fuller was informed by his friend William Ryley the elder (an archivist and herald) of the Pilkington version, which explained the armorial motto 'Now thus'
as the utterance of the disguised ancestor, imitating a flail, and the story was
reinforced for him by the testimony of a 'country man'. By the late nineteenth
century this temporally portable tale had been transplanted to the civil war era.[156]
Further south, the Norman tales were often closely linked with the environment,
rather than with particular families. The colour of the soil at Battle near

[154] K. Nessler, *Geschichte der Ballade Chevy Chase* (Berlin, 1911). Joseph Addison singles out *Chevy Chase* as 'the favourite ballad of the common people of England', recalling Sir Philip Sidney's praise for it: *Spectator*, 70 (21 May 1711), ed. Bond, i. 297–8.
[155] Northumberland RO ZAN M13/F9 (George Mark, fragmentary 'History of Northumberland', written c.1730), unfoliated.
[156] Arthur Agarde, 'Of the Antiquity, Variety, and Reason of Motts [Mottoes]', and Joseph Holland, 'Of the Same', in Thomas Hearne, *A Collection of Curious Discourses*, ed. J. Ayloffe, 2 vols. (1775), i. 262, 264; *The History of the Worthies of England*, ed. J. Nichols, 2 vols. (1811), i. 542; J. H. Round, *Peerage and Pedigree: Studies in Peerage Law and Family History*, 2 vols. (1910; facs. repr. 1970), i. 316.

Hastings, which looked reddish after rain, was explained as residual dye from the livery of the Conqueror's troops.[157] One of the correspondents to *The Spectator* mentions having often heard in his home county of Kent 'how the Kentish men evaded the Conqueror, by carrying green boughs over their heads'.[158]

The enemy of choice often followed geographical lines. The Scots were much mentioned in the north, the Anglo-Saxons and Normans in the south-west—'as great as the devil and the earl of Kent', referring to the memory of the Saxon Earl Godwin, was a proverbial expression long before Swift satirized it in his *A Complete Collection of Genteel and Ingenious Conversation* (1738).[159] The Welsh periodically figured in the western and north-western border shires that had seen Owain Glyndwr's revolt under Henry IV. In 1687 the discovery by Cheshire workmen of a large stone, under which were several bones and 'the figure of a man' led several local gentry to speculate on their origins. Sir John Crewe, referring to himself in the third person, was among them, and was later instrumental in having them ceremonially reburied in 1701 in an earthen pot, complete with verses by himself and others to mark the reinterment of this ancient unknown soldier. As to the skeleton's identity, Crewe's friend Mr Wittar of Frodsham had 'seen a manuscript (in whose hands is forgot by him) that in old time in some of the Edw. time then king was fought a great battle at the town of Hellesby betwixt the English & Welsh, and that both their commanders was slain, and that one was buryed in the forest near Manly's Wall'.[160]

It was the Danish invasions, however, that recur most often as a topic in popular discourse, especially in those areas which suffered the worst of their ravages between the ninth and the eleventh centuries.[161] There is little evidence of a continuous tradition of Dane stories throughout the Middle Ages, and it has been suggested that the Danes as a popular topic may have originated in late fifteenth-century learned literature. This is a salutary reminder both that the oral and the literate cannot be easily disentangled, and that a long pedigree cannot be automatically assumed for beliefs any more than for great families.[162] Whatever their origins, however, more references to the Danes occur in popular lore of the sixteenth and seventeenth centuries than to any other invading host, from the Romans to the Normans. Indeed, the term was sometimes used generically (and confusingly) to include any invading host, rather as the 'Goths' or 'Scythians' often provided a generic tag for migratory nations in learned culture's account of the remote European past. One early Stuart traveller would refer to William I's conquest of

---

[157] Childrey, *Britannia Baconica*, 57–8.   [158] *Spectator*, 284 (25 Jan. 1712), ed. Bond, iii. 9.

[159] Jonathan Swift, *Swift's Polite Conversation*, ed. E. Partridge (New York and Oxford, 1963), 168.

[160] Cheshire RO DAR/J/2, unfoliated commonplace book of Sir John Crewe, note near end of volume.

[161] The late thirteenth-century poem *The Lay of Havelok the Dane* (which involves a heroic Danish prince who delivers both his own kingdom and England from the tyranny of usurping earls), for example, appears to have originated in Lincolnshire and never penetrated far beyond the east Midlands: *The Lay of Havelok the Dane*, ed. W. W. Skeat, EETS ES 4 (1868), introduction; Coss, 'Aspects of Cultural Diffusion', 62.

[162] Fox, *Oral and Literate Culture in England 1500–1700*, 243–4.

the 'Danes' at Hastings in 1066.[163] Thomas Fuller, drawing on the Jacobean etymologist Richard Verstegan, dismissed as 'fond opinion' the belief 'among some of the common people' that names ending in the suffix 'son' were of Danish origin.[164]

It is perhaps significant that John Leland, the first and most thorough recorder of early sixteenth-century traditions, has far more to say about Danish incursions than he does of Normans or Anglo-Saxons. The atrocities of which his interviewees reminded him included the destruction of monasteries and the depopulation of villages, though it is possible that in the former case people may have been reminded of the Danes by the all too recent event of the Henrician dissolution, while in the latter more recent depopulations due to enclosure, famine, or plague may have been projected back on to a remote ancient enemy. Sometimes, in fact, more recent events were conflated or associated with the Danes. In one Devon community, Kingsteignton, the inhabitants told Leland 'how their town hath been defacid by the Danes, and of late tyme by the Frenchmen', which might mean either the Normans or more recent French coastal incursions. Elsewhere in the same shire he found the church of Axminster to be locally famous for the burial of a number of Danes slain under King Athelstan, probably at the battle of Brunanburgh in AD 937.[165] Sixteenth-century inhabitants of Manchester averred that because their ancestors had fought the Danes valiantly, they had been rewarded with the name Manchester or 'city of men'. Camden, who was more sympathetic to such opinions than most of his seventeenth-century successors, gently points out to his reader, 'But full little knowe the good honest men, that Mancunium was the name of it in the Britans time, so that the etymologie thereof, out of our English tongue, can by no meanes seeme probable.'[166] Nearly two centuries later the traveller Jeremiah Milles discovered that the citizens of Southampton had vivid memories of the plunder of their town in the year 980.[167]

Whether many of the sites associated by locals with the Danes did in fact derive from that period is of little consequence here. The remarkable fact is how strongly people 'remembered' events so remote. Since at least the beginning of the fifteenth century the inhabitants of Coventry had celebrated their ancestors' overthrow of Danish tyranny in the Hocktide play; suppressed as superstitious in 1561, it was revived at Kenilworth in 1575 for the benefit of Queen Elizabeth and her host, the earl of Leicester. Public performances of the play, which conflates distinct historical events such as the massacre of Danes on St Bruce's night 1002 and the death of Harthacnut in 1042, were resumed in 1575. In 1591

---

[163] *A Relation of a Short Survey of the Western Counties*, 29.

[164] Thomas Fuller, *The History of the Worthies of England*, ed. J. Nichols, 2 vols. (1811), i. 65.

[165] *Leland's Itinerary*, i. 119, 121, 225, 243; Briggs, *Dictionary of British Folk-Tales*, B.II, p. 10. The stones on Exmoor included one with Danish runes, and the village of Hubblestow was believed to have been the site of a battle in which the Danes had lost their banner and their captain: Childrey, *Britannia Baconica*, 29. For a Trinity Sunday ritual linking Athelstan's victory over the Danes to the village of Newnton, Wiltshire, see Aubrey, *Remains of Judaisme and Gentilisme*, 136.

[166] Camden, *Britain*, 746–7.

[167] BL MS Add. 15776 (travel notes of Jeremiah Milles), fo. 254ʳ.

performances of 'the destrucion of Jerusalem' and of 'the Conquest of the Danes' on midsummer's day were authorized by the common council as a grudging concession to the populace at the same time that maypoles were removed; the plays at least could be said to be 'grounded on story'.[168] Dramatic representations of Danish atrocities crept easily from civic pageantry to elite theatre, in plays such as *Edmund Ironside*, first performed in the 1590s and revived in the middle of the next century.[169]

Residual hatred of the Danes survived even the depredations of the civil war, and the addition of an entirely new tradition of stories about rampaging round-heads or cutthroat cavaliers.[170] In the 1670s Richard Blome recorded a number of anti-Danish beliefs, which he generally accepted, including the assertion of inhabitants of Bolsover, Derbyshire, that two large trenches had originally been Danish garrisons.[171] In some places, a strong memory of the Danes exists today, as the evidence of regional dialects attests. An old person in the West Country today may still call a red-headed boy 'a proper little Dane'. Red heads have often been disliked both because of their biblical connection with Judas Iscariot (who is supposed to have had red hair) and because this colour of hair later became associated with the 'buccaneering Danes, whose red-haired offspring everywhere remains', as Daniel Defoe put it by way of lampooning the xenophobia of the 'true-born Englishman'.[172]

In the sixteenth and seventeenth centuries, many such Danish connections centred on burial mounds. On the road to Stevenage in Hertfordshire at the end of the sixteenth century were a number of heaps of earth which were popularly believed to contain the remains of Englishmen killed fighting the Danes about 829; a nearby place was and is still today known as Dane End. Throughout the seventeenth century stories of 'a tirable battle there foughten betweene the Saxons and the Danes' two miles north-east of Gloucester gave the location the name Battle Bridge, while the place name Camden was said to derive from 'Camp-Dane', a place used by the Danes as fortification.[173] The hillocks on Swadling Downs, about four miles from Canterbury, in the parish of Chartham, were known in the early eighteenth century as the 'Danes banks'. The discovery of coins, bones, and weapons by a

[168] Sharp, *A dissertation on the pageants or dramatic mysteries*, 12, 125–7, 131; *REED: Coventry*, ed. Ingram, 215, 233, 271–6 for Hock-Tide and the Danes; Phythian-Adams, *Desolation of a City*, 172.

[169] I. Ribner, *The English History Play in the Age of Shakespeare* (Princeton, 1957), 242 ff. Other episodes of remote antiquity given public, popular renditions include the story of Ferrex and Porrex. Sir Daniel Fleming paid 10s. to travelling players performing a version of this outdoors on what must have been a frosty Westmorland day (30 Dec. 1662): Hist. MSS Comm., *Twelfth Report* (1890), part 2, p. 372.

[170] For several Cromwellian tales, including some believed by folklorists to have been passed down directly from 'eyewitnesses', see Briggs, *Dictionary of British Folk-Tales*, B.II, pp. 25–7, 52–3.

[171] Blome, *Britannia*, 51, 78, 196. Blome's account also lists a number of towns which had heroically withstood Danish sieges.

[172] K. Palmer, *Oral Folk-Tales of Wessex* (Newton Abbot, 1973), 58–9; Sharp, *A dissertation on the pageants or dramatic mysteries*, 31; Briggs, *Dictionary of British Folk-Tales*, B.II, p. 17; Daniel Defoe, 'The True-Born Englishman', in *The Earlier Life and the Chief Earlier Works of Daniel Defoe*, ed. H. Morley (1889), 191.

[173] John Norden, *Speculum Britanniae pars: the discription of Hartfordshire* (1598), 3; Bodl. MS Top. Glouc. c. 3 (Abel Wantner, 'History of Gloucester'), fos. 147^r, 203^v.

local landowner, Charles Fagg, in June 1730, in one of these banks or barrows provided confirmation of the belief in a long-ago historic battle.[174]

Often such places were associated with a specific historical figure from the period of the invasions, such as Alfred, Edmund, or Athelstan, the image of whom adorned a wall in Beverley church, where he was believed to have donated the 'free stool', a stone chair which offered sanctuary to any fleeing felon. Various wells associated with Athelstan, including one at Startforth, near Newcastle, provided a focus for Dane stories in Northumberland. According to the Startforth tale, Athelstan was supposed to have camped nearby. Having found no water for his troops, the king had prayed for it. He then stuck a spear into the rock, 'whence the water hath continued to flow ever since'. In the early eighteenth century, when this story was recorded, the well was 'greatly frequented' by visitors. The citizens of Wantage in Berkshire similarly took pride in their town because it had been the birthplace of that 'scourge of the Danes', Alfred, and a brick-paved pool located there was known as 'King Alfred's Pool' from before that time until well into the twentieth century.[175]

Casual finds of objects like bones and weapons invited Dane stories, as did certain types of vegetation. The rural folk of Bartlow End, Essex, unearthed soldiers' bones in the sixteenth century, which they ascribed to a battle against the Danes, probably that of Assandun (now known to have been Ashingdon in the southeast of the county) at which Edmund Ironside was defeated by Cnut. A plant with red berries known as 'Danewort' was plentiful there, and the locals, who called the plant 'Danes-bloud', believed that the plants signified the number of Danes slain there. Camden noted that they even believed that the plants 'blometh from their blood'.[176] Both these terms, however, appear to have originated no earlier than the sixteenth century.[177] Similar traditions attached to the Daneweed in a field named Dunstall or 'Danestall' near Hexton, Hertfordshire, where locals celebrated Hock Monday with cakes and ale into the reign of Elizabeth, believing that the weed was so plentiful 'because the Danes bloud, there spilt, did bring up this weed, which here (as in some other places) will not be destroyed'.[178] Certain fields near Checkley parish church in Staffordshire were called 'Nakedfields' in

[174] SAL, Minute Book 1718–32, p. 255.
[175] *The English Travels of Sir John Percival and William Byrd II: The Percival Diary of 1701*, ed. M. R. Wenger (Columbia, Mo., 1989), 105–6; M.R., *Memoirs of the Life of Mr Ambrose Barnes . . .*, ed. W. Longstaffe, Surtees Soc., 50 (1866), 26–7; Blome, *Britannia* (1673), 42. The *Bartholomew Gazetteer*, 71, notes 'Dane' place names in Cheshire, Lancashire, Staffordshire, East Sussex, Leicestershire, Norfolk, Hampshire, Derbyshire, Devon, and Gloucestershire, as well as other features such as Dane's Brook on the Devon-Somerset border.
[176] Camden, *Britain*, 452; Childrey, *Britannia Baconica*, 29.
[177] Fox, *Oral and Literate Culture*, 246.
[178] Camden, *Britain*, 452; Childrey, *Britannia Baconica*, 29. At Cerne Abbas in Dorset in the nineteenth century a labourer was discovered cutting the figure of a giant into the turf. He explained to visitors that this was the image of a Danish giant who had led an invasion of the coast 'about a hundred years' earlier and who had been beheaded by locals while lying on the hill to sleep: Briggs, *Dictionary of British Folk-tales*, B.I, p. 611, citing A. L. Gomme, *Gentleman's Magazine Library: English Traditional Lore* (1885). The Cerne giant, and the similar 'Long Man' of Wilmington, East Sussex (restored from an earlier figure in 1874), are visible today.

the late seventeenth and early eighteenth centuries because the fallen victims of
a battle against the Danes had been left naked and unburied for some time. The
Staffordshire antiquary who reported this story, Richard Bolton, commented that
'what ground there may be for this tradition I know not'.[179]

A SENSE OF THE REAL?

Local legends might receive a helping hand from interested visitors, concerned
to anchor architecture, topography, and local language firmly to a documentable
past. In his discussion of Danish 'lows' or mounds, Richard Bolton noted the
relative paucity of such traces of the great 'slaughter' of Danes at Tettenhall. Locals
claimed the place had been a Danish fortification, but Bolton went further.
Although the old roads were hard to trace, having been interrupted by plough
lines,

> the foundations being dayly dug up by the former to mend the highways, make inclos-
> ures, and pavements, and then all made levell by the plough, which together with the
> large hinges for the doors, an antique dagger, and other things that have been found here,
> and some of the stones squared makes one rather thinke it some ruinous citty, then a
> fortification onely.

He concluded that the site was in fact the Danish city of Theotenhall, razed by
Edward the Elder in AD 910 according to the *Anglo-Saxon Chronicle*. At nearby
Wednesfield, where traces of another such great battle had recently disappeared,
Bolton noted the survival of the low in the place name Southlowfield 'which has
lately had a windmill sett upon it, the low before being there within memory'.
Close by was Northlowfield which had also once had a low 'tho' now it be quite
gone'. In these cases, the educated visitor was prepared to elucidate local tradition and dialect in the context of documentable events. Elsewhere he was less
easily persuaded. The local belief at Wilbrighton that the Romans had called the
place Villam Brittonum was not substantiated by sufficient physical remains to
make it convincing, so that 'one may question whether this tradition have not
been broached of later yeares, by some fond conceited etymologist'; in his view,
the conclusions of an over-enthusiastic antiquary had fed back into local lore and
established sheer linguistic speculation as 'fact'.[180]

Richard Bolton's ambivalence towards explanations of local phenomena issuing from both local tradition *and* learned philology, like George Mark's above-
mentioned willingness to accept a fantastic tale about the Scots, or Dugdale's defence
of a pruned-down Guy of Warwick, traceable to 'certain authors of good

---

[179] Bodl. MS Top. Staffs. e. 2 (Richard Bolton, 'A View of Staffordshire', 1707–21), p. 189.
[180] Ibid. p. 187; *The Anglo-Saxon Chronicles*, trans. A. Savage (New York, 1983), 115. Bolton drew
his manuscript topography principally from earlier surveys such as the then unpublished Elizabethan
chorography by Sampson Erdeswicke (a contemporary copy of which is Bodl. MS Gough Staffs. 4)
and Robert Plot's *Natural History of Stafford-shire* (Oxford, 1686), but he added contributions of his
own.

credit',[181] are a warning against positing too firm a division between 'historical' elite views of the past and 'mythical' oral traditions, ballads, and folk tales. Like the opposite position that romanticizes traditions as unchanged and impermeable vestiges of centuries-old folk memory, this is a naive judgement. It presumes that there is an inherent quality to certain stories that makes them more believable than others, as opposed to a set of external intellectual criteria, such as canons of evidence, that can be developed to judge all such stories against each other. To quote Paul Veyne once again, 'There is no such thing as a sense of the real.'[182]

The literate and educated, for all that they might publicly scoff at vulgar beliefs about the past, were entirely capable of accepting local explanations, particularly where they filled a complete vacuum in the written sources. Abel Wantner, a citizen of Gloucester who completed his unpublished history of the city and its environs in 1714, was willing to accept oral traditional sources if they concerned objects or structures that no longer survived, and he 'documented' two missing chapels in this way.[183] The eighteenth-century inscription to a fifteenth-century panel in the South Range of the Bodleian Library quadrangle suggests that the two figures represented are William of Scotland doing homage to Henry II; they almost certainly represent St Thomas of Canterbury at the feet of Louis VII of France. The framers of the inscription, probably clergymen themselves, chose to invent and perpetuate in brass an explanation for the panel, even though they recognized in the same inscription that the adjoining one *did* feature Henry II doing penance before the shrine of the murdered archbishop. The invention of tradition can occur at all social levels and for a variety of purposes.[184]

This chapter has pointed out some of the main contours of popular beliefs about history, which are part, but not the whole, of the broader 'sense of the past' that is the subject of this book. It is possible to make some cautious generalizations at this juncture. The first is that visual stimuli such as landscape, edifices, and other objects were critical to both the creation and preservation of popular perceptions of the past, since they often provided not only the *explanandum* about which a story arose, but also the specific performative occasion for telling that story in response to questions from the curious. This should not be very surprising given both the prominence of such features on local horizons, and the parallel development of a more acute sense among the learned of how the past ought properly to look when represented in books or in buildings. The second observation is that popular beliefs about the past were part of an intellectual commons, not a battlefield. It is certainly true that elite inclinations to sort, historicize, and even dismiss certain examples of local belief—essentially enclosing and selectively cultivating that commons—became more consistent and firmly pressed from the seventeenth century on. It is also the case, as noted in the preceding chapter, that

[181] Dugdale, *Antiquities of Warwickshire*, ed. Thomas, i. 374–5.
[182] Veyne, *Did the Greeks Believe in their Myths?*, 27.
[183] Bodl. MS Top. Glouc. c. 3 (Wantner, 'History of Gloucester'), fo. 282ʳ.
[184] Royal Commission on Historical Monuments, *City of Oxford* (1939), 4.

local memory was at risk of being overwhelmed by a print-based historical culture which expanded its influence considerably after the Restoration. Against this there were countervailing tendencies: elite reluctance wholly to depart from popular beliefs about the past; the critical role of certain learned works, the Bible and Foxe's *Acts and Monuments* among them; and the long lives of many collectable ballads whose words and images resounded across social and economic lines. And one must acknowledge, too, the importance of divisions—gender, locality, religion, and political connection—that cut across the grain of social and educational affiliation.

There are in short a number of continuities and connections between popular beliefs about the past and the literary legends and stories that both rivalled and influenced them. Such cross-fertilization between elite and popular history dates back to the medieval chronicles.[185] It did not disappear in the early modern period, but the relationship assumed a different form. Many of the stories, jests, and anecdotes noted above did not fit easily into the categories of formal historical writing now commonly read and written by the educated. This tension mounted in the seventeenth century for two distinct but connected reasons. First, the dominance of neoclassical models in formal historiography, initially in the period from 1590 to 1625 and more profoundly after the Restoration, made a point of emphasizing the dignity and *gravitas* of history, now a manor-house with (at least in theory) little room for the quirky, the curious, the anecdotal, and the trivial. A single quotation from Queen Anne's first biographer, Abel Boyer, neatly sums up a century of English thought about the 'proper' character of historical writing: 'the gravity and dignity of history excludes all low and vulgar expressions, mean jests, clenching witticisms, trivial proverbs, and such like trash'.[186] It was a tone that would be sounded repeatedly in the urban historiography of the eighteenth century, which increasingly repudiated the local and legendary in favour of the national, and emulated the 'civilized' discourse of enlightenment society.[187] The second and broader reason has to do with the oral provenance of much of this kind of material. Oral sources, as the next chapter suggests, were subjected to much greater critical scrutiny as the relations between the written and the spoken, the documentary and the remembered, the authoritative and the testamentary, continued to evolve.

[185] Jackson, *The International Popular Tale*, 117, esp. for Welsh chroniclers as a source of European folk tales.

[186] Abel Boyer, quoted in P. Hicks, *Neoclassical History and English Culture from Clarendon to Hume* (1996), 11.

[187] For the change in urban historical writing see Sweet, *Writing of Urban Histories*, esp. pp. 100–27; even antiquarian histories tended increasingly to stress recent building and improvement, and current national prominence, rather than ancient glories and the legends attending them.

CHAPTER TEN

Oral Tradition

Where there is no penman to record the memorable acts and passages of times,
the memory of them is swallowed up in the gulfe of oblivion.

(Sir Thomas Widdrington, *Analecta Eboracensia*, c.1660[1])

IT IS OFTEN overlooked that early modern antiquaries relied to a great extent
not only on manuscript and archaeological material, but also on a variety of
oral sources ranging from popular traditions to the personal recollections of the
aged. The purposes of this final chapter are to examine more closely the uses to
which oral traditions were put between 1500 and 1700; to explore the changing
attitudes of the recorders to the content and sources of such traditions; and to
offer an interpretation of their declining status as historical sources in the
seventeenth century and their eventual exile to the wilderness of folklore and
vulgar error. I shall argue that this decline can be attributed to a number of
contemporaneous developments. These include changing attitudes to historical
evidence as *historical* evidence (what historians of history are usually interested
in); broader reconceptualizations of the nature of truth; the related, widening division between learned and popular cultures; and the evolving agenda of antiquarian
research.

The subject of oral traditions has recently attracted the attention of several
students of early modern social history.[2] Yet most accounts of English antiquarianism have little to say on the topic, either ignoring oral traditions altogether
or summarily dismissing them as an example of lingering medieval credulity in
otherwise forward-looking scholars. The reason why this should be so is clear

---

[1] BL MS Egerton 2578, fo. 8ᵛ (also included in the printed edition by C. Caine, 1897). The present
chapter is a revised version of my article, 'The "Common Voice"': History, Folklore, and Oral Tradition
in Early Modern England', *Past and Present*, 120 (Aug. 1988), 26–52. I am grateful to Prof. Michael
Hunter for a helpful critique of the original essay, and to Dr Adam Fox for several useful exchanges
on the subject.

[2] See especially A. Fox, 'Remembering the Past in Early Modern England: Oral and Written Tradition',
TRHS, 6th ser., 9 (1999), 233–56; id. *Oral and Literate Culture in England* (Oxford, 2000); P. Burke,
Popular Culture in Early Modern Europe (1978), 91–115; B. Reay (ed.), *Popular Culture in Seventeenth-
Century England* (1985), introduction and *passim*. For the general position of oral tradition in
European culture after the Renaissance, Giuseppe Cocchiara's classic study, first published in 1952,
remains useful, especially for the period after 1700: *The History of Folklore in Europe*, trans. J. N. McDaniel
(Philadelphia, 1981), 2–3, 203–5. For the fate of oral culture in the nineteenth century, see D. Vincent,
'The Decline of the Oral Tradition in Popular Culture', in R. D. Storch (ed.), *Popular Culture and
Custom in Nineteenth-Century England* (1982), 20–47, and id. *Literacy and Popular Culture: England
1750–1914* (Cambridge, 1989), 181 ff.

enough: most modern historians place little stock in oral sources when they study anything more remote than their grandparents' generation. We have, in increasing volume as the past approaches the present, a multitude of books, documents, letters, manuscripts, coins, funeral urns, paintings, and maps from which to reconstruct history. Such 'hard' evidence is to be preferred, where it can be found, to the 'soft' evidence of folk tale, unwritten and undatable local custom, and ancestral tradition, because only the former is both tangible and more easily verifiable through reference to other sources. But the early modern antiquary could not always be so fussy.

FORMS OF EARLY MODERN ORAL TRADITION

Recent scholars such as Ruth Finnegan have argued against making universalizing claims about the 'nature' or form of oral tradition, or about the manner in which it reacts when it comes into contact with writing.[3] Early modern oral traditions were much more informal and far less structured than the modern, performative African traditions to which they bear a superficial resemblance.[4] Nor is there anything in English oral tradition that rivals the contemporary Inca dynastic memory that the Spaniard Cieza de León found in Peru. This included a story 'that the Indians who told it to me say that they heard [it] from their ancestors, who in like manner heard it in the old songs which they received from very ancient times'. These were presented in public ritual performances around images of previous rulers, and principally concerned the events of their reigns, entrusted successively by each king to 'three or four old men, known for their intelligence and ability, who were instructed to retain in their memory all the events that happened in the provinces . . . so that the history of the reign might be had in remembrance in after times.'[5] Garcilaso de la Vega, 'El Inca', the mestizo historian who described the Inca empire's origins and fall at the beginning of the seventeenth century, similarly reported how the Incas and other Peruvian peoples 'invented endless stories of the origin and beginning of their earliest ancestors'. Seventeenth-century readers of Garcilaso, whose *Royal Commentaries* was first translated into English by Paul Rycaut in 1688, would have learned that the Incas preserved entire speeches, embassies, and accounts of military feats in their memories, 'taught by tradition to their successors and descendants from father to son'. *Amautas* or 'sages' turned these into longer, didactic stories, and

[3] R. Finnegan, *Literacy and Orality: Studies in the Technology of Communication* (Oxford, 1988), 87–91, 144–6.

[4] On the African 'griots', descendants of those first reported by Ibn Battuta in the fourteenth century, see T. A. Hale, *Griots and Griottes: Masters of Words and Music* (Bloomington and Indianapolis, Ind. 1998), esp. pp. 59–113.

[5] Pedro de Cieza de León, *La chronica del Peru* (Anvers, 1554), trans. and ed. C. R. Markham as *The Travels of Pedro de Cieza de Leon, A.D. 1532–50, Contained in the First Part of his Chronicle of Peru*, Hakluyt Soc., 33 (1864), part 2, pp. 5, 17, 32.

harauicus or poets made 'short compressed poems, embracing a history, or an embassy, or the king's reply'.[6] Numerical facts of births, deaths, and numbers killed in particular battles were recorded on a monthly basis in *quipus* or knots, the Inca equivalent of statistics. Garcilaso's commentary on these methods of commemorating the past, though admiring of his Indian ancestors' ingenuity, reveals doubts about their accuracy impressed upon him by his Spanish upbringing:

Thus they remembered their history. But as experience has shown, all these were perishable expedients, for it is letters that perpetuate the memory of events. But as the Incas had no knowledge of writing, they had to use what devices they could, and treating their knots as letters, they chose historians and accountants, called *quipucamayus* ('those who have charge of the knots') to write down and preserve the tradition of their deeds by means of the knots, strings, and colored threads, using their stories and poems as an aid.[7]

The weakness of this system was that, without genuine Western-style writing, those who did not have possession of the oral traditions were in no position to make sense of the knots. Moreover, oral cultures have little sense of a relative past and either do not assign dates to events in their tradition, or forget large parts of the past. The transmitters of such traditions thereby 'telescope' their own history and provide a chronology which, though it is comprehensible to the members of their group, will mislead outside observers conditioned to dealing in firm dates. Cieza found something like this in the recitation of Inca traditions during the public *taquis*, wherein cowardly, lazy, or vicious kings were ordered not to be mentioned.[8] Datelessness is a frequent, though not invariable, feature of English traditions about the past, and this would not assist in their longer-term adoption by a historical culture oriented towards precise chronology. Garcilaso's own ambivalence towards tradition and his repeated appeals to the 'authority' of printed Spanish histories resembles in many ways the rejection of tradition that would occur in seventeenth-century England.[9]

[6] Garcilaso de la Vega, *The Royal Commentaries of Peru, in two parts*, trans. P. Rycaut (1688); I cite from *Royal commentaries of the Incas, and general history of Peru*, trans. Harold V. Livermore (Austin, Tex. 1966), 49, 62, 89, 130.

[7] Ibid. 332.

[8] *The Travels of Pedro de Cieza de Leon*, ed. Markham, pt. 2, p. 29. On 'telescoping' and other aspects of chronology, see D. Henige, *The Chronology of Oral Tradition* (Oxford, 1974); J. Vansina, *Oral Tradition: A Study in Historical Methodology*, trans. H. M. Wright (Chicago, 1965); cf. Vansina's revisions to this work, 'Once Upon a Time: Oral Traditions as History in Africa', *Daedalus*, 100 (1971), 442–68, and a more thorough rethinking in his *Oral Tradition as History* (1985); R. Finnegan, 'A Note on Oral Tradition and Historical Evidence', *History and Theory*, 9 (1981), 196–201.

[9] D. A. Brading, 'The Incas and the Renaissance: *The Royal Commentaries* of Inca Garcilaso de la Vega', *Journal of Latin American Studies*, 18 (1985), 1–23; R. L. Kagan, 'Clio and the Crown: Writing History in Habsburg Spain', in R. L. Kagan and G. Parker (eds.), *Spain, Europe, and the Atlantic World: Essays in Honour of John H. Elliott* (Cambridge, 1995), 73–99; F. Salomon, 'Chronicles of the Impossible: Notes on Three Peruvian Indigenous Historians', in R. Adorno (ed.), *From Oral to Written Expression: Native Andean Chronicles of the Early Colonial Period* (Syracuse, NY, 1982), 9–21; this essay notes the disparity between the native Andean's idea of a 'relación' and the superimposed Spanish version of the *crónica*.

A British example that comes close to Inca traditions is the *eisteddfodau* of the Welsh bards. Briefly revived under Elizabeth and again in the early eighteenth century, these were praised by the poets Henry Vaughan and Michael Drayton for providing an unbroken oral narrative of the past. In Drayton's view, tradition preserved the history of the long-dead British bards and Druids, and was far more durable than the corruptible book:

> For, when of ages past we looke in bookes to reade,
> Wee retchlessly discharge our memory of those.
> So when injurious time, such monuments doth lose
> (As what so great a worke, by time that is not wrackt?)
> Wee utterly forgoe that memorable act:
> But when we lay it up within the minds of men,
> They leave it their next age; that, leaves it hers agen.
> So strongly which (me thinks) doth for tradition make,
> As if you from the world it altogether take,
> You utterly subvert antiquitie thereby.[10]

But with the possible exception of the *eisteddfodau*, which were a Welsh national rather than a genuinely local practice, there were no 'village remembrancers', men assigned the task of transmitting a stable, 'official' local tradition to succeeding generations.[11] The memories of old people on matters of boundaries, property, and custom were a much more informal resource, as noted above. They were also, most often, traditions of stasis ('since time out of mind'), rather than change, and their status as information depended entirely on the disposition of the judicial bodies that employed them as evidence. There were, however, specific beliefs associated with particular places and events, and, at least initially, Tudor antiquaries regarded these as useful evidence.

[10] *Works of Henry Vaughan*, ed. L. C. Martin, 2nd edn. (Oxford, 1957), 696 (Henry Vaughan to John Aubrey, 9 Oct. 1694); Michael Drayton, *Poly-Olbion*, x, lines 234–58, 267–77 ff., in *Works of Michael Drayton*, ed. J. W. Hebel, K. Tillotson, and B. H. Newdigate, 2nd edn., 5 vols. (Oxford, 1961), iv. 207 ff. J. E. Curran Jr., 'The History Never Written: Bards, Druids, and the Problem of Antiquarianism in *Poly Olbion*', *Renaissance Quarterly*, 51 (1998), 498–525. Cf. John Selden's note (*Poly-Olbion*, ed. cit., p. 83) on the *eisteddfod* (which Selden calls a *stethva*). Significantly, Selden (who ordinarily had no use for oral sources) thought that such a *formalized* type of tradition, involving a complete, orderly narrative, would assist historical accuracy by allowing regular correction of inaccuracies by the witnesses to public recitations of community history. The mid-Tudor antiquary and fierce defender of British antiquity Sir John Price used Welsh manuscripts to support the historicity of Geoffrey of Monmouth, but he also made appeal to oral tradition to attack Polydore Vergil in his *Historiae brytannicae defensio* (published posthumously in 1573): J. W. Binns, *Intellectual Culture in Elizabethan and Jacobean England: The Latin Writings of the Age* (Leeds, 1990), 183. The Winchester antiquary John Trussell referred to Druid doctrines as *non literis sed tradita memoria fuit*, which a later annotator of his manuscript rendered as 'the truth of history transfered by tradition'. Hants. RO W/K1/11/1, fos. 9ʳ, 17.

[11] R. Suggett, 'Vagabonds and Minstrels in Sixteenth-Century Wales', in A. Fox and D. Woolf (eds.), *The Spoken Word: Oral Culture in Britain, 1500–1850* (Manchester, 2002), 138–72. On the eighteenth-century revival of the *eisteddfodau*, see G. H. Jenkins, *The Foundations of Modern Wales, 1642–1780* (Oxford, 1987), 229–31, 241–53. For a comparable Scottish example, see James Kirkwood, *A Collection of Highland Rites and Customes*, annotated by Edward Lhwyd and ed. J. L. Campbell (Cambridge and Totowa, NJ, 1975), 55, from Bodl. MS Carte 269.

THE 'COMMON VOICE'

The types of oral evidence exploited by Herodotus, the 'father of history' in the fifth century BC continued to provide a rich source of information for historians and chroniclers through some two millennia after his travels.[12] Many medieval chroniclers used evidence garnered from eyewitnesses to events, as well as traditional tales that were often associated with miracles, or with the cult of a particular saint. Eadmer, writing at the end of the eleventh century, based his *Historia Novorum* on 'things which I have seen with my own eyes and myself heard'. William of Malmesbury reported what he had 'heard from credible authority' and borrowed from old songs to fill out gaps in the written record, while Orderic Vitalis frequently passed on things he had 'learned from the oldest monks and from other people he encountered'.[13] In most cases, medieval writers exercised due caution in accepting reports, though they generally accepted those which came from men of blameless character: thus Orderic could report without hesitation the testimony of 'a trustworthy man of upright life' while remaining sceptical of many miraculous tales when he himself had seen no 'solid proof of any such things'.[14] Gerald of Wales referred often to 'vulgar tradition', and was impressed by the ability of the Welsh to commit their royal genealogies to memory. It was precisely these memorized traditions which spawned romances such as Geoffrey of Monmouth's *Historia Regum Britanniae* and vernacular chronicles such as the *Brut*. At the end of the fifteenth century, William Worcestre sought information on places of interest from monks, hermits, and, on occasion, common people. On visiting Bristol in 1480, Worcestre recorded that one 'Dynt, by craft a pumpmaker of the city of Bristol, told several men that he had heard from old people who used to tell him

---

[12] M. I. Finley, 'Myth, Memory and History', *History and theory*, 4 (1965), 279–302; A. Momigliano, 'Historiography on Written Tradition and Historiography on Oral Tradition', in his *Studies in Historiography* (1966), 211–20, at p. 214. Modern oral historiography is dealt with in P. Thompson, *The Voice of the Past: Oral History* (Oxford, 1978) and D. Henige, *Oral Historiography* (New York and Lagos, 1982). The theoretical debates on the historical relationship between oral tradition and writing are of only secondary concern here, but it is worth noting at least the following division of opinion. An older school, led by Albert B. Lord and reinforced by subsequent writers such as Marshal McLuhan, sets oral societies in stark contrast to literate ones and romanticizes the democratic qualities of the former. More recent scholars such as Ruth Finnegan have pointed out both that societies which are exclusively literate or illiterate are very rare, and that genuinely oral societies are not necessarily inherently democratic as McLuhan claimed: R. Finnegan, *Oral Poetry* (Cambridge, 1977). Rosalind Thomas has similarly pointed out that ancient Athens was an oral society in many respects but also relied on record-keeping, while reminding us that the written histories of classical Greece were largely based on oral tradition: R. Thomas, *Oral Tradition and Written Record in Classical Athens* (Cambridge, 1989), 2–3. Useful surveys may be found in B. A. Rosenberg, 'The Complexity of Oral Tradition', *Oral Tradition*, 2 (1987), 73–90; and J. Goody, *The Interface between the Written and the Oral* (Cambridge, 1987), esp. pp. 59–109.

[13] *Eadmer's History of Recent Events in England*, trans. G. Bosanquet (1964), 1; William of Malmesbury, *Chronicle of the Kings of England*, trans. J. A. Giles (1847), 4; *The Ecclesiastical History of Orderic Vitalis*, ed. M. Chibnall, 6 vols. (Oxford, 1969–80), iii. 7, 291. R. Crosby, 'Oral Delivery in the Middle Ages', *Speculum*, 11 (1936), 88–110, remains a useful overview of medieval orality.

[14] Orderic, *Ecclesiastical History*, ii. 19, iv. 243, 261. The destruction of many irreplaceable documents by Danish incursions also forced him to heed 'the oral traditions of old men'. See B. Stock, *The Implications of Literacy* (Princeton, NJ, 1983), 76.

that they had seen a tree called in English a hawthorn growing in the High Street in the place where the splendid Cross stands.'[15]

By the time John Leland, the first important Tudor antiquary, conducted his own tours during the reign of Henry VIII he had extensive precedent for seeking out and recording oral information. He differed from medieval writers only in the degree to which he made the traditional nature of much of his evidence explicit. It was not that Leland was 'credulous' and did not know better than to rely on oral testimony. On the contrary, he knew very well that the manuscripts, books, and archives to which he devoted most of his career as a humanist did not by themselves provide a sufficiently full record of the past.[16] When Leland ascribed information to an oral source, he frequently used the phrase *in hominum memoria*. In general this denoted for contemporaries the memory of men living—what we would call oral history—rather than received tradition.[17] At Queen Camel, or Camallat, Somerset, he reported the recent discovery of Roman coins, adding, 'Ther was found *in hominum memoria* a horse shoe of sylver at Camallate.' At Lostwithiel he discovered that 'in tyme of memorie of men lyving' the local stone bridge had gradually sunk deeper and deeper into the sand.[18] Leland was not uncritical of the information that he garnered, and he discriminated among his sources. The ideal subject was an articulate, literate man who had lived in an area for some time: monks, priests, and merchants, for example. Visiting Bewdley in Worcestershire, he 'asked a merchant there of the ancientnesse of the towne'. The merchant replied that it was a new town, whose liberties were granted by Edward IV, a fact that Leland could not have gathered by looking at its considerably older buildings.[19] He prefaced his account of the history of

---

[15] Gerald of Wales (Giraldus Cambrensis), *The Itinerary through Wales and the Description of Wales*, ed. W. L. Williams (1908), 19, 33, 109, 128, 157–8; William Worcestre, *Itineraries*, ed. J. H. Harvey (Oxford, 1969), 119, 193, 199–201, 261, 331. C. S. L. Davies has commented usefully on the somewhat misleading notion of 'credulity' in the primarily oral late medieval environment, pointing out that 'men were too conscious of the limitations of their own experience to dismiss a tale too readily': *Peace, Print and Protestantism* (1977), 38; cf. L. Febvre, *The Problem of Unbelief in the Sixteenth Century: The Religion of Rabelais*, trans. B. Gottlieb (Cambridge, Mass. 1982), 438–51. An early attempt to interpret English Renaissance responses to the marvellous, while remaining almost entirely at the level of elite culture and concerned principally with the natural rather than the historical world, is of relevance here: M. Doran, 'On Elizabethan "Credulity": With Some Questions Concerning the Use of the Marvellous in Literature', *Journal of the History of Ideas*, 1 (1940), 151–76.

[16] C. E. Wright, 'The Dispersal of the Monastic Libraries in the Sixteenth Century', in F. Wormald and C. E. Wright (eds.), *The English Library before 1700* (1958), 148–75; T. D. Kendrick, *British Antiquity* (1950), 49, 53–5, 63; M. McKisack, *Medieval History in the Tudor Age* (Oxford, 1971), 11. On the deplorable condition of the public records until the late sixteenth century and its only very slow improvement thereafter, see R. B. Wernham, 'The Public Records in the Sixteenth and Seventeenth Centuries', in L. Fox (ed.), *English Historical Scholarship in the Sixteenth and Seventeenth Centuries* (1956), 11–30.

[17] *The Laboriouse Journey and Serche of Johan Leylande for Englandes Antiquities*, ed. John Bale (1549), now republished in *Leland's Itinerary*, vol. i, pp. xxxvii–xliii; *Joannis Lelandi Antiquarii de Rebus Britannicis Collectanea*, ed. Thomas Hearne, 3 vols. in 4 pts., plus 2 vols. of appendices (Oxford, 1715), which also includes a number of Leland's miscellaneous and poetical works.

[18] *Leland's Itinerary*, i. 151, 206; for other examples, see ibid. i. 143, 156, 163, 186, 254, iii. 27, v. 73, 100. Queen Camel also had strong Arthurian traditions, reported by Leland, which derived from the conflation of its Cadbury Castle with Camelot.

[19] Ibid. ii. 88.

Gloucester Abbey by stating his source: 'these notable things following I learned
of an ould man, made lately a monke of Gloucester'. Often he suspected that a
recent building had replaced a more ancient one on the same or a different site.
It was no chronicle but the testimony of its monks which told him that 'the old
Abbey of Bardeney [Lincolnshire] was not in the very same place wher the new
ys, but at a graunge or dayre a myle of'.[20]

But besides the opinion of the learned and literate, another sort of oral testimony rated highly by Leland's standards. This was the 'common voice' or 'common fame': what almost everyone in the area agreed had happened in the past.
Leland may have made the error of taking each individual testimony as an independent source, but he had little reason to doubt what people who had lived
in an area all their lives concurred upon, unless he had external evidence which
contradicted or clarified it. He happened upon a small pool in rural Carnarvon-
shire, 'wher they say that Idwalle Prince of Wales was killid and drounid'.[21] At
Oxenhall, near Darlington in Durham, locals recalled the long-standing tradition
of a 'horrible noyse' in which the earth had raised itself up and then collapsed,
leaving a huge crater, which country folk called 'Hell Kettles'. Leland suspected
that this was the earthquake of 1179, recorded in twelfth-century chronicles,
an opinion later endorsed by his Jacobean reader, William Burton.[22] William
Harrison, in discussing the same site in 1577, noted that locals believed the souls
of sinners were 'seethed' in this 'bottomless hole', a belief discredited in good Royal
Society fashion in the 1690s, when Jabez Kay tested its depths on behalf of
Edmund Gibson, editor of the 1695 edition of Camden's *Britannia*.[23] The common voice was sometimes to be trusted, at other times dismissed. At Winchelsea,
by Leland's time a decayed town, the common voice blamed French and Spanish
raids for the end of better days when the town had twenty aldermen, all 'mar-
chaunts of good substaunce'. This he recorded without further comment. But in
Rutland, where the 'commune fame' was that one Rutter had been given as much
land as he could ride around in one day on a wooden horse, which he did by
magic, thereby founding the tiny county, Leland was more sceptical. 'This is very
like a lye,' he wrote with some understatement, 'and more lykelihod it is that for
Rotherland, or Rutherland, it is shortely caullid Rutlande.'[24]

[20] *Leland's Itinerary*, v. 36.

[21] Ibid. iii. 76, 83; cf. iv. 4. Defoe would also use the phrase 'common fame' to denote accepted facts
about a community's past, nearly two centuries later: *A Tour Thro' the Whole Island of Great Britain*,
ed. G. D. H. Cole, 2 vols. (1927), i. 281; cf. ii. 460 for Defoe's reference to 'the voice of the people'.

[22] William Burton, *The Description of Leicester Shire* (1622), 270, citing the MSS of the *Collectanea*,
vol. i, fo. 418 (ed. Hearne, i. 327). Defoe makes no mention of this tradition. He believed that the
Hell Kettles were 'nothing but old coal pits filled with water by the river Tees': *Tour*, ii. 657.

[23] *Camden's Britannia* (1695), col. 774; Harrison, 'The Description of Britaine', in R. Holinshed, *The
First and Second Volumes of Chronicles* (1587), 130. Traditions regarding this site and the earthquake
continued into the nineteenth century: J. Weston, *Albion: A Guide to Legendary Britain* (1985), 333.

[24] *Leland's Itinerary*, iv. 89, 113, 124, 127; cf. i. 30, 110, 276, ii. 66, 75. Variants of the Rutter story
occur elsewhere: for a similar tradition in Dunster, Somerset, where 'a grand lady obtaind of her husband so much ground for the inhabitants' as she could compass barefoot in a day, see BL MS Stowe
1048 ('Observations of Warwickshire'), fo. 68ᵛ (vol. reversed).

The Elizabethan and early Stuart antiquaries who developed the genre of chorography adopted Leland's approach to oral sources just as they followed him in his study of monastic manuscripts.[25] William Lambarde found that many tales of the Kentish past had survived in both oral and written forms. He recounted the tales of popish impieties in St Nicholas's chapel near Hythe, putting in writing 'some such of them as I have learned, either by the faithfull report of honest persons that have seen and known the same, or els out of such written monuments as be yet extant and ready to be shewed'.[26] Of all the Elizabethan antiquaries, Lambarde came closest to putting his finger on the problem that most frustrates the oral historiographer today, that of 'feedback', which occurs when writing influences, distorts, or even creates outright an oral tradition.[27] Lambarde came across a good example of this in the folk tale surrounding Earl Godwin of Wessex, the father of King Harold II. According to tradition, Godwin choked to death on a piece of bread, shortly after which his land sank into the sea. What Lambarde suspected was not the integrity of the honest people he spoke to, but the origins and purity of these particular tales. 'Neither were these things continued as memorie, by the mouthes of the unlearned people only, but committed to writing also, by the hands and pens of monks, frears, and others of the learned sort.' Over the centuries the written version had so completely infested the traditional version that it gave the tales an unwarranted and misleading credibility, 'so that in course of time, the matter was past all peradventure, and the things beleeved for undoubted veritie'.[28]

William Camden knew the island of Britain in much less detail than Lambarde knew his native county, and like Leland he was forced to exploit the common

---

[25] There is much literature on the development of the chorographies, none of it dealing with the matter at issue here: among recent treatments, see A. McRae, *God Speed the Plough: The Representation of Agrarian England, 1500–1660* (Cambridge, 1996), 231–61; G. Parry, *The Trophies of Time* (Oxford, 1995); R. Helgerson, *Forms of Nationhood: The Elizabethan Writing of England* (Chicago and London, 1992). S. A. E. Mendyk, *'Speculum Britanniae': Regional Study, Antiquarianism, and Science in Britain to 1700* (Toronto, 1989), as its subtitle suggests, comes closest to discussing the relations between antiquarianism and knowledge, but its definition of the latter is too narrow and is also linked to the same positivist model of the development of historical methods that has seriously distorted the history of history as a whole.

[26] William Lambarde, *A Perambulation of Kent* (1576), 173. Leland had accepted as authoritative the memory of informants who had read old books or records: *Leland's Itinerary*, i. 12.

[27] D. Henige, ' "The Disease of Writing": Ganda and Nyoro Kinglists in a Newly Literate World', in J. C. Miller (ed.), *The African Past Speaks* (Folkestone, 1980), 240–61; Finnegan, *Literacy and Orality*, 117–20, for Polynesian examples. A good nineteenth-century instance of feedback comes from James Henry Dixon's collection of ballads and songs published in 1846. Following in the tradition of earlier gatherers of popular songs such as Ritson and Percy, Dixon transcribed one ballad, *The Bold Pedlar and Robin Hood* (included in no previous collection) which he thought of 'considerable antiquity, and no doubt much older than some of those inserted in the common garlands'. He took this from the oral recitation of 'an aged female in Bermondsey [Surrey]' who in turn had heard her grandmother sing it. The old woman claimed that it had never been printed, but Dixon soon discovered several copies at a bookseller's stall. *Ancient Poems, Ballads, and Songs of the Peasantry of England*, ed. J. H. Dixon, Percy Soc. 17 (1846), 71.

[28] Lambarde, *Perambulation*, 105. For an Oxfordshire example, an oral tradition noted by White Kennett as originating in an error in the 1607 Latin edition of Camden's *Britannia*, see Fox, *Oral and Literate Culture*, 242–3.

memory in order to remedy his ignorance. Though he 'poored upon many an old rowle and evidence', he felt no shame in admitting that he had also wandered over England and 'conferred with the most skillful observers in each country'.[29] Like Leland, he spoke both to the common folk and to learned residents who had themselves garnered morsels of local lore, generally attempting to verify their statements with reference to a document such as the Antonine Itinerary, a crucial source for the identification of Roman towns.[30] As in Leland's case, the traditions encountered by Camden frequently derived from the perception of local people that at some time in the past their community had enjoyed a level of economic prosperity and commercial or political importance now greatly declined, but of which ruins and other antiquities remained to testify. These beliefs were thus by-products of the broader sensitivity to environmental and material change with which this book began. In Croydon, the inhabitants pointed out a place where 'in old time' a royal house had once stood. The tiny village of Overburrow (or Burrow), Lancashire, had a tradition that it had once been a large city until a famine reduced it to poverty. 'This tradition', Camden observed, 'they received from their ancestours, delivered as it were from hand to hand unto them.' Camden thought the locals might be correct, for the plenitude of engraved stones and Roman coins, and the chequerboard paving pattern, suggested that this had once been a Roman camp. Here, physical evidence supplied the chronology lacking in the tradition, while Camden's documentary source, the Antonine Itinerary, provided further reinforcement and suggested possible Roman names for the place.[31] Of the foundation of the college at Bunbury, Cheshire, Camden wrote that he had been orally informed that this had been established by the Egerton family; subsequent 'autenticall proofe' revealed instead that Sir Hugh Calvely had founded it in 1388.[32] Camden's inclusiveness of oral information was so considerable that in 1695 it was argued in one legal dispute that *Britannia* 'amounted to as much as the sayings of an old man'.[33]

Other travellers and topographers, many of them more dependent on local information than the learned antiquaries, continued to report orally based data, primarily concerning buildings, inscriptions, landscape features, and the history of local families, well into the seventeenth century. A lieutenant on tour in the western counties in 1635 recorded numerous traditions and beliefs in his travel diary, noting with disappointment that he could 'neither see nor hear' any information

---

[29] Camden, *Britain*, 'To the Reader'.

[30] F. J. Levy, 'The Making of Camden's *Britannia*', *Bibliothèque d'humanisme et renaissance*, 27 (1964), 70–97; Stuart Piggott, 'William Camden and the *Britannia*', *Proceedings of the British Academy*, 37 (1951), 199–217.

[31] William Camden, *Britain*, trans. P. Holland (1610), 302, 590, 753; for some other examples, see pp. 194, 428, 525, 587, 590, 753, 795.

[32] Bodl. MS Smith 19 (Camden's 'A Suplement of the Topographicall Description of Britain published MDCX'), p. 18, a correction intended for p. 687 of Holland's 1610 edition.

[33] R. W. Baker, *The Hearsay Rule* (1950), 108–9, discussing the case of Steyner v. Burgesses of Droitwich (1695). Ironically, while the principle of the admissibility of sayings by deceased ancient persons was granted in this instance, the *Britannia* itself was excluded on the grounds that to give credence to it would be to afford similar status to other historians 'and there would not be any certainty'.

concerning the benefactors of Ely Cathedral, 'but onely those old and weather-beaten kings, in their durable freestone robes, whose statues are mounted on the west frontispiece of this fabricke'.[34] Marching with the royalist forces in 1645, Richard Symonds took down various descriptions of church monuments and arms, many newly destroyed by the ravages of the civil war. The unnamed statue of a bishop at Llangothlyn church, Denbighshire, was called 'Bishop Cuthlyn' by the locals; Worcestershire people provided him with similar information. Thomas Gerard, describing South Petherton in Somerset, recorded of a long-vanished palace that he was 'beholding to histories to tell us [there] was one here, and to tradicion to point out the place, for the very footeings of it are soe farr lost that noe man would ever believe a pallace stood in that place'. The Elizabethan biographer John Smyth noted the memories, then a century old, of the final skirmish between the feuding Lords Berkeley and Lisle in 1469 at Nibley, Gloucestershire, where he was the Berkeleys' long-serving estate steward. Smyth still heard locals

relate the reports of their parents, kinsfolks and neighbours present at this skirmish, some with the one lord, and others with the other; and of such as carryed victualls and weapons to some of those companies . . . and afterwards climbed up into trees, (being then boys of twelve and sixteen yeares,) to see the battle.[35]

Like the popular beliefs about the past of which it was a major vessel of transmission, oral tradition was very closely tied to objects and visible features, either natural or man-made. If they vanished, the popular memory often disappeared within a generation or two, or became vague as to details. Hearne would note at the beginning of the eighteenth century that the fall or destruction of churches led to the rapid forgetting of the benefactions behind them, and his contemporary Browne Willis found only the barest tradition of the medieval abbey at Winchcombe destroyed after the Reformation.[36] A hundred years earlier, when Sir John Oglander took up his inheritance on the Isle of Wight in 1607, he set about excavating the great Cistercian abbey that had once stood on his lands. But he had difficulty locating its foundations. 'I went to Quarr, and inquyred of divors owld men where ye greate church stood.' One Father Pennie, 'a verye owld man' told him that the foundations were to be found in a nearby cornfield, but Oglander's attempts to dig them up proved unsuccessful.[37] William Burton was luckier; he found a vivid memory of the battle of Bosworth field among its locals early in the seventeenth century, a memory reinforced by discoveries in 1602 of a 'great store' of armour, arrowheads, and weapons on a nearby enclosed field.

[34] Anon. (attrib. to one Lieutenant Hammond), *A Relation of a Short Survey of the Western Counties made by a lieutenant of the military company in Norwich in 1635*, ed. L. G. W. Legg, *Camden Miscellany*, 16, Camden Soc., 3rd ser., 52 (1936), 91.

[35] BL MS Harl. 944 (Richard Symonds's observations), fos. 30[r], 58[r]; Thomas Gerard, *The Particular Description of the County of Somerset*, written c.1632, ed. E. H. Bates, Somerset Rec. Soc., 15 (1900), 115; John Smyth, *The Berkeley Manuscripts*, ed. J. Maclean, 3 vols. (Gloucester, 1883–5), ii. 114.

[36] Both examples cited in Fox, *Oral and Literate Culture*, 219.

[37] S. Piggott, 'Antiquarian Thought in the Sixteenth and Seventeenth Centuries', in Fox (ed.), *English Historical Scholarship*, 105.

This was both oral tradition and oral history, since Burton had the testimonies of some ancient men who had seen the battle fought, 'of which persons my selfe have seene some, and have heard of their discourses, though related by second hand'.[38] The inhabitants of Hornchurch in Essex told John Weever that their parish church, formerly a priory, had originally been called 'Whore-church'. It had received its modern, more decorous name by the grace of 'a certaine King, but by what king they are uncertaine'.[39]

THE WRITTEN RECORD AND THE BEGINNINGS OF REACTION

Like the artefacts studied in previous chapters, traditions circulated both among the inhabitants of local communities and beyond their boundaries through antiquaries and other travellers. In this way they entered the pool of historical knowledge available for inclusion in the works of the learned and for repetition or discussion by educated readers. The process of circulation itself changed very little in the two centuries between Leland and Stukeley. What profoundly shifted, however, was the intellectual status of tradition relative to other types of historical source. There are signs as early as the end of the sixteenth century of a growing discomfort with the use of oral traditional evidence. Some of this is no doubt attributable to a wider Protestant distrust of 'unwritten verities'. Throughout Elizabeth's reign, the orientation of established religion towards the authority of Scripture and away from 'tradition' (in the specific sense of the received practices and prescriptions of the medieval Church) sharpened hostility towards assertions about the past not based on written texts.[40] This remained a theme in religious controversies during the next century: both Bishop Joseph Hall in 1628 and Archbishop John Tillotson two generations later denounced the appeal to oral tradition in the religious sphere.[41] The Catholic position on the traditional basis of religion generally ran to the contrary, the polemicist John Sargeant deeming 'tradition oral and practical to be the rule of faith'.[42]

---

[38] Burton, *Description of Leicester Shire*, 47.

[39] John Weever, *Ancient Funerall Monuments* (1631). A visual reference to the name of the parish of Hornchurch (though with no trace of the Whore-church tradition) was placed on the eastern gable of the chancel at St Andrew's church; by 1610 there is reference to 'points of lead fashioned like horns' (cf. *VCH, Essex*, vii. 48) and some form of horns has been fixed there ever since. M. K. McIntosh, *A Community Transformed: The Manor and Liberty of Havering, 1500–1620* (Cambridge, 1991), 226. John Aubrey encountered a rival tradition at Hornchurch in the 1670s, according to which the name derived from the horns of a hart having been kept in the church for several centuries: *Anecdotes and Traditions Illustrative of Early English History and Literature*, ed. W. J. Thoms, Camden Soc., os 5 (1839), 106.

[40] Ironically, as Linda Colley points out, much of the belief about Catholic atrocity that circulated in the early nineteenth century and proved an obstacle to Catholic emancipation was in the form of oral tradition: *Britons: Forging the Nation, 1707–1837* (New Haven, 1992), 333.

[41] These and other examples are given in A. Fox, 'Custom, Memory and the Authority of Writing', in P. Griffiths, A. Fox, and S. Hindle (eds.), *The Experience of Authority in Early Modern England* (London and New York, 1996), 89–116, at p. 91.

[42] John Sargeant, *Sure Footing in Christianity, or Rational Discourses on the Rule of Faith* (1665), mentioned in *The Journal of James Yonge [1647–1721] Plymouth Surgeon*, ed. F. N. L. Poynter (1963), 159.

Yet differing Protestant and Catholic positions on Scripture versus tradition do not provide sufficient explanation for the shift in attitude, since they did not automatically carry over into other spheres such as the secular past. Moreover, there is no reliable correlation between Catholicism and a predisposition to accept tradition in contexts where religious truth was not at stake. Camden, a Protestant, inclined to use them liberally, while among the earliest explicit critics of tradition as a historical source one finds his two contemporaries Sampson Erdeswicke, the son of a Staffordshire papist, and Thomas Habington, a Worcestershire recusant. Erdeswicke expressed reservations about a local tradition concerning a monument at Burton Abbey in Staffordshire, 'which monument, the common fame (of the unskillful) reports to have been of the first founder Wilfricus [i.e. Ulfricus] Spot, and that cannot in any wise be so'. Since the monument was made of alabaster, fashioned into armour of the post-Conquest period, 'something like to our new monuments', Erdeswicke thought it no older than the reign of Edward III, though he admitted that it might be a fourteenth-century reconstruction of an earlier monument to the founder or another benefactor.[43] Habington, a Catholic exiled to his county after the Gunpowder Plot, admitted that written sources such as heraldic pedigrees were 'often farced with untruthes', yet he consistently preferred written evidence to traditions 'reported by the vulgar' and inveighed against those who relied upon them.[44] John Stow, born in the 1520s and at best ambivalent about reformed religion, makes surprisingly little use of tradition in his *Survey of London*, though this may be because the London environment provided a richer source of written and architectural evidence than did many rural parishes.[45]

Many other early critiques of oral tradition or endorsements of the superiority of the written word can be adduced from the late Elizabethan and Jacobean antiquaries. In Great Yarmouth, Henry Manship (the sometime town clerk whom we have already met as a reformer of record-keeping) went to some lengths to follow the origins of the town only through its documents, supplemented on occasion by information from recent books like Camden's *Britannia* and John Speed's *Theatre of the empire of Great Britaine*, and by his own 'reasonable conjecture'. He thought the pursuit of his or any town's remotest beginnings a lost cause, as unseeable as the head of a river, even if, like a river, one knew it had to have a head. He made no effort in this regard to fill in the blank with oral tradition.[46]

---

[43] Sampson Erdeswicke, *A Survey of Staffordshire* (1717), 169–70 (mispaginated as p. 180), 214.

[44] Thomas Habington, *A Survey of Worcestershire*, ed. J. Amphlett, 2 vols., Worcestershire Historical Soc. (Oxford, 1893–9), i. 468–70, ii. 34, 226–7, 242; BL MS Add. 28564, fo. 236ᵛ (Habington to Symon Archer, 7 Dec. 1635).

[45] John Stow, *The Survey of London*, ed. H. B. Wheatley (1912; repr. 1980), 176, for a rare instance where Stow repeats a story told by his father and another old man. Many London traditions and customs had already found their way into script, thanks to the city's well-established practice of chronicle-writing and record-keeping.

[46] Henry Manship, *The History of Great Yarmouth*, ed. C. J. Palmer (1854), 20; the sole exception to his reliance on documents, which was already anticipated in the earlier collections of his older contemporary Thomas Damet (above, Ch. 8) is Manship's repeating of the story of a relatively recent great catch of mackerel of which he heard 'very credibly reported' (ibid. 97).

364 The Past Remembered

Elsewhere in East Anglia, Robert Reyce found no written evidence of mineral discoveries in old Suffolk. He had heard 'that in ancient time there was a mine of gold oare', but this struck him as 'an unprobable heare say'. The people of Tottenham High-Cross in Middlesex attributed the refusal of an old walnut tree to grow to the burning of a religious martyr on the site, but whether this was a Marian or an earlier martyr remained unknown. The tale's vagueness was too much for William Bedwell: 'But who it was, and when it should be done, they cannot tell, and I finde no such thing in our stories upon record, and therfore I do not tell this for a truthe.'[47] Reginald Bainbrigg praised his friend and fellow North Country antiquary, John Denton of Cardew, for his study of the antiquities of Carlisle, a work which 'goes by no hearesaies, but by ancient recordes'.[48]

In the seventeenth century, a further influence on the declining interest in and growing mistrust of oral sources would emerge in legal thinking, especially in the work of jurists such as John Selden and Sir Matthew Hale. Common lawyers in general were well acquainted with the study and criticism of oral testimony. Hale himself was an early exponent of the notion that the formal swearing of a witness did not *ipso facto* make that witness credible, and that only moral rather than absolute certainty was ever possible with regards to things past.[49] It is true that the English judicial system steadily relied upon—and generated—increasing quantities of written evidence, case records, and legal reports. But the transition to a system dependent predominantly upon the written rather than the spoken word was neither sudden nor thorough, and it encountered a good deal of resistance along the way.[50] 'All courts of justice', commented Bishop Burnet, 'proceed upon the evidence given by witnesses; for the use of writings is but a thing more lately brought into the world.'[51] As we have seen, human memory was accepted as valid evidence in cases of property and land disputes, and the same was true for the very recent past involved in criminal proceedings.

Increasingly, however, such testimony ran into scepticism deriving from the belief that an illiterate witness was *ipso facto* an unreliable witness.[52] Jurors were

[47] Robert Reyce, *Suffolk in the XVIIth Century*, ed. F. Hervey (1902), 26 f.; William Bedwell, *A Brief Description of the Towne of Tottenham High-Crosse* (1631), sig. E[v].

[48] T. H. B. Graham, 'Analysis of the Denton Pedigree', *Transactions of the Cumberland and Westmorland Antiquarian and Archaeological Society*, NS 34 (1934), 1–16; C. W. James, 'A Copy of John Denton's MS in the Possession of the Earl of Leicester at Holkham', ibid., NS 23 (1923), 103–8.

[49] B. J. Shapiro, *Probability and Certainty in Seventeenth-Century England* (Princeton, 1983), 180–6.

[50] The short-lived statute 11 Hen. 7 c. 3 (1495), for instance, represents an early, unsuccessful, attempt by the Crown to avoid the use of a grand jury in non-capital cases by allowing prosecutions on information; it was repealed in 1509: T. A. Green, *Verdict According to Conscience* (Chicago, 1985), 115–16.

[51] Gilbert Burnet, *Some Passages of the Life and Death of . . . John Earl of Rochester* (1680), 74; Shapiro, *Probability and Certainty in Seventeenth-Century England*, 183–4; id. *A Culture of Fact: England, 1550–1720* (Ithaca, NY, 2000), 8–33.

[52] Juries were often criticized, perhaps wrongly, in the later seventeenth and the eighteenth centuries, for their members' alleged credulity, which was generally linked to low social status and marginal literacy; a character in *Humphry Clinker* refers to them as 'illiterate plebeians, apt to be easily misled': P. J. R. King, ' "Illiterate Plebeians, Easily Misled": Jury Composition, Experience and Behavior in Essex, 1735–1815', in J. Cockburn and T. Green (eds.), *Twelve Good Men and True* (Princeton, 1988), 254, 278–80, 302. King points out that this putative illiteracy and low degree were often only relative, jury members being drawn, even at quarter sessions, from the middling sort of farmers and artisans.

expected to be able to discern believable from unbelievable and, according to Hale, were permitted to pronounce verdict against testimony if they lacked faith in a witness.[53] The mechanics of a criminal jury system which still depended heavily upon verbal information and accusation, and on memory or even hearsay as evidence, ensured that those skilled in the law were obliged to develop critical standards for evaluating the spoken and written word alike. It was the later seventeenth century that first adumbrated the 'hearsay rule' for juries, according to which jurors with prior knowledge of an event were required to be sworn as witnesses, and could no longer simply act upon information known only to themselves. The testimony of witnesses was at the same time weighted in favour of direct knowledge of events, with third-party information given only corroborative status, and by the 1720s it was more or less accepted that 'a mere hearsay is no evidence'.[54] Lawyers, unlike jurors, were also first and foremost students of the documentary and legible. During the sixteenth century, textbook study gradually supplanted the legal readings that had formed the basis of the law student's education for centuries, much to the grief of Sir Edward Coke.[55] Those lawyers who were influenced by the best of Continental learning and philological rigour, and who turned from the practice of law to legal history, were even less likely than the majority of the profession to place great faith in, let alone actively pursue, oral evidence in their researches.

The heralds were also familiar with oral testimony and its hazards. Like the lawyers, they were unable to dispense with it but had come by 1600 to prefer the document or artefact to personal testimony, and it is not surprising that a well-known 'historical controversy' of Elizabeth's later reign revolved in large measure around the value of oral evidence in the verification of family genealogies. When Ralph Brooke, the aggressive York herald, attacked William Camden for a number of genealogical errors in the early editions of *Britannia*, he was attacking Camden's method as much as any specific factual errors. Brooke was concerned that Camden was insufficiently skilled in the study of such documents and that he took too much on 'hearsay'.[56] Camden was unquestionably the greater scholar of the two, and his attractive personality tempts us to defend him against

---

[53] P. Lawson, 'Lawless Juries? The Composition and Behavior of Hertfordshire Juries, 1573–1624', in Cockburn and Green (eds.), *Twelve Good Men and True*, 119 ff., 142.

[54] Baker, *The Hearsay Rule*, 9–10. However, note the continued admission of hearsay throughout the eighteenth century in cases of pedigree or descent: ibid. 98–108 and above, Ch. 3 (p. 78n.20).

[55] Edward Coke, *The First Part of the Institutes of the Lawes of England* (1628), fos. 280r–v; cf. George Buck's comments on lectures and readings, already in decline when he wrote in the 1610s: *The Third Universitie of England*, appended to John Stow, *Annales*, ed. Edmund Howes (1631), 1074. On legal education at this time see L. A. Knafla, 'The Law Studies of an Elizabethan Student', *Huntington Library Quarterly*, 32 (1969), 221–40; R. J. Schoeck, 'Lawyers and Rhetoric in Sixteenth-Century England', in J. J. Murphy (ed.), *Renaissance Eloquence: Studies in the Theory and Practice of Renaissance Rhetoric* (Berkeley and Los Angeles, 1983), 274–91.

[56] Ralph Brooke, *A Discoverie of Certaine Errours Published in the Much-commended Britannia* (1594), 'To Maister Camden'. Camden replied in 'Ad Lectorem', appended to the 1600 edition of *Britannia*; F. J. Levy, *Tudor Historical Thought* (San Marino, 1967), 157; W. Rockett, '*Britannia*, Ralph Brooke, and the Representation of Privilege in Elizabethan England', *Renaissance Quarterly*, 53 (2000), 475–99.

the cantankerous Brooke. Yet it is worth remembering that, when this controversy began in the 1590s, Brooke had been a herald for over a decade and had acquired a good deal of experience in sifting through genealogical evidence, oral and written. This was experience that Camden (who became a herald only in 1597, and was at this point still a London schoolmaster) manifestly lacked, for all his prodigious classical learning and Continental connections.

The Brooke–Camden dispute fumed on for three decades, leading finally to an attack by one of Camden's own protégés, Augustine Vincent, on Brooke's 1619 *Catalogue* of the nobility.[57] When Vincent published his own *Discoverie of Errours* in 1622, a year before Camden's death, the formidable antiquary John Selden intervened. Selden, a lawyer like Matthew Hale (his junior by a generation) provided a commendatory epistle that amounted to a brief manifesto of historical research methodology, synthesizing the techniques of the legal philologist and the herald. Selden praised Vincent's industry and diligence in reading not only published authors, but also 'the more abstruse parts of history which lie hid, either in private manuscripts, or in the publick records of the kingdom'. He extolled the use of Exchequer documents and of judicial records; he commended the great libraries of his day—the Royal, Cottonian, Bodleian, and several others. But of oral sources, even the ones that Vincent himself must surely have encountered on his heraldic visitations, Selden said not a word.[58]

The library-bound Selden was no peripatetic antiquary, so his experiences in dealing with tradition, in particular rural tradition, would have been rather limited. Even so, his private views on popular sources may in fact have been more ambivalent than this hard-headed endorsement of the written text suggests. He had a taste for ballads and is said to have remarked that 'there was more truth in them than there was in many of our historians'.[59] His posthumously published *Table-talk* similarly asserts that 'More solid things do not show the complexion of times so well, as ballads and libels', while also endorsing both proverbs and tradition.[60] But his published remarks ran in the opposite direction, and their influence can be felt in the antiquarian writings of the middle and later seventeenth century, the authors of which were all acquainted with Selden's works. The great Anglo-Saxon scholar William Somner frequently cited oral tradition in his early work, *The Antiquities of Canterbury*. At one point he found that common tradition was so unequivocal that it rendered citations from the records

---

[57] Ralph Brooke, *A Catalogue and Succession of the Kings, Princes, Dukes, Marquesses, Earles, and Viscounts of the Realme of England Since the Norman Conquest to this Present Yeare 1619* (1619).

[58] John Selden, 'To my Singular Good Friend, Mr Augustine Vincent', in Vincent, *A Discoverie of Errours in the First Edition of the Catalogue of Nobility Published by Ralph Brooke, Yorke Herald, 1619* (1622), sigs. a–a^v; cf. the preface to the second, enlarged edition of Selden's *Titles of Honor* (1631) for similar comments.

[59] Anthony Wood, *Athenae Oxonienses*, ed. P. Bliss, 4 vols. (Oxford, 1813–20), iii, col. 366 and n.; *The Diary of Abraham de la Pryme, the Yorkshire antiquary*, ed. C. Jackson, Surtees Soc., 54 (1870), 67, where Selden's remark is quoted. The remark is credible given Selden's family connections to oral culture: he is supposed to have been the son of a Sussex minstrel or fiddler.

[60] *Table-talk: being the discourses of John Selden, Esq.*, ed. R. Milward, 2nd edn. (1698), 93, 153, 155.

unnecessary. 'Because tradition keepes it yet in memory with some', he could afford to cite only one record as additional proof. For Somner, however, oral tradition was to be used as a last resort, and even then it required further verification: 'as a thing uncertaine I leave it with a *fides penes lectorem esto*, untill further enquiry shall inable me to give him better satisfaction'.[61]

Similar examples of the priority accorded to written materials can be found throughout the remainder of the seventeenth century. The Cheshire engraver Daniel King, who wrote the introduction to a collective investigation of Cheshire antiquities entitled *The Vale-royall of England*, thanked his friends for providing information 'either of their own knowledge, or the relation of their elders'. The actual authors of the book, however, relied almost entirely on written sources (which by this time increasingly included the works of earlier and con-temporary scholars), clearly distinguishing between the questionable authority of 'old tales' and the more convincing evidence in 'writers both ancient and modern'.[62] Richard Butcher corrected a number of traditions that he found in Stamford, many of which had been reported by Leland or Camden.[63] Dugdale seems to have believed that what did not survive in manuscript or inscription was lost for ever. In *The History of St Paul's Cathedral*, he comments that 'the dismall ruins' of some tombs in the cathedral 'have put an end to any future discovery, that can be made of them'. His own *Antiquities of Warwickshire* quotes from Selden's letter to Augustine Vincent and wholeheartedly adopts Selden's bias in favour of the written. Dugdale could report oral traditions for amusement, but he took a pedantic, almost malicious, delight in correcting or disproving them from the manuscript sources that he knew so well. Tradition told him that Richard Boughton, sheriff of Warwick, had died at Bosworth field in 1485, but inquisitions *post mortem* revealed that Boughton had been killed two days before the battle, probably in a preliminary skirmish.[64] He was less scrupulous on this point when not writing for publication. The notes of his journey about the fens in 1657 mention the tradition that 'Audrey Causey' had been built by William the Conqueror while he besieged the Isle of Ely. They also record the belief at Littleborough Ferry on Trent that a Roman station had once been there

[61] William Somner, *The Antiquities of Canterbury* (1640), 34–5; Somner also notes (p. 62) that as reputable a medieval historian as Bede derived information from 'tradition of his elders'.

[62] Daniel King, *The Vale-royall of England or, the County Palatine of Chester Illustrated* (1656), 2, 118. Anthony Wood records (on information from Dugdale, who denounced King, the son of a baker, as 'a most ignorant, silly fellow') that the true authors were William Webb, William Smith, Samuel Lee and the regicide James Chaloner: *Athenae Oxonienses*, ed. Bliss, iii, col. 503; *DNB*, *sub* 'King, Daniel'; the section by Smith was completed in the 1590s.

[63] Richard Butcher, *The Survey and Antiquitie of the Towne of Stamford, in the County of Lincolne* (1646), 26, 27; cf. Camden, *Britain*, 534; *Leland's Itinerary*, iv. 89.

[64] Sir William Dugdale, *The History of St Paul's Cathedral in London* (1658), 48; Dugdale, *The Antiquities of Warwickshire* (1656), preface and p. 66. Dugdale did, however, settle at least one pedigree dispute by reference to 'divers aged people': K. Thomas, 'Age and Authority in Early Modern England', *Proceedings of the British Academy*, 62 (1976), 1–46, at p. 234. For earlier examples of the use of oral evidence for family genealogy, see Thomas Westcote, *A View of Devonshire in 1630* (Exeter, 1845), xvi, 449; Richard Carew, *The Survey of Cornwall* (1602), fo. 117.

'as tis sayd', a supposition in this case supported by regular discoveries of Roman coins.[65]

Dugdale's attitude reveals a widening but not unbridgeable gap between scholarly and popular views of the past, in which oral sources were relegated to second-class evidence or were quoted only for interest, but were not dispensed with altogether. By the 1640s, the document and the inscription had achieved an unquestionable priority over the common voice. The distance between a methodical student of records such as Dugdale and a talented amateur like Sir Thomas Browne is equally apparent. Browne's brief study of monuments in Norwich Cathedral, the *Repertorium*, owed a great deal to oral evidence, largely because Browne's documentary knowledge was thinner than that of a Dugdale or a Selden. Browne unhesitatingly reported information given him orally by two ancient cathedral officials. Some of this information was personal recollection; the rest was traditional. Sir Thomas thought that many bishops might have been buried in the cathedral, 'and wee find it so asserted by some historicall accounts, butt there remaining no historie or tradition of the place of their enternement, in vayne wee endeavour to designe and poynt out the same'. Rather than let perish the memory of some inscriptions no longer extant, he 'tooke the best account I could of them at the Kings returne from an understanding singing-man of 91 yeares old and sett them downe in a booke'. Yet even Browne distanced himself from his vulgar sources, and devoted one of his most celebrated treatises to the repudiation of popular errors, believing the common people to be 'the most deceptible part of mankind'.[66] Citing Browne as his example a few decades later, Edward Lhwyd, who was proposing a natural history of Wales, issued a folio sheet of heads of questions in 1697 to which he wished gentry to return answers. His categories included natural history (foliage, rocks, plants, rivers), Roman antiquities, architecture, medieval and other artefacts and, finally, the 'vulgar errors' of the ignorant.[67] This movement of popular beliefs out of the category of source and into that of subject of study is an important point to which we will return further on.

TRUST, TRUTH, AND AUTHORITY

It is very tempting to see in the reactions of document-oriented lawyers, humanist-trained philologers, and sceptical heralds the principal cause of the

---

[65] BL MS Lans. 722 (Dugdale's Itinerary into the Fens, 1657), fos. 29[r], 37[v]. It is perhaps also worth observing that the thicket of citations from manuscript sources in the margins of his *Baronage of England*, 2 vols. (1675–6), thins considerably as its successive family accounts approach his own time, in contrast to the accounts themselves, suggesting considerable—and undeclared—use of oral information.

[66] Thomas Browne, *Repertorium, or Some Account of the Tombs and Monuments in the Cathedrall Church of Norwich, 1680*, in *Works of Sir Thomas Browne*, ed. G. Keynes, 4 vols. (1964), iii. 123–42; *The Letters of Sir Thomas Browne*, in *Works*, iv. 373–4 (Browne to John Aubrey, 24 Aug. 1672); Browne, *Pseudodoxia Epidemica*, ed. R. Robbins, 2 vols. (Oxford, 1981), i. 15 and *passim*. Most of the 'vulgar errors' Browne discusses are, however, errors of the educated, with classical and literary rather than popular origins: Doran, 'Elizabethan "Credulity"', 159.

[67] E. Lhwyd (or Lhuyd), *Parochial Queries in Order to a Geographical Dictionary, a Natural History &c. of Wales* (1697), 1–4.

devaluation of oral tradition as a legitimate historical source during the seventeenth century. Certainly the influence of Selden and others in this regard was considerable, since they did in fact set up rubrics of method that would be adhered to by the antiquaries and historians of the second half of the century and beyond. It should also be noted that the changing tactics of the Restoration and Augustan antiquaries, from Aubrey to Lhwyd, Woodward, and eventually Stukeley, in the direction of observation and comparison, rendered oral sources useless for most purposes, both because they could 'explain' only individual objects rather than assist in their categorization, and also because many objects so studied, unlike churches and ruined castles, had origins lying well before the span of human memory.

But we are in danger of tracing back a false pedigree of historical method along purely intellectual lines. Other factors need to be considered. Foremost among these are the cultural underpinnings of trust and authority—that is, of the right to be believed. This, scholars such as Steven Shapin and Lorraine Daston have shown, was itself in flux during the seventeenth century. 'Far from embracing the ideal of the interchangeable observer,' writes Daston, 'seventeenth- and eighteenth-century scientists carefully weighted observation reports by the skill and integrity of the observer.'[68] Elsewhere, she has suggested that the word 'fact' in its modern sense of a datum of experience (as opposed to the older sense of a 'deed' or 'act') first entered usage in English about the time of Bacon, and 'the most important factor in the ready acceptance of Baconian facts, despite their strangeness and/or irreplicability, was trust, extended almost *carte blanche* to at least a small circle of respected colleagues or informants'.[69] Shapin's study makes much the same point, arguing that 'truth' in the seventeenth century was not a free-standing absolute but a relative and movable value, attachable to statements of empirical or inductive fact when the speaker or writer was deemed worthy of belief. A variety of circumstances and factors could intrude themselves on the way to acceptance of a particular claim as true, such as the claimant's gender. The lack of contemporary acceptance of the scientific ideas of the duchess of Newcastle thus may have had as much to do with her sex as with any intrinsic lack of coherence with reality, or faults in logic. Above all, social status and reputation were critical in endowing truth-claims with authority.[70] The experimental culture of the Royal Society was dominated by men whose claims to credibility were supported by their gentility or nobility. Since most experiments were not repeated for verification, the word of a gentleman thus played a

[68] Daston places the origins of what she calls 'aperspectival objectivity' in the later eighteenth century, seeing it as deriving from moral and aesthetic philosophy rather than the natural sciences: Daston, 'Objectivity and the Escape from Perspective', *Social Studies of Science*, 22, special issue on the social history of objectivity (1992), 597–618, esp. p. 610.

[69] Daston, 'Baconian Facts, Academic Civility, and the Prehistory of Objectivity', *Annals of Scholarship*, 8 (1991), 337–63, quotation at p. 349; cf. Shapiro, *Culture of Fact*, 49–62; M. Poovey, *A History of the Modern Fact: Problems of Knowledge in the Sciences of Wealth and Society* (Chicago, 1998), 7–21.

[70] For the contemporaneous role of reputation in ensuring trust or 'credit' in the economic sphere, and at all social levels, see C. Muldrew, *The Economy of Obligation: The Culture of Credit and Social Relations in Early Modern England* (New York, 1998), 148–57.

significant role in defining what should be believed. At the same time, lying and cognitive unreliability were also becoming increasingly associated with the poor and servile, a theme prominent in seventeenth-century courtesy literature.[71]

By the time of Robert Boyle and the early Royal Society, arguments from fact were fast supplanting more traditional scholastic and Renaissance arguments from authority. The 'canons of human testimony' that Zachary Coke, following the Continental logician Bartholomew Keckermann, adumbrated in his 1654 *Art of Logic*, are an odd mixture of the old and new. On the one hand, Coke continued to venerate oldness in a thoroughly unmodern way. His fifth canon had it that 'old testimony is worth more than new'. His eighth, that 'testimonies historical, of approved historians, are firm' was a formal assertion already well out of step with the sort of scepticism towards *all* historical knowledge that was occasionally mooted in the sixteenth century, and that became all the more common as readers became increasingly aware of contradictions of detail, to say nothing of partisanship and ideology. On the other hand, Coke made social distinctions in the ranking of sources of testimony—that of 'skillful artizen' being preferable to that of an unskilful one, 'however famous otherwise'; and he limited the probative authority of Church Fathers to 'theological conclusions' only, not to 'humane'.[72]

The rhetoric of argumentation was, in certain spheres of knowledge, beginning to consider the massive citation of authorities (as opposed to direct first-hand evidence) as having a secondary and informative value only, rather than possessing probative power in itself: Bacon's natural history called for the abandonment of what he collectively called 'philology'. A few decades later Boyle would make a show of *not* using 'passages in classick or other authors, that may either give some authority to our thoughts' where reason or first-hand experience would be more compelling; where he appealed to other writers at all it was as supportive 'witnesses' not as decisive 'judges'.[73] The rethinking of what sorts of argument had persuasive value thus links our earlier account of the transition in attitudes to antiquity and ancestry very directly to the declining status of oral tradition considered as a species of argument from the past.

A distinction was often drawn between truth, which was unitary, and falsehood, which had many different voices. The very multiplicity of testimony that previously seemed to attest to the truth of a statement—Leland's 'common voice', for example—had come by the late Elizabethan period to be seen as a

---

[71] S. Shapin, *A Social History of Truth: Civility and Science in Seventeenth-Century England* (Chicago, 1994), 74–95. For women, the additional criterion of sexual honour or 'honesty' was a factor in evaluating credit-worthiness: L. Gowing, *Domestic Dangers: Women, Words, and Sex in Early Modern London* (Oxford, 1996), 128–9.

[72] Zachary Coke, *The Art of Logic* (1654), 163–4; I owe this reference to Richard Serjeantson. Only three years earlier Thomas Hobbes had distinguished deference towards the great men of the past from belief in the historians who reported their deeds: 'If Livy say the Gods made once a cow speak, and we believe it not; we distrust not God therein, but Livy.' Thomas Hobbes, *Leviathan*, bk. 1, ch. 8, ed. M. Oakeshott (Oxford, 1946), 42.

[73] Boyle, *Certain Physiological Essays, written at Distant times, and on sevral occasions* (1661), 28–9.

liability. Richard Hooker, borrowing from Galen, thought it unreasonable that opinions be accepted on the basis of rumour and report purely because they were repeated several times, and Restoration writers such as Stillingfleet and Boyle picked up on this theme in connection with religion and natural philosophy.[74] Problems also arose from the circumstances in which an event was observed and from the nature of the event itself. Witnesses examined long after a particular occurrence such as a crime or murder were known to be less accurate and more likely to conflict on details than those examined immediately after, in contrast to the more general consensus they produced on general points of enduring custom. This is a point that has been supported by modern psychological investigations of the reliability of eyewitness testimony, which note that violent events or sudden changes are less accurately recalled by witnesses than routine or mundane, non-disruptive matters.[75]

Those who still wanted to be able to accept some statements as true without conducting experiments or making observations themselves thus had to steer a course between the sucking vortex of credulity and the even more threatening dragon of extreme doubt. In order to work out an effective compromise between error and truth in areas such as eyewitness testimony, lawyers and judges began to work out early ideas of 'probability', a word that in turn connects etymologically with the 'probity' of witnesses. Barbara J. Shapiro has demonstrated that a concern with probability connected a wide spectrum of activities from the law to history, literature, and religion.[76] In a similar vein, Steven Shapin suggests that the concept of 'moral certainty' was adumbrated by Boyle and other Restoration authors not only to establish what could be believed but also to protect against the opposite threat of complete doubt, the sort of pyrrhonist scepticism of *any* truth that could be found in the French *libertin* tradition from la Mothe le Vayer to Bayle.[77] Boyle conceded that for certain areas of knowledge, including law, commerce, religion, and history, testimony (whether written or oral) was the principal source of knowledge, since truth concerning these matters could not be self-evident. 'It is by this we know, that there were such men as Julius Caesar and

---

[74] Hooker, cited in Shapin, *Social History of Truth*, 232–3; for an older account of Boyle's views (which regrettably separates his scientific and religious views), see H. Van Leeuwen, *The Problem of Certainty in English Thought 1630–80* (Leiden, 1963), 91–106.

[75] 'It is by now a well-established fact that people are less accurate and complete in their eyewitness accounts after a long retention interval than after a short one': E. F. Loftus, *Eyewitness Testimony* (Cambridge, Mass., 1979), 53; Loftus shows that perception of a violent event is *less* accurate than of an ordinary, unemotional one (p. 31). Cf. I. M. L. Hunter, *Memory* (1957), 169–75. Matters of trust in social interaction are raised on the basis of a discussion of courtroom procedure in A. Brannigan and M. Lynch, 'On Bearing False Witness: Credibility as an Interactional Accomplishment', *Journal of Contemporary Ethnography*, 16 (1987), 115–46: 'Even when there may be good reason to question the "truthfulness" of someone's conduct, everyday interaction does not offer many occasions to undertake such inquiries in an open and unambiguous way' (p. 116).

[76] Shapiro, *Probability and Certainty in Seventeenth-Century England, passim*; J. A. I. Champion, *The Pillars of Priestcraft Shaken: The Church of England and its Enemies, 1660–1730* (Cambridge, 1992), 42–6.

[77] Shapin, *Social History of Truth*, 214; R. H. Popkin, *The History of Scepticism from Erasmus to Spinoza*, rev. edn. (Berkeley, Calif., 1979).

William the Conqueror, and that Joseph knew that Pharaoh had a dream, which the Egyptian wise men could not expound'. But testimony was not self-evident and needed to be evaluated by reason, according to strict criteria which included the moral reputation of the witness.[78]

The philosopher John Hardwig has argued in connection with modern knowledge that 'In most disciplines, those who cannot trust cannot know.' Trust indeed precedes evidence as the basis of knowledge. Certain authors are recognized as 'authorities' in their subjects today, and we accept certain types of documentary evidence as better than or more reliable than others on the basis of our trust in their authenticity, which in turn can derive from their authorship, chronology, or provenance.[79] Peter Dear has made a similar point about both natural philosophy and history in the early modern period. Aside from his reputation as a scholar or a gentleman, the mark of authority in many historians, so far as eighteenth-century readers were concerned, was the author's lack of 'interest' in lying or twisting the truth.[80] This was the 'impartiality' claimed by post-civil war historians such as Rushworth, Nalson, Fuller, and Clarendon, their writings compromised by the ideological baggage of the events they described and the inclinations of their readers. So long as they could be shown not to be grinding personal axes or pursuing obvious self-promotion, a degree of trust could be reposed in their accounts.[81]

The activities of the Royal Society, many of whose members had antiquarian interests arising from the more comprehensive virtuoso habits of the earlier seventeenth century, played a direct role in the ranking of written testimony over oral, just as they ranked the claims of gentlemen over those of the humbler sort. In 1699 a member of the Royal Society attempted to work out a mathematical formula with which to compare the reliability of oral and written testimony, and found that the written document would 'not lose half of its certainty' for 7,000 years. 'Oral tradition', he remarked, was in contrast 'subject to much casuality' and would lose much of its reliability within two decades.[82] This attempt at

---

[78] Robert Boyle, *The Christian Virtuoso*, quoted in Van Leeuwen, *Problem of Certainty*, 98.

[79] J. Hardwig, 'The Role of Trust in Knowledge', *Journal of Philosophy*, 88 (1991), 693–708.

[80] P. Dear, 'From Truth to Disinterestedness in the Seventeenth Century', *Social Studies of Science*, 22, special issue on the social history of objectivity (1992), 619–31, esp. p. 625. In contrast to extreme pyrrhonism about knowledge of the past as represented by Henry Cornelius Agrippa in the early sixteenth century and Pierre Bayle in the late seventeenth, 'most people, who simply wanted to do the best they could with what was available, were happy with more or less elaborate rules for determining lack of bias in historical writers. And disinterestedness was the most important characteristic a historian could have.'

[81] J. H. Preston, 'English Ecclesiastical Historians and the Problem of Bias, 1559–1742', *Journal of the History of Ideas*, 32 (1971), 203–20; Champion, *Pillars of Priestcraft Shaken*, 32–52.

[82] Anon., 'The Credibility of Human Testimony', *Philosophical Transactions of the Royal Society*, 21 (1699), 359–65. The term 'oral tradition' figures in common parlance by the early eighteenth century: apologizing to his friend the Revd George Plaxton for merely sending oral greetings of respect via a third party instead of writing a proper letter, Francis Skrimsher of Forton wrote 'it is highly unbecoming my duty and obligations for Mr Wisdon to carry hence only a few oral traditions of respect'. Staffs. RO D593/K/1/1/7 (Skrimsher to Plaxton, 24 Dec. 1714).

a quantitative measure of the credibility of testimony thus makes a distinction between recent memory and remote tradition, the former being proportionately more reliable. Thus William Stukeley was able to justify the irony—which he himself did not recognize—of searching in Grantham and neighbouring villages for biographical materials on the society's most distinguished late fellow, Sir Isaac Newton; he found some of his missing information 'among antient people, from their own knowledge or unquestionable tradition'.[83]

Perhaps even more significant than these attempts to work out a basis for evaluating testimony was the society's adoption of an explicit analogy between true 'civil history' of the Baconian variety and true science, emanating from the same fount. In his 1667 *History of the Royal Society*, Thomas Sprat made clear his view that the inductive method of natural philosophy, which was supposed to rid the scholarly world of metaphysical error, had in the writing of history an exact parallel. History, he optimistically projected, would itself achieve a new perfection under the restored monarchy following centuries of 'naked breviaries' by monks and city magistrates (a passing shot at the chronicles), just as it had peaked in Augustan Rome following the late republican civil wars. He even conceded that 'Of all the labors of mens wit, and industry, I scarce know any, that can be more useful to the world, then civil history', calling for a history of the troubled 1640s on Baconian principles.[84] Most compelling, however, is his likening of the new natural philosopher to the civil historian, an 'exploder' of the historical errors contained in romances:

In this there is a neer resemblance between natural and civil history. In the civil, that way of romance is to be exploded, which heightens all the characters, and actions of men, beyond all shadow of probability . . . The same is to be affirm'd of natural history. To make that only to consist of strange, and delightful tales, is to render it nothing else but vain, and ridiculous knight-errantry . . . The first may be only compar'd to the fables of *Amadis*, and the *Seven Champions*: the other to the real *histories* of Alexander, Hannibal, Scipio, or Caesar.[85]

This treatment does not address oral testimony or oral tradition as such, and in fact Sprat goes on to concede that this is only an analogy since the subjects of science and history 'do not cross each other'.[86] But it is further evidence of the notion that it was the duty of the upright, learned scholar to preserve history from the fabulous, an attitude that comes across more and more clearly from the 1660s to the 1730s. Half a century after Sprat this opinion is well established in the efforts of the Catholic antiquary Charles Eyston to disprove traditions related by a

---

[83] Nichols, *Literary Illustrations*, iv. 25 (Stukeley to Richard Mead, 16 June 1727).
[84] T. Sprat, *The History of the Royal Society*, ed. J. I. Cope and H. W. Jones (St Louis, Mo., 1958), 29, 43.
[85] Ibid. 214–15. Sprat returns to this analogy between civil history/fable and good and bad philosophy at p. 414.
[86] Ibid. 325.

Glastonbury innkeeper concerning Joseph of Arimathaea.[87] The remarks of Eyston's editor, the formidable Thomas Hearne, in themselves constitute a devastating critique of traditional evidence redolent of Royal Society principles:

Tho' the vulgar are generally uncapable of judging of antiquities, yet there are hardly any of them, but are very attentive, when things of this nature are talked of, especially if the discourse happens to be of the church which themselves are parishioners. Hence 'tis, that there are so many old stories of the original of some churches, and of their being translated from one place to another. Whatever foundation there might have been at first for such stories, they have, however, been mightily improved by the constant additions that have been made to them, as cannot otherwise but happen, when history is only convey'd by tradition. There is not the least probability in some of these stories; and yet the most incredible of them are often times listened to with greater attention, than to the most rational and solid discourses in divinity.

Hearne noted that the 'vulgar' tended to forget the details surrounding churches when these fell or were destroyed, an interesting perception of the collective forgetting of irrelevant details of the past which modern oral historians call 'structural amnesia'. He himself had encountered many curious local tales, but these only reinforced his rigid distinction between 'uncertain tradition' and the 'authenticke chronicles' of which he was a tireless transcriber and editor.[88]

The comments of Augustan antiquaries, heralds, and historians lend further weight to the impression that the written record had, by 1700, elbowed oral tradition aside as an acceptable historical source. But there is more to the decline of oral tradition than this. The remarks of Hearne, Dugdale, and others, and even of relatively sympathetic writers like Browne and Wood, suggest the emergence of a *social*—as distinct from a merely *intellectual*—bias against such sources. To an extent, this had always been there. Leland himself had preferred priests to peasants, while at the end of the sixteenth century Sir William Wentworth advised his son, the future earl of Strafford, to beware the tales of servants, even 'auncyentt honest servants', because 'such men do mistake and misreport matters for wantt of lerning and sounder judgementt, though they be honest and meane truth'.[89] But while specific traditions were often questioned by Tudor antiquaries, there is little evidence prior to 1600 of a more general hostility to 'vulgar' traditions *because* they were vulgar, as opposed to being merely in conflict with a written source. The tone of dismissal had also sharpened since Camden's sympathetic reference to the 'good honest men' of Manchester and their tale of Danish resistance.[90]

---

[87] [Charles Eyston], *A Little Monument to the Once Famous Abbey and Borough of Glastonbury*, in *The History and Antiquities of Glastonbury*, ed. Thomas Hearne (Oxford, 1722), 1–2, 80, 104; *A Relation of a Short Survey of the Western Counties*, 79, for an earlier report on the Glastonbury legends, c.1635.

[88] *History and Antiquities of Glastonbury*, ed. Hearne, pp. vii–viii, xiv, xxvi. On structural amnesia, see J. A. Barnes, 'The Collection of Genealogies', *Rhodes-Livingston Journal: Human Problems in British Central Africa*, 5 (1947), 48–56; J. Goody and I. Watt, 'The Consequences of Literacy', in J. Goody (ed.), *Literacy in Traditional Societies* (Cambridge, 1968), 32–3.

[89] *Wentworth Papers 1597–1628*, ed. J. P. Cooper, Camden Soc., 4th ser., 12 (1973), 15.

[90] Camden, *Britain*, 746–7.

The England of the later seventeenth century had become much more radically stratified, economically, socially, and culturally, than that of two centuries
earlier. Elite forms of entertainment, literature, and art had grown increasingly
remote from popular forms throughout the seventeenth century. Although there
remained considerable cross-fertilization between the two (the ballad collections
of Wood and Pepys, for example), the historical tastes of gentle and aristocratic
readers had evolved sufficiently over two centuries to allow relatively little room
to vulgar memories and tales.[91] At the very end of our period, William Stukeley,
who regularly repeated elite oral traditions, especially those involving his own
family, was considerably more sceptical of their popular cousins. In his 'Iter
Oxoniense' (c.1710), he noted on the Rollright Stones (overlooking Long Comp-
ton on the border of Warwickshire and Oxfordshire) that nearby was a single
large stone, nine feet high, 'called King Stone by the country people'. He notes
the 'many fabulous storys related of 'em by the neighbours', and locals annually
had, by old custom, a picnic in a square cut out of the grass by the King Stone.[92]
At virtually the same time, the very first number of the *Spectator* contained Addison's
mock-characterization of his own origins in an estate which according to 'the
tradition of the village where it lies, was bounded by the same hedges and ditches
in William the Conqueror's time that it is at present, and has been delivered down
from father to son whole and entire, without the loss or acquisition of a single
field or meadow, during the space of six hundred years'.[93]

The social bias against tradition's credibility was reinforced, paradoxically, just
as often by those who accepted it grudgingly as by those with stronger antipathies.
A good example of this comes from a satirical piece in another early eighteenth-
century periodical, *The Guardian*, in which the ancient topos of barbers being
the best sources of information is mocked. Wanting to know the history of a particular place, and especially what had happened in the civil war, the pseudonym-
ous author sought out

a certain barber, who for his general knowledge of things and persons, may be had in equal
estimation with any of that order among the Romans. This person was allowed to be the
best historian upon the spot; and the sequel of my tale will discover, that I did not chuse
him so much for the soft touch of his hand, as his abilities to entertain me with an account
of the Leaguer Time, as he calls it, the most authentick relations of which, thro' all parts
of the town, are derived from this person.[94]

[91] Charles Sackville, sixth earl of Dorset (1643–1706) was another famous collector of ballads, referred
to by Addison in *Spectator*, 85 (7 June 1711), ed. D. F. Bond, 5 vols. (Oxford, 1965), i. 363. Paradoxically, ballads which likely *did* derive ultimately from oral sources increasingly legitimized themselves
by anchoring their tales in an implied written text. Thus the ballad, recorded by Elias Ashmole in the
late seventeenth century, and which recounts the murders of Lewes and Edmund West by two sons
of George, Lord Darcy, in the 1550s cites as its authority 'historyes of olde': thereby a written version
of an oral ballad is vested with the mantle of writing: Bodl. MS Ashm. 48, fos. 31ʳ–35ᵛ.
[92] Bodl. MS Top. gen. e. 61(Stukeley, 'Iter Oxoniense'), fo. 76ʳ (vol. reversed); H. Bett, *English Myths
and Traditions* (1952), 41–3; L. Spence, *Minor Traditions of British Mythology* (New York, 1972), 139–41.
[93] *The Spectator*, 1 (1 Mar. 1711), ed. Bond, i. 1–2.
[94] *The Guardian*, 50 (7 May 1713), ed. J. C. Stephens (Lexington, Ky., 1982), 196.

A real-life example of information accepted grudgingly and with apologies comes from the Hanoverian traveller Jeremiah Milles, who was prepared to believe an innkeeper's information about Roman walls in Wales because, despite his humble station, he 'seemed to be a sensible man; pretty well acquainted with the country, and in all appearance not a Romancer'.[95]

Perennial early modern concerns for social order, felt most intensely in the century between the accession of Elizabeth and the Restoration, contributed to a deepening suspicion of much popular discourse, complete with its occasional memories of local folk heroes and even rebellions against authority. This cultural division did not close with the return of an uneasy and tenuous stability following the tumultuous 1640s and 1650s. The association of oral traditions with socially marginal groups (ballad-singers and strolling players, for instance) and with the 'gossip' of old women, did nothing to endear them to the educated, who increasingly began to lump all such popular discourse under the same category which embraced superstitions and 'vulgar errors'.[96] Even the majority of harmless, amusing tales from the past, expressed in colourful rural language, could irritate refined Augustan sensibilities.

The implications for historical knowledge of this reshaping of truth are not difficult to see. Documents were certainly preferable to oral tradition because they represented a kind of ultimate authority, testable and often externally verifiable. But oral testimony about the past, even the remote past, could still be acceptable if it came from trustworthy (that is, educated or propertied) sources. This helps to explain the continued willingness of antiquaries and historians throughout the eighteenth century to accept the word of learned informants on points of detail about history, even as second-hand sources for information that could be found independently in manuscripts. This is the sort of trust that permits us now to rely on reputable historians' works without personally rechecking every fact they cite. One scholar's miscellaneous recollections might become another's reference tool. Biographical writers such as Fuller would rely on the information of other 'credible' persons throughout the seventeenth and eighteenth centuries.[97] Dugdale was convinced that a family deed, no longer extant, had once existed because 'one Mr Mathew Manwaring of Namptwich (a very old man)' could recount having shown it several decades earlier to the Elizabethan antiquary Sampson Erdeswicke.[98] Champion Branfill, an Essex gentleman, vaguely recalled hearing of a monument in Kelvedon church to the Petty family, in whom William

---

[95] BL MS Add. 15776 (travel notes of Jeremiah Milles), fo. 152ʳ.

[96] Joshua Childrey's *Britannia Baconica* (1661), for example, is an early attempt 'for the use of the vulgar', though mainly to teach them to believe new scientific and natural discoveries instead of their own superstitions (pref. sig. Aᵛ). On the concept of vulgar error, see K. Thomas, *Man and the Natural World: Changing Attitudes in England, 1500–1800* (1983), 70–81.

[97] Fuller, for example, reported of the Cambridge poet William Alabaster that at the performance of his tragedy *Roxanna* 'a Gentle-woman present thereat' had gone mad because of the play and never recovered her senses: 'Reader I had it from an Author whose credit is sin with me to suspect': *The History of the Worthies of England*, ed. J. Nichols, 2 vols. (1811), ii. 353 (*sub* 'Suffolk').

[98] Dugdale, *Life, Diary and Correspondence*, 209.

Holman was interested. The puzzle of some missing manuscripts was solved for Anthony Wood with the aid of an elite oral tradition nearly a century old. The manuscripts had disappeared in the mid-sixteenth century from the Merton College library. Wood had heard, from a scholar named John Wilton, that Thomas Allen, the Jacobean antiquary of Gloucester Hall, had in turn told him years earlier 'that old Garbrand the bookseller, that lived where Bowman the bookseller doth now, bought them of the college'. Allen had purchased several of the manuscripts as a young man, and his collections passed at his death to the Bodleian, where Wood soon found them.[99]

Family oral traditions survived among the elite, sometimes across more than two generations. Although people rarely survived into their grandchildren's adulthood, James Whitelocke heard an account from his wife's grandfather of the latter's baptism, at the time of the monastic dissolution, as told to him by his own father.[100] William Stukeley recorded in his memoirs many remarks about his grandfather William (1623–75), who had died twelve years before the great antiquary's own birth: 'I have heard my father say that he was mighty fond of making ex tempore jokes', he noted, and 'My aunt Dodson once repeated to me some verses which he made upon a great eclipse of the sun which were not contemptible.'[101] Young scholars learned from their parents, from older colleagues, and from strangers of their own social position. The commonplace book of William Johnson, a fellow of Clare College, Cambridge, in the 1650s, contains numerous anecdotes related to him by acquaintances. Johnson put a series of 'once upon a time' tales together in one section of the book, some of which derived from his reading but others from conversation. Many tales are taken second- or third-hand. 'In ffrance, studying ye law I learned of a scholler this story who had it from the gentleman himselfe', Johnson noted next to his rendition of one tale.[102] The author of an unpublished letter of advice to a newly matriculated Oxford student urged his protégé to study Scripture regularly, citing an anecdote he had heard of a 'good old Churchman' who had read the Bible from start to finish annually for eighty years.[103]

This double standard for oral sources was not unique to England. All over western Europe a combination of epistemological scepticism and socially based distaste was targeting the traditional selectively, in particular when it issued from common mouths. Jacques Revel has commented that 'To be denounced for error or false belief now meant to be socially discredited. Popular beliefs were no longer the sign of epistemological nonconformity, as they had been in the preceding stage;

---

[99] Essex RO D/Y/1/1/42 (Champion Branfill to William Holman, 9 Nov. 1720); for a similar example of papers heard of but not seen, see Essex RO D/Y/1/1/87 (Thomas Cox to Holman, 15 Dec. 1716); Wood, *Life and Times*, i. 424.

[100] *Liber Famelicus of Sir James Whitelocke, a Judge of the Court of King's Bench, in the Reigns of James I and Charles I*, ed. J. Bruce, Camden Soc., os 70 (1858), 24.

[101] Bodl MS Eng. misc. c. 533 (Stukeley notes), fos. 1ᵛ, 2ʳ.

[102] Bodl. MS Top. Camb. e. 5 (commonplace book of William Johnson, 1652–63), fos. 38ᵛ–41ʳ.

[103] Bodl. MS Top. Oxon. d. 344 (Anon., 'Letters of advice to a young Gentleman', written 1684–5), fo. 7ᵛ.

they had become the source of obfuscation and misunderstanding.'[104] First Bayle and then Voltaire would declaim against tales and legends reported from oral sources. According to Boyle, tradition was nothing but 'the assertion of two or three persons repeated by a numberless throng of credulous people'.[105] So far as Voltaire was concerned, reliance on tradition represented a fundamental failure of historiography from the era of Herodotus to his own day. Lorraine Daston has pointed out that in mid-seventeenth-century France, at least, there was a close connection between the discounting of popular tradition, much of it oral, and legal measures that inverted medieval jurisprudence's preference for oral over written testimony (and especially for oral testimony by witnesses over written testimony composed well after the fact). 'The belief that written testimony, even of an event centuries remote, counted as more reliable than the oral testimony of an eyewitness reflected changing canons of both legal and, especially, historical evidence', Daston argues. Learned writings increasingly became the corrective to popular beliefs, and this had obvious implications for diminishing the evidentiary force of oral tradition, their principal vessel of transmission. [106]

THE SELECTIVE USE OF ORAL TRADITION, 1640–1730

Although oral sources never entirely disappeared from the antiquaries' fishing-pond, references to them become steadily sparser as the seventeenth century wanes. There is no reference to tradition in the manuscript collections, written in the early 1650s, of the Suffolk antiquary Philip Candler, though he frequently noted broken or eradicated inscriptions; the same may be said for the church notes of Hannibal Baskervile of Sunningwell, Berkshire. Elias Ashmole relied very little on oral evidence for his *Antiquities of Berkshire*, though he could not resist repeating a graphic traditional tale, recorded in the writings of Anthony Wood, of the 'murder' of Sir Robert Dudley's unfortunate wife, Amy Robsart, a century earlier.[107] Wood himself, though reluctant to lean too heavily on tradition, thought that it should not always be dismissed out of hand. At a rural Oxfordshire church he found an old monument the inscription of which was 'gone and quite out of remembrance'. The 'country people' told Wood that it commemorated 'one, or three, daughters' who had been 'antiently co-heires of this lordship'. An air of

---

[104] J. Revel, 'Forms of Expertise: Intellectuals and "Popular" Culture in France (1650–1800)', in S. L. Kaplan (ed.), *Understanding Popular Culture: Europe from the Middle Ages to the Nineteenth Century* (Berlin, New York, and Amsterdam, 1984), 256–73, esp. p. 262.

[105] Pierre Bayle, *Pensées diverses* (Rotterdam, 1683), cited in Cocchiara, *History of Folklore in Europe*, 62, who points out that Bayle, like Browne, paradoxically ended up making a major collection of that which he affected to despise.

[106] L. Daston, *Classical Probability in the Enlightenment* (Princeton, 1988), 320–1, including the opinions of Bayle and Voltaire.

[107] Bodl. MS Tanner 324 (Suffolk collections), fos. 1–143ᵛ *passim*; H. Baskervile, 'Certaine Remembrances of monuments yt I have seene in some churches', Bodl. MS Rawl. D. 859, fos. 89ᵛ–92ᵛ; Elias Ashmole, *The Antiquities of Berkshire*, written c.1666, 3 vols. (1719), i. 52, ii. 486. For Wood's version of the story as told him by friends, see Bodl. MS Wood D. 4, fos. 99–100ᵛ.

willingness to believe hangs about his treatment of the traditions surrounding a sacred well near Seacourt:

If I should tell you of the enriching of a towne hereabouts by the continuall resort to this place, you would perhaps scarce beleive me; and yet it is a constant tradition among the good people here ... All which, you'll say, *comming from the mouths of rusticks,* may be accounted noe truer then the tales of Robin Hood and Little John. But, however such constant tradition from each other among them may have something in the bottome thereof of truth; though much of it lost by the longinquity of time since acted.[108]

A highly sceptical Georgian observer such as Jeremiah Milles thought reasonable the tradition that William the Conqueror had landed at Bulverhythe, five miles from Hastings, rather than at Hastings itself, the site of the famous battle. He was less impressed by local claims that William had dined at Bulverhythe on a certain large stone, and by the tradition that Hastings itself was named for a Danish pirate.[109]

Other writers, who avoided oral traditions as a general rule, cited them incidentally on particular points. Sporadic references can be found in the works of Robert Plot (Oxfordshire), Robert Thoroton (Nottinghamshire), Sir Peter Leycester (Cheshire), Silas Taylor (Harwich and Dovercourt), James Wright (Rutland), Henry Chauncy (Hertfordshire) and Robert Atkyns (Gloucestershire).[110] White Kennett was prepared to accept a traditional story if he could find some corroborating evidence in documents or ruins. The rigorous Ralph Thoresby distrusted the yarns of the vulgar but nevertheless turned to tradition as an aid in reconstructing the state of the parish church of Leeds on the eve of the Reformation, two centuries earlier. He could even refer to a certain family's pedigree as 'only conjectural (though highly probable) from Tradition &c.'.[111] The revisers of Camden's *Britannia* in 1695 actually used traditions to clarify or

---

[108] Anthony Wood, 'Survey of the Antiquities of the City of Oxford' (written 1661–6), in *Wood's City of Oxford,* ed. A. Clark, 3 vols., Oxford Historical Soc., xvii, xix, xxxvii (Oxford, 1889–99), i. 325; cf. i. 186, 215–16, 248–9, 426 (emphasis added). Wood's friend and contemporary Nathaniel Greenwood (fellow of Brasenose 1654–81) compiled his own record of the monuments, epitaphs, and arms in Oxford parish churches in 1658, with no reference at all to oral traditions: Bodl. MS Top. Oxon. e. 286 ('Nathaniel Greenwood, his booke'), fos. 1–142.

[109] BL MS Add. 15776 (travel notes of Jeremiah Milles), fo. 208ʳ.

[110] Robert Plot, *Natural history of Oxford-shire* (Oxford, 1677), 325–6, 337, 341, 351–2; Robert Thoroton, *The Antiquities of Nottinghamshire* (1677), ed. John Throsby, 3 vols. (Nottingham, 1790–6; repr. 1972), i. 103, ii. 27, 167; Sir Peter Leycester, *Historical Antiquities* (1673), 249–50, and his 'A short view of Greate Brettaine and Ierland ffrom the beginning' (written 1670 and the source for book 1 of his *Antiquities*), Cheshire RO DDX 180; Silas Taylor (alias Domville), *The History and Antiquities of Harwich and Dovercourt, Topographical, Dynastical and Political,* written c.1676, ed. Samuel Dale (1730), 16, 81; James Wright, *The History and Antiquities of the County of Rutland* (1684), 1 (William Stukeley, the annotator of the Bodleian Library copy (shelfmark Gough Rutland 3), also noted (p. 62) traditions from the area as late as 1734; Sir Henry Chauncy, *The Historical Antiquities of Hertfordshire* (1700), 32; Sir Robert Atkyns, *The Ancient and Present State of Glostershire* (1712; repr. 1974), 214, 248, 503.

[111] White Kennett, *Parochial Antiquities,* ed. B. Bandinel, 2 vols. (Oxford, 1818), i. 36, 56, ii. 156, 284, 295; Ralph Thoresby, *Ducatus Leodiensis: or, the Topography of the Ancient and Populous Town and Parish of Leedes* (1715), 81, 106; cf. his *Vicaria Leodiensis: or, the History of the Church of Leedes in Yorkshire* (1724), 51; *The Diary of Ralph Thoresby, F.R.S.,* ed. J. Hunter, 2 vols. (1830), i. 89–90.

correct their great predecessor, and they were even able to exploit the writings of European antiquaries, such as Olaus Wormius, to bring a comparative approach to the study of rural folk tales.[112] The early eighteenth-century student of cathedral antiquities, Browne Willis, also reported local traditions, some of which had originated only in the preceding century.[113]

If we turn from published works of famous scholars, who were increasingly cautious about hitching their reputations to the cart of unprovable local traditions for all the world to see, and look instead at the private correspondence of local antiquaries and at their unpublished notes, a rather different picture emerges. This demonstrates considerably greater ambivalence towards tradition, and a greater willingness to trust in it as a supplement to gaps in the record. Thomas Ford, an antiquary with a particularly strong distaste for vulgar error, described the 'Weeping Cross' near Bodicote, Oxfordshire, with reference to two conflicting traditions, the first that the town's inhabitants had been obliged to carry their dead to nearby Adderbury 'because (as they say) their own church yard (which is ample enough) is not consecrated'. The cross had apparently been used time out of mind to rest caskets on during the burial procession, providing another occasion for 'weeping'. Ford was less willing to accept the second explanation, that the cross had been the point at which Banbury mothers had said farewell to the children going to London as apprentices. This seemed 'less probable, yett because asserted by many with great assurances I shall not omitt to insert it'.[114] In a similar case, Benjamin Orwell, writing to William Holman in 1724, was cautious but curious in reporting what might be a vanished church near Great Chesterford:

About 2 miles from the Town, close to the Road leading from thence to Neumarket, is a place called Sunkin Church: of which I never could meet with any account from any author. The Inhabitants are told (but it is only Tradition) that there a church sunk into the ground: I have gon to the place and could find stones and mortar; some building there has been ... perhaps a Crosse or ffort, or mark for the bounds of the countys of Essex and Cambridgeshire. I can't think it a Church. I write this because perhaps some of your Ancient Historians may give some light into it. It seems to have taken up about a Rod of ground.[115]

Browne Willis's collections for his *Antiquities of Buckinghamshire* record of Chetwode the tradition that their parish church was a priory before the dissolution, while at the parish church of Ivinghoe in the same county was an effigy 'which

[112] *Camden's Britannia*, ed. Edmund Gibson (1695), cols. 355, 802, 814; compare Camden, *Britain* (1610), 439.
[113] Browne Willis, *A Survey of the Cathedrals of York, Durham, Carlisle, Chester, Man, Lichfield, Hereford, Worcester, Gloucester and Bristol*, 2 vols. (1727), i. 17, 22, ii. 694; cf. Willis's *A View of the Mitred Abbeys*, in *Joannis Lelandi Antiquarii de Rebus Britannicis Collectanea*, ed. Hearne, appendix, vol. ii, p. 166. Willis's contemporary, Samuel Gale, thought that the man-made mound in Catterick, near the site of a Roman encampment, that the inhabitants called 'Palat Hill' was simply a corruption of 'Palatin[e] Hill'. Bodl. MS Top. gen. c. 66 (fragmentary diary of Samuel Gale, undated), fo. 29ʳ.
[114] CUL MS Mm. 6.50 (Covel correspondence), fos. 194–5 (Ford to John Covel, 12 Aug. 1697).
[115] Essex RO D/Y/1/1 (unfoliated Holman letters, Neville-Prideaux volume, Orwell to Holman, 16 June 1724); cf. Essex RO D/Y/1/1/87 (Cox to Holman 14 Dec. 1716) for another example.

all the inhabitants say is a cardinall'.[116] Even 'Honest Tom' Martin of Palgrave, an exceptionally uncompromising sceptic, went actively hunting for traditions that might explain the two stone coffins on the north aisle of Burford church once all recourse to documents had failed.[117]

Many early eighteenth-century landowners and citizens could not resist the temptation to memorialize the traditions of their communities for posterity, unproven or otherwise. In 1705 an anonymous inhabitant of Tottenham, who was not a native of the place, wrote such an account of the parish to render it 'what civil returns I can' for its hospitality to him, in part because other writers had no good guide, though a chorography of the town had been published by William Bedwell in 1631. He noted, however, that reliance on oral information was a risky necessity for those not well acquainted with a community. 'Strangers who cannot stay long in a place and must take many things upon trust or hearsay . . . may be misled by vulgar reports or conjecture and give an erroneous or at best but a dubious account of what they publish for truth.'[118] Samuel Dale of Braintree, normally a harsh critic of error, speculated to William Holman that an unidentifiable grave marked by a brass plate at his parish church was perhaps that of a chantry founder, 'but who he was we have no tradition, nor is there any remembrance here any further then by the escocheons carved on the beams of the roof'. A field trip to Raine church revealed only one gravestone, which 'hath no inscription remaining, but the tradition is, that it's for one Mr Thomas Woods, whose daughter Marie was the wife of John Goodday of Braintree'.[119]

Another, rather different, form of oral tradition also remained largely immune from contempt, namely the proverb.[120] Local proverbs invited speculation as to their origins throughout the Restoration and eighteenth century. Sir Peter Leycester, the respected historian of Cheshire, also wrote a 'short view of greate Brettaine and Ierland ffom the beginninge' in 1670, expressing curiosity as to a saying such as 'Every man is not born to be the vicar of Bodon', which he ventured might be a reference either to the living's profitability, 'or else of the learning & piety of some former vicar there'.[121] The general hostility to oral tradition as a historical source did not extend to popular wisdom as contained in proverbs, however traditional, since they were not generally the sort of oral utterance that could be used as evidence for a particular historical fact and since, too, they were much more free-floating and usually less tied to particular localities.

[116] Bodl. MS Willis 6 (c.1710–20), fo. 35ʳ; MS Willis 2 (c.1710), fo. 22ᵛ.

[117] Bodl. MS Top. gen. e. 85 (Thomas Martin of Palgrave, 'Some Remarks and Observations taken in a Journey from Eton near Windsor to Oxford', 1724), p. 5.

[118] Bodl. MS Gough Middlesex 5 (dated 1705, with a continuation dated 1710), fos. 1–25.

[119] Essex RO D/Y/1/1/97 (Dale to Holman, 11 Apr. 1712). It should be noted that recent traditions such as this are rarely identified as to source, making a gentry rather than popular origin a distinct possibility. The information provided to Holman by the Revd Samuel Adamson on a chapel at Northend, Great Waltham, was derived from 'trustees or feoffes who take care of the chapel' who were of respectable if not gentle status: ibid. D/Y/1/1/5 (Adamson to Holman, 14 May 1723).

[120] Fox, Oral and Literate Culture, ch. 2.

[121] Leycester, 'A short view', Cheshire RO DDX 180, fo. 54ᵛ. Browne Willis collected numerous 'country proverbs' in the early 1700s, arranging them alphabetically by county: Bodl. MS Willis 2, fos. 84ʳ⁻ᵛ.

This made them easily adaptable to writing, like the classical adages and commonplaces printed by Erasmus and other humanists. James Howell, the first Historiographer Royal, was an admirer of nobility and learning whose political works regularly deplore the many-headed monster, yet he had a sufficiently high regard for the 'people's voice' as handed down in proverbs to bother assembling a collection of such wisdom.

> The Peeples voice, the Voice of God we call
> And what are Proverbs but the peeples voice?
> Coin'd first, and current made by common choice,
> Then sure they must have weight and truth withall.
> They are a publick heritage entayld
> On every nation, or like Hireloomes nayld,
> which passe from Sire to Son, and so from Son
> Down to the Granchild till the world be done;
> They are Free-Denisons by long Descent,
> Without the grace of prince or parlement,
> The truest commoners, and inmate guests,
> We fetch them from the Nurse and Mothers brests;
> They can prescription plead gainst King or Crown,
> And need no Affidavits but their own . . .[122]

Howell was followed in 1670 by the great naturalist John Ray and in 1732 by the physician Thomas Fuller.[123] Yet even proverbial wisdom, by the end of the seventeenth century, was becoming subject to a social bias, and, by the middle of the eighteenth century, a minority position that held such knowledge as conservative, vulgar, and out of step with polite society, was rapidly permeating the attitudes of elite commentators, such as the earl of Chesterfield, who denounced 'proverbs, and vulgar aphorisms' as inappropriate to 'a man of fashion'.[124]

TRADITION INTO FOLKLORE

I suggested in earlier chapters that as print spread through the countryside local communities were gradually caught up in a national historical tradition that competed with popular beliefs and often syncretistically affected them with

---

[122] Preface to James Howell: 'Of Proverbs and Adages', in his Παροιμιογραφια. Proverbs (1659); Fox, *Oral and Literate Culture*, 133 ff.; A. Walsham, *Providence in Early Modern England* (Oxford, 1999), 96–106, on the frequency of oral episodes containing cautionary tales of divine punishment.

[123] John Ray, *A Collection of English Proverbs* (Cambridge, 1670); Thomas Fuller, M. D., *Gnomologia: Adagies, Proverbs, Wise Sentiments, and Witty Sayings, Ancient and Modern, Foreign and British* (1732). We find a similar enthusiasm in the normally snobbish Addison for another traditional form, 'the songs and fables that are come from father to son, and are most in vogue among the common people of the countries . . . An ordinary song or ballad that is the delight of the common people, cannot fail to please all such readers as are not unqualified for the entertainment by their affectation or ignorance.' *Spectator*, 70 (21 May 1711), ed. Bond, i. 297–8.

[124] Fox, *Oral and Literate Culture*, 169.

extraneous material from learned culture.[125] That many popular beliefs about the past have survived at all is owed to Restoration and eighteenth-century antiquaries who forswore oral tradition as a source for details of local history (unlike most of their Tudor predecessors) but were often willing to preserve it for other ends. In other words, they no longer wished to record it so much as to filter and channel it, confining its impact on historical awareness to the margins and footnotes of learned texts built on written documents. Alternatively, some of them hived it off altogether into the earliest examples of works specifically devoted to what we would now call 'folklore', beginning with Browne's *Pseudodoxia epidemica* (principally about natural rather than historical beliefs) and John Aubrey's *Remains of Gentilisme and Judaisme*. In some ways, this simply carried forward the ethnographic strand in sixteenth-century chorographies and in early modern travel literature, studying beliefs and traditions less for the sake of history than to understand a popular culture that seemed increasingly alien, even anachronistic. The result was the preservation of much oral lore about the past in printed form, now safely quarantined from true history.

Perhaps no one better illustrates the changing relationship between history, folklore, and tradition than John Aubrey himself, who has generally been underrated both as an antiquary and as an ethnographer.[126] As a boy, Aubrey 'did ever love to converse with old men, as living histories', rather as Maurice Halbwachs, in the early part of the twentieth century discusses having learned of the Paris commune and the Second Empire from 'a good old woman, full of superstition and prejudice'. Aside from works such as the *Remains*, much of Aubrey's *Brief Lives* derives from oral testimony. His unfinished study of the antiquities of Surrey (which does not incline to the archaeological methods of his comparable work on Wiltshire) in some ways resembles earlier works such as *Britannia* in its mixture of the oral and the documentary. At Petersham he encountered the familiar tradition of a vanished religious house, and at Stretham a recumbent figure in white marble, said by tradition to be John of Gaunt.[127] At Addington the inhabitants spoke much of their town's ancient prosperity; a similar nostalgia existed at Ewell, though 'History being silent in this affair' Aubrey believed that 'little can be depended on our weak conjectures'.[128]

---

[125] A suggestive parallel may be drawn from the fate of traditional folk carols which ceased to be created in the seventeenth century and were ultimately superseded by the text hymnbooks of Isaac Watts and others: A. L. Lloyd, *Folk Song in England*, rev. edn. (1969), 134–8; cf. V. Gammon, '"Babylonian Performances": The Rise and Suppression of Popular Church Music, 1660–1870', in Eileen and Stephen Yeo (eds.), *Popular Culture and Class Conflict, 1590–1914* (Brighton, Sussex, 1981), 62–88.

[126] M. Hunter, *John Aubrey and the Realm of Learning* (1975), 39–40, 154–70, has been to date the most persuasive attempt to rehabilitate Aubrey as a pan-sophic scholar.

[127] John Aubrey, *The Natural History and Antiquities of the County of Surrey*, written 1673–92, 5 vols. (1719; Scolar Press facs. edn., Dorking, 1975), i. 53, 82, 190, 201; M. Halbwachs, *The Collective Memory*, trans. F. J. Ditter and V. Y. Ditter (New York and London, 1980), 62.

[128] Aubrey, *Natural History . . . of Surrey*, ii. 39, 219–20. For another version of this tradition, see Bodl. MS Top. gen. e. 80, fo. 1ʳ ᵛ, Edward Steele of Bromley's parish notes, c.1710. Steele was more credulous with regard to tradition than Francis Taverner, the Jacobean antiquary of Hexton, Herts., who lived a century earlier and whose works Steele liberally transcribed into his own collections. Taverner's

Aubrey's fascination with the supernatural, with prophecies, apparitions, and ghosts, also made him rather more open than most of his Restoration contemporaries to anecdotes and traditions that could not be documented, in contrast to the more stringent stance taken by his younger contemporary, Thomas Sprat.[129] Recalling the thunderclouds that he had seen gather minutes after the execution of Christopher Love, the Presbyterian conspirator, in 1651, Aubrey added the 'report' of a similar incident in 1685.[130] No less believable, because he had heard it from 'persons of honour' was the tradition that Protector Somerset had observed 'a bloody sword come out of the wall', prophesying his own decapitation, or the parishioners' tale, endorsed by Aubrey's friend Pepys, that the bells of St Mary Overy had originated in the ruined abbey of Merton in Surrey.[131] Yet the significant feature here is surely Aubrey's emphasis on the social status of his informants; he was much less credulous of the sayings of 'vulgar people' than of educated sources such as the Welsh assize judge George Johnson, 'a serious person, and *fide dignus*', on whose word he accepted an account of a skeleton found in a quarry. Aubrey repeats the story of Thomas and Edith Bonham of Great Wishford, Wiltshire, who had produced seven children at one birth, because he found it written in the parish register by the parish's curate, Roger Powell, in 1640.[132] A tale connected with conjuring up apparitions, from Henry VIII's reign, came to Aubrey from his maternal grandfather, who had in turn heard it from 'old father Davis'.[133]

Much of the information that Aubrey records falls into the category of colourful and entertaining, but there is absolutely no evidence that he believed all that he wrote down, any more than a modern anthropologist either accepts his subjects' information at face value or disregards it entirely. Just as Aubrey discounted the transformation of St Oswald into 'St Twasole' in eastern Gloucestershire and parts of Wiltshire, so he remained sceptical of tales of fairies, elves, giants, and historical personages, all of which issued from popular sources. 'The vulgar

---

view of a tradition at Hexton, with reference to a vanished castle, was distinctly sceptical: 'if that had byn soe, then some remaynes of the foundations of brick or stone would have byn plowed up. And some chronicle or record would have mentioned who were the builders or at some tyme since Lords thereof'. Bodl. MS Top. gen. e. 80, fo. 127ᵛ.

[129] Sprat, *History of the Royal Society*, 6 and elsewhere.

[130] John Aubrey, *Miscellanies upon Various Subjects*, 4th edn. (1857), 45.

[131] Ibid. 72, 77–8, 112–13; Aubrey, *Natural History . . . of Surrey*, i. 226. Cf. Sir John Percival, *The English Travels of Sir John Percival and William Byrd II: The Percival Diary of 1701*, ed. M. R. Wenger (Columbia, Mo. 1989), 44, for an oral tradition concerning the history of Chelmsford, accepted by Percival because it came from John Ouseley (1645–1708), rector of Panfield, near Braintree. Daniel Featley believed an account of the appearance of an apparition before a Knight of the Bath, Sir Thomas Wise, primarily because of the latter's 'ancient descent', but also because of Wise's 'large revenues', which enhanced Featley's willingness to accept an unlikely tale: Bodl. MS Rawl. D. 47 (Featley papers), fo. 42ᵛ (Featley to Archbishop Abbot, n.d.) also printed in Wood, *Athenae Oxonienses*, ed. Bliss, iii, cols. 166–8.

[132] John Aubrey, *The Natural History of Wiltshire*, ed. J. Britton, Wiltshire Topographical Soc. (1847), 71 (both the skeleton and the Bonham story); Aubrey, *Miscellanies*, *passim*, for stories variously fostered on such authorities as Elias Ashmole and Sir William Dugdale.

[133] Aubrey, *Remains of Gentilisme and Judaisme*, ed. J. Britten (1881), 52.

have a tradition', he noted of Blechingley, 'that I know not what duke of Buckingham was arrested by a royal precept in one of the galleries here.'[134] In the vestry of Frensham church he viewed a huge cauldron 'which the inhabitants say, by tradition, was brought hither by the fairies, time out of mind' from a nearby hill. Aubrey believed the cauldron to be an ancient utensil from the era of pre-Christian revels, and he could scarcely conceal his amusement at the traditional explanation: 'These stories are verily believ'd by most of the old women of this parish, and by many of their daughters, who can hardly be of any other opinion; so powerful a thing is custom, joyn'd with ignorance.'[135]

Aubrey was convinced not just that traditional tales could legitimately be preserved without being believed, but also that there was some urgency in so doing. He was nearly unique among his contemporaries in observing that they had declined in popularity even among the common people since his childhood. Aubrey even offered a remarkably perceptive explanation for this decline, which he associated with increasing literacy in the countryside (and especially with the growth in female literacy) occasioned by the mid-century turmoil. 'In the old, ignorant times, before women were readers,' he observed, 'the history was handed downe from mother to daughter.' Aubrey's nurse had given him the history of England 'from the Conquest downe to Carl. I in ballad', and rural folk had told him many old tales as he grew up. Since then, however, such stories had been disappearing. 'Before printing, Old wives' tales were ingeniose; and since printing came in fashion, till a little before the civill warrs, the ordinary sort of people were not taught to reade.' From the 1640s and 1650s, however, books had become more common, 'and most of the poor people understand letters; and the many good bookes, and variety of turnes of affaires, have putt all the old fables out of doors'. Aubrey unquestionably overstated the degree to which print had destroyed an oral culture of ballads and tales: the growing number of broadsides and chapbooks could reinforce as much as undercut spoken versions of those stories. Yet there is a kernel of truth to his observation, at least in so far as the *subject* of these oral tales are concerned. Those that continued to weave tales of the past now devoted increasing attention to recent affairs such as the civil war, giving proportionately less emphasis to the deeds and personalities of more remote times. It was thus not print on its own but memories of Oliver and tales of the past two centuries that 'frighted away Robin-good-fellow and the fayries'.[136] There were indeed sufficiently horrific new events of national or regional importance to make the

---

[134] Aubrey, in *Anecdotes and Traditions*, ed. Thoms, 83, 87; Aubrey, *Natural History . . . of Surrey*, iii. 87; *Wiltshire. The Topographical Collections of John Aubrey, F.R.S.*, ed. J.E. Jackson (Devizes, 1862), 417.

[135] Aubrey, *Natural History . . . of Surrey*, iii. 366–7. Aubrey compared this belief to similar traditions about Camelot or Queen Camel in Somerset.

[136] Aubrey, *Remains of Gentilisme and Judaisme*, 67–8; id. *Natural History . . . of Surrey*, iii. 93, 99, 102, 106, 115–16. Half a century later, Lewis Theobald thought that such stories lingered like an infection, spread by the 'garrulity of nurses and servants', whence they travelled 'from the cottage to the farm, from the farm to the Squire's Hall': *The Censor*, 3 vols. (1717), i. 75–6. On old wives' tales, see Fox, *Oral and Literate Culture*, 173–212.

supernatural give ground to the historical in ballad and tradition alike. Where Aubrey remembered the fairies, the young Thomas Babington Macaulay a century and a half later heard 'tales of terror' in Somerset, the oral remains of Sedgemoor and the Bloody Assizes.[137]

Although Aubrey exaggerated the extent to which rural literacy had improved in his lifetime, his explanation supports the arguments advanced earlier in this book about the implications of print for local memory. The 'variety of turnes of affaires' in the second half of the seventeenth century undoubtedly gave birth to a new stock of stories that may have superseded traditions of longer standing. By the early eighteenth century, yarns from the Great Rebellion were sufficiently commonplace at all levels of society to merit satire in the literary periodicals. The unknown author of an essay in *The Guardian* commented that everyone at the inns of court seemed to have lost a relation at Marston Moor or Edgehill, and that he was having recourse to written history to help him understand these tales, spending his time reading Rushworth and Clarendon because each of the members 'has a story which none who has not read those battles is able to taste'.[138] *The Tatler* tells us of the ancient members of the Trumpet club, civil war veterans most of them, including Major Matchlock, 'who served in the last civil wars, and has all the battles by heart. He does not think any action in Europe worth talking of since the fight of Marston-Moor; and every night tells us of his having been knock'd off his horse at the rising of the London 'prentices.'[139] During his short-lived emigration to New England in the 1680s, the publisher John Dunton had stayed with an ex-roundhead near Boston, who exhausted him with recollections of his glory days. 'Captain Marshal is a hearty old gentleman, formerly one of Olivers souldiers, upon which he very much values himself; he had all the *History of the Civil Wars* at his fingers ends, and if we may believe him, Oliver did hardly any thing that was considerable without his assistance.'[140] Henry Prescott, the Chester diarist who was normally fond of sitting up late with his history books, his friends, and his liquor, endured the reminiscences of an old man's adventures at the battle of Preston and his wife's confinement by guards to her house.[141] One of Joseph Addison's correspondents complains of the 'dull

---

[137] Macaulay quoted in R. Palmer, *A Ballad History of England* (1979), 36. One example of a modern oral tradition which appears to date right back to the civil war links the death of John Hampden (of wounds sustained at Chalgrove) with a local charity: the versions vary, but the story tells how he spent the night before the battle in Watlington at an inn, today known as the Hare and Hounds. After Hampden's death, officers appeared looking for a trunk of his with soldiers' pay. This was not found, but soon after the innkeeper, one Robert Parslowe, yeoman, began to buy land, presumably with the missing money. When he died, he left a charitable bequest which continues today and is locally believed to be founded on Parslowe's guilty conscience. *The Diary of Bulstrode Whitelocke 1605–1675*, ed. R. Spalding (Oxford, 1989), 147 n. 1.

[138] *The Guardian*, 44 (1 May 1713), ed. Stephens, p. 178.

[139] *The Tatler*, 132 (11 Feb. 1710), ed. D. F. Bond, 3 vols. (Oxford, 1987), ii. 266.

[140] John Dunton, *Life and Errors* (1705), 175.

[141] *The Diary of Henry Prescott, LL.B., deputy registrar of Chester Diocese*, ed. J. Addy, J. Harrop, and P. P. McNiven, 3 vols., Rec. Soc. of Lancashire and Cheshire, vols. 127, 132, 133 (Chester, 1987–97), ii. 308 (28 Apr. 1711), 516 (24 June 1716).

generation of story-tellers', gentlemen who bore their fellows at coffee-houses and clubs with prolix accounts of battles and other events, which 'murder time'.[142]

It was in this anecdotal form, suitable for conversation, entertainment, or illustration, rather than as history, that some writers continued to garner oral traditions into the eighteenth century, their attentiveness much greater if they were themselves attached to the place whence the traditions arose. Richard Gough's history of Myddle is replete with traditions and the recollections of 'antient persons'.[143] Abraham de la Pryme enjoyed talking with his parishioners as much as reading. His many informants included other antiquaries and parsons as well as poorer folk. When noting the death of 'Old Richard Baxter' in 1694 he added a character of the great puritan 'as far as my accounts can reach, as well oral as printed'. The 'oldest parishioners' in the village of Caistor gave him much information about an old Roman road 'commonly call'd amongst them the High Street Way'.[144] Yet Pryme was, despite his relative isolation, no country bumpkin himself but a fellow of the Royal Society and a promising young scholar in touch with the leading antiquaries of his day. He had one foot in the world of rural tradition and another in that of Augustan scholarship.

Daniel Defoe had few such local ties and was no historian, despite his vast publication of journalistic lives and memoirs. His usage of oral tradition was motivated very clearly by a desire to bring national customs and points of interest back out of the realm of the learned chorography and natural history and make it attractive to a wide audience. With Defoe's *Tour thro' the Whole Island of Great Britain*, first published in three volumes between 1724 and 1727, we have come almost full circle. Defoe's frequent accounts of traditional tales and of the recollections of country folk connect him with Leland and Camden, and with the folkloric and ethnographic interests of Aubrey half a century earlier, rather than with the documentary zeal which by now fired the souls of historians and antiquaries. The difference is that no one (including himself) regarded Defoe as a serious scholar. Intent on writing for the entertainment of a wide audience, Defoe persistently denies any claim to the title of antiquary: his task is to describe Britain's towns, countryside, and people as these appear in the present. It was precisely this lack of deep concern for the scholarly side of English antiquities, coupled with a boundless curiosity about everything he encountered, that allowed Defoe to adopt Leland's interest in local lore, and to share his caution towards specific points of tradition rather than the general scepticism and distaste of a century of scholars, from the recusant Thomas Habington to the non-juror Thomas Hearne.[145]

---

[142] *Spectator*, 371 (6 May 1712), ed. Bond, iii. 309; for another example of old men swapping tales of the civil wars, no. 497 (30 Sept. 1712), ed. Bond, iv. 262.

[143] Richard Gough, *The History of Myddle*, ed. D. Hey (Harmondsworth, 1981), 54, 56, 77, 81, and *passim*.

[144] *Diary of Abraham de la Pryme*, 47, 71, 79 ff.

[145] Defoe, *Tour*, i. 116, ii. 429–30; for other examples, cf. ibid. i. 16, 188, 216, 243, 257, 278, ii. 452, 463, 634, 662, 768.

Defoe's book appeared at virtually the same time as another work which similarly marks an Aubreyesque interest in popular traditions about the past, and much else, for their own sake, namely Henry Bourne's *Antiquitates vulgares*.[146] The work of a sometime glazier's apprentice turned curate, the influence of Bourne's book was relatively slight in the first half of the century, when it had to contend with the dismissive attitude of periodicals such as the *Gentleman's Magazine*. This denounced tales of ghosts, based on 'a motley mixture of low and vulgar education' provided by nurses, and stories of cities 'famous for their antiquity and decays'.[147] In the later eighteenth century, however, it once again became fashionable to study popular traditions, superstitions, and practices, again if only for their quaintness, under the rubric of 'popular antiquities'. At the same time, European writers such as Rousseau were also commenting on the detrimental effects of writing and on the innate superiority of speech.[148] In France, Jacques Revel has shown, popular culture began to be understood by French intellectuals as 'a social artifact produced in particular conditions, not as the negative product of a system of invalidation'. In short, they began to approach it with something like the detachment of anthropologists, their interests eventually culminating in the use of oral sources by as respected a post-Napoleonic historian as Jules Michelet.[149] Across the Channel, coinciding with the new-found interest in ballads of Bishop Thomas Percy and Francis Grose's attention to vulgar speech, John Brand's investigations into this subject were able to pick up where Bourne had left off. This pointed the way towards a more systematic study of folklore in the Victorian era, when students such as W. Carew Hazlitt, who in turn edited and updated Brand, listened afresh to the 'common voice'. From there the road leads fairly directly to twentieth-century folklorists while also forking out into the local history and popular cultural studies of the past two or three decades.[150]

Although the nature and the context of historical writing and research had changed profoundly in two centuries, there is a certain resemblance between the sixteenth-century view of tradition and that of one Victorian collector, Robert Chambers, according to whom 'the value of popular tradition as evidence in antiquarian inquiries cannot be disputed, though in every instance it should be received

---

[146] Henry Bourne, *Antiquitates vulgares; or, The antiquities of the common people* (Newcastle, 1725); R. Sweet, *The Writing of Urban Histories in Eighteenth-Century England* (Oxford, 1997), 19.

[147] *Gentleman's Magazine*, 2 (Oct. 1732), 1001–2. Another writer thought ballads, that other popular vehicle for history, as 'the bane of all good manners and morals, a nursery for idlers, whores, and pickpockets, a school for scandal, smut and debauchery, and ought to be entirely suppressed, or reduced under proper restriction': ibid., 5 (Feb. 1735), 93.

[148] N. Hudson, *Writing and European Thought 1600–1830* (Cambridge, 1994), 92–114; id. 'Constructing Oral Tradition: The Origins of the Concept in Enlightenment Intellectual Culture', in Fox and Woolf (eds.), *The Spoken Word*, pp. 240–55.

[149] Revel, 'Forms of Expertise', 267; for Michelet and oral history, see Thompson, *The Voice of the Past*, 41 f.

[150] Cocchiara, *History of Folklore in Europe*, 145–50, on Ritson, Percy, and the revival of interest in ballads.

with the greatest caution'.[151] And an even more positive attitude would be taken by Kenneth Beacham Martin, ex-sailor and historian of the Cinque Ports, in 1832, who opined that

Oral tradition must have had some source more worthy of credit than the love of the marvellous, or the idle inventions of mankind; and in days long past it was regarded with extreme veneration; the names and places of things were carefully preserved, and transmitted from generation to generation, as an unfailing register of sudden casualties and extraordinary events.

He professed a high degree of faith in the reliability of his own ancestors:

My grandfather, also, was fond of reciting to us all he knew of ancient traditions from his father, who was a doctor and a scholar; and as my venerable ancestor was born in the reign of Queen Anne, and remembered Dover before the innovations of the first American war, which levelled some of its old ruins to erect batteries, we were highly interested by his descriptions.[152]

Martin's defence of tradition is romantic and fanciful, but at the dawn of nineteenth-century historicism and of the rebirth of interest in local antiquities, he had recognized the status that tradition had once held as a historical source.[153] Once again it is instructive to turn to a more famous literary representation of antiquarianism from the same decade, Sir Walter Scott's *The Antiquary*. Jonathan Oldbuck may be closer to the kind of balance between hard-edged critical scholarship and interest in legitimate traditions that characterized the late eighteenth and nineteenth centuries (and also the sixteenth—Oldbuck quotes from Leland). He regards Edie Ochiltree, the mendicant ex-soldier, as a 'rascal', a lingering specimen of the 'mendicant who . . . was the news-carrier, the minstrel, and sometimes the historian of the district'. He nevertheless prizes Edie's stock of 'old ballads and traditions' rather more highly than the fake Celtic lore in *Ossian* much admired by his bellicose highland nephew, Hector M'Intyre. Oldbuck has a particular distaste for stories of ghosts and fairies, as opposed to historical

[151] John Brand, *Observations on Popular Antiquities, Chiefly Illustrating the Origins of Our Vulgar Customs, Ceremonies, and Superstitions*, ed. H. Ellis, 2 vols. (1813); see esp. ii. 259–72 for beliefs connected with wells, fountains, and other places of interest; W. Carew Hazlitt, *Brand's popular antiquities of Great Britain. Faiths and Folklore; a Dictionary of National Beliefs, Superstitions and Popular Customs, Past and Current, with their Classical and Foreign Analogues, Described and Illustrated*, 2 vols. (1905); R. Chambers, 'Tradition and Truth', in *The Book of Days: A Miscellany of Popular Antiquities*, 2 vols. (Edinburgh, 1869), i. 337; T. S. Knowlson, *The Origins of Popular Superstitions and Customs* (1930), is largely derived from Brand.
[152] K. B. Martin, *Oral Traditions of the Cinque Ports and their Localities, compared with Antiquarian Researches, Natural Causes, and their Effects* (1832), 1, 12, 23.
[153] Nineteenth-century authors of popular historical works, and in particular of textbooks for children, often hedged about the traditional with the phrase 'it is said', permitting them to make considerable use of material that one of their number, Charlotte Mary Yonge, referred to as 'the beautiful, half-traditionary stream that flows along beside the graver course of our history'. C. M. Yonge, preface to *The Kings of England* (1852), quoted in R. Mitchell, *Picturing the Past: English History in Text and Image 1830–1870* (Oxford, 2000), 76. Charles Dickens, in *A Child's History of England*, 3 vols. (1852–4) was most reluctant to give up a good story in the face of historical facts: see Mitchell, *Picturing the Past*, 80.

ballads; he nearly tosses his servant Caxon out a window for claiming to see a ghost, but as Edie himself tells us, the laird will listen all day to tales of William Wallace, David Lindsay, and Blind Harry. We find him later in the story enthusiastically recording ' "a historical ballad" . . . "a genuine and undoubted fragment of minstrelsy!" ' of a sort that could be accepted as authentic by Percy or Ritson. Moreover, Oldbuck is not as wise as he pretends, a fact recognized by the aged beggar: 'he wad believe a bodle to be an auld Roman coin, as he ca's it, or a ditch to be a camp, upon ony leasing that idle folk made about it'. And as Edie himself admits, 'I hae garr'd him trow mony a queer tale mysell, gude forgie me.'[154]

ORAL TRADITION AND THE TRANSFORMATION OF HISTORICAL CULTURE

The vicissitudes in the fate of oral tradition over several centuries bring us back to the general mutations in historical culture between 1500 and 1730, and especially to the break that, I have suggested, occurred in the mid-seventeenth century. It is a story less of a single, linear development than of change, adaptation, and rediscovery. Above all, it is a further illustration of the shifts in the social and epistemological attitudes that underlie adjustments of genre, such as the detachment of history and scholarship from folklore, and modifications in historical method. It was certainly the later seventeenth-century antiquaries, heralds, and philologists themselves who exiled the oral from mainstream historiography by discounting its value, helping to push local memory outside the broader, national historical tradition and into the graveyard of rural antiquarianism. But they would not have done so if the general tendency of English culture had not been leaning increasingly towards the expulsion of popular tradition from civilized discourse, and towards doubting the information it contained because it came from vulgar mouths. The derisory treatment of both traditions and their tellers by scholars such as Hearne mirrors the attitude of his educated contemporaries to the finders of physical antiquities, the low men and women in the 'archaeological economy'.

The neglect of oral sources from the middle of the seventeenth century was thus not the mark of methodological progress magically conjured up by humanist philology, but a function of the increasing availability and reliability of written material, of which philology and the enshrinement of the documentary in print were simply by-products. The written and visible may render the remembered and spoken unnecessary, but where the past exists only in the mouths of the people, the modern folklorist, the student of African history, and the recorder of working-class memories must still turn to the 'common voice'. If such evidence is now treated with a more rigorous degree of scepticism and is checked and rechecked against external sources, it is not simply because modern practitioners

---

[154] Walter Scott, *The Antiquary* (Edinburgh, 1886), 44, 157, 208–9, 367.

are free of credulity but because they often have more with which to work. Those Tudor and Stuart antiquaries, from Leland and Camden through Aubrey, who balanced scepticism in recording traditions with an attitude of inclusiveness and respect, deserve our gratitude, but not just for the reasons that are usually mentioned. They helped to keep open not one road to the past, but two.

Conclusion

ENGLISH MEN AND women living at the middle of the sixteenth century were certainly well aware that both their own country and the wider world had a past. Those who were interested in history had a small number of books to which they could turn—predominantly the ancients and the Tudor chronicles. They also had wider access to oral traditions, ballads, and popular tales. By Daniel Defoe's time, oral tradition was no longer intellectually respectable, and the popular beliefs that it conveyed were now widely held to be little better than vulgar error. In place of these repositories of the past, one could now turn to a much wider range of books spread across a number of different genres. But the past could also be found elsewhere. It decorated homes and gardens; it filled museums and galleries, both at home and abroad; and it lay scattered about the countryside in the landscape and in man-made monuments, the true origins of some of which were only just then being surmised.

As a socially circulated commodity, the past itself also had a different value in 1700 than it had in the sixteenth and early seventeenth centuries. Aspects of it had clearly achieved higher status—in the form of 'historical knowledge'—as a source of entertainment, a means of education, and a subject of polite discussion. At the same time, the past had lost some of its power to authorize individual behaviour and validate social practices in a world that increasingly planned for present needs and future contingencies. Argument from tradition, custom, or antiquity still packed a punch, but there was less weight behind it, and more ways to parry the blow.

Various disputes of the early eighteenth century, many of which lie at some remove from narrowly historiographical concerns, testify to this. Perhaps the best known was the conflict between a Whig or contractarian view of monarchy in which alteration of the dynastic line was permissible if in the public interest, and a Tory position which insisted on an indefeasible hereditary succession. The differences are ones of emphasis, rather than exclusive choice of one mode of argumentation over another, but they are very clear. Though they, too, could produce historical examples (of popish atrocity or imperial despotism), exponents of the Whig view argued mainly from necessity and pragmatism. Those taking the Tory (and eventually Jacobite) position might similarly make arguments from present exigency, but the force of their case rested heavily on an appeal to centuries of historical practice, punctuated by disastrous medieval and especially seventeenth-century cautionary tales of the violation of the hereditary principle (which in fact was of much more recent origin than generally credited) and of the doctrine of obedience to an anointed sovereign. They thereby echoed earlier discourses of succession, in particular those of the 1590s, as an ageing, childless queen was unsuccessfully pressed to name an heir. Those late Tudor discussions had been voiced in unison in the reign of Elizabeth with the memory of fifteenth-century baronial conflicts, colourfully depicted in verse and drama. The issues were more vigorously contested in the reigns of William III and Anne, despite recent memories of civil wars more terrible still. The compromises of 1689 and 1714 would cling relentlessly to the shell and rhetoric of hereditary right, but invest the power to alter such claims in the king-in-parliament through legislation.[1] A parallel tendency towards argument from reason rather than from tradition can be seen in the religious sphere. Where sixteenth-century religious polemic had often relied on the validity of 'unwritten verities' and continuous practices (the Catholic position) or the unassailable truth of revelation in Scripture alone on matters essential to salvation (the mainstream Protestant position), discussions two centuries later were more likely to turn on acceptance or rejection of a combination of logic and historical criticism.[2]

The progressive circumscription of prescriptive rights by statute in the eighteenth century represents a further discounting of the authoritative—as opposed to the illustrative or decorative—power of the past. By the end of the century, that tendency had reached its extreme in rationalism, radicalism, and jacobinism, and a reaction, perhaps inevitable in the wake of the French Revolution and another European regicide, set in. But Edmund Burke, the most prominent British exponent of that reaction, could scarcely return to an early Tudor appeal to tradition which saw all social and political arrangements as absolutely timeless and immutable, and which denied any possibility of progress in the human sphere while also assuming the inevitability of natural decay. He could not even return, quite, to a Cokean notion of an evolving but self-consistent ancient constitution, though the same legal traditionalism enunciated by Coke and Sir Matthew Hale can be shown to underlie Burke's thought.[3] As a conservative Whig he had to settle for defending the Revolution Settlement and its legal institutions as the product of long-standing judicial and legislative wisdom, certainly accrued over several centuries, but not originating in the depths of an unfathomable antiquity. Burke made a compelling case for the return of the past to the council table as accumulated experience and collective national wisdom. But even his powerful oratory and prose could not restore it to sovereignty over political action. There is no doubt that radical change retained a strong capacity to unnerve those facing it, especially if its visible consequences were demonstrably violent or socially disruptive. Rural protests against enclosure, defences of local custom, and

[1] H. Nenner, *The Right to be King* (Chapel Hill, NC, 1995), 6–12, 165–70.

[2] H. Van Leeuwen, *The Problem of Certainty in English Thought 1630–80* (Leiden, 1963), esp. pp. 26–30; G. R. Cragg, *Reason and Authority in the Eighteenth Century* (Cambridge, 1964), 62–92. For a more recent account of thought about tradition in religious matters, see J. M. Levine, 'From Tradition to History: Chillingworth to Gibbon', in A. T. Grafton and J. H. M. Salmon (eds.), *Historians and Ideologues: Essays in Honour of Donald R. Kelley* (Rochester, NY, 2001), 181–210.

[3] J. G. A. Pocock, 'Burke and the Ancient Constitution: A Problem in the History of Ideas', in his *Politics, Language and Time* (New York, 1973), 202–32.

Luddite reaction to industrialism all provided reminders of this. They were responses to changes—generally imposed from above—that flew in the face of shared experience. On the other hand, conservative, incremental change was much more likely to gain silent acceptance among the politically or socially powerful than it had been in the sixteenth century. Mere novelty or innovation, taken as any departure from past practice, had, in most everyday contexts, lost its capacity to frighten all but the most obscurantist of minds.

One reason for this development is that the differences between past and present had become more obvious—and over progressively shorter periods. With this awareness of the ever-increasing frequency of change came a degree of desensitization to its consequences, and a certain comfort level—not universally shared—with the notion that not all change was *ipso facto* evil. In the first part of this book I argued that contemporary comments express a heightened sense of change, and an awareness of distance not only from the remote past (as noted by Renaissance humanists), but also from the past of only a few years, or even months, previously. Mutability was a known and oft-lamented fact of life in the sixteenth and seventeenth centuries. The difference in 1700 is that most people had realized that they could live with it, and many positively embraced it. One is less likely to fear a process that one can understand, and short-term change, previously the realm of fortune's random wheel or of direct but inscrutable providential intervention, was now increasingly represented as meaningful and comprehensible, even predictable and economically manageable. It was also, now, narratable. The printed media that emerged in the seventeenth century, from the newsbook to the daily newspaper, reflect this foreshortening of time, a shrinkage of the period within which meaningful change could be perceived and recounted.[4] Domestic timepieces became more commonplace in the seventeenth century—Samuel Pepys would fuss over his new pocket watch like an executive with an electronic calendar today.[5] Within the private and domestic realm, the advent of the diary as a commonplace record of the individual's experience of short-term change is a further sign of a shift in cognitive attitude that warrants further study.[6] The seventeenth century was perhaps the first to experience that 'acceleration of history' which has increased exponentially over the century just ended, hand in hand with what one commentator has called 'a growing belief in a right, a capacity, and even a duty to change'.[7]

The past remained a boundless sea from which could be fished limitless examples for imitation, but it was also now seen, in the form of history, as a cumulative story, its individual events and personalities leading up to—but also

---

[4] For more on this theme see my essay, 'News, History and the Construction of the Present in Early Modern England', in B. Dooley and S. A. Baron (eds.), *The Politics of Information in Early Modern Europe* (London and New York, 2001), 80–118.

[5] Pepys, *Diary*, vi. 101 (13 May 1665).

[6] S. Sherman, *Telling Time: Clocks, Diaries, and English Diurnal Form, 1660–1785* (Chicago, 1996).

[7] P. Nora, 'Between Memory and History: Les Lieux de Mémoire', *Représentations*, 26 (1989), 7–25, at p. 8.

subordinate to—the present. Action in the present no longer needed to imitate, much less replicate, action in the past, even when the origins of the situation requiring action could be traced back to that past. The function of literary history-writing as a 'mirror' on the present and the pool of abstractable examples certainly endured, the very portability and quotability of historical episodes finding a new home in civilized conversation and correspondence. But reference to 'History' as a connected series of yesterdays, culminating in the contemporary world, became much more commonplace. In historiographical terms we have moved from the *Lives and Sayings of the Philosophers*, Machiavelli, and the *Mirror for Magistrates* to Clarendon's *History of the Rebellion*, Kennett's *Complete History of England*, and eventually Hume's *History of England* and Gibbon's *Decline and Fall*. In explanatory terms, we have moved from a time that linked temporally separate and disparate events by analogy, to one that historicized even recent occurrences, while habitually tracing modern customs and institutions back, step by step, to their origins. In linguistic terms, we have moved from a historical field ordered by metaphor to one governed by metonymy, leaving behind a world in which events and people are twinned with remote, detemporalized analogues, and entering one in which they are understood more readily by reference to their immediately contiguous causes and consequences.

Having described some of the contexts within which discussion of the past occurred, and noted shifts in thinking around certain key issues connected with the conception of the past, such as antiquity, change, innovation, and family ancestry, much of the book has explored the ways in which specifically historical knowledge of various sorts made its way through early modern society. Antiquarianism, that branch of historiography which first became interested in the origins and developments of 'things' as opposed to the representation of great events, flourished in the later sixteenth and seventeenth centuries as the otherness of the past became more and more apparent. By 1700 it was still, taken as a literary genre, something of a cadet branch, separate from narrative historiography, but few readers would by then have failed to recognize its close kinship: 'history and antiquities' is a common combination in booksellers' advertisements and library catalogues.[8] Yet if the activity of antiquarianism seems methodologically and temperamentally closer to the research of the modern academic than does the rhetoric of most seventeenth-century narrative historians, we should remember that the study of the physical remains of the past also did much else. It promoted a strongly visual sense of history (and especially of a previously under-represented secular history). This in turn doubled back to affect antiquarian methodology, steering it towards direct observation, comparison, and classification. It encouraged an impulse to collect and display physical pieces of the past. Antiquarian enthusiasm was not the monopoly of a select group of scholars. In its more popular form, it helped to create the historic site, transforming the location of any significant historical event into a virtual portal back to the event itself,

[8] D. R. Woolf, *Reading History in Early Modern England* (Cambridge, 2000), chs. 6 and 7.

its land, artefacts, and monuments tangible survivals from that past which could be *literally* as well as intuitively grasped in the present. The full implications of this can be seen in the eighteenth century, when sentimental reaction to place and monument features more prominently in diaries and correspondence. 'Gothicism', and especially Romanticism, would bring an even more powerful sense of immediacy, but the beginnings of emotive reaction to specific sites is already observable in some of the comments discussed in Chapters 5 and 6.

Antiquarianism inspired several generations of local clergy and gentlemen to take a serious interest in their familial, provincial, and national pasts, but the character of that interest, too, changed during the seventeenth century. The increasingly sophisticated philological and numismatic skills that the more learned scholars developed, and the more subtle approach to archaeological study that arose between William Camden's time and William Stukeley's, are correctly noted as significant intellectual developments. Many of these antiquaries also preserved for posterity a parallel past to that contained in histories, the past of local memory and popular belief, conveyed in anecdotes, rituals, ballads, and oral traditions. The role of memory as a vessel of past events was eroded significantly by the advent of print culture, by the growing dominance of the written record, and by the crystallization of a national historical narrative. Popular beliefs about the past, many of them purely local, had long been the product of a dynamic interaction between elite literary culture and local memory and tradition. This interaction was itself being strained by the late seventeenth century as the contents of such beliefs, and often the very language in which they were expressed, were now deemed inappropriate to polite society, and were instead associated with an ignorant and superstitious multitude. Oral tradition was perhaps the most important vehicle of popular beliefs about the past; yet, with some exceptions, it had been virtually eliminated from the respectable scholar's toolkit by 1700. Augustan antiquaries, the successors of the very scholars who had committed many popular tales to writing in the first place, now relegated the subjects of such tradition to the status of folklore and vulgar error. From providing Leland with a 'common voice', a useful guide to what had happened where the written record did not run, the words of illiterate and semi-literate labourers and shepherds were now deemed intellectually less reliable than those of elite informants. Any fact or assertion deriving from spoken tradition, especially if it reached back more than a generation, could routinely be presumed to possess less historical worth than one founded on document or artefact.

This view became ingrained in the scholarship of the eighteenth, nineteenth, and twentieth centuries, notwithstanding occasional revivals of interest in the oral past such as that which commenced towards the end of the eighteenth century. The same social bias that led the Augustans to diminish the place of the rude discoverers of the tangible past of artefacts, the base point in the 'archaeological economy' described in Chapter 7, also figured in their sneering dismissal of a past remembered and spoken by precisely these sorts of people. The final result of this was a historical past in some ways broader than that to which sixteenth-century people could gain access, and in others much narrower. Broader, from the vantage point of learned culture, because history now embraced many topics not previously treated by historians, and because it was now readily available in hundreds of British and European printed books. Narrower, because it had ruled much of the traditional past out of 'History' proper, and abandoned it to occasional treatment in the writings of parochial antiquaries operating for the most part on the fringes of the scholarly community.

It was therefore left to local populations to preserve their own traditions, stories, and songs. In this they were sometimes assisted by parochial antiquaries and, less frequently, by more prominent scholars such as John Aubrey. This task of preservation, too, was rendered more difficult by the ubiquity of print and by the growing hegemony of an orthodox account, a master-narrative of political and religious history. In this account, authors frequently argued over the causes and consequences, good or ill, of this or that significant event or personality, but rarely disagreed as to which events or personalities had significance. There are certainly signs of this meta-narrative in the sixteenth century, especially in accounts of the Tudor accession or of the liberation from popish tyranny, and the number of historical episodes around which discussion could revolve grew considerably in the crucible of the seventeenth century. By the early nineteenth century, the outlines, reliefs, and major landmarks of 'British history' were clearly established and have stayed that way for the better part of two centuries. Political opinions could be almost routinely measured by attitudes to particular episodes and figures, simply because those events had earned by consensus the legitimizing tag 'historical'.[9] Thus the lingering memory of the civil war and of all encroachments on the Crown since then could provide a litmus test of political and social attitudes for a Victorian novelist such as Trollope. The dean of Bobsborough in the second Palliser novel, *The Eustace Diamonds*, holds reactionary views that reflect his perspective on two centuries of English history. 'It was bad to interfere with Charles, bad to endure Cromwell, bad to banish James, bad to put up with William. The House of Hanover was bad. All interference with prerogative has been bad. The Reform bill was very bad.'[10]

The year 1730 has been a convenient if arbitrary end-point for this study, but it represents little by way of finality, for the processes described herein were by no means complete in that year. The rest of the eighteenth century witnessed further literary change, notably the success of history's most potent rival among the genres, the novel, and the *modus vivendi* of fiction and history in the great

[9] On nineteenth-century historical writing see in particular the following: T. Lang, *The Victorians and the Stuart Heritage: Interpretations of a Discordant Past* (Cambridge, 1995); S. Bann, *The Clothing of Clio: A Study of the Representation of History in Nineteenth-Century Britain and France* (Cambridge, 1984); J. W. Burrow, *A Liberal Descent: Victorian Historians and the English Past* (Cambridge, 1981); A. D. Culler, *The Victorian Mirror of History* (New Haven, Conn., 1985); R. Jann, *The Art and Science of Victorian History* (Columbus, Ohio, 1985). Cf. R. Mitchell, *Picturing the Past: English History in Text and Image 1830–1870* (Oxford, 2000); V. E. Chancellor, *History for their Masters: Opinion in the English History Textbook, 1800–1914* (Bath, 1970).
[10] Anthony Trollope, *The Eustace Diamonds*, ed. D. Skilton (Edinburgh, 1990), 29.

literary historians from Hume through Macaulay. This reconciliation occurred when historians, fixated on defending their claims to truth and impartiality during the partisan debates of the first half of the eighteenth century, began in the second to borrow the sentimental and evocative language of fiction.[11] Then, in the first decades of the nineteenth century, novelists themselves made the historical past a site of narrative.[12] Beginning with Sir Walter Scott's *Waverley* and its hero's encounter with the Young Pretender, the historical novel's fictional characters participate in actual events and mingle with recreated 'real' people. By the time of Thackeray's Henry Esmond, fifty years later, we are given an imagined Augustan world in which the likes of Addison, Steele, General Webb, Lord Mohun, and the duke of Marlborough are vividly portrayed and threaten to overwhelm the more central but imaginary characters.[13] *The History of Henry Esmond* is a relatively late entry in the field, but it is a prototype for hundreds of modern books, plays, and films along similar lines in which real persons are introduced, often in minor roles, to appeal to the audience's historical sense and amuse it with the imaginative possibilities of such fictional encounters.[14]

One of the earliest historical novels, Scott's *The Antiquary*, carries with it especially strong echoes of some of the themes treated in the present book, including the clash between gentry refinement and vulgar error, here embodied in the central character, Jonathan Oldbuck.[15] The fictional life of the Laird of Monkbarns lies several decades removed from the chronological boundaries of this study, but in many ways his milieu is that of the earlier Scottish antiquary he so admires, Alexander Gordon (1692–1754), himself a figure from the very end of our period. We have already witnessed Oldbuck's disparagement of local excavations of antiquities by 'fools, boors, and idiots'. He is equally sceptical (in contrast to his naive friend and fellow antiquary Sir Arthur Wardour) of local legends. Only briefly does the prospect of hearing a genuine oral tradition arouse Oldbuck's interest, and then because it runs into a time where the documentary record is utterly silent. This is in stark contrast to local Scottish tales and beliefs that he dismisses as barbaric superstition because they conflict with written history. Though Oldbuck is the creation of a Romantic novelist, he himself is no Romantic. He has no particular feel for the medieval or the wild, preferring his Roman ruins and seals, a further indication that he himself is somewhat out of

---

[11] See especially L. Braudy, *Narrative Form in History and Fiction: Hume, Fielding, & Gibbon* (Princeton, 1970); and M. S. Phillips, ' "If Mrs Mure be not Sorry for Poor King Charles": History, the Novel, and the Sentimental Reader', *History Workshop Journal*, 43 (1997); id., *Society and Sentiment: Genres of Historical Writing in Britain, 1740–1820* (Princeton, 2000).

[12] A. Fleishman, *The English Historical Novel* (Baltimore and London, 1971), 16–36; R. Chapman, *The Sense of the Past in Victorian Literature* (London and Sydney, 1986), 17–33.

[13] In a sense, we have come 180° with the early nineteenth-century historical novel from the Elizabethan history play. In the latter, real historical characters were central, fictional characters such as Prince Hal's ruffian companions peripheral figures introduced as plot devices or comic relief. By Scott's time, the 'real' characters are secondary to the fictional ones; *Henry Esmond* shifts the balance back towards the historical characters.

[14] A. Sanders, *The Victorian Historical Novel 1840–1880* (1978), 102–4.

[15] Sir Walter Scott, *The Antiquary* (Edinburgh, 1886).

step with 'this Gothic generation'. He declaims against architectural offences, which he attributes to a conflation of the Vitruvian orders in the reign of James I.[16] Oldbuck similarly draws a line separating fiction from history (an ironic statement given its placement within a historical novel). He encourages his younger friend Lovel to write an 'old-fashioned historical poem' on the British defeat of Agricola—an event that never happened—because a poet is free to 'defeat the Romans in spite of Tacitus'.[17]

Jonathan Oldbuck recognizes, correctly, that the genuine achievements of an artisan are as admirable a point from which to trace one's origins as the more conventional gentry lineage valued by his literary near contemporary, Jane Austen's Sir Walter Elliot, baronet. Oldbuck is no treasurer of ancient pedigrees traced through Banquo back to Kenneth MacAlpin or Fergus MacFerquhard. On the contrary, he is proud to trace his lineage back no further—nor socially any higher—than a sixteenth-century German printer. An honest tradesman and Protestant founder of the modern media universe presents a more attractive ancestry than a series of legendary Scottish kings or supposititious medieval barons.[18] Like some of the seventeenth-century commentators who evinced scepticism towards outlandish claims of aristocratic lineage, and disdain of the pretensions therein, Oldbuck at least implicitly sees that ancestry is less like a tree than, as modern genetics would put it, a pool.

As historians, we should see our disciplinary ancestry in much the same way. Without discounting the achievements of the Greats, this book has been an attempt to move the history of history away from admiration of its 'family tree' towards consideration of a much larger cultural gene pool, one that includes a number of hereditary traits now recessive but not extinct. Our own historiographical predilections sprang from local discussions of custom and memorized tradition as much as from advanced documentary scholarship, even if the latter is the genetically dominant feature of today's academy. The current vogue for a social and cultural history focused on the material, anecdotal, and mundane, and the postmodern questioning of boundaries between history and fiction, show that those recessive genes in historiography's past have a strong capacity to resurface.

Strong gene pools are more likely to emerge where there is extensive cross-breeding. It is a serious error to assume that modern historical method and its practitioners have in their intellectual ancestry only the noteworthy figures of the historiographical past. It is similarly mistaken to suppose that the great works of history written in earlier periods were composed in a social vacuum. The historical past became such an important fixture of English culture during the early modern period not only because a narrow strand of humanist scholarly practice was picked up and spun on from generation to generation, but also because the past was a much more commonplace commodity that circulated in a variety of ways across and between social levels. The freedom of that circulation, however,

---

[16] Ibid. 144, 177.   [17] Ibid. 130.
[18] Ibid. 50; D. Brown, *Walter Scott and the Historical Imagination* (1979), 47–67.

was increasingly constrained by changing intellectual presumptions and by a hardening of social boundaries, at the very time when historical knowledge was achieving a status within educated ranks unprecedented in any earlier period of English civilization. In a sense, the horizontal circulation of knowledge of the past expanded dramatically in the course of the seventeenth century while the opportunities for its vertical circulation, while certainly not closed off, were increasingly determined by elite intellectual selectivity and by the boundaries of an emergent national history.

In the final analysis, it mattered less that the sixteenth and seventeenth centuries produced some political histories of lasting worth such as Clarendon's *History of the Rebellion,* or even some formative works of erudite scholarship such as Camden's *Britannia,* Selden's *Historie of Tithes,* and Lhwyd's *Archaeologia Britannica,* than that these works were widely read and discussed (together with a great many more now forgotten) among the nation's literate elite and that their subjects became coin of the civilized realm. Modern historical methods indeed emerged in part because critical skills and sensible principles of interpretation were transmitted over time, from one historian to another: from Polydore Vergil to Camden, from Selden to Gibbon, and thence through the nineteenth century up to Maitland and onward to Elton. But it surely happened also because an intellectual and social environment existed that encouraged such knowledge to be discovered in the first place and then widely disseminated. It would be nonsense to claim that provincial antiquaries like the Blundells of Little Crosby, or William Holman of Halstead contributed as much as William Camden or William Stukeley to the methods of modern scholarship. Yet the keen interest of hundreds of Blundells and Holmans, and the participation of the far humbler folk who furnished them with artefacts and stories, cannot be ignored. Indeed, it is hard to see how, without them, the public interest in the past that has suffused our social life from the seventeenth century to the present could ever have come about, and with it the historiographical enterprise that such interest continues to support.

INDEX

Peers are indexed by family name; titles such as 'Sir' are not recorded in the index except for purposes of distinguishing similar names.

(*Page numbers in italics refer to illustrations*).

Lightning Source UK Ltd.
Milton Keynes UK
08 March 2011

168846UK00007B/9/A